Baedeker's
Switzerland

Baedeker's

SWITZERLAND

Imprint

354 colour photographs

18 maps, 7 ground plans, 33 town plans, 44 sketches and drawings, 1 large road map.

Text: Madeleine Cabos, Prof. Dr Wolfgang Hassenpflug, Hans Rathgeb, Christine Wessely and Vera Beck.

Editorial work: Baedeker-Radaktion (Madeleine Cabos).

General management: Dr Peter Baumgarten, Baedeker Stuttgart.

Cartography:
Gert Oberländer, Munich.
Christoph Gallus, Lahr.
Hallwag AG, Bern (map of Lichtenstein).
Mairs Geographischer Verlag, Ostfildern-Kemnat (large road map).

English translation: James Hogarth, David Cocking, Julie Waller.

Source of illustrations:
Most of the photographs were provided by the Schweizerische Verkehrszentrale (Swiss National Tourist Office) in Zurich and Frankfurt am Main, the cantonal tourist organisations and local travel bureaux and information offices, as well as the Liechtensteinische Fremdenverkehrszentrale (Liechetenstein National Tourist Office) in Vaduz (2); Anthony (2), Baumgarten (4), Bodan AG (1), Cabos (283), Cern (1), Fetzer (1), Globetrotter (1), Historia (8), Linde (3), de Morsier (1), Säntis Luftseilbahn Schwägalp (2), Sawade (1), Schweizerische Käseunion (1), Stetter (2), Ullstein (4).

Following the tradition established by Karl Baedeker in 1844, sights of particular interest and hotels and restaurants of exceptional quality are distinguished by either one or two asterisks.

To make it easy to find on the accompanying map the places listed under the "A to Z" section, each has been given a map co-ordinate in red: e.g., Zürich **D1**.

Only a selection of hotels and restaurants can be given: no reflection is implied, therefore, on establishments not included.

In a time of rapid change it is difficult to ensure that all the information given is entirely accurate and up to date, and the possibility of error can never be entirely eliminated. Although the publishers can accept no responsibility for inaccuracies and omissions, they are always grateful for corrections and suggestions for improvement.

1st English edition
© Baedeker Stuttgart
Original German edition

© 1991 The Automobile Association
United Kingdom and Ireland

© 1991 Jarrold and Sons Ltd
English language edition worldwide

US and Canadian Edition
Prentice Hall Press

Distributed in the United Kingdom by the Publishing Division of The Automobile Association, Fanum House, Basingstoke, Hampshire, RG21 2EA.

The name *Baedeker* is a registered trademark
A CIP catalogue record for this book is available from the British Library.

Licensed user:
Mairs Geographischer Verlag GmbH & Co., Ostfildern-Kemnat bei Stuttgart

Reproductions: Erder Repro GmbH, Ostfildern-Scharnhausen

Printed in Italy by G. Canale & C. S.p.A. – Borgaro T.se – Turin

ISBN 0–13–094822–5 US and Canada
    0–7495–0277–0 UK

Contents

Principal Sights at a Glance

Preface

This Pocket Guide to Switzerland is one of the new generation of Baedeker guides.

These guides are designed to meet the needs of the modern traveller. They are quick and easy to consult, with the principal sights described in alphabetical order and useful details shown in the margin.

Each guide is divided into three parts. The first gives a general account of the country, its geography, climate, flora and fauna, population, prominent personalities and so on; in the second part the principal sights are described, and the third part contains a variety of practical information designed to help visitors to find their way about and make the most of their stay. For the reader's convenience this practical information, like the main part of the guide, is arranged in alphabetical order.

The new guides are abundantly illustrated and contain a series of specially drawn plans. In a pocket at the back of the book is a large road map, and each entry in the main part of the guide gives the coordinates of the square on the map in which the place concerned can be found. Users of this guide, therefore, will have no difficulty in finding the places they wish to visit.

Facts and Figures

For long one of the world's great tourist countries, Switzerland contains Introduction within a relatively small area an extraordinary abundance of natural beauties and interesting attractions, and at the same time, in spite of the country's varied geographical pattern and the differences in language, religion and way of life among its inhabitants, offers an admirable example of unity in diversity. The 4000 m/13,000 ft peaks of the High Alps and the lesser summits of the Pre-Alpine regions began to attract the first modern tourists – mainly British – during the 19th c. Since then Switzerland has developed into a Mecca for visitors of every nationality and every age and condition, who find here accommodation to suit every taste from modest to luxurious, modern tourist facilities and a hospitable welcome.

General

Switzerland

© Baedeker

Situated in the south of Central Europe, Location Switzerland is mainly a mountainous country. Its landlocked position, with no direct access to the sea and once a commercial disadvantage, is compensated for by its location in the very centre of the Alps and thus in the centre of Europe itself. As the crow flies, some 250 km/150 miles separate the southern tip of Switzerland from the nearest sea-port of Genoa. The rail journey from Luzern in central Switzerland to Genoa is 430 km/270 miles and culminates in the Gotthard Tunnel 1156 m/3800 ft above sea level. The trip by water between Geneva and the mouth of the Rhône measures some 640 km/400 miles, and the rail journey 510 km/320 miles, as it winds its way over a 375 m/1230 ft difference in altitude. The Rhine is the only route to the sea for ships, representing a voyage of 800 km/500 miles from Basle to Rotterdam. Switzerland's northernmost point lies 47° 48' 35" north at Oberbargen in the canton of Schaffhausen, and its southernmost at Chiasso in the canton of Ticino, at 45° 49' 8" north. Thus, its maximum distance from north to south is about 220 km/140 miles. From west to east, between Chancy near Geneva (5° 57' 24" east) and the easternmost peak of the Grisons at Fiz Chavalatsch (10° 29' 36" east) the country measures over 348 km/215 miles. The local time difference is 18 minutes and nine seconds.

With an area of 41,293.2 sq. km/15,943 sq. miles, the country is about the Area same size as the Netherlands (41,160 sq. km/15,892 sq. miles), larger than Belgium (30,514 sq. km/11,781 sq. miles), but rather smaller than Denmark (43,069 sq. km/16,629 sq. miles), and about a sixth of the size of the United Kingdom (244,000 sq. km/94,208 sq. miles).

Switzerland has a common frontier with five neighbouring countries. The total length of its frontiers is 1881.5 km/1169 miles – 363 km/226 miles with the German Federal Republic, 165 km/103 miles with Austria, 41 km/25 miles with Liechtenstein, 741 km/460 miles with Italy and 572 km/355 miles with France.

Switzerland is made up of three geographical regions of different size – the Alps (some 60% of the total area), the Mittelland (30%) and the Jura (10%). Of the total area 46% is occupied by meadowland and pasture, 25% by

◀ *The Bernina group from the Piz Languard*

forest and 6% by arable land. Thus 77% of the country's area has been brought into productive use and is densely populated; the remaining 23% is unproductive land in the mountains, but these empty regions provide magnificent recreation areas for holidaymakers and nature-lovers.

Geography and Geology

Geographical divisions

Geographically Switzerland is made up of three very dissimilar parts. The south-eastern half of the country consists of the Alps; to the north-west are the Jura mountains, and between these two mountain regions is the lower-lying Mittelland, extending from Lake Geneva in the south-west – where the Jura beyond the rift valley of the Rhône abuts on the Alpine chain – to Lake Constance in the north-east, beyond which lies the German Alpine foreland region. The total area of the country is divided fairly equally between the Jura and Mittelland on the one hand and the Alps on the other – one half well cultivated and densely inhabited, the other offering the grandeur and beauty of the high mountains.

Jura

The Swiss Jura extends in long rolling crests and much-weathered ridges from the south-west, around Geneva, where it adjoins the similarly formed and oriented chains of the French Pre-Alpine region, to Schaffhausen in the north-east, where Randen (912 m/2992 ft) and the volcanic Hegau form a transition to the Swabian Jura.

The limestone chains of the Jura reach their highest points in Swiss territory – Mont Tendre, 1679 m/5509 ft, and La Dôle, 1677 m/5502 ft – and fall steeply down to the Mittelland. Between the Lac de Neuchâtel and the Doubs valley near Besançon there are some twenty successive chains, their highest points rising only slightly above the uniform ridges in the

Geographical Regions of Switzerland

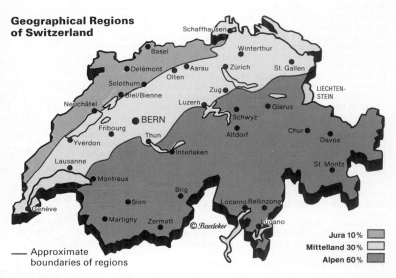

— Approximate boundaries of regions

Jura 10%
Mittelland 30%
Alpen 60%

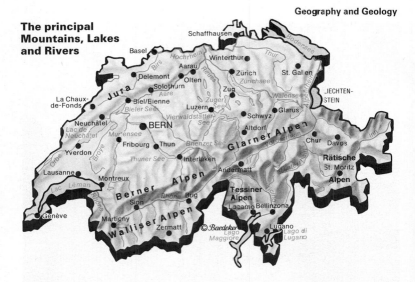

The principal Mountains, Lakes and Rivers

Schaffhausen · Basel · Hochrhein · Bodensee · Thur · Winterthur · Aarau · Reuss · Zürich · St. Gallen · Delemont · Olten · Zug · Zürichsee · Jura · Solothurn · Aare · Zuger See · Walensee · LIECHTENSTEIN · La Chaux-de-Fonds · Biel/Bienne · Luzern · Glarus · Bieler See · Vierwaldstätter See · Schwyz · Glarner Alpen · Neuchâtel · BERN · Altdorf · Chur · Davos · Lac de Neuchâtel · Murtensee · Fribourg · Thun · Brienzer See · Rätische · Yverdon · Broye · Thuner See · Interlaken · St. Moritz · Orbe · Andermatt · Alpen · Lausanne · Montreux · Alpen · Berner · Sion · Brig · Tessiner Alpen · Lago · Bellinzona · Lac Léman · Rhône · Genève · Martigny · Walliser Alpen · Zermatt · © Baedeker · Lago Maggiore · Lugano · Lago di Lugano

form of gently rounded hills. The chains are frequently cut by gorges (known as "Klus", from the Latin claudere = to close or cut off), through which the river flowing down a longitudinal valley finds its way into the next valley, continuing through further gorges until it emerges from the mountains. Here the slopes covered with beautiful forests and the summits with pastureland and scrub open up to reveal in their light-coloured bands of rock the folding to which the strata have been subjected (most strikingly seen in the Val Moutier and the Gorges de Court).

From the west the Burgundian Jura, flatter but still wave-like in form, advances into Swiss territory in the plateaux of La-Chaux-de-Fonds and the Franches Montagnes and is known as the Jura plateau. A weak build-up of synclines coupled with marked erosion produced the sandstone plateaux of the Franches Montagnes, creased with wooded ridges (resistant layers of friable limestone) and flat hollows. The long gorge of the Doubs river, which here forms the frontier, flows between steep wooded rock walls 400 m/1300 ft below the edges of the plateau, is particularly beautiful. *Jura plateau*

Between Basle and Brugg the Jura, only a few hundred metres high, forms tabular plateaux. In the Oligocene Age the unfolded Mesozoic strata were broken down into numerous ice floes, pierced by deep valleys, some widened by erosion, which now frequently serve as important mountain roads. *Jura table*

Mittelland

The Swiss Mitteland (c. 400–800 m/1312–2625 ft), which rises gradually from the Jura to the foot of the Alps, belongs to the Molasse Trough i.e., the accumulation basin which was filled by the Alpine rivers with detritus during the Alpine folding in the Tertiary Age. This resulted in a number of flat sediment layers being deposited on the crystalline mountain floor. A fresh-water lake was left by the arm of the sea which reached from South Germany to Lyons during the time of the Alpine folding; it later became part of the sea again, only to silt up and end up as a lake once more. As a *Molasse*

11

Bernese Oberland: between First and the Wetterhorn

result, the Molasse displays the following structure: lower sea, lower fresh-water, upper sea and upper fresh-water Molasse. The detritus deposited by the Alpine rivers in the foothills led to the formation of pockets of debris and deltas, where initially heavy boulders and gravel were deposited, followed by sand and finally clay materials. With the help of mainly chalky binding materials this rubble became compressed into new layers of stone, which together reach a massiveness of almost 3000 m/10,000 ft. Near the Alps the conglomerate "nagelfluh" was formed, sand became sandstone and mud produced a marl mixture. Through these conglomerates the same rivers later cut their way once more, widening and deepening their channels to form valleys. The hills between them are remnants of the older rocks which have resisted erosion. The Tertiary rocks, however, are covered almost everywhere with a mantle of pasture and arable land, peatbogs and lakes, with small areas of woodland on the hills.

In the western part of the Mittelland the heights have a gently rounded tabular form ("le plateau suisse"), like, for example, Mont Jorat (932 m/3058 ft/) above Lausanne. To the east they are mostly in the form of long and fairly uniform ridges, the flanks of which have been worn smooth by the glaciers of the last Ice Age, such as the Pfannenstiel (853 m/2799 ft) near Zurich and the Lindenburg (881 m/2891 ft) in the Aargau. The Napf group, built up by the original rivers Rhine and Aare, (1411 m/4629 ft) and the Töss hills (Hörnli, 1136 m/3727 ft) lay outside the glaciated area and were exposed to continual erosion by running water; in consequence, they now show a much-dissected pattern of alternating ridges and furrows.

The final Alpine folding movement affected the neighbouring foreland region, thrusting the Helvetian layers over the southernmost Molasse strata, which in turn became buried by or were folded into the Alps. The rounded peaks of the Molasse which were thus forced upwards have since been largely eroded away, however. Some remnants of these folds, however, survive in the nagelfluh beds which can be seen rising towards the north on the Rigi (1800 m/5900 ft), Rossberg (1584 m/5197 ft) and Speer

(1954 m/6411 ft). From the summits of these rocky heights there is a view over the intervering uplands to the distant chains of the Jura.

During the various Ice Ages the Molasse surfaces were almost completely covered by the moraines of the Alpine glaciers. Many side and end moraines remain in the form of high, long-shaped hills. The wide valley areas around Winterthur, Zurich, Burgdorf, Berne and Geneva are traversed by moraines left by the last great Ice Age, which lasted until about 10,000 B.C.. These moraines appear mostly as undulations across the valleys or along the hillsides and frequently bounding the lower ends of lakes. With its variety of landscape pattern the Mittelland is a region of great attraction, even on cloudy days when the view of the Alps is cut off.

Moraines

The Mittelland is the most densely settled part of Switzerland, with almost all its larger towns and more than three-quarters of its total population. However, it is also a highly developed agricultural region.

Alps

Even though 58% of the country lies in the centre of the Alps it in fact accounts for only one-seventh of their total area. The longitudinal valleys of the Rhône and young Rhine, together with the transverse valleys of the Reuss and Ticino, divide the mountainous backbone of Europe into a north-eastern chain (Alpstein–Toggenburg, the Glarus, Schwyz and eastern Uri Alps), the north-west Alps (western Urn, Unterwalden, Berr, Fribourg, Vri Vaud Alps) and the southern Alps (Valais, Ticino and Grisons Alps). The average height of these young folded mountains is about 1700 m/5600 ft; some one hundred peaks reach 4000 m/13,000 ft or more. The highest point in Switzerland is the Dufour Peak in the Monta Rosa massif (Valais canton), which is 4634 m/15,209 ft above sea level.

The formation of the Alpine range commenced in the Palaeolozic Age, about 300 million years ago. When molten granite flowed upwards during the Carboniferous period and solidified as cooled magma into granite, this produced a mountain in Hercynian form. Today, largely hidden under later layers of stone, the central massifs which pushed up during the formation of the Alps (e.g. Aiguilles-Rouges and Mont Blanc massif in Lower Valais, the Aare and Gotthard massif in the central Alps) still bear witness to this ancient crystalline base. In the Mesozoic Age, when the sea covered everything and eroded the "original Alps", a long-reaching valley was created. Over a period of some 160 million years its bottom became covered by material swept in by the rivers and limestone and dolomite accumulated in the peaks and troughs thus formed. The Helvetian section of the trough included the northern coastal region, the central ocean area was embraced by the Pennines and the southern coastal strip by the eastern and southern Alps. In the Chalk Age, towards the end of the Mesozoic period, the coastal floe in the southern Tethys moved northwards, probably as a result of strong undercurrents: the formation of the mountain range had begun.
Due to the resistance from the northern mainland mass there was a folding, elevation and shifting of the sediment from the Pennine region to the Helvetian deposit area. As the land surface arched upwards horizontal folds extended even further and covered other stone masses over a large area, thus producing the characteristic tabular construction found in many parts of the Alps. The Mesozoic sediments, originally extending over 500 km/300 miles from north to south, became forced together and on top of one another in various phases until they ended up as mountains 150 km/90 miles in width. The result was an extremely complex system of layers and inversions. Constant weather erosion acted against the formation of the mountains, thus making geological relationships even more difficult to diagnose in many places. The erosion also reduced the strain on the subsoil, so that in the central Alps isostatic equilibrium movements

The formation of the mountains

13

Monte Rosa massif, with the highest peak in Switzerland

resulted in the crystalline base piercing the surface in some places. As the granite and gneiss masses pushed upwards they formed the Central Massif. The Helvetian deposits which were also involved in the formation of the mountains became stratified and their brow pushed up against the Molasse foothills.

Magnificent scenery

The Alps, which from a distance appear to be a uniform chain, are in fact deeply indented by many valleys, terrasses, passes, chains and corridors, indicating that they were formed by Pleistocene glacier masses. On the north side of the mountain mass are the Pre-Alps, long limestone chains which in many places rise above the Mittelland in sheer rock walls. Running parallel to one another, they are broken up by wide, deep valleys extending down from the High Alps (for example, at Montreux, Thun, Lucerne, Rapperswil and Rorschach-Bregenz).

Even the Pre-Alps offer magnificent scenery, with light grey limestone peaks rearing above green upland pastures and dark pine forests. In spite of much erosion and weathering the violent folding of the strata still reveals the gigantic wave-like structure of the rock formations which follow one another in close succession northwards – particularly impressive in the Säntis ridges (2504 m/8216 ft) and Pilatus (Tomlishorn, 2132 m/6995 ft). Elsewhere massive limestone mountains tower up, such as Tödi (3614 m/11,858 ft), Selbsanft (3026 m/9928 ft) and Glärnisch (Bächistock, 2915 m/9564 ft) which enclose the canton of Glarus. To the south of the Pre-Alps, forming a magnificent backdrop, are the glaciated summits of the High Alps, which slope down on the south, almost without transition, to the North Italian plain. On this side there are no limestone Alps preceding the main massif of ancient rocks.

The Alpine world of Switzerland is brought within reach by a dense network of roads and railways. Nature has created a pattern of valleys which provide access to the mountains and make possible the extension of human settlement to considerable altitudes. The valleys extend far into the

Vierwaldstättersee: Basin of the prehistoric Reuss glacier

mountains on a fairly gentle gradient. The fall of the rivers is sufficient, however, to enable them when the water level is high to bring down great quantities of rock debris which cover the whole floor of the valleys. The sides of the valleys are cut by deep gorges and gullies, filled after heavy rain by rushing mountain streams which also carry down quantities of weathered rock and debris, surging over their banks and any man-made barriers. The hillsices below these gullies, formed by the destructive force of nature, are indebted to nature also for their fertility.

The Alpine valleys were given their characteristic form during the Ice Age. Perhaps 20,000 years ago they were filled with great seas of ice reaching almost to the summit ridges of the mountains. and under the pressure of the ice the rock debris which had been carried down on the floor of the valleys took on a more or less pronounced U shape. Above the steep sides of these trough valleys are found terraces which are probably the remains of earlier valley floors (e.g. the Lauterbrunnen valley and Lake Uri). The side valleys were less deeply indented than the main ones, since the glaciers they contained were smaller, and in consequence their floors lie high above the main valley. The streams flowing down these "hanging valleys" tumble over the edge in the form of waterfalls (Giétro, in the Valais Alps; Giessbach near Brienz; Trümmelbach and Staubbach, Lauterbrunnen; Reichenbach, near Meiringen; falls in the Ticino valleys) or emerge from a dark enclosed gorge (Trient gorge, Valais; Medel gorge, Disentis). The floor of the main valley does not fall in a regular gradient but in stages or "steps". The drop between one step and another may be no more than a few metres, but is usually several hundred metres. The head of the valley is frequently a cirque enclosed by high rock walls.

Almost all the larger Alpine valleys have lakes near the foot of the mountain. Essentially, these are merely elongated basins within the valley, such as the 38 km/24 miles long Lake Lucerne which is a section of the Reuss valley. The bottom of the lake frequently goes down almost to sea-level

Ice Age formation

Lakes

15

and, in some cases, to considerably below sea-level as in Lake Maggiore. Smaller lakes are found right up to the highest stages in the valleys; sometimes, as on the Engstligenalp, they have been filled up by rock and soil and are now pastureland. The lakes were originally formed either by glacier action during the Ice Age or by a sinking of the mountain mass after the formation of the valleys which reversed the gradient at the mouth of a valley, thus damming the river and creating a lake.

The Swiss lakes, like the mountains, have become popular holiday areas, providing visitors during the warm periods of the year with bases from which they can make excursions into the mountains, the Mittelland and the towns; bathing is possible in most Swiss lakes. Switzerland has a total of 1484 natural lakes, the two largest of which, Lake Geneva and Lake Constance, are shared respectively with France and with Germany and Austria. In addition there are 44 man-made lakes, created for the purpose of producing hydroelectric power, which contribute to the beauty of the landscape in many areas. The largest of these is the Sihlsee in the canton of Schwyz (11 sq. km/4 sq. miles), while the Grande-Dixence dam in the canton of Valais is the highest gravity dam in the world (285 m/935 ft).

High mountains   Switzerland has none of the plateau-like high mountains found, for example, in Scandinavia. The various valley systems, each usually meeting on the summit ridge with a corresponding system on the other side, are separated by sharp ridges of variegated profile. The main rock mass is broken up by Kare – corries formed on the flanks of the ridge by small glaciers – into jagged arêtes and rugged towers and pinnacles. Where two corries meet on opposite sides of the ridge they form a breach in the summit line (Lücke, Joch, Furka, Fuorcia) between the towering peaks on either side.

Most of the high peaks are pyramids of crystalline rock with sharply defined edges, their varying form reflected in a variety of designations such as Horn, Stock, Dent, Aiguille, Piz, Becca, Poncione, etc. The rugged forms of the mountains are shaped not only by the action of rain and snow but by the daily variation in temperature, which has a particularly destructive effect at the highest altitudes. During the day the rock is heated by the sun and then sharply chilled during the night. In consequence the St Gotthard group, for example, is riven by deep clefts, and many ridges and summits are formed only of loosely bedded blocks, buttresses and tabular formations.

The differences in height between individual peaks in a group appear greater from below than they are in reality: there are only a few giant peaks which stand out from the rest, dominating the landscape. From a high viewpoint, on the other hand, hundreds of peaks fit together into a total picture: at these altitudes the view extends to distances at which differences in height of a few hundred metres are of little significance. Only the very highest peaks, including Mont Blanc, Monta Rosa, the Weisshorn, the Finsteraarhorn and Bernina, rise commandingly above the mass of mountains which appear to sink down from these few giants.

The geographical centre of the Swiss Alps is the St Gotthard massif, the water-tower of Europe, with the sources of the Rhine, the Rhône, the Reuss and the Ticino. The highest peaks in the Alps, however, are to be found in Valais, the Bernese Oberland and Grisons.

Alpine passes   The numerous passes in the Alps have since time immemorial provided means of passage through the mountains. During the Ice Age the sea of ice reached up to heights of over 2000 m/6560 ft in the interior of the Alps, and consequently the glaciers were able in places to gouge out a passage over the summit ridges and to enlarge it into a broad saddle. The ice-smoothed ridges of rock, the little lakes of clear dark water and the jagged peaks, unaffected by ice action, which rise above them give the St Gotthard, Bernina, Grimsel and other passes an atmosphere of Arctic desolation.

Many of the Alpine passes have a long history, which in some cases goes back to Roman times. The San Bernardino pass (Chur-Bellinzona) is almost always open throughout the winter. A drive over one of the great Alpine

Glacial Giants: The Gorner . . .　　　　*. . . and Findeln glaciers*

passes in good weather is a tremendous experience; and with the excellently maintained pass roads day trips are possible over many passes. In winter (November to May or June) many passes are closed. The Swiss Alps can be traversed from east to west by way of the Oberalp and Furka passes, via Andermatt; and the journey from Chur into Valais takes only a few hours, either by road or by rail.

The original sea of ice which many millenia ago covered the whole of the Mittelland and filled the Alpine valleys almost to the summit ridge of the mountains has left behind it about 140 glaciers, some of them steadily retreating, others still growing. The total area of all the Swiss glaciers is 1556 sq. km/601 sq. miles. The three largest are in Valais – the Aletsch glacier (area 117.5 sq. km/45 sq. miles, length 23.6 km/15 miles – the longest in Europe), the Gorner glacier at Zermatt (area 63.7 sq. km/25 sq. miles, length 14.5 km/9 miles) and the Fiesch glacier (area 39 sq. km/15 sq. miles, length 14.7 km/9 miles). The great majority of glaciers, however, are no more than a few dozen square kilometres in area.

Glaciers

At altitudes approaching 3000 m/10,000 ft and above the snow is largely permanent, since in the low air temperatures prevailing at these altitudes there is little melting. The layers of new snow change into the thinner but more compact layers, called "firn" or "névé", which in turn, under the weight of successive annual falls, becomes granular – but still stratified – glacier ice. The snow-line (the lower boundary of perpetual snow) lies between 3200 and 2500 m/10,500 and 8200 ft. The firn accumulates particularly at the heads of the highest valleys, where hundreds of metres of firn and ice may build up, forming the origin of the glaciers in the proper sense. Particularly characteristic of Switzerland are the "valley glaciers", some of which extend over several "steps" in the valley and may reach down almost to the 1000 m/3300 ft mark (Lower Grindelwald Glacier). Most of these glaciers, however, end at heights of between 1500 and 2000 m/5000 and 6500 ft, although they reach down to more than 1000 m/3300 ft below the snow-line.

More numerous than the valley glaciers, however, are the "mountainside glaciers" or "corrie glaciers" (Hanggletscher, Kargletscher) – glaciers clinging to the feared upper slopes, occupying hollows in the mountainside which are known as "corries" (Kare). On warm summer days parts of these overhanging glaciers frequently break off and thunder down into the valley in the form of avalanches.

Variations in the rate of movement in the glaciers (the central part having the fastest pace, up to 200 m/660 ft a year) lead to the formation of crevasses, which open and close according to the pulling action or the pressure of the ice. At the steeper places the glacier is broken up by large deep transverse crevasses which transform it into a chaos of vertical ice walls and towers, known by the Savoyard term "sérac". Where the bed of the glacier becomes wider, on the other hand, longitudinal crevasses open up. Wide glaciers of this kind may bear the designation of Eismeer ("sea of ice") and are usually flanked by lateral crevasses formed by friction against the sides of the valley, which frequently impede access to or return from the glacier. The rock debris which falls into the crevasses is carried down with the stones from the firn area to the melting tip of the glacier, where it emerges together with the ground moraine, material abraded by the movement of the glacier and splintered fragments of the rock bed. Still more rock debris is carried down by the moraines proper which run down the edges, and often also the middle, of the glacier. All this detritus eventually forms the horseshoe-shaped terminal moraine or is carried farther down by the melt water.

Avalanches

Snow is also carried down from the mountains by avalanches. In winter these take the form of dry "dust avalanches" generated by wind; in spring come the real avalanches, in which compact masses of ice break away and hurtle down into the valley. In the steep-sided transverse valleys of the Reuss and the Aare and in the Valais Alps great masses of avalanche snow can still be seen on the valley floor in summer, covered with stones and reddish earth and with foaming mountain streams running through them in a tunnel. The protective measures taken against avalanches (barriers, walls, lines of posts, belts of trees) can be seen particularly in the Upper Valais, in the Bedretto valley, on the St Gotthard railway and on the Albula railway at Bergün.

Watersheds

The main Swiss rivers – the Rhine, the Rhône, the Aare, the Reuss and the Ticino – rise in the St Gotthard area. The catchment areas of Swiss rivers are as follows: Rhine 36,494 sq. km/14,090 sq. miles (of which 8531 sq. km/3294 sq. miles are outside Switzerland), Rhône 10,403 sq. km/4017 sq. miles (3456 sq. km/1334 sq. miles), Inn 2150 sq. km/830 sq. miles (358 sq. km/138 sq. miles), Ticino 1616 sq. km/624 sq. miles, Poschiavino 238 sq. km/92 sq. miles.

67.7% of Swiss waters drain into the Atlantic, 27.9% into the Mediterranean and 4.4% into the Black Sea. The mean annual flow of the Rhine at Basle is 1026 cu. m/36,228 cu. ft per second.

The unique panorama of the Swiss Alps is shaped by two dozen peaks over 4000 m/13,000 ft, all first climbed between 1811 (Jungfrau, 4158 m/13,642 ft) and 1865 (Matterhorn, 4478 m/14,692 ft), and some 70 mountains rising to over 3000 m/10,000 ft. With three fifths of its area occupied by mountains, Switzerland ranks as Europe's "No. 2 Alpine state", first place being taken by Austria, where the Alps cover more than two-thirds of the country.

Climate

Taken as a whole, the populated areas of Switzerland have a cool, temperate and always humid climate; the higher mountainous regions, however, display many variations including icy climates. Broadly there are three climatic zones: in the northern side of the Alps (Jura and Mittelland), the inner Alpine region and the southern foot of the Alps.

Eight regional climate stations in Switzerland

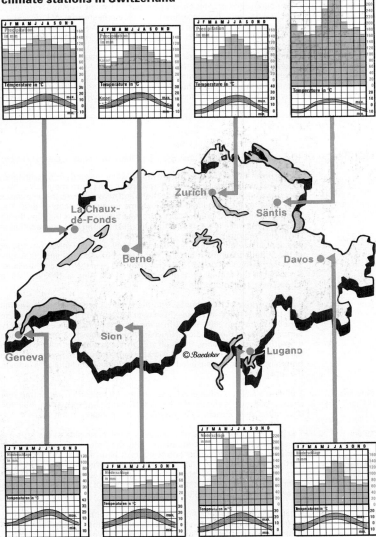

Explanations in text

Drawn by Prof. Dr. Wolfgang Hassenpflug

Climate

Climatic diagrams The climates experienced in the above regions are illustrated on page 19 by means of climatic diagrams of various places showing the annual range of temperature, precipitation and periods of sunshine (reading from left to right; J = January, D = December). The blue rain/snowfall columns show the precipitation (in mm) per month, as shown on the blue scale at the side. Temperatures are shown as an orange-red band. The upper edge corresponds to the average maximum day temperature, the lower the average minimum night temperature. The corresponding temperature figures can be read off the red scale at the side.

For the Jura region the climatic values for La-Chaux-de-Fonds have been chosen, for the Mittelland those of Bern, Geneva and Zurich, whilst for the inner Alpine region Säntis (climate in the upper mountains), Davos (mountain climate) and Sion (dry climate of the inner Alps) have been used, together with the climatic values of Lugano to illustrate the southern foot of the Alps.

North side of the Alps (Climatic stations: Bern, La-Chaux-de-Fonds, Geneva, Zurich)

On the north side of the Alps the prevailing westerly winds bring with them moist Atlantic air masses. Forced upwards by the Jura mountains, they cool down and produce cloud formations and heavy rain. As the air masses flow down to the Mittelland the air warms up again, becomes drier and there is less rain and cloud. As they proceed further across the Alps the air masses climb once more, resulting in increased cloud and precipitation in the higher regions of the Mittelland near to the Alps.

The annual rainfall in the Jura is between 1500 and 2000 mm/60 and 80 in, in the Mittelland where it adjoins in the east between 800 and 1000 mm/ 32 and 40 in, and 1000 and 1500 mm/40 and 60 in in the higher Mittelland. On average the rainfall on the north side of the Alps is 1200 mm/48 in spread over 140 days in the year.

Jura From the edges of the mountains to the inner parts the temperatures fall and the precipitation increases (from over 1200 mm/48 in per annum at the edges to more than 2000 mm/80 in in the upper regions). While the January temperatures on the east side (Neuchâtel) remain above freezing point and vine-growing is possible, the high trough valleys are extremely cold in winter (temperature reversal). The lowest temperatures in Switzerland are normally found in a basin filled with cold air in the Neuchâtel Jura – not in the Alps.

Mittelland The western and north-eastern parts of the Mittelland lie within the rain shadow of the Jura and the Black Forest (Geneva: 852 mm/34 ins over 104 days in the year, Zurich: 1136 mm/45 in over 134 days in the year).

Periods of sunshine The periods of winter sunshine enjoyed on the north side of the Alps are conspicuously short in comparison with the inner and southern Alps (Zurich 37 hours in December and 46 hours in January). The valley bottoms are then drowned under a deep sea of mist and suffer lower temperatures than the sunny uplands above the cloud cover (temperature reversal/inversion). Near the edge of the Alps the blankets of mist often lift for days on end, so this is a more pleasant place to stay.

Föhn A particular feature of the Alpine climate is the "föhn". This occurs mainly in spring and autumn, when a depression north of the Alps sucks air from a summit ridge south of the Alps. These comparatively moist and foggy air masses cool off as they ascend the southern side, forming clouds and heavy rain (as happens on the Jura when the wind blows from the west). Because of the warmth released by condensation the air cools only slightly as it rises, but its temperature is raised by 1° C for every 100 m/328 ft as it descends the northern side. Accompanied by squalls and storms, it then falls down into the valleys as an increasingly warm, dry and cloud-free wind. The edge of the cloud dispersal, the so-called "föhn wall", remains stationary above the central Alps, while to the north appears a band of blue sky, the "föhn window". The stronger the föhn the deeper it penetrates into the valleys and the Alpine foothills. Often it affects only the upper Mittelland (for example, in the canton of Appenzell), and the valleys remain under cold masses of air. The föhn is at its strongest in the "föhn lanes", that is in the great Rhône, Reuss or Rhine valleys leading out of the Alps; for example, it is felt in Altdorf on 64 days in the year.

The effects of the föhn are many: it increases the average temperatures (Altdorf has a January temperature almost 2° higher than Winterthur, which is at the same altitude but on the other side of the mountain); it encourages the ripening of the fruit in the fields (warms the grapes); it melts the snow, as much on some days as it would take the sun 14 days to do; it causes a lot of damage through storms and spreading fire, especially in villages of timber construction. Not least is its effect on the well-being of the human body. For example, during föhn weather conditions, there are increases in migraine attacks, blood circulation problems and extreme changes in mood.

Inner Alps (Climatic stations: Säntis, Davos, Sion)

Overall, the Alps show marked differences in climate between north and south. As a result the inner Alpine valleys, especially the upper ones, being higher and protected on all sides, have a unique climatic character, quite different from that of the outer valleys and lowlands.

Generally, as you go higher the temperature falls by 0.5° C per 100 m/328 ft, but by less in winter, or even the other way round where temperature reversal prevails. Humidity, cloud and rainfall, on the other hand, increase with altitude, while the deep valleys are very dry. The wettest region in all Switzerland (the peaks around Mönchsgrat and Monte Rosa, with an annual rainfall of up to 4100 mm/160 in) lies scarcely 40 km/25 miles from the driest (Visp in Valais, with only 529 mm/21 in). **Temperatures and precipitation**

The proportion of the precipitation which falls as snow also increases the higher you go (Lugano 5%, Davos 40%, Säntis 72% and, at heights above 3,500 m/11,500 ft, 100% of the annual fall). Falls of fresh snow total 5 m/16 ft in Davos and as much as 19 m/62 ft in Säntis. At an altitude of 700 m/2300 ft the snow remains for three months, whilst at 1800 m/6000 ft it remains for eight and at 2500 m/8200 ft for more than ten months. At above 2800 m/ 9200 ft in the northern Alps and 3300 m/10,800 ft in the southern Alps the snow remains all through the year.

It is true, of course, that less falls in the valleys and basins of the inner Alps than in the northern foothills, but nevertheless the night temperatures there, especially when there is a blanket of snow, drop well below freezing point and in fact reach temperatures normally experienced only in the peak regions. The intervening slopes are less cold, so the main health resorts lie on mountain terraces and midway up the slopes.

In winter there is a minimum of cloud and rain or snow, with long periods of sunshine, at a time when the lowlands are often completely overcast. Heat and ultra-violet rays noticeably increase, as the air is very dry. **Periods of sunshine**

Wind speeds remain low. In summer the sun and heat from the upper sides of the valleys give rise to a valley wind which blows up the slopes and causes clouds to form above the peaks during the morning. During the evenings and nights, on the other hand, the cooled masses of air roll downhill towards the valleys in the form of a mountain wind, while the clouds disappear above the peaks. Generally, the valley wind is characteristically stronger than the mountain wind. The strength of the wind is clearly demonstrated in, for example, Valais, by the clumps of trees bent over to point up the mountainsides (wind deformity). **Winds**

Therapeutic
factors

Because of their climatic attractions and therapeutic benefits the inner Swiss Alps are particularly suitable for health cures, especially in winter. The different combinations of climate to be found in the many spas means there is an excellent choice to meet individual therapeutic needs. The climatic diagram for Davos, for instance, shows a marked increase in hours of sunshine from February to March, so that although there will be sharp frosts at night and low air temperatures by day you can still count on getting a tan in the warm sunshine.

Southern foot of the Alps (Climatic station: Lugano)

Temperatures
and periods of
sunshine

The southern foot of the Alps (Ticino) lies in the lee of the prevailing north-westerly winds. This is where the air masses, which brought rain and snow to the northern side of the Alps and to the central heights, make their way downhill again, resulting in reduced precipitation and cloud. In particular, the period of winter sunshine is greater than anywhere else in the country, even more than in Davos, and is exceeded only on some peaks such as on the Säntis. The predominantly mild, sunny and mist-free winter produces vegetation some of which has an almost Mediterranean look about it, even though the heat and aridity typical of the Mediterranean climate are lacking. In summer, six to seven days in each of the months of July and August are sultry. The nights, however, are always pleasantly cool and the fresh lake breezes on sunny days and the cool north winds ensure a pleasant atmosphere.

Precipitation

The fall of rain and snow at the southern foot of the Alps is about one-third higher than that on the northern side of the Alps (1800 mm/72 in per annum instead of 1200 mm/48 in), with the greatest amounts falling in summer. Conversely, however, the number of hours and days when it rains or snows is smaller in the south than in the north (Lugano 107, Zurich 134 days per annum). In fact, a large part takes the form of intensive, thundery showers lasting only a short time. As a result, the summer months with the heaviest rainfall are also those blessed with the longest periods of sunshine. When there is a föhn in the northern Alps there is heavy rain on the southern foot of the mountains.

Flora and Fauna

The plants of Switzerland are abundant and varied. From the sub-tropical warmth of Lake Lugano to the snow-clad regions of the High Alps, the country has areas belonging to every zone of plant life in Europe. Particularly notable for its variety of form and splendour of colour is the Alpine flora, which contrives to exist and to flourish in the most rigorous climatic conditions, with temperatures which may rise to 40° C (104° F) during the day and freeze hard when the rocks cool down at night. Among the species are rhododendron, gentian, Alpine pansy, primula, globe-flower, silver thistle, soldanella, martagon lily, Alpine aster, and in the rockier regions edelweiss, Alpine poppy, glacier buttercup and a variety of saxifrages.

Protected Plants

Of Switzerland's more than 3000 flowering plants and ferns 160 are fully or partially protected by law. A federal law provides for the protection of plants and their habitat, but the executive regulations are the responsibility of the cantons, since the plants vary from area to area. Fully protected plants may not be picked or uprooted; in the case of partially protected plants picking is permitted within reasonable limits, but such plants or flowers may not be sold or supplied commercially.

Fauna

The animal life of Switzerland is very similar to that of other Central European countries. The country's stock of game includes some 110,000 roe deer, 70,000 chamois, 20,000 red deer, 9000 ibex and 100 recently established sika deer from Asia. Stocks of pheasants, hares and partridges are released every year. Marmots are to be found all over the Alps.

Among the species protected by federal law are: hedgehog, beaver, brown bear, otter, wild cat, lynx, ibex, black grouse, capercaillie, hazel hen, eagles, falcons, owls, nutcracker, jackdaw, Alpine chough, turtledoves and rock doves, swans, curlew, black-tailed godwit, sandpipers, rails (except the coot), snow finch and numerous less common species.

Protected Animals

Regulations on shooting and fishing vary from canton to canton. More than half the cantons issue individual shooting licences (some 20,000 of which are in force); the others lease particular areas to shooting clubs.

Shooting and Fishing

The height limits for plants, animals and human settlement vary according to climatic conditions. In the northern Alps vines are grown in certain areas up to 550 m/1800 ft, and above this is the zone of deciduous forest, which in these areas can be regarded also as the highest level of agricultural use of the land. In favourable situations the beech grows at levels of 1500 m/5000 ft or over; and this is also the height reached by permanent human settlements, mostly small villages, which are more commonly found on the sheltered fringes of the valley floor than on hillsides or hill terraces. The growing of corn, which was once practised in these areas with rather meagre results, was almost completely abandoned in the 19th c. In consequence, increased attention has been given to the flower-spangled pastures and the fruit-trees which grow at heights up to 900 m/3000 ft.

Height Zones

The next zone, some 1300 to 1700 or 1800 m/4300 to 5600 or 6000 ft, is dominated by coniferous forest, with patches of mountain pasture, which is cut in summer, in the clearings. Deciduous trees are represented by the beautiful maples which grow around the log huts and barns of the mountain-dwellers.

At altitudes between 1600 and 1700 m/5250 and 5600 ft the dense forest ceases, and only the sturdiest spruces and stone pines survive in proud

Alpine marmots

isolation. The last outposts of the forest are alders and mountain pines. The lower-growing plants flourish in the summer warmth of the soil, the tough short-stemmed species form a vigorous mantle of turf. This is the real "Alp", the mountain pasture to which the stock is brought in summer and on which the herdsmen have their characteristic huts.

Higher still there are only meagre strips of grass between the areas of scree and the rocky crags. Then the patches of firn and the remains of avalanches become increasingly numerous, and between 2800 and 3000 m/9200 and 9850 ft the snow-line is reached. Even in the zone of perpetual snow, however, plant life does not completely disappear. The glacier buttercup is found at heights of over 3000 m/9850 ft, and even on the high tops lichens cover the sunny rock faces with their patterns of colour.

In Valais and the Engadine all these various zones reach unusually high, owing to the favoured climate of these areas as a result of the upthrust of the mountain masses and to the warm and dry conditions in their sheltered valleys. In these areas there are still cornfields as well as pastureland, and, exceptionally, rye and potatoes are grown as high as 1900 m/6200 ft (Chandolin).

In Ticino vines are grown on stone and timber frames up to a height of some 600 m/2000 ft, and early flowering almonds and peaches and chestnuts are cultivated up to 1000 m/3300 ft. Above this is a zone of spruce, larch and stone pine; then, as on the north side of the Alps, the mountain pastures begin at 1800 m/6000 ft and the snow at 2800 m/9200 ft.

Swiss National Park

The Swiss National Park, in the canton of Grisons, is a federal plant and animal reserve with an area of 159 sq. km/61 sq. miles.

Population

General

The historical development of Switzerland, during which influences from the neighbouring areas of German, French and Italian culture mingled with survivals from the Roman and pre-Roman periods, is reflected in the composition and characteristics of its population.

Languages of Switzerland

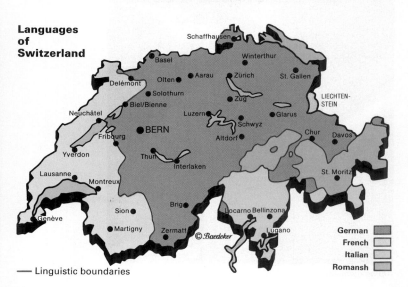

German
French
Italian
Romansh

—— Linguistic boundaries

24

At the present time the country has over 6.5 million inhabitants, with an annual growth rate of 0.7%; some 15.2% of the resident population are foreigners.

The overall population density is 157 per sq. km/406 per sq. mile. In accordance with the nature of the countryside, however, the population is spread unevenly across the country. The most densely populated part is the Mittelland (250 per sq. km/648 per sq. mile), where the cantons of Zug, Nidwalden and Ticino have shown the most marked growth during the past decade, whereas the cantons of Basel-Land, Neuchâtel and Schaffhausen have suffered the greatest reductions. These changes arise from the recession on the one hand, coupled with a general trend towards moving out of the cities and into the surrounding countryside. The root causes of this phenomenon, the very opposite of the classical flight from the land found elsewhere, lie in the tendency for more and more service industries (banks, insurance companies and office buildings) to move out of the towns and cities, together with a radical increase in land prices and the growing noise of traffic in the city centres. Although the large cities remain fairly big (Zurich 357,000 inhabitants. Basle 177,000, Geneva 159,000, Bern 142,000), more than half the total population lives in "new towns" or urban regions (more than 10,000 inhabitants). In the Alpine regions, for obvious geographical reasons, the density is very low (about 30 per sq. km/78 to the sq. mile).

Population Density and Spread

Since population growth has not kept pace with economic development Switzerland has had to bring in foreign labour, mainly from Italy and Spain. A big increase in their numbers produced a fear in the seventies of "swamping", leading to a tightening of the regulations governing immigration and the granting of citizenship. The law relating to foreigners passed in 1980 created a new legal concept in Swiss foreign policy, together with changes in the periods in which seasonal workers may stay in the country. In 1981 the so-called Mitenand-Initiative, which had as its aim an improvement in the position of foreigners working in Switzerland, suffered defeat after a referendum set up for the purpose. In April 1987 a fresh referendum approved the revision of the law governing asylum and foreigners.

Foreigners

A striking indication of the heterogenous population structure is the multilingual character of the country. Some three-quarters of the Swiss speak German, a fifth French, 4% Italian and 1% Romansch or Rhaeto-Romanic. All four languages are recognised for official purposes throughout the country.

Language

Although in schools and in correspondence in the German-speaking parts of the country standard German is used, with the occasional form peculiar to Switzerland, the spoken language is a quite distinctive tongue, Schwyzerdütsch or Swiss German, derived from the old Alemannic (West Germanic) language and diversified into a series of local and regional dialects. The use of Schwyzerdütsch is deliberately cultivated, and on radio and television, and even in the political and military fields, it is strongly preferred to standard German at every level including the highest.

"Swiss German" (Schwyzerdütsch)

The Swiss forms of French (in western Switzerland or Suisse Romande) and Italian (in the canton of Ticino and some valleys in Grisons) differ only slightly – mainly in intonation – from standard French and Italian. A notable feature of Swiss French (as of Belgian and Canadian French) is the divergent formation of certain numbers (70 = septante instead of soixante-dix, 80 = huitante or octante instead of quatre-vingts, 90 = nonante instead of quatre-vingt-dix).

French, Italian

Rhaeto-Romanic, a language derived from Vulgar Latin which is spoken in a number of dialectal forms in Grisons, has also been officially recognised

Rhaeto-Romanic or Romansch

25

since 1938 as an independent language. The main dialects of Romansch are Surselvian, Sutselvian, Surmeirian and the forms spoken in Unterhalbstein, Oberhalbstein, Oberengadin and Unterengadin (the Upper and Lower Engadine).Closely related to these dialects are the Ladin and Friulian spoken in South Tirol. The general written language of Rumantsh Grischun, developed in 1982 by Prof. H. Schmid, represents a compromise between the main idioms of Surselvian, Ladin and Surmeirian.

Religious beliefs   Another result of differing development in the various parts of the country is the diverse pattern of religious belief. Today 44% of the population are Protestants (protesting the special form of Protestantism established by Zwingli and Calvin) and 48% Roman Catholics. 0.3% belong to the Old Catholic Church of Christ, the same number as those of the Jewish faith.

Government and Society

Confoederatio Helvetica (Swiss Confederation)

The official (Latin) designation of the Swiss Confederation is Confoederatio Helvetica: hence the letters CH to be seen on Swiss cars and in Swiss post codes.

The name of the country (in German "Schweiz", French "Suisse", Italian "Svizzera", Romansch "Svizera") comes from the canton of Schwyz, and was originally applied only to central or inner Switzerland, i.e. the three cantons of Uri, Schwyz and Unterwalden, which laid the foundations of the Confederation when they formed a perpetual alliance on the Rütli meadow by Lake Lucerne in 1291. From the 14th to the 16th c., as the number of cantons joining the alliance increased, the term confederation (Eidgenossenschaft) was preferred; but in the end the designation of Schweiz or Switzerland became generally accepted. The official name of the state, Swiss Confederation, combines both forms.

Swiss Flag

The Swiss National Flag depicts a white cross on a red ground: the arms of the cross are of equal length, each arm being one-sixth longer than it is broad.

Reversing the colours produces the flag of the Red Cross, the organisation which came into being in 1863–1866 as a result of the efforts of Henri Dunant.

Federal Constitution

It may at first appear surprising to an outsider that a state which has developed out of a medley of different ethnic groups should have become the very symbol of stability and harmony; but on closer observation it will be seen that the Swiss communes, the cantons and the Confederation as a whole owe their democratic strength to this very diversity and to the preservation of a federal structure which has eschewed the centralisation of authority. An essential element in Swiss attitudes, too, is the proverbial neutrality of Switzerland, stemming from the Peace of Paris of November 1815.

Extensive rights of self-government, practical participation in the reaching of political decisions and the basic human rights and freedoms are the foundations of Swiss democracy.

The federal constitution of 1848 converted the previous federation of states into a single federal state with a common postal service, army, legislature and judiciary and without any customs or commercial barriers. The new form of union was then approved by all the then existing cantons.

Communes

The smallest unit in the administrative structure is the Commune, of which there are over 3000. They are independent bodies which settle their own budgets and fix their own taxes. The communal or municipal councils are directly elected, usually for a four-year term.

Cantons

Since Jan. 1st 1979 Switzerland has had 26 cantons (20 full cantons and six half-cantons: see page 28), whose independence is enshrined in the

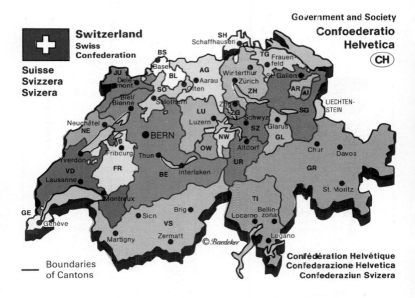

Switzerland
Swiss Confederation

Suisse
Svizzera
Svizera

Government and Society

Confoederatio
Helvetica
(CH)

Boundaries
of Cantons

Confédération Helvétique
Confederazione Helvetica
Confederaziun Svizera

Area and Population

	Cantons	Area in sq. km (sq. miles)	Population (1990)		Cantons	Area in sq. km (sq. miles)	Population (1990)
AG	Aargau	1405 (542)	472,000		Unterwalden:		
AR	Appenzell-Ausserhoden	243 (94)	49,300	NW	Nidwalden	276 (107)	31,000
				OW	Obwalden	491 (190)	27,600
AI	Appenzell-Innerrhoden	172 (66)	13,100	SG	St Gallen	2014 (778)	403,900
				SH	Schaffhausen	298 (115)	69,800
BL	Basel-Land	428 (165)	225,800	SZ	Schwyz	908 (351)	103,400
BS	Basel-Stadt	37 (14)	194,300	SO	Solothurn	791 (305)	219,500
BE	Berne	6050 (2335)	925,500	TG	Thurgau	1013 (391)	192,400
FR	Fribourg	1670 (645)	194,700	TI	Ticino	2811 (1085)	277,200
GE	Geneva	282 (109)	363,600	UR	Uri	1076 (415)	33,500
GL	Glarus	685 (264)	36,600	VS	Valais	5226 (2018)	232,600
GR	Grisons	7106 (2744)	166,500	VD	Vaud	3219 (1243)	550,300
JU	Jura	837 (323)	64,700	ZG	Zug	239 (92)	81,600
LU	Lucerne	1492 (576)	306,100	ZH	Zurich	1729 (668)	1,131,500
NE	Neuchâtel	797 (308)	156,200	CH	Swiss Confederation	41,293 (15,943)	6,523,400

The Cantons of the Swiss Confederation

 Aargau (AG)
Canton since 1803
Capital: Aarau

 Appenzell-Ausserrhoden (AR)
Half-canton since 1513
Capital: Herisau

 Appenzell-Innerrhoden (AI)
Half-canton since 1513
Capital: Appenzell

 Basel-Land (BL)
Half-canton since 1501
Capital: Liestal

 Basel-Stadt (BS)
Half-canton since 1501
Capital: Basle

 Berne (BE)
Canton since 1353
Capital: Berne

 Fribourg (FR)
Canton since 1481
Capital: Fribourg

 Geneva (GE)
Canton since 1815
Capital: Geneva

 Glarus (GL)
Canton since 1352
Capital: Glarus

 Grisons (GR)
Canton since 1803
Capital: Chur

 Jura (JU)
Canton since 1979
Capital: Delémont

 Lucerne (LU)
Canton since 1332
Capital: Lucerne

 Neuchâtel (NE)
Canton since 1815
Capital: Neuchâtel

 Nidwalden (NW)
Half-canton since 1291
Capital: Stans

 Obwalden (OW)
Half-canton since 1291
Capital: Sarnen

 St Gallen (SG)
Canton since 1803
Capital: St Gallen

 Schaffhausen (SH)
Canton since 1501
Capital: Schaffhausen

 Schwyz (SZ)
Canton since 1291
Capital: Schwyz

 Solothurn (SO)
Canton since 1481
Capital: Solothurn

 Thurgau (TG)
Canton since 1803
Capital: Frauenfeld

 Ticino(TI)
Canton since 1803
Capital: Bellinzona

 Uri (UR)
Canton since 1291
Capital: Altdorf

 **Valais** (VS)
Canton since 1815
Capital: Sion

 Vaud (VD)
Canton since 1803
Capital: Lausanne

 Zug (ZG)
Canton since 1352
Capital: Zug

 Zurich (ZH)
Canton since 1351
Capital: Zurich

Unterwalden

Landsgemeinde (local parliament) in Glarus

constitution. They are real states with their own constitutions, legislatures, executives and judiciaries. Legislative power rests with the people or with a parliament elected by them (Great Council, Cantonal Council, Provincial Council). The cantonal executive is known as the Governing Council, the Smaller Council, the State Council or the Permanent Committee.

In the cantons of Appenzell, Glarus and Unterwalden the cantonal assembly ("Landesgemeinde") of local citizens still meets frequently in the open air to exercise the votes enjoyed by each participant.

The coats-of-arms of the individual cantons can be seen, for example, on car licence-plates and cyclists' tax-discs.

The Swiss cantons are incorporated in the "Confederation", which has a two-chamber legislature, the Federal Assembly, French, consisting of the National Council, which represents the people, and the Council of States composed of representatives of the cantons. The 200 seats in the National Council are distributed among the cantons in proportion to population, with a minimum of one seat for each canton or half-canton. Each full canton sends two and each half-canton one member to the Council of States. The decisions of the Federal Assembly come into effect only after both chambers have approved them by a majority vote.

Federal Assembly (Legislative)

Executive power is in the hands of the Federal Council consisting of seven members elected by a joint meeting of both chambers of the Federal Assembly for a four-year term. In the selection of members attention is paid to the interests of linguistic, ethnic and geographical minorities. No canton may have more than one member of the Council.

Federal Council (Executive)

The Federal President is chosen from the ranks of the Federal Council and holds office for a year, during which he continues to be responsible for his ministerial department. The Federal Council renders an account of its activity annually to the Federal Assembly.

Federal President

Education and Science

Basic Rights

Every Swiss elector (from the age of 20) is entitled to participate in the affairs of his commune by virtue of the basic rights guaranteed by the constitution – equality before the law, freedom of conscience and religious belief, freedom of establishment, freedom of the press, freedom of association and freedom of trade.

The people of Switzerland can exert an important degree of influence on national policy through the mechanisms of the "initiative" and the "referendum". An amendment in the constitution can be effected by an initiative of at least 100,000 votes. At least 50,000 voters or eight cantons can demand the approval of a federal law passed by both chambers or of generally binding federal decisions by means of a plebiscite (known as a facultative referendum). Any change in the constitution must be approved by a majority of the people and the Council of States (obligatory referendum).

Defence of the Realm

The federal army is a militia based on universal military service between the ages of 20 and 50. After serving their time members of the forces keep their equipment (including weapons) at home and must take part in periodic shooting practice and put in an annual period of training. There is no provision for performing civilian service in place of military service.

Swiss Guard

A relic of earlier centuries when many Swiss took service with other states is the Swiss Guard, which still serves as the Papal guard in the Vatican City in Rome.

International organisations

Numerous international organisations have their headquarters in neutral Switzerland. Although, following a referendum in 1986, the country is not a member of the main United Nations Organisation, it does belong to almost all the important independent subsidiary organisations of UNO. For example, the following bodies have their headquarters in Geneva: the Food and Agriculture Organisation (FAO), the General Agreement on Tariffs and Trade (GATT), the International Labour Organisation (ILO), the World Health Organisation (WHO), the United Nations Educational, Scientific and Cultural Organisation (UNESCO), the United Nations Industrial Development Organisation and numerous UNO sub-bodies (UNICEF, United Nations Development Programme, United Nations Environmental Programme, etc.). Switzerland is also a member of the European Free Trade Association (EFTA), the Council of Europe and the Organisation for Economic Cooperation and Development (OECD). Since 1977 Switzerland has had a free trade agreement with the European Community (EC).

Geneva is also the seat of the International Committee of the Red Cross, the members of which are all Swiss citizens. This institution is responsible for upholding the four Geneva Conventions, promotes humanitarian international law and organises help in the event of natural catastrophes.

Education and Science

General

"Head, heart and hand" were the three elements identified by the Swiss educationalist Johann Heinrich Pestalozzi (1746–1827) as requiring training; and the objectives which he set out so clearly not only influenced the development of the Swiss school system but also aroused wide international interest – forming the basis, for example, of Wilhelm von Humboldt's reform of the Prussian educational system in 1810. Johann Wolfgang von Goethe, who visited Switzerland three times, expressed the view that this was where "thought based on sound common-sense" originated.

During the early medieval period the main centres of education and culture were the episcopal sees (Sion, Chur, Geneva, Lausanne, Basle, Konstanz, now in Germany) from the 6th c. onwards, followed later by the monastic houses (St Maurice, St Gallen: Reichenau, in Germany). At the height of the Middle Ages the cultural importance of the towns increased. Powerful new impulses came from the Councils of Constance (1414–18) and Basle

University of Zurich . . .   *. . . University of Geneva*

(1431–39). Basle was also the centre of Swiss humanism, and Erasmus was active here between 1521 and 1529. The humanists were the first to show an awareness of national identity. The Reformers Ulrich Zwingli (1484–1531) in Zurich and Jean Calvin (1509–64) in Geneva gave fresh stimulus to intellectual and religious life in Switzerland. Later the Enlightenment directed the main currents of thought, in Switzerland as in other countries, towards the exact sciences.

Education was slow in reaching the broad mass of the population. In the early days it was in the hands of the Church, and the ability to read and write was until the High Middle Ages a privilege reserved for a small élite. The need for a wide expansion of basic education came to the fore only at the Reformation and Counter-Reformation, with the vigorous new impulses which they gave to human thought. Then, in the 18th and 19th centuries, the Swiss educational systems advanced and developed under the influence of Jean-Jacques Rousseau (1712–78) and the great educationalist Johann Heinrich Pestalozzi. **School System**

The Swiss constitution of 1848 assigns the main responsibility for education to the cantons, which share it with the communes. A constitutional amendment making education a joint responsibility of the Confederation and the cantons was rejected by a national referendum in 1972. Only vocational training falls within the competence of the Confederation.

Switzerland also has some 350 private and boarding schools, many of them with an international reputation. Some of these – like some of the Swiss universities – run special holiday courses for both Swiss and foreign students.

Higher education is also, in general, the responsibility of the cantons. The Confederation is responsible only for the Federal Colleges of Technology in Zurich (opened 1855) and Lausanne (opened in 1853 as a private college for road and civil engineers and taken over by the Confederation in 1969). There are cantonal universities at Basle (founded 1460), Berne (1834), **Universities**

31

Fribourg (1889), Geneva (1873), Lausanne (1890), Neuchâtel (1909) and Zurich (1833), together with the School of Economic and Social Sciences in St Gallen (1899). There is also a private Theological Faculty (1878) in Lucerne.

The massive increase in student numbers has strained the resources of the cantons responsible for universities, and has led these cantons to put forward claims for federal aid and for contributions from other cantons related to the number of students from those cantons. In addition to the universities there are numbers of technical colleges throughout the country. The total number of students at Swiss higher educational establishments is some 77,000, including 11,000 foreign students.

Research and Development

As the OECD noted in a report, expenditure on research in Switzerland is well above the international average. There is a well-established division of function between public and private agencies, with the state accepting responsibility for the running of academic institutions, while the main costs of research, particularly in the natural sciences, are borne by the private sector. The state is thus unable to exert any major influence on research and development. Here, as in other fields of Swiss life, the trend towards decentralisation can be observed.

Swiss Nobel Prize Winners

1901	Henri Dunant	Nobel Peace Prize
1902	Elie Ducommun	Nobel Peace Prize
1902	Albert Gobat	Nobel Peace Prize
1909	Theodor Kocher	Medicine
1913	Alfred Werner	Chemistry
1919	Carl Spitteler	Literature
1920	Charles-Eduard Guillaume	Physics
1937	Paul Karrer	Chemistry
1939	Leopold Ružička	Chemistry
1945	Wolfgang Pauli	Physics
1946	Hermann Hesse	Literature
1948	Paul Müller	Medicine
1949	Walter Rudolf Hess	Medicine
1950	Tadeusz Reichstein	Medicine
1975	Vladimir Prelog	Chemistry
1978	Werner Arber	Medicine
1986	Heinrich Rohrer	Physics
1987	Karl Alexander Müller	Physics

Economy

General

Switzerland is poorly supplied with minerals and raw materials, and accordingly was compelled from an early stage to turn to the processing industries, commerce and the services sector. The market is characterised by a wide range of products, the result of decentralisation, high quality products and widely distributed capital wealth.

The country possessed scarcely 3.3 million wage-earners in 1987 (of whom 23% were foreigners, including seasonal workers and international commuters), 55.5% being in the service industries. While the number of new jobs in the service sector has continued to increase since the seventies, those in manufacturing industry and agriculture have fallen, just as in other European countries. Only 6.5% still work in agriculture. 38% continue in industry, but additional automation, transferring production to more cost-favourable countries and structural streamlining all lead to a relative reduction in the numbers of industrial workers in absolute terms. In 1986 the Gross National Product increased to 254,510 million Swiss francs, a nominal increase of 4.8% compared with the previous year; in real terms, i.e. after allowing for inflation, the growth was only 0.7%. The number of unemployed, which in 1984 stood at 35,100, the highest since the thirties, fell to under 25,000 by 1987, while the number of jobs on offer increased by 50% to around 12,000 over the same period.

Nestlé headquarters in Vevey

In spite of the difficulty of communication in this mountainous land – a
handicap for a country so heavily dependent on imports – Switzerland's
principal source of income is industry, which employs 38% of the working
population and accounts for around 40% of the GNP. This industry, however, mainly medium and small firms with high quality, individual products, is distributed all over the country, with none of the industrial con-
centrations found in Britain, Germany or Belgium. Even industrial focal
points like Basle, St. Gallen, Zurich, Winterthur and La Chaux-de-Fonds are
poles apart from the traditional idea of dirty and pollution-ridden factory
towns. However, the fact that risks to the environment exist here too was
demonstrated by two serious chemical accidents which occurred recently
in the Basle area, at the firms of Sandoz and Ciba-Geigy, causing con-
tamination to the Rhine as far as the North Sea.

In comparison with other European countries Swiss industry operates
under most unfavourable conditions. The country's land-locked situation
increases freight costs; the high living standard calls for high wages; and
production costs are higher because of the lack of local raw materials and
fuels. Faced with these difficulties, Swiss industry must compete in foreign
markets not by offering lower prices but by the quality of its products.
Economically, Switzerland is one of the group of Western European industrial countries which depends essentially on exchanging its finished products for raw materials and foodstuffs from other countries.

The main branches of industry are the highly developed and highly export-
orientated chemicals and pharmaceuticals (concentrated mainly in the
Basle area), engineering and armaments (Zurich, Winterthur, Oerlikon,
Schaffhausen, Baden, Geneva), metalworking, instruments and apparatus,
leather, plastics and textiles, the graphic trades and foodstuffs.

The traditional watchmaking industry (concentrated in La Chaux-de-
Fonds) is also of great importance. In spite of its quartz technology, the
tremendous growth in digital electronics meant that, at the end of the
seventies, the Swiss watch industry found itself in serious competition with

Industry

*Modern Swiss
watch designs*

33

Swiss Banking company in Basle   *Upland cattle on the Julier Pass*

foreign suppliers (especially Japan). Changes in manufacturing methods (e.g., fully-automatic production based on the modular construction system) and new projects such as the "Swatch" made by the SMH Group (Société Suisse de Microélectronique et d'Horlogerie) have meant that sales figures have markedly increased again since the middle of the eighties.

Industrial products account for some four-fifths of Switzerland's total exports. The largest industrial firms include Nestlés (foodstuffs) in Cham and Vevey, Ciba-Geigy (chemicals and pharmaceuticals), Roche (chemicals and pharmaceuticals) and Sandoz (chemicals and pharmaceuticals) in Basle, Brown Boveri (electrical engineering) in Baden, Alusuisse (metal-working) in Chippis and Zurich, Sulzer (engineering) in Winterthur, Oerlikon-Bührle (engineering, armaments) and Jacobs (foodstuffs) in Zurich and Holderbank (cement) in Glarus.

Energy

In the field of energy Switzerland is again almost wholly dependent on imports. Electric power is an exception: some 61% of electrical energy (net output 1986: 54,419 million kilowatt-hours) comes from nearly 450 hydro-electric power stations, some 37% in the country's five nuclear power stations and only 2% from oil-fuelled thermal power stations. Roughly a third of the output is available for export. Alternative sources of energy come from a large number of solar-energy installations, electrical heat pumps, wind-generators and bio-gas plants. A national referendum taken in the spring of 1988 agreed to restrict the use of nuclear energy.

Services sector

The services sector continues to grow in importance. Catering for the Swiss desire for material security, the country boasts an established insurance industry formed of companies which enjoy an international reputation and obtain the bulk of their premium income from abroad.

Particular mention must be made of the many, newly-formed service institutions in the administrative sphere which – partly in close collabora-

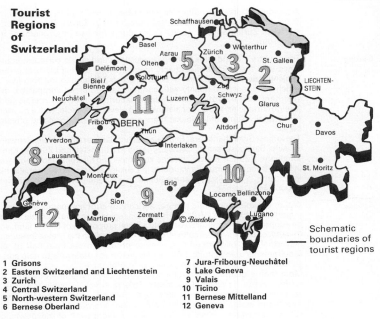

Tourist Regions of Switzerland

Schematic boundaries of tourist regions

1 Grisons
2 Eastern Switzerland and Liechtenstein
3 Zurich
4 Central Switzerland
5 North-western Switzerland
6 Bernese Oberland
7 Jura-Fribourg-Neuchâtel
8 Lake Geneva
9 Valais
10 Ticino
11 Bernese Mittelland
12 Geneva

tion with industry, partly fully independently – offer highly complex financial plans for building, production and organisational projects.

The biggest insurance companies in Switzerland include the Zurich, the Swiss Re, Vita, Helvetia Personal Accident and Pensions Company (Helvetia Unfall und Rentenanstalt) in Zurich, Winterthur Insurance and Winterthur Life in Winterthur, Basle Insurance, Basle Life and Patria Life in Basle.

The biggest commercial firms in the Transport and Services sectors are: PTT (postal and communications services) in Bern, Danzas (haulage) in Basle, Kühne & Nagel (haulage) in Pfäffikon, SBB (railways) with its headquarters in Bern, Swissair (air services) in Zurich, Panalpina (haulage) in Binningen, Wienerwald Schweiz (hotels and restaurants) in Feusiberg, Publicitas (press advertising) in Lausanne, Kuoni (travel agency) in Zurich and Adia Interim (temporary employment agency) in Lausanne.

The industrial and services sector form the framework for trade and commerce which, given the high level of imports and exports, also plays a very important part in the economy. The balance of trade is still in deficit, but exports have shown a marked expansion since 1985 (mainly consumer durables such as watches, aircraft, medical instruments and apparatus machinery for paper-making and printing, yarns and textiles) mainly as the result of increased demand from the United States and the EEC countries. The biggest commercial companies include Migros (foodstuffs and non-food goods) in Zurich, Co-op (foodstuffs and non-food goods) in Basle, AMAG (motor vehicles) and Jelmoli (chain of department stores) in Zurich, Usego (foodstuffs and non-food goods) in Egerkingen, Globus (chain of

Commerce and Trade

department stores) and Siber Hegner (international trading company) in Zurich, Shell Switzerland (petroleum products) in Zurich, Denner (foodstuffs) in Zurich as well as VOLG (products for use in agriculture) in Winterthur.

Banking

The country's world-wide trading connections and stable currency, combined with the strict confidentiality maintained by the banks, have given banking a dominant position in Switzerland. In addition to the "big five", which are concerned mainly with commercial and credit companies, investment administration and trade in securities, precious metals and foreign currencies, the cantonal banks also play a major role, with a quarter of the total volume of business; there are also regional, local and private banks.

The largest Swiss banks are: Schweizerischer Bankverein in Basle, Schweizerische Bankgesellschaft, Schweizerische Kreditanstalt and Zürcher Kantonalbank in Zurich, Schweizerische Volksbank and Kantonalbank von Bern in Bern, Banque Cantonale Vaudoise in Lausanne, Luzerner Kantonalbank in Lucerne, St Gallische Kantonalbank in St Gallen and Crédit Foncier Vaudois in Lausanne.

Agriculture

Within the total economic picture, agriculture is of comparatively small importance (4% of the GNP). The mountain regions are unfavourable to the development of agriculture, with only a small proportion of usable land, so that reasonably intensive cultivation is possible only in the Alpine foreland. Nevertheless, Switzerland contrives to produce more than half of its requirements of foodstuffs. In spite of government measures to help agriculture the drift from the land gives rise to problems.

More than a quarter of the total area of the country is unproductive. A further quarter is covered by forest, 70% of which is publicly owned, pastureland occupies around 46%, with only 6% of the country's area devoted to arable farming. These proportions are mainly a reflection of climatic conditions, which are favourable to the growth of meadowland and pasture. Most of the farm holdings are small: only some 30% are larger than 25 acres/10 hectares. Stock-farming is the most important branch of agriculture, and Swiss breeds of cattle are sought after in many countries in the world.

The principal type of agricultural produce is milk, and Swiss cheeses (Emmental, Gruyère, etc.) take first place in the country's exports of foodstuffs. Wheat, barley, oats, maize, sugar-beet and potatoes are being grown in increasing quantities. Vines grow in the sunniest and mildest parts of Switzerland – Valais, southern Ticino, on Lake Geneva and the Lac de Neuchâtel and in the transverse valley of the Rhine.

Tourism

Since the end of the 19th c. the tourist trade has been one of Switzerland's major sources of income, and latterly its importance in the economy as a whole has steadily increased. In recent years the decrease in purchasing power of the dollar has led to a fall in the number of tourists from the USA. Today some 33% of foreign visitors to Switzerland come from West Germany, followed by those from the USA, Britain, France, Italy, Holland and Belgium. In 1987 the Swiss Tourist Board recorded 34.6 million overnight stays by foreign tourists, together with 40 million such stays by Swiss people who had decided to spend their holidays in their own country.

On the Rütli meadow, scene of the foundation of the Confederation ▶

History

<table>
<tr><td>Stone Age</td><td>Finds of Palaeolithic material in caves (e.g. below the Ebenalp in the canton of Appenzell and at the Schweizerbild crag in the canton of Schaffhausen) point to the presence of primaeval hunters in Switzerland during the Ice Age. In the Neolithic period the commonest form of settlement was the lake village built on piles, first identified in Lake Zurich in 1853.</td></tr>
<tr><td>Bronze and Iron Ages</td><td>In the Bronze Age (c. 2500–800 B.C.) and Early Iron Age the area of human settlement expands, and cultural links are established with the neighbouring regions to the north and east.</td></tr>
<tr><td>400–58 B.C.</td><td>About 400 B.C. the Celts advance into Switzerland from the west. The period takes its name from a Celtic island stronghold discovered at La Tène, near Neuchâtel. The Helvetii, a Celtic tribe, seek to move into southern France, but are defeated and driven back by Julius Caesar at Bibracte in Burgundy (58 B.C.).</td></tr>
<tr><td>15 B.C. to A.D. 455</td><td>The Romans' campaigns of conquest over the Alps (first roads over the passes) are completed with the subjugation of Rhaetia, in the western Alpine region, in 15 B.C. There follows a period of peaceful colonisation under Roman rule, which comes to an end only about A.D. 455 with the incursion of the Alemanii into northern Switzerland and the settlement of the Burgundians (who soon become Romanised) in western Switzerland.

(Roman Remains in Switzerland: see map on page 39.)</td></tr>
<tr><td>5th–9th c.</td><td>About the turn of the 5th and 6th centuries the Alemanii and Burgundians are conquered by the Franks. Switzerland now becomes part of the Frankish kingdom and, under Charlemagne, of the Holy Roman Empire. After the fall of the Frankish Empire the noble families of Zähringen, Habsburg, Kyburg and Savoy establish separate domains which seek to achieve independence.</td></tr>
<tr><td>1098</td><td>Count Berthold of Zähringen is granted the imperial protectorate (Reichsvogtei) of Zurich.</td></tr>
<tr><td>1218</td><td>After the death of the last of the Zähringen family, Berthold V, the Zähringen possessions fall to the Counts of Kyburg. Berne, Zurich and Solothurn become free Imperial cities.</td></tr>
<tr><td>1231</td><td>Uri, an area of importance through its situation on the St Gotthard route, is granted "immediacy" (Reichsunmittelbarkeit: self-government in direct subordination to the Emperor) by Henry, son of the Emperor Frederick II.</td></tr>
<tr><td>1240</td><td>Schwyz is also granted immediacy by the Emperor Frederick II.</td></tr>
<tr><td>1264–1291</td><td>Count Rudolf III of Habsburg (German Emperor from 1273) wins power over large parts of Switzerland. Strict rule by governors from outside the area.</td></tr>
<tr><td>1291</td><td>After Rudolf's death the forest cantons of Uri, Schwyz and Unterwalden form the "Perpetual Alliance" which is the germ of the Confederation. By the "Rütli Oath" they promise mutual assistance in the struggle for their traditional rights and against the dynastic policy of the Habsburgs, with the object of maintaining the self-government and independent jurisdiction of the rural communities and towns and achieving the status immediacy. When the Habsburgs try to bring Switzerland back under Austrian rule in 1439 the Confederation breaks free of the Empire.</td></tr>
</table>

The Romans
in Helvetia

Roman remains
in Switzerland

1 Geneva *(Genava)*: Town walls, villa; museum
2 Nyon *(Noviodunum*: Columns; museum
3 Ste-Croix: Roman road
4 Baumes: Columns, altar
5 Yverdon *(Eburodunum)*: Fort; museum
6 Orbe *(Urba)*: Mosaics
7 Ursins: Temple
8 Ferreyres: Kilns
9 Lausanne *(Lousonna)*: Mosiac pavement, remains of fortifications; museum
10 Moudon *(Minnodunum)*: Inscriptions
11 St-Saphorin: Remains of walls, milestone with inscription
12 Massongex *(Tarnaiae)*: Mosiac pavement, inscriptions
13 St-Maurice *(Acaunum)*: Milestone, gateway; museum
14 Martigny *(Octodurum)*: Theatre, milestone, remains of columns
15 Great St Bernard *(Summus Poeninus)*: Temple, Roman road; museum
16 Avenches *(Aventicum)*: Theatre, temple, remains of town
17 Fribourg: Mosaic pavement; museum
18 Sion *(Sedunum)*: Milestone, inscriptions; museum
19 Pierre Pertuis *(Petra Pertusa)*: Rock gateway with inscription
20 Studen *(Petinesca)*: Temples, gate tower
21 Berne: Theatre, temples, remains of town; museum
22 Solothurn *(Saloaurum)*: Fort; museum, lapidarium
23 Schauenburgerflüe: Temple
24 Liestal: Aqueduct; museum
25 Munzach: Villa, mosaics
26 Augst *(Augusta Raurica)*: Remains of town; museum
27 Kaiseraugst *(Castrum Rauracense)*: Fort

28 Hauenstein: Roman road
29 Pfärichgraben: Watch-tower
30 Bürkli: Remains of fortifications
31 Stelli: Watch-tower
32 Wittnau: Remains of fortifications
33 Olten: Villa, fortifications; museum
34 Zofingen: Mosaic pavement
35 Bözberg: Roman road
36 Schwaderloch: Watch-towers
37 Brugg: Fort; museum
38 Windisch *(Vindonissa)*: Theatre, military camp, aquaduct
39 Lenzburg: Theatre
40 Sarmenstorf: Villa
41 Wettingen: Inscription
42 Baden *(Aquae Helveticae)*: Baths; museum
43 Koblenz: Watch-tower, inscriptions
44 Zurzach *(Tenedo)*: Fort, inscriptions; museum
45 Rümikon: Watch-tower
46 Weiach: Remains of fortifications
47 Schleitheim-Salzbrunnen *(Juliomagus)*: Bath; museum
48 Seeb: Villa
49 Zurich *(Turicum)*: Remains of fortifications; museum
50 Stein am Rhein: Fort; museum
51 Stuetheien: Villa
52 Pfyn *(Ad Fines)*: Fort
53 Winterthur *(Vitudurum)* Fort, temple, inscriptions; museum
54 Irgenhausen: Fort
55 Ufenau: Temple
56 Arbon *(Arbor Felix)*: Fort; museum
57 Stralegg: Watch-tower
58 Filzbach: Watch-tower
59 Sargans: Villa
60 Julier (Guglia) pass: Remains of columns
61 Stabio: Altar

History

History leading up to the Perpetual Alliance	The meeting on the Rütli, Wilhelm Tells great feat and the destruction of the castles of Zwing-Uri, Sarnen, etc. are vividly described in the "Federal Chronicle" of Obwalden – an account which is probably based on historical facts, though we possess it only in a much revised version of about 1470. Later chroniclers, in particular Ägidius Tschudi of Glarus (*c.* 1570), who did not possess the text of the 1291 alliance, erroneously dated the rising to the reign of King Albrecht (1307–08). Schiller's play "Wilhelm Tell" (1804) was based on Tschudi's account.
1315	The forest cantons defeat the Habsburg forces in the Battle of Morgarten, south of the Ägerisee (Nov. 15th). Renewal of the Perpetual Alliance at Brunnen (Dec. 9th).
1332–1353	The Confederation is enlarged to eight members by the admission of the Habsburg territory of Lucerne in 1332, the Imperial city of Zurich in 1351, Glarus and Zug in 1352 and the Imperial city of Berne in 1353. Tension with Austria leads to further fighting.
1367–1471	Formation of the "Three Leagues" in Rhaetia. To defend themselves against oppression by the nobility the common people form a series of alliances – the "League of God's House" (1367), in which the lead is taken by the Chur church; the "Upper League" or "Grey League" (1395, renewed at Truns in 1424); and the "League of the Ten Jurisdictions" (1436). In 1471, at Vazerol, they become the "Three Perpetual Leagues".
1386	Victory of the Confederates at Sempach over Duke Leopold III of Austria, who is killed in the battle (July 9th). Sacrificial death of Arnold von Winkelried ("A road to freedom").
1388	Defeat of the Austrians at Näfels in the canton of Glarus.
1394	In the "Twenty Years Peace" Austria renounces its claims to sovereignty over the forest cantons of Lucerne, Glarus and Zug.
1403–1474	By adroit tactics the Confederation gains additional territories, some of them (Appenzell, Aargau, Thurgau and a number of places between the Walensee and Lake Constance) as "associated territories" which are not admitted to the Confederation but form defensive alliances with it.
	Valais breaks away from Savoy and becomes an associated territory. The Confederation acquires influence in Upper Ticino. St Gallen, Schaffhausen and Mulhouse in Alsace ask for the Confederation's protection.
1436–1450	In the "Old Zurich War", which arises out of a conflict between Zurich and Schwyz, the Confederation once again finds itself involved in a confrontation with Austria, which now seeks the support of France. On Aug. 26th 1444 the Confederates are defeated at St Jakob an der Birs by an army of French mercenaries (the "Armagnacs"), but defeat the Austrians at Ragaz in 1446. Under a peace treaty in 1450 they retain possession of the territories they hold.
1474	Peace with Austria (March), which once again recognises the territories held by the Confederates. Alliance between the Confederates and Louis XI of France (Oct.). Both agreements are directed against Charles the Bold of Burgundy, who is seeking to encircle the Confederates in the Black Forest and Upper Rhine area and in Vaud.
	The treaty with France is the first agreement for the provision of Swiss mercenary troops to a foreign power – the beginning of a practice which later, in the Milanese campaigns, leads to Swiss fighting Swiss.
1476–1477	Burgundian War, in which the Confederation fights on the side of Austria against Charles the Bold. Charles marches on Berne, but is defeated by the

Swiss at Grandson (Mar. 2nd 1476) and Murten (June 22nd 1476) and is killed in the Battle of Nancy on Jan. 15th 1477. Swiss mercenaries fighting for Duke René of Lorraine play a considerable part in this victory. Berne and Fribourg acquire territory in Vaud.

At the Battle of Giornico by the Ticino river the Confederates defeat the Milanese, who renounce their claim to the Livine valley.   1478

Fribourg and Solothurn are admitted into the Confederation.   1481

Grisons enters into a loose association with the Confederation.   1497/98

Swabian War, in which the Confederation and Grisons are allied against Austria and the Swabian League. In the Calven defile, near Taufers, a Grisons force of 6000 men defeats an Austrian army of 12,000 (May 22nd). Victory of the Confederates over the Swabian League at Dornach (July 22nd). In the Peace of Basle (Sept. 22nd) the Confederation in effect breaks free of the Holy Roman Empire.   1499

Basle and Schaffhausen join the Confederation.   1501
After the admission of Appenzell in 1513 the composition of the Confederation, which now has 13 members, remains unchanged until 1798.

Milanese campaigns. The Confederates, originally involved only as mercenaries (with Swiss fighting against Swiss), later take part in the campaigns as an independent power. After the victory won by François I of France at Marignano (Sept. 13th–14th 1515) the Swiss are left in an untenable position and give up mercenary service. The Confederates assert their possession of Ticino, and Grisons holds on to the Valtellina, conquered by them in 1512, retaining it until 1797.   1500–1515

Peace with France (Nov. 29th). The Confederates thereafter abandon their role as a belligerent power and declare their complete neutrality.   1516

Ulrich Zwingli (born 1484 in Wildhaus, killed at the Battle of Kappel in 1531) begins his reforming work as priest at the Great Minster in Zurich.   1519

The Reformation is adopted in Zurich, Schaffhausen, St Gallen, Basle, Berne and Grisons; the four forest cantons, Zug, Fribourg, Solothurn and Valais remain Catholic.   1523-1528

The First Kappel War, arising out of religious conflicts, ends in a peace favourable to the Reformed faith.   1529

Second Kappel War. Defeat and death of Zwingli in the Battle of Kappel, north of Zug, against the original (Catholic) cantons (Oct. 11th). The peace treaty gives each territory the right to choose its own faith.   1531

Berne is appealed to for help by Geneva, under threat from Savoy. The Bernese conquer the Savoyard territory of Vaud and impose the Reformed faith. The Confederation thus attains approximately the same area as present-day Switzerland.   1536

The theologian Jean Calvin (1509–1564), having fled from Paris, pursues his work as a Reformer in Geneva. The town becomes the great centre of Calvinism, which then spreads to France, the Netherlands, Brandenburg, Hungary, Britain and North America. (The French term "Huguenot" is a corruption of "Eidgenosse" or "Confederate".)

The Counter-Reformation and the exacerbation of religious differences lead to an internal split within the Confederation. Ludwig Pfyffer (1524–1594) makes Lucerne the centre of the Catholic territories.   1543–1586

History

1618–1648	Switzerland remains neutral in the Thirty Years War. Only Grisons, disturbed by party strife, is involved in the conflict, since the strategic importance of the Alpine passes within its territory draws Austrian and Spanish forces and a French army commanded by the Duc de Rohan into the area. Thanks to the bold efforts of Colonel Georg Jenatsch (1596–1659); however, the country succeeds in regaining its independence. In the Peace of Westphalia Switzerland is recognised as a European State.
18th century	The patchwork of separate units that makes up the Confederation remains, politically and constitutionally, in the pattern achieved at the time of the Milanese campaigns. The lack of any all-embracing state authority is reflected in the continuing religious, party-political and social tensions. At the same time, however, there is a flowering of intellectual life, linked with that of the neighbouring countries of France and Germany (Haller, Bodmer, Breitinger, Lavater, Pestalozzi, Rousseau, etc.).
1790–1797	The influence of the French Revolution makes itself felt; uprisings against aristocratic and patrician rule. Loss of the Valtellina (1797).
1798	France occupies the whole of Switzerland, dissolves the old Confederation and establishes the Helvetian Republic, a unified state on the French model. Geneva, the Jura and the former free Imperial city of Mulhouse (in Swiss hands since 1515) are annexed to France.
1803	Under the Mediation Acts (mainly the work of Napoleon) Switzerland again becomes a confederation of equal cantons, now nineteen in number, with the addition of Aargau, St Gallen, Grisons, Ticino, Thurgau and Vaud to the previous thirteen. Geneva and Valais remain French. Napoleon constructs the road over the Simplon pass.
1813	Dissolution of the Medication Acts following the fall of Napoleon.
1814–1815	At the Congress of Vienna the number of cantons is increased to 22 by the addition of Geneva, Valais and Neuchâtel. Under the Bundesvertrag (Federal Agreement) a new constitution is introduced: the 22 cantons are now recognised as sovereign bodies (Aug. 1815). Peace of Paris (Nov. 1815): the perpetual neutrality of Switzerland is guaranteed. Customs-free zones established on the frontiers of Geneva.
1830–1839	A Liberal Movement ("Regeneration") in many cantons and attempt to achieve a liberal revision of the federation; this fails in the face of conservative opposition.
1845	The Catholic and conservative cantons of Lucerne, Uri, Schwyz, Unterwalden, Zug, Fribourg and Valais form a separate federation, the Sonderbund.
1847	Sonderbund War, which soon ends, after no serious fighting, in the defeat of the Sonderbund.
1848	Adoption, by national referendum, of a new federal constitution: the federation of states becomes one Federal State.
1864	Geneva Convention. On the initiative of Henri Dunant (1828–1910) an international agreement on the conduct of war on land is signed in Geneva (Aug. 22nd: formation of Red Cross).
1870	Switzerland remains neutral in the Franco-Prussian War.
1874	Revision of the federal constitution to increase both the unity of the Confederation and the independence of the cantons. The federal government is assigned responsibility for foreign policy, the army and economic affairs (currency, railways, postal services) and partial responsibility for justice.

On the outbreak of the First World War the Swiss army is mobilised, but the country's neutrality is fully preserved. During the war Switzerland takes in wounded and sick prisoners of war from both sides. | 1914–1918

First meeting of the League of Nations in Geneva (May 15th). Switzerland becomes a member of the League after a national referendum (May 18th). | 1920

During the Second World War Switzerland again remains neutral, but gives aid to those of any nation who need it. | 1939-1945

Switzerland becomes a member of UNESCO. | 1948

Switzerland becomes a member of the Organisation for European Economic Cooperation (OEEC). | 1950

Switzerland joins the European Free Trade Association (EFTA). | 1960

Switzerland becomes the 17th member of the Council of Europe. | 1963

Women are granted the right to vote and stand for election in federal elections. | 1971

Switzerland signs a free trade agreement with the European Community (EC). | 1972

Regional referenda on the establishment of a new canton of Jura. | 1974–1975

Economic agreement with the Soviet Union (Jan. 12th). The formation of the new canton of Jura is approved in a national referendum (Sept. 24th). | 1978

The new canton of Jura becomes a member of the Confederation as the République et Canton du Jura (Jan. 1st). | 1979

A national referendum rejects a proposal for the separation of church and state. Queen Elisabeth II becomes the first British Head of State to visit Switzerland (May). On Sept. 5th the new 16.3 km/10 mile long road tunnel through the St Gotthard is opened to traffic. | 1980

In a referendum a majority votes for a constitutional measure by which the equality of men and women will be legally established. | 1981

Demolition of the Autonomous Youth Centre (AJZ) in Zurich (Mar. 20th). The Foreigners Law, aimed at improving the standing of foreign citizens, is rejected by referendum (June 6th). | 1982

Pope John Paul II makes a pastoral visit to Switzerland June 11th–17th. By a plebiscite the Principality of Liechtenstein becomes the last country in Europe to give women the vote. Although Franz Joseph II remains the titular head of the Principality, the business of government is transferred in August to his son, Hans Adam. On Oct. 2nd a woman is elected for the first time to the Federal Government of Switzerland. | 1984

Following a referendum, tolls are introduced for motorways (highways) in Switzerland. The meeting of the US President Reagan and the Soviet Party Chief Gorbachev in Geneva (Nov. 19th–21st) creates world-wide interest. | 1985

Following a referendum (Mar. 16th) 75% of the electors vote against Switzerland's joining UNO. Chemical accidents in the Ciba-Geigy and Sandoz firms lead to pollution of the Rhine and the air near Basle and in the adjoining area. The National Council resists sanctions against South Africa (mid-Dec.). | 1986

The revision of the laws concerning refugees and foreigners is approved in a referendum (Apr. 5th). | 1987

1988

Parliament resolves in May to build no more nuclear power stations in Switzerland. Introduction of the concept of "Rail and Bus 2000" which proposes a thorough modernisation of Swiss railways and public transport.

In June the government in Berne approves a budget of some 55 million Swiss francs to celebrate in 1991 the 700th anniversary of the Swiss Confederation. The extensive programme of festivities which is planned will take the form of a trilogy related to the founding of the Confederation in 1291, with the "Celebration of the Confederation" (excursion to the Rütli mountain on the eve of the public holiday, song and dance in Schwyz on Aug. 1st, traditional "Seenacht" party in Brunnen on Aug. 2nd–3rd, ending with an ecumenical church service on the day of prayer). Also planned are the "Celebration of the Four Cultures" in west Switzerland, a "Culture Carousel" (free and applied art, literature, music, films, theatre, dancing), conferences and seminars under the heading of "Culture Forum", artistic activities linked to "Action Meeting 1991" and the "Celebration of Solidarity: Switzerland's Place in the World", with three symposia in Grisons. A fourth symposium "Switzerland on the Threshold of the New Century" in the canton of Ticino looks forward to the "Regional Exhibition 1998 in Ticino", as well as a wide programme of events celebrating the 150th anniversary of the Swiss canton.

In Ecône the traditionalist Bishop Lefébvre consecrates four of his priests as bishops, contrary to the wishes of the Vatican.

Dr J. P. Delamuraz is elected Federal President by a majority vote (Dec.).

1989

Immediate resignation of the cabinet member Elisabeth Kopp following a breach of the Official Secrets Act (Jan. 12th). Her successor is the member for Lucerne, Kaspar Villiger (Feb. 1st).

State visit to Poland by the Swiss Foreign Minister René Felber. Bilateral questions form the theme of the talks (Feb.).

Official Swiss protest to the government of El Salvador following its failure to clarify the circumstances surrounding the death of Jürg Weis, a member of the Swiss Consulate for Central America.

Federal President Delamuraz confirms before the European Parliament Switzerland's readiness to assist in the reconstruction of Europe. Important areas of co-operation include protection of the environment, the provision of financial services and the education sector (Feb.).

Discussions are held on the New Trans-Alpine Railway (NEAT) and attempts to transfer the heavy north–south traffic from the roads on to the railways (Mar.).

The planned construction of the Kaiseraugst nuclear power station near Basle is turned down by both houses of parliament. Both houses also decide to reject a private member's bill for a national referendum on "Switzerland without an army" (Mar.). Although, in a referendum in Nov., a majority of the people were against the abolition of the Swiss army, one third were in favour – a surprisingly high figure.

Art and Culture

Cultural Life and Museums

Switzerland is a turn-table of lively cultural exchange. Foreign artists have always come to the country to live and work, while at the same time the Swiss have made important contributions to the international art scene with artists such as Paul Klee, Alberto Giacometti, Le Corbusier or Jean-Luc Godard.

Cultural Life

The fullness and variety of Swiss cultural life is largely the product of the four different languages found in the country – not to mention the numerous dialects – each of which has its own important cultural spheres. Added to this is the fact that while the cantons are mainly responsible for overall cultural policy, the local communes, each with its own peculiarities, have developed a considerable degree of cultural autonomy. The Federation aims mainly at a balance between the regions, preserving the landscape (nature reserves), historical monuments and other testimonials to Swiss culture, as well as promoting the arts.

The "Pro Helvetia" foundation set up in Zurich in 1939 is devoted to protecting Swiss culture within the country and spreading its name abroad.

Cultural collections are displayed in over 600 museums large and small throughout the country. The most important include the Swiss National Museum in Zurich and the art museums in Basle, Berne, Geneva and Zurich. Private enterprise must be thanked for some superbly equipped collections, such as the Oskar Reinhart exhibition "Am Römerholz" in Winterthur, the Abegg Foundation in Riggisberg, the Rietberg Museum in Zurich and the Thyssen-Bornemisza Collection (Villa Favorita) in Lugano-Castonola in the canton of Ticino.

Museums

Permanent important historical museums are to be found at Berne and Basle, while Technorama in Winterthur and the International Clock and Watch Museum in La-Chaux-de-Fonds are examples of those devoted to science and technology. Also especially worthy of mention are the Swiss Musical Automata Museum in Seewen (canton of Solothurn) and the Musée Baud in L'Auberson (canton of Waadt), the Postal, Telegraph and Telephone Museum in Berne, the Swiss Transport Museum in Lucerne and last but not least the Open Air Museum at Ballenberg near Brienz, in which rural houses from all over the country are on display. Local collections of domestic and regional history are also gaining in importance in all parts of the country.

For items of special interest the Swiss Historical Art Company ("Schweizerische Gesellschaft für Kunstgeschichte") issues monographs under the serial heading "Swiss Art Guides".

History of Art

The history of Swiss culture is as varied and manifold as the landscape of Switzerland. This region of passage, this land of four languages, has been open at all times to influences from the wider world, and it is not surprising, therefore, to find that its art and architecture in particular show affinities with those of the neighbouring countries of Germany, Austria, France and Italy. But these creative impulses operated in both directions, with architects from Ticino and the Italian-speaking Grisons making a major contribution to the development of Baroque architecture in Rome and South Germany in the 16th and 17th c., and Austrian and South German architects creating the finest Baroque buildings in Switzerland in the 17th and 18th c.

General

Accordingly Switzerland's numerous works of art and architecture show no distinctively national style; and the federal structure influenced by the linguistic and ethnic differences, the absence of any princely houses to act as patrons, and other factors; all these inhibited the development of any major national centre of artistic creation.

The art and culture of Switzerland are predominantly centred on the commune, the valley or the region. With few exceptions (Ferdinand Hodler) Swiss artists of international reputation have established their fame outside Switzerland, for example the Ticinese architects Francesco Borromini and Carlo Maderna (who designed the nave of St Peter's in Rome), Alberto Giacometti and Le Corbusier, who opened up new dimensions of sculpture and architecture while working in Rome, and Othmar Ammann, the engineer who built the George Washington Bridge in New York.

Stone Age

Implements and animal bones dating from the Palaeolithic period were found in the Wildkirchli cave on the Ebenalp, and the prehistoric material in the excellent All Saints Museum in Schaffhausen points to occupation during the Ice Age.

The Neolithic period (c. 3000 B.C.) is represented in Switzerland by traces of the Cortaillod culture and Michelsberg culture (belonging to the Western European cultural sphere), probably left by a Pre-Indo-European population which already practised arable and stock farming (tulip-shaped cups, mostly black undecorated ware).

Bronze and Iron Ages

In the Bronze Age (from c. 2500 B.C.) the Alpine regions, paricularly in Grisons, were settled up to altitudes of 2000 m/6500 ft. In sheltered situations on the shores of lakes (e.g. Lake Zurich) pile-dwellings have been found. In the Bronze Age and Early Iron Age (the Hallstatt culture) there is evidence of cultural links with the regions to the north and east. The Iron Age inhabitants of Grisons and Ticino were the Rhaetians, while central Switzerland was settled from about 450 B.C. by Celts.

They developed the Late Iron Age La Tène culture (c. 450–50 B.C.), named after the site at Lac de Neuchâtel. The characteristic feature of La Tène art is its ornament, partly vegetable and partly abstract and showing strong Etruscan influence. Highly stylised human and animal heads are also found.

In the Late La Tène period art degenerated completely and the decoration of plane surfaces was abandoned.

Roman Occupation

In 15 B.C. the Romans completed their conquest of Rhaetia. Thereafter major Roman settlements were established, particularly in western Switzerland.

Avenches (*Aventicum*): The town flourished in the 1st and 2nd c. A.D. but was destroyed by the Alemanni in 260. Considerable remains survive – a theatre seating 10,000, fragments of the 6 km/4 mile circuit of walls, the forum baths, the Corinthian column known as the "Cigognier". Artifacts can be seen in the local museum.

Lausanne (*Lousonna*): Bust of Marcus Aurelius in the Archaeological Museum.

Nyon (*Noviodunum*): Columns in the Bourg-de-Rive park.

Geneva (*Genava*).

St Maurice (*Acaunum*).

Martigny (*Octodurum*): Remains of a Roman amphitheatre.

Sion (*Sedunum*)

Windisch (*Vindonissa*): Roman camp and remains of an amphitheatre seating 10,000. Rich collection of material in Vindonissa Museum, Brugg.

Kaiseraugst (*Augusta Raurica*): Large theatre and remains of several temples, a basilica and an amphitheatre. Museum.

Notable remains of Roman pass roads can be seen on the Julier (Guglia), Septimer (Sett), Splügen and Great St Bernard passes.

Remains of Roman settlements in Nyon . . .   . . . and in Avenches

With the beginning of the Great Migrations the Alemanni penetrated into northern Switzerland in 455, and the Burgundians, who became Romanised at a very early stage, settled in the south-west (linguistic boundary between French and German). By 534 the Franks had conquered the whole country.

The Great Migrations

During the medieval period the French-, German- and Italian-speaking parts of Switzerland pursued their separate development, influenced respectively by France, Germany and Italy but nevertheless retaining a certain cultural independence.
Christianity now became the main cultural force, particularly in Valais and Grisons.
Examples of pre-Carolingian architecture can be seen in a number of places, particularly at St-Maurice, Disentis (a Benedictine abbey founded about 720 by St Sigisbert) and Chur (8th c. crypt in the 12th c. church of St Lucius; St Martin's church, 8th c.).

Middle Ages

The Carolingian period is represented by an abundance of buildings, including the choir of St John's church at Moutier (Grisons). The church, originally founded in 780, was rebuilt in Late Gothic style at the end of the 15th c. It is notable for its frescoes, some of them revealed only about 1950 (now in the National Museum, Zurich), which give some impression of what the original abbey church of St Gallen must have been like.
Also of the Carolingian period are the octagonal baptistery of Riva San Vitale on Lake Lugano; parts of the Augustinian abbey of St-Maurice in Valais, the oldest monastic house in Switzerland, founded about 515 (4th c. chapel, devastated by the Saracens about 940; famous treasury, with Merovingian works of art including reliquaries, an Oriental ewer enamelled in gold and a Roman vessel of sardonyx; 11th c. Romanesque tower); and St Martin's church at Zillis (Early Romanesque nave and tower, Late Gothic choir; unique painted ceiling of 1140, a magnificent example of very early figural painting).

The Carolingian Period

Church of St-Pierre-de-Clages

Benedictine Abbey of Payerne

The Benedictine abbey of Einsiedeln was founded in 934 on the site of the hermitage of St Meinrad (murdered in 861). The library contains very beautiful illuminated manuscripts.

Abbey of St Gallen

The Benedictine abbey of St Gallen was founded by St Othmar on the site of a hermitage established by the Irish missionary monk St Gall or Gallus about 612. In the 9th c. it rose to considerable economic prosperity and enjoyed a great cultural flowering (dissolved 1805). Its school and library made it one of the leading intellectual centres of the Alpine region (Ekkehart, Notker Balbulus, Notker Labeo).

About 820 the famous plan of the abbey of St Gallen (now in the abbey library at St Gallen) was drawn up. This shows the detailed layout of a medieval monastic establishment with a double-choired church and a complete range of conventual buildings. The plan is not to scale, and probably represents the proposed layout for the 9th c. abbey, none of which has survived.

The abbey library, with its magnificent interior architecture, contains a rich store of valuable manuscripts and incunabula (ivory book-covers by Tutilo, c. 900; "Psalterium Aureum", 9th c.; Folchard Psalter, c. 860–70; "Casus Monasterii Sancti Galli", by Ekkehart IV, 11th c.; 13th c. manuscript B of "Nibelungenlied", etc.).

Romanesque

The Benedictine abbey on the island of Reichenau, founded in 724, was one of the leading cultural centres of the early medieval period from the 9th to the 11th c. (miniatures, wall-painting), the influence of which was particulary strong in northern Switzerland. A notable establishment in this area was the Benedictine abbey of All Saints at Schaffhausen. The minster (1087–1150), a pillared basilica with a single tower, a flat roof and (since its restoration) a sparsely decorated interior, is an outstanding example of Romanesque architecture (12th c. cloister with elegant arcades). All saints was a daughter house of the Cluniac abbey of Hirsau in the Black Forest.

Murten: Medieval town moat in the Törfliplatz

Of the Benedictine abbey of Muri (Aargau), founded by the Habsburgs in 1027 (dissolved 1841, largely destroyed by fire in 1859), parts of the east and west ends and the Romanesque three-aisled crypt survive. The "Acta Murensia" are informative on the early period of the abbey, and a Middle High German Easter play has also been preserved.

About the year 1000 a small Romanesque church showing Lombard influence, with fine frescoes, was built at Spiez; and the churches at Amsoldingen and Romainmôtier also date from the 10th to the 11th c. The church of St-Pierre-de-Clages (11th–12th c.), in Valais, is one of the finest Romanesque churches in Switzerland.

The Benedictine abbey of Engelberg in the canton of Obwalden, founded about 1120 (church and conventual buildings rebuilt by Kaspar Moosbrugger in 1730–1737 after a fire), became noted in the time of Abbot Frowin (1143–1178) for its scriptorium and school of painters. The abbey library (open to men only) contains valuable illuminated manuscripts, incunabula and miniatures.

Also of the 12th c. are the two fine Romanesque churches of Giornico San Nicolao (three-aisled crypt) and Santa Maria di Castello, and part of the Château of Neuchâtel (west wing). The Grossmünster in Zurich was built between the 11th and 13th c. (fine double crypt of 1100; nave stripped of its interior decoration at the Reformation).

Other examples of Romanesque architecture are the 11th c. three-aisled pillared basilican church (fine porch) of the Benedictine abbey of Payerne (founded during the Cluniac reform movement of the 10th c., dissolved in 1536); the 12th c. church of St-Jean, a pillared basilica with Carolingian work in the nave and a Gothic choir, in the picturesque little town of Grandson; the 12th c. collegiate church and the Tour de la Reine Berthe, a relic of the Church of St-Martin, in St-Imier; and the Cistercian abbey of Hauterive (Fribourg), showing Burgundian influence, which was founded by Guillaume de Glâne about 1138 and dissolved in 1848 (the church in

Romanesque-Gothic transitional style, c. 1160; Romanesque cloister; fine stained glass of 1332).

Other examples of the Romanesque-Gothic transitional style of the 12th and 13th c. are the Cathedral of Chur (crypt 6th and 12th c.); the five-aisled minster of Basle, which dates in its oldest parts from the 9th c. and was replaced at the end of the 12th c. by a new structure mingling the most varied influences with earlier Ottonian architectural traditions (remodelled in Gothic style 1356; richly carved Romanesque capitals; remains of Late Romanesque pavements and frescoes; Late Gothic choir-stalls of the late 14th c.); and the church of the former Cistercian abbey of Kappel on the River Albis (13th–14th c.).

Impressive examples of Romanesque sculpture can be seen in the Grossmünster of Zurich (seated figure of Charlemagne in crypt; copy on south tower). Notable also are the richly varied capitals in the choir of the church of Notre-Dame de Valère (12th–13th c.) in Sion, which is built on Roman foundations. The famous St Gallus doorway in the minster in Basle (originally on the west front, now in the north transept: 1170–1200), the earliest major figured doorway in German-speaking territory, has rich sculptured decoration, including figures of the Four Evangelists and the Wise and Foolish Virgins and representations of Christ as Judge of the world and the Last Judgment in the tympanum. It appears to have been based on Italian and Provençal models, like the south doorway of the conventional church (12th–13th c.) in the little town of St-Ursanne.
The National Museum in Zurich has a large collection of Romanesque sculpture in wood.

Romanesque Sculpture

During the Gothic period the art and architecture of the towns begins to develop, although the appeal of the buildings of this period frequently lies in their picturesque effect rather than in their architectural quality.
Throughout the 15th c. Switzerland remained open to influences from outside the country. Only Basle, with its University (founded in 1460), evolved a distinctive intellectual culture of its own. The altar by Konrad Witz in Geneva (1444), with the first representation of the mountains as seen by the artist, marks the beginning of landscape painting.
The political successes of the Confederates in the Burgundian wars also created the basis for a distinctively Swiss development of art and architecture. Each town now took on a character of its own, building the town halls, gates and fortifications still to be seen in Murten, Romont, Solothurn, Schaffhausen and many other towns. The finest urban ensembles which have survived from this period are Berne and Fribourg, the charm of which is enhanced by their situation or peninsulas rising high above the river valleys.

Gothic

Notable among the Gothic churches is the church of the Cistercian abbey of Wettingen, founded in 1227 and dissolved in 1841 (richly carved choir-stalls of 1604; fine 16th–17th c. stained glass in cloister). To this period also belongs the cathedral of Notre-Dame in Lausanne (dedicated by Pope Gregory X in 1275), in Early Burgundian Gothic style, with five towers, fine sculptured decoration in the Apostles' Choir (13th c.) and on the main doorway (16th c.) and a rose window containing beautiful 13th c. stained glass. The cathedral of St-Pierre in Geneva, built between the 12th and 14th c. and a Protestant church since the Reformation, has notable capitals in the Romanesque-Gothic transitional style and beautiful Late Gothic choir-stalls.
The minster in Basle was rebuilt in Gothic style in 1356 after an earthquake. The west front, between St George's tower (1428) and St Martin's tower (1500), is decorated with magnificent 13th c. sculpture, including a figure of the Emperor Henry II holding a model of the church. The double cloister,

Gothic Church Building

◀ Neuchâtel: Monumental tomb of the Counts of Neuchâtel

built on Romanesque foundations, dates from the 15th c. The Rathaus of Basle, in Late Burgundian Gothic style with a brightly painted façade and arcades, was built between 1504 and 1521. The parish church of Winterthur was built between 1264 and 1515, though the towers date only from the 17th and 18th c.

The cathedral of St Nicholas in Fribourg dates from the 14th and 15th c. and has magnificent sculpture of that period above the principal doorway (Apostles; the Angelic Salutation; Last Judgment in tympanum); it contains a beautiful choir screen and choir-stalls, stained glass and a famous organ.

The Late Gothic minster of Berne, a three-aisled pillared basilica without transepts, was begun in 1421 to the design of the Ulm architect M. Ensinger. The richly decorated west doorway has a Last Judgment, with numerous figures, in the tympanum. The side walls are embellished with frescoes of 1501 (restored); the nave and choir have reticulated vaulting with fine roof bosses bearing coats of arms; choir-stalls (1523) in Renaissance style; beautiful stained glass by Hans Acker (1441–1450).

The Rathaus of Berne was built in 1406–1416 in Late Burgundian Gothic style. The clock tower with its astronomical clock of 1530 dates from the 15th century, but has undergone much subsequent rebuilding. Also of great interest are the old streets and lanes of Berne with their charming fountains, including the Banner-Carrier fountain of 1542 and the Ogre fountain of 1540.

The cathedral of Notre-Dame-du-Glarier in Sion was rebuilt in the 15th c.; it contains fine Gothic tombs. The beautiful Gothic parish church of Moudon has fine choir-stalls of 1502, and the town also possesses three castles, the Tour de Broye (12th c.), the Château de Rochefort (1595) and the Château de Billens (1677).

Other buildings showing the influence of French models are the Gothic castles of western Switzerland – at Champvent (a massive 13th c. stronghold), Grandson (Vufflens-le-Château, one of the most imposing castles in Switzerland, 14th–15th c.), Lucens (a massive structure of the 15th–16th c., with a 13th c. round tower, now the Conan Doyle Museum) and Chillon, near Monyteux (founded in the 9th or 10th c., present structure 13th c.; rock-cut dungeons, large church, court hall, living quarters, etc.: cf. Byron's poem "The Prisoner of Chillon").

At Sion is the ruined Château de Tourbillon, once an episcopal stronghold (built 1294, burned down 1788).

The only structures in southern Switzerland which can be compared with these massive fortresses are the three castles of Bellinzona, built in their present form by the Dukes of Milan in the 15th c. and in 1503 given the names of the three original cantons of Uri, Schwyz and Unterwalden. In German Switzerland the castles are on a considerably more modest scale, for example the Habsburg (c. 1020), ancestral seat of the Austrian Imperial House, or the Kyburg, which first appears in the records in the 11th century (restored 1925).

Gothic
Sculpture

The finest examples of Gothic sculpture are to be seen in the cathedrals of Lausanne and Fribourg and in the Collegiate Church of Notre-Dame-de-Valère in Sion, a three-aisled pillared basilica of the 12th–13th c. with its original interior furnishings, a carved wood altar of the 16th c. and a 15th c. organ still in working order. In the collegiate church in Neuchâtel is the tomb of the Counts of Neuchâtel (1372) with its fifteen painted effigies, the most magnificent funerary monument in Switzerland.

Stained Glass

The beautiful stained glass produced in Switzerland during this period has unfortunately survived only in a very small number of examples – e.g. in the minster in Berne, the choir of the Gothic conventual church of Königsfelden (14th c.) and the cloister of the Cistercian abbey of Wettingen. A

Gothic castle of Vufflens-le-Château

secular form of stained glass is represented by the "Schweizerscheiben" (stained glass panels) in the National Museum in Zurich.

After the defeat of Charles the Bold of Burgundy the enhanced political standing of the Confederation was matched by a greater degree of independence in art and architecture. The towns now increased in importance, and secular building played a much more prominent part in comparison with religious building. These developments coincided with the coming of the Renaissance to Switzerland.

Renaissance

The architecture of this period can be seen at Murten, with its completely preserved circuit of walls, its timber wall-walk, its arcades and its picturesque fountains; at Romont, also with handsome walls and towers; at Solothurn; and in Fribourg, Berne, Lucerne and Schaffhausen.

The decorative arts flourished during this period, which has left some beautifully decorated interiors – e.g. in the house built by Georg Supersaxo in Sion in 1505 (panelled banqueting hall with carved and painted ceiling), the richly appointed palace built for Colonel Freuler in Näfels in 1642-1647 (panelled rooms, Winterthur stoves: now the Glarus Cantonal Museum) and the Ital-Reding house in Schwyz, and above all in the canton of Grisons. Many churches were equipped with new choir-stalls and pulpits at this period, for example at Muri, Wettingen and Beromünster.

Decorative Arts

The painting of the 15th and 16th c. ranks as one of the high points of Swiss art. A particularly notable figure who worked at Basle in the first half of the 15th c. was Konrad Witz (1400–1444), one of the great masters of Late Gothic painting. He broke away from the "soft" style and became the first artist to depict real landscapes (Lake Geneva) and was the founder of Swiss landscape painting ("St Christopher" *c.* 1435; altar of 1444 in Museum of Art and History, Geneva). Of his 20 surviving panel-paintings thirteen belong to the Basle "Mirror of Salvation" altar (*c.* 1435).

15th and 16th c.
Painting

Urs Graf (1485–1527), who also worked as a goldsmith, depicts the life of the landsknechts (mercenary soldiers), which he knew from personal observation, in vigorous and often overcharged drawings and woodcuts (Museum of Art, Basle).

Niklaus Manuel, known as Deutsch (1484–1530), was a draughtsman of exceptional quality who also depicted scenes from the life of the landsknechts in a rather Mannerist style, as well as altarpieces, mythological pictures and frescoes.

Hans Leu the Younger (1490–1531) was another of the early Swiss landscape-painters, showing affinities with the work of the Danube school. Hans Asper (1499–1571) was another painter who also produced woodcuts.

Jost Amman (1539–91), who worked mainly in Nuremberg, produced an extraordinary number of woodcuts covering the whole range of subject-matter then in vogue (historical, military and hunting scenes; armorials; illustrations to rhymes by Hans Sachs).

Tobias Stimmer (1539–1584) was one of the leading Swiss painters of the Late Renaissance (portraits; vividly coloured paintings on the façade of the Haus zum Ritter in Schaffhausen (1485), the originals of which are now in All Saints Museum).

Hans Fries (1465–1520), working mainly in Basle, Fribourg and Berne, is known principally for his altarpieces, painted in glowing colours. The Berne and Zurich Masters of the Carnation also devoted themselves mainly to religious themes.

Hans Holbein the Younger (1497–1543), a native of Augsburg, worked for many years in Basle (Public Art Collection, Basle). In scale and variety his output can be compared only with that of Dürer, and as a portrait-painter he is unequalled. Most of his wall-paintings have unfortunately been lost. His woodcuts are also of the highest quality ("Dance of Death", c. 1525).

Bernardino Luini painted frescoes in the church of Santa Maria degli Angioli in Lugano in 1529. The cathedral of San Lorenzo in that town, with a marble façade of about 1515, is an early example of Renaissance architecture in Ticino.

Baroque

After the end of the Thirty Years War there was a great burst of building activity – mainly by the Catholic Church, then concentrating all its resources on the Counter-Reformation, but also by princes and great nobles. During the Baroque period no huge and imposing secular buildings were erected in Switzerland, but mainly fine town houses and small country houses, particularly around Berne, Basle, Geneva, Solothurn and Fribourg. Almost all the house fronts in Berne were rebuilt at this time.

Protestant Church Building

Protestant churches built during this period included a number of small country churches, the Church of the Holy Ghost in French baroque style, in the Bubenbergplatz in Berne (1726–1729), the Temple de la Fusterie in Geneva and the temple in Neuchâtel. The parish church in Yverdon was built in 1755–1757 (the Town Hall in 1769–1773), a beautiful church at Morges in 1776.

Catholic Church Building

The Catholic Church did a great deal of building in the first half of the 18th c., and most of the monastic houses were rebuilt or altered. In contrast to protestant building, however, it followed Italian rather than French models: Cathedral of St Ursen, Solothurn (1763–1773) and Jesuit churches in Solothurn (1680–1689) and Lucerne (1666–1677; Rococo interior 1750). The South German type of Baroque hall-church is also found, for example in the church (built 1705, with a sumptuous interior) of the Benedictine abbey of Rheinau (founded in the 9th c., dissolved in 1862).

Vorarlberg School of Architecture

From the 1680s onwards three families of architects belonging to the Vorarlberg school – the Beers, the Thumbs and the Moosbruggers – developed an indigenous form of Baroque which displaced the Italian style. Several generations of these families worked in Switzerland. Peter Thumb

(1681–1766) and Johann Michael Beer built the three-aisled hall-church of St Gallen (1755–1766), and Peter Thumb was also responsible for the famous abbey library at St Gallen (1758–1761), which already shows strong Rococo influence. The principal work of Kaspar Moosbrugger (1656–1723) was the rebuilding of the abbey and church of Einsiedeln (1704–1723), a masterpiece of Baroque form and boldly contrasting spatial sequences. The interior of the church was the work of two Bavarian brothers, Cosmos Damian and Egid Quirin Asam, who had been trained in Rome but cast off the influence of Roman Baroque and created theatrical architectural forms which sought to achieve an indissoluble unity between space, light, colour and plastic and architectural movement.

The Ticinese architects Carlo Maderna or Maderno (1556–1629: nave of St Peter's, Rome) and Carlo Fontana (1624–1714) were among the great masters of the Roman Baroque.

18th c. Painting

Although in the first half of the 18th c. sculpture, painting and decorative art were completely subordinate to architecture, towards the end of the century they achieved a greater degree of independence.

The poet and painter Salomon Gessner (1730–1788) illustrated his famous "Idylls" with delicately etched vignettes, and painted small gouaches and watercolours which depicted mythological scenes and landscapes.

Jean-Etienne Liotard (1720–1789), who worked in many different countries, produced charming pastels.

Anton Gaff (1736–1813) was exclusively a portrait painter, notable particularly for his likenesses of leading intellectual figures of the day (Bodmer, Bürger, Gellert, Lessing, Schiller, Wieland, etc.).

Johann Heinrich Füssli (1741–1825), known in Britain as Henry Fuseli, worked first in Italy and later became Keeper of the Royal Academy in London. He specialised in the dramatically Baroque and the fantastically horrific ("The Nightmare").

Neo-classism

The Neo-classical period is represented in Swiss architecture by handsome mansions built for the wealthy middle classes (e.g. Talacker, Zurich), the church at Heiden and the Town Hall of Altdorf (1805–1808).

An important Neo-classical painter was Angelica Kauffman (1741–1807), most of whose work was on mythological, allegorical and religious themes. She was a prominent member of the group of German artists working in Rome and produced a famous portrait of Goethe. Johann August Nahl the Younger, a pupil of the German artist J. H. Tischbein, painted mythological and historical pictures.

Historicism

During the second half of the 19th c. the Swiss government commissioned a number of major buildings, including the massive Bundeshaus in Berne, in the style known as Historicism or Neo-Renaissance, with the Bundesterrasse rising 164 ft/50 m above the Aare on its huge retaining walls, the Swiss National Museum in Zurich and various administrative buildings, railway stations, etc.

19th c. Painting

The painting of this period was of higher quality than its architecture. Among painters working in French Switzerland were Alexandre Calame (1810–1864), noted for his paintings of the mountains, François Diday (1802–1877) and Barthélemy Menn (1815–1893); in German Switzerland Albert Anker (1831–1910), Frank Buchser (1828–1890), Max Buri (1868–1915), Hans Sandreuter (1850–1901: sgraffito work, stained glass, watercolours) and the etcher Albert Welti (1862–1912: stained glass in Bundeshaus, Berne, 1901-1903).

A painter who exerted wide influence was Arnold Böcklin (1827–1901), who alternated between the two extremes of gay joie de vivre and profound melancholy ("Island of the Dead").

Giovanni Segantini (1858–1899), a native of Trento, painted the mountains of the Upper Engadine (Segantini Museum, St Moritz), but also produced pictures of symbolic content ("The Dead Mothers").

Ferdinand Hodler (1835–1918) gave fresh impulses to painting, developing beyond the naturalism of the late 19th c. and setting up in sharp opposition to Impressionism. His monumental murals, "Retreat of the Swiss after the Battle of Marignano" and "Departure of the Jena Students, 1813", gave fresh direction to historical painting (National Museum, Zurich; Museum of Art, Berne; Museum of Art and History, Geneva).

The Lausanne-born painter and graphic artist Félix Vallotton (1865–1925) worked mainly in Paris (landscapes; Art Nouveau).

In the middle of the First World War the Dadaist movement was launched in Zurich, where the pacifist Hugo Ball opened the Cabaret Voltaire in 1916 as a meeting-place for Dadaists.

Cuno Amiet (1868–1961) was influenced by the Impressionists and Neo-Impressionists, and also by Gauguin. Other notable painters of this period were René Auberjonois (1872–1957), Augusto Giacometti (1877–1947), Heinrich Altherr (1878–1947), Alfred Heinrich Pellegrini (1881–1958) and Hans Erni (b. 1909).

The painter and graphic artist Paul Klee (1879–1940), who had affinities with the Surrealists and was a member of the "Blauer Reiter" group, worked at the Bauhaus in Weimar, Dessau and Düsseldorf. His pictures, usually of small size and endearing themes, often have a droll humour and an enigmatic charm ("The Twittering Machine").

20th c.
Sculpture

Among sculptors of this period are Carl Burckhardt (1876–1928: "Amazon", 1923), Hermann Haller (1880–1950) and Alexander Zschokke (b. 1894).

Alberto Giacometti (1901–1966) sets his figures, lean and emaciated, in empty space, thus emphasising their vulnerability ("L'Homme qui marche"). After 1930 he became associated with the Surrealist movement.

Jean Tinguely (b. 1925) has produced major works in the field of kinetic sculpture ("meta-mechanisms" and "machine sculpture" such as the huge "Heureka" in Zürichhorn Park) and self-destroying sculpture ("La Vittoria", a golden phallus over 26 ft/8 m high).

20th c.
Architecture

Among leading Swiss architects of the 20th c. are Karl Moser (1860–1936): St Anthony's Church, Basle, 1927, Adolf Wasserfallen (b. 1920) and Jean-Claude Steinegger (b. 1930). Max Bill (b. 1908) was one of the pioneers of modern architecture in Switzerland; he was also a sculptor, producing abstract plastic works.

The architect who left his mark on the century, however, was Le Corbusier (Charles-Edouard Jeanneret, 1887–1965). Trained under Josef Hoffmann and Peter Behrens, he established a new style of housing and a new pattern of urban living in his "unité d'habitation", a form of residential accommodation which went beyond the normal functions of a house, which he criticised as a mere "machine for living in". Almost all his work was done abroad: in Switzerland there are the Immeuble Clarté in Geneva (1930–1932) and the Centre Le Corbusier in Zurich (1966).

Modern architecture in Switzerland finds expression mainly in churches and schools, but also in offices and industrial buildings with glass and steel being the main building materials.

Modern Trends
in Art

Of the artists active in Switzerland since the Second World war, representing a variety of trends which run parallel to and influence one another, only a brief selection can be mentioned. Wilfried Moser (b. 1914) produces collages, assemblages and sculpture intended for walking and climbing on. André Thomkins (1930–1985: "holograms"), a strikingly original draughtsman, shows affinities with surrealism. Roland Werro (b. 1926) creates coloured objects, monochrome bas-reliefs and mobile sculpture. Christian Megert (b. 1936) loves mirror constructions and light-kinetic objects, as does Christian Herdeg (b. 1952: "light sculpture"). Karl Gerstner (b. 1930) creates "colour sound", pictures with gradations of colour in exactly calculated degrees. Fritz Glarner works in the field of "relational painting". Franz Gertsch (b. 1930, originally belonging to the "peinture

Hipped-roof farmhouse near Berne

naïve" school, is the only Swiss Hyper-Realist. Peter Travaglini (b. 1927) is a Pop artist ("Zip-Fastener", 1970), as is Urs Lüthi (b. 1947). Gérald Minkoff (b. 1937) produces video tapes, and Alex Sadowsky experiments with Surrealist and metaphysical films.

Modern Swiss graphic art also has considerable achievements to its credit, and Switzerland occupies one of the leading places in the field of commercial art and advertising. Notable among contemporary graphic artists is Celestino Piatti (b. 1922), best known for his expressive book-covers. *Modern Graphic Art*

Switzerland's rich artistic heritage is studied and interpreted by its art historians and other scholars. The Swiss Society of Art History (Gesellschaft für Schweizerische Kunstgeschichte) publishes a regionally arranged inventory of works of art and architecture in Switzerland, "Die Kunstdenkmäler der Schweiz". *Cultural Heritage*
The protection of historical and artistic monuments (Denkmalpflege) is the responsibility of the federal and cantonal authorities, with increasing support from the communes and private sources.

The Buildings of Switzerland

Swiss domestic buildings show a carefully cherished individuality of style, with differences and contrasts not only between town and country but also between different parts of the country. Common to all Swiss, however, is the idea that in building a family home they are building for more than one generation, so that the house must be a substantial and durable structure. Swiss towns and villages are notable for their trim and well-kept appearance, and flowers are much in evidence in squares, on fountains and on houses. Town halls and other public buildings, and private houses as well, match the country's high standard of living, and are almost invariably well maintained and cared for.

Barn with "mice stones" on roof, Valais   *Typical façade in Obertoggenburg*

Many buildings have paintings, either old or modern, on their façades – a practice which was originally a great speciality of the Engadine. In eastern Switzerland projecting oriel windows have long been a popular feature. Many Swiss towns and villages offer attractive pictures of streets and lanes and sometimes whole quarters built in uniform style. The picturesque little town of Stein am Rhein with its old painted façades is particularly notable in this respect.

The strong sense of local awareness found in the small Swiss communities means that there is wide support for the conservation of their architectural heritage. Perhaps the most distinctive contribution made by Switzerland to European architecture is its varied range of farmhouses and other rural houses, differing widely from region to region. Local styles are determined by climatic conditions and local needs, but also by a firm attachment to comfort and cosiness. Local differences are reflected principally in the disposition of the masses, the distribution of the living and working quarters and the roof structure.

Engadine bay window

The Open-Air Museum of Rural Life now in course of development at Ballenberg, near Brienz, is designed to show the variety of house types by selected examples.

Rural House Types

Travellers in the 17th c. were already remarking on the handsome houses of the Swiss peasants and the degree of comfort – extraordinarily high by the standards of the day – which they enjoyed. The independent Swiss of today still show a great pride in them.

Every part of Switzerland, indeed almost every valley, has its own distinctive type of house. It is only possible, therefore, to mention the most important types out of this wide range.

Knutti House in Därstetten, Bernese Oberland

In the Appenzell region, with its relatively high rainfall, the house and farm buildings are brought together under a single roof. The fronts of the houses, built of timber, are frequently broken by continuous rows of windows.

Appenzell

In north-eastern Switzerland, a region of deciduous forests, the houses are predominantly half-timbered, with whitewashed panels in the interstices of the framing.

North-eastern Switzerland

In the Jura the houses are massive stone-built structures, broad-based, with saddle roofs which frequently come far down over the walls.

Jura

Around Berne and in the Emmental the houses are predominantly of timber, with deep hipped roofs and the barn usually adjoins the living quarters.

Berne, Emmental

In the Bernese Oberland, as in other mountain regions with large coniferous forests, the "log-cabin" method of building is preferred, the walls being constructed of horizontally laid tree-trunks. The house is separate from the farm-buildings and can thus achieve considerable architectural dignity.

Bernese Oberland

Characteristic of Valais are its timber-built houses of several storeys with flat gables and stone-built kitchen premises, and its store-houses built on piles, with flat stones at the top of the piles to keep rodents out.
In the area of Lake Geneva the rear of the house, with deep eaves, faces on to the street.

Valais and Lake Geneva

The houses of the Engadine differ sharply from those of other parts of Switzerland, showing both Germanic and Latin influence. The timber core of the house is surrounded by masonry walls, with sgraffito decoration on the façade (see "Switzerland from A to Z": Engadine).

Engadine

Ticino

In Ticino the houses are very similar to those found over the frontier in Italy. The walls are of undressed stone, the roof (which projects only slightly over the walls) of stone slabs.

Literature

Earliest Literary Works

The earliest literary activity in Switzerland dates back to the Carolingian period, when the abbey of St Gallen (founded in 613) was a centre of intellectual life. Notable figures who worked at St Gallen were Notker Balbulus (*c.* 840–912), whose "Gesta Karoli Magni" is one of the finest narrative works of the Middle Ages, and the historian Ekkehart (*c.* 980–1060).

The period of chivalry is reflected in the works of the epic poet Hartmann von Aue (*c.* 1200) and the minnesingers Johannes Hadlaub of Zurich (first half of the 14th c.) and Otau de Grandson.

In the age of humanism Aegidius (Gilg) Tschudi (1505–1572) of Glarus wrote his "Helvetian Chronicle", which became a standard work. Economic themes and contemporary criticism were the hallmarks of the works of the doctor Paracelsus (1493–1541). Some leading figures of the Reformation, including Ulrich Zwingli (1484–1531) were also writers of some note.

18th century

Swiss literature reached its full development, however, only in the 18th c. The Bernese poet, doctor and scientist Albrecht von Haller (1708–1777) wrote a poem, "Die Alpen", contrasting the beauty of the mountains and the natural life of the mountain people with the unhealthy life of the towns. The Geneva-born Jean Jacques Rousseau (1712–1778), who spent most of his life in France, was one of the great revolutionary influences of his day, preaching a "return to nature" and preparing the way for the French Revolution with his doctrine of liberty and equality of men. His ideas on politics, education and literature were equally fertile in stimulation, and

William Tell statue

J. J. Rousseau: "Back to Nature"

influenced both the German "Sturm und Drang" period of the 1770s and the French Romantic movement of 50 years later.

Johann Jakob Bodmer (1698–1783) and Johann Jakob Breitinger (1701–1776), both of Zurich, ran a moral and aesthetic weekly "Discourse der Mahlern" ("Discourses of the Painters") which influenced the development of German literature. Other Zurich writers whose reputation extended beyond the bounds of Switzerland were the lyric-poet, etcher and landscape painter Salomon Gessner (1730–1788), Johann Caspar Lavater (1741–1801) and Heinrich Pestalozzi (1746–1827). Johannes von Müller (1752–1809) of Schaffhausen wrote a "History of the Swiss Confederation", which gave Schiller the inspiration for his play "Wilhelm Tel ". Ulrich Bräker (1735–1798) also achieved some reputation abroad with his autobiography "Life History and Natural Adventures of the Poor Man in Toggenburg".

Western Switzerland produced three of its notable writers during this period in Germaine de Staël-Holstein (1766–1817), born in Paris but descended from an old Geneva family, who became one of the forerunners of the French Romantic movement under the name of Mme de Staél; Benjamin Constant de Rebecque (1767–1830) of Lausanne; and Léonard de Sismondi (1773–1842) of Geneva. From Italian Switzerland there was Francesco Soave (1743–1806).

In the 19th c., under the influence of the Romantic movement, national and regional themes came increasingly to the fore.

19th century

Jeremias Gotthelf (Albert Bitzius, 1797–1854), a native of Murten who became pastor of Lützelflüh, takes a high place in Swiss literature with his simple but profoundly human stories of peasant life in Emmental.

The writings of Gottfried Keller (1819–1890) and Conrad Ferdinand Meyer (1825–1898), both of Zurich, are an enduring contribution to literature in the German language.

Johanna Spyri (1827–1901), best known for her children's stories ("Heidi"), also wrote short stories and novels on regional themes.

The literature of Rhaeto-Romanic Switzerland began with Conradin de Flugi about 1845. The most notable Romansch writer is Giachen Caspar Muoth (1844–1906), known principally as an epic poet but also of importance as a lyric poet and philogist.

The first generation of 20th c. writers must include the names of Robert Walser (1878-1956), a master of the inward approach, and Albin Zollinger (1895–1941). The latter found a great admirer in Max Frisch (b. 1911 in Zurich), whose novels and tales are grouped around the Swiss theme. He has made important contributions to literature world-wide, as has the author Friedrich Dürrenmatt of Berne (b. 1921), whose works for the stage have gained him a reputation extending far beyond the frontiers of Switzerland. Plays such as "Andorra" and "Biedermann und die Brandstifter" ("The Fire-Raisers") by Max Frisch and Dürrenmatt's "Der Besuch der alten Dame" ("The Visit") and "Die Physiker" ("The Physicists") and novels such as Frisch's "Stiller" and "Mein Name sei Gantenbein" occupy a high place in contemporary German Literature.

20th century

Carl Jakob Burckhardt of Basle (1891–1974) made a considerable contribution to international understanding by his work as an art historian and essayist.

Carl Spitteler (1845–1924) from Liestal, as an innovator of epic poems and author of psychological novels, was awarded the Nobel Prize for Literature in 1919.

The outstanding writers in French and Italian were respectively Charles Ferdinand Ramuz (1878–1947), whose prose on the Vaud region was the first in the local dialect to gain true recognition and who collaborated with the composer Igor Stravinsky in writing the "Histoire du Soldat", and Francesco Chiesa (1871–1973), of Sagno (near Chiasso), who established his place in Italian literature in spite of the fact that his work was deeply rooted in his native Ticino.

Literature

The writer and art-historian Piero Bianconi (b. 1899) produces impressive descriptions of the wild mountains of Ticino.

A number of younger writers, including Otto F. Walter (b. 1928), Adolf Muschg (b. 1934), Hugo Loetscher (b. 1929), Peter Bichsel (b. 1935), Beat Brechbühl (b. 1939), Urs Widmer (b. 1938), Gerold Spät (b. 1939) and E. Y. Meyer (actually Peter Meyer, b. 1946) concern themselves with the problems of contemporary life, usually from a critical point of view. Hansjörg Schneider (b. 1938) and Manfred Schwarz (b. 1932) have made their mark as dramatists while Jürg Federspiel (b. 1931) writes tales and novels.

The literature of French Switzerland concerns itself less with social and political problems, and concentrates more on inner conflicts. The masters of this "inwardness" include Gustave Roud from the Vaud region (1897–1977), whose influence can be seen in the work of Philippe Jaccottet (b. 1925).

Jacques Chessex (b. 1934), from French-speaking Switzerland, won the French Prix Goncourt in 1973 for his novel "L'Ogre", and Georges Boorgeaud (b. 1914) was awarded the Prix Renaudot in 1974. While the work of Maurice Chappaz (b. 1916) shows a new and unique vitality, Georges Haldas (b. 1918) is one of the most relentless analytical thinkers of his time. Important essayists include Gonzague de Reynold (1880–1970) from Fribourg and the non-conformist Denis de Rougemont (1906–1985).

Of the literary critics, special mention must be made of Jean Starobinski (b. 1920) and Marcel Raymond (1897–1981).

Among the main female literary figures hailing from French-speaking Switzerland are Monique Saint-Hélier (actually Betty Briod, née Ymann, 1895–1955), Cathérine Colomb (actually Marie-Louise Reymond, 1893–1965), S. Corinna Bille (1912–1979), Alice Rivaz (b. 1901), Yvette Z'Graggen (b. 1920) and Anne Cunéo (b. 1936).

In Grisons literature in the Romansch language, which has tended not to spread far because of the small area involved, has made a considerable breakthrough in the 20th c. The most important writers from this part of Switzerland include the traditionalist Peider Lansel (1863–1943) from the Engadine, Alexander Lozza (1880–1953), whose lyrics are closely linked to folklore and nature, the master story-teller Gion Fontana (1897–1935) and Cia Biert (b. 1920) from the Münster valley, with his humorous tales. Andri Peer (b. 1921) is the originator of the contemporary Engadine lyric. Of the more modern writers mention must also be made of Gian Belsch (b. 1913), Tista Murk (b. 1915) and Gion Depiazes (b. 1918).

In recent years literature in dialect has developed with fresh vigour in every part of Switzerland.

Foreign authors
Switzerland has given asylum to many foreign writers subject to persecution in their own countries on political or racial grounds. The most prominent of the German authors who found a home in Switzerland during the Nazi period were Thomas Mann and Carl Zuckmayer. More recently writers and scientists from the Eastern bloc have found a refuge in Switzerland, notably Alexander Solzhenitsyn from the Soviet Union and Ota Šik from Czechoslovakia.

Theatre

Switzerland's theatrical life can trace its origins back to the 10th c. religious plays performed in the German language. Towards the end of the 19th c. the popular theatre received a special boost. Some of the patriotic festival productions introduced at that time, such as the popular William Tell plays in Altdorf and Interlaken, are still regularly enacted today.

The "Great World Theatre" by Calderón de la Barca, held every 10 years in Einsiedeln (next one in 1995) has become famous far beyond Switzerland itself.

Every 25 years since the end of the 18th c. the "Fête des Vignerons" takes place in French Switzerland (last one was in 1977), to give thanks to the farmers and wine-producers.

The performances by the "Theâtre du Jorat", which was founded in 1903 in Mézières near Lausanne, also form a part of the true popular theatre.

Internationally famous are Switzerland's great playhouses in Basle, Berne, Geneva and Zurich. A considerable contribution to the establishment of these came from the large number of German authors, playwrights and directors who were obliged to emigrate to Switzerland before and during the Second World War, such as Bertolt Brecht.

Playhouses

The contemporary theatre, which for a long time was dominated by the works of Max Frisch and Friedrich Dürrenmatt, has received fresh creative impulses from "Living Theatre" and "Open Theatre".

Although the bulk of state subsidies goes to the larger theatres the number of small playhouses and experimental theatres is continually growing. The most successful of these are in the German-speaking regions, especially the theatre on the Hechtplatz in Zurich, the Zähringer workshop-theatre and the Gaskessel Youth and Culture Centre in Bern, the "Kulturtäter" and Théâtre de Poche in Biel, the Fauteuil ("Armchair") and Zum Teufel ("To the Devil") theatres in Basle, the basement theatre by the Müller Gate in St Gallen, the Little Theatre on the Bundesplatz in Lucerne, the Upper Valais Basement Theatre in Brig and La Claque and Spatz & Co. in Baden.

Small theatres

In French-speaking Switzerland the Compagnie des Faux-Nez in Lausanne, founded in 1948, and the Centre Dramatique Romand have made a name for themselves. Swiss and foreign plays are included in the programme of the Théâtre de Carouge, Théâtre de l'Atelier and Nouveau Théâtre in Geneva, while the Théâtre Populaire Romand is above all else a popular theatre which involves the audience, and therefore often performs at schools.

Swiss cabaret artists of note are Elsi Attenhofer, Voli Geiler, Walter Morath, Franz Hohler and "Emil" Steinberger; Bernard Haller from western Switzerland is working successfully in Paris.

Cabaret and Mime Artists

Mention should also be made of the world-famous artiste and clown Grock (real name Adrian Wettach, 1880–1959), the pantomimes of the "Mummenschanz" group, the solo artistes Kaspar Fischer and Dimitri, the "clown of Ascona", who also founded the theatre and school of acting in Verscio in the canton of Ticino.

Music

An independent school of Swiss music first came to the fore in the 19th c. The names of the composers of this period, however, have largely fallen into oblivion.

In the early 20th c. the belated Romantic Othmar Schoeck (1886–1957) was a composer of some quality, and Willy Burkhard (1900–1955) – not to be confused with Paul Burkhard (1911-1977), the composer of musicals – made a name for himself.

Contemporary Music

The leading Swiss composer is Arthur Honegger (1892–1955), who was born in France, lived for many years as one of the principal members of the Groupe des Six and died there. Among his chief works are five symphonies (including the "Symphonie Liturgique" and "Deliciae Basilenses"), a number of symphonic poems ("Pacific 231", "Rugby"), the scenic oratorios "Judith", "Jeanne d'Arc au Bûcher" and "Le Roi David", and an impressive Christmas cantata, with a final section in which Christmas carols in various European languages are skilfully mingled.

Frank Martin (1890–1974), a native of Geneva, was also an exponent of 12-tone music (dodecaphony), and taught for some years at the Cologne

63

Academy of Music. In addition to symphonic music (Concerto for seven wind instruments, strings and drums) he also composed much choral and chamber music.

Another contemporary composer of more than regional significance is Heinrich Sutermeister (b. 1910), whose opera "Titus Feuerfuchs" received its first performance during the Brussels Exhibition of 1958. Volkmar Andreae (1879–1962), who was conductor of the orchestra of the Tonhalle-Gesellschaft from 1906–1949, wrote operas and choral works as well as orchestral and chamber music. Rolf Liebermann (b. 1910), from Zurich, was for many years manager of the Hamburg State Opera and until 1980 Director-General of the Paris Opéra. As a composer he works mainly in the 12-tone technique. The Bernese opera, ballet and instrumental composer Gottfried von Einem (b. 1918) has put to music works by Büchner, Kafka and Dürenmatt, among others. The world-famous oboist Heinz Holliger (b. 1939) has also made a name for himself as an avant-garde composer.

Opera Houses

Although Switzerland is a relatively small country, it has a remarkable number of good opera companies, orchestras, conductors and soloists. The Zurich Opera is one of the largest and finest opera-houses in German-speaking territory, and the Grand Théâtre in Geneva and the Municipal Theatre in Basle also enjoy a considerable reputation.

Orchestras, Conductors and Instrumentalists

The best-known orchestras in Switzerland are the Orchestre de la Suisse Romande, the Tonhalle-Orchester of Zurich, the Basle Symphony Orchestra, as well as the chamber orchestras of Basle, Zurich and Lausanne, the Camerata of Berne and the Festival Strings of Lucerne.

Swiss conductors of international reputation include Ernest Ansermet, Paul Sacher, Edmond de Stoutz, August Wenzinger, Silvio Varviso, René Klopfenstein, Charles Dutoit, Armin Jordan, Michel Corboz and Robert Denzler (1892–1972); among instrumentalists there are Heinz Holliger (oboe), Ursula Holliger (harp), Peter-Lukas Graf and Aurèle Nicolet (flute) and Karl Engel and Adrian Aeschbacher (piano).

In addition, many musicians from countries all over the world have made Switzerland their home, among them Paul Kletzki (1900–1973), Andor Foldes and Nikita Magaloff. During the 19th and 20th c., too, many composers took advantage of Swiss tolerance and generosity in cultural matters and came to live in Switzerland in order to escape the censorship or persecution to which they were exposed in their own country (Wagner, Stravinsky, Hindemith, etc.).

Light Music and Jazz

In the fields of light music and jazz a considerable number of individual performers and groups have achieved reputations outside Switzerland, such as Teddy Staufer, Cedric Dumont, Hazy Osterwald, George Gruntz, Pierre Favre Franco and Flavio Ambrosetti, the Tremble Kids Jazz Group, Vico Torriani and Pepe Lienhard. Internationally popular, too, are the annual jazz festivals in Montreux and Willisau, as well as the folk and rock festival in Nyon.

Folk Music

The folk music of the Alpine regions – yodelling, Kuhreigen (round dances), dance tunes such as the ländler, etc. – is popular and performed with committed enthusiasm throughout the whole of Switzerland.

Films

The critical differences in Swiss films lie in their basic themes. While the German-speaking contributions are mainly documentaries, the emphasis in French-speaking Switzerland has always been on feature films. It was in the latter sphere that many of the great film-makers, such as Claude Goretta, Michel Soutter, Jean-Jacques Lagrange, Jean-Luc Godard (who worked almost solely in France) and Alain Tanner, who was honoured in Cannes for his film "Années lumiere", experienced their first successes.

International recognition was also found by such films as Yves Yersin's "Les Petites Fugues", "It Happened in Broad Daylight", the filming of Dürrenmatt's "The Promise" with Gert Fröbe and Heinz Rühmann, "The Boat is Full" by Markus Imhof, which impressively describes the refugee problem during the Second World War, "A Swiss named Nötzli" and "The Swissmaker", a best-seller by Rolf Lyssy, which analyses the typical Swiss man in a humorous manner. Other well-known Swiss film-makers of the modern generation are Daniel Schmid, Jacqueline Veuve, Francis Reusser, Richard Dingo and Kurt Gloor.

Folklore

Present-day Switzerland is still rich in traditional celebrations which have been lovingly nurtured over the centuries. Relics of pagan times are very apparent in numerous customs relating to late winter and Shrove Tuesday. The people really "go to town" with religious feasts and processions.
The Swiss national pride is clearly demonstrated in the old, traditional communal elections, the Rütli shoots and other popular events. In addition there are many specifically Swiss sports which have developed from competitive games held among the farming communities.

General

On New Year's Eve, especially in the German-speaking region, figures disguised in fancy costumes parade through the streets, symbolising the end of the Old Year and the time of darkness.
Well into Lent, indeed right up to the beginning of spring, the numerous Shrove Tuesday customs continue the symbolic battle between winter and spring. Atavistic fertility rites and pagan natural beliefs are reflected in the numerous masks worn by wild characters named according to the region they hail from, such as "Butzi", "Wildma", "Bärzeli" or "Roitschäggädä'. Well-known is the "Baseler Fasnacht", which begins at four in the morning

New Year and Shrove Tuesday Customs

Engadine . . .

. . . Appenzell costumes

65

Schwingen: Swiss wrestling

on the Monday after Ash Wednesday with the "Morgenstraich" (morning stroll) and lasts until the following Thursday. Before daybreak the various Shrovetide carnival guilds, known as "cliques", parade through the old town, accompanied by loud music played on pipes and drums. This is followed on the Monday afternoon by the official parade, in which the masked members of the individual cliques wear their own unique-costumes. They are accompanied by floats on which various satirical scenes are performed. The noisy celebrations continue on the Tuesday, when the "Guggenmusiken" parade with drums and wind-instruments. The time-difference between this and the German "Karneval" is explained by the fact that the Swiss shrovetide follows the Julian Calendar.

Another old spring custom is the "Eieraufleset" (picking up the eggs), in which the egg is a fertility symbol representing the victory of spring over winter.

Processions

Swiss traditions are rich in processions. In Ticino, the region strongly influenced by Roman culture, Holy Week processions are held in many towns, sometimes (such as in Mendrisio) depicting representation of scenes from the Passion.

At the beginning of April in the canton of Glarus the "Näfelser Fahrt", in which the Capucin monks take part, is held to remind the people of Glarus of their victory over the Austrians on April 9th 1388. The "Stoos Pilgrimage" in Appenzell has similar origins. In many places in the canton of Lucerne around Ascension Day the so-called "Ascension Ride" is celebrated, a procession which harks back to pre-Christian traditions for the blessing of the fields. The most beautiful and impressive processions take place at the time of the Feast of Corpus Christi in those regions with a mainly Roman Catholic population and on such occasions beautiful traditional costumes are worn.

Historical
Festivals

There are a vast number of historical festivals reflecting the Swiss love of freedom and willingness to bear arms when necessary. Magnificent

Cattle coming down from Alpine pasture

parades in historical costume commemorate the battles of Morgarten (1315), Sempach (1386), Näfels (1388; see above), Murten (1476) and Dornach (1499). Many are the festivities held by rifle clubs and military celebrations such as the "Rütli shooting contest" in Uri, the "Zurich Boys' Shoot", the "Thun Shoot", the "Women's Shoot" in the canton of Lucerne and others. Perhaps the best-known historical celebration is the "Geneva Escalade", which commemorates the successful repulsion of an attack by the Savoyards in 1602.

A living testimonial to the way the Swiss view democracy is found in the communal assemblies (landsgemeinde), at which the representatives of the citizens are elected by public vote.

Communal Assemblies

The Swiss National Day, celebrated throughout the country with torchlight processions, fireworks and shooting contests, is August 1st. This "Bundesfeier" revives memories of the year 1291, when the representatives of the three "original cantons" of Schwyz, Uri and Unterwalden swore the "Rütli Oath", promising mutual assistance in their struggle for their traditional rights, thus laying the foundations of the Confederation. In 1991 there is to be a big programme of festivities to mark the 700th Jubilee.

National Day

There are three sports which are specifically Swiss, known respectively as "Schwingen", "Hornussen" and "Steinstossen".

Sports

Schwingen is a kind of wrestling, in which each combatant grasps the other's short trousers made of strong twill and tries to throw him to the ground.

In Hornussen the batting side tries to hit a kind of puck about the size of a man's hand, as far as possible with the "Hornuss", a flexible club nearly 2 m/6½ ft long with a hardwood head. The "Abtuer" (fielders), armed with big wooden shingles, try to catch the Hornuss before it hits the ground.

In Steinstossen the object is to hurl a stone weighing 83½ kg/184 pounds as far as possible. The record is about 3½ m/11½ ft.

Folklore

Folk Music

Yodelling plays a major role in folk music. Most Swiss yodelling is improvised without an established format, unlike that practised in Upper Bavaria or Austria. Yodelling was a traditional method of communicating from one Alpine pasture to another, and this was also the original function of the alphorn made from the hollowed-out trunk of a mountain pine, usually about 3½ m/11½ ft. long. The characteristically soft sound carries a surprisingly long way. The accordion ("Schwyzörgeli" or "Handörgeli", with a chromatic keyboard) is widely played. Flag-wavers ("Fahnenschwinger") often accompany the bands playing folk-music.

Alpine Festivals

Farming traditions are also reflected in many customs, especially in the Alpine festivals. In early summer the "Alpaufzug" (Alpine Parade) celebrates the move of cattle up to the mountain pastures. A similar custom, especially in the canton of Valais, is the "Kuhkampf" (cow fight), in which cows fight for positions within the herd. The victor is the leader for the coming year. When summer ends the cheese produced on the mountain pasture is distributed to the individual farmers, who draw lots to decide how it is to be allocated.

Winter Festivities, Markets.

In autumn many vintage and grape festivals are held in the wine-producing regions. This is also the season of markets, the best known of which are the onion markets in Berne and Biel.

Jass

The Swiss people's favourite card game is "Jass", played with 36 cards in four colours.

Local Crafts

Local crafts also flourish in the form of rural paintings, embroidery, wood-carving and hand-weaving.

On the way to the St Gotthard ▶

Switzerland A to Z

Aarau D1

Canton: Aargau (AG)
Altitude: 388 m/1273 ft
Population: 16,000

Situation and general

Aarau, capital of the canton of Aargau since 1803, lies on the River Aare under the southern slopes of the Jura. With Late Gothic houses dating from the period of Kyburg rule, their street fronts colourfully remodelled in Baroque style, it is known as the "town of gables and gardens". In addition to its role as an administrative and cultural centre it also has a variety of industry (manufacture of instruments, iron and steel works, optical industry, bell-casting).

History

Founded about 1240 by the Counts of Kyburg, Aarau soon passed into the hands of the Habsburgs. In 1415 it came under Bernese rule, and in 1798 became for six months capital of the Helvetian Republic. In the 18th c. the Swiss national gymnastic, shooting and singing associations were founded or held their first meetings in Aarau.

Sights

The well-preserved old town, built on a prominent rocky hill above the Aare, has many gabled houses with carved decoration (ornamental and figured) on the roofs and painted shingle fronts. The Rore tower (1240) is the oldest part of the Rathaus (Town Hall), which was enlarged about 1520 and remodelled in Baroque style in 1762. The Late Gothic parish church (Stadtkirche: Protestant), a pillared basilica, was built in 1471–78. Both these buildings are in the Halde, the best preserved old street in the canton, with houses ranging in date from the 16th to the 19th c. Here, too, is the Upper Tower (Oberer Turm, 1270). Its clock dates from 1532 and still strikes daily. On the south side of the tower is the painting "Dance of Death" by Felix Hoffman.

The Schlössli was originally a castle keep (11th c.). The Grossratsgebäude, seat of the cantonal parliament, is the finest Neo-classical building in Aargau (1826–28). From the new bridge over the Aare (Neue Aarebrücke,1949) there is a fine view of the old town. Also of interest are the Municipal Museum (Stadtmuseum Alt-Aarau) in the castle and the Art Gallery, as well as the Aargau Museum of Nature and local interest.

Aarau: Fountain of Justice

Surroundings

Good walking in the Aare valley, the Jura and Mittelland hills. In the wooded Roggenhausen valley are a wildlife park and a nature trail, and in Schachen an interesting aviary.

Schloss Wildegg

10 km/6miles north-east on road 5 lies Wildegg (alt. 357 m/1171 ft), at the foot of the Kestenberg, with saline springs containing iodine (water available only bottled). Above the town to the north (1.5 km/1 mile by road) stands the imposing Schloss Wildegg (alt. 433 m/1421 ft: 12th and 17th c.; now open to the public as a museum). The Schaerer-Citterio Weapon Collection and the Erlach House have been open to visitors since 1988. The latter was built by Albrecht von Effinger in 1825 in Biedermeier (early Victorian) style for his half-sister Sophie von Erlach-von Effinger.

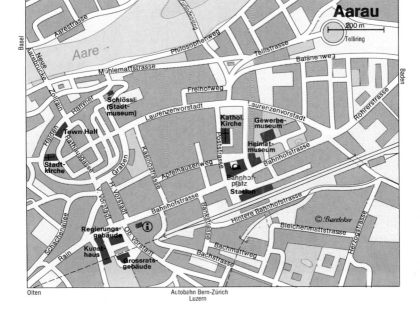

On the left bank of the Aare, a little way downstream, is Schloss Wildenstein, now an old people's home.

5.5 km/3 miles farther downstream we come to Bad Schinznach (alt. 355 m/1165 ft), an elegant spa established in 1694 (closed in winter), with sulphurous water (34° C–93° F) which is effective in the treatment of rheumatism and metabolic disorders; beautiful park (restaurant) and golf course.

Bad Schinznach

Beyond Bad Schinznach, on the left, a steep narrow road ascends (2.5 km/ 2 miles) to the ruins of the Habsburg (alt. 513 m/1683 ft: inn), on the Wülpelsberg. The castle, built about 1020 was in the 12th and 13th c. the seat of the Counts of Habsburg, one of whom, Rudolf III, was elected King of Germany in 1273 and thus became the founder of the Imperial dynasty of Habsburg. From the 24 m/79 ft-high tower there are superb views. The castle can also be reached from Brugg (see p. 96) on a steep and not very good road (3.5 km/2 miles).

Habsburg ruins

East of Aarau by way of Buchs is Lenzburg (alt. 400 m/1312 ft), a little town of 7000 inhabitants well known for its food-preserving factories (particularly fruit preserves). Above the old town with its unspoiled 17th and 18th c. houses rises the Burgberg (512 m/1680 ft: road to top) crowned by the large Schloss Lenzburg (11th–16th c.), now the property of the town of Lenzburg and the canton of Aargau (cantonal historical museum). To the west or the Staufberg (520 m/1706 ft: view), is a Gothic pilgrimage church with 15th c. stained glass.

*Lenzburg

To the west of the motorway access road are the foundations of a Roman theatre of the 1st c. A.D. discovered in 1964 and restored in 1970–1972.

Aarau: the Old Town

Lenzburg Castle

8 km/5 miles north-east on the Baden road, in the old country church of Wohlenschwil, is the Swiss Country Museum (Bauernmuseum: house types, costumes, weapons).

Adelboden   C2

Canton Bern (BE)
Altitude: 1357 m/4452 ft
Population: 3500

Situation

The village of Adelboden, a popular altitude and winter sports resort in the Bernese Oberland, lies in a sheltered situation on the west side of the Engstligen valley at the end of a road from Lake Thun. Along the east side of the wide valley with its scatter of huts rises the Lohner chain; to the south is the Wildstrubel.

Townscape

This attractive mountain village is famed for its scenic beauty, its many charming old farmhouses, and its hotels and chalets scattered about on sunny terraces. On the south wall of the church (1433) is a late 15th c. painting of the Last Judgment.

Climbs

Via Hahnenmoos up the Laveygrat (2254 m/7395 ft: 3½ hours, not particularly difficult); via Schermtanne up the Albristhorn (2765 m/9072 ft: 5½ hours, for experienced climbers only); from the Engstligenalp in 5½–6 hours, with guide, up the Wildstrubel (the east peak, Grosstrubel, 3253 m/10,673 ft), with magnificent views (west peak climbed from Lenk in the Simmental); from the Engstligenalp by way of the Engstligenrat to the Gemmi pass (4–5 hours, with guide: see p. 243)

Good downhill runs from the Fleckli (1862 m/6109 ft: two lifts from Boden), on the Engstligenalp (1940 m/6365 ft: three lifts; accessible by cableway); from the Kuonisbergli (1731 m/5679 ft; two lifts from Boden); from the Schwanfeldspitz (2029 m/ 6659 ft; lift; accessible by cableway); from the Luegli (2080 m/6824 ft) and from Lavey (2200 m/7220 ft; chair-lift from Geils) and on the Hahnenmoos (1957 m/6421 ft: lifts from the Simmental; combined "ski pass" with Lenk; accessible by cableway from Geilsmäder). Also ski-jumping, cross-country skiing, skating (rink with artificial ice) and curling (indoor and outdoor rinks).

Surroundings

There are about 200 km/125 miles of signposted walks. A chair-lift, 1268 m/ 4160 ft long, ascends in 8½ minutes to the Tschentenalp, on the east side of the Schwanfeldspitz (2029 m/6657 ft: restaurant), from which there are magnificent views of the Lohner and Wildstrubel. A road runs 3.5 km/ 2 miles west up the Allenbach valley to the Schermtanne inn.

A narrow road branches off the road to Frutigen (on right, after the second bend), runs south up the Engstligen valley and passes through Boden to the hamlet of Unter dem Berg, at the Lower Engstligen Falls (6 km/4 miles), from which a cableway takes us up past the Upper Engstligen Falls to the Engstligenalp (1940 m/6365 ft: Berghaus Bärtschi, 15b. Berghotel Oester, 40b.), a former lake basin at the foot of the Wildstrubel. A bus runs south-west up the Gilbach valley to Geils. Cableway from Geilsmäder (1707 m/5601 ft) to the Hahnenmoos pass (1957 m/6421 ft: Berghotel 15b.). Chair-lift 1650 m/5414 ft long from Geils to the Laveygrat (2200 m/7218 ft) and a chair-lift from Geils to Luegli (2080 m/6824 ft), both operating only in winter. From Hahnenmoos it is a 45 minutes' descent to the Bühlberg restaurant (1660 m/5446 ft), from which a road leads down (6 km/4 miles, with steep bends) to Lenk in the Simmental (see entry), or alternatively along the valley by cableway.

Aigle   B2

Canton: Vaud/Waadt (VD)
Altitude: 420 m/1378 ft. Population: 6500

The small town of Aigle is situated in the Chablais on the banks of the Rhône, surrounded by the well-known vineyards of the Vaud Fendant.

The history of Aigle goes back to the Bronze Age. Ruled by Savoy from 1076, this small market town was conquered by Berne in 1476 and remained in its possession until the independence of Vaud was declared in 1798.

Sights

A stroll through the Fontaine quarter and the picturesque Rue Jerusalem with its old houses connected by covered arcades is to be recommended. The main shopping street is the Rue du Bourg (pedestrianised). Other attractions include the market square, the medieval church of St Jacques, where the reformer G. Farel (1489–1565) once preached his sermons, and the old clock tower.

Renowned as one of the most important castle sites in Switzerland the 12th c. Schloss Aigle, surrounded by vineyards, towers above the town. It has a square keep, numerous small towers and a balcony from which boiling pitch was poured down. This former residence of the Bernese provincial

Aigle Castle

Wine-press in the Museum of Viniculture

governors served as the district prison until 1972 and today houses an important viticultural museum.

Altdorf   D2

Canton: Uri (UR)
Altitude: 458 m/1503 ft
Population: 8000

Situation

Altdorf, capital of the canton of Uri, a little town with a long and eventful history, lies 3 km/2 miles south of the outflow of the Reuss into Lake Uri in a wide plain at the mouth of the Schächen valley; it is the starting-point of the road over the Klausen pass. It is here that William Tell is supposed to have shot at the apple on his son's head.

History

The parish is believed to have been established in the 10th c., although its first appearance in the records is only in 1223. After the struggle to shake off Habsburg rule the place acquired political and economic importance as capital of the territory of Uri, which until 1439 was self-governing in direct subordination to the Emperor.

Sights

*Tell
Monument

In front of the Rathaus (Town Hall, 1805–08) and a medieval tower house is the Tell Monument (by Richard Kissling, 1895). To the east is the Tell theatre (1925), in which Schiller's "Wilhelm Tell" is performed by Altdorf towns-people. Also of interest are the parish church of St Martin (rebuilt 1801–10), the Uri Historical Museum (founded 1892), the Suvorov house and the Capuchin friary.

The Historical Museum, (Gotthardstrasse 18), founded in 1892, contains a cultural collection from the Canton of Uri (wooden sculpture, altars, embroidery from the 15th–18th c., costumes).

Surroundings

3 km/2 miles away on the road to the Klausen pass is Bürglen (alt. 552 m/ 1811 ft: pop. 3600), one of the oldest settlements in Uri, built on detritus deposited by the Schächenbach, which here flows into the Reuss. Parish church (1684), with Romanesque crypt and substructure of the tower. Bürglen is supposed to have been the home of the mythical William Tell, whom Schiller's plays made the greatest figure in Swiss legend. The Tell chapel (1582) is said to occupy the site of Tell's house, and a stone cross beside the bridge marks the spot where Tell is traditionally believed to have been drowned while rescuing a child from the Schächenbach in his later years. There is a Tell Museum in a Romanesque tower adjoining the church.

Bürglen

1.5 km/1 mile south of Altdorf, on the left bank of the Reuss, is Attinghausen (alt. 469 m/1539 ft; pop. 1200), with the remains of a castle in which Freiherr von Attinghausen, who features in Schiller's play, died in 1321.

From Altdorf a road runs via Seedorf (alt. 437 m/1434 ft) at the south-west tip of Lake Uri. At the end of the village, directly on the lake, stands the pinnacled Schloss a Pro, which was built for the Knight Jacob (1556–60) of the same name. Nowadays the castle houses the Uri Mineral Museum (slide shows).

*Schloss a Pro

From Isleten to the delightfully situated village of Isenthal (10k m/6 mi es: alt. 778 m/2553 ft; pop. 600), the starting-point for the ascent of the Urirostock (2932 m/9620 ft; 6–7 hours, with guide; cableways).

*Urirostock

14 km/9 miles south by way of Erstfeld (alt. 475 m/1558 ft: station on the St Gotthard line) is Amsteg (552 m/1811 ft), a beautifully situated village and

Amsteg

Altdorf: William Tell Monument   *Schloss a Pro, on Lake Uri*

summer holiday resort at the mouth of the Maderanertal, here spanned by a 53 m/174 ft-high viaduct carrying the St Gotthard railway; cableway (1440 m/4725 ft long: 7 minutes) up the Arniberg (1392 m/4567 ft).

*Maderanertal   A road to the left leads into the Maderanertal, one of the most beautiful of the Alpine valleys, watered by the rushing Kärstelenbach. A steep mountain road, with many bends, climbs (4 km/2 miles) to Bristen (797 m/2615 ft), from which there is a cableway to the Golzernsee (1410 m/4626 ft) and a rough track which leads in 2½ hours up to the magnificently situated Hotel Schweizer Alpenclub (1354 m/4442 ft), a good base for climbers and hillwalkers (e.g. to the Oberalpstock, (3330 m/10,926 ft); 8–9 hours, with guide).

Andermatt   D2

Canton: Uri (UR)
Altitude: 1444 m/4738 ft
Population: 1600

Situation   Andermatt lies in the wide Urseren valley at the junction of four important Alpine roads, which with the exception of the access road from the Reuss valley are closed for between four and six months in the year. The old village has developed into an ideal base for walkers and climbers and a popular winter sports resort.

History   The Urseren valley was settled from the Valais, and the oldest parts of Andermatt and Hospental still show Valaisian features. The people of the valley were long subject to the authority of Disentis abbey, but achieved independence in 1382, with their own constitution and their own amman (chief magistrate) and the village is still a separate district within the canton of Uri.

Sights

The Baroque church of St Peter and Paul dates from 1695 (Rococo interior). On the mountainside is the little 13th c. church of St Columban (dedicated to the Irish monastery saint). From the Mariahilf chapel, above the village to the south, there are far-ranging views of the Bäzberg (2550 m/8367 ft), the Furka pass, with the Muttenhorn (3103 m/10,181 ft), and the Badus (2931 m/9617 ft).

Surroundings

Urschner   The five-hour walk along the Urschner Höhenweg from Andermatt to
Höhenweg   Tiefenbach is recommended.

Gernstock   There is a cableway up to the Gernstock (2963 m/9721 ft; length 4036 m/13,240 ft; height difference 1525 m/5003 ft; time 12 minutes; magnificent views).

*Devil's Bridge   Road 2 runs north up the wide Urseren valley (Bear Hunters' Valley), a massive Alpine trough flanked by high mountains, some of them snow-capped, and by scree-covered slopes, and watered by the streams which feed the Reuss. The road crosses the Devil's Bridge (Teufelsbrücke 1402 m/4600 ft), built in 1955-56, which spans the Reuss at a waterfall 30 m/98 ft high. The bridge, 86 m/282 ft long, inherited its name from an old 15th c. bridle-path bridge at the same spot. A stone cross 12 m/39 ft high commemorates the fighting in September 1799, when General Suvorov's Rus-

An arctic impression: the Totensee (dead lake) on the Grimsel Pass

sians, coming from the St Gotthard pass, defeated the French force which attempted to bar their way. To the right, on the old road, is the Teufelsbrücke restaurant.

The road passes through the Teufelswand ("Devil's Wall") in a short tunnel, and leaving a parking place (fine views) and five sharp bends (Schöllenen restaurant) returns to the right bank of the river of the Spänngi bridge (1234 m/4049 ft).

It then enters the Schöllenen (probably from Latin "scala"=ladder), a wild gorge enclosed between precipitous granite walls, and after another four sharp bends (fine views) crosses to the left bank again on the Vordere Brücke. Thereafter it crosses the Göschenen-Reuss and continues to wind sharply downhill on the St Gotthard road to the village of Göschenen.

*Schöllen gorge

Göschenen (alt. 1115 m/3658 ft) is magnificently situated at the junction of the Göschenen-Reuss with the Reuss, which issues from the Schöllenen gorge. It lies near the north entrance to the 15 km/9 miles long St Gotthard tunnel (see p. 355) and has a large railway station. The builder of the tunnel, Louis Favre, died of a stroke in the tunnel in 1879, shortly before its completion, and is buried in Göschenen churchyard.

Göschenen

To the west an attractive road ascends the beautiful Göschenen valley to a reservoir on the Göschener Alp (9.5 km/6 miles). 7 km/4 miles from Göschenen, on the right is the Göschener Alp inn (1715 m/5627 ft), and 2.5 km/2 miles beyond this, in a magnificent mountain setting, the Dammagletscher inn (1795 m/5889 ft) with a large parking place. Above the inn, from a reservoir (75 million cu. m/2648 million cu. ft), there is a superb view of the Dammastock and its glacier. The Göschenen Alp is the starting-point of a variety of rewarding climbs: to the Lochberg (3088 m/10,132 ft: 4½ hours, with guide), the Dammastock (3633 m/11,920 ft: 5–6 hours, with guide), the Susterhorn (6½ hours, with guide).

*Göschenen valley

The winding Grimsel road

The road continues down the bare mountainside and once again crosses to the right bank on the Schöni Bridge (981 m/3219 ft). Below, on the right, lies the Teufelstein ("Devil's Stone"), a massive boulder which was moved 127 m/417 ft upstream in 1973, during the construction of the St Gotthard road tunnel. The road passes the village of Wattingen and crosses to the left bank of the Reuss, with the Rienzenstock (2964 m/9725 ft) on the right and the magnificent Dammafirn (névé) on the left.

Wassen

5 km/3 miles from Göschenen we reach Wassen (934 m/3064 ft), a beautifully situated village at the junction with the road over the Furka pass. From the terrace in front of the church (1734), which stands on higher ground, there are superb views of the valley in both directions.

**Circuit of three passes

This circuit (a round trip from Wassen) of the Susten, Grimsel and Furka passes offers a breathtaking experience, combining splendid Alpine scenery with the tremendous technical achievements of the road engineers.

*Susten road

The newest of the three roads, the boldly engineered Susten road (No 11), built between 1938 and 1946, runs up from Wassen through the wildly beautiful Meiental, goes over the Susten pass in a tunnel (2224 m/7297 ft) just under the summit and descends the Gadmen valley, passing close to the Stein glacier, to Innertkirchen, where it leaves the magnificence of this high Alpine valley for a gentler landscape of pastureland and orchards.

*Grimsel road

The Grimsel road (No 6), built in 1891–94, which links the Bernese Oberland with Upper Valais (the Upper Rhône valley) and the Furka, starts from Innertkirchen (626 m/2054 ft), in a beautiful setting of forest and Alpine meadows, and runs up the attractive Hasli valley. Above Guttannen this becomes narrower and wilder, until at Handegg the trees disappear altogether and the road continues to climb through a bare rocky wilderness. past massive dams and narrow fjord-like reservoirs. From the Grimsel pass (2165 m/7013 ft), the lowest of the three passes, the road runs down, with many hairpin bends, to Gletsch (1763 m/ 5784 ft), in the Upper Rhône valley.

From here the Furka road (No 19), built in 1864–66, leads up through the bare upper reaches of the valley, passes immediately under the Rhône glacier and continues up to the Furka pass (2431 m/7976 ft), the highest point on the trip. It then continues down into the Urseren valley through scenery of a different type, with rugged mountains of uncompromising bulk.

*Furka road

All three roads are well built and excellently engineered, particularly the Susten road (minimum width 6 m/20 ft, well-cambered bends, maximum gradient 8%). The Grimsel road, with its many bends, has been modernised (4–7 m/13–23 ft wide, maximum gradient 9%). The Furka road (improved 1960–63; 4–8 m/13–26 ft wide) is the steepest of the three (10%); the stiffest gradients are mostly on the bends, and in the thinner air at this altitude they make particularly heavy demands on the engine of a car. The round trip involves an ascent of some 3600 m/11,812 ft with about 60 sharp bends. Motorists who are unused to Alpine driving should exercise particular care. All three passes are usually open from mid June to mid October (emergency telephones).

*Susten road

The Susten road, branching off the St Gotthard road at Wassen, runs uphill at a moderate gradient, with an attractive view of Wassen church to the rear. In 0.5 km/¼ mile it winds its way through two tunnels, between which is another view of Wassen. The road then crosses the gorge of the Meien- reuss on a high concrete bridge, from where there is a view of Titlis (3239 m/10,627 ft) ahead. At the Leggistein tunnel on the St Gotthard railway the road takes a left-hand turn, beyond which one has a view of the Fleckistock (3420 m/11,221 ft) and Stücklistock (3309 m/10,857 ft). Soon after this it goes through a third tunnel and runs high up on the mountainside above the gorge of the Meienreuss, with a panorama of the valley. After a total of 5.5 km/3 miles the road comes to the group of houses and the church at Meien (1300 m/4265 ft), beautifully situated at a point where the valley opens out. Beyond this point, in the upper reaches of the Meiental, an area of Alpine pasture enclosed by steep mountain walls, the road continues uphill on a moderate gradient above the left bank of the Meienreuss; from here one can see the jagged peaks of the Wendenhorn and Fünffinger- stöcke at the head of the valley. In another 3 km/2 miles a road goes off on the left and runs down into the valley to the hamlet of Färnigen, on the old bridlepath to the Susten pass.

Meiental

8.5 km/5miles farther on, at Gorezmettlen, the road crosses the stream flowing down the Kleinalp valley from the Kleiner Spannort and then climbs higher up the slopes of the Meiental, now wild and desolate, with a view of the summit of the pass and the Sustenhorn, with the Rüttifirn and Kalchtalfirn. The Sustenstübli inn is passed on the right of the road. Beyond this, to the left, there is a magnificent panorama, looking backwards down the valley; ahead to the left, is the summit of the pass, from which the jagged crest of the Fünffingerstöcke extends to the right towards the Wendenhorn (3023 m/9918 ft) and Grassen (2946 m/9666 ft). Then follow two bends and a short tunnel leading up to the Susten pass (2259 m/7412 ft), under which the road passes in a tunnel 325 m/1066 ft long (alt. 2224 m/7297 ft). Just beyond the far end of the tunnel are a large parking place and a small lake, from which there is a rewarding climb (5 minutes) to the summit of the pass (restaurant), the boundary between the cantons of Uri and Berne, with views of the imposing chain of mountains north of the

*Susten pass

Andermatt

Meiental (highest point Titlis, 3239 m/10,627 ft), the group formed by the Gewichtenhorn (3425 m/11,327 ft) and the Tierberge (3444 m/11,300 ft) rearing up above the Stein glacier, the Himmelrank gorge and, in the background, the tunnels on the Susten road and the Gadmerfluh.

Beyond the pass the road – still scenically and technically magnificent but now showing more variety of scenery – runs down in two sharp bends, offering superb close-up views of the Stein glacier and its drainage lake immediately below. It then passes through the Himmelrank gorge, with seven tunnels or arches in the rock, and takes a left-hand bend down to the Hotel Steingletscher (1866 m/6122 ft), on the Alp Stein. From here there is first a road (3 km/2 miles) to the Steinlimmi glacier (summer skiing centre), and then a footpath (20 minutes) to the mighty Stein glacier, also a climb of 7 hours (with guide) to the summit of the Sustenhorn (3504 m/11,497 ft: superb views). From the Steingletscher Hotel the road descends the Wendental on the stony slopes of the Gschletterwald, through wild and rugged scenery, passing through five tunnels and under a sheer rock face, with a backward view of the Sustenhorn, of which there is a further glimpse after a left-hand bend. It then continues to wind its way down, with continually changing prospects of the Tierberge and Gewichtenhorn to the south and the precipitous walls of the Wendenstöcke and Gadmerfluh to the north. In another 5 km/3 miles it crosses a stream, and soon after this traverses another tunnel into a left-hand bend (turning-place), and through three more tunnels and round two bends to the Wendenwasser bridge over the stream of the same name. It then continues down the Gadmental, the valley of the Gadmer Wasser. The scenery becomes gentler, with fresh green pastureland and woods of maple and stone pine. Ahead can be seen the Wetterhorn (3701 m/12,143 ft).

* Himmelrank

* Stein glacier

Gadmen

Gadmen (alt. 1207 m/3960 ft) is a straggling little village in a picturesque situation under the steep rock faces of the Gadmerfluh.
The road continues downhill on a gentle gradient, passes through a tunnel, crosses the gorge of the Gadmer Wasser on the high Schwendi bridge and winds its way down to the mouth of the Trift valley, from where one can see the Trift glacier. It then crosses back to the right bank of the Gadmer Wasser and comes into the commune of Nessental (930 m/3051 ft) which gives its name to the lower part of the valley where fruit-trees abound. The road then runs down on a uniform easy gradient to Mühletal (837 m/2746 ft), at the mouth of the Gental, a valley running down from the Engstlenalp (toll road 11.5 km/7 miles); the stream is crossed on the Rossweidli Bridge. Then on to Wiler (4.5 km/3 miles: alt. 740 m/2428 ft). Beyond this point there is another fine view of the mountains, a fter which the road winds down into the wide valley of the Aare and arrives at Innertkirchen (626 m/2054 ft), a holiday resort surrounded by lush Alpine meadows.

Innertkirchen

From Innertkirchen the road to the Grimsel goes gradually uphill in the wooded and steadily narrower Oberhaslital above the right bank of the Aare, with beautiful vistas of the mountains ahead. In another 2.5 km/ 2 miles, beyond the huts on the Aussere Urweid (716 m/2349 ft), a narrow stretch of road above the gorge-like valley bears left around a wall of rock and passes through the short Zuben tunnel, under a waterfall, into the Innere Urweid (760 m/2494 ft: inn). 1 km/½ mile farther on the road runs through another short tunnel in a rocky spur of the Tönende Fluh, after which the valley opens out a little. At the hamlet of Boden (876 m/2874 ft) the road crosses the river and winds its way up the wooded mountainside, with four hairpin bends, to Guttanen (1060 m/3478 ft), the last village in the Oberhaslital, under the precipitous Ritzlihorn (3282 m/10,768 ft), which every year sends its dreaded avalanches tumbling down into the Spreitlaui valley. The crystal museum at Wirzen in Guttanen has examples of crystals from the Hasli valley and other regions of Switzerland.

Guttanen

The Grimsel Lake

*Grimsel road

The Grimsel road proper, which begins at Guttanen, follows a fairly straight and gentle course up the valley for a kilometre or so, begins to climb more steeply through the forest and crosses the river on the Tschingel bridge (1140 m/3740 ft). It then passes rugged black crags and massive accumulations of debris which bear witness to the violence of the avalanches and the rushing torrents, returns by the Schwarzbrunnen bridge to the left bank (1217 m/3993 ft) and continues around the rocky bulk of the Stäubender. The compensation reservoir of the Handegg I hydro-electric station is passed on the left (1309 m/4295 ft). Then two sharp bends carry the road up through a further stretch of forest to the Handegg (Handeck) saddle, 150 m/492 ft higher up. From a wider length of road there is a view of the Handegg falls, in which the grey-green waters of the Aare mingle with the silvery Aerlenbach, emerging below the road, and plunge into the chasm 46 m/151 ft below. Soon after this, off the road to the right, is the Hotel Handeck (1404 m/4607 ft). From here a cableway (for industrial use only) ascends the east side of the valley to the Gelmersee (1849 m/6067 ft), an artificial lake formed by a dam 35 m/115 ft high. The Grimsel road follows the valley bottom, strewn with boulders, and then winds its way, with sharp bends, up the granite mountainside, worn smooth by the glaciers, to the Kunzentännlen Alp (1616 m/5302 ft), where the last firs disappear, giving place to dwarf pines and rhododendrons. To the right, below, is the Handegg I hydro-electric station with its lake; to the left, higher up, the Gerstin glacier; straight ahead the dam of the Räterichsboden reservoir, up to which the road now winds its way (one hairpin bend). Above, to the right, is the Räterichsboden reservoir (1767 m/5798 ft), which the road skirts, with a view of the Grimselsee dam; near the end of the lake it passes through a short tunnel. The road then climbs again (to the right, below, a fine view of the Räterichsboden lake), and after two hairpin bends at the massive Seeuferegg dam, reaches the Grimselsee (1909 m/6263 ft), a fjord-like lake

*Handegg falls

Räterichsboden reservoir

*Grimselsee

extending for 5.5 km/3 miles to the Unteraar glacier (nature reserve). A road on the right (0.8 km/½ mile) leads by way of the Seeuferegg dam (325 m/1155 ft long, up to 42 m/138 ft high) to the Grimsel hospice (hotel and restaurant, 1960 m/6431 ft on the Granite ridge of Nollen, with a view of the Spitallamm (258 m/846 ft long, up to 114 m/374 ft high) and a magnificent view over the lake of the Zinkenstock, the Finsteraarhorn and the Agassizhorn. There is a rewarding walk from the hotel (2–3 hours) to the Unteraar glacier.

*Oberhasli
power stations

The Oberhasli hydro-electric scheme (1925-54) comprises four separate power stations. The Handegg I station (90,000 kW), built in 1925-32, uses the water of the Grimselsee (100 million cu. m/3531 million cu. ft), formed by the Seeuferegg and Spitallamm dams, which is carried in a 5 km/3 mile-long tunnel to a subsidiary reservoir, the Gelmersee (13 million cu. m/459 million cu. ft) and the power station 540 m/1772 ft below. The Innertkirchen station (192,000 kW) uses water from Handegg I, which is conveyed to it in a tunnel 10 km/6 miles long. The Handegg II station (60,000 kW), built in 1947–50, obtains its water from the Räterichsboden lake (27 million cu. m/953 million cu. ft) and the small Gauli reservoir in the Upper Urbach valley. The power station (underground) is at Handegg. The Oberaar station (31,000 kW), built in 1950–54, uses water from the Oberaarsee, formed by a dam 525 m/1723 ft long and 105 m/345 ft high; the underground power station is between the Grimselsee and Räterichsboden. An expansion of the power station is planned for the 90s, with the construction of a new dam.

*Grimsel pass

*Kleines
Siedelhorn

From the Seeuferegg dam the Grimsel road skirts the east end of the Grimselsee and then climbs on a moderate gradient (four sharp bends), with magnificent views to the rear (Grosser Schreckhorn, to the west, 4080 m/13,386 ft). 3.5 km/2 miles farther on is the Grimsel pass (2165 m/7103 ft; Hotel Grimselblick, 80b.), on the boundary between the cantons of Berne and Valais, with beautiful views of the Valais Alps, particularly the Gries glacier. Rewarding climb (2½ hours) of the Kleines Siedelhorn (2768 m/9082 ft; fine panorama). From the top of the pass a beautiful but narrow private road (alternating one-way traffic) runs 6 km/4 miles west to the Oberaarsee (58 million cu. m/2048 million cu. ft), with a car park and the Berghaus Oberaar (hotel and restaurant, 12b., camp-site; alt. 2340 m/7678 ft). A little farther on, to the right, are the Hotel Grimselpass Höhe (30b.) and the Totensee (2144 m/7034 ft), whose name ("Lake of the Dead") commemorates the bitter fighting here between Austrian and French forces in 1799. Various crystals from the region are exhibited in the crystal cavern at Grimsel.

Gletsch

The road descends the steep slope of the Meienwang in six sharp bends, with views of the Rhône glacier and the windings of the Furka road: to the left the Galenstock and Dammastock, to the south-east the Pizzo Rotondo. It then comes to Gletsch (1763 m/5784 ft) at the lower end of the debris-covered valley, which a century ago was blanketed for more than half its area by the Rhône glacier.

*Furka road

*Rhône glacier

In Gletsch the Furka road crosses the Rhône and then climbs (three sharp bends) up the south side of the valley and follows the slope, with fine views of Gletsch and the Grimsel road to the rear and of the Rhône glacier ahead. At the head of the valley the road crosses the narrow-gauge Furka railway, the middle section (completed 1927) of the line from Lake Geneva to Lake Constance by way of the Rhône and Rhine valleys ("Glacier express" from Zermatt to St Moritz). The road then crosses the Muttbach bridge and climbs steeply (five hairpin bends) up the north side of the valley, with beautiful views of the Rhône glacier and of Gletsch far below. In 7 km/4 miles the car park of the Belvedere restaurant (2272 m/7454 ft), is reached. From here it is only a few minutes walk to the Rhône glacier, between the

View of the Rhône Glacier from the Furka road

Grosses Furkahorn (3217 m/10,555 ft) and the Gerstenhörner (3184 m/10,447 ft), which hangs over the side of the valley in a formidable cataract of ice (charge for access: interesting artificial cave hewn from the glacier).

The road continues to climb (two steep bends), with a magnificent view of the Rhône glacier to the rear, and to the right, above the Gratschluckt glacier, of the Grosses Muttenhorn (3103 m/10,181 ft). In 2.5 km/2 miles the road reaches the Furka pass (2431 m/7976 ft). The Furka ("Fork") is a saddle, falling steeply away on each side, between the Kleines Furkahorn (3026 m/9928 ft; 2 hours north) and the Blauberg (2757 m/9046 ft; 1½ hours south), both offering easy and rewarding climbs. It forms the boundary between the cantons of Valais and Uri and affords magnificent views, extending north-east to the Urseren valley and the Oberalp pass and west to the Bernese Alps (Finsteraarhorn) and the Valais Alps (Weisshorn). Rewarding climb, to the north, of the Galenstock (3583 m/11,756 ft; 5 hours, with guide), which commands extensive views.

* Furka pass

Since 1983 the Swiss art exhibitor Marc Hostettler has invited artists to show their "Furka art" on the Furka pass every spring. Nature determines the end of the event, the first snow being the signal to dismantle the exhibition. Among the artists who have shown work here are Rémy Zaugg, Gianni Colombo, Per Kirkeby, Stanley Brown, Caniel Buren and Ian Hamilton Finlay.

Furka art

500 m/1641 ft farther on is the Hotel Furkablick (30b.). The road then continues downhill, high up on the bare north face of the Garschental, a valley constantly threatened by avalanches, with the Furka-Reuss flowing down below. Views of the Siedeln glacier and the sharp pinnacles of the Bielenhorn (2947 m/9669 ft). Then by way of the Tiefentobel gorge (to the left a waterfall) to the Hotel Tiefenbach (2109 m/6920 ft; 20 b.). 1.5 km/1 mile farther on at the Ebnetenalp (2010 m/6595 ft), where the road takes a sharp bend to the right, there are magnificent views of the Urseren valley and the

Realp

*Pizzo Rotondo

Wyttenwasser valley, which now opens up to the south, with Piz Lucendro (2964 m/9725 ft). Now down the rounded slopes of Fuchsegg (nine sharp bends) to the valley bottom and the little village of Realp (1547 m/5076 ft), the name of which is derived from "riva alpa" (riva,"stream"; alpa,"mountain pasture"). To the south-east is Pizzo Rotondo (3192 m/10,473 ft; 8 hours, with guide), the highest peak in the St Gotthard group.

The road now follows a level and almost straight course down the wide Urseren valley, between the river Furka-Reuss and the Furka railway, which is crossed in another 3 km/2 miles. From this point the road becomes narrower. Ahead can be seen the square tower of Hospental castle. 6 km/4 miles from Realp is Hospental (1484 m/4869 ft; bypass), an old village (from hospitum, "hospice") situated at the point where the Furka-Reuss and Gotthard-Reuss join to form the Reuss, a popular health and winter sports resort. It is dominated by a church (1705–11) and 13th c. castle tower. From here follow road 2 to Andermatt.

Appenzell   E1

Cantons: Appenzell-Ausserhoden (AR, main town: Herisau)
Appenzell-Innerrhoden (AI, main town: Appenzell)

Situation and general

This attractive Pre-Alpine region in eastern Switzerland, just south of Lake Constance, reaching its highest point in the Säntis (2504 m/8216 ft) in the Alpstein range, is the only Swiss canton which is completely surrounded by another canton (St Gallen). It is subdivided into two independent half-cantons, established in 1597 following democratic votes in the two religious communities, Appenzell-Ausserrhoden being Protestant and Appenzell-Innerrhoden Roman Catholic. The division also reflects a geographical difference; Innerrhoden consists mainly of the Alpstein and Säntis massifs, while Ausserrhoden takes in the upland region to the north of the Säntis

The town of Appenzell

range. Both the half-cantons reach their most important political decisions at the Landsgemeinde, the annual meeting, held in the open air, of all the men of the community.

In the Middle Ages Appenzell belonged to the Prince-Abbot of St Gallen, but at the beginning of the 15th c. it broke away after a valiant and determined struggle for independence, and in 1513 became the last canton in the 13-member confederation, which received no further accessions until the French Revolution. The canton owed its prosperity in earlier centuries to its flourishing textile industry, and many villages still have handsome houses with curved gables dating from this period. History

According to legend the devil once flew over the region with his sack full of towns and villages. A sharp rock from Mt Säntis tore a hole in his bundle, through which thousands of houses fell and were scattered over the countryside, this being the reason for the typically wide dispersal of settlements. Folk art is deeply rooted in Appenzell traditions; in Innerrhoden in particular an ancient culture characteristic of these upland pastoral regions is still very much alive. Naïve peasant painting is to be seen everywhere in the canton, and other old crafts still practised are the making of bell harness and coopering. Folk music played by string bands (violins, cellos, double basses, dulcimers) and the elegant local costumes also play an important part in the ancient traditions of the sociably disposed people of Appenzell. Folk art and customs

The annual general meeting of the Landsgemeinde is an impressive experience for any visitor who is fortunate enough to be present. On the last Sunday in April all citizens entitled to vote – men over the age of 20 – make their way wearing swords, to the square where the meeting takes place. The men of Ausserrhoden meet alternately in Trogen, headquarters of the cantonal court and the cantonal police, and in Hundwil. The men of Innerrhoden, carrying their swords as evidence of their right to vote, meet in the cantonal capital, Appenzell. The landamman (chief magistrate) and other members of the cantonal government are elected by show of hands and solemnly sworn in on the spot. Every citizen has the right to speak, and can put forward a proposal for legislation or constitutional amendment. Landsgemeinde

Appenzell is served by good roads and by narrow-gauge railways. The Appenzellerbahn runs from Gossau, in the Unterland, via Herisau and Urnäsch to the town of Appenzell, and from there to Weissbad and Wasserauen; the Gaiserbahn links St Gallen and Altstätten with Appenzell, and there are other lines from Rorschach, St Gallen and Rheineck to Heiden, Trogen and Walzenhausen. Transport

Around Mt Säntis

The highest peak in the Alpstein massif, which consists of three ranges lying between the Rhine valley, Toggenburg and the Vorderland of Appenzell, is the Säntis (2504 m/8216 ft), a mountain much favoured by hill-walkers, climbers and those who prefer to make the ascent by cableway. From the summit there are panoramic views of the Vorarlberg, Grisons, Glarus and Uri Alps and across Lake Constance and far into Southern Germany (Swabia). To the north-west of the peak the boundaries of the two half-cantons and of the canton of St Gallen meet.

From the Schwägalp (1283 m/4210 ft; inn, 64b.) a cableway runs up, with only two intervening supports, to the Säntis (upper station 2476 m/8124 ft; length 2307 m/7569 ft, height difference 1193 m/3914 ft, time 10 minutes; restaurant and inn, 20b.). The ascent on foot takes 3½ hours from the Schwägalp and 4–5 hours from Wasserauen.
The railway line from St Gallen via Herisau (11 km/7 miles; change trains) terminates at Urnäsch (23 km/14 miles), from where there is a bus to the *Säntis

Schwägalp (11 km/7 miles; 30 minutes). The road from St Gallen to Urnäsch (32 km/20 miles passes through the villages of Stein and Hundwil.

Urnäsch

Urnäsch (alt. 826 m/2710 ft; pop. 2300) is the largest in area and one of the oldest communes in Appenzell-Ausserrhoden. The village square with its trim wooden houses reflects the people's attachment to tradition, and Urnäsch is widely known for its rustic dances, New Year celebrations and other traditional observances. It has a museum of Appenzell traditions and a local museum. Footpaths lead into the surrounding hills.

From Urnäsch it is 14 km/9 miles to Appenzell. The road comes in 4 km/ 2 miles to Jakobsbad (alt. 876 m/2874 ft; chalybeate spring), from which there is a cableway up the Kronberg (1663 m/5465 ft: length 3223 m/10.575 ft, height difference 772 m/2533 ft, time 8 minutes; restaurant). 2 km/1 m le beyond this is Gonten (alt. 903 m/2963 ft).

Appenzell

Appenzell (alt. 789 m/2589 ft; pop. 5000) has been since 1597 capital of the Roman Catholic half-canton of Appenze I Innerrhoden. The town centre is well preserved, with fine old traditional houses. Interspersed among the painted wooden houses are stone buildings dating from the 16th c., n- cluding the Town Hall (local museum), the Schloss and the parish church of St Mauritius (nave of 1823). Also of interest are the Landesgemeindeplatz, the square on which the annual meeting of the community takes place, the churches of the nunnery and the Capuchin friary, Retonio's museum of mechanical musical instruments, the "Blaues Haus" private museum and the show cellar for Appenzeller cheese, belonging to the Züger firm.

Appenzell is the terminus of the Gaiserbahn from St Gallen and a station on the Appenzellerbahn from Gossau, which runs via Weissbad (alt. 820 m/2690 ft; pop. 1500) to Wasserauen (alt. 872 m/2861 ft). *Gaiserbahn, Appenzellerbahn*

There is a cableway to Ebenalp (1644 m/5394 ft; inn), from which it is a 10- minute walk down through a 75 m/82 yard-long cavern to the Wildkirchli (1477 m/4864 ft; inn), a chapel in a cave which was inhabited by hermits from 1658 to 1853. In 1904 Palaeolithic implements and animal skeletons were found here. From Wasserauen there is a pleasant walk (1 hour) to the Seealpsee (1146 m/3760 ft) and from there to the Meglisalp (1520 m/4987 ft; inn) with its little church of "Maria zum Schnee". *Ebenalp *Wildkirchli*

Brülisau

Brülisau (alt. 922 m/3025 ft; pop. 700), the terminus of a postal bus service (Swiss postal buses convey both passengers and mail), has a cableway up the Hoher Kasten (1794 m/5886 ft), from which there is a geological trail to Staubern. A road leads from the Brülitobel gorge to the Sämtisersee and Fählensee (mountain inns). Other good climbs are up Fähnern (1506 m/4941 ft), with a little lake, the Forstseeli, and by way of the steep "Zahme Gocht" up the Alpsigel (1662 m/5453 ft).

In the Vorderland of Ausserrhoden

Herisau

Herisau (alt. 778 m/2553 ft; pop. 15,000), capital of the half-cantor of Ausserrhoden, lies at the junction of the St Gallen – Wattwil (Bodensee –

◄ *Ascending the Säntis by cable-car*

Toggenburg – Bahn) and Gossach – Urnäsch – Appenzell (Appenzeller-bahn) railway lines, and has a postal bus service to Hundwil – Teufen – Speicher – Trogen and Schwellbrun. The straggling little town has a beautiful square amd is a local market and industrial focal point.

A good impression of the character of the half-canton can be gained on the drive from Herisau to St Margrethen (49 km/30 miles), via Waldstatt, Teufen (18 km/11 miles), Trogen (25 km/16 miles), Heiden (35 km/22 miles) and Walzenhausen. The road crosses a number of deep gorges, including the Hundwiler Tobel near Waldstatt (concrete viaduct with a span of 105 km/345 ft).

Hundwil

Hundwil (alt. 793 m/2602 ft; pop. 1000; inn) has handsome old houses in the characteristic local style and a 13th c. church. The Hundwiler Höhi (1305 m/4282 ft), with a mountain inn, is a favourite local excursion.

Stein

1 km/½ mile beyond Hundwil we turn off the road to Appenzell (8 km/5 miles) to reach Stein (alt. 823 m/2700 ft; pop. 1050) where daffodils, a protected species, bloom in March. Tourists can visit a model cheese factory opened in 1978.

*Appenzeller model cheese factory

About 4500 litres of fresh milk are delivered daily from the surrounding farms with the same amount again brought by tanker from more distant farms so that about 9000 litres of unpasteurised milk are processed daily.

Production of Appenzeller cheese

The milk is first sieved, tested and weighed. If the milk needs to be stored before the next process it is cooled and stored in large vats at 10° C/50° F. The fat content of Appenzeller cheese is regulated to exactly 50% of the dry mass so some of the milk is skimmed in centrifuges.
The skimmed and full cream milk then flow over a heat exchanger, where it is heated, into the so-called cheese kettle, which contains about 600 litres of milk. The milk is constantly stirred as it is heated to a temperature of 32° C/90° F, at which it coagulates, and the rennet and the lactic acid bacteria (natural coagulants and fermentation additives) are added. The cheese then begins to ferment and after about 30–40 minutes it coagulates to form curds, which are broken up with the cheese sieve. The resulting crumbs – small lumps the size of maize kernels – separate from the whey. After the initial process has finished the curds are gently heated and stirred constantly until the necessary thickness has been reached.
During the next stage the lumpy mixture is siphoned up with the whey and poured into the pressing tub, where it is formed into blocks of cheese which are cut into pieces and shaped. The remaining whey is squeezed out of the fresh cheeses, which are turned several times.
The whey is completely skimmed of cream, after it has passed over the heat exchanger and through the centrifuge, before it enters the whey tank. It still contains protein and minerals and provides a valuable source of nutrition for pigs.
The temperature is regulated in the drying-room where the cheeses begin to form a crust. The salt dip promotes the formation of a perfect crust and determines the flavour and storage properties of the cheese.
The cheese is allowed to ferment and ripen naturally in cellars with a temperature of 14–15° C/57°–59° F and a relative humidity of over 90%.
About five to seven weeks after manufacture the cheeses reach the retail trade, where they are stored and subjected to further quality controls relating to texture, hole formation, colour, appearance and smell.
The cheese-dealer regularly bastes the cheese with the so-called "Sulze", made from white wine, herbs and spices (a secret traditional recipe), which

gives the "Appenzeller" its typical flavour and special aroma. After 3½–5 months the cheese is ripe and ready for sale.

Teufen

Teufen (alt. 837 m/2746 ft; pop. 5500) a favourite residential town a few kilometres from St Gallen, is situated on the southern s opes of the Fröhlichsegg (1003 m/3291 ft; 20 minutes to top; restaurant). In the handsome square stands an interesting church built in 1778 by the family of a local builder, Hans Ulrich Grubenmann. Domestic industry (embroidery, weaving).

*Fröhlichsegg

Beyond Teufen lies the pretty village of Bühler (alt. 828 m/2717 ft; pop. 1700), with trim houses in the local style.

Bühler

Gais

Gais (alt. 933 m/3061 ft; pop. 2400) is a popular health resort with one of the prettiest squares in the region (typical houses with curved gables). This was the first resort to offer the whey cure – medical treatment involving the medicinal properties of milk. There is a school of folk art. From the top of the Gäbris (1247 m/4091 ft; 1 hour; inn) there are magnificent views in all directions (road closed on Saturdays and Sundays).

4 km/2 miles above Gais, on the Stoss pass (938 m/3078 ft; inn) are a chapel and a monument commemorating the victory of 400 Appenzellers over 3000 Austrians in 1405.

Stoss

5 km/3 miles north-east of Teufen the health resort of Speicher (alt. 926 m/3038 ft; pop. 3350), is an idyllic village, to the north of which is the Vögelinsegg (959 m/3146 ft). Here stands a monument commemorating the Appenzellers' victory over the Abbot of St Gallen in 1403 and there are extensive views of the Lake Constance area.

Speicher

Trogen

Trogen (alt. 903 m/2963 ft; pop. 1950), the terminus of the St Gallen – Speicher – Trogen tramway, houses the cantonal court and the cantonal school. In the centre of the village is the Landsgemeindeplatz, the elegant square in which the cantonal assembly meets in even-numbered years (in Hundswil in odd-numbered years); the square is surrounded by fine 18th c. houses, a church built by Grubenmann in 1779 and the Town Hall.

South-west of Trogen is the Pestalozzi Children's Village for orphans of many nationalities, founded by the Zurich philosopher Walter Robert Corti in 1946.
From Trogen a beautiful minor road leads via the Ruppen (1010 m/3314 ft; inn) into the Rhine valley.

Pestalozzi
Children's
Village

Heiden

Another winding road (14 km/9 miles) runs via Wald and Scheidegg (side roads to Rehetobel and Oberegg) to Heiden (alt. 806 m/2644 ft; pop. 4000), a popular health resort in a park-like setting high above Lake Constance (rack-railway (cog-railway) from Rorschach, 7 km/4 miles in 25 minutes), where a monument stands to Henri Dunant, founder of the Red Cross, who lived in Heiden from 1887 until his death in 1910. This village has recently been declared a protected area and is a prime example of Biedermeier style.

Dunant Museum

Arosa

Wienacht	To the north, via Grub, lies the village of Wienacht (alt. 734 m/2408 ft) with the Tobel vineyards.
Rheineck, Walzenhausen, Oberegg	From Rheineck there is a rack-railway (1898 m/6227 ft long; 6 minutes to Walzenhausen (alt. 673 m/2208 ft; pop. 2000) above Lake Constance, and Oberegg (alt. 880 m/2887 ft; pop. 2500), an enclave of Innerrhoden, 3 km/ 2 miles south-west of which is the St Anton viewpoint (1121 m/3678 ft).
Schönengrund	Between Herisau and Wattwil, on the Wasserfluh road, is Schönengrund (alt. 836 m/2743 ft), which has a chair-lift up Hochhamm (length 1345 m/4413 ft, height difference 328 m/1076 ft, time 15 minutes). On a ridge
Schwellbrunn	of hills is the highest holiday village in Ausserrhoden, Schwellbrunn (alt. 966 m/3169 ft; pop. 1200).

Arosa   E2

Canton: Grisons (GR)
Altitude: 1740–1890 m/5709–6201 ft
Population: 2700

Situation	The popular summer and winter resort of Arosa seems in a world of its own, lying as it does in a sheltered hollow in the high valley of the Schanfigg, surrounded by mountains, well away from the main traffic routes of the Grisons. The road from Chur, almost 1200 m/3937 ft below, to Arosa is 30 km/19 miles long and has many bends; there is also a narrow-gauge railway, opened in 1914, which takes just under an hour to reach the resort.
History	The first settlement in the Arosa valley, then accessible only by troublesome bridle-paths, was initiated about 1220 by the monasteries of Churwalden and Sankt Luzi in Chur, and soon afterwards the population was

Arosa in winter

increased by some families brought in from the Valais by the Barons of Vaz. From 1320 to 1851 Arosa belonged to the parish and commune of Davos, but thereafter became an independent commune. In the 15th c. the village had a population of only 150. The little village church was built in 1490. In 1575 most of the mountain pastures were sold to the town of Chur, which still owns some land in the commune. By 1850 the population had fallen to no more than 50. In 1875, however, the post road from Chur to Langwies was constructed, and in 1890 it was extended to Arosa; in 1880 the Seehof hotel was built to provide accommodation for visitors. By the turn of the century Arosa had made a name for itself as a health resort, and in 1913 it ranked briefly as the leading resort in the Grisons. By 1930 the population had risen to 3724. The first ski school was opened in 1933, and the first three cableways were constructed in 1939.

Townscape

With excellent facilities for walkers and climbers in summer and skiers in winter, provision for a great variety of sports and more than 150 km/93 miles of footpaths, Arosa has developed into a leading resort. Other features of interest are the Late Gothic church (1493) in Inner-Arosa and the Schanfigg Local Museum (history of iron-mining and winter sports). In summer a miniature railway operates at the Arosa Kulm Hotel. Driving is prohibited in the town after dark.

Arosa is an attractive town, with hotels dispersed about the beautiful sheltered valley and numerous small lakes. The tree-line passes through the resort, so that the skiing areas are almost completely open. The road from Chur runs from the Obersee (Upper Lake, 1740 m/5709 ft; rowing boats), beside the railway station, above the Untersee (Lower Lake 1694 m/5558 ft, in a charming wooded setting, past the Kursaal (gaming casino) and up above the tree-line to the Alpine meadows of Inner-Arosa, sloping gently uphill.

To the north is the mountain village of Maran, a favourite objective of walkers, reached on the "Eichhörnliweg" (Squirrel's Path). There are easy mountain walks over the Strela pass to Davos and by way of the Aroser Weisshorn to the Parpaner Weisshorn. — Maran

Cableways from Arosa station to the Mittlere Hütte (2013 m/6605 ft) and the Weisshorn (2653 m/8704 ft; 15 minutes, restaurant) and from the lower station "Am Wasser" (1830 m/6004 ft) to the Hörnligrat (2493 m/8180 ft; 15 minutes; mountain hut, serviced). — Cableways

Natural and artificial ice rinks (curling); toboggan run; cross-country skiing; ski-bob runs; ski-lifts on Tschuggen, Plattenhorn (2318 m/7605 ft), Hörnli, Carmenna (2177 m/7143 ft) and Alp Prätschli. The most popular ski runs are on the Weisshorn (2657 m/8718 ft), Brüggerhorn (2429 m/7970 ft; chair-lift) and Hörnli (2497 m/8193 ft); on all three are serviced ski huts. — Winter sports

Surroundings

Magnificent footpaths through the pine-forests and flower-spangled Alpine meadows: north over the Maran plateau to Alp Prätschli (2000 m/6562 ft; ski-lift), 1 hour from Inner-Arosa past the Schwellisee (1919 m/6296 ft) to the romantic Aelplisee (2192 m/7192 ft), 1¾ hours; from the Untersee up the Welschtobel gorge to the waterfalls on the Alteinbach, 1 hour.
The best climbs are the Aroser Weisshorn (2653 m/8704 ft), 2½ hours by way of the Mittlere Hütte, easy, and the Aroser Rothorn (2984 m/9791 ft), 4 hours, rather more difficult, with superb views.

Ascona   D2

Canton: Ticino (TI)
Altitude: 196 m/643 ft
Population: 5000

Situation and general

Thanks to its beautiful situation in a mist-free bay on Lake Maggiore, sheltered from the north winds, and to its sub-tropical vegetation, Ascona has developed from a little fishing village into one of Switzerland's most popular holiday resorts, excellently equipped for visitors. It has long hours of sunshine and a mild winter. The main areas of activity from spring into autumn are the picturesque town, a pedestrian precinct with numerous little shops, art galleries and antique dealers, and the piazza on the lake.

*Townscape

History

A prehistoric cemetery excavated in 1952 provided evidence of a Bronze Age settlement here (*c.* 800 B.C.). The town was "discovered" by a group of vegetarians and nature-worshippers who settled on Monte Verità before and during the First World War. The artists' colony of Ascona attracted such leading figures as Lenin, Leoncavallo, Isadora Duncan, J. C. Jung and Rudolf Steiner, and later residents included the writers Remarque and Herman Hesse and the painters Paul Klee, M. von Werefkin and Jawlensky.

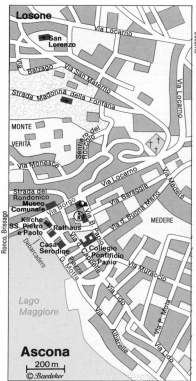

Ascona: Lakeside promenade

Baroque decoration on the Casa Serodine

In the 1930s many refugees found a home on Lake Maggiore. The extensive modern development has unfortunately swallowed up the old village.

Sights

The Collegio Pontificio Papio (1584) has one of the finest Renaissance courtyards in Switzerland (two-storey loggias). In the church of Santa Maria della Misericordia (1399–1442), belonging to a Dominician Monastery, is a cycle of late Gothic frescoes.

Collegio
Pontificio Papio

Casa Serodine (1620), now known as Casa Borrani, has a sumptuous façade of Baroque stucco (a frieze of mythical creatures and bible scenes).

Casa Serodine

The parish church of SS Pietro e Paolo (first referred to in 1264; rebuilt in the 16th c.), a pillared basilica with lateral aisles, has a high altar painting by Giovanni Serodine (1633) "Coronation of the Virgin".

In the Via Borgo (No. 34) the Museo Communale has an important art collection including works by Marianne von Werefkin (1860–1938), Richard Seewald (1896–1976), Otto Niemeyer-Holstein, Maurice Utrillo, Paul Klee, Hermann Hesse and Fritz Pauli. (Special exhibitions during the summer months.)

Paintings are also exhibited in the Casa Beato P. Berno, a typical Ticinese Baroque house (now a craft centre) and in the Casa Anatta, Monte Verità, are documents about the history of the mountain. To the south lies the large lido, an 18-hole golf-course and the airport.

St Peter and St Paul

Surroundings

The road to Verbania (No. 13) follows the steep north-west shore of Lake Maggiore (see entry). To the right, high above the lake, is the picturesque village of Ronco; to the left are two small islands, the Isole di Brissago or dei Conigli ("Rabbit Islands"), on the larger of which is an interesting Botanic garden of Mediterranean flora. 3.5 km/2 miles away is Port Ronco, where a minor road from Ronco joins on the right.

**Lake
Maggiore

3.5 km/2 miles is Brissago (alt. 219 m/719 ft), a popular summer resort (bathing lido), also noted for the manufacture of cigars ("Brissago", a long thin Virginia cigar). The town is charmingly situated at the foot of Monte Limidario (2189 m/7182 ft), on the lower slopes of which are beautiful gardens with Mediterranean plants and vineyards. 2 km/1 mile beyond Brissago, at the little Lombard-style Renaissance church of the Madonna del Ponte (1528), is the Italian frontier.

Brissago

Baden

D1

Canton: Aargau
Altitude: 385 m/1263 ft
Population: 15,000

The health resort of Baden has long been an important market town. The picturesque old town, the core of the medieval settlement, lies in the Limmat defile under the Lägern hills; downstream is the spa, with its 19 sulphur springs (48° C/118° F), already used for medicinal purposes in Roman times. To the west of the spa, where the valley opens out, are the newer parts of the town, with large industrial plants, (Brown-Boveri).

Situation and general

Known to the Romans as Aquae Helvetiae, Baden became in the Middle Ages the country's leading curative resort, the hot sulphurous water (1000

History

Baden, on the Limmat

cu. m/35,310 cu. ft daily) being piped up from a great depth. The town's central situation and its political activity made it a place of importance in the old Confederation, and the Diet frequently met here. The first hydro-electric power station was brought into operation in Baden in 1892.

Sights

At the entrance to the fine old town, to the north, stands the 15th c. Bruggerturm (54 m/177 ft high). A little way south-east is the Roman Catholic parish church (built 1457–70, remodelled in Baroque style in 1612–98 and in Neo-classical style in 1813–29), and facing it, to the north, the Stadthaus (Town Hall), with the Council Chamber (reconstructed in 1497) in which the Diet met between 1424 and 1712. The Swiss Children's Museum (29 Ölrainstrasse), situated about three minutes from the station, gives an insight into the history and manufacture of toys (open Wed.,Sat. and Sun.). A covered wooden bridge (1810) leads across the Limmat to the Landvogteischloss (rebuilt 1487–89), the old governor's residence, which now houses the Historical Museum. On a crag to the west of the old town (road and rail tunnel) is the ruined castle of Stein, formerly a Habsburg seat.

Children's Museum

Historical Museum

Kappelerhof

At Kappelerhof power station a small technical museum has impressive exhibits from the pioneering age of electricity production.

*Brown Art Collection

The opening of the Brown Art Collection is planned for early 1990. Around the turn of the century Sidney and Jenny Brown began to compile a comprehensive collection of paintings of English artists, the Munich school and French impressionists. The last surviving member of the family, John A. Brown, left the house and collection to the town of Baden on his death in 1987. The collection includes works by Cézanne, Gauguin, Monet, Degas, Sisley, Bonnard, Van Gogh and Renoir.

The spa is beautifully laid out with gardens, and has a Kursaal, with a gaming room, restaurant, inhalatorium (establishment where sulphur

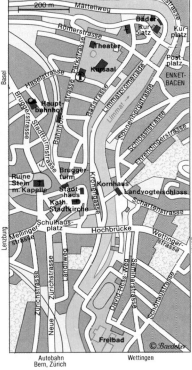

Baden: Old Town, with Bruggerturm

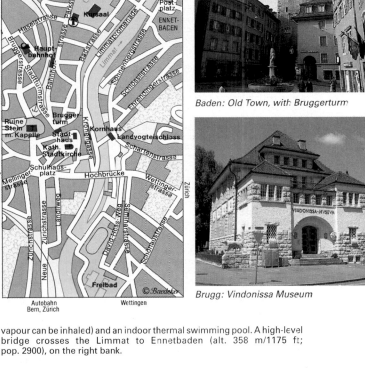

Brugg: Vindonissa Museum

vapour can be inhaled) and an indoor thermal swimming pool. A high-level bridge crosses the Limmat to Ennetbaden (alt. 358 m/1175 ft; pop. 2900), on the right bank.

Surroundings

Baden is a good base for walks and climbs in the Lägern hills. 2¼ hours from Ennetbaden rises the Burghorn (863 m/2832 ft), the highest point in these eastern outliers of the Jura (views of the Alps and Black Forest); ½ hour east above the Limmat bridge, is Schartenfels (467 m/1532 ft; restaurant), and 2 km/1 mile west Baldegg (572 m/1877 ft; restaurant), with a view of the Alps.

South of Baden the largest commune in the Aargau, Wettingen (alt. 395 m/1296 ft; pop. 19,500), was once a sleepy little wine-growing village, which has developed since the last war into a favourite residential town. In the bend of the Limmat is the best preserved Cistercian monastery in the country, now a teachers' training college. The abbey (founded 1227) has superb Late Renaissance and Rococo decoration, finely carved choir-stalls and in the cloister some of the best stained glass in Switzerland (182 roundels with coats of arms and figures, 13th–17th c.). The extensive

Wettingen

*Cistercian monastery

95

renovations to the exterior and the redevelopment of the cloister and chapter-house were completed in 1988. Refurbishment of the interior is planned for 1990 and should last about three years.

Brugg

10 km/6 miles north-west of Baden lies Brugg (alt. 355 m/1165 ft), an old town of 7000 inhabitants and an important traffic junction near the confluence of the Aare, the Reuss and the Limmat. As the name indicates it grew up around its bridge, near which are the Black Tower (Schwarzer Turm, 11th c.) and the Town Hall. In the old-world main street (No. 39) stands the house in which the educationist Heinrich Pestalozzi (1746-1827) died; his grave is at Birr, 7 km/4 miles south. The Vindonissa Museum contains a rich collection of material from the Roman fort of Vindonissa (A.D. 1, now called Windisch).

*Königsfelden
convent

The Zurich road (No. 3) passes the former convent of Königsfelden (on left), founded in 1308 by Elisabeth , widow of the German King Albrecht I, on the spot where he was murdered by Duke Johann of Swabia. The convent was converted into a mental hospital in 1866–72. The choir of the Gothic church has magnificent 14th c. stained glass.

Windisch

1 km/½ mile beyond this is Windisch (alt. 366 m/1201 ft; to the left of road), on the left bank of the Reuss, the site of Roman Vindonissa. On the road to Lucerne, which goes off on the left just before the village, are remains of a large amphitheatre which could seat 10,000 spectators.

Basle   C1

Canton: Basel-Stadt (BS)
Altitude: 256 m–282 m/840–925 ft
Population: 180,000

**Situation and
Townscape

Basle (German Basel, French Bâle), Switzerland's second largest city, lying close to the French and German frontiers, has been an independent half-canton (Basel-Stadt) since 1833, the other half being Basel-Land. The city is built on both sides of the Rhine, which here takes a sharp turn northward between the Swiss Jura and the Black Forest to enter the Upper Rhine plain; upstream from Basle the river is known as the High Rhine (Hochrhein). Gross-Basel (Great Basle), the city's commercial and cultural centre, lies on the higher left bank; Klein-Basel (Little Basel), where most of its industry is situated, on the flat right bank.

General

Situated on the Swiss frontier and at an important river crossing, Basle soon developed into an important commercial town. Its heavy commercial traffic is now served by two large railway stations and the Rhine harbour (Rheinhafen) at Kleinhüningen, 3 km/2 miles north of the city on the right bank of the river (shipping exhibition, "Our Way to the Sea"; viewing terrace on the grain elevator, 55 m/180 ft high). At St Louis, 9.5 km/6 miles north-west in French territory, is the Basle-Mulhouse airport (restaurant), which is to be expanded into an International-European airport in the 1990s.
The city's main industries are the manufacture of chemicals and pharmaceuticals, machinery and electrical equipment; it also has numerous banks.

History

In the second half of the 1st c. B.C. the hill on which the Minster now stands was occupied by a Celtic settlement, remains of the ramparts of which have been found in the Rittergasse. The proximity of the Roman town of Augusta Raurica, founded in 44 B.C. (see p. 113), led to the establishment of a Roman military station on the hill in 15 B.C. The name Basilia ("royal fortress") first appears in the records in A.D. 374, and soon after that date there is a reference to Basle as the see of a bishop. In the 10th c. the town belonged to Burgundy, and in 1025 it became part of the German Empire. A long history

Basle: View across the Rhine to the Minster

of conflict with the house of Habsburg ended in 1501 when the town joined the Swiss Confederation. In 1529 it went over to the reformed faith. The university, founded by Pope Pius II in 1460, became, thanks to the presence of Erasmus from 1521 onwards, the principal centre of humanism, and its fame was maintained by a series of distinguished scholars and teachers in later periods: the physician Paracelsus lived in Basle in 1527–28, the mathematicians Jakob and Johann Bernoulli taught in the university in the 17th and 18th c., the cultural and art historian Jakob Burckhardt from 1844 to 1893, the philosopher Friedrich Nietzsche from 1869–1879. Among the artists connected with Basle were Hans Holbein the Younger (b. 1497 in Augsburg, d. 1543 in London), who spent many years in Basle between 1515 and 1538, and the 19th c. painter Arnold Böcklin (b. Basle 1827, d. Fiesole 1901).

Museums, Galleries, etc.

Antiquities, Museum of (Antikenmuseum)
and Ludwig Collection,
St-Alben-Graben 5;
Nov.–Apr.: Tue.–Sun, 10–12 and 2–5;
May–Oct.: Tue.–Sun. 10–5.

In the city

Art Collection, Public
(Öffentliche Kunstsammlung),
St-Alben-Graben 16;
Tue.–Sun. 10–5.

Art Gallery
(Kunsthalle),
Steinberg 7;
daily 10–5
Wed. 10–9.30.

Basle

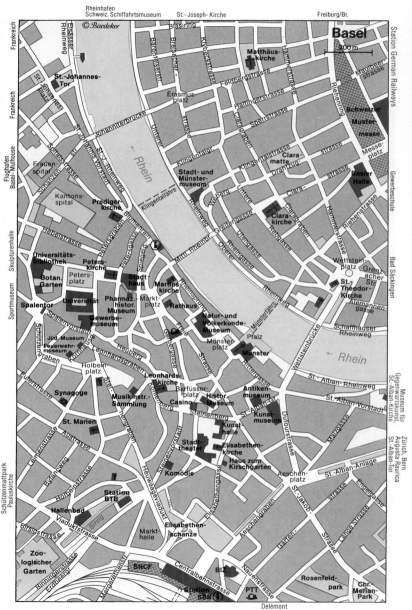

Basle Mission, Exhibition on
(Ausstellung der Basler Mission),
Missionsstrasse 21;
Mon.–Fri. 8–12 and 2–6.

Caricature and Cartoon Collection
(Sammlung Karikaturen und Cartoons),
St-Alban-Vorstadt 9;
Wed. and Sat. 4–6.30; Sun.2–5.

Childhood and Toy Museum
(Museum Kind und Spielzeug),
Oelrainstrasse 29;
Wed. and Sat. 2–5; Sun. 10–5.

City and Minster Museum
(Stadt- und Münstermuseum),
Unterer Rheinweg 26;
Tue.–Sat. 2–5,
Sun. 10–5.

Contemporary Art, Museum of
(Museum für Gegenwartskunst),
St-Alban-Tal 2;
Mon., Wed.–Sun. 10–12 and 2–5.

Firemen's Helmet Museum
(Feuerwehrhelmmuseum),
Kornhausgasse 18;
Sun. 2–5.

Gymnastics and Sport, Swiss Museum of
(Schweizerisches Turn- und Sportmuseum),
Missionsstrasse 28;
daily 2–5,
Sun. also 10–12 midday.

Historical Museum
(Historisches Museum),
(Barfüsserkirche);
Barfüsserplatz;
Mon., Wed.–Sun. 10–5.

Industrial Museum
(Gewerbemuseum),
Spalenvorstadt 2;
Nov.–Apr.: daily 10–12 and 2–5
May–Oct.: Tue.–Sun. 10–5.

Jewish Museum of Switzerland
(Jüdisches Museum der Schweiz),
Kornhausgasse 8;
Mon. and Wed. 2–5,
Sun. 10–12 and 2–5.

Kirschgarten, Haus zum
Elisabethenstrasse 27;
Nov.–Apr.: Tues.–Sun. 10–12 and 2–5,
May–Oct.: Tue.–Sun. 10–5.

Musical Instruments, Collection of Old
(Sammlung alter Musikinstrumente),
Leonhardsstrasse 8;
Wed. and Fri. 2–5,
Sun. 10–12 and 2–5.

Natural History and Ethnography, Museum of
(Natur- und Völkerkundemuseum)
Natural History Museum (Naturhistorisches Museum),
Augustinergasse 2;
Nov.–Apr.: Tue.–Sun. 10–12 and 2–5,
May–Oct.: Tue.–Sun. 10–5.

Swiss Folk Museum (Schweizerisches Museum für Volkskunde),
Münsterplatz 20;
Open as above

Museum of Ethnography (Museum für Völkerkunde),
Augustinergasse 2;
Open as above.

Paper Museum
(Basler Papier- und Buchmuseum),
St-Alban-Tal 35–37,
Tue.–Sun. 2–5.

Pharmacy, Swiss Museum of the History of
(Schweizerisches Pharmaziehistorisches Museum),
Totengässlein 3;
Mon.–Fri. 9–12 and 2–5.

Rathaus
(Council House),
Marktplatz;
Visits by appointment.

Sculpture Gallery
(Skulpturhalle),
Mittlere Strasse 17;
Tue.–Sun. 10–12 and 2–5.

University Library
(Universitätsbibliothek),
Schönbeinstrasse 20;
issue of books on loan Mon.–Fri. 10–5,
catalogue and reading rooms Mon.–Fri. 8.30–7.30, Sat. 8.30–4.30.

In the
surrounding
area

Augusta Raurica,
Roman House and Museum,
Augst;
Nov.–Apr.: daily 10–12 and 1.30–5,
Mar.–Oct.: daily 10–12 and 1.30–6.
Closed Mon. morning.

Rhine Shipping Exhibition
(Rheinschiffahrtsausstellung),
Rheinhafen
Kleinhüningen,
Wiesendamm 4;
Mar.–Oct.: daily 10–12 and 2–5,
Nov.–Feb.: Sat. and Sun. 10–12 and 2–5.

Village and Toy Museum
(Dorf- und Spielzeugmuseum),
Riehen, Baselstrasse 34;
Wed. and Sat. 2–5,
Sun. 10–12 and 2–5.

Description of the Town

Gross-Basel (Great Basle) and Klein-Basel (Little Basle) are linked by six bridges over the Rhine. From the Mittlere Rheinbrücke (Middle Rhine Bridge, 1905), on the position of the first bridge in Basle, built in 1225, there is a fine view of the Minster. Upstream from this bridge are the busy Wettsteinbrücke (built 1879, widened 1937), the Schwarzwaldbrücke (Black Forest Bridge, 1973), which is designed for through traffic and the Eisenbahnbrücke (Railway Bridge), together with the dam of the Birsfelden hydro-electric power station. Downstream are the Johanniterbrücke (built 1882, rebuilt 1934). There are also three ferries, driven by the current, with no motors.

Gross-Basel, on the left bank of the Rhine, still preserves in the central area some features reminiscent of an old Imperial city, in spite of its many modern buildings and its busy commercial activity.

Around the Market Square

The Mittlere Brücke leads into the Marktplatz (Market Square), which is dominated by the brightly painted Rathaus (Council House). The main building, with arcades, is in Late Burgundian Gothic style (1504–21); the new wing to the left and the tall tower on the right are 19th c. additions. The clock is the work of the Master Wilhelms (1511/1512). The wall-paintings in the attractive courtyard are in part the work of Hans Bock (1608–11: restored). The statue (1574) on the outer staircase represents the legendary founder of the town, Munatius Plancus. Visitors can see the two council chambers (the Regierungsratsaal with its impressive wood panelling and the Grossratsaal, which contains 15 coat-of-arms of the Swiss cantons).
*Rathaus

A little way west, at the corner of the Marktplatz and Freie Strasse is the Renaissance Geltenzunfthaus (1578), the guild-house of the wine merchants. In the same street (No. 25) the guild-house of the locksmiths (Ruman Faesch 1488), charmingly decorated in Baroque style in 1733, now houses a restaurant. The guild-house of the Hausgenossen (No. 34), has attractive wall-paintings.
Freie Strasse

A little way west, at Stadthausgasse 13, we find the Rococo Stadthaus (Town House, 1771), and at Totengässlein 3 the Swiss Museum of the History of Pharmacy.
Stadthaus
History of Pharmacy Museum

North-west of the Marktplatz is the little Fischmarkt, with a Gothic fountain (reproduction: original in Historical Museum).
Fish market fountain

*Minster

South-east of the Marktplatz the long Münsterhügel (Minster Hill) rises above the Rhine (reached from St-Alban-Graben by way of Rittergasse). The spacious Münsterplatz, on the site of the Roman fort, is an elegant 18th c. square.
Minster hill

The Minster stands on the highest point of the hill, dominating the city with its two slender spires, its masonry of red Vosges sandstone and its colourful patterned roof. The oldest parts of the building date from the 9th–13th c. It was rebuilt in Gothic style after an earthquake in 1356, and was a cathedral until the Reformation. The high altar and much of the furnishings were destroyed by militant Protestants in 1529. The church's greatest treasures were concealed in the vaulting of the sacristy and escaped destruction, but were sold when the canton was divided into two in 1833 and are now partly in the Historical Museum in Basle and partly dispersed among other museums throughout the world.
History

Basle

The West Front

The west front and towers are entirely Gothic, with the exception of the lower part of the north tower (St George's tower), which dates from the end of the 11th c. St George's tower, with its elegant upper part and spire, is 64.2 m/211 ft in height, the south tower (St Martin's), completed in 1500, is 62.7 m/206 ft high.

The sculptured friezes above the main doorway depict prophets in the outer frieze, roses in the middle one and dancing angels in the inner one. To the right of the doorway is a figure of the "Prince of this world" dallying with one of the Foolish Virgins: from the front he looks like a fine young man, but his back is crawling with adders and noxious vermin symbolising corruption. To the left of the doorway are depicted the founder of the church, the Emperor Henry II, with a model of the building, and the Empress Kunigunde. Farther out, under the towers, two mounted saints represent St George (left) and St Martin (right) and above the latter are a clock and a sundial. On the central gable the figures of the founders appear again, and above them, enthroned and bearing the infant Jesus, is the Virgin (to whom the church is dedicated).

*St Gallus Doorway

The St Gallus doorway in the north transept (12th c.), with numerous Romanesque figures showing an archaic severity of style, is one of the oldest figured doorways in German-speaking territory. Between the slender columns on either side of the doorway are four figures, two on each side, identified by their symbols (the ox, the lion, the eagle and the angel) as Luke, Mark, John and Matthew. To right and left of the Evangelists are six tabernacles with representations of the Six Works of Mercy; above them are John the Baptist with the Lamb of God (left) and John the Evangelist; and above these figures again are two angels with the trumpets of the Last Judgment. The tympanum above the doorway depicts the Wise and Foolish Virgins, with Christ enthroned above them as the Judge of the world, flanked by Peter and Paul, who present to him the foundress and the sculptor. The large rose window above the St Gallus doorway symbolises the Wheel of Fortune. The choir, the lower part of which is Romanesque,

Basle: the Minster . . .   *and Façade of the Town Hall*

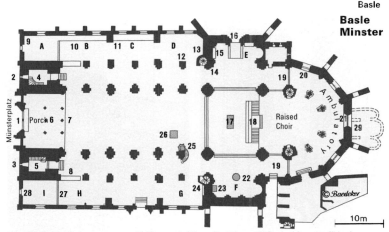

has round arches borne on capitals with rich foliage decoration surmounted by figures of animals. In the paving east of the choir are lines showing the plan of a 9th c. external crypt which was discovered in 1947.

Interior

The church, which was carefully investigated and restored between 1963 and 1975, is 65 m/213 ft long by 32.5 m/107 ft across, with double lateral aisles; the outer aisles were originally a series of interconnected chapels. The raised choir is surrounded by an ambulatory, and under it is the crypt. The Gothic organ gallery was originally a rood-screen which until 1852 separated the chancel from the nave. In front of the pulpit, under glass, is a piece of the Late Romanesque pavement (12th c.). The Romanesque capitals in the nave and ambulatory are very fine. On the north side of the ambulatory is the sarcophagus of Anna von Hohenberg, wife of Rudolf of Habsburg, and her young son Karl (d. 1271).

Most of the interior furnishings were destroyed in 1529 by Protestants at the Reformation. The elaborately decorated High Gothic altar was the work of Hans von Nussdorf, builder of the Minster (1486). In the outer north aisle are a number of tombs and the monument of Erasmus, who died in Basle in 1536. The panel near here depicting eight scenes from the martyrdom and death of St Vincent of Saragossa and another panel depicting the Apostles in the outer south aisle date from the 11th c. and may be by the same sculptor. The choir-stalls, now at the entrance and the crossing as well as in

Basle

Museum of Art: "The Burghers of Calais"   *"Shrovetide Fountain", by J. Tinguely*

*Crypt

the choir, are of the late 14th c. The Crypt, which can be entered from either side of the choir, contains the tombs of bishops of the 10th to the 13th c. and other monuments. The Romanesque frieze on the piers shows fabulous themes, hunting scenes and interlace ornament. The ceiling frescoes depict scenes from the life of the Virgin, the childhood of Christ and the lives of St Martin of Tours and St Margaret. On either side of the altar, formerly dedicated to the Virgin, are life-size Romanesque statues of bishops, dated by an inscription to 1202. On the right-hand side of the altar recess, also identified by an inscription, is Bishop Adalbero, builder of the earlier cathedral of 1019. Under the crossing are a collection of lapidary material and the recently excavated walls of a still earlier church of the early 9th c.

Cloister

The very beautiful double cloister (entrance from Rittergasse), built in the 15th c. on Romanesque foundations, contains many monuments ranging over a period of five centuries, including that of the mathematician Bernoulli (d. 1705). The south tower can be climbed; access from inside the church. Behind the Minster is the Pfalz ("Palace"), a terrace 20 m/66 ft above the Rhine with fine views of the river and the Black Forest hills.

Around the Münsterplatz

Museum of Natural History and Ethnography

In Augustinergasse, which runs north-west from the Münsterplatz, is a Neo-classical building (left) by Melchior Berri 1844–1849 which houses the Museum of Natural History and Ethnography (Natur- und Völkerkunde-museum). The Natural History Museum, situated at the front of the building, contains a display cabinet from the 18th c. At the rear is the Museum of Ethnography with exhibits from Melanesia and Oceania; the collections are the result of the museum's own expeditions. Just a few yards away in Rollerhof stands the Swiss Folk Museum (textiles, traditional paintings, European masks).

Augustinerstrasse is continued by the Rheinsprung, which descends to the Mittlere Brücke, passing the old University on the left. In Martinsgasse, which runs parallel to the Rheinsprung on the side away from the river, are two very elegant patrician houses, the Blaues Haus (Blue House) and Weisses Haus (White House), built between 1763 and 1770 for wealthy silk-merchants. At the west end of the Minster Hill, in a square with a fountain, stands St Martin's church (consecrated 1398), the oldest parish church in Basle.

St Martin's church

**Public Art Collection (Plans of floors see pp. 106–107)

From the Minster, Rittergasse, lined by handsome Rococo houses, runs south-east into St-Alban-Graben. At the corner of Dufourstrasse in a bu Id-ing designed by R. Christ and P. Bonatz (1932–36), is the Public Art Collec-tion or Museum of Art (Kunstmuseum), which contains the finest collect on of pictures in Switzerland, including both old masters and modern art, and also a Print Cabinet.

Museum of Art

On the first floor are the old masters, from Konrad Witz to Holbein the Younger (both well presented), and a collection of French and Dutch pic-tures presented by Professor Bachofen. The second floor houses an out-standing collection of 19th and 20th c. art, including Impressionists, Expressionists and Surrealists (Gauguin, Van Gogh, Corot, Corinth, Cézanne, Braque, Kokoschka, Picasso, Kandinsky, Léger, Chagall, Paul Klee, Juan Gris, Dali, Max Ernst), together with 20th c. works and special exhibitions.

Items of particular importance include the Heilspiegel (Mirror of Salvation) Altar by Konrad Witz (d. c. 1447), portraits by Holbein (16th c.), a "Cruci-fixion" by Mathias Grünewald (d. 1528), paintings by Niklaus Manuel-Deutsch (d. 1530) and Rembrandt ("David with Goliath's Head", 1627), Böcklin's "Island of the Dead" (earliest version, 1880) and works by Ferdi-nand Hodler (1853–1918).

Between St. Alban Graben and Theaterstrasse

At 5 St-Alban-Graben is the Museum of Antiquities (Antikenmuseum) and Ludwig collection with Greek works of art from 2500 to 100 B.C. and Roman and other Italian art from 1000 B.C. to A.D. 300 (including some items on loan) and an educational department. The growing collection made the creation of a "museum island" necessary between St-Alban-Graben and Luftgässlein. Four buildings and annexes different in style, function and date of origin surround a picturesque courtyard in the shade of a mighty lime tree. In 1988 the collection, comprising over 2000 items, was put on view in its new setting.

Museum of Antiquities and Ludwig Collection

To the west of the Museum of Art, on the left-hand side of the street cal ed Steinenberg, stands the Art Gallery (Kunsthalle, with restaurant), used for special exhibitions. At the far end of the street, on the right, is the Municipal Casino (Stadtcasino: restaurant), with a wall-painting by A. H. Pelligrini (1940).

Art Gallery

The Municipal Theatre (Stadttheater, 1975) with its "state-of-the-art" tech-nology dominates Theaterstrasse. The irregular-shaped building with its curved roof enjoys a high reputation among German-speaking theatres. There is an unusual "Carnival Fountain" (Fasnachtsbrunnen) 1977 by Jean Tinguely.

Municipal Theatre

In Elisabethenstrasse, to the east of the Theatre, one of the finest of Basle's patrician houses, the Haus zum Kirschgarten (No. 27, 1777–1780, built in early Classical style by J. U. Büchel) contains 25 rooms furnished in 18th c. style (including toys, porcelain, etc.).

Haus zum Kirschgarten

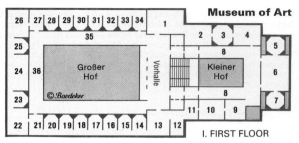

Museum of Art

I. FIRST FLOOR

GROUND FLOOR (not shown)
Entrance courtyard: Sculptures by
August Rodin ("The Burgers of Calais"),
Alexander Calder, Hans Arp and Eduardo
Chillida; temporary exhibitions,
engravings (over 100,000 examples);
study and reading room of the library
lecture hall; museum café.

FIRST FLOOR

1–13 *German and Swiss painting of*
15th and 16th c.
  1 Romanesque wall-paintings
  2 Konrad Witz
  3 School of Witz (1450–80)
  4 Hans Fries, Hans Holbein the Elder
    ("Death of the Virgin")
  5 Holbein the Elder, Lucas Cranach
    the Elder
  6 Hans Baldung, Cranach, Niklaus
    Manuel-Deutsch ("Judgment of
    Paris")
  7 Mathias Grünewald, Albrecht
    Altdorfer, Baldung ("Death and the
    Maiden", "Death and the
    Woman"), Hans Leu
  8 Hans Holbein the Younger
    (selection of drawings)
  9 Ambrosius Holbein, Hans Holbein
    the Younger (double portrait of
    Jakob Meyer zum Hasen,
    burgomaster of Basle, and his
    wife; portrait of Bonifacius
    Amerbach; portraits of Erasmus)
  10 Holbein the Younger, religious
    paintings ("Dead Christ", "Last
    Supper", panel of the Passion)
  11 Holbein the Younger, late portraits
    ("Family Group")
  12 Hans Bock the Elder (also Dutch
    painting of the 15th–17th c.)
  13 Tobias Stimmer, Bock; El Greco

12, 14–21 *Dutch painting of the*
15th–17th c.
  12 Quentin Matsys, Katharina von
    Hemessen, Frans Floris
  14 Jan Breughel the Elder, Joos de
    Momper, Tobias Verhaecht, etc.
  15 Rembrandt ("David presenting
    Goliath's Head to King Saul"),
    Pieter Lastman, Govert Flinck,

Leonhard Bramer, etc.
16–17 Flemish and Dutch landscapes:
    David Teniers the Younger, Jan
    van Goyen, Salomon van Ruysdael,
    Jacob van Ruisdael, Frans Post
  18 Adriaen Brouwer, Teniers, Adriaen
    van Ostade, Paulus Potter, etc.
  19 Jan van der Heyden, Pieter de
    Hooch, etc.
  20 Nicolaes Maes, Casper Netscher
  21 Jan van de Velde III, Willem van
    Aelst, Jan Fyt, etc.

22–23 *18th c. painting*
  22 Hyacinthe Rigaud, Anton Graff,
    Hubert Robert, Johann Heinrich
    Füssli (Fuseli), etc.
  23 Swiss Alpine and landscape
    pictures: Caspar Wolf

24–25 *Romantic Neo-classicism*
  24 Peter Birman, Joseph Anton Koch
    ("Macbeth and the Witches"),
    Charles Gleyre
  25 Ferdinand von Olivier, Friedrich
    Overbeck, Moritz von Schwind,
    Carl Gustav Carus, Emilie Linder
  26 Early 19th c. Swiss landscapists

27–34 *19th c. French painting*
  27 Théodore Géricault, Eugène
    Delacroix, Camille Corot
    ("Italienne à la Fontaine")
  28–34 Gustave Courbet, Edouard Manet,
    Auguste Renoir, Camille Pissarro,
    Claude Monet, Edgar Degas ("Le
    Jockey blessé"), Paul Cézanne
    ("Montagne Sainte-Victoire"), Paul
    Gauguin ("Ta Matete"), Vincent
    van Gogh
  29 *German painting of the*
    19th c. (second half)
    Hans von Marèes ("Self-Portrait in
    High Hat")

35–36 *19th c. Swiss painting*
  35 Ferdinand Hodler ("The Valiant
    Wife", Lake Geneva from
    Chexbres")
  36 Anselm Feuerbach ("Self Portrait",
    "Death of Pietro Aretino"), Arnold
    Böcklin ("Fight with Centaurs",
    "Island of the Dead", "Odysseus
    and Calypso", "The Plague")

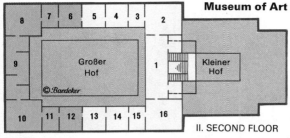

Museum of Art

II. SECOND FLOOR

SECOND FLOOR

20th c. painting and sculpture

1 Pop art

2 Pablo Picasso ("Pains et compotier aux fruits sur une table", "L'aficionado", "Le poète", "Femme à la guitare")

3 "Les Fauves" art group around Henri Matisse ("La Berge", "La Danse" La Musique")

4 Henri Rousseau ("The Customs Officer", "La muse inspirant le poète", "Primeval landscape with setting sun"), Georges Roualt

5 Georges Braque ("Violon et cruche", "Le Portugais"), Juan Gris ("Le Violon")

6 The Blue Rider group, Orphism, Futurism

7 Marc Chagall ("Portrait de ma fiancée en gants noirs", "The Stockdealer")

8 Fernand Léger ("La femme en bleu", "Eléments mécaniques", "La femme et l'enfant")

9 Expressionism, New Functionalism: Paula Modersohn-Becker ("Self Portrait"), Lovis Corinth ("Ecce Homo"), Franz Marc ("Destiny of Animals"), Oscar Schlemmer ("Four Figures in space – Roman", "Frauentreppe"), Oskar Kokoschka ("Storm"), Max Beckmann ("Nice in Frankfurt"), Otto Dix ("The Artist's Parents")

10 Alberto Giacometti ("Self Portrait", "Palais à 4 heures du matin", "La Place")

11 Paul Klee ("Villa R", "Senecio", "Old Sound", "Ad marginem", "Rich Harbour"

12 De Stijl; Constructivism: Piet Mondrian ("Composition aux couleurs gris"); Theo van Doesburg ("Composition XII en blanc et noir"); El Lissitzky ("Proun 1 D"); Làszlò Moholy-Nagy ("Construction LIV"); Georges Vantongerloo ("Construction $Y=axy-bxx+cx$"); Antione Pevsner ("Construction surface développable") Hans Arp ("Cloud Arrow", relief); Sophie Taeubner-Arp ("Moving picture circle")

13 Dadaism, Surrealism: Salvador Dali ("The Burning Giraffe"); Max Ernst ("La grande forêt")

14 Robert Rauschenberg, Cy Twombly, Jaspar Johns

15 Ecole de Paris: Joseph Beuys ("Scene of the Fire", "Woman Throwing Discus")

16 *Modern American painting* Franz Kline, Barnett Newman, Clyfford Still, Mark Rothko, Frank Stella, Claes Olderburg, Andy Warhol, Carl Andre, Donald Judd, Sol Le Witt, Sam Francis ("Meaningless Gesture" on the staircase)

The Museum's largest collection of *20th c. Swiss painting and sculpture* (including Jean Tinguely, etc.) can be displayed only in selected groups, varying from time to time.

Around the Barfüsserplatz

In the busy Barfüsserplatz is the 14th c. Barfüsserkirche (church of the barefoot friars), which now houses the Historical Museum, with an important collection on the history of culture and art (renovated 1975–81; cellars constructed and reconstruction of the rood screen). Notable exhibits in the nave of the church are the Late Gothic tapestries and the "Lällenkönig" ("Babbling King"), a crowned head with a movable tongue and eyes, once the emblem of Gross-Basel (17th c.). In the aisles are weapons and furnished rooms, in the choir religious art, in the crypt the Minster treasury.

*Barfüsser-kirche, Historical Museum

Above the west side of the church rises St Leonard's church (Leonhardskirche), rebuilt between 1480 and 1512 and restored in 1965. The crypt is Romanesque; the choir dates from the 13th–14th c. The former monastery adjoining the church, known as the Lohnhof, is now occupied by the police.

Spalenvorstadt

From the Steinenberg we go north-west along Kohlenberg and Leonhardsgraben. To the left in Kornhausgasse (No. 8), is the Jewish Museum of Switzerland. We then come into the Spalenvorstadt, which can also be reached from the Marktplatz up a picturesque flight of steps. At the near end of this on the right (No. 2), is the Industrial Museum (Gewerbemuseum: periodic special museums). Farther along on the left is the Spalenbrunnen, a fountain also known as the Holbein fountain (after Holbein and Dürer: original in Historical Museum).

Jewish Museum of Switzerland

Industrial Museum

In the centre of this part of the town is the tree-shaded Petersplatz, on the east side of which stands St Peter's church (Peterskirche), rebuilt at the time of the Council of Basle (15th c.), with a gallery running round the nave and reticulated vaulting in the choir from an earlier building (14th c.); interesting frescoes in the Eberler chapel and the nave. In front of the church is a bronze bust of the poet J. P. Hebel (b. Basle 1760). On the north side of the square is the handsome Wild'sches Haus (1763) and on the west side the Botanic Garden of the University. Beyond this a concrete building (1965) houses the rich University Library (Universitätsbibliothek), with numerous incunabula and manuscripts dating from the time of the Council of Basle (1431–87).

St Peter's Church

On the south side of Petersplatz stands the new university building (1938–46) by the Zurich architect Roland Rohn. At the entrance is a mosaic by Walter Eglin depicting scenes from daily life and in the corridors are pictures and busts of famous personalities and scientists, including one of Pope Pius II who founded the university in 1460. The great hall (Aula) contains ten stained glass windows and its beautiful courtyard has a water-lily pond.

University

To the west of the University is the Spalentor (1370), a fortified gate which marks the end of the old town. The town gate, once part of the old town walls, has stood alone since their destruction in the 19th c. On the left there is an old letter box by M. Berri (1801–1854) with the emblem of the Basle pigeon.

*Spalentor

At 28 Missionsstrasse is the Swiss Museum of Gymnastics and Sport with exhibits relating to different sports, including the Olympic Games and the Swiss sports of "Hornussen" and "Schwingen".

Swiss Museum of Gymnastics and Sport

◀ *The Spalentor, at the end of the Old Town in Basle*

Basle Zoo

↕ Entrance/exit
← Exit only
00 Toilets
P Car Parks

1 Main entrance and director's office
2 Kiosk (books)
3 Fishes, penguins, reptiles
4 Aquatic birds
5 Somali wild asses, bongos
6 Brown bears, Malayan bears, spectacle bears, polar bears
7 Zebras, ostriches, flamingos
8 Orangutans, gorillas, chimpanzees, woolly monkeys, smaller monkeys
9 Birds from all continents
10 Waterfowl and waders
11 African and Indian elephants
12 Elephant arena
13 Otters, civets, ratels
14 Waders and waterfowl
15 Lions, tigers, panthers, fossas, servals
16 Okapi, giraffes, kudos, kangaroos
17 Rhinoceroses, pigmy hippopotamuses, tapirs
18 Parrots
19 Penguins
20 Barbary sheep, Himalayan thars
21 Reindeer
22 Birds of prey (golden eagle, bateleur eagle, vulture, raven)
23 Covered seating
24 Sea-lions
25 Owls (snowy owl, eagle-owl)
26 Marmots, porcupine, agouti
27 Sardinian wild sheep
28 Wolves
29 Camels, llamas, pigmy zebus
30 Wild pigs, musk-oxen, bison
31 Children's zoo (ponies, pigmy goats, domestic animals)

© Baedeker

Dorenbachviadukt

Predigerkirche	At the foot of Petersgraben, which runs down to the Rhine from Petersplatz, is the Predigerkirche (Dominician church), a long building of the 14th–15th c. with a graceful roof turret. Opposite is the house in which the poet Johann Peter Hebel (1760–1826) was born (plaque).
St Antonius Kirche	In the north-west of the city St Anthony's church (St Antoniuskirche) was in its day a pioneering example of concrete architecture (fine windows).

South of the old town

Railway station, Basle SBB	On the south side of the old town, behind the Elisabethenschanze with the Strasbourg monument of F. A. Bertholdi, is the main railway station (Bahnhof SBB), built 1905–1909 by Emil Faesch and Emanuel La Roche. The imposing Neo-baroque façade with its high concourse is framed between domed towers. Adjoining it is the Centralbahnplatz (underground passage with shops, information bureau and café) surrounded by big hotels.
BIZ	Nearby stands the circular tower block (architect Burckhardt; 1977) of the Bank for International Settlements (Bank für Internationalen Zahlungsausgleich, BIZ), which was founded in 1930 at the Hague Conference and today is at the centre of the international gold and currency markets as well as the European money market.

To the west in the Birsig valley is the large and interesting zoo (Zoologischer Garten; restaurant), affectionately known as the Zolli by the people of Basle. Founded in 1874 with 510 European animals it contains mainly exotic species. It comprises a vivarium (fishes, penguins, reptiles), a bear enclosure with different species, an excellent monkey house (1970 orangutans, gorillas, proboscis monkeys, etc.), an aviary (1927) with indigenous and exotic birds, birds of prey, an antelope house and children's zoo. The zoo has been particularly successful in breeding rhinoceros. The elephants put on a performance in a special arena and give rides to children.

*Zoo

St-Alban-Vorstadt

To the east of the old town a stroll through the old town brings you to the square St-Alban-Tor, with its lower part finished in bulging stone blocks. An old town gate, it dates from the 13th c. when it was part of the fortifications. It was altered in 1871 with the addition of the watch house on the side facing the Rhine, being completely restored in 1976.

St-Alban-Tor

At No. 9 St-Alban-Vorstadt the constantly changing collection of caricatures and cartoons by famous artists is a source of amusement.

Collection of Caricatures and Cartoons

The Mühlenberg runs down to the old St Alban's monastery under the town walls. Part of its Romanesque cloister is preserved in a neighbouring house.

St Alban's monastery

To the east on the Gewerbebach an old Gallician paper mill has been turned into the Museum of Writing, Printing and Paper demonstrating the individual processes.

Basle Paper Mill

Not far away stands the Museum of Contemporary Art (Museum für Gegenwartskunst), an old paper mill with modern extensions (1980 Katharina and Wilfried Steib). Works on display range from c. 1960 and the contemporary part of the Emanuel Hoffmann collection. Especially noteworthy are works by Stella, Beuys, Chagall, de Chirico, Dali, Braque, Mondrian, Klee, Arp, Pevsner, Giacometti, Moore and Tinguely. There is an attractive trip across the Rhine to Klein-Basel by ferry.

Museum of Contemporary Art

Klein-Basel

In Klein-Basel a tree-lined promenade runs along the bank of the river, affording fine views of the old town. At 26 Unterer Rheinweg, a little way north-west of the Mittlere Brücke, is the City and Minster Museum (Stadt- und Münster Museum), notable particularly for its collection of sculpture from the Minster.

City and Minster Museum

In Claraplatz stands the Roman Catholic St Clara Kirche, a light-coloured roughcast building with a small turret. The Gothic nave has 19th c. additions by Amadeus Merian. The choir contains the Sunday Cross from Basle Minster.

St Clara Church

Near the Wettstein bridge is the St-Theodor-Kirchplatz, in which is the Late Gothic St Theodore's church (14th c.). Noteworthy are the sandstone font (c. 1500), the choir with a wall tabernacle (16th c.) and the old choir windows (c. 1375). Between the square and the river we find the old Carthusian monastery which has served as a monastery since 1669.

St Theodore's Church

One of the main traffic arteries of Klein-Basel is the Riehenring, along which extend the buildings of the Swiss Trade Fair (Schweizer Mustermesse) and the European World Trade and Congress Centre (EWTCC). Swiss trade fairs have a long history. Some of the most important international fairs include ART (20th c. art fair), the Swiss Trade Fair, Basle Autumn Fair, ELSM

Swiss Trade Fair, European World Trade and Congress Centre (EWTCC)

Augusta Raurica: a Roman theatre

(European Clock and Watch Fair) and Nuclex, an international trade fair for the nuclear industry.

A little way east, at the Vogelsangstrasse 15, is the Technical College (Gewerbeschule, 1961), which has a column by Hans Arp in the courtyard. North-east is the Art Nouveau building of the Baden Railway Station (Badischer Bahnhof), the German Railways (DB) terminus. The allegorical statues above the entrance are by C. Burckhardt.

Beyond the railway line , along the little River Wiese, is situated the popular Lange Erlen Zoo (Tierpark: cafés).

Baden Railway Station

In Riehen, a desirable residential area of Basle, are the Village and Toy Museum and probably the only Cat Museum.

Riehen, Cat Museum

Surroundings

Boats leave from the Mittlere Brücke for trips on the Rhine or around the port installations; boats to Rotterdam from St Johann, Elsässerrheinweg.

From Basle to Kaiseraugst

Leave Basle on the east and join the motorway (N2/N3) which crosses the Rhine. After crossing the river Birs we arrive in 3.5 km/2 miles at the exit for the Basle suburb of Birsfelden, on the north bank of the Rhine. Here there are port installations and a power station built in 1950–55 (visitors' gallery). We continue along the south edge of the Hard forest and through a tunnel, beyond which the southern slopes of the Black Forest can be seen on the left. 6.5 km/4 miles: Liestal-Augst exit. 6 km/4 miles south is Liestal; 1 km/ ½ mile north is Augst (alt. 275 m/902 ft), on the left bank of the Ergolz, which

Augst

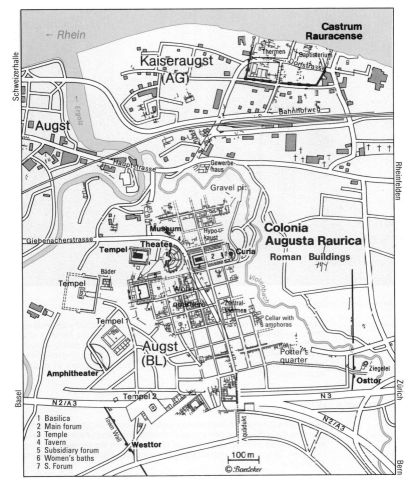

Map legend:
- Castrum Rauracense
- Kaiseraugst (AG)
- Augst
- Schweizerhalle
- ← Rhein
- Ergolz
- Thermen
- Baptisterium
- Dorfstrasse
- Bahnhofweg
- Hauptstrasse
- Gewerbe-haus
- Gravel pit
- Rheinfelden
- Giebenacherstrasse
- Museum
- Hypo-kaust
- Colonia Augusta Raurica
- Roman Buildings
- Tempel
- Theater
- Curia
- Bäder
- Tempel
- Wohn-quartiere
- Violenbach
- Zentral-Thermes
- Cellar with amphoras
- Tempel
- Augst (BL)
- Potter's quarter
- Ziegelei
- Amphitheater
- Osttor
- Basel
- Tempel 2
- N 2/A 3
- N 3
- Town Wall
- Aquädukt
- N 2/A 3
- Zürich
- Bern
- Westtor

1 Basilica
2 Main forum
3 Temple
4 Tavern
5 Subsidiary forum
6 Women's baths
7 S. Forum

100 m
© Baedeker

here flows into the Rhine and forms the boundary between the cantons of Basel-Land and Aargau. In Griebenbacherstrasse a Roman museum has exhibits from Augusta Raurica and the silver treasure from Castle Kaiseraugst.

0.5 km/½ mile uphill from the town (signposted) is the site of the Roman colony of Augusta Raurica, founded about 27 B.C., with a large theatre and the remains of several temples. At the near end of the site, on the left, is a reconstruction of a Roman house (1953–57) containing a museum. To the right is the theatre (restored: performances in summer), and beyond this to the east the site of a temple, the main forum and a basilica. On a hill west of the theatre are the remains of a large temple, and to the south a residential district. South-west of the main complex is an amphitheatre discovered in 1959.

*Augusta Raurica

Goetheanum in Dornach

Kaiseraugst

1 km/½ mile north-east of Augst beyond the Ergolz, beautifully situated on the banks of the Rhine, the little town of Kaiseraugst has the remains of a Roman fortified post. On the Rhine is the Augst-Whylen power station (1907–12), which has a dam 212 m/696 ft long, and the Kaiseraugst nuclear power station which was finally halted in 1989 after years of strong opposition.

From Basle via Dornach to Liestal

Leave from the main railway station on Münchensteiner Strasse and after crossing the railway line take a road on the left; then, soon afterwards, keep straight ahead through the suburb of Neuewelt with the recreational park

Grün 80

"Grün 80" (playground and lake), which is dominated by the stone statue of a dinosaur.

Münchenstein

Over the Birs 6 km/4 miles lies Münchenstein (alt. 540 m/1772 ft) where there is a coach and sledge museum of Basle's Historical Museum in a barn.

Arlesheim

After 2 km/1 mile is Arlesheim (alt. 340 m/1116 ft), with a church built in 1681 and remodelled in Rococo style in 1760 (Silbermann organ of 1761) and many country houses. On the wooded hill above the town are Burg Reichenstein (alt. 480 m/1575 ft) and Schloss Birseck (private property), formerly the residence of the Prince-Bishops of Basle.

*Dornach, Goetheanum

Only 1 km/½ mile farther lies Dornachbrugg (alt. 295 m/968 ft) with a Capuchin friary. It is separated by 1 km/ ½ mile from Dornach (alt. 300 m/984 ft), a pretty village, to the north of which is the Goetheanum, a massive concrete structure in Expressionist style. After the first Goetheanum with its wooden twin cupolas was destroyed by fire the Anthropological Society

Allschwill: Local museum   *Bottmingen: medieval moated castle*

founded by Rudolf Steiner (1861–1925) designed a second in 1924, which was constructed after his death by E. Aisenpreis. It houses the urns containing the remains of Rudolf Steiner, Christian Morgenstern and others (conducted tours). On a hill to the east are the ruins of Dornach Castle.

From Dornach the road winds uphill through wooded country for 7 km/ 4 miles to Gempen (alt. 672 m/2205 ft) side road on left ascending the Gempenfluh (765 m/2510 ft), with magnificent views of the Jura and the Rhine, extending beyond Basle to Strasbourg.

*Gempenfluh

From Gempen the road winds its way down for 10 km/6 miles east to Liestal (alt. 330 m/1083 ft), chief town of the half-canton of Basel-Land. In the 13th c. Town Hall is the gold cup of Charles the Bold, Duke of Burgundy, which was captured at Nancy in 1477. The "Dichtermuseum" (Writers' Museum) has mementoes of the Nobel Prize winner Carl Spitteler (1845–1924), who was born in Liestal, Georg Herwegh and others. At the end of Rathausstrasse is the picturesque Oberes Tor (Upper Gate). North-west of the town, at Munzach, are the remains of a Roman villa (mosaics, etc.). 5 km/3 miles north via the holiday resort of Bienenberg (alt. 431 m/1414 ft) is Bad Schauenberg (468 m/1536 ft); both places have brine baths.

Liestal

From Basle to Laufen through the Birsig valley

Leave Basle by Oberwiler Strasse. Near the zoo take the Hohestrasse towards Allschwil (3 km/2½ miles). Near the parish church of St Peter and Paul are several half-timbered buildings including a local museum.

Allschwil

Returning to the zoo take the main road heading south for 2 km/1 mile to Binningen (alt. 285 m/935 ft) where there is a restaurant in Schloss Binningen, a former moated castle which is first mentioned in 1229 and also the smaller Schloss Holee with a stepped gable and tower (lookout terrace).

Binningen,
Monteverdi Car
Collection

The Monteverdi Car Collection in Oberwilerstrasse is interesting, a car museum of unique Swiss cars (100 cars and Europe's largest collection – 8000 – of model cars).

Bottmingen

Bottmingen (295 m/968 ft), 2 km/1 mile to the north also has a medieval moated castle. The only castle with a lake in north-west Switzerland it dates back to the 14th c., but was renovated in the 18th and 20th c. (restaurant). There are interesting Baroque statues in the hall and a ceiling painted by Isaak Merian (18th c.).

Flüh

10.5 km/6½ miles via Oberwil (alt. 515 m/1690 ft), Therwil (alt. 309 m/1014 ft) with a fine church and Ettingen we reach Flüh (alt. 381 m/1250 ft), just on the French frontier, with a chalybeate spring. On a hill beyond the frontier is the ruined castle of Landskron (546 m/1791 ft). Beyond Flüh the road climbs sharply. 2.5 km/2 miles: Mariastein (alt. 515 m/1690 ft) has a Benedictine abbey on a steep-sided crag which was founded in 1645, dissolved in 1874, and reoccupied by Benedictines in 1941; there is also a pilgrimage church (1648–55) and the cave of Maria im Stein.

Laufen

The road runs up on to the western slopes of Blauen and then descends steeply to (9 km/6 miles) Laufen (alt. 358 m/1175 ft), a little town of 3500 inhabitants on the south side of the hill. Two town gates belonging to the old fortifications, the Baslertor and the Obertor; St Catherine's church (1698); palace of the Prince-Bishops, now the Prefecture. Large limestone quarry.

Bellinzona

E2

Canton: Ticino (TI)
Altitude: 230 m/755 ft
Population: 18,200

Castello Grande: the oldest fortress in Bellinzona

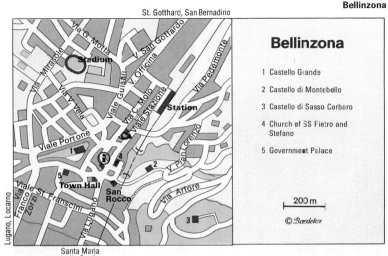

Bellinzona

1 Castello Grande

2 Castello di Montebello

3 Castello di Sasso Corbaro

4 Church of SS Pietro and Stefano

5 Government Palace

200 m

© Baedeker

Three important North-South routes – the roads over the Alpine passes of St Gotthard, San Bernardino and Lucomagno – meet in the valley of the Ticino, and could in the past be closed by a barrier across the road at Bellinzona. The town thus occupied a key strategic situation for many centuries, and this led to its selection as the cantonal capital in 1878. It is now an educational focal point as well as the seat of cantonal administration. The town is still dominated by its three castles, an impressive example of a medieval defensive system which, together with a double circuit of walls, were built by the town's Milanese rulers in the second half of the 15th c.

Situation and general

The region was occupied by Rome for five centuries, from about 30 B.C to A.D. 450. Bellinzona itself first appears in the records in A.D. 590. In 1242 it fell into the hands of Milan, ruled by the Visconti family and later by the Sforzas. In 1503 the Confederates established the governor's headquarters in the castles. In 1803 Bellinzona became part of the new canton of Ticino.

History

Sights

The main features of interest in Bellinzona are the three castles. The oldest Castello Grande, (known in the 14th c. as Castel Magnum, in the 17th c. as Burg Uri or Altdorf and in 1818 as San Michele), was constructed above a Roman castle. The Torre Bianca (27 m/89 ft) and the square Torre Negra 28 m/91 ft) form the most ancient part of the five defences. Situated 50 m/164 ft above the town the castle boasts wonderful views.

*Castello Grande

The Castello di Montebello, (originally Castello Piccolo, later Burg Schwyz and in the 19th c. San Martino), stands on the east side of the town, where the old town walls divided. It is the most interesting of the three as an example of the art of fortification (originally centred on the keep, with a 13th c. palace and courtyard and further structures built between 1460 and 1480), which now contain a historical and archaeological museum.

*Castello di Montebello

The square-shaped Castello di Sasso Corbaro (known as Burg Unterwalden and in the 18th c. S. Barbara), also called Castello di Cima by the

*Castello di Sasso Corbaro

117

Bellinzona

Bellinzona: Castello di Montebello . . .   *. . . and collegiate church*

Bellinzonese, was built in less than six months in 1479 following the Battle of Giornico to reinforce the defences of the Ticino valley (230 m/755 ft above the town). It houses the Ticino Museum (arts, crafts local costumes).

*Collegiate church of SS Pietro and Stefano

The Roman Catholic Collegiate church SS Pietro and Stefano dates back to 1424. This fine Renaissance building was largely rebuilt in 1517 by Tomaso Rodari, master builder of Como Cathedral in Italy. The rich Baroque interior and façade were added in the 17th–18th c. The marble high altar is decorated with a representation of the Crucifixion (1658) by either Simone Peterzano or Tintoretto.

Historic Old Town

There is an interesting former Franciscan church S. Maria della Grazie with magnificent wall paintings by the Lombard artists working in Ticino (16th c.), the Palazzo del Governo (1738–43, altered 1867–69) and the old town which retains its Lombard character with its picturesque little streets, arcades, old doorways and wrought-iron balconies that inspired the English writer John Ruskin and the painter J. M. William Turner.

Villa dei Cedri

The art museum in the Villa dei Cedri has sculptures and paintings by early 20th c. Swiss artists and more recently by the 16th c. Italian Francesco da Basano.

Civica Galleria d'Arte

In the Civica Galleria d'Arte are exhibits by Augusto Sartoni (1880–1957), Giovanni Genucchi (1904–1979) and Mario Marioni (1910–1987).

Ravecchia

In the outlying district of Ravecchia (1.5 km/1 mile south), off the road to the left, is the Romanesque church of San Biagio (St Blaise), with fine frescoes of the 14th–15th c.

Berne

Canton: Berne (BE)
Altitude: 540 m/1772 ft
Population: 142,000

The Swiss capital, Berne (German spelling Bern), is also capital of the country's second largest canton and a university town. The old town, dominated by the Minster (or basilica), is built on a sandstone ridge encircled on three sides by the Aare, flowing in a valley 35–40 m/115–131 ft deep. High-level bridges link it with the high ground on the right bank and with the newer parts of the city. The charming older part of Berne still preserves its original layout. The houses, with their arcades on street level (6 km/4 miles of arcades altogether) and their projecting roofs, reflect the prosperity of the citizens of Berne in the 18th c. Most of the attractive fountains, painted in lively colours, were the work of Hans Gieng (1540–45).

Situation and General

*Townscape

The industries of Berne include textiles, machinery, chocolate, pharmaceuticals, foodstuffs, the graphic trades and electrical equipment, and it also has a considerable trade in agricultural produce. Over 12% of its working population are employed in administration, the highest proportion of all Swiss towns.

THe town is believed to have been founded on its excellent defensive site by Berthold V of Zähringen in 1191. The bear on the Bernese coat-of-arms, together with the bear-pit, commemorate the legend according to which a bear was the first animal to be killed by Berthold V in the year in which the city was founded. After the Zähringen dynasty died out the Emperor Frederick II granted Berne self-government and its own law court. In the Battle of Laupen (1339) the Bernese, led by Rudolf von Erlach, defeated the Burgundian nobility. In 1353 Berne became a member of the young Confederation, in which the military prowess of its citizens enabled it to play a

History

Berne: The Old Town above the Aare valley

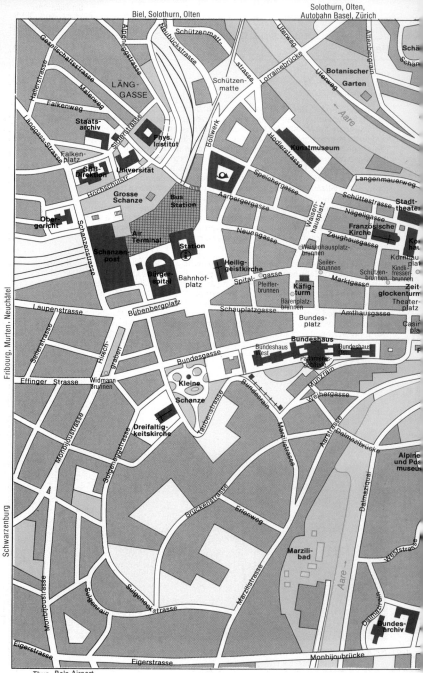

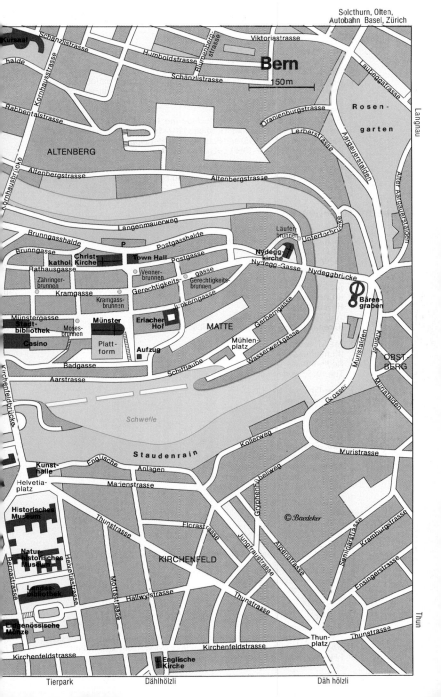

Solothurn, Olten,
Autobahn Basel, Zürich

Viktoriastrasse

Bern

50m

Schänzlistrasse
Humboldtstrasse
Schänzlistrasse

Kursaal
halde
Kornhausstrasse
Rabbentalstrasse

Oranienburgstrasse
Lerberstrasse

Rosen-
garten

Langnau

ALTENBERG
Altenbergstrasse
Altenbergstrasse

Alter Aargauerstalden
Aargauerstalden

Kornhausbrücke
Langenmauerweg

Läufer-
brunnen
Untertorbrücke

Brunngasshalde
Brunngasse
Rathausgasse
Postgasshalde
Postgasse

Nydegg-
kirche
Nydegg-Gasse
Nydeggbrücke

P
Christ
kathol. Kirche
Town Hall

Vennel-
brunnen
Gerechtigkeits-
gasse
Gerechtigkeits-
brunnen

Zähringer-
brunnen
Kramgasse
Kramgass-
brunnen
Unkerngasse

Bären-
graben

Gerbergasse

Münstergasse
Stadt-
bibliothek
Münster
Moses-
brunnen
Erlacher
Hof

MATTE

Muristalden

Kleiner Muristalden

OBST
BERG

Casino
Platt-
form
Aufzug
Mühlen-
platz
Wasserwerkgasse

Badgasse
Schifflaube

Aarstrasse

Grosses

Muristalden

Schwelle

Staudenrain
Kollerweg

Muristrasse

Kirchenfeldbrücke

Englische
Anlagen
Marienstrasse

Kunst-
halle
Helvetia-
platz

Gryphenhübeliweg

Alpenstrasse

© Baedeker

Seminarstrasse

Kramburgstrasse

Ensingerstrasse

Historisches
Museum
Thunstrasse
Florastrasse
Jungfraustrasse

Natur
historisches
Museum
Helvetiastrasse

KIRCHENFELD

Landes-
bibliothek
Bernastrasse
Mottastrasse
Hallwylstrasse
Thunstrasse

Thunstrasse

Eidgenössische
Münze

Thun-
platz
Thunstrasse

Thun

Kirchenfeldstrasse
Englische
Kirche

Tierpark
Dählhölzli
Däh hölzli

leading role. In 1528 the Reformation came to the town and by 1536 Berne was the largest city state north of the Alps.

Since 1848 Berne has been the seat of the Federal Council and Federal Assembly; it is also the headquarters of important organisations including the Universal Postal Union (since 1874) and the international copyright and railway unions, and of an institute attached to the University for research into tourism.

Notable people born in Berne include the 18th c. scholar Albrecht von Haller, the writer Jeremias Gotthelf (1797–1854) and the painters Ferdinand Hodler (1853–1918) and Paul Klee (1879–1940). The famous physicist Albert Einstein (1879–1955) published his Theory of Relativity in Berne.

Berne was awarded the honour of being judged the best European City in Bloom by "Entente Florale" and accepted by UNESCO as a world cultural centre.

Museums, Galleries, etc.

Alpine Museum
(Schweizerisches Alpines Museum),
Helvetiaplatz 4;
Summer: Mon. 2–5, Tue.–Sun. 10–5.
Winter: Mon. 2–5, Tue.–Sun. 10–12 and 2–5.

Art Gallery
(Kunsthalle),
Hevetiaplatz 1;
Tue. 10–9, Wed.–Sun. 10–5.
(Open only during temporary exhibitions).

Art, Museum of
(Kunstmuseum),
Hodlerstrasse 12;
Tue.10–9, Wed.–Sun. 10–5.

Bear-Pit
(Bärengraben),
Nyddegbrücke;
Apr.–Sept. 7–6,
Oct.–Mar. 8.30–4.

Botanic Gardens
(Botanischer Garten),
Altenbergrain 21;
Outdoors: Mon.–Fri. 7–7, Sat., Sun. 8–5.30.
Indoors: Mon.–Sun. 8–11.30 and 2–5.

Bundeshaus
(Parliament),
Bundesplatz;
conducted tours: weekdays at 9, 10, 11, 2, 3 and 4;
Sun. 9, 10, 11, 2 and 3
(except during sittings of Parliament and on public holidays).

Cast Collection of Berne
(Bernische Abguss-Sammlung)
Mattenege 10;
Sat. 10–12.

Clock Tower
(Zeitglockenturm);
1 May–31 Oct.: daily until 4.30 guided tours including astronomical clock (about 1 hour). Meeting point: east side of tower. Numbers limited.
1 Nov.–30 Mar.: guided tours by arrangement.

Einstein House (Einstein-Haus),
Kramgasse 49;
1 Feb.–30 Nov.: Tue.–Fri. 10–5, Sat. 10–4.

Historical Museum of Berne
(Bernisches Historisches Museum),
Helvetiaplatz 5;
Tue.–Sun.10–5.

Käfigturm
(Information Centre for the Canton of Berne)
Marktgasse 67;
Tue.–Sun. 10–1, 2–5, Thurs. 6–9.

Kornhaus
Industrial Museum (Gewerbemuseum),
Swiss Gutenberg Museum,
Zeughausgasse 2;
Tue.–Sun. 10–12 and 2–5, Thur. also 6–9 p.m.

Minster
Münsterplatz;
Mon.–Sat. 10–12 and 2–5, Sun. 11–12 and 2–5.
Ascent of the tower: Mon.–Sat. 10–11.30 and 2–4.30.
Nov.–Easter: Tue.–Fri. 10–12 and 2–4, Sat. 10–12 and 2–5, Sun. 11–12.
Tower: Tue.–Fri. 10–11.30 and 2–3.30, Sat. 10–11.30 and 2–4.30, Sun. 11–11.30.

Municipal Archives (Stadtarchiv),
Falkenplatz 4;
Mon. 1.30–5, Tue.–Thur. 7.45–12 and 1.30–5, Fri. 7.45–5.

Municipal and University Library
(Stadt- und Universitätsbibliothek).
Casinoplatz;
issue of books on loan Mon.–Fri. 10–12 and 2–6, Sat. 10–12;
reading room Mon–Fri. 8 a.m–9 p.m., Sat. 8–12.

Municipal Zoo, Dählhölzli
(Dählhölzli Städtischer Tierpark),
Dalmaziquai 149;
Vivarium Summer; Mon.–Sun. 8–6.30. Oct.: Mon.–Sun. 9–5.30.
Winter: Mon.–Sat. 9–12 and 1–5, Sun. 9–5.

National Library
(Schweizerische Landesbibliothek),
Helvetiastrasse;
issue of books Mon., Tue., Thur. 11–12 and 1–4,
Wed. 11–12 and 2–8, Sat. 9–2;
reading room Mon., Tue., Thur., Fri. 9–12 and 1–6.
Wed. 9–12 and 1–8, Sat. 9–2.

Natural History Museum
(Naturhistorisches Museum),
Bernastrasse 15;
Mon.–Sat. 9–12 and 2–5, Sun. 10–12 and 2–5.

Nature Reserve, Elfenau
(Stadtgärtnerei Elfenau);
Indoor houses - winter: Mon.–Sat. 8.30–11.45 and 1.30–5, Sun. 8.30–4.30.
Summer: normal working hours.

Postal Museum
(Schweizerisches PTT Museum),
Helvetiaplatz 4;
Summer: Mon. 2–5, Tue.–Sun. 10–5.
Winter: Mon. 2–5, Tue.–Sun. 10–12 and 2–5.

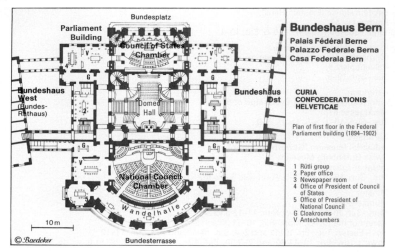

Bundesplatz

Parliament Building

Council of States Chamber

Bundeshaus West (Bundes-Rathaus)

Bundeshaus Ost

Domed Hall

National Council Chamber

Wandelhalle

10 m

© *Baedeker*

Bundesterrasse

Bundeshaus Bern

Palais Fédéral Berne
Palazzo Federale Berna
Casa Federala Bern

CURIA
CONFOEDERATIONIS
HELVETICAE

Plan of first floor in the Federal Parliament building (1894–1902)

1 Rütli group
2 Paper office
3 Newspaper room
4 Office of President of Council of States
5 Office of President of National Council
G Cloakrooms
V Antechambers

Rathaus
(Town Hall),
Rathausplatz;
seen by prior arrangement, tel. 64 48 34.

Schulwarte, Berner
Helvetiaplatz 2;
Mon.–Fri. 10–12 and 2–5.30.

Description of the town

Bubenbergplatz

Bürgerspital

Heiliggeistkirche

The hub of the city's traffic is the long Bubenbergplatz. On its north side stands the handsome Bürgerspital (Municipal hospital, 1734–42; now an old people's home), built around two courtyards. To the right is the Heiliggeistkirche (church of the Holy Spirit: Protestant), in French Baroque style, built 1726–29.

From here it is a short distance south along Christoffelgasse into the broad Bundesgasse, in which are the Bundeshaus and the Kleine Schanze.

Around the Bundesplatz

Bundeshaus

In the Bundesplatz (vegetable and flower market on Tuesday and Saturday mornings) is the Renaissance-style Bundeshaus (Parliament building), standing on the edge of the high ground above the river. The domed central block (by H. Auer, 1896–1902) contains the two chambers of the Swiss Parliament (open to visitors), the meeting-places of the National Council and the Council of States; in the east wing (also by Auer, 1888–92) and west wing (by F. Studer, 1851–57) are various Federal agencies and the Federal library.

From the Bundesterrasse, which rests on massive retaining walls, there are fine views of the river Aare 48 m/157 ft below (funicular into valley) and of the Alps beyond.

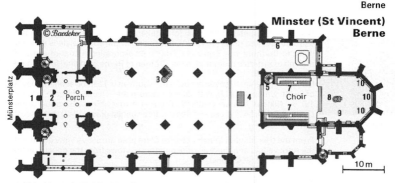

1 Main doorway (1490–95), with 45 figures (copies: originals in Historical Museum)
2 Organ (1726–30)
3 Pulpit (1470)
4 Communion table from Lausanne Cathedral
5 Stone staircase, a relic of the rood-screen
6 North Doorway
7 Double rows of choir-stalls (1523–25)
8 Font (1524)
9 Sedilia (c. 1435)
10 Stained glass windows of choir (1441–50 and 1868)

Another popular viewpoint, with an orientation table, is the Kleine Schanze (Little Redoubt; restaurant) to the west, a relic of the old fortifications. In the gardens are a monument to Oskar Bider, who made the first flight over the Alps in 1913, and a monument (1909) commemorating the foundation of the Universal Postal Union.

*Kleine Schanze

Between Theaterplatz and Münsterplatz

To the east of the Bundesplatz in the Theaterplatz are the Hauptwache (guard House), a small pillared hall of 1767, and the Hôtel de Musique (1771), once the fashionable assembly rooms of Berne. On the south-east corner of the square, at the end of the Kirchenfeld bridge, is the Casino (1906–09), an assembly and concert hall with a restaurant and large lookout terrace. To the north is the horseshoe-shaped site of the Municipal and University Library (Stadt- und Universitätsbibliothek), which was built in 1755 as the Corn Exchange but renovated in 1787–92 as the library by Sprüngli and Schmid.

Hôtel de Musique

From here Münstergasse (market for meat and dairy produce on Tuesday and Saturday mornings, every 1st Saturday in the month a craft market of hand-made goods) leads to the Münsterplatz, where stands the Moses Fountain (c.1545). The so-called late Baroque Stiftsgebäude (Albrecht Stürler, 1748) is the seat of the Cantonal government.

Münstergasse

*Minster

The Late Gothic Minster (dedicated to St Vincent), a three-aisled pillared basilica without transept, was begun in 1421 to the design of Matthäus Ensinger of Ulm, but the tower was not completed until 1893, with the addition of the octagonal upper section and the open-work spire.

The west doorway is richly decorated with sculpture (now copies); in the tympanum is a Last Judgment (originally 1495) containing a large number of figures, and on the side walls are paintings (1501, restored) of the Fall and the Annunciation.
The nave and the choir have reticulated vaulting with fine 16th c. bosses (coats-of-arms).

*West Doorway

Berne

Interior

Modern stained glass

The finely carved choir stalls (1523) were the first Renaissance work of art in Berne. In the apse are a Gothic font (1524), sedilla (15th c.: on right) and beautiful stained glass (1441–50). At the end of the south aisle is a monument to Berthold von Zähringen (1601), incorporating a coat-of-arms; at the end of a marble memorial to the 702 men of Berne who died fighting the French in 1798.

In the Matter chapel (seventh bay in the south aisle) can be seen the Dance of Death window (1917), with 20 scenes from the "Dance of Death" (1516–19) by Niklaus Manuel-Deutsch. There is a magnificent Baroque organ (1726–30) with 5404 pipes and fine modern stained glass (1947) in the south aisle.

From the tree-planted Minster terrace there is an attractive view down into the Aare valley; and there are fine panoramic views from the gallery on the Minster tower (254 steps).

Between Junkerngasse and Bärengraben

Erlacherhof

From here Junkerngasse, lined with arcaded houses once occupied by the old patrician families of Berne, runs towards the east end of the old town. At No. 47 is the handsome Erlacherhof (1749–52), now the seat of the State President.

Nydeggbrücke

Junkerngasse joins the wide Nydegg-Gasse, at the far end of which is the Nydegg bridge (1840–44) over the Aare gorge; the principal arch of stone has a span of 55 m/180 ft and stands 26 m/85 ft above the river. On the left, just before the bridge is the little Nydegg church, built in 1494 on the site of an Imperial stronghold (restored 1956).

Bärengraben

On the far side of the bridge is one of Berne's great popular attractions, the Bear-Pit (Bärengraben), a deep circular den in which bears, the heraldic animal of Berne, have been kept since 1480.

Berne: Church of the Holy Ghost . . .   *and the Parliament Building*

From the road running up to the right (Muristalden) there is a fine view of the Minster and the old town. Above the bridge to the left is the beautiful Rose-Garden (Rosengarten), with views of the Aare and the old town. Just downstream from the Nydegg bridge at the end of the old Untertorbrücke (1461–87), in Läuferplatz are Berne's first town hall and the Läuferbrunnen ("Runner Fountain", 1543).

From the Nydegg bridge to the Bubenbergplatz

From the Nydegg bridge a series of picturesque streets (Nydeggsgasse, Gerechtigkeitsgasse, Kramgasse, Marktgasse and Spitalgasse), with many antique shops and art galleries, runs along the whole length of the old town for a distance of 1700 m/1860 yards to end in the Bubenbergplatz.

The Gerechtigkeitsgasse is lined on both sides by arcades and elegant shops. In the middle of the street is the Justice Fountain (Gerechtigkeitsbrunnen, 1543) probably by Hans Gieng of Freiburg, with Justitia (since 1988 a copy) as the image of justice. The original statue was destroyed in 1986 and has been carefully restored in the Historical Museum.

* Gerechtigkeitsgasse

At the far end of Rathausgasse, on right, leads to the Rathaus (Council House, the seat of the Great Council of the canton and of the Town Council), in Late Burgundian Gothic style, built in 1406–16, much altered in 1866 and restored in the original style in 1939–42. In the square in front of the Rathaus stands the Banner-Carrier or Venner fountain (1542).

Rathaus

The continuation of the Gerechtigkeitsgasse, the Kramgasse, also lined with arcaded houses, has three fountains – the Kramgassbrunnen (1778), the Simsonbrunnen (Samson fountain, 1544) and the Zähringerbrunnen (1544) which shows the heraldic animal in jousting costume.

* Kramgasse

The world-famous physicist, humanist and Nobel prize winner, Albert Einstein, lived at 49 Kramgasse from 1902–1909 before emigrating to the United States. The house has been open to the public since 1979. In 1905 alone he wrote six epoch-making treatises, discovered quantum light, for which he was awarded the Nobel prize sixteen years later, and produced his "General Theory of Relativity", thereby revolutionising contemporary concepts of space, time and mass.

Albert Einstein House

The Kramgasse ends at the Clock Tower (Zeitglockenturm or Zytgloggeturm), a notable Berne landmark, frequently rebuilt (the present stone tower with its pointed spire is 15th c.) which was the west gate of the town until about 1250. On the east side of the tower is an astronomical clock (1527–30), with mechanical figures which perform four minutes before every hour.

* Clock Tower

Beyond this is the busy Marktgasse (pedestrian precinct), with old guildhouses, arcades, shops and two more fountains, the Schützenbrunnen (Marksman fountain) and Anna-Seiler-Brunnen, both of about 1545. At the far end of the street is the Käfigturm ("Cage tower", 13th and 17th c.), which was once one of the town gates from 1250 to 1350.
Beyond it is the Bärenplatz, from which the Spitalgasse (pedestrian precinct), with the Pfeifferbrunnen (Piper's fountain, 1545), continues to the Bubenbergplatz.

* Marktgasse

Käfigturm

Between Kornhausplatz and the railway station

This line of streets cuts across two of the town's principal squares. In front of the Clock tower is the Kornhausplatz, in which stands the curious Kindlifresserbrunnen ("Child Eater Fountain" or Ogre Fountain, with the figure of an ogre devouring a child) of about 1540.

Berne: Late-Gothic façade of the Town Hall   Clock tower and Zähringer Fountain

Kornhaus

On the west side of the square we see the handsome Kornhaus (1711–16), with high-vaulted wine cellars (restaurant); on the first floor are the Industrial Museum and the Swiss Gutenberg Museum. It is due to be refurbished in the early 1990s as a cultural and social centre.

French Church

Behind it the French church (Französische Kirche), originally a Dominician foundation (13th c.), has frescoes by the Berne "Master of the Carnation". In the north-west corner of the square, at the end of the iron bridge called the Kornhausbrücke , is the Municipal Theatre (Stadttheater, 1903).

Bärenplatz

Waisenhaus-
platz

To the south of the Käfigturm the charming little Bärenplatz (pedestrian precinct: flower and vegetable market Tuesday and Saturday mornings) was once a bear-pit; to the north is the large Waisenhausplatz (partly pedestrianised), at the far end of which stands the elegant old Orphanage (Waisenhaus) of 1782, now the police headquarters

*Museum of Art

To the west of this, in the Hodlerstrasse (No. 12), the Museum of Art (Kunstmuseum), built in 1879, with a plain windowless extension of 1935, contains a large collection of Swiss art, pictures by Italian masters of the 14th–16th c. and works by French artists of the 19th and 20th c. Among the older Swiss masters represented are the "Master of the Carnation" (Paul Löwensprung d. 1499) and Niklaus Manuel-Deutsch (1484–1530), one of the leading Swiss painters of the Early Renaissance: among modern artists Karl Staufer (1857–91) and Ferdinand Hodler (1853–1918). Notable also are the Paul Klee Collection with over 2500 of Klee's works, and the Rupf Collection of Cubist art (Braque, Gris, Léger, Picasso, Kandinsky, Feininger, etc.). The Print Cabinet contains works by both Swiss and foreign artists.

Main Railway
Station

The main railway station, in Bahnhofplatz, below the Grosse Schanze, was completely rebuilt between 1957 and 1974, with the tracks running underground for a distance of 200 m/656 ft (tourist information office, shopping, restaurants, café, car park, bus station). In the Christoffel underpass are remains of the fourth medieval defensive system (foundation of walls, round towers, remains of a bridge).

Elevators and flights of steps lead up from the station to the Grosse Schanze, the principal bastion in the old fortifications (built 1634, demolished 1834), now a park commanding extensive views.

Grosse Schanze

On the north-west side are the University, founded in 1834 (present buildings 1899–1930, with a monument to the Berne doctor and poet Albrecht von Haller (1708–77) in front of it, and the headquarters of the Swiss federal Railways (SBB-Direktion). To the left, beyond Schanzenstrasse, is the Supreme Court (Obergericht, 1909).

University

From Kornhausplatz the Kornhausbrücke (1898, a graceful iron bridge 48 m/157 ft high with a span of 115 m/377 ft, leads over the Aare into the newer part of the town. On a little hill immediately beyond the bridge, on the left, is the Schänzli, once an outer work in the town's defences, now occupied by the Kursaal (café-restaurant, concert hall, casino), from the terrace of which there is a magnificent view of Berne and the Alps.

Kornhausbrücke

Schänzli

Below the hill to the west are the Botanic Garden and the Lorraine bridge, a concrete structure of 1928–29 which links the Lorraine district of the town with the area around the station.

Botanic Garden

South of the Old Town

From the south side of the old town the Kirchenfeld bridge a two-arched iron bridge built 1882–83, crosses the Aare to the residential district of Kirchenfeld, the central feature of which is Helvetiaplatz, a large square around the Telegraph Union Monument (1922) and surrounded by museums. To the left is the Art Gallery (Kunsthalle, 1918), which puts on special exhibitions of contemporary art. To the right are the Berner Schulwarte (1933), with a rich collection of teaching material and a library on education, and the Swiss Alpine Museum (1934), which presents a fascinating picture of the Swiss Alps, covering their scientific study, communications, mapping and climbers (large relief model of the Bernese Oberland). In the same building is the Swiss Postal Museum, illustrating the history of the Swiss postal service, with a large collection of stamps.

Kirchenfeld Bridge

*Swiss Alpine Museum

Swiss Postal Museum

On the south side of Helvetiaplatz the Historical Museum of Berne (1892–94) is built in the style of a 16th c. castle, with collections of prehistoric material, folk art and traditions, ethnography and various types of decorative and applied art. Of particular interest are the Burgundian room, with trophies won at the Battle of Grandson in 1476 (weapons, tapestries, embroidery), the Henri Moser Charlottenfels Collection weapons and objets d'art from the Islamic East), the Lausanne cathedral treasury and late medieval tapestries.

*Historical Museum of Berne

Beyond the Historical Museum, in Bernastrasse, are (No. 5) the Swiss Riflemen's Museum and (No. 15) the Natural History Museum (Naturhistorisches Museum, 1933), with excellently displayed collections of geology, mineralogy, palaeontology and zoology (series of dioramas of African mammals in the B. von Wattenwyl Collection; dioramas of the animals of other regions; collection of rock-crystal; collection of antlers; zoological laboratory).

Natural History Museum

Still farther south rises the massive building occupied by the National Library (Landesbibliothek, 1929–32). Thormannstrasse continues south to the Dählhölzli, in a bend of the Aare, with the Tierpark (nature park and zoo:

Swiss National Library

Sampson Fountain in the Kramgasse   *Berne: Historical Museum*

restaurant). Footpath along the river (15 minutes) to the Elfenau nature reserve.

Surroundings of Berne

Bremgartenwald   To the north-west, between the town and the Aare, is a large wooded area, the Bremgartenwald, now encroached on by the motorway.

Halen   On the north side of the Aare, near the Halenbrücke, the interesting modern residential district of Halen (1959–61), is surrounded by the forest.

Walensee   To the north-west of the Bremgartenwald lies the Walensee, an artificial lake 15 km/9 miles long formed by the damming of the Aare (motor-boat trips, rowing boats).

Ascent of Gurten

Leave on the road to Belp, which runs south-east to the suburb of Wabern (alt. 556 m/1824 ft), 3.5 km/2 miles away. From here (car park) a funicular

Gurten   ascends in 5 minutes to the summit of the green hill of Gurten (861 m/2825 ft). At the upper station, Gurten-Kulm (843 m/2766 ft), are the Gurten-Kulm Hotel, a large garden restaurant (view of Berne) and a miniature railway. From the Ostsignal (857 m/2812 ft: 10 minutes' walk east) and the Westsignal (856 m/2809 ft: 3 minutes west) there are superb views of the Bernese Alps.

Through the Gürbe valley

From Wabern it is 3.5 km/2 miles to Kehrsatz (alt.573 m/1880 ft; bypass), with a 16th c. Schloss, now a state girls' reformatory.

From here the direct road runs through the beautiful Gürbe valley (to the left Schloss Oberried, now a boys' school), via the neat little town of Belp (alt. 526 m/1726 ft), at the foot of the Belpberg (894 m/2933 ft , which has a picturesque 16th c. castle and a series of Gothic frescoes (1455–60) in the church of St Peter and Paul. | Gürbetal Belp

Then on to Toffen where there is a museum of veteran cars and motor-cycles in the Gürbestrasse and a medieval Baroque castle (1671). The castle in neighbouring Rümligen is also of Baroque style (18th c.); the last owner was the well-known Bernese Madame de Meuron. Past Seftigen, contin-uing over the ridge between the Gürbe and Aare valleys, the road reaches Thun (see entry) on the lake of the same name. | Toffen

Alternatively take a road on the right to Kehrsatz, and after a short distance uphill turn left into a ridge road which runs above the Gürbe valley (exten-sive views), passing below Zimmerwald, where the formation of the Third International (the Communist International Organisation) was discussed at a conference in September 1915 attended by Lenin. | Zimmerwald

The road runs sharply downhill to (12 km/7 miles) Riggisberg (alt. 768 m/2520 ft), a little town of 2000 inhabitants (Abegg Collection of textiles and decorative art). From here via Gurnigel (alt. 1153 m/3783 ft: winter sports) to Schwefelbergbad (see p.185). Beyond this turn left (road on right to Gurnigel) 4.5 km/3 miles: Burgistein (775 m/2543 ft) under a prominent 16th c. castle (813 m/2667 ft). | Riggisberg Burgistein

2.5 km/2 miles: Wattenwil (604 m/1982 ft), below the Staffelalp (983 m/3225 ft: far-ranging views; inn; 3 km/2 miles by road). Continue through the Gürbe valley for 4 km/2 miles to Blumenstein (661 m/2169 ft), with a 14th c. church (beautiful stained glass in choir) and a chalybeate spring (impreg-nated with iron). Finally, 4.5 km/3 miles, we reach Oberstocken (672 m/2205 ft), at the foot of the Stockhorn, from which there are extensive views. | Wattenwil

From Berne to Fribourg via Schwarzenburg

In Köniz (575 m/1887 ft; pop. 32,000) a visit to the Morillongut country seat (1832) and the former Augustinian Provost St Peter and Paul s a must. The notable Romanesque church (Gothic choir with 14th c. glass and wall-paintings) was taken over by the Teutonic knights in 1226. | Köniz

About 5 km/3 miles farther on the road cuts across the deeply cut valley of the Scherlibach. Another 10 km/6 miles to Schwarzenburg (795 m/2608 ft) where there is a castle of 1573, the 15th c. little church of Maria Magdalena with a shingle-covered 17th c. clock tower and the Swiss short-wave radio transmitter. | Schwarzenburg

From here road 74 leads west towards Fribourg through an upland region with far-reaching views, crossing the gorge of the Sense River on a covered wooden bridge (1.3 km/1 mile north, above the right bank of the river the ruins of the Imperial castle of Grasburg). Via Heitenried, 13 km/8 miles, (760 m/2494 ft) is Tafers (655 m/2150 ft) with its notable church (oldest part 9th–10th c.; altered in 16th, 18th and 20th c.). After only a few kilometres the church towers of Fribourg are visible. | Tafers

Bernese Oberland   C2/D2

Cantons: Berne (BE) and Valais (VS)

The Bernese Oberland is that part of the Swiss Alps lying between Lake Geneva and the River Reuss; it rises above the 4000 m/13,124 ft mark in the Finsteraarhorn (4274 m/14,023 ft), the Aletschhorn (4195 m/13,764 ft). the Schreckhorn (4078 m/13,380 ft), the Mönch (4099 m/13,449 ft) and the Jungfrau (4158 m/13,642 ft). | Situation

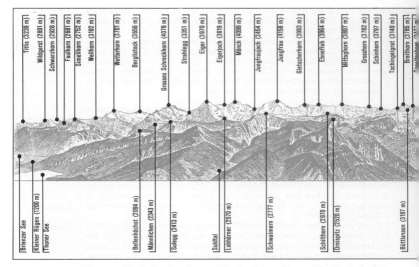

| Lakes and Rivers | The massif is drained on the north by the Saane, Simme, Kander and other rivers, on the south by the Rhône, which is fed by the Aletsch glacier and Rhône glacier and by its right-bank tributaries. The Rhône forms the southern boundary of the Bernese Oberland until it flows into Lake Geneva. Below the north side are Lake Thun and Lake Brienz. The principal gateway to the mountains of the Bernese Oberland is Interlaken. |

History

The regions bordering the Bernese Oberland have a long history of human settlement, as is shown by the Stone Age and Bronze Age material and the Roman remains which have been found by excavation, as well as by churches dating from before the year 1000. For many centuries the villages in the Bernese Oberland were wholly dependent on their stock-farming and pastoral economy, but the time came when the beauties of mountain scenery began to be appreciated. In the latter part of the 18th c. Goethe visited the Lauterbrunnen valley, and during the Romantic period there was an enthusiastic interest in natural beauty. This period too saw the beginning of modern mountaineering; the Jungfrau was climbed in the early years of the 19th c., and other peaks represented a challenge to climbers. Perhaps the best known of these is the Eiger, the north face of which was long regarded as unclimbable. The first successful ascent was in 1938 (by Heckmair, Vörg, Harrer and Kasparek), and the first winter ascent in 1961 (by Hiebeler, Kinshofer, Almberger and Manhardt).

Communi-
cations

The main north-south route through the Bernese Oberland is the 14.6 km/ 9 mile railway tunnel under the Lötschberg; the busiest road is the one which runs over the Grimsel pass from Brienz to Gletsch, at the foot of the Rhône glacier.

****Culture and Landscape**

The Bernese Oberland has a number of major tourist resorts which are among the oldest established in Switzerland. Alexander von Humboldt,

Panorama from Niesen (2362 m – 7750 ft)

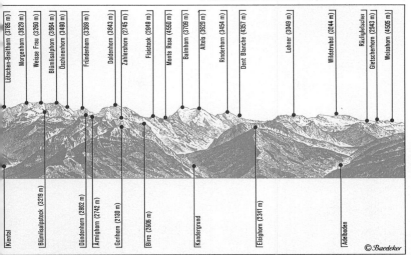

© Baedeker

Goethe, Kleist and Brahms were regular visitors to Lake Thun, the site of three famous castles, which today house Historical Museums. The neighbouring Lake Brienz is equally attractive. Interlaken, as the name suggests, lies on an alluvial delta between the two lakes. Lenk, Adelboden and Grindelwald, among others, were already attracting many visitors in the 19th c., and up to the First World War the region became the haunt of the nobility and successful artists from all over Europe. Today the Bernese Oberland, with its magnificent scenery and its excellent and steadily expanding facilities for winter sports, is perhaps still the best-known holiday region in Switzerland and it is not without good reason that it is often described as "The playground of Europe".   *Lake Thun*   *Lake Brienz*

Summer in the Bernese Oberland means walking, hiking and climbing in magical countryside on well marked paths. A number of routes of varying difficulty await the climber while the lakes are a sailor's paradise.   *In Summer*

In winter the region is a skier's paradise offering marvellous pistes for both beginners and experienced skiers. With almost 500 km/310 miles of routes the Bernese Oberland is a paradise for long-distance skiers. For non-skiers there are excellent indoor and outdoor facilities for curling, ice-skating, tennis and swimming.   *In Winter*

The finest mountains, and those affording the best views, are well provided with cableways and elevators – e.g. the Jungfraujoch (3545 m/11,635 ft) with Europe's highest cableway station. On the route to the "Top of Europe" one can enjoy unique views of the Alpine glaciers of the Swiss Alps (see Jungfrau region), e.g. the Eismeer (3160 m/10,371 ft), the Eigerwand (2865 m/9403 ft), the First (2168 m/7115 ft), the Schilthorn (2971 m/9751 ft) and others.   ***Jungfrau region**

The most impressive panoramic view is to be had from the 2362 m/7750 ft high Niesen, which rises above the south-west side of Lake Thun and can be reached by funicular from Mülenen. From the summit there is a panorama taking in Lakes Thun and Brienz, the 4000 m/13,124 ft peaks of the Jungfrau massif and the Valais Alps to the south.   **Niesen*

Spiez Castle on Lake Thun   *Typical 18th c. timber house in Bönigen*

Bernina Pass   E2/F2

Canton: Grisons (GR)
Altitude: 2323 m/7622 ft

One of the most rewarding routes through the Alps is the one which runs
from St Moritz over the Bernina pass and down the Poschiavo valley into
Italy, and usually remains open throughout the year for both road and rail
traffic. The pass is not only the watershed between the Engadine and the
Valtellina but also the boundary between Rhaeto-Romanic (referring to the
language and culture peculiar to south-eastern Switzerland and the Tyrol)
and Italian culture. The road, already being used in the 13th c. and built in its
modern form between 1842 and 1865, traverses magnificent mountain and
glacier scenery.

Situation and general

The journey from St Moritz to Tirano in Italy goes over the 58 km/36 miles
long pass road, via Pontresina (8 km/5 miles) to the Bernina pass (24 km/15
miles), and then via Poschiavo (17 km/11 miles) to Tirano (34 km/21 miles).

Communications

By rail on the Rhätische Bahn, the journey takes 3½ hours (the highest
railway over the Alps). A tourist attraction is the Bernina-Express from Chur
via the pass to Tirano, which can also be combined with the Glacier-
Express (see Practical Information, Railways).

The road crosses the plateau via Samedan (airport) and Celerina, and
begins to climb at Punt Muragl (cableway up Muottas Muragl: see p. 315).
At Pontresina there are views up Val Roseg to the right and Val Languarc to

◀ *View from the Eiger over Grindelwald and First*

Walking to the Boval hut above the Morteratsch glacier

Morteratsch Glacier

the left. 4.5 km/3 miles farther on a road goes off on the right to the Hotel-Restaurant Morteratsch (45 minutes climb from here to the Morteratsch glacier, 35 minutes up Chünetta). From the sharp bends at Montebello there are superb views of the Morteratsch glacier, Piz Palü (3905 m/12,812 ft), Bellavista (3827 m/12,556 ft), Piz Bernina (4049 m/13,285 ft) and Piz Morteratsch (3751 m/12,307 ft).

Two of Switzerland's finest cableways start from special stations on the Bernina railway.

**Diavolezza

The Diavolezza (2973 m/9754 ft), one of the most popular skiing areas in the Alps, is reached by a cableway starting just beyond Bernina Suot (length 3625 m/11,894 ft, height difference 883 m/2897 ft, time 10 minutes). The Diavolezza-Haus (2977 m/9768 ft), situated opposite the giant peaks of the Bernina group, affords magnificent views. From here there are numerous paths leading into the mountains, including the "Diavolezza-Tour", one of the easiest glacier walks (3 hours, with guide), going from the Diavolezza-Haus by way of the Pers and Morteratsch glaciers to the Morteratsch Hotel. Summer skiing.

*Piz Lagalb

Piz Lagalb (2959 m/9708 ft: lower station Curtinatsch 2090 m/6857 ft, upper station 2896 m/9502 ft: restaurant, with panoramic view): wildlife park, view into the Valtellina. The cableway, 2381 m/7812 ft long, runs up from Curtinatsch (Bernina-Lagalb) in 8 minutes.

Bernina Hospice

The Bernina Hospice (2309 m/7576 ft: 40b.) is a good walking and climbing base. Two lakes, Lej Nair (Black Lake, 2222 m/7290 ft) and Lej Pitschen (2220 m/7284 ft), fed by springs, drain northward into the Inn; they are separated by a masonry dam from the Lago Bianco (White Lake, 2230 m/7317 ft), an artificial lake supplying the Brusio hydro-electric station. From the Alp Grüm (2091 m/6861 ft: railway station) there is a fine view of the Palü glacier (Alpine garden). Nature-lovers can observe many species of birds, from the golden eagle to the rock swallow, from the pigmy owl to the snow finch.

The Bernina road now leaves the railway track, which runs over the Alp Grüm and down into the Val di Pila, and climbs past the Lago della Crocetta to the Bernina pass (Italian Passo del Bernina, 2323 m/7622 ft), with the desolate landscape of ice-worn rocks commonly found on the high passes and beautiful views on both sides. From here the road runs sharply downhill in short bends and then descends in four hairpins, with magnificent views down into the valley, into the Val Agoné, the highest part of the Poschiavo valley. At La Motta a road branches off on the left over the Forcola di Livigno pass (2315 m/7596 ft) into the Val di Livigno, in Italy (3.5 km/2 miles to the frontier, then 15 km/9 miles to Livigno: large skiing area, customs-free zone).

*Bernina Pass

5.5 km/3 miles from the pass is La Rösa (1878 m/6162 ft), a picturesque little mountain village at the foot of Piz Campasscio. Then downhill above a wooded gorge, with beautiful views, followed by two sharp bends down to Sfazù (1666 m/5466 ft: restaurant) and over the Wildbach at the mouth of the beautiful Val di Campo (on left), a valley gouged out by a glacier (narrow mountain road, 8 km/5 miles, maximum gradient 13%). 4 km/2 miles beyond La Rösa, on the left, is the Pozzolascio restaurant (1530 m/5020 ft), near a small lake.

Val di Campo

The road continues high up on the wooded mountainside, soon affording an excellent view of the Poschiavo valley. On the opposite slope (view restricted by trees) are the boldly engineered bends of the Bernina railway. 10 km/6 miles from La Rösa, at San Carlo (1095 m/3593 ft), the road reaches the floor of the Poschiavo valley (Italian Valle di Poschiavo). Before the village is a hydro-electric station belonging to the Brusio complex.

Valle di Poschiavo

From the Poschiavo valley into the Valtellina

The 34 km/21 miles long Poschiavo valley, which descends from the Bernina pass to Tirano in the Valtellina, is a region of southern vegetation and Italian life-style. It remained part of the canton of Grisons after the cession to Italy of the Valtellina, which belonged to the Grisons from 1512 to 1797. In 1987 the valley was subject to catastrophic floods, but repairs were completed within a year.

The road on the south side of the Bernina pass is now of a good standard. In 17 km/11 miles it comes to Poschiavo (1014 m/3327 ft: pop. 3600), the central area of population in a commune made up of six separate villages. Sights include the 17th c. Town Hall with Romanesque tower, the Late Gothic church of San Vittore (15th–16th c.) and the Baroque church of Santa Maria Presentata (17th–18th c.) with a beautiful ceiling painting in the nave from 1770. Not far from the Piazza are the elegant patrician houses. Colourful façades characterise the Spaniola quarter, which was settled in the 19th c. by emigrants returning from Spain.

4 km/2 miles beyond Poschiavo is the summer holiday resort of Le Prese (alt. 965 m/3166 ft) on the Lago di Poschiavo.

Le Prese

The commune of Brusio (alt. 740 m/2428 ft: pop. 1340), which takes in the seven villages between the Lago di Poschiavo and the frontier, is an area of lush southern vegetation. The principal village is dominated by the towers of its 17th c. church.

Brusio

The road continues through tobacco plantations and forests of chesnut-trees to Campascio (630 m/2067 ft) and Campocologno (553 m/1814 ft), the last place in Switzerland (customs), with the Brusio power station (33,000 kW).

From the frontier crossing at Piatta Mala the road leads into the Valtellina. The Village of Madonna di Tirano (438 m/1437 ft) has a famous pilgrimage church (1503–33). The road now forks: to the right it runs down the Valtellina and continues via Sondrio and around Lake Como to Lugano (120 km/75 miles: see entry); the road to the left runs up the valley to the old town of Tirano (429 m/1408 ft: pop. 8000), straddling the River Adda, with old patrician houses of the 15th–17th c.

Madonna di Tirano

Tirano

Biel/Bienne   C1

Canton: Berne
Altitude: 440 m/1444 ft
Population: 58,000

Situation and general

This bilingual town (Biel in German, Bienne in French), with two-thirds of its inhabitants speaking German and one-third French, is the capital of the Swiss watchmaking industry. Several hundred small and medium-sized firms are engaged in the manufacture of watches and watch parts in the town, which is also a place of considerable commercial activity. The residential districts are mainly on the lower slopes of the Jura hills, which here slope down to the lake. In recent years the town has also made a name for itself as a convention capital.

History

The town was founded about 1220 by the Prince-Abbot of Basle and remained under the rule of successive Prince-Abbots until 1792. From 1798 to 1815 it belonged to France; thereafter it was incorporated in the canton of Berne and is now the second largest town in the canton.

Sights

Rathaus

The upper town with its historic old buildings is well preserved. In the Burgplatz are the Late Gothic Rathaus (Town Hall: built 1530–34, renovated 1676) and the Theatre, originally the armoury (1589–91; in front of the Rathaus stands the Justice fountain (1714).

*Zunfthaus der Waldleute

From here the Burggässli leads to the Ring, a square surrounded by arcaded houses. The old Zunfthaus der Waldleute (Guild-House of the Foresters, 1559–61) is now occupied by the Kunnstverein (Society of Arts). The Late Gothic parish church (1451–92: Protestant) has 15th c. stained glass and wall-paintings. In the Obergasse are the 16th c. Angel fountain and the former inn Zur Krone (1578–82), with a tablet commemorating Goethe's stay there in 1779. In the Rosiusplatz are towers and part of a moat belonging to the old fortifications, the old Clock tower (rebuilt on this site in 1843) and the Technikum (Technical College).

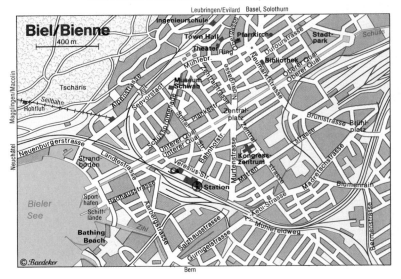

Biel/Bienne: Guild house of Foresters . . .   . . . and the Devil's Fountain

The Omega Museum (43, Rue Stämpfli) has a clock collection ranging from the first watches to NASA's latest time measuring equipment. Viewing by appointment only.

In the Seevorstadt, a street running down to the lake, is the Schwab Museum (closed Mondays), with material of the prehistoric period (lake-dwellings), Iron Age and Roman period. To the south are the railway station and the modern Congress Hall in the Zentralstrasse (1961–66: swimming pool).

Congress Hall

Surroundings

From the north-western Jura hills above the town there are panoramic views of the Bernese Alps and the Mittelland, with the lakes. 2.5 km/2 miles from Biel on the Delémont road (No. 6) a narrow road branches off on the left and in 4.5 km/3 miles reaches Magglingen (French Macolin: alt. 875 m/2871 ft; pop. 2700), with the Federal School of Gymnastics and Sport; easy hill-walking in the surrounding area.

Magglingen

There are cableways from Biel to Magglingen (length 1694 m/5558 ft, time 9 minutes) and to Leubringen/Evilard (length 933 m/3061 ft, time 6 minutes).

In the Taubenlochschlucht, a gorge 2 km/1 mile east of the outlying district of Bözingen, the folding of the strata caused by the geological upheavals of the past can be observed in the rock face.

Taubenloch-schlucht

The wine villages around the lake

The Bieler See (Lake Biel) or Lac de Bienne (alt. 429 m/1408 ft: area 39 sq. km/15 sq. miles), forms the boundary between two geological regions, the limestone formations of the Jura and the molasse (soft greenish sandstone) of the area around the lakes. On the north side of the lake the slopes

Lake Biel

Erlach Castle

of the Jura fall steeply down, with the German-speaking villages of Tüscherz, Twann and Ligerz, once belonging to Burgundy, set amid vineyards at the foot. The shore on the south side, less visited by tourists, is flatter, and in prehistoric times was occupied by numerous lake-dwellings built on piles. At the south end of the lake lies the popular resort of St Peterinsel (St Peter's Island), the south-east side of which is the haunt of large numbers of waterfowl.

Regulation of the River Aare

In 1878, as a result of the control of the River Aare, the level of the lake was lowered by some 2 m/7 ft. The Aare, which had previously flowed past the lake 7 km/4 miles to the east, was then diverted into the lake by the construction of a canal at Hagneck and brought back to its original bed by another canal from Nidau to Büren. As a result soil and debris carried down by the river were deposited in the lake.

Vine-growing

A circuit of the lake provides an opportunity of seeing the beautiful scenery of its shores and a series of attractive little towns and villages, in the largest vine-growing area in the canton of Berne. Three-quarters of the area is planted with the white Chasselas grape, a fifth with the red Pinot Noir. The local method of wine-making, involving early racking (separation of the wine from the sediment or "lees"), produces fruity wines of high carbonic acid content, mainly sold as Twanner, Schafiser and Erlacher, which are much sought after. Vines are also grown at Ligerz, Tüscherz, Vingelz, Tscugg, La Neuveville and Alfermée and on St Peterinsel. There is a Museum of Viticulture in Ligerz and visits to wine-making establishments can be arranged through the Informations- und Propogandastelle für Bieler-See-Weine, CH-2514 Ligerz.

A walk along the "wine route" from Biel to Tüscherz and Twann (2 hours), returning from Twann by boat or continuing on foot to Ligerz (½ hour), is a memorable experience. The road around the lake runs south-west via Vingelz and the old Burgundian settlement of Alfermée to the wine village

The Blanche-Eglise (white church) of La Neuveville

of Tüscherz (alt. 435 m/1427 ft; pop. 2800), which has a railway station and landing stage and continues to Twann (French Douanne: 434 m/1424 ft; pop. 900), a sleepy little village of narrow winding streets and old houses which has preserved its medieval character. Excavations here in 1974–76 revealed remains of the earliest farming settlements (between 3000 and 2000 B.C.).

Twann

The next village is Ligerz (French Gléresse: 433 m/1421 ft; pop. 500; Wine-Growing Museum), from which there is a cableway to Prêles (Prägelz) on the Tessenberg (length 1200 m/3937 ft, height difference 379 m/1243 ft, time 7 minutes); from the terrace below Mont Chasseral there are superb views. Good walking among the vineyards, through the Twannbach gorge and to Schernelz.

Ligerz

The last Bernese commune on the lake is La Neuveville (German Neuenstadt: 438 m/1437 ft; pop. 3900), the "Montreux of the Jura", with narrow streets, old gates and towers which belonged to the town's fortifications and a thousand-year-old church, the Blanche Eglise, with a wooden ceiling and Gothic frescoes (restored 1988/89). The road now enters the canton of Neuchâtel.

La Neuveville

The first place beyond the cantonal boundary is Le Landeron (433 m/1421 ft; pop. 3400), a medieval market town with house fronts of the 16th and 17th c. The largest flea-market in Switzerland, the Fête de la Brocante, is held here annually in September.

Le Landeron

Continuing along the south side of the lake, the next town is Erlach (433 m/1421 ft; pop. 1050) with an old castle which is now a cantonal school hostel. The administrative district of Erlach also includes the farming and vine-growing villages of Vinelz and Lüscherz.

Erlach

The most popular excursion on the lake is to St Peterinsel (alt. 435 m/1427 ft: Hotel), a place of idyllic beauty. Once an island it can be reached from

St Peterinsel

Biel or La Neuville by boat, or (since the 19th c. regulation of the River Aare) on foot from Erlach on the "Heidenweg". The inn was originally a Cluniac priory (founded 1120, dissolved 1530); the room in which Rousseau stayed in 1765 is shown to visitors. The return route from Erlach crosses the Aare canal and just before Biel reaches Nidau (alt. 430 m/1411 ft; pop. 8400), which is separated from Biel only by the Zihl canal, and is the starting point of the Nidau-Büren canal; thus in effect Nidau lies on an artificial island.

Aarberg

Aarberg (alt. 455 m/1493 ft; pop. 3300) 11 km/7 miles south of Biel, a unique little medieval town, was founded about 1220, and was for centuries one of the countries most important road junctions. Its main features of interest are the Stadtplatz with its ring of well-to-do citizens' houses and the old wooden bridge over the Aare. The castle (end of 17th c.) contains a gallery of coats-of-arms from over 80 provincial governors.

Lyss

Lyss (alt. 444 m/1493 ft; pop. 8300: swimming pool and ice rink): walks along the Alte Aare, the old course of the river (rich flora and fauna).

Büren an der Aare

Büren an der Aare (alt. 443 m/1453 ft; pop. 2900), a little town, bright with flowers, lying between the Aare and the forest, with many fine old buildings. The town hall (c.1500) and the provincial governor's castle from 1620 with picturesque Gothic stepped windows are worth visiting.

Val Bregaglia   E2

Canton: Grisons (GR)

Situation and general

The Val Bregaglia (in German Bergell) is a wild and romantic gorge, enclosed between towering granite mountains, which descends in a series of terrace-like steps from the Majola pass (1815 m/5955 ft) to the Italian town of Chiavenna (333 m/1093 ft), 32 km/20 miles south-west. The high valley of the River Mera, which eventually flows into Lake Como, begins by falling steeply down from the pass (the watershed between the Val Bregaglia and the Engadine) and then descends to Chiavenna in six stages, the first four of which are within the canton of Grisons. The oddly shaped crags, buttresses and pinnacles of this mountain world are a climber's paradise, and the picturesque villages with their old patrician houses are a reminder of the long history of this region, which began in Roman times.

Beyond the pass the road leads down in a series of 13 hairpin bends, with gradients of up to 9%, into the green valley below.

Casáccia

The highest village in the valley is Casáccia (1458 m/4784 ft; pop. 60), from which the old bridle-path, one of the busiest routes through the Alps in medieval times, crossed the Pass da Sett (Septimer pass) to Bivio in the Sursés (Oberhalbstein) valley. The ruined Turratsch watch-tower and the 16th c. hospice are relics of these earlier days. A cableway 2500 m/8203 ft long belonging to the hydro-electric station which supplies power to Zurich (available for the transport of visitors by prior arrangement) leads up to the Albigna reservoir (2163 m/7097 ft: dam 115 m/377 ft high.

Vicosoprano

Vicosoprano (1067 m/3501 ft; pop. 400) was originally the chief settlement in the valley. Sixteenth century patrician houses; Senwelenturm, a 13th c. tower 23 m/75 ft high; courthouse, with torture chamber; Town Hall (1584); church (1761).

Stampa, Ciäsa granda

Stampa (994 m/3261 ft; pop. 180), a village which straggles along the road, was the home of the Giacometti family of artists. In the Ciäsa Granda (the "large house") is a fascinating museum devoted to the Val Bregaglia (collection of minerals, a weaving room, elegant living rooms and domestic utensils).

View of the upper valley of the Mera from the Maloja Pass

The following defile, La Porta, marks the boundary between the Alpine and the more southerly parts of the valley; it was fortified in Roman times.

The hamlet of Promontogno (821 m/2694 ft) has a church (Nossa Donra), which dates in part from the 12th c., and a ruined castle (Castelmur).

From here a rewarding excursion (3 km/2 miles) can be made to Soglio (1090 m/3576 ft; pop. 210) on a road which branches on the right and runs through a chesnut wood. The village was the ancestral home of the Salis family and has three palaces (16th–18th c.) which belonged to them. From the village, huddled around the tall tower of its church on a natural terrace above the valley, there are magnificent views of the Sciora group and the Val Bregaglia.

*Soglio

22 km/14 miles from the Majola pass the road reaches the Italian frontier at Castasegna (697 m/2287 ft; pop. 220), a trim village of southern aspect surrounded by luxuriant vegetation and the beautiful chesnut wood of Brentan. Underground hydro-electric power station (50 by 25 m/164 by 82 ft).

Castasegna

The Italian town of Chiavenna lies at the junction of the Spluga (Splügen) and Majola pass routes. The Roman Clavenna occupied a key strategic position, as its name (from clavis, "key") implies. From 1512 to 1797 it was in the Grisons. Its principal church, San Lorenzo, has an octagonal baptistery (font of 1156).

Chiavenna

Brig

C2

Canton: Valais
Altitude: 684 m/2244 ft
Population: 10,000

Brig

Situation and general

The historic little town of Brig, on the south bank of the Rhône, is the capital of the German-speaking upper Valais (Oberwallis) and an important junction on the Simplon, Lötschberg, Furka-Oberalp and Brig-Visp-Oberalp railways. It has a number of notable buildings and is also the starting-point of the great roads over the Simplon, the Furka and Nufenen passes.

History

Brig was already of importance in Roman times as a staging point on the north side of the Simplon pass. Its name comes from its situation between two bridges (over the Rhône and the Saltina). It later became the see of a bishop, and enjoyed a period of great prosperity in the time of Kaspar Jodok Stockalper (see below).

Sights

*Stockalperschloss

The most notable building in Brig is the Stockalperschloss, the finest Baroque palace in Switzerland, which the town bought from the Stockalper family in 1948. Since then it has been thoroughly renovated and restored by a trust, with financial assistance from the Federal government, the canton and the town. This imposing structure, dominated by three square gabled towers, was built by the great Valais merchant Prince Kaspar Jodok Stockalper von Thurm (1609–91), who had occupied all the leading positions in the land. The palace, built between 1658 and 1678, pointed the way towards a great flowering of the baroque in Valais. It now houses, in addition to the family library of the "King of the Simplon" and 12,000 documents, the archives of the Upper Valais Historical Society, the Valais Institute (Walser-Institut) and the Museum of the Upper Valais (May–October). Also here are the Matza and Jadok galleries which both have special exhibitions.

Near the palace are the collegiate church of Spiritus Sanctus (1675–85) and the Gothic St Antony's chapel. Also of interest are the Fernanda Stockalper house (18th c.) opposite the palace, the Wegener house (17th–19th c.) and the Theiler house in Simplonstrasse.

*Pilgrimage church of Unsere liebe Frau

West of Brig, on the Glisacker, stands the pilgrimage church of Unsere liebe Frau (c.1540), representing the final phase of medieval architecture (Gothic and Renaissance), which contains the finest works of art in this part of Switzerland.

Also of interest are the monument to Dr Ernest Guglielmetti (known as "Dr Goudron" – i.e. "Dr Tar"), inventor of the asphalt-surfaced road (in the Marktplatz to the north of the Stockalperschloss) and the fountain commemorating the Peruvian aviator Geo Chavez, who flew over the Simplon for the first time in 1910 (in Sebastianplatz).

Surroundings

Brigerbad

On the north bank of the Rhône is Brigerbad (alt. 655 m/2149 ft; pop. 185) with the first thermal swimming bath in a cave (air-conditioned, 38–42° C/100–108° F) and the largest open-air thermal baths in the country.

Visp

9 km/6 miles south-west is Visp (alt. 660 m/2165 ft), a little town of 4000 inhabitants beautifully situated at the mouth of the Vispa valley, up which runs the road to Zermatt and Saas Fee. Remains of town walls; old houses with coats-of-arms. On a crag above the Vispa is a large church of 1761 with a Romanesque tower, and higher up the hill St Martin's church (1651, altered 1963), with an arcaded porch.

Visperterminen

A road winds its way up the east side of the Vispa valley, through the highest vineyards in Europe (700–1200 m/2297–3937 ft: "Heidenwein", "heathen's wine"), for 10.5 km/7 miles to the village of Visperterminen (1340 m/4397 ft), surrounded by a network of irrigation channels. From the

Brig: Stockalperschloss   *Church of St Hilarius in Mörel*

village a path, with Stations of the Cross, climbs to the pilgrimage chapel of the Visitation (17th c.: old organ). Chair-lift from Visperterminen to Giw (1925 m/6316 ft).

About 14 km/ west is Raron (640 m/2100 ft) with a pretty 16th c. castle church where the poet Rainer Maria Rilke lies buried.   Raron

At the foot of the Aletsch glacier

To the north of Brig extends a magnificent glacier region. Between the Riederhorn (2230 m/7317 ft) and the Eggishorn (2937 m/9636 ft), a natural terrace exposed to the sun, from which the land falls steeply away, forms a transition to the Rhône valley. From Brig there are various routes to the Aletsch glacier which offer attractive day or half-day outings, with the help of cableways and lifts.

From Brig-Naters there is a good road up to Blatten (1332 m/4370 ft; pop. 50), a typical little Valais mountain village, from which there is a cableway (length 1780 m/5840 ft, height difference 766 m/2513 ft, time 6 minutes to Belalp (2080 m/6824 ft). From here a footpath (½ hour) leads to the Belalp Hotel (D, 30b.), at the foot of the Sparrhorn and above the western tip of the Aletsch glacier.   Blatten   Belalp

7 km/4 miles up the Rhône valley from Brig is Mörel (800 m/2625 ft; pop. 600), formerly a post station and now a base for walks and climbs on the Riederalp. There are two cableways, one running up in two stages via Ried (length 3055 m/10,123 ft, height difference 1155 m/3790 ft, time 25 minutes) to the Riederalp, the other to the Greicheralp (length 2798 m/9180 ft, height difference 1141 m/3744 ft, time 15 minutes) with a continuation to the Moosfluh (length 1817 m/5962 ft, height difference 451 m/1480 ft, time 12 minutes), directly above the Aletsch glacier. From the Riederalp there is a   Mörel

The Great Aletsch glacier

chair-lift (length 1053 m/3455 ft, height difference 299 m/981 ft, time 7 minutes) to the Hohfluh, from which there is a splendid walk down to the Riederfurka (2064 m/6772 ft). A well constructed road leads from the mountain station of the cableway Rieder-Alp–Moosfluh, along the Bettmerhorn to Lake Märjelen, and offers spectacular views of the Aletsch glacier and the surrounding peaks over 4000 m/13,000 ft.

**Aletsch glacier

The Aletsch glacier is a unique feature of great magnificence - the largest stretch of firn (ice formed from snow) in the Alps and in Europe (area 170 sq. km/66 sq. miles, length 22 km/14 miles). Its catchment area extends from the south side of the Bernese Alps, around the Jungfrau, to the almost level Konkordiaplatz (see below), where the ice is some 800 m/2625 ft deep, and from there southwards to the Aletschwald (nature reserve), one of the highest forests of stone pines in Europe.

Villa Cassel, Riederfurka

The Aletsch area offers magnificent opportunities for walkers and climbers. The Villa Cassel on the Riederfurka was the first office for the protection of nature established by the Schweizer Bund für Naturschutz (Swiss Association for the Protection of Nature: exhibition, Alpine garden).

*Riederalp

The real gateway to the Aletsch glacier and the Aletschwald is the Riederwald (1950 m/6398 ft; pop. 300) which is accessible by three cableways from Mörel. The highest golf course in Switzerland (9 holes) is situated here. Popular attractions include guided glacier walks, excursions over the high mountain path from the mountain station Riederalp/Moosfluh to Lake Märjelen and the weekly cheese show at the Alpine museum. The well established pistes of the Riederalp are an ideal skiing area in winter with guaranteed snow (ski school offering courses in ski acrobatics). Particular features of interest are the Riederalp chapel (1679) and the Blausee (Blue Lake; restaurant, Alpine trout farm).

*Bettmeralp

There is a pleasant, almost level, walk to the Bettmeralp (1950 m/6398 ft; pop. 150). The picturesque little mountain village, around the chapel of

Maria zum Schnee (1679), is a popular resort both in summer and in winter, with excellent walking (walking, fishing and tennis weeks; glacier walks; climbing school). From the Rhône valley the Bettmeralp can be reached via Betten (10 km/6miles from Brig) on a cableway (length 2610 km/8563 ft, height difference 1120 m/3675 ft, time 10 minutes).

The Aletsch area can also be reached from Fiesch, 18 km/11 miles east of Brig (1050 m/3445 ft; pop. 700). Fiesch, which first appears in the records in 1203, has a chapel with an altar of 1704. There is a large health and holiday complex for young people, opened in 1966 (1050b., SB, gymnasium).

Fiesch

From the Eggishorn (2916 m/9600 ft) there are panoramic views in the Upper Valais. A cableway (length 4795 m/15,732 ft, height difference 1807 m/5929 ft, time 13 minutes) ascends to the Kühboden and from there to the summit (magnificent view of the Aletsch glacier). Under the north face of the Eggishorn is the Märjelensee (Lake Märjelen; 2345 m/7694 ft: nature reserve).

*Eggishorn

8 km/5 miles north-east of the Eggishorn is Konkordiaplatz (2840 m/9318 ft: Swiss Alpine Club hut; guide required).

*Konkordiaplatz

A new-style holiday resort can be found at Breiten ob Mörel, 8 km/5 miles up the valley from Brig (900 m/2953 ft; pop. 80). This centrally managed resort on a sunny terrace above the valley of the infant Rhône is the only brine spa in the Alps (water at 33° C/91° F, with a well-equipped treatment and fitness facility (heated SB, SP) and its own farm (cheese dairy of 1713).

*Breiten ob Mörel

Brunnen

D1/2

Canton: Schwyz (SZ)
Altitude: 440 m/1444 ft
Population: 6300

The popular summer resort of Brunnen has a magnificent situation at the right-angled bend in Lake Lucerne formed by the Urner See (Lake Uri) and the Gersauer Becken (Gersau basin), at the beginning of the Axenstrasse (opened 1865), on the road over the St Gotthard. Since the construction of a bypass road it is a pleasantly quiet resort, with splendid views of the lake, the Seelisberg (with the Rütli Meadow) and the Bürgenstock. Above the wide Muota valley rise the two characteristically shaped horns of the Mythen; above the deep rocky trough of the Urner See towers the massive Urirotstock, almost 3000 m/9843 ft high; and to the rear of the Gersau basin is Pilatus, rising to over 2000 m/6562 ft.
The first reference to the town is in the Einsiedeln chronicles in 1217, but its traditions go much further back.

Situation and general

Sights

The historic Bundeskapelle (Federal Chapel), built in 1632 by Landamman Heinrich von Reding, has an altarpiece by Justus van Egmont (1642), a pupil of Rubens. Late Baroque parish church of St Leonhard (1661, restored 1978) in Ingenbohl. Memorial to the composer Othmar Schoeck, a native of Brunnen (1959). Crypt dedicated to the foundress of the convent of the Sisters of Charity of the Holy Cross (1975).

Surroundings

From the Axenstrasse a steep road runs up to the natural terrace at the foot of the Fronalpstock (1922 m/6396 ft). 3 km/2 miles: Morschach (alt. 645

Fronalpstock
Morschach

147

Brunnen

At the north end of Lake Uri . . .   . . . lies Brunnen

Bürgernstock – Hotels

m/2116 ft: pop. 550) has a superb view of the lake and the mountains,
concerts, a forest park and a swimming pool.

From here it is 1 km/½ mile to the Axenstein (708 m/2323 ft: nurses' home),
an excellent viewpoint.

*Axenstein

The first stage of the "Weg der Schweiz". "Swiss Way", was completed in
October 1988. It is to lead around Lake Uri (completion date planned for
1991 for the 700th anniversary of the Confederation) with its impressive
scenery and historical references making it typical of the canton.

Swiss Way

Bürgenstock

D2

Canton: Nidwalden (NW) and Lucerne (LU)
Altitude: 878–1132 m/2881–3714 ft

The Bürgenstock is a limestone ridge 10 km/6 miles long and between 1.5
and 3 km/1 and 2 miles broad, covered with forests and Alpine meadows,
which forms a peninsula in Lake Lucerne. Its north side rises steeply to a
height of 500 m/1641 ft above the lake; the south side slopes more gently
down to the Stans valley.

Situation

This select health resort and magnificent viewpoint can be reached by road
from Stansstad (5 km/3 miles) or from the landing-stage of Kehrsiten-
Bürgenstock (30 minutes from Lucerne) by funicular (944 m/3097 ft, gradient 45%, 7 minutes). At the upper station of the Bürgenstock funicular,
the oldest in Switzerland (opened in 1888), are the Bahnhofsrestaurant, the
Park-Hotel and the Palace Hotel; 300 m/328 yards south-west is the Grand
Hôtel, the furnishing of which include a notable collection of pictures.

General

Tour

(2 hours: strongly recommended). Starting from the hotels, walk along the
Felsenweg on the Hammetschwand cliffs (30 minutes) to the Hammetschwand lift, which runs up the vertical rock face to the upper station (restaurant) at 1115 m/3580 ft.
Take the lift down again and continue on the Felsenweg, the finest stretch of
which begins here: 20 minutes to the Honegg-Känzeli, and from there
another 30 minutes, past the Kurhaus Honegg and the golf-course, back to
the hotels.

*Felsenweg

Hammet-
schwand

The narrow road which runs from the hotels by way of the Honegg saddle
to Ennetbürgen can be used by cars only from the Kurhaus Honegg.

La Chaux-de-Fonds

B1

Canton: Neuchâtel (NE)
Altitude: 997 m/3271 ft
Population: 37,000

Situated in a high valley in the Jura, the town of La Chaux-de-Fonds (rebuilt
on a regular plan after a fire in 1794) is the capital of the Swiss watchmaking
industry, which was first established here about 1705 (several hundred
firms: visitors can occasionally tour some of the establishments). The town
is home of the Théâtre Populaire Romand, the only professional acting
troupe of West Switzerland, and an important centre of Esperanto. La
Chaux-de-Fonds was the birthplace of the Romantic painter Léopold
Robert (1794–1835), of the famous pilot and automobile manufacturer
Louis Chevrolet (1878–1941), the poet and writer Blaise Cendrars (Frédéric

Situation and
general

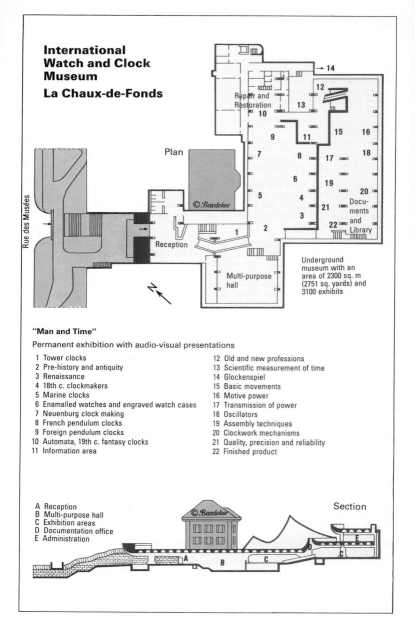

International Watch and Clock Museum
La Chaux-de-Fonds

Plan

© Baedeker

Rue des Musées

Repair and Restoration

14
12
13
10
9
11
15
16
7
8
18
17
6
19
5
4
20
3
21
Documents and Library
2
22
1
Reception

Multi-purpose hall

Underground museum with an area of 2300 sq. m (2751 sq. yards) and 3100 exhibits

"Man and Time"

Permanent exhibition with audio-visual presentations

1 Tower clocks
2 Pre-history and antiquity
3 Renaissance
4 18th c. clockmakers
5 Marine clocks
6 Enamalled watches and engraved watch cases
7 Neuenburg clock making
8 French pendulum clocks
9 Foreign pendulum clocks
10 Automata, 19th c. fantasy clocks
11 Information area

12 Old and new professions
13 Scientific measurement of time
14 Glockenspiel
15 Basic movements
16 Motive power
17 Transmission of power
18 Oscillators
19 Assembly techniques
20 Clockwork mechanisms
21 Quality, precision and reliability
22 Finished product

A Reception
B Multi-purpose hall
C Exhibition areas
D Documentation office
E Administration

Section

© Baedeker

A
B
C
D
E

La-Chaux-de-Fonds: Glockenspiel outside the International Clock Museum

Sauser, 1887–1961) and the famous architect Charles-Edouard Jeanneret, better known as Le Corbusier (1887–1965).

Illuminated ski trails, lifts from town, cross-country skiing, ski-bob run, indoor and outdoor ice rinks, tobogganing, ski school.

Wintersports

Sights

In Rue du Progrès is a Technical college, with a watchmaking school. At 29 rue des Musées the International Watch and Clock Museum (Internationales Uhrenmuseum: partly underground) takes as its theme "Man and Time", displaying the history of timekeeping from the Egyptians to the latest achievements of modern technology. It also has a workshop for the restoration of old watches and clocks which make its services available to collectors generally, a documentation office and library, audio-visual apparatus and a multi-purpose hall which is used for special exhibitions.

**International Watch and Clock Museum

Other interesting museums are the Museum of Art and Ethnography at 33 Rue des Musées, the Historical Museum at 11 Rue de la Loge and the Natural History Museum at 63 Avenue Léopold-Robert. The Hairdressing Museum (Musée de la Coiffure) in Rue de la Balance has a notable collection on the subject of hair care.
The Protestant church, built in 1794 after plans by M. Perret-Gentil, was rebuilt in 1921 after a fire.

Museums

Surroundings

8 km/5 miles south-west is the modern industrial town of Le Locle (alt. 925 m/3035 ft), second only to La Chaux-de-Fonds as a hub of the watchmaking industry, which was founded in 1705 by Daniel Jean-Richard (monument at Post Office). In front of the Watchmaking school stands a monument to the

Le Locle

La Grande Fontaine . . .   *. . . and Musée des Beaux Arts*

first director of the school, J. Grossman (1829–1907), a native of the watch-making town of Glashütte in Saxony. In the Rue Marie-Anne Calame (No. 6) the Museum of Art has works by Swiss artists of the 19th and 20th centuries.

In the Château des Monts are a Watch and Clock Museum, with an interesting collection of watches and clocks and 35 automata, ranging in date from the 16th c. to the 19th c., and a small historical museum.

*Col-des-Roches, Mill Museum

Near the town at Col-des-Roches the underground river Bied was harnessed as far back as the 16th c. The mills built into the mountains processed flour, hemp and flax for 200 years before the water became necessary for the new electricity works. The mills were forgotten and fell into disrepair until they were restored in 1973 by a preservation society, with the aim of establishing the Musée National de la Meunerie. (Open to visitors: April–Oct., Sat. and Sun.)

Chur (Cuera/Cuoira)   E2

Canton: Grisons (GR)
Altitude: 587 m/1926 ft
Population: 33,500

Situation and general

Chur, capital of the Grisons canton and oldest town in Switzerland, has developed into a considerable intellectual and cultural attraction thanks to its excellent strategic situation at the end of some of the most important passes through the Alps and also its mild climate. The town, known in Romansch as Cuera or Cuoira, grew up around the episcopal residence of the bishops of Chur (who are first mentioned in the records in 452), and became an important staging-point on the trade routes through the Alps. It is also the terminus of international railway lines and the starting-point of the Rhätische Bahn (narrow gauge) to St Moritz, the Chur–Arosa line and

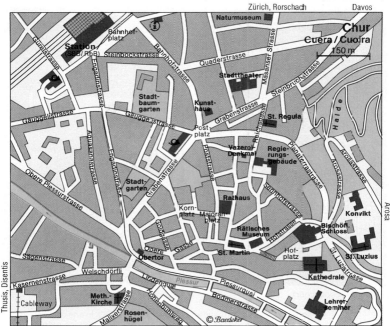

the "Glacier Express" to Zermatt, the Bernina-Express to Tirano (Italy) and the Furka–Oberalp line to Brig. There is a postal bus service from Chur via Lenzerheide to St Moritz (see Practical Information, Railways). The post stage-coach connection "Grand Cañon Express" from Chur through the Upper Rhine Valley to Laax is becoming increasingly popular.

Excavation has shown that the sight was occupied about 3000 B.C. In 15 B.C. after their conquest of Rhaetia (an ancient Alpine district), the Romans made this the chief town of Rhaetia Prima. The name is derived from the Celtic "kora" or "koria" (tribe, clan). In 284 Chur became the provincial capital, about 450 the see of a bishop. In the 12th c. the bishops of Chur were granted the status of princes of the Empire, but the Reformation deprived them of their secular authority. When the canton of Grisons was established in 1803 Chur became its administrative capital.

History

Sights

The town is situated on the River Plessur, which here flows into the Rhine. It is dominated by the picturesque Bishop's Court (Bischöflicher Hof), an extensive group of buildings surrounding the Hofplatz, on the site of a Roman fort.

Bishop's Court

The cathedral, dedicated to the Assumption, is a Romanesque and Gothic building of the 12th and 13th c. (choir consecrated 1178, church 1272) with fine monumental sculpture and a richly decorated interior ranging in date from the Carolingian period to the Baroque.
Inside the cathedral the carved altar, by Jakob Russ of Ravensburg (1486–92), is the finest Late Gothic altar in the country, and there are notable

*Cathedral

153

Chur (Cuera/Cuoira)

Chur: Episcopal court

figured capitals in the nave and crypt (6th and 12th c.). In one of the aisles is the tomb (gravestone), discovered in 1960, of the Swiss patriot Jürg Jenatsch (b. 1596, murdered 1639), who fought for the return of the Valtellina region to the Grisons canton. In the choir is a fine triptych of 1492.

*Cathedral Museum
The Cathedral Museum displays the valuable Cathedral treasury, including the relics of St Lucius (2nd c.) and a 4th c. seal.

Bishop's Palace
The Bishop's Palace (1732–33), an elegant Baroque building, has an imposing façade (stucco decoration). In the medieval Marsöl tower are the Bishop's chapel (17th c.) and a library.

*St Lucius church
Above the cathedral to the east are the former monastic church of St Lucius, with a round Carolingian crypt (8th c.), a seminary for the training of priests and a theological college.

*Old Town Regierungsplatz
Below the Bishop's Court is the Old Town, with interesting old buildings of the 15th–17th c. In the Regierungsplatz are the Vazerol monument, commemorating the union of the three Rhaetian leagues in 1471, and the Regierungsgebäude (Government Building), known as the "Graues Haus" (Grey House), with the cantonal chancery, the chamber in which the Little Council meets, the cantonal library and the state archives.

Reichsgasse
In the Reichsgasse is the Rathaus (Town Hall), built in 1465, with the Citizens' Council Chamber (1538: 17th c. tiled stove), and the Town Council Chamber (1494: collection of precious stones). The trapezoid roof and the cross vaulting of the Town Hall are of 16th c. origin. In the Romantik Hotel are Swiss horse-drawn carriages, harnesses and bells from the 19th c.

St Martin's church
At the end of the Reichsgasse St Martin's church (Protestant: originally 8th c., rebuilt in Late Gothic style 1476–91) has stained glass by A. Giacometti (1917). The fountain of the same name (1716), in front of the church, depicts

Chur: High Altar in the Cathedral...   *... and St Martin's Well*

a Roman soldier; it was erected in 1910 by A. Bianci as a copy of the original by F. Hundertpfund, which is lost.

Above the church to the east, we find the Buolsches Haus (1674–80), now housing the Rhaetian Museum (Rätisches Museum: material of early historical period, cultural history, folk art). **Rhaetian Museum**

In the middle of the town is the Postplatz, from which the Bahnhofstrasse and Grabenstrasse run respectively north-west and north-east to south-west. In the Bahnhofstrasse is the Art Gallery (Kunsthaus: pictures of the 18–20th c., including works by Giovanni, Augusto and Alberto Giacometti, Giovanni Segantini and Angelika Kaufmann; closed Mondays). **Postplatz. Art Gallery**

In Masaner Strasse is the Natural History Museum (Naturhistorisches Museum: also a national park museum; collections of rock and minerals and common species of animals). **Natural History Museum**

To the north-east is the Grossratsgebäude (Great Council Building), converted in 1958 from the old Armoury, which also houses the Municipal Theatre (Stadttheater).
South-east of the Postplatz is the Fontanaplatz, with a monument to Benedikt Fontana, leader of the men of Grisons in the Battle of the Calven gorge in 1499. **Fontanaplatz**

Surroundings

From the south side of the town a cableway ascends in two stages to Brambrüesch (1600 m/5250 ft), from which there ia a chair-lift to the Dreibüdenstein (2180 m/7153 ft): walks and climbs on Pizokel and up Calanda (2806 m/9206 ft: wide views). **Calanda**

4.5 km/3 miles from Chur on the Lenzerheide road is Bad Passugg (alt. 780 m/2559 ft: Hotel Kurhaus), which has chalybeate (iron-bearing) springs in **Bad Passugg**

155

the Rabiosa gorge (drinking-fountain). The road continues via Praden (1160 m/3806 ft) to the health resort of Tshiertschen (1343 m/4406 ft: pop. 200; two ski-lifts). From here it is a 2 hours' climb to the Churer Joch (2038 m/6687 ft) and a rewarding 3 hours' walk to Arosa (equally good in the reverse direction). Arosa: see entry.

Lake Constance D1/E1

Within Germany, Switzerland and Austria
Cantons: Thurgau (TG) and St Gallen (SG)

Situation and general

Lake Constance, (in German the Bodensee), lying below the northern edge of the Alps, with its shoreline shared between Switzerland, Germany and Austria, is by far the largest lake in Germany, the third largest lake in Central Europe (after Lake Balaton and Lake Geneva) and the second largest of the lakes bordering the Alps. From south-east to north-west it is divided into the Obersee, extending from Bregenz Bay to Eichhorn (Constance), and the much narrower, shorter and shallower Überlinger See, between the Bodanrück and Linzgau, and Untersee.

The Untersee is separated from the main lake by a strip of land which is traversed by the Rhine at Konstanz. At its northern end it splits into the Gnadensee, between the island of Reichenau and the Bodanrück, and the Zeller See, between the Höri and Mettnau peninsulas in Radolfzell Bay.

The whole of the southern shore of the lake is in Switzerland, much the greater part of it (running south-east to beyond Arbon) belonging to the canton of Thurgau and the rest (from the vicinity of Rorschach to the Old Rhine) to St Gallen.

History

Evidence of the ancient fauna of the region has been found in the form of animals' bones (mammoths, bison, reindeer, deer, wild horses, bears, etc.), and, in caves in the Thayngen area (canton of Schaffhausen), particularly in the Kesslerloch, works of art dating from the Late Palaeolithic period (c. 10,000 B.C.) – engravings on reindeer antlers, figures of wild horses, a carving of a musk-ox's head, etc. Many traces of human settlement in the Mesolithic period (c. 8000–5000 B.C.) have been identified around the lake; and occupation during the Late Neolithic and Early Bronze Age (c. 3000-2000 B.C. (attested by the pile-dwellings – huts occupied by hunters, fishermen and farmers - found, for example, at Ermatingen on the Untersee and between Botighofen and Seedorf on the Obersee. Remains of these houses, built on piles to provide protection from flooding, can be seen at low tide a short distance from the shore of the lake. Since the water level was 2–3 m/7–10 ft lower at the time the houses were built they would originally have been on dry land. There are also remains of whole villages of pile-dwellings dating from the Early Iron Age (c. 800 B.C.).

The land around Lake Constance was originally Celtic territory, into which the Romans penetrated in the 1st c. B.C. Among Roman foundations on the Swiss shore of the lake was "Arbor Felix" (Arbon). In the 3rd c. A.D. the Alemanni, a Germanic tribe from the north, thrust into the western Lake Constance area. The region was Christianised by Iro-Scottish monks including Columban and his disciple Gallus, who preached here about the year 610, and the 8th c. saw the foundation of the abbey of St Gallen, which developed into a major cultural hub whose influence extended far beyond the region. In the Appenzell war (1403–08) the confederation of towns on Lake Constance supported the Abbot of St Gallen against the mountain peasants, who suffered a defeat at Bregenz in 1408.
Constance, a member of the Swabian League, lost all rights of sovereignity in the Thurgau under the Treaty of Basle at the end of the Swabian war (1498–99).

Kreuzlingen: Night festival on the lake . . .   . . . and the Seeburg

Facts and figures about Lake Constance

Constance (lighthouse) lat. 47°39' north, long. 9°10' east;
Bregenz (lighthouse) lat. 47°30' north, long. 9°44' east.
Mean water level: 395 m/1296 ft (with fluctuations, so far unexplained,
unconnected with seasons or weather conditions). This change of water
level, which occurs at regular intervals in calm weather, resembles the ebb
and flow of the sea, yet occurs 26–38 times in 24 hours and varies only a few
centimetres.
Geographical
situation

Although the borders between the countries neighbouring Lake Constance
are not distinct, the respective areas are approximately as follows: Germany 55%, Switzerland 34% and Austria 11%.
Sovereign
territory

Total area: 545 sq. km/210 sq. miles (Obersee and Überlinger See together
480 km/185 sq. miles, Untersee 65 sq. km/25 sq. miles).
Area

Greatest length: between Bregenz and Stein am Rhein 76 km/47 miles (as
the crow flies 69 km/43 miles).
Between Bregenz and the mouth of the Stockacher Aach 63 km/39 miles;
longest direct line over water, from Hard to near the mouth of the Aach,
60 km/37 miles. Between Bregenz and Constance 46 km/28 miles.
Length

Greatest width: between Kressbronn and Rohrschach 14.8 km/9 miles
Width

Greatest depth: in the Obersee (between Fischbach and Uttwil) 252 m/327
ft, in the Überlinger See 147 m/482 ft, in the Untersee 46 m/151 ft (Zeller See
26 m/85 ft, Gnadensee 22 m/72 ft). New depth measuring works are in
progress.
Depth

Circumference at half-tide level: total 263 km/163 miles, of which 168
km/104 miles (64%) are in Germany, 69 km/43 miles (26%) in Switzerland
and 26 km/16 miles (10%) in Austria.
Circumference

Lake Constance

Volume of water	Average volume of water: total 48,430 million cu. m/1,710,163 million cu. ft, Obersee and Überlinger See together 47,600 million cu. m/1,680,756 million cu. ft, Untersee 830 million cu. m/29,307 million cu. ft.
Tides (at Constance tide-gauge)	Mean high water (end June/beginning July) 440 cm/173.2 inches (highest recorded, beginning September 1817, 623 cm/245.3 inches). Mean low water (end February) 280 cm/110.2 inches (lowest recorded this century, end March 1972, 237 cm/93.3 inches).
Visibility	Visibility from surface: annual average c. 7.50 m/25 ft (in January down to 12 m/39 ft).

*The Swiss side of Lake Constance

Kreuzlingen

Kreuzlingen (alt. 404 m/1326 ft; pop. 17,000), sister city to the German town of Constance, is separated from that town only by the line of the frontier, which does not follow the Rhine but runs through the built-up area at some distance from the river. The town's name comes from a relic of the True Cross which is preserved in the conventual church.

In the Hauptstrasse is the former Augustinian convent (since 1844 occupied by the Thurgau teachers' training college) built by Michael Beer in 1640–53 to replace an earlier monastic house destroyed during the Thirty Years' War and remodelled in Baroque style in 1765. St Ulrich's church, well restored, together with the rest of the conventual buildings, after a fire in 1936, has notable ceiling frescoes, a fine organ and a grille by Jakob Hoffner (1737). A representation of the Agony in the Garden (in the north lateral chapel) preserves 280 of its original 322 figures (1720–40), and a large Gothic cross bears a figure of Christ with natural hair.

In the Tenants' house of Schloss Girsberg the Thurgau Doll Museum was opened in 1988, the oldest of its kind in the country containing over 300 dolls and old-fashioned children's toys.

Seeburg park — To the north of the town, by the lake, lies the ivy-clad Seeburg, built in 1598 as a country residence of the bishops of Constance, largely destroyed during the Thirty Years' War, rebuilt in 1879–94 and now occupied by the military. The park contains a reserve for fallow deer and wildfowl.

Waterworks — 1 km/½ mile east of the Seeburg, at the Fischerhaus camping site and restaurant, is a waterworks, and just offshore is a fountain, visible far and wide when it is working (illuminated at night).

Rosenegg Heimatmuseum, Observatory — South-west of the former convent stands the Rosenegg Heimatmuseum (Bärenstrasse 6) with weapons, documents and furniture from Kreuzlingen and the surrounding area. Still farther south-west, in Bernrain, are an observatory and a Baroque pilgrimage chapel.

*Conny Island — A good 12 km/7 miles south-west on the main road to Frauenfeld, near Lipperswil is the recreational park of Conny Island with a dolphinarium, children's zoo and many amusements.

Untersee

Tägerwilen — The road west from Kreuzlingen towards the Untersee arrives first at the village of Tägerwilen (alt. 406 m/1332 ft) with the church of SS Cosmas and Damian. 1.5 km/1 mile south, above the village, Schloss Castell or Chastel, was built in 1661 near the palace of the bishops of Constance, which was destroyed in 1499; it was rebuilt between 1878 and 1894. Tägerwilen was the birthplace of Hermann Müller (1850–1927), who produced the Müller-Thurgau grape (a cross between Riesling and Sylvaner) which bears his name.

Steckborn: Turmhof Castle

To the north, on the Rhine, in the picturesque Gottlieber district of the town (alt. 398 m/1306 ft), stands a palace built in 1251 as a subsidiary residence of the bishops of Constance (enlarged 1480, rebuilt in Neo-Gothic style 1837–38), in which Jan Hus, his fellow Hussite Jerome of Prague and Anti-Pope John XXIII were imprisoned in 1415; the palace now belongs to the singer Lisa della Casa.

Gottlieben

There are a number of handsome half-timbered houses, including the Drachenburg and the Waaghaus or Weigh-House (both 17th c.), as well as the so-called Burg (Castle) and Haus Rheineck.

A local speciality is the pastry called "Gottlieber Hüppen".

Ermatingen (alt. 397 m/1303 ft: pop. 2000), 4 km/2 miles farther west an old fishing village (attractive half-timbered houses and the Fishing Museum), is also a holiday resort, situated on the Staad or Stad peninsula (on which remains of pile-dwellings have been found).

Ermatingen, Lake Constance Fishing Museum

Farther west again, beautifully situated opposite the island of Reichenau (2 km/1 mile: ferry), is Mannenbach (alt. 405 m/1329 ft), above which stands Burg Salenstein (505 m/1657 ft: originally 11th c., restored 1842).

Mannenbach-Salenstein

On a terrace to the east is Schloss Arenenberg (458 m/1503 ft: Napoleonic Museum, closed November to March), built 1540–46, with later alterations. From 1830 until her death in 1837 this was the residence of Napoleon's step-daughter Queen Hortense de Beauharnais, whose son Louis Napoléon, later Napoléon III, spent his childhood here. In 1906 the Empress Eugénie, Napoléon III's widow, presented the castle to the canton of Thurgau as a memorial to her husband.

*Schloss Arenenberg

Above Mannenbach to the west is the ruined castle of Sandegg (517 m/1696 ft: views), and 500 m/1641 ft farther south Schloss Eugensberg (544 m/1785 ft: private property), built in 1820 for Eugène de Beauharnais, Napoleon's stepson and brother of Queen Hortense.

The road continues through the quiet resort of Berlingen (alt. 398 m/1306 ft), with a Town Hall of 1780, to Steckborn (404 m/1326 ft: pop. 4500), an

Steckborn

Lake Constance

Schloss
Turmhof

ancient little town on a peninsula in the Untersee which is a popular holiday resort (picturesque half-timbered houses). The Turmhof, a castle on the lakeside, built about 1320 (17th c. domed tower and corner turrets) by Diethelm von Castell, Abbot of Reichenau, houses a local museum (contains Neolithic, Roman and Alemannian exhibits, Steckborn ceramics, examples of wrought-iron and turned wood from the 18th and 19th c.: closed in winter). The Town Hall dates from 1667 and has a collection of weapons on the first floor (open weekdays). The Town church (1776), a plain Baroque building by F. A. Bagnato, has extensive wide views from the tower. The Roman Catholic Jakobuskirche (St James's church) was built in 1963.
At the south-west end of the town is the Bernina sewing-machine factory, with a sewing-machine museum.

Obersee

The road south-east from Kreuzlingen along the Obersee arrives in 2.5 km/ 2 miles at the village of Bottighofen (alt. 398 m/1306 ft), which is attractively situated amid fruit orchards and has a well-equipped boating harbour.

Münsterlingen

1.5 km/1 mile beyond this is Münsterlingen (398 m/1306 ft), a hotel resort situated on a peninsula. The church of the Benedictine convent (rebuilt 1709–16), now a cantonal hospital, has a fine Baroque interior, and since 1968, when the lake last froze, has housed the 16th c. bust of St John the Baptist, which traditionally transfers between Hagnau and Münsterlingen whenever the lake freezes.

Romanshorn

The road continues through Kesswil and Uttwil, both with fine half-timbered houses, to Romanshorn (399 m/1309 ft: pop. 8200), a lakeside resort which is also the largest port on Lake Constance and the base of the Swiss lake steamers (shipyard of Swiss Federal Railways).
To the north of the Bundesbahnhafen (Federal Railways harbour) lies the Seepark, with the Old Church. The Schloss (now a hotel) dates in its present form from 1829. In the lake, to the north, is the "Inseli", a rocky islet.

Arbon

The next town of any size is Arbon (alt. 398 m/1306 ft: pop. 12,300), a port and an industrial town situated on a peninsula, occupying the site of the Celtic settlement of Arbona and the Roman Arbor Felix. St Gallus died here about 645. From 1285 to 1798 the town was held by the Bishops of Constance.
North-west of the Alter Hafen (Old Harbour) and the Schlosshafen is the Roman Catholic parish church of St Martin (choir 1490, nave 1788; Madonna of 1525). Farther north-west is the 16th c. Schloss, built on the foundations of a Roman fort of A.D. 294, with a seven-storey tower originally dating from 400, which contains a local historical museum (closed in winter). Other features of interest are the Römerhof (c. 1500), the chapel of St Gallus (originally 10th c.; 14th c. frescoes) and the lakeside promenade 3 km/2 miles long.

Steinach

Horn
Rorschach

From Arbon the road continues to Steinach (alt. 400 m/1312 ft), a fishing village with a Baroque parish church and a large granary (the "Gred") of 1473. Horn (398 m/1306 ft), an enclave belonging to the enclave of Thurgau, boasts a castle which belonged to the Landgrave of Hesse, and Rorschach (p. 342), the old port of St Gallen.

Altenrhein

Farther east is Altenrhein, on the delta of the Old Rhine. Here is the hangar of the FFA aircraft and car factory (Flug-und Fahrzeugwerke Altenrhein: formerly the Dornier works) and the base from which the old Dornier flying-boats took off in the 1920s.

Rheineck

South-east of the mouth of the Old Rhine is Rheineck (400 m/1312 ft: pop. 3000), the attractive little Swiss frontier town on the banks of the idyllic Old

Rhine. Rheineck has arcaded streets, and old town gate, a Town Hall of 1555, a Late Gothic and Baroque church (Protestant), two imposing 18th c. town houses, the Löwenhof and the Custerhof, and a ruined castle (views).

Walzenhausen

From here a narrow-gauge rack railway runs up (1.9 km/1 mile, taking 6 minutes) to Walzenhausen (682 m/2238 ft), a hillside village in a commanding situation high above Lake Constance which is also a health and winter sports resort.

St Margrethen

3.5 km/2 miles south-east of Rheineck is St Margrethen (402 m/1319 ft: pop. 5000), a rail and road junction on the Swiss-Austrian frontier (customs) situated on the Old Rhine in a fertile fruit-growing region. It is also a spa (Kneipp treatment). St Margaret's chapel, a cemetery church dating from 1090, has frescoes and Late Baroque altars. Directly next to the motorway is the large "Rheinpark" shopping centre.

To the south-west is Schloss Bergsteig, to the west Schloss Vorburg (open to visitors).

Pleasant walks to the hill villages (good views) in the St Gallen and Appenzell areas.

Crans-Montana C2

Canton: Valais (VS)
Altitude: 1500–1680 m/4922–5512 ft
Population: 4500

Situation

The popular holiday and winter sports area of Crans-Montana lies north-west of the little town of Sierre in the Rhône valley. It is reached by any one of three roads from the Rhône valley or by a funicular from Sierre.

Crans-sur-Sierre

The attractive resort of Crans-sur-Sierre (1480–1500 m/4856–4922 ft), to the west, lies around a number of small lakes, the Etangs de Lens. For over 45 years the resort has been equally famous in summer for its "Open" on the two splendid golf courses (9 and 18 holes), hang-gliding, hot air balloon meetings and other sporting events as for its marvellous skiing in winter. From Crans a cableway 4480 m/14,699 ft long ascends in 25 minutes, via Merbé (1900 m/6234 ft) and Cry d'Err, to Bella Lui (2543 m/8344 ft: restaurant), from which there are superb views. Another cableway, roughly parallel to the first, takes 13 minutes to reach Chetzeron (2100 m/6890 ft), from which there is a ski-lift to the Cry d'Err.

Montana

The popular mountain and winter sports resort of Montana (1500 m/4922 ft), 1.5 km/1 mile to the east on Lac Moubra, lies on a natural terrace covered with forests and Alpine meadows 1000 m/3281 ft above the Rhône valley, sheltered by the mountains to the north, and has a mild, dry mountain climate. A cableway 540 m/1772 ft long climbs in 3 minutes to the Grand Signal (upper station 1712 m/5617 ft), from which there are ski-lifts to Verdet (1875 m/6152 ft) and the Cry d'Err. Another cableway, 2500 m/8203 ft long, runs up in 12 minutes to the Cry d'Err (2263 m/7425 ft: restaurant)

Vermala

Above Montana, 1.5 km/1 mile north, is Vermala (1670 m/5479 ft), with a ski-jump. From Vermala-Zaumiau a cableway 2545 m/8350 ft long goes up via Les Marolires to the Swiss Alpine Club's Cabane des Violette (2208 m/7244 ft: restaurant), from which another cableway (3243 m/10,640 ft long) continues to the Plaine Morte (2927 m/9603 ft), above the south end of the Plaine Morte glacier (summer skiing).

Aminona

10 km/6 miles north-east of Montana is Aminona (1437 m/4415 ft), a popular winter sports resort with a group of tower-block hotels, from which there is a cabin cableway 2410 m/7907 ft long to the Petit-Mont-Bonvin (2411 m/7910 ft: numerous ski-lifts). Access to the pistes of Crans-Montana is via the Violettes, La Tza and La Barma.

Anzère

The mountain station of Anzère, separated from the deep valley of the Lienne, lies about 8 km/5 miles west of Crans. This modern village, with its

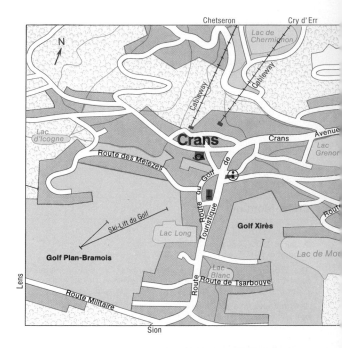

Crans-Montana: Violettes ski area

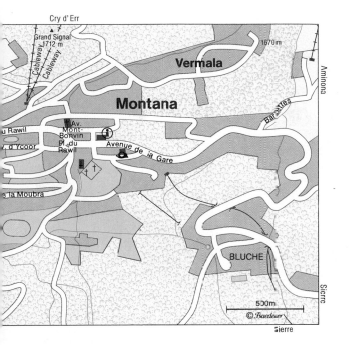

typical large chalets, is surrounded by excellent long-distance courses and pistes of varying levels of difficulty.

Short training lifts in the valley, numerous lifts on the Cry d'Err (2207 m/ 7241 ft: cableways from Crans and Montana), Chetzeron (2100 m/6890 ft: cableway from Crans) and Bella Lui (2543 m/8343 ft: cableway from Cry d'Err). Summer skiing in the Plaine Morte glacier area (3000 m/9843 ft: cableway from Violettes). Many ski-trails with lifts between Violettes (2208 m/7244 ft: cableway from Vermala-Zaumiau) and Petit-Mort-Bonvin (2411 m/7910 ft: cabin cableway from Aminona). There is splendid long-distance skiing between Crans, Montana and Vermala. National teams from all over Europe train on the high slopes of the Plaine Morte glacier. An artificial ice rink, curling, tobogganing and famous Swiss ski schools are also to be found here.

Winter sports

Davos

E2

Canton: Grisons. Altitude: 1560 m/5118 ft. Population: 12,300

Davos, a high valley extending 16 km/10 miles south-west from the Wolf-gang pass and traversed by the Landwasser, is the second largest com-mune in Switzerland (254 sq. km/93 sq. miles) – larger than the canton of Zug. The twin settlements of Davos Platz and Davos Dorf have increased their population five-fold over the last 100 years and have now united to form a built-up area 4 km/2 miles long. Surrounded by forest-covered mountains and sheltered from rough north and east winds, Davos enjoys a climate (bracing but not excessively so, with plenty of sunshine and dry air) which has made it one of Switzerland's leading summer and winter resorts.

Situation and general

Cableway from Weissfluhjoch to the summit of the Wiessfluh

The foundations of Davos's fame as a health resort were laid by a Mannheim doctor, Alexander Spengler, who prescribed mountain air for his tuberculosis patients and brought the first summer visitors here in 1860 and the first winter visitors in 1865.

Communications

Since 1890 Davos has been linked with the Rhine valley (Chur) by the Rhätische Bahn (Rhaetian Railway), and since 1909 with the Albula valley and the Engadine. There are postal bus services from Davos over the Flüela pass to Susch/Süs (only in summer), to Clavadel and Sertig Dörfli (in winter only to Clavadel) and into the Dischma valley (in winter only as far as Teufi), and from Davos Glaris to Monstein. Local bus operators run services between Davos Platz, Davos Dorf, Davos Wolfgang and Dörfji (near which is the lower station of the Pischa mountain railway). There are numerous cableways and lifts and a wide range of facilities for sport and entertainment.

History

The name of Davos (in the form Tavauns, which later became Dafaas) appears for the first time in 1160, in a document in the episcopal archives in Chur. In 1289 14 families from the Valais established households here. After the death of the last member of the Toggenburg family in 1436 the League of the Ten Jurisdictions was formed. In 1649 Davos purchased its freedom from Austrian sovereignty. A large ice-rink (24,000 sq. m/28,704 sq. yards) for the world figure-skating championships and the European speed skating championships was opened in 1899, and in the same year the Davos-Scatzalp toboggan run came into operation.

Sights

Davos Platz

The chief place of the valley is Davos Platz (1560 m/5118 ft),the only old buildings in which are the parish church of St John the Baptist (1481; nave 1280–85, restored 1909), with a window in the choir by Augusto Giacometti

Davos – panorama

(after 1928), and the adjoining Rathaus (Town Hall: restored 1930), with the panelled "Great Chamber" (Grosse Stube) of 1564.

Above here, in the post office building is the Ernst-Ludwig-Kirchner Museum, opened in 1982, which contains oil-paintings, sketches and documents by the artist Kirchner (1880–1938) who lived in Davos-Frauenkirch from 1917–1938.
Adjoining the indoor swimming pool (Hallenbad) stands the modern Congress House (Kongresshaus, 1969).

Ernst-Ludwig-Kirchner Museum

In Davos Dorf (1563 m/5128 ft) is the 14th c. church of St Theodulus At Museumstrasse 1 is the Old Prebend House (Altes Pfrundhaus), the only surviving example of an old burgher's house, which is now occupied by a local museum (Heimatmuseum). The Gemeindehaus (communal house) of Davos Dorf was built by Jürg Jenatsch in 1643 (altered 1886).

Davos Dorf

Bathing beach on the Davoser See; indoor and outdoor swimming pools (Hallenbad, Gartenbad) in the Kurpark. There is a 18-hole golf course on Davos Platz. Natural ice-rinks (22,000 sq. m/26,312 sq. yards: the largest in Europe), with areas for figure and speed skating, ice-hockey and curling; artificial ice-rink (1800 sq. m/2153 sq. yards), open in summer as well as winter: curling). Beautiful Kurpark (bandstand). 55 cableways and lifts with a total capacity of 55,000 persons, giving access to extensive mountain-walking and skiing areas. Toboggan run, Schatzalp-Davos. Davos is famous for the International Ice Hockey Tournament for the Spengler Cup, curling tournaments, skating events, ski races. "walking" weeks and its music festival.

Recreation and sport

Swiss Research Institute (Physical and Meteorological Observatory and World Radiation Centre, Institute of Medical Climatic and Tuberculosis Research, Laboratory of Experimental Surgery, Osteosynthesis Study Group); Federal Institute of Snow and Avalanche Research, Weissfluhjoch/Davos.

Scientific institutes

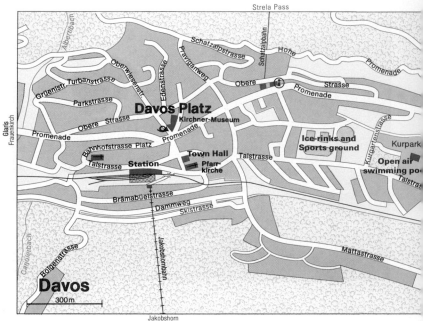

Surroundings

Davoser See   A favourite walk from Davos is to the Davoser See, a natural lake (area 0.59 sq. km/0.23 sq. mile) which supplies a hydro-electric power station (walk around the lake 1½ hours).

Walks   The footpath called the Hohe Promenade (level walk of 2.5 km/2 miles from Davos Dorf to Davos Platz) leads to Wolfgang (1631 m/5351 ft) and Laret (1525 m/5004 ft), to the north-east, and to Frauenkirch (1532 m/5026 ft), Spinabad (1465 m/4807 ft), Schmelzboden (1590 m/5217 ft: Mining Museum) and Wiesen (1421 m/4662 ft) to the south-west.

To Parsenn and Weissfluhjoch

*Davos-Parsenn-Bahn

Weissfluhjoch

This is a renowned skiing area and also excellent walking and climbing country. The mountains on the west side of the Davos valley were made conveniently accessible by the opening in 1931 of the Davos-Parsenn-Bahn, a funicular 4106 m/13,472 ft, time 25 minutes). From the Höhenweg station (2 km/1 mile: 2219 m/7281 ft) there are magnificent mountain walks without any real climbing. The funicular continues up to the Weissfluhjoch (2663 m/8737 ft: restaurant), with views of the Silvretta and Flüela groups, from Piz Buin to the Tinzenhorn. From the upper station there is a cableway to the summit of the Weissfluh (2844 m/9331 ft: restaurant), from which there are superb views in all directions. There is also a cableway from the Weissfluhjoch to the Parsenn hut (2200 m/7218 ft: reataurant), 2 hours' walk from Wolfgang.

Panoramaweg   One of the finest paths in the area is the Panoramaweg, which runs from the Parsenn hut through the Meierhoftäli valley to the Höhenweg funicular

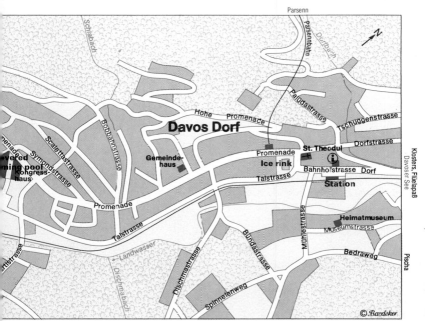

Parsenn

Davos Dorf

Hohe Promenade

Gemeinde-
haus

Promenade
Ice rink

St. Theodul
ⓘ

Dorfstrasse

Bahnhofstrasse Dorf

Talstrasse

Station

Promenade

Talstrasse

Landwasser

Heimatmuseum

Museumstrasse

Bedraweg

Spinnelenweg

Klosters, Flüelapaß
Davoser See

Pischa

© Baedeker

station and from there through the Dorftäli and under the Schiahörner to
the Strela pass. From the Parsenn hut it is a half-hour's walk to the Gotschnagrat (2285 m/7497 ft).

From Davos Platz the Schatzalpbahn (funicular, length 716 m/2349 ft,   *Schatzalp
height difference 301 m/988 ft, time 5 minutes) ascends to the Schatzalp
(1861 m/6106 ft: hotel and restaurant); on foot 1–1½ hours. 350 m/1148 ft
north of the Berghotel is the Schatzalp Alpine Garden (Alpinium), which
contains 7550 plants and 550 species and sub-species (free admission with
funicular ticket).
From the Schatzalp a rewarding walk via the Podestatenalp, Lochalp and
Grüenalp leads to Davos (2¼ hours). The Schatzalp-Davos toboggan run is
2.5 km/2 miles long with well-cambered bends.

The Strela pass (2350 m/7710 ft), reached by the Schatzalp-Strela cableway   Strela pass
(length 1760 m/5775 ft, height difference 488 m/1601 ft, time 10 minutes;
restaurant), passes larches over a thousand years old. From the Strela
pass a cabin cableway (opened 1981) ascends to the lower station of the
Haupteräli Ski-lift which goes up to the Weissfluhjoch.

The Jakobshorn and the eastern valleys

There are also pleasant walks and climbs on the left side of the valley. A
cableway constructed in 1954 runs up to the Ischalp (1931 m/6336 ft:
restaurant), and from there to the Jakobshorn (2590 m/8498 ft: restaurant ,   *Jakobshorn
from which there are splendid panoramic views. From here a waymarked
path runs down through groves of rhododendrons to the Ischalp (1¼
hours). Ski-lifts from the Ischalp serve the Brämebüel skiing area (2477
m/8127 ft). Another footpath from the Ischalp leads in 45 minutes to the

Clavadeler Alp (1971 m/6467 ft) and from there in another 45 minutes to Clavadel (1664 m/5460 ft: postal bus), one of the sunniest spots in the valley. The walk from Davos Platz to Clavadel and back takes between 2 and 3 hours.

Clavadel

In summer the postal bus runs up the Sertig valley to Sertig Dörfli (1861 m/ 6106 ft: restaurant), in a superb mountain setting (a popular trip with walkers, plant-lovers and animal lovers).

*Sertig Dörfli

The magnificent walking and winter sports area on the Rinerhorn, a few kilometres south of Davos, can be reached by taking the chair-lift from Davos-Glaris to Jatzmeder (2045 m/6710 ft: restaurant), from which it is 1½ hours climb to the summit of the Rinerhorn (2528 m/8294 ft).

Rinerhorn

A short distance beyond Glaris a by-road branches off on the left to the little village of Monstein (1626 m/5335 ft), idyllically situated on a sunny terrace on the mountainside, where the old German dialect of the Upper Valais is still spoken.

*Monstein

The Dischma valley is the longest (12 km/7 miles) of the valleys on the left side of the Davos valley. On the right bank of the Dischmabach is a narrow road, on the left bank a pleasant footpath. The timber buildings to be seen here are typical of the older Davos. The last village in the valley is Dürrboden (2007 m/6585 ft: inn), which can be reached on foot in 3–4 hours from Davos Dorf. Postal bus in summer to Dürrboden, in winter to Teufi.

Dischma valley

The Flüela valley is another good walking and skiing area (nature reserve). The road from Davos Dorf crosses the Flüelabach (waterfall, 5 minutes' walk) and comes in 4 km/2 miles to Dörfji (1303 m/5916 ft: bus station, restaurant), from which the Pischabahn (length 2030 m/6660 ft, height difference 680 m/2231 ft, time 6 minutes) serves Pischa (2485 m/8153 ft: inn). From there it is a climb of 1½–2 hours to the summit of the Pischahorn (2980 m/9777 ft).

Dörfji
*Pischabahn

Over the Flüela pass into the Engadine

The shortest route from the Rhine valley to the Lower Engadine goes from Landquart through the Prättigau to Davos Dorf and from there over the Flüela pass to Susch. The Flüela pass road between Davos and Susch (27 km/17 miles), opened to traffic in 1867, is between 5.5 and 7 m/18 and 23 ft wide, with gradients of up to 10%. In winter the road is closed for 40 days, on average, due to the risk of avalanches. This problem should be solved in the future by the construction of a new tunnel (see "Vereina-Bahn").

Flüela pass road

From Dörfji (1815 m/5955 ft: restaurant), from which there is a beautiful view to the rear of the Weissfluh, one can reach Tschuggen 7 km/4 miles south-east (1941 m/6368 ft: holiday centre, 100 chalets; in summer postal bus service from Davos), amid magnificent expanses of rhododendrons and stone pines. 13 km/8 miles beyond this is the Flüela pass (2383 m/7819 ft: mountain inn), the highest mountain pass in the Grisons, 3¾ hours on foot from Davos Dorf. Beyond the pass, at the head of the lower Engadine, Susch (1438 m/4718 ft: pop. 200), straddles the Inn and the Susasca.

Tschuggen

*Flüela pass

Susch

Construction began in 1988 of a tunnel which is designed to avoid using the Flüela pass in future between Davos and Unterengadin. A 19 km/11 mile long tunnel is being excavated between Klosters and Susch/Lavin, through which the motor-rail "Vereina-Bahn" will travel.

Vereina-Bahn

◀ *Susch in the Inn valley*

Delémont C1

Canton: Jura (JU)
Altitude: 430 m/1411 ft
Population: 12,500

Situation
Delémont (in German Delsberg), the largest town in the Jura and capital of the newest Swiss canton, is an important railway junction on the Berne-Basle and Delle-Paris lines and the starting point of many postal bus services. It lies in the wide valley of the Sorne, which here flows into the Birs.

History
Delémont first appears in the records in 782 as a market village, and again in 1212 as a town founded by the Prince-Bishop of Basle. It was granted a municipal charter in 1289. After the Reformation it was a favourite residence of the bishops of Basle. From 1815 it was the chief town of a district in the canton of Berne, and in 1978 it became capital of the new canton of Jura.

Sights

As an important industrial, cultural and tourist area Delémont has developed into a modern town without losing its old-world character. The main features of interest are the church of St-Marcel (1762–66), a three-aisled basilica built over an earlier cruciform structure; the château of the Prince-Bishops (1716–21); the 13th c. Archive tower; the Grand'rue, the wide main street; five large fountains; and the Musée Jûrassien (local history, prehistoric and Roman material).

Surroundings

Vorbourg
Fortress
There are many places of interest in the immediate surroundings of the town, including the fortress of Vorbourg, an early medieval fortification, to the north-east of the town. The adjoining pilgrimage church of St-Maria,

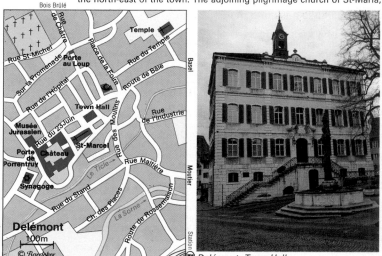

Delémont: Town Hall

which was consecrated by Pope Leo IX in the 11th c., has an interesting 16th c. high altar.

To the west of Delémont is the Château de Domont, dating from the middle of the 16th c.

Château de Domont

Also to the west of Delémont a hilly region extends towards the French frontier. An interesting route into the Ajoie takes in the renowned medieval small town of St-Ursanne and Porrentruy. Heading south-west one comes to the scenic Franches Montagnes (see Jura) before reaching the town of Saignelégier, famous for its horse-breeding. There are other interesting excursions into the wildly romantic Jura, south-west towards Lake Geneva.

Jura

Disentis/Mustér

D2

Canton: Grisons (GR)
Altitude: 1140 m/3740 ft
Population: 2500

The holiday resort Disentis (accent on first syllable: Romansch Mustér) lies in a wide green valley on the upper reaches of the Surselva at the junction of the Upper Rhine with the Medelser Rhein or Mittelrhein (Middle Rhine). The development of summer tourism in Disentis is due mainly to the building of the former Hotel Disenterhof (1870), which as a bathing and spa hotel utilises the waters of the St Placidus spring. This health and winter sports resort has over 150 km/93 miles of walks of varying difficulty, and offers the visitor attractions such as river trips, tennis, mountain excursions on the Glacier-Express, well-prepared pistes and long-distance runs for the skier.

Situation and general

Sights

Above the town is a Benedictine abbey founded by St Sigisbert about 720 and almost completely rebuilt at the end of the 17th c.; the abbey dominates the valley with its fine conventual buildings and St Martin's church (Vorarlberg Baroque, 1696–1712); it contains a collection of artistic and historical interest.

Benedictine Abbey, St Martin

Surroundings

Cableway (2060 m/6759 ft, 5 minutes) from Funs (1228 m/4029 ft) north-west to Caischavedra (1842 m/6044 ft); from there ski-lifts to the slopes of Piz Ault (3027 m/9932 ft).

Over the Lucomagno (Lukmanier) pass to Biasca (65 km/40 miles)

The road runs south from Disentis and climbs, with moderate gradients, through the Höllenschlucht (Hell's Gorge), a magnificent wooded defile. It then continues uphill, with numerous bends, and passes through a number of tunnels, between which there are views to the rear of Disentis Abbey and later impressive views of the foaming waterfalls in the gorge below.

*Höllenschlucht

Curaglia (alt. 1332 m/4370 ft), with a church of 1672 (Late Gothic altar) is situated at the mouth of the Val Plattas, which runs down from Piz Medel (3210 m/10,532 ft: 7 hours with guide); to the east there is a rewarding climb (3½–4 hours) up Piz Mauraun (2897 m/9505 ft), from Monte Rosa to the Ortles (Ortler) group, and of the nearer Tödi group in the Glarus Alps.

Curaglia

*Piz Mauraun

Disentis, with the Benedictine Abbey of St Martin

Platta

Platta (1380 m/4528 ft), a straggling village (church with Romanesque tower) in an open part of the Val Medel.

Acla

Acla (1476 m/4843 ft: off the road to the right), with a chapel. The scenery now becomes wilder; Fumatschfalls, 30 m/98 ft high, on the Medelser Rhein. To the rear there is a view of the valley around Platta, with the Tödi massif rearing up beyond the Vorderrhein.

Santa Maria Lake

From Pardatsch (or Perdatsch), 1556 m/5105 ft, a hamlet with a small chapel, the road continues uphill under Piz Curvet (2248 m/7376 ft) to Sogn Gion (1615 m/5299 ft), a former hospice. It then climbs a lonely Alpine valley, with tumbles of rock, areas of sparse pasturage and rhododendrons. To the right are the pointed summit of Tgiern Sogn Gion (2677 m/8783 ft) and Piz Ganneretsch (3040 m/9974 ft). In 8 km/5 miles the Santa Maria lake (formed by a dam completed in 1967) can be seen below the road on the right. On the old road on the west side of the lake, at Santa Maria (1842 m/6044 ft), was the old hospice of "Sancta Maria in Luco Magno" which gave its name to the pass. Above the west side of the lake is Piz Rondadura (3016 m/9895 ft; 3½ hours), to the east the dark slaty peak of Scopi (3187 m/10,457 ft; 4–4½ hours).

Lucomagno pass

The Lucomagno pass (Romansch Cuolm Lucmagn, German Lukmanierpass: 1920 m/6300 ft), with an inn, a large stone figure of the Virgin and a chapel, is the lowest road crossing of the central ridge of the Swiss Alps, over which there was already considerable traffic in medieval times. It is flanked on the left by Scopi and on the right by Scai (2676 m/8780 ft). The pass marks the boundary between the cantons of Grisons and Ticino.

Pizzo Curvo

The road descends from the pass through a rocky valley, following the left bank of the Brenno, which is fed by numerous streams flowing down from Scai and Pizzo Lucomagno. To the left are the rock walls of Pizzo Curvo (2510 m/8235 ft). Then it continues through an area of high Alpine mea-

dows with scattered summer chalets. Ahead can be seen the Rheinwaldhorn (3406 m/11,175 ft).
4.5 km/3 miles beyond the pass, on the right, is the Aquacalda inn (1730
m/5850 ft; Albergo del Paso, 20b.), surrounded by a forest of stone pines,
with a beautiful waterfall on the Brenno.

The road traverses the Alpine meadows of the Piano di Segno, passing
above the huts of Campra, continues down the north side of the beautiful
Valle Santa Maria, high above the Brenno, and then through a wooded
gorge, passes close to the Albergo Grande Venezia and comes to the
former hospice of Camperio. The road now leaves the Valle Santa Maria
and runs down the Val Blerio, high up on the south side of the valley, with
magnificent views of the valley itself, the precipitous buttresses of the
Rheinwaldhorn, the Cima di Pinaderio and the Cima Giù (2369 m/7773 ft),
and Olivone in its fertile valley, with the jagged granite peak of Sosto
rearing above it.
5.5 km/3 miles beyond Camperio there is a rewarding drive along a road
which branches off on the left and after traversing a tunnel 1490 m/4889 ft
long, which bypasses the narrow Gola di Sosto, reaches the mountain
village of Campo Blénio (1228 m/4029 ft, 4.5 km/3 miles north, situated at
the meeting of three valleys. Beyond this, 1.5 km/1 mile up the Val Cama-
dra, is Ghirone (1302 m/4270 ft), with a very picturesque old church; then
3 km/2 miles east up the Val Luzzone to a large artificial lake (1590 m/5217 ft).

Valle Santa
Maria

*Val Blenio

Campo Blénio

The main road continues down to the village of Olivone (Romansch Uor-
scha, 893 m/2930 ft), a summer holiday resort beautifully situated at the
junction of two arms of the Brenno under the massive pyramid of Sosto
(2221 m/7278 ft), surrounded by fruit trees. It has a fine old house, still
inhabited, the Casa Cesare Bolla (c. 1500), once the residence of the governor, and an interesting local museum. Beyond Olivone the road to Biasca
winds its way down the fertile Val Blénio, on the left bank of the Brenno, to
the valley floor.

Olivone

Aquila (788 m/2585 ft), with neat houses in the Ticinese style, lies at the foot
of the Colma massif, which reaches its highest point in the Cima di Pinaderio (2490 m/8170 ft).
From here there are alternative routes to Dongio: either on a narrow
by-road (5 km/3 miles longer) which runs above the right bank of the
Brenno through a series of pretty villages and chestnut groves (at Pru-
giasco, 7.5 km/5 miles), detour on right, 30 minutes, up to the little Romanesque church of San Carlo Negrentino, with 13th–16th c. frescoes); or on
the main road, which climbs up the left bank of the Brenno and beyond
Dongio turns into the Val Soia, running down from the Rheinwaldhorn
(3406 m/11,175 ft).

Aquila

Torre (770 m/2526 ft) is prettily situated on a terrace, and here a southern
vegetation of vines, mulberries and walnut-trees begins to feature more
prominently in the landscape.

Torre

Farther down the valley, on the hillside to the left, is the village of Lottigna
(695 m/2280 ft), the chief place in the Val Blenio, beautifully situated at the
foot of Simano (2580 m/8465 ft), with a church of the 15th and 17th
centuries.
Beyond this there is a superb view down the valley, with a view of the
pyramidal peak of Sosto to the rear. Acquarossa (538 m/1765 ft), is a spa
(mineral spring, 25.5° C,78° F).

Lottigna

Dongio (470 m/1542 ft) is a long straggling village surrounded by vineyards
and orchards, where the by-road from Aquila comes in. To the south-west,
on the other side of the Brenno, stands the chapel of San Reigio, with
Romanesque wall-paintings.

Dongio

Malvaglia (375 m/1230 ft), lies at the mouth of the deep Malvaglia Valley,
with the church of San Martino (originally Romanesque, altered in 1603:

Malvaglia

173

Semione

beautiful campanile). A narrow mountain road runs 10.5 km/7 miles up the Val Malvaglia, passing an artificial lake, to Madra (1086 m/3563 ft).

Opposite Malvaglia, on the right bank of the Brenno, is the village of Semione (402 m/1319 ft), with the ruined castle of Seravalle (12th–14th c.). In the Casa San Carlo is the Museo di Minerali with fossils and minerals from Ticino and other areas of the country.

Below Malvaglia the valley becomes wider and more regular, with large areas of tumbled rocks on the valley bottom. Below the narrow mouth of the Val Pontirone the road skirts the Buzza di Biasca, a great mass of debris the result of a tremendous landslide in 1512. The place from which the rock broke away can be seen high above the road on Pizzo Magno (2298 m/7540 ft).

Biasca

At Biasca (305 m/1001 ft) we join the road from the St Gotthard (see entry), which runs down the Ticino valley to Bellinzona (see entry).

Einsiedeln   D1

Canton: Schwyz (SZ)
Altitude: 905 m/2969 ft
Population: 9600

Situation and general

The famous Swiss pilgrimage destination of Einsiedeln, situated in a high valley of the Pre-Alps between Lake Zurich and Lake Lucerne, has been a great focus of religion and culture for more than a thousand years, and its magnificent conventual buildings are one of the peak achievements of Baroque architecture. The Gnadenkapelle (chapel of Grace) with its Black Virgin, draws large numbers of pilgrims every year, and many visitors are also attracted by the quiet and beauty of the abbey's setting. For the winter sports enthusiast there are six ski-lifts and about 52 km/32 miles of long-distance runs.

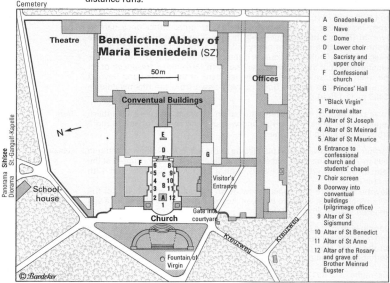

Einsiedeln

The Benedictine Abbey of Maria Einsiedeln

The famous "Grosse Welttheater" (Great Theatre of the World) by Calderón de la Barca has been performed here several times since 1924 (planned for 1992).

In 934 Eberhard, Dean of Strasbourg Cathedral, founded a community of hermits in the "Dark Forest" above the hermitage of a monk from Reichenau, Meinrad, who had been murdered in 861; and Duke Hermann of Swabia and his wife Reginlinde granted the monastic settlement enough land to provide for its maintenance. In 937 Einsiedeln was made a royal abbey, and its abbot became a prince of the Empire. The buildings were destroyed by fire on five occasions, in 1029, 1226, 1465, 1509 and 1577. The Reformer Ulrich Zwingli was for a time a secular priest at Einsiedeln. In 1639 the first peace negotiations between France and Bavaria during the Thirty Years War were conducted here. The building history of the abbey covered the whole range from Romanesque through Gothic to Baroque. Einsiedeln later developed into an important area of intellectual activity, with a flourishing printing and publishing industry. It is the administrative heart of the district of the same name, which comprises the "quarters" of Bernau, Egg, Eutal, Gross, Trachslau and Willerzell.

History

Sights

The Benedictine Abbey of Maria Einsiedeln, built by the lay brother Kaspar Moosbrugger (1656–1723) of Au in the Bregenzerwald, is the finest example of Vorarlberg architecture in Switzerland. The conventual buildings, laid out in a regular square around four courtyards, cover an area of 34,000 sq. m/40,664 sq. yards. The twin-towered church (1719–35) is a sumptuous Baroque building, with ceiling frescoes by the Asam brothers of Bavaria (the largest fresco in the country), and a wrought-iron choir screen (1684), designed to give the effect of perspective. The Gnadenkapelle (Chapel of Grace), rebuilt in 1815–17 in Neo-classical style after its destruction by the

**Benedictine Abbey of Maria Einsiedeln

French in 1798, contains the carved wooden figure of the "Black Virgin", (15th c.). The library possesses 150,000 volumes, 1300 manuscripts produced in the great medieval scriptorium here and 1200 incunabula. The Princes' Hall (Fürstensaal: entrance from the south side of the conventual buildings), with stucco decoration by M. Roncati (1704–05), is used for special exhibitions.

Bethlehem
Diorama

Near the square outside the abbey is the Bethlehem Diorama, a representation of the manger in Bethlehem with 500 carved wooden figures. A little way beyond this a circular building houses a Panorama of the Crucifixion (originally 1893, reconstructed after a fire in 1960).

Surroundings

Sihlsee

An attractive feature of the surrounding area is the Sihlsee (alt. 892 m/2927 ft), an artificial lake 9 km/6 miles long and just over 1 km/½ mile wide on average (area when full 10.85 sq. km/4 sq. miles, depth 25 m/82 ft) completed in 1934, the first stage in the Etzelwerk hydro-electric complex. The road along the west side of the Sihlsee comes in 13 km/8 miles to Unteriberg (alt. 931 m/3055 ft: pop. 1450). 2 km/1 mile beyond this is Oberiberg (1123 m/3685 ft: pop. 550).

*Hochybrig

5 km/3 miles farther south again is Weglosen (parking garage), from which there is a cableway up to the holiday and sports facility of Hochybrig (Weglosen-Seebil), at the foot of the Drusberg and the Forstberg, a recently developed walking and skiing area (1600–2200 m/5250–7218 ft: restaurant, chair-lifts, ski-lifts).

*Grosser
Mythen

11.5 km/7 miles south-west of Einsiedeln in the Alptal is the little hamlet of Brunni (996 m/3268 ft; pop. 330), from which there is a cableway up Holzegg: good walking country, starting-point for the climb of the Grosser Mythen (1902 m/6240 ft: mountain inn; wide views), Ibergeregg, Haggenegg and Hochstuckli. From the Ibergeregg pass (1406 m/4613 ft: inn) there is a pleasant walk to Rickenbach, from which a cableway 2446 m/8025 ft long runs up to the Rotenfluh (1565 m/5135 ft).

To the north is the Etzel pass, with St Meinrad's chapel (poor road to Pfäffikon), from which a footpath (20 minutes) climbs to the Etzel-Kulm (959 m/3146 ft: inn). Near the Teufelsbrücke (Devil's Bridge) in the Sihl valley is the house in which the scientist and doctor Theophrastus Paracelsus (1493–1541) was born.

Emmental   C2

Canton: Bern (BE)

Situation and
general

The Emmental (Emme valley), renowned for its cheese, is a fertile farming region extending east from Berne towards the Napf (1408 m/4620 ft), with a characteristic way of life which was described in the works of the 19th c. novelist Jeremias Gotthelf (Albert Bitzius), who was pastor at Lützelflüh. Until about 1800 it was thought that good cheese could be made only from the milk of the Alps; but the first cheese dairies in the valleys were then established in the Emmental, and the excellent cheese produced there is now exported far and wide. A model Emmentaler cheese dairy is planned to open in Affoltern.

Lakes and rivers

The Kleine Emme (Little Emme) rises on the Giswilerstock and flows down through the Mariental and Entlebuch valley to join the Reuss after a course of 58 km/36 miles. The Grosse Emme (Great Emme) rises on the Hohgant (2197 m/7208 ft), north of Lake Brienz and flows through the Emmental to join the Aare east of Solthurn after a course of 80 km/50 miles.

Burgdorf: Zähringer Castle

The Emmental is a region of gently rolling country with a long tradition of good farming with many farms having belonged to the same families for centuries. Although traditional values are deeply rooted, the farmers of the Emmental have been among the pioneers of modern agriculture in Switzerland. The farmhouses have a distinctive character – substantial and well-built, with arcades, an abundance of flowers and often elaborate carved decoration – as have the barns and the little houses for the grandparents, and the inns with the old traditional names, the "Bear" and the "Lion", the "Star" and the "Crown". The region offers endless walking opportunities off the beaten track.

*Culture and Landscape

The Emmental is the shortest route from Berne to Lake Lucerne. Road 10 runs from Berne to Langnau (30 km/19 miles) and from there via Wolhusen to Lucerne (92 km/57 miles).

Communications

Burgdorf (alt. 533 m/1749 ft; pop. 16,000), a fine town north-east of Berne, is the real gateway to the Emmental. 10th c. castle of the Zähringen family, with three towers (now a historical museum); Late Gothic parish church (1490: organ gallery with sandstone tracery); fine old guild-houses; picturesque arcaded market and cantonal technical college.
Following its conversion in 1991 the 18th c. granary is to house the Swiss Museum and Institute for Folk Music and Musical Instruments, the Swiss Costume Collection, the Swiss Confederation Yodelling room and a large collection of musical equipment. Ethnological collections are also on show in Kirchbühl. There is an attractive marked walk from Binzberg to Wynigen.

Burgdorf

Engadine   E2/F2

Canton: Grisons (GR)

The Engadine (in German Engadin, in Romansch Engiadina) is the valley of the Inn (in Romansch En), enclosed between mighty mountain chains and

Situation and general

177

flanked by flower-spangled Alpine meadows and magnificent forests of larch and stone pine on the steep hillsides. The village houses are solid white-washed structures, often with sgraffito decoration, painting, handsome oriel windows or elaborate window grilles. The population is Rhaeto-Romanic and predominantly Protestant. Since 1938 the old Ladin place-names have been in official use.

**Culture and Landscape

*Upper
Engadine

From the Majola pass (1815 m/5955 ft), the boundary between the Engadine and the Val Bregaglia (see entry), the road runs north-east through the Upper Engadine, with its clear air and extensive views, to the international resort of St Moritz (see entry) and two smaller resorts, popular both in summer and in winter, Celerina, where the road to the Bernina pass branches off, and Samedan. It then continues to La Punt (road on left to Albula pass) and the old-world village of Zuoz, once the chief settlement in the Engadine. Beyond S-chanf it runs through a defile at Puntota to enter

*Lower
Engadine

the Lower Engadine, where the valley becomes narrower and more densely forested.

**Swiss
National Park

After passing through Zernez, where the road through the Swiss National Park (see entry) to the Ofen pass and the Stelvio pass diverges to the right, the Engadine road turns north for 6 km/4 miles to reach Susch, where the road to Davos over the Flüela pass branches off on the left.

From here we continue down the Lower Engadine, running under the south side of the magnificent Silvretta group, with a series of wild side valleys nestling on its sunny southern slopes. Throughout the centuries the old Imperial road (Reichsstrasse) avoided the impenetrable valley and ran through the upper villages.

*Guarda

A narrow side road leads via steep hairpin bends to the linear village of Guarda (1600 m/5251 ft), which was awarded the Wakker Prize in 1975 for its harmonious architecture.

Engadine House

The inns and guest houses of Guarda provide a prime example of the traditional Engadine house, which from the 14th c. has combined both house and stable under one roof. The "Suler" below the round arched doorway serves as the entrance to the barn and the lobby to the living-room, with the "Stüva" (parlour, lounge), the "Chadafö" (kitchen), and the "Chaminada" (pantry). Above these last two rooms are the bedrooms ("Chombra"), access to which is usually via stairs from the parlour. In addition there is a winch and more "Giodens" or "Gebens" (rooms) for the young men. Occasionally there is a finely panelled upper room. The external appearance is characterised by the mortar-coloured walls with inward-sloping window openings and a large door. The influence of neighbouring Tirol is clearly visible in the fascinating and varied wall decorations. Every style is reflected from Gothic to Rococo and Neo-classical to Naïve, and typical decorative features include oriel windows, window grilles and heraldic animals.

*Ardez

The neighbouring village of Ardez also has many examples of typically decorated houses of the Lower Engadine region, with charming sgraffiti, oriel windows and gables. A notable example is the Clalgüna house.

Lavin, Ftan

The hamlets of Lavin and Ftan-Pitschen also have wonderful farmhouses in Engadine style.

Bad Scuol-
Tarasp-Vulpera

The valley then opens up again, and the road reaches the Bad Scuol-Tarasp-Vulpera group of resorts (see entry), with Tarasp Castle on its precipitous crag dominating the scene.

Beyond Scuol the valley becomes wilder and more solitary, with the few villages (Sent, Ramosch, Tschlin) perched high above the road on the

Traditional Engadine house . . .

. . . with decorated façade

. . . such as the Clalgüna-Haus in Ardez . . .

. . . or in Guarda

green meadows on the sunny side of the valley. The scenery becomes still more forbidding in the wooded Finstermünz defile beyond the last Swiss Village (Martina), in which, at the hamlet of Vinadi, the old frontier fortifications can still be seen. Here a boldly engineered road leads into the Samnaun valley, where secluded villages attract many visitors both in summer and in winter.

Landeck
The road now crosses the Austrian frontier into Tirol and continues down the Inn valley, between the Samnaun group and the western ridge of the Ötztal Alps. After passing through Stuben-Pfunds and Prutz it comes to Landeck, where it meets the road from the Arlberg pass.

Engelberg D2

Canton: Obwalden (OW)
Altitude: 1050 m/3445 ft
Population: 3400

Situation and general
The little town of Engelberg with its abbey, in a sunny basin under the north face of Titlis, is a popular winter and summer resort lying well away from the main traffic routes. Since 1815 it has been an enclave of the half-canton of Obwalden. It is a region of varied scenery; good walking country with hills and lakes, and with a number of cableways providing easy access to the mountains.

History
The Benedictine abbey was founded in 1120, and its abbot held independent sway over the territory. In 1798 the town was released from ecclesiastical authority and became part of the canton of Obwalden.

Sights

Benedictine Abbey
At the upper end of the town is the Benedictine abbey, founded about 1120, which ruled the whole valley until 1798. The handsome church, designed by Kaspar Moosburger, and the square complex of conventual buildings were rebuilt in 1730–37 after a fire. Rich library (men only admitted), with valuable manuscripts, incunabula and minatures.

Also of interest are the adjoining charnel-house and below the village the chapels St Jakob in Espen (17th c.) and Maria im Horbis (17th c.) at the so-called "end of the world". To the south, on the left bank of the Aawasser, are beautiful gardens surrounded by forest.

Recreation and sport
Swimming (indoor and open-air pools), walking (walkers' railcards for mountain railways and cableways), riding, tennis, summer skiing (ski-lift at upper station of Titlisbahn, 3020 m/9909 ft). Skating rinks, curling rink, toboggan run from the Gershnialp (3.5 km/2 miles), hobby courses.

Mountain railways and cableways
Terminus of narrow-gauge railway from Lucerne via Stans (1 hour); cableways Engelberg-Gerschnialp (length 528 m/1733 ft, height difference 264 m/868 ft, time 4 minutes); Engelberg-Trübsee (length 2195 m/7204 ft, height difference 531 m/1742 ft, time 6 minutes); Trübsee-Stand-Kleintitlis (length 3465 m/11,369 ft, height difference 1220 m/4003 ft, time 14 minutes); Trübsee-Joch pass (length 1459 m/4787 ft, height difference 439 m/1440 ft, time 13 minutes); Engstlensee-Joch pass (length 1631 m/5351 ft, height difference 273 m/896 ft, time 10 minutes); Rindertitlis-Laubersgrat (length 1183 m/3883 ft, height difference 385 m/1264 ft, time 8 minutes); Engelberg-Brunni (length 1193 m/3914 ft, height difference 582 m/1910 ft, time 6 minutes).

Climbs
Titlis (3239 m/10,627 ft), usually starting either from the Trübsee Hotel or from Kleintitlis; Hutstock (2680 m/8793 ft: 6 hours; wild goats); Schlossberg (3155 m/10,351 ft: 8 hours); Engelberger Rotstock (2820 m/9252 ft:
*Urirotstock
6 hours, with guide); Urirotstock (2932 m/9620 ft: 8–9 hours, with guide).

View of Engelburg below the Spannort group

The first stage of the Benedictine Way is from Engelberg village centre v a **Benedictine**
Brunni/Ristis (1600 m/5251 ft), Alp Stafel (1694 m/5560 ft) and Walenalp to **Way**
Wolfenschiessen (guest houses). It continues by cableway to Haldiwald
(1400 m/4595 ft) or by cabin cableway to Schmidsboden (1215 m/3988 ft)
climbing down the Underrist-Hütti to Dallenwil (inn).

Surroundings

Titlis (3239 m/10,627 ft), covered by eternal snow and ice, is the highest **⁎Titlis**
viewpoint in central Switzerland, offering a unique panorama of the Alps
(ice cave, glacier trail). Restaurants on Titl s and in Stand (2450 m/8038 ft).
Cableway Engelberg-Titlis (45 minutes).

The highest experimental solar power station at Stand came into operation **Solar power**
in 1988 with energy being produced by a bank of solar panels. With a **station**
nominal output at present of 2.3 kW. an annual output of between 3000 and
3500 kWh is expected.

From Engelberg there is a funicular to the Gerschnialp (1266 m/4154 ft), and **Trübsee**
from there a cableway by way of the steep Pfaffenwand to the Trübsee
Hotel (1792 m/5880 ft); descent in 2 hours via the Trübseealp. From Trübsee
by chair-lift (or on foot in 1¼ hours) to the Joch pass (2215 m/7267 ft: ski
hut), and from there a bridle-path (1 hour) to the Engslensee (1852 m/6076
ft), in a magnificent mountain setting, and on to the Engstlenalp (1839 **⁎Engstlenalp**
m/6034 ft), one of the finest areas of Alpine pasture in the country (rich
flora, superb views) and the Melchsee.

Other rewarding walks are to the Bergli (1341 m/4400 ft): to the Surenenal p
and Tätschbach Falls (1090 m/3576 ft: restaurant); and by the Herrenrüti
grazings to the Nieder-Surenenalp (1260 m/4134 ft: restaurant) and the
Arnialp.

Entlebuch   D2

Canton: Lucerne (LU)

Situation and general

The quickest route between Lucerne and Berne by either road or rail (92 km/57 miles) is through the valleys of Entlebuch and Emmental. The region drained by the Great and Little Emme extends from the Brienzer Rothorn to the Napf: a land of many legends, it has preseved much of its traditional character, but what was once the home of woodcutters and charcoal-burners is now a favourite holiday area. From the borders of the cantons of Lucerne and Berne in the Emmental low passes lead through the hills to Lake Thun and Obwalden.

From Lucerne the road follows the Kleine Emme (Little Emme) by way of Emmenbrücke and the old market village of Malters to Wolhusen (20 km/12 miles), the gateway to the Entlebuch valley. The picturesque village of

Entlebuch

Entlebuch (alt. 684 m/2244 ft; pop. 3500) lies above the Entlen, a torrential stream which flows into the Kleine Emme here. It has a parish church founded about 900 with an elegant Rococo interior and a tower of the 13th–14th c.

Schüpfheim

Schüpfheim (alt. 719 m/2359 ft; pop. 3800) is the chief town in the district of Entlebuch, with an eventful history as the place of execution of the Governor of Wolhusen. It is the starting-point of the panoramic road which runs

Flühli

via Flühli (883 m/2897 ft; pop. 1500), the principal commune in the Marientäl, which also includes the holiday resort of Sörenberg, on the road to Giswil (1159 m/3803 ft; ski-lifts). From Sörenberg there is a cableway up the Brienzer Rothorn (length 2740 m/8990 ft, height difference 1040 m/3412 ft, time 8 minutes); and access to other walking and skiing areas is provided by a chair-lift from the Eisee to the Rothorn (length 1061 m/3481 ft, height difference 298 m/978 ft, time 11 minutes) and a cableway to the Rossweid (length 1457 m/4780 ft, height difference 305 m/1001 ft, time 8 minutes). Escholzmatt (853 m/2798 ft) marks the watershed between the Entlebuch valley and the Emmental.

Marbach, Marbachegg

A minor road goes off to Marbach (871 m/2858 ft; pop. 1300), from which there is a cableway to the Marbachegg (1470 m/4823 ft), with extensive views of the Bernese Alps.

Flims   E2

Canton: Grisons (GR)
Altitude: 100 m/3609 ft
Population: 2400

Situation and general

The summer and winter resort of Flims lying on a south-facing terrace 500 m/1641 ft above the Vorderrhein, consists of the original mountain village of Flims Dorf and the hotel development of Flims Waldhaus to the south. The high plateau with its extensive forests and its beautiful lake, the Caumasee, is magnificent walking and climbing country.

This easily accessible resort – reached by leaving the motorway at Reichenau, 10 km/6 miles west of Chur and taking a road which runs up to Flims in 12 km/7 miles – lies on the great mass of debris resulting from the biggest landslide of the last Ice Age in Switzerland. The debris covers an area of 40 sq. km/15 sq. miles, reaching 14 km/9 miles downstream and 6 km/4 miles upstream, and blocks the Vorderrhein valley for a distance of 15 km/9 miles between Kästris and Reichenau. The landslide brought down at least 12,000 cu. m/423,720 cu. ft of rock.

There is a wide choice of recreational activities including classical concerts and traditional plays, excursions and sporting events such as the Alpine triathlon, mountain bike racing, moonlight skiing and hot air balloon week.

Flims, in the skiing area of the "White Arena"

Sights

The village of Flims (Romansch Flem), under the Flimserstein (Crap da Flem, 2696 m/8846 ft), has a Late Gothic church (1512). The "Schlössli" (1682) is now the headquarters of the commune (Gemeindehaus). 2 km/ 1 mile east is the old German settlement of Fidaz (1178 m/3865 ft), with wooden houses (an unusual case of the adoption of a Rhaeto-Romanic practice).

Flims, Schlössli

2 km/1 mile south of Flims Dorf is Flims Waldhaus (1103 m/3619 ft), a modern resort with hotels and holiday houses.

Flims Waldhaus

Chair-lift (1400 m/4595 ft in 20 minutes) by way of Alp Foppa to Alp Naraus; from there cableway (2200 m/7218 ft in 7 minutes) to Cassonsgrat. Cableway from Flims Dorf to Startgels (1590 m/5217 ft); from there Grauberg-bahn at 2230 m/7317 ft, near the Berghaus Nagiens (2128 m/6982 ft). Cableway (height difference 1100 m/3609 ft, time 10 minutes) to Crap Sogn Gion (2228 m/7310 ft; restaurant).

Cableways

(Experienced climbers only with guides). Piz Segnes (3102 m/10,178 ft; 8 hours) by way of the Segneshütte (2130 m/6989 ft; service). Vorab (3030 m/9941 ft; 6 hours), with magnificent views of the Tödi group.

Climbs

Several ice-rinks; curling rink; toboggan run (3 km/2 miles) from Alp Foppa; skiing on Alp Foppa (1425 m/4675 ft) and Alp Naraus (1840 m/6037 ft; restaurant), and on Cassonsgrat (2678 m/8787 ft; inn) and Alp Nagiens; ski-lifts; cross-country skiing. Flims-Laax–Fellers "Weisse Arena" ("White Arena"; see below), with summer skiing on the Vorab.

Winter sports

Surroundings

From Waldhaus beautiful forest tracks run south-west (1 hour) to Salums (1015 m/3330 ft; restaurant) and south-east (1 hour) past the delightful

Salums

Caumasee   Caumasee, in the heart of the forest (1000 m/3281 ft; small funicular to shore), to Conn (990 m/3248 ft; restaurant); from both places there are superb views of the gorge of the Vorderrhein.
From Flims Dorf to the Cresta-See (850 m/2789 ft), on the Rhine valley road in the direction of Trin.

Flimserstein   Ascent of the Flimserstein (4½–5 hours): from Flims Dorf via Fidaz and Bargis (1550 m/5086 ft; from here bear left uphill) to Alp Sura (3 hours; 2102 m/6897 ft); then over the Alpine meadows to the highest point (1¾ hours; 2696 m/8832 ft), with magnificent views to the north of Ringelspitz (Piz Bargias, 3251 m/10,667 ft) and the Trinserhorn (Piz Dolf, 3028 m/9935 ft).

Laax   5 km/3 miles west of Flims on the road to Ilanz (12 km/7 miles; postal bus) is the village of Laax (alt. 1016 m/3333 ft; pop. 610), which in the time of King Rudolf of Habsburg (13th c.) was the seat of a county, with the right to hold a market and self-government. There is a Baroque church (1675) and the local museum has an intersting local history collection.

*Weisse Arena   Laax, Flims and Fellers (Romansch Falera, alt. 1213 m/3980 ft) – where
Falera   remains of a Middle Bronze Age settlement and cult site were found – together form the famous "Weisse Arena" ("White Arena"). An extensive winter sports region, it has recently been developed as a huge skiing complex, one of the largest in the Alps, more than 140 sq. km/54 sq. miles in area. Since November 1978, with the provision of facilities for access to the Vorab glacier area (3025 m/9925 ft), it has been possible to ski here all year round. There are more than 52 trails, with a total length of some 220 km/137 miles, reached with the aid of two cableways. One cabin cableway, six chair-lifts and seven ski-lifts, which have a total capacity of 33,000 persons per hour.

Crap Sogn Gion   From Mulania a cableway (length 4200 m/13,780 ft, height difference 1100 m/3609 ft, time 10 minutes) runs up to Crap Sogn Gion (2228 m/7310 ft), the starting-point of the Laax skiing and climbing area, with a modern mountain restaurant seating 600 and an indoor swimming pool.

Fribourg   C2

Canton: Fribourg (FR)
Altitude: 550–630 m/1805–2067 ft
Population: 40,000

Situation and   Fribourg (in German Freiburg), capital of the canton of the same name, is
general   the great stronghold of Catholicism in Switzerland, seat of the Bishop of Lausanne, Geneva and Fribourg and of a Catholic University. One of the finest old medieval towns in Switzerland, it lies on the River Sarine (German Saane), which flows in a deep valley through the Mittelland. The Auge and Bourg quarters leading to the upper town are picturesquely situated, like Berne, above the rocky banks of a bend in the river; in the lower town are the districts of Neuveville on the left bank and Planche on the right bank. Fribourg was founded by Duke Berthold IV of Zähringen in 1157 and joined the Confederation in 1481.

Sights

**Old Town

Town Hall   In the middle of the old town is the Place de l'Hôtel de Ville, where the Town Hall (Hôtel de Ville or Hôtel Cantonal), built 1501–1522 by Gylian and Hans

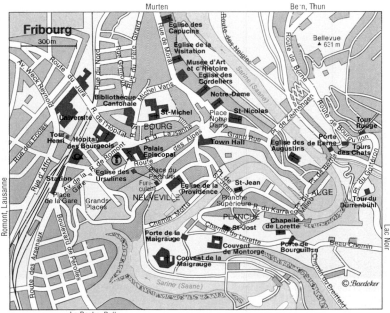

Felder the Younger, has an octagonal clock-tower (lantern added 1642) and two attractive arched friezes above the entrance (1881 Charles Iguel). The interior has Louis XVI style panelling and Gothic 16th c. windows by Martin Gramp decorate the "Hall of the Lost Steps".

The adjoining Baroque-Classical Stadthaus (addition to Town Hall) was built 1730–31 by Hans Fasel.

Stadthaus

To the east of the Town Hall stands the Cathedral of St Nicholas (Gothic, 14th and 15th c.) on the former site of a Romanesque building. Its front tower measures 76 m/249 ft and above the main doorway are fine 14th and 15th c. sculptures (Apostles, Angelic Salutation; Last Judgment in the tympanum). At the south door is a 14th c. representation of the Three Kings.

*Cathedral

Notable features of the interior are the pulpit, font (1498), choir screen (1474) and choir-stalls (15th c. Antoine Peneys), modern stained glass by Joseph de Mehoffer, a famous organ by Alois Mooser and the treasure in the sacristy.

In the adjoining Place Notre-Dame (Samson fountain by Hans Gieng, 1547, original in museum) is the 12th c. church of Notre-Dame, the oldest church in the town (altered 1787 and 1853) with a Baroque-Classical Façade.

Church of Notre-Dame

Immediately north is the Franciscan friary with a church (Eglise des Corde-liers; choir 1281, nave 1745–46) which contains some notable works of art, including an altarpiece by the "Master of the Carnation" (1481), a predella with a painting by Hans Fries, "The Death of the Usurer" (1506), and a carved and gilded wooden triptych (c. 1513).

Franciscan friary

Beyond this, to the north-west, the Musée d'Art et d'Histoire in the old Ratzehof houses sculpture and painting from the 10th to the 19th c. At the

Musée d'Art et d'Histoire

185

View of the Old Town of Fribourg

end of Rue de Morat, which continues north-west, is a well-preserved old town gate, the Porte de Morat (1414).

Place Georges-Python

From the Place de l'Hôtel-de-Ville we go up the busy Rue de Lausanne or the Route des Alpes (views) to Place Georges-Python (610 m/2001ft), at the top of a funicular from Neuveville (Place du Perthuis). On the east side of the square stands the Bishop's Palace (Palais Episcopal). Higher up, to the north, are the Albertinium, a seminary, the Cantonal and University Library (Bibliothèque Cantonale) and the Jesuit church of St Michel, with the tomb of St Peter Canisius (Hundlinger, 1521–97), the "first German Jesuit".

University

To the west, beyond the railway, is the University (by Dumas and Honegger, 1941), with an art collection and a museum of natural history and ethnography. The great hall is decorated with 17th c. tapestry.

Station quarter

To the south-west of the upper town is the newer district around the station, with the Grand' Places, from which there is a beautiful view of the old town and the Sarine valley.

Beer museum

To the west of the station in the Avenue Beauregard a beer museum was opened in July 1988 in the cellars of the Cardinal brewery by the Blanc-pain Foundation exhibiting photographs, documents and utensils connected with the history of brewing.

Quartier de Pérolles

St Bartholomé's chapel

From the nearby Place de la Gare the Avenue de Pérolles runs south through the Pérolles quarter, with the church of Christ the King (1954), to the Pont de Pérolles. To the west of Avenue de Pérolles the 16th c. chapel of St Bartholomé (restored 1970) has fine stained glass.

Neuveville

In Neuveville, in the lower town, are two attractive fountains – in Place du Perthuis (alt. 553 m/1814 ft; funicular to upper town) the Fontaine du

Fribourg Cathedral: font . . .   *. . . and organ*

Sauvage (1627), and at the end of Rue ce la Neuveville the Fontaine de la Prudence (1550); Gothic house fronts.

Auge

In the old-world Auge-quarter, which a so has fine 16th c. fountains, is a former Augustinian convent, on a peninsula in the bend o' the Sarine. The church, dedicated to St Mauritius, dates from the 13th c. but was rebuilt in the 16th and 18th c. The conventual buildings now house the Cantonal Archives, with more than 30,000 parchment documents, the oldest dating from 928.

Augustinian convent

From Auge a covered wooden bridge, the Pont de Berne (1580), leads to the Place des Forgerons, on the right bank of the Sarine, with the Fontaine de la Fidélité (by Hans Gieng, 1553). To the north are the Porte de Berne (13th–14th c., restored 1660), the Tour des Chats (1383) and the Tour Rouge (1250).

Place des Forgerons

Planche

In the Planche area of the lower town, on the right bank of the Sarine, is the church of St-Jean (1529; later enlarged). Above Planche are the Couvent de Montorge and two chapels (see below).

St-Jean

South-west of Planche, on the Banks of the Sarine, is the Couvent de la Maigrauge, a Cistercian nunnery with a church built before 1300.

Maigrauge

Surroundings

Circuit on the right bank of the Sarine: 4.5 km/3 miles from the cathedral cross the river on the Pont du Zähringen and turn right past the Tour Rouge;

Round trips

*Pont du Gotteron — cross the Pont du Gotteron, with a fine view of the town, and continue past the Tour du Dürrenbühl to the west end of the village of Bourguillon (alt. 658 m/2159 ft; church of 15th–18th c.); then sharp right along the Beau Chemin to the Porte de Bourguillon, beyond which, to the right, is the chapel of Notre-Dame de Lorette (1648), with a view of the town; beyond this, to the right, the chapel of St-Jost (1684) and, to the left, the Capuchin friary of Montorge, founded in 1626; then down into the Planche quarter, returning to the upper town either by way of the Pont du Milieu and Auge or by the Pont St-Jean and Neuveville.

Lorette chapel

Capuchin friary Montorge

From Fribourg to Hauterive

Leave Fribourg by Avenue du Midi. In 3 km/2 miles the road crosses the Glâne, a short distance above its junction with the Sarine, on a bridge above the gorge of the river. 2 km/1 mile beyond the bridge a road goes off on the left and runs 2 km/1 mile south to the Cistercian Abbey of Hauterive (inn), in a bend of the Sarine. The church (1160), in the purest Cistercian style, has fine stained glass (1332) and richly carved choir-stalls (1480).

Cistercian Abbey of Hauterive

To the Schwarzsee and Schwefelbergbad

A beautiful run (22 and 33 km/17 and 21 miles south-east) through the Fribourg Pre-Alps. The road runs via Bourgouillon and Giffers (alt. 767m/2517 ft) to Plaffeien (18 km/11 miles; 851 m/2792 ft), where it enters the valley of the Sense and the Fribourg Alps. 4 km/2 miles: Zollhaus (902 m/2959 ft), at the junction of the Warme and the Kalte Sense. From here a road to the left leads to Schwefelbergbad (below); the road to the right ascends the valley of the Warme Sense to the Schwarzsee (1048 m/3438 ft; Hotel Gypsera, D, 25b.), a lake surrounded by beautiful wooded hills. From the north end of the lake a chair-lift 1436 m/4712 ft long runs up in 14 minutes to the Riggisalp (1500 m/4922 ft). From Kaiseregg (2189 m/7182 ft; 3½ hours from the lake) there are magnificent views; good skiing (ski-lifts).

Zollhaus

Schwarzsee

From Zollhaus the road to Schwefelbergbad leads east up the valley of the Kalte Sense by way of the Sangernboden (1005 m/3297 ft). 10 km/6 miles: Schwefelbergbad (1398 m/4587 ft), with sulphurous springs, in a beautiful wooded setting at the foot of the Ochsen (2190 m/7185 ft; 2½ hours; view) and Gantrisch (2177 m/7143 ft). These mountains form a skiing area much favoured by the People of Berne (many ski huts; ski-lifts from Schwefelbergbad to 1700 m/5578 ft on the north face of the Ochsen).

Schwefel-bergbad

Geneva   B2

Canton: Geneva (GE)
Altitude: 337 m/1237 ft
Population: 158,000

Situation and general

Geneva (in French Genève; in German Genf), the city of Calvin and the centre of the Reformation, lies in the extreme western tip of Switzerland at the south-west end of Lake Geneva (in French Lac Léman). The town is built on morainic hills of varying height on either side of the swiftly flowing Rhône, which here flows out of the lake and is joined on the south-west side of the town by its tributary the Arve, coming down from the Savoy Alps. Lying between the Jura to the north-west and the limestone ridges of Mont Salève and the Voirons to the south-east, Geneva enjoys a magnificent situation on the largest of the Alpine lakes, within sight of the majestic peak of Mont-Blanc. As a hub of European cultural life in which French savoir-vivre and Swiss solidity are happily combined, the venue of international meetings on the highest level, as well as conventions and exhibitions of all

The "Jet d'Eau", a landmark of Geneva

kinds, and not least as a major financial, commercial and industrial city, Geneva has a lively and cosmopolitan atmosphere which makes it perhaps the most attractive town in Switzerland and the one that attracts the greatest number of visitors. Evidence of its dynamic growth during the last few decades is provided by the large amount of new building in the city itself and in the surrounding area, where a number of residential suburbs and satellite towns of considerable importance have grown up.

The first human settlements in this area were established at the foot of   History
Mont Salève at the end of the Ice Age: then about 2500 B.C. a large village of pile-dwellings grew up in the area of the modern port. The first fortified settlement on the hill now occupied by the old town is believed to have been an oppidum (town) belonging to a Celtic tribe, the Allobroges, who were first conquered by the Romans in 120 B.C. The first known reference to the town under the name of Geneva occurs in the "Commentaries" (I, 7) of Julius Caesar, who in 58 B.C. caused the strategically important bridge over the Rhine to be destroyed in order to hinder the advance of the Helveti into Gaul. In A.D. 443 the town became the Burgundian capital: in 534 it fell into the hands of the Franks. At the end of the 9th c. it passed to the second Burgundian kingdom, and together with Burgundy became part of the Holy Roman Empire in 1033.

The long continued conflicts between the Bishops (later Prince-Bishops) of Geneva, the Counts of Geneva and the Counts (later Dukes) of Savoy for control of the town were ended by the Reformation, to which Geneva firmly adhered. In 1536 Jean Calvin (1509–64) fled from Paris to Geneva and joined forces with the Reformer Guillaume Farel (1489–1565), who had been preaching the new faith in the town since 1532. Calvin acquired great influence in both ecclesiastical and state affairs, particularly after his return in 1541, when he established a theocratic régime based on strict and often intolerant church discipline. Through his foundation in 1559 of an Academy mainly designed to train Reformed theologians he turned the commercially minded town towards an interest in intellectual matters.

Geneva

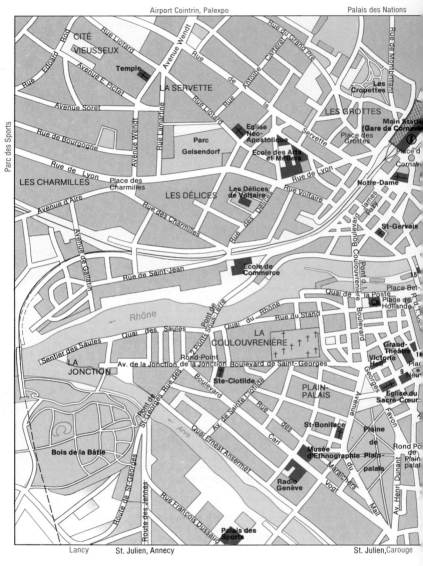

1 Palais de Justice
  (Justizgebäude)
2 Collège de St-Antoine
  (Gymnasium)

3 Musée des Instruments
  Anciens de Musique
  (Museum für historische
  Musikinstrumente)

4 Musée d'Art et d'Histoire
  (Kunstmuseum)
5 Ecole des Beaux-Arts
  (Kunstschule)

6 Athénée (Athenäum;
  Bibliothek, Wechselausstellungen)
7 Monument de la Réformation
  (Reformationsdenkmal)

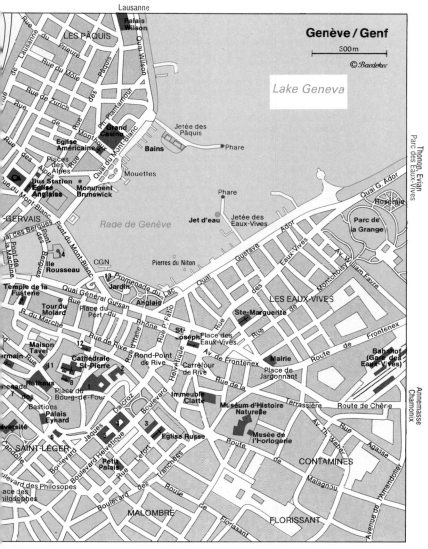

Temple de l'Auditoire
Kirche ausländischer Protest.)
Conservatoire de Musique
Musikkonservatorium)

10 Musée Rath
(Wechselausstellungen)
11 Ancien Arsenal
(urspr. Kornhalle)

12 Temple de la Madeleine (Kirche der
deutschschweizerischen Reformierten)
13 Monument National
(„Helvetia" & „Geneva")

14 Sitzbild von
Jean-Jaques Rousseau
15 Tour de l'Ile
(Historischer Inselturm)

191

In 1602 Geneva beat off an attempt by the Duke of Savoy to capture the town (the "Escalade", 11–12 December). The town was occupied by the French in 1798, and until 1813 was the administrative capital of the French department of Léman. In 1814 Geneva became the 22nd canton to join the Confederation. The International Committee of the Red Cross was established in Geneva in 1865, and from 1920 to 1946 it was the headquarters of the United Nations.

Geneva was the birthplace of Jean-Jacques Rousseau (1712–78), the writer and philosopher whose ideas had so much influence on the French Revolution.

**Townscape   The townscape of Geneva, though undramatic, is full of variety. On a steep-sided hill on the left bank of the Rhône rises the old town, dominated by the cathedral, with its picturesque old streets, flights of steps, fountains and historic buildings. On the west, south and east it is surrounded by a ring of imposing buildings and broad streets on the line of the old fortifications. The business life of the city is concentrated in the area below the old town to the north and in Saint-Gervais, formerly an outlying suburb. On both sides of the lake are elegant promenades and extensive parks and gardens. In the northern part of the town are the main railway station, industrial establishments, craft workshops and residential areas. Most of the international organisations have their headquarters still farther north, in spacious park-like grounds.

Geneva is the capital of the smallest Swiss canton, the République et Canton de Genève. It is almost entirely surrounded by French territory (free trade zones) and is connected to the rest of Switzerland only by the lake and a narrow corridor along the north-west shore of the lake. It has two small enclaves around Céligny in the canton of Vaud.

Boat services   (Not all operating during the winter.) Regular steamer services to places on the lake, run by the Compagnie Générale de Navigation sur le Lac Léman (CGN; head office in Lausanne-Ouchy; branch office in Geneva, "Le Bateau", Jardin Anglais); round trips and cruises; shuttle services and short trips in the port area and round about by the Mouettes Genevoises (motor-launches).

Museums, Galleries, etc.

Bibliotheca Bodmeriana
21 Route de Guignard,
Cologny;
Tue.–Sun. 2–6.

Cabinet des Estampes
(Print Room),
5 Promenade du Pin;
Tue.–Sun. 10–12 and 2–6.

CERN
(European organisation for nuclear research),
Bus from Cornavin station.
Guided tours by prior arrangement (minimum age 16),
Sat. 9.30 and 2.30 (tel. 83 40 52).

Château de Coppet
March–October daily except Mon. 10–12 and 2–6.

Château de Voltaire,
Ferney-Voltaire (France);
Sat. afternoons in July and August only.

Collection Barbier-Muller,
4 rue de l'Ecole de Chimie;
Tue.–Sat. 2.30–5.30.

Collection Baszanger,
6 Petite Corraterie;
weekdays 10–12 and 2.30–6.

Collection Baur,
8 rue Munier-Romilly;
daily except Mon. 2–6.

Collection Tatiana Zoubov,
2 rue des Granges;
part of the tour of the old town "le tour de la vieille ville", departs from the
Hôtel de Ville (Town Hall) at 5 p.m. or by prior arrangement.

Conservatoire et Jardin Botaniques,
Route de Lausanne;
Botanical collections:
Mon.–Fri. 7.45–12.30 and 1–5.
Botanic garden:
daily 7 a.m. to 6.30 p.m., winter 8–5.

Hôtel de Ville,
2–2 bis rue de l'Hôtel-de-Ville;
conducted visits only as part of organised city tours.
Cantonal archives Mon.–Fri. 9–12 and 2–5.

Institut et Musée Voltaire,
25 rue des Délices;
Mon.–Fri. 2–5.

Musée d'Art et d'Histoire,
2 rue Charles-Galland;
Tue.–Sun. 9–5.
Salle des Casemates:
special exhibitions.
Cabinet des Dessins:
by appointment (tel. 29 00 11).

Musée de l'Ariana,
10 Avenue de la Paix;
at present closed.

Musée de l'Athènée,
2 rue de l'Athènée;
Tue.–Fri. 10–12 and 2–6, Sat. until 5, Sun. 10–12.

Musée de l'Automobile Jean Tua,
3 rue Pestalozzi;
by appointment only (tel. 33 31 84).

Musée de Carouges,
2 Place de la Sardaigne, Carouge;
Tue.–Sun. 2–6.

Musée de l'Horlogerie et de l'Emaillerie,
15 Route de Malagnou;
daily 10–12 and 2–6,
closed Mon. mornings.

Musée de l'Ordre de Malte,
Commanderie de Compesières;
by appointment (tel. 71 10 04).

Musée des Instruments Anciens de Musique,
23 rue Lefort;
Tue. 3–6, Thur. 10–12 and 3–6, Fri. 8–10 p.m., or by appointment
(tel. 46 95 65).

Musée des Régiments Suisses au Service Etranger,
Château de Penthes,
18 Chemin de l'Impératrice;
daily except Mon. 10–12 and 2–6.

Musée d'Histoire des Sciences,
128 rue de Lausanne;
April–October daily 2–6.

Musée d'Histoire Naturelle,
11 Route de Malagnou;
at present closed for renovation.

Musée du Vieux Genève,
6 rue de Puits-Saint Pierre
(Maison Tavel);
Tue.–Sun. 10–5.

Musée et Institut d'Ethnographie,
65–67 Boulevard Carl-Vogt;
Tue.–Sun. 10–5.

Musée Historique de la Réformation/Musée Jean-Jacques Rousseau,
Bibliothèque Publique et Universitaire
(Salle Lullin);
Mon.–Fri. 9–12 and 2–5, Sat. 9–12.

Musée Philatélique des Nations Unies,
Palais des Nations,
Bâtiment E, Porte 39;
Mon.–Fri. 9–11 and 2–4.

Musée Rath,
Place Neuve;
Tue.–Sun. 10–12 and 2–6, Mon. only 2–6.

Observatoire,
Sauverny;
special exhibitions.
Library (tel. 55 26 11).

Palais des Nations (ONU/UNO);
conducted tours only (Entrance 7) every hour, daily
15 May–30 September 9.15–12 and 2–5.15
1 October–14 May 9.15–12 and 2–4.15.
See also Musée Philatélique des Nations Unies.

Petit-Palais,
2 Terrasse Saint-Victor;
Tue.–Sun. 10–12 and 2–4.30.

Temple de l'Auditoire
(John Knox Chapel),
Place de la Taconnerie;
March–October daily 2–5,
November–February 2–4.

Temple de Saint-Pierre
(Cathedral),
Cour Saint-Pierre;
daily 9–12 and 2–5;
service on Sunday at 10.
Archaeological site: Tue.–Sun. 10–1, 2–6.

Cathedral of St Peter, Geneva
Temple de Saint-Pierre · Genève

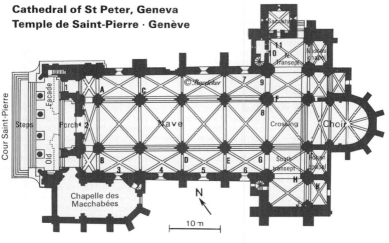

Chapelle des
Macchabées

N

10 m

1 Entrance
2 Organ
3 Gravestone of the Huguenot Théodore Agrippa
  d'Aubigné (1552–1630)
4 Tablet commemorating the first oecumenical
  service (20 February 1946)
5 Tablet commemorating the restoration of Genevese
  independence (31 December 1813)
6 Choir-stalls (from the Chapelle des Florentins,
  destroyed)
7 Tablet commemorating the Calvinist Reformation
8 Pulpit
9 Calvin's chair
10 Steps to N tower
11 15th c. door

NOTABLE CAPITALS
a Lions, dancers and acrobats
b Daniel in the lions' den
c Angels fighting with dragons
d Salome dancing in front of her father; demons,
  themes from the Apocalypse
e Melchizedek with bread and wine; Abraham's
  sacrifice
f Sirens; monks' heads with lions' bodies
g Ornamental motifs with human figures and animals;
  geometric arabesques
h Partridges billing and cooing, with grapes; acanthus
  ornament
j Orpheus charming birds
k Christ at Emmaus

Description of the town

One of Geneva's busiest traffic arteries is the Pont du Mont-Blanc (1862; rebuilt 1969), the first of its eight bridges over the Rhône, spanning the river at the point where it leaves Lake Geneva. At the southern end is the entrance to a car park under the riverbed. Between this bridge and the next one, the Pont des Bergues, lies the Ile Rousseau, with a statue of Jean-Jacques Rousseau (by Pradier, 1834). Then come the Pont de la Machine (pedestrian bridge; under it a dam) and the double Ponts de l'Ile (until the 19th c. the only bridge), crossing an island in the Rhône on which stands the Tour de l'Ile, a relic of the medieval fortifications.

Pont du Mont-Blanc

Ile Rousseau

Lower town

The Lower Town or "Rues Basses", lying between the south bank of the Rhône and the old town, is the city's main business and shopping quarter. the busiest streets are the Rue du Rhône and a succession of streets which run parallel to it – Rue de la Confédération, Rue du Marché, Rue de la Croix-d'Or (these last two for pedestrians only) and Rue de Rive – with a series of squares (originally landing-stages), passages and cross streets linking the two. Opposite the island in the Rhône is Place Bel-Air, around which are a number of banks. Farther east is Place de la Fusterie, in the

Rue du Rhône

Temple de la Fusterie	middle of which stands the Temple de la Fusterie, a Neo-classical structure built by J. Vennes in 1713–15 as a Protestant church and restored in 1975–77 for use as an ecumenical facility.
Tour du Molard	Along Rue du Rhône, at the corner of Place Molard, is the Tour du Molard (built 1591, several times altered or restored), the remnant of an old arcaded building, with a bas-relief of 1920, "Genève Cité de Refuge".

*Temple de Saint-Pierre

History
: On the highest point of the old town (Vieille Ville: alt. 404 m/1326 ft), occupying the site of a Roman temple and a number of earlier churches of the 4th–5th c. onwards, rises the Temple de Saint-Pierre, the post-Reformation name of the Cathedral of Saint-Pierre, a Romanesque church with Gothic elements which was built between about 1150 and 1232, with later alterations, particularly to the exterior. The two principal towers, never completed, date from the 13th c.; the metal spire over the crossing was built only in 1895, replacing a tower destroyed by fire in the 15th c. The original west front and doorway were replaced in 1749–56 by a portico of six Corinthian columns – a piece of stylistic nonconformity which does not, however, interfere with the unity of the interior. Extensive restoration of the church was carried out in 1888–98 and in 1974–79.

*Interior
: The interior of the cathedral (total length 64 m/210 ft) is of impressive effect with its harmonious proportions and the austere simplicity characteristic of Calvinist churches. The nave, with the aisles divided off by massive clustered piers, has a gallery, blind arcading and triforium; the transepts are short and narrow; the choir, with no ambulatory, ends in a semi-circular apse.

*Choir-stalls
: Against the walls of the aisles, in the second bay, are the gravestones of ecclesiastical and lay dignitaries of the 15th and 16th c., originally set into the ground. In the fifth bay are Late Gothic choir-stalls with delicate carving from the destroyed Chapelle des Florentins. In front of the last pillar on the wall of the north aisle is the "Chaise de Calvin", a triangular chair said to have been used by the Reformer.

In the transepts are chapels: in the north-east corner the plain Nassau chapel, north-west of the choir the Rohan chapel, with the tomb (1889) of Duc Henri de Rohan (1579–1638), leader of the French Protestants in the reign of Louis XIII.

Choir
: The simple choir with blind arcading, dates from the 12th c.: the stained glass windows are copies of the 15th c. originals, now in the Musée d'Art et d'Histoire (which also has the surviving parts of the high altar, painted by Konrad Witz).

*Capitals
: The large gallery above the entrance houses a modern organ (1962–65) with 6000 pipes. The late Romanesque and Early Gothic capitals on the clustered piers of the nave and the pillars on the walls and windows of the aisles and in the choir and transepts are notable for their artistic quality and their variety of theme.

The recently opened archaeological excavations below the cathedral reveal an extensive underground labyrinth, evidence of early Christian settlement on the hill.

Chapelle des Macchabées
: Adjoining the south-west corner of the cathedral is the Chapelle des Macchabées (1406, with later alterations in 1898; restored 1939–40), a superb example of High Gothic religious architecture, with beautiful window traceries.

Around the cathedral

Temple de l'Auditoire
: On the south side of the cathedral the former church of Notre-Dame (originally early 13th c.) has been called since the Reformation the Temple de

Grand Théâtre, the opera-house cf Geneva   *Arcaded courtyard of the Hôtel de Ville*

l'Auditoire, in which Calvin. Beza and John Knox preached. Partly rebuilt in the 19th c., it is now used by Scottish. Dutch, Italian and Spanish Protestants (John Knox Chapel; restored 1959; exhibition of historical documents).

To the west of the cathedral the peaceful tree-shaded Cour Saint-Pierre has a number of historic old houses, the most elegant of which is the Maison Mallet (Louis XV style, 1721).

Cour Saint-Pierre

South-east of the cathedral in the picturesque Place du Bourg-de-Four, on the site of the Roman forum, stands the handsome Palais de Justice, built 1707–12, which has housed the law courts since 1860.

*Place du Bourg-de-Four

South-west of the cathedral is the Hôtel de Ville (15th–17th c.), seat of the cantonal government, which has a ramp without steps, leading to the upper floors. The Tour Baudet contains the cantonal archives. On the ground floor of the south-east wing is the Alabama room, in which the first Geneva Convention (on the Red Cross) was signed in 1864.

Hôtel de Ville

Facing the Hôtel de Ville is the Old Arsenal, a former 16th c. granary which served as a weapons arsenal in the 18th c. Restored in 1971, it now houses the State archives.

State Archives

Here is the beginning of the Grand' Rue (pedestrians only), the well-preserved main street of the old town, with house fronts of the 15th–18th c. (at No. 40 the birthplace of Jean-Jacques Rousseau).

Grand' Rue

South-west of the Hôtel de Ville, reached through a pillared gateway, is the Promenade de la Treille, lined with chestnut-trees (views of Mont Salève and the Jura).

Promenade de la Treille

From the Arsenal the narrow Rue du Puits-Saint-Pierre leads north: at No. 6 is the Maison Tavel, the oldest private house in Geneva (first mentioned in the records 1303, rebuilt 1334). Today it houses the Musée du Vieux Genève

* Maison Tavel

Reformation Monument: Farel, Calvin, Bèze and Knox

with a model of the town of Geneva in 1850 before the walls were destroyed (scale 1:250; 1880–1896; A. Magnin) along with doors, carved inn and shop signs, bells, chairs and other exhibits from the town's history.

Place Neuve

Below the old town, to the south-west, is the Place Neuve (equestrian statue of General Dufour).

Grand Théâtre
Musée Rath
Conservatoire de Musique

On the north side stands the Grand Théâtre (Opera House, 1874–79), with the Musée Rath (1826: exhibitions) on the right, and the Conservatoire de Musique (1858: annual music competition) on the west side. South-east of the square the Promenade des Bastions, is graced by old trees and busts of prominent citizens of Geneva.

*Reformation monument

Against the wall under the Promenade de la Treille can be seen the Reformation Monument (Monument de la Réformation, 1917). In the middle are figures of Calvin, Guillaume Farel, Théodore de Bèze or Beza and John Knox, and on either side are the statesmen who promoted the cause of the reformed faith and bas-reliefs with scenes from the history of the Calvinist Reformation, while at the ends are memorials to Luther and Zwingli.

University

On the south side of the Promenade des Bastions is the University, housed in its present buildings since 1873, which developed out of the Academy founded by Calvin in 1559 for the training of Reformed theologians. The Library in the east wing was founded in the 15th c., and contains some 1,200,000 volumes, a collection of portraits of leading theologians, scholars, writers and statesmen, 6000 valuable manuscripts, a Rousseau Museum (manuscripts, books, compositions, etc.) and a Reformation Museum.

Palais Eynard

At the east end of the Promenade des Bastions is the elegant Palais Eynard (1821: municipal reception rooms), and to the south-east of this the Neoclassical Palais Athénée (art gallery; 1864).

Palais Athénée

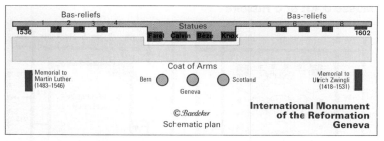

Bas-reliefs — Bas-reliefs
1536 — Statues — Farel Calvin Bèze Knox — 1602

Coat of Arms
Memorial to Martin Luther (1483–1546) — Bern ○ ○ ○ Scotland — Memorial to Ulrich Zwingli (1418–1531)
Geneva

© Baedeker
Schematic plan

International Monument of the Reformation Geneva

On the upper part of the rear wall of the monument, on either side of the central figures, is an inscription in large Roman lettering, POST TENEBRAS LUX ("After darkness comes light"), the motto of the Genevese Reformation. On the plinth of the central group is the Christian emblem IHS. At the ends of the wall are inscribed the two most important dates in the history of Geneva – **1536** (adoption of the Reformed faith and introduction of compulsory schooling) and **1602** (the "Escalade").

STATUES
of the Genevese Reformers **Guillaume Farel** (1489–1565), **Jean Calvin** (1509–64) and **Théodore de Bèze** (1519–1605) and the Scottish Reformer **John Knox** (1505–72)
On either side of the main figures:

A Frederick William of Brandenburg (1620–88), the Great Elector
B William I, the Silent, of Nassau-Orange (1533–84)
C Admiral Gaspard de Coligny (1519–72), leader of the French Protestants
D Roger Williams (1603–83), the English settler in New England who fought for freedom of conscience in the North American colonies
E Oliver Cromwell (1599–1658)
F István (Stephen) Bocskay (1557–1606), Prince of Transylvania, the Hungarian statesman

BAS-RELIEFS of important events in the history of the Reformation:

1 The Great Elector issues the Potsdam Edict of 1685, offering asylum to Protestants driven from France by the Revocation of the Edict of Nantes
2 The States General in The Hague vote for the independence of the Netherlands (26 July 1581)
3 Henry IV of France signs the Edict of Nantes granting religious toleration (13 April 1598)
4 The Reformation is preached to the people of Geneva in the presence of envoys from Berne (22 February 1534)
5 John Knox preaches the Reformation in St Giles' Cathedral, Edinburgh (1565)
6 The Pilgrim Fathers sign a covenant on the "Mayflower" for the righteous colonisation of North Africa (11 November 1620)
7 The Lords and Commons present the Bill of Rights, providing for the establishment of constitutional monarchy, to William and Mary (13 February 1689)
8 Stephen Bocskay presents to the Hungarian Diet in Košice (Slovakia) the Vienna peace treaty which secures religious freedom for the kingdom of Hungary (13 December 1606)

West of the University, beyond the spacious Plaine de Plainpalais, is the Museum of Ethnography (65–67 Boulevard Carl-Vogt), with a collection of more than 30,000 items from all over the world, only about a fifth of which can be displayed. In the front garden two Indian totem poles (19th c.) from Alaska have been erected.
Facing the museum rises a tower block with the headquarters of Radio Genève (radio and television).

Plaine de Plainpalais
Museum of Ethnography

At the south-east end of the hill on which the old town is built is the Promenade St-Antoine, a former bastion, below which is the Collège St-Antoine, founded by Calvin in 1559, now one of the eight cantonal secondary schools.

Promenade de St-Antoine

*Musée D'Art et d'Histoire

Facing it to the south, between the Boulevard Jacques Dalcroze and Boulevard Helvétique, on a lower level, the Musée d'Art et d'Histoire has rich collections of applied art and archaeology, a collection of weapons and a

Geneva

Museé d' Art et d' Histoire

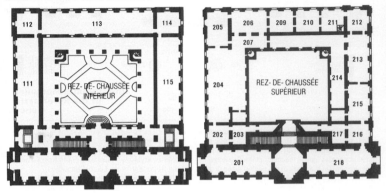

LOWER GROUND FLOOR (Rez-de-Chaussée Inférieur)

111 Egypt: steles, reliefs, sarcophagi and mummies.

112 Near East; gravestones, vessels, bronzes, ceramic and gold articles (various regions).

113 Greek sculpture, vases and jewellery.

114 Etruscan art – pottery, ceramics and sculptures, urns, small bronzes (figure of Heracles).

115 Ancient Rome:
works of art and everyday objects, mainly from the Geneva area, fine marble head of Augustus.

UPPER GROUND FLOOR (Rez-de-Chaussée Supérieur)

Applied Art

212 Ecclesiastical Art of the Middle Ages: sculptures in wood, stone and ivory; enamel ware from Limoges, windows from the Cathedral of Saint-Pierre, Geneva (end of 15th c.) and from Saint-Fargeau, France (13th c.), capitals from Geneva Cathedral (11th c.), Madonna from Saas, Wallis (early 14th c.).

211 "Sallis J.-J. Rigaud": sculptures, furniture, ceiling (15th c.), tapestries from Tournai (c. 1470), Swiss glass (16th c.)
Access to the rooms of the Château of Zizers in the mezzanine, rooms 306–300.

210 "Salle du Conseil d'Etat": carved wooden ceiling (early 18th c.) from the old council chamber of the Hôtel de Ville; furniture, tables (18th c.); Florentine marble table (16th c.).

209 "Salon de Cartigny": carved wooden ceiling (end of 18th c.) from the Château de Cartigny, near Geneva, by the Geneva sculptor Jean Jaquet (1754–1839); furniture, pastel drawing (end of 18th c.).

206/207 "Salle Renaissance": stucco work, articles of marble, bronze and ivory (Italy, France, 14th–16th c); French embroidery (c. 1580).

205 "Salle d'honneur" of the Château of Zizers (Grisons) (c. 1680): musicians' gallery, painted ceiling, doors, furniture, weapons (15th–17th c.).

204 European Weapons and Armour (15th–18th c.): guns, guillotine (1799), fine collection of pistols; windows from Sainte-Pierre (end of 15th c.).

202, 203 Silver from Geneva, the rest of Switzerland and France (18th c.).

201 Contemporary Art: special exhibitions sponsored by AMAN (Association of a Modern Art Museum).

Collection of Antiquities

218 Prehistoric articles: utensils, weapons, handmade articles, jewellery, principally from the Geneva region; especially a bronze helmet (950–750 B.C.) from Fillinges, Savoy.

213–217 Being converted for special exhibitions.

MEZZANINE (Entresol)

300, 301 Special exhibitions.

301, 308 Numismatic collection, Byzantine art.

302 "Salle des étains": pewter from Geneva and other regions of Switzerland (16th–19th c.).

303 "Belle chambre": room from the Château of Zizers, tiled stove.

304 "Chambre peinte": room from the Château of Zizers (Regency style).

306 "Salle Anna Sarasin": coffered ceiling, stove from Winterthur.

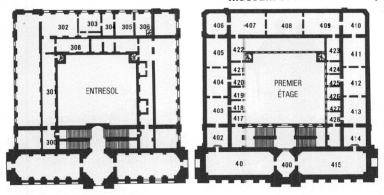

FIRST FLOOR (Premier Étage)

Pictorial Art

Paintings and sculpture including panels by Ferdinand Hodler symbolising the Swiss cantons. A commission on the occasion of the National Exhibition of 1896.

400 Peristyle: special exhibitions.

401 Paintings of the German, Flemish, French and Italian schools. Notable paintings: winged altarpiece by Conrad Witz (b. Rottwell c. 1400–10, d. Basle or Geneva c. 1446), a triptych from Maria Stein Monastery, Upper Rhenish school, portraying the "Miraculous Draught of Fishes"; Juan de Flands (d. 1519): "Beheading of John the Baptist"; Fontainebleau school: "Sabina Poppaea" (c. 1570); Andrea Vaccaro (c. 1598–1670): "Triumph of David". Outstanding sculptures: "The Virgin in Majesty" (Auvergne), (c. 1150–80), "St John the Evangelist" (South Germany or Frankish, c. 1480), "Archbishop Giving Blessing" (Rhineland (?), c. 1460).

402 "Foundation Baszanger": Dutch and Flemish painting (15th–17th c.).

403 Dutch painting (16th–17th c.)

404 French and Italian paintings of the 17th–18th c.: Nicolas Régnier (c. 1590–1667), Mattia Preit (1613–99), Charles le Brur (1619–90) and Jean-Baptiste Oudry (1686–1755).

417, 418 Room with pictures of the Flemish type and Dutch portraits of the 17th c.

419 Dutch masters, painting in the Italian manner. Notable are two paintings by Nicolaes Berchem (1620–83): "The Miraculous Child" and "Abraham Receives Sarah from the hands of Abimelech".

420 French paintings of the 17th c.; noteworthy "The Visitation" by Philippe de Champaigne (1602–74).

421 Italian painting of the first half of the 18th c.

422 Pastels by Jean-Etienne Liotard (1702–89), wooden ceiling by the sculptor Jean-Jaquet, sculptures, furniture (18th c.).

405 First and foremost French portraits of the 18th c. (Nicolas de Largillière, 1656–1746; Maurice-Quentin de La Tour, 1704–88); among them a portrait of Didero by Levitzky, a likeness of Rousseau by La Tour and a bust of Voltaire by Jean-Baptiste Lemoyne (1704–78).

406 Paintings by Jean-Etienne Liotard; furniture of the 18th c.

407 Paintings from Geneva of the second half of the 18th c.: Jean-Pierre Saint-Ours, Pierre-Louis de la Five.

408 Paintings and sculpture from Geneva from the end of the 18th and from the first half of the 19th c.: Jacques-Laurent Agasse (1737–1849), Adam-Wolfgang Töpffer (1766–1847), James Pradier (1790–1852).

409 Paintings from Geneva of the 19th c François Diday (1802–77) and Alexandre Calame (1810–4).

423, 424 Temporary exhibitions of the Cabinet des Dessins.

410 Room entirely devoted to Camile Corot (1736–875).

425–428 Room devoted to the pioneers of modern painting (Centre Bruno Lussato).

425 Works by Sonja Delaunay, Paul Klee (1879–1940), Fernand Léger (1831–1955) and Le Corbusier (1887–1965).

426 Works by Kurt Schwitters (1887–1948).

427 Works by Hans Richter (1902–69). Hans Arp (1887–1966) and Alexancer Rodtschenko (1891–956).

428 Works by Russian Constructionists.

413 Swiss paintings from the beginning of the 20th c.: Giovanni and Augusto Giacometti, Cuno Amiet (1868–1961), Edouard Vallet, Albert Trachsel and Hans Berger.

414 Paintings by Félix Vallotton (1865–1925).

415 Room devoted to sculpture from the end of the 19th c. and of the present day Auguste Rodin (1840–917), August Rodo, Antoine Bourdelle (1861–929), Henri Laurens (1885–1954), Alexander Archipenko (1887–1964), Hans Arp, Albert Giacometti, Max Bill (b. 1908), Henri Presset, Jean Tinguely (b. 1925), Robert Müller (b. 1920), César (b. 1921), Bernhard Luginbühl (b. 1929).

The *Cabinet des Dessins*, with about 10,000 drawings and sketches of various schools, can be visited by appointment.

Jardin Anglais: "Helvetia and Geneva"   *Brunswick Monument*

fine picture gallery. On the lower ground floor Greek and Roman art treasures are displayed, together with Middle Eastern and Eastern Mediterranean antiquities, Greek, Roman and Etruscan pottery and Egyptian funerary art. On the main ground floor is the museum's collection of antiquities, with material from Geneva and the surrounding area ranging in date from the Paleolithic and the Iron Age through Roman and Gallo-Roman times to the Middle Ages. There are also objets d'art of the Gothic and Renaissance periods on display.

*Picture collection

On the first floor the museum's picture collection includes Italian, Flemish and Swabian old masters, works by Flemish, Dutch and French artists of the 16th–18th c. and pictures of the 18th and 19th c. Geneva school.

East of the Old Town

Ecole des Beaux-Arts
*Petit Palais

The Ecole des Beaux-Arts (Art School) behind the Museum to the southwest, houses the collection of graphic art of the Cabinet des Estampes at 5 Promenade du Pin. A little way south is the Petit Palais (2 Terrasse St-Victor), a private museum of modern art.

Russian church

To the east of the Museum of Art and History, beyond the Boulevard Helvétique, stands the Russian Church (1866), with nine gilded domes. Nearby, at 23 rue Lefort, is the Musée des Instruments Anciens de Musique (Museum of Old Musical Instruments) and at 8 rue Munier-Romilly the private Collection Baur (Far Eastern art).

Collection Baur

Muséum d'Histoire Naturelle

Farther east, at 11 Route de Malagnou, the important Musée d'Histoire Naturelle (Natural History Museum) contains informatively displayed collections and a specialised library. Of particular interest are the dioramas of regional fauna on the ground floor and the large fossils and palaeontological and mineralogical collections on the third floor.

Immediately east of the museum, at Route de Malagnou, is a mansion housing the Musée de Horlogerie et de l'Emaillerie (Museum of Watch-making and Enamels).

Musée de
l'Horlogerie et
de l'Emaillerie

In a heavily built-up area below the Natural History Museum to the south-west rises the Immeuble Clarté, the only building of any size in the country designed by the Swiss architect Le Corbusier (along with his cousin P. Jeanneret). The outer walls, mainly of glass, of this block of apartments (1930–32) have no load-bearing function, being suspended from a steel skeleton.

Immeuble Clarté

On the south bank

On the south side of the lake (the Rive Gauche) the Promenade du Lac runs east from the Pont du Mont-Blanc, flanked by the Jardin Anglais (large flower clock, café), with the Monument National (figures of "Helvetia" and "Geneva"), erected in 1869 to commemorate Geneva's entry into the Confederation (1814). From here Quai Gustave-Ador leads north-east, following the shore of the lake (commercial and boating harbour). In the lake are two erratic boulders known as the Pierres du Niton ("Neptune's Stones"), on the larger of which is a Swiss Ordnance Survey reference point (373.6 m/1226 ft a.s l.).

Jardin Anglais

Pierres du Niton

Beside the Jetée des Eaux-Vives, the breakwater enclosing the harbour (beacon), is the Jet d'Eau, a mighty jet of water which soars up to a height of 145 m/476 ft (1360 HP pump).

*Jet d'Eau

Farther along the lakeside road, on the right, are the Parc de la Grange (rose-garden) and the Parc des Eaux-Vives (restaurant), both with beautiful mature trees and flower-beds. Beyond this are the yacht harbour and the Genève-Plage bathing area.

Parc de la
Grange
Parc des
Eaux-Vives

On the north bank

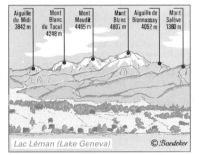

Aiguille du Midi 3842 m / Mont Blanc 4248 m / Mont Maudit 4465 m / Mont Blanc 4807 m / Aiguille de Bionnassay 4052 m / Mont Salève 1380 m

Lac Léman (Lake Geneva) © Baedeker

On the north side of the lake (the Rive Droite) the Quai de Mont-Blanc extends north-east from the bridge, with a view of the Mont-Blanc chain (particularly fine in the late afternoon in clear weather). At the landing stage in front of the Hôtel Beau Rivage the Empress Elizabeth of Austria (b. 1837) was assassinated by an Italian anarchist in 1898.

*Quai de
Mont-Blanc

Beyond this is the imposing Brunswick monument, a mausoleum modelled on the Scaliger tombs in Verona, which was built for Duke Karl II of Brunswick (1804–73), who left his money to Geneva.

Brunswick
Monument

Beyond this again are the modern Grand Casino and the Jetée des Pâquis (breakwater; bathing area, beacon). From here Quai Wilson runs north past the large Palais Wilson in which the League of Nations met from 1925 to 1936, to the beautiful lakeside parks of Mon Repos and La Perle du Lac (Museum of the History of Science, summer only; restaurant).

Grand Casino

Palais Wilson
Mon Repos, La
Perle du Lac

From the Pont du Mont-Blanc Rue du Mont-Blanc goes north-west past the Hôtel des Postes (on right: the main Post Office, with a special philatelic

Rue du Mont-
Blanc

department) to the main station, the Gare de Cornavin (Swiss and French Railways), with underground shopping passages and Geneva's tourist office.

Quartier Les Grottes | Beyond the railway line, to the west, is the Quartier Les Grottes, a model example of sympathetic restoration. Extensive and innovative renovation is planned with grants available in order to help preserve the character of the quarter and to allow the existing residents to remain.

Temple de Saint-Gervais | South of the station, extending towards the lake, is the old watchmaking quarter of Saint-Gervais, in the midst of which is the Temple of Saint-Gervais; the present church (Protestant) dates from the 15th c. (tower 1435).

Institut et Musée Voltaire | To the west of Saint-Gervais, in the district of Les Délices, we find the little property of the same name where Voltaire lived from 1755 to 1765, when he moved to Ferney, across the frontier in France. The mansion (1730–35, enlarged by Voltaire), set in a small park, is now occupied by the Institut et Musée Voltaire, with relics and mementoes of Voltaire.

International Organisations Quarter

International Organisations based in Geneva

A selection in alphabetical order: names and abbreviations in French and English

Accord Général sur les Tarifs Douaniers et le Commerce
General Agreement on Tariffs and Trade (GATT)

Alliance Internationale du Tourisme
International Touring Alliance (ITA)

Alliance Réformée Mondiale (ARM)
World Alliance of Reformed Churches

Alliance Universelle des Unions Chrétiennes de Jeunes Gens
World Alliance of Young Men's Christian Associations

Alliance Universelle des Unions Chrétiennes Féminines
World Alliance of Young Women's Christian Associations

Association Européenne de Libre-Echange (AELE)
European Free Trade Association (EFTA)

Bureau Internationale d'Education (BIE)
International Bureau of Education (IBE)

Bureaux Internationaux Réunis pour la Protection de la Propriété Intellectuelle (BIRPI)
United International Bureaux for the Protection of Intellectual Property

Centre Européen de la Culture (CEC)
European Cultural Centre (ECC)

Comité Intergouvernmental pour les Migrations Européenes (CIME)
International Committee for European Migration (ICEM)

Comité International de la Croix-Rouge (CICR)
International Committee of the Red Cross (ICRC)

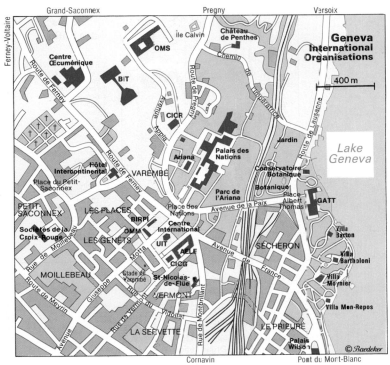

Geneva International Organisations

Commission Économique pour l'Europe
Economic Commission for Europe

Conférence des Nations Unies sur le Commerce et le Développement
United Nations Conference on Trade and Development (UNCTAD)

Conseil Œcuménique des Eglises (COE)
World Council of Churches (WCC)

Fédération Luthérienne Mondiale (FLM)
Lutheran World Federation (LWF)

Haut Commissariat pour les Réfugiés
High Commissariate for Refugees

Ligue des Sociétés de la Croix-Rouge
League of Red Cross Societies

Organisations des Nations Unies (ONU)
United Nations (UN)
(European headquarters: main headquartes in New York)

Organisation Européenne pour la Recherche Nucléaire (CERN = Centre
Européen pour la Recherche Nucléaire)
European Organisation for Nuclear Research

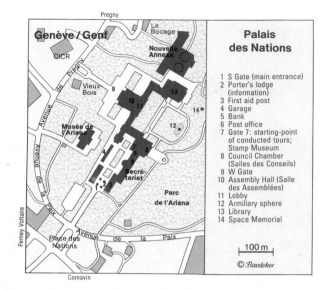

Palais des Nations

1 S Gate (main entrance)
2 Porter's lodge (information)
3 First aid post
4 Garage
5 Bank
6 Post office
7 Gate 7: starting-point of conducted tours; Stamp Museum
8 Council Chamber (Salles des Conseils)
9 W Gate
10 Assembly Hall (Salle des Assemblées)
11 Lobby
12 Armillary sphere
13 Library
14 Space Memorial

100 m

© *Baedeker*

Organisation Internationale du Travail (OIT)
International Labour Organisation (ILO)
Executive agency:
Bureau International du Travail (BIT)
International Labour Office

Organisation Météorologique Mondiale (OMM)
World Meteorological Organisation (WMO)

Organisation Mondiale de la Santé (OMS)
World Health Organisation (WHO)

Union Européenne de Radiodiffusion (UER)
European Broadcasting Union (EBU)
Administrative headquarters of EUROVISION
(technical services in Brussels)

Union Internationale des Télécommunications (UIT)
International Telecommunications Union (ITU)

Union Internationale des Transports Routiers
International Road Transport Union

Union Interparlementaire (UIP)
Inter-Parliamentary Union (IPU)

Around the Place des Nations

The Place des Nations, 2 km/1 mile north of the Pont du Mont-Blanc, is a busy traffic intersection around which are the headquarters of many international organisations.

Varembé, International Organisations

South of the square in the district of Varembé are a series of modern buildings occupied by a variety of important institutions. Between the Chemin des Colombettes and the Avenue Guiseppe-Motta are the United

Palais des Nations: seat of the United Nations

International Bureaux for the Protection of Intellectual Property (BIRPI: by
P. Braillart, 1962) and the World Meteorological Organisation (WMO/
OMM)): by E. Martin, 1956). Between Avenue Guiseppe-Motta and Rue de
Vermont is the International Telecommunications Union (ITU/UIT), a six-
sided tower block by Bordigoni (1958). At the corner of Rue Varembé and
Rue de Montbrillant is the Centre International, housing numerous in-
ternational associations; and closely adjoining are the European Free
Trade Association (EFTA: by Grand, Praplan and Fischer, 1969), with a
beautiful inner courtyard, and the new International Conference Centre and
Press House (CIGC: by A. and F. Gaillard and A. Camenzind, 1971).
Also in this area is a modern Roman Catholic church, Saint-Nicolas-de-Flüe
(by Bouvier and V. and J. Malnati, 1967), which was visited by Pope Paul VI
in 1969.

*Palais des Nations

North-east of the Place des Nations, in a large area of parkland sloping
down towards the lake, stands the Palais des Nations a monumental
complex of buildings clad in light-coloured marble.

This area, which now enjoys extraterritorial status with full judicial, fiscal
and postal rights, was formerly part of the Parc de l'Ariana, which was
bequeathed to Geneva by P. G. Revilliod in 1890. In 1929 the town handed
over the area, 200,000 sq. m/239,200 sq. yards in extent, to the League of
Nations, which had held an architectural competition in 1927–28 for the
design of new headquarters.

Parc de l'Ariana

The most modern and progressive designs were those put forward by Le
Corbusier and P. Jeanneret and by H. Meyer and K. Wittwer, but these were
rejected and the choice fell instead on the rather ponderous designs sub-
mitted by an international group of architects – C. Broggi (Italy), F. Flegen-
heimer (Switzerland), C. Lefèvre and H. P. Nénot (France) and J. Vago

History of the
building

(Hungary). The buildings were erected between 1929 and 1937, and the League of Nations (hitherto housed in the Palais Wilson) was able in 1936 to transfer its headquarters to the new Palais des Nations, which was formally inaugurated in 1938 under the presidency of the Aga Khan. In 1940 the League of Nations ceased to operate, since after the exclusion of the Soviet Union it was no longer an effective international instrument, and it was dissolved in 1946 to give place to the United Nations Organisation (UNO/ONU), founded at San Francisco on 24 October 1945. The United Nations Organisation (at present with 159 members) has its main headquarters in New York but has established its European headquarters in the Palais des Nations. Conducted tours: Entrance 7.

The extensive complex of buildings (25,000 sq. m/29,900 sq. yards), the second largest in Europe (after the Palace of Versailles), consists of three main sections. In the middle is the main range of buildings, with a wing at each end enclosing a terrace courtyard facing the lake; in this section are the Assembly Hall, Council Chamber, conference rooms and library. To the south is the Secretariat building, and to the north a higher block of offices completed in 1972, with a front wing (conference rooms) topped by two large polygonal domes.

The Palais des Nations has a total of some 30 conference rooms and 1100 office rooms, its own printing office with 36 polycopiers and 6 offset machines, a restaurant, a snack bar and a number of refreshment bars. The interior is comfortable and equipped with the most modern technical services. The large assembly halls have simultaneous interpretation facilities, enabling speeches to be translated into and out of the five official languages of the United Nations (English, French, Spanish, Russian and Chinese). The lavish decoration of the various halls and rooms was donated by different countries. The following are of particular interest:

Salle des Assemblées

Assembly Hall (Salle des Assemblées), a square chamber with seating for over 2000, the largest in the Palais, used for meetings of the United Nations and its associated organisations. The curtains, of raw silk, were a gift from India. It is preceded by the Salle des Pas Perdus (Lobby), with a view of the Alps from the east side. The floor is of Finnish granite, and the walls are faced with Swedish marble. The two heavily gilded bronze doors at the ends, brought back from Italy by Napoleon, were presented to the League of Nations by Clemenceau.

Salle des Conseils

Council Chamber (Salle des Conseils), with seating for 500. The wall and ceiling painting (by J. M. Sert, 1934–36) was a gift from Spain. Carried out in sepia on a gold ground, it depicts four related themes – technical, social and medical progress and, as a hope for the future, the abolition of war. In the middle (opposite the window side) is "Victors and Vanquished", and on the ceiling "Solidarity of the Five Continents". In this chamber was held the 1955 Four-Power Conference on the reunification of Germany (Eisenhower, Bulganin, Eden, Faure).

In the ante-chamber are three bas-reliefs by Eric Gill inspired by Michaelangelo.

Other rooms

Room III: birch and pearwood panelling; "Ship on a Calm Sea", a picture by the Genevese painter Barraud. Room V: decoration by an English artist, W. Allom; architectural motifs on the doors. Room VI: decoration presented by Switzerland (frescoes by K. Hügin; events from Swiss history on the insides of the doors). Room VII: decoration by Porteneuve. Room VIII: clad with wood inlay by a Dane, Petersen. Room IX: Panelled with beautifully grained stinkwood from South Africa. Room X: presented by Latvia (black intarsia oak floor). Room XI: by Mutters (Holland), with leather wall covering. Room XII: presented by Italy (used for showing films). Room XIV: by M. Simon.

Library

The library, donated by John D. Rockefeller Jr, was founded in 1920, and now possesses some 750,000 volumes and numerous manuscripts and

Double space-monument outside the Palais de Nations

letters from outstanding internat onal figures. The stamp museum cis-plays rare and interesting United Nations issues.

Between the wings of the main rar ge of buildings is the Cour d'Honneur, a spacious terrace which merges into the park, with a magnificent view of the lake and the Alps. In the middle is a bronze armillary sphere with gilded signs of the Zodiac, by the American sculptor Paul Manship, presented by the Woodrow Wilson Foundation n 1939.

Cour d'Honneur

On a marble terrace near the Library wing is a Space Memorial symbolising the conquest of space. The 26 m/85 ft high sculpture (architect Alexannder N. Kolchin, sculptor Jurij G. Neroda) was presented by the Soviet Unior in 1971.

Space Memorial

Around the Palais des Nat ons

The Château de Penthes, north o³ the Palais des Nations (18 Chemin de l'Impératrice), houses the Musée des Régiments Suisses au Services Etran-ger (Museum of Swiss Regiments in Foreign Service).

Château de Penthes

Above the Palais des Nations, to the west, stands the Ariana, a building in Italian Renaissance style erected in 1877–84 for the Geneva writer and philanthropist P. G. Revill od (1817–90). With a sumptuously appointed interior, it now houses the International Academy of Ceramics and a rich collection of ceramics and porcela n begun by Revilliod (temporarily closed for refurbishment).

*Ariana

To the south-east, lying between the Route de Lausanne and the Geneva-Lausanne railway line and between the Avenue de la Paix to the south and the Chemin de l'Impératrice to the north lies the Jardin Botanique a botanic garden established in 1902, with glasshouses (exotic plants, etc. , a

Jardin Botanique

fine Alpine garden, a small animal enclosure (fallow deer, llamas, peacocks, cranes, parakeets) and a refreshment pavilion (summer only).

Conservatoire Botanique

On the east side of the Route de Lausanne is the Conservatoire Botanique, with an excellent specialised library and famous herbaria (in the garden pavilion), new greenhouses and an aviary.

Villa Vieux-Bois

From the Place des Nations the broad Avenue de la Paix extends north in a wide curve, passing the Ariana on the right and the Soviet embassy on the left. Opposite the west entrance to the Palais des Nations is the attractive villa, Vieux-Bois, which houses the Geneva Hotel School restaurant.

Comité International de la Croix-Rouge

On higher ground to the north-west is the imposing headquarters of the International Committee of the Red Cross (Comité International de la Croix-Rouge). The International Red Cross, founded in 1864 on the initiative of Henri Dunant (1828–1910) and managed exclusively by Swiss citizens, is dedicated to pursuing humanitarian aims on the international level (e.g. by the register of prisoners of war and missing persons which it has maintained since 1916). The various national organisations (Red Cross, Red Crescent, Red Lion, Red Sun) belong to the League of Red Cross societies, which is also based in Geneva.
The Musée de la Croix-Rouge, opened in November 1988, has information on the history of the organisation.

Centre Œcumenique

A little way along the old road to Ferney is the Centre Œcumenique (Ecumenical Centre), Headquarters of the World Council of Churches, the Lutheran World Federation, the Reformed World Federation and other non-Catholic associations.
The World Council of Churches, first discussed at the Edinburgh World Missionary Conference in 1910 and founded in its present form at Amsterdam in 1948, is composed of more than 220 Protestant, Orthodox, Old Catholic and Anglican churches and maintains contacts with other Christian denominations, (in particular with the Roman Catholic Church; Papal visits 1969 by Pope Paul VI, 1984 by John-Paul II).

World Health Organisation

North-west of the Ecumenical Centre (1 km/½ mile from the Palais des Nations) is the headquarters of the World Health Organisation (Organisation Mondiale de la Santé; WHO/OMS: 1962–66, by J. Tschumi, P. Bonnard, H. Curchid and P. Cotty), also known as the Palais de la Santé.
The World Health Organisation, founded in 1948, succeeded the International Office of Public Health, established in Paris in 1907. It is concerned with health care on an international basis, epidemic control, the training of doctors and other health care personnel, etc., and is active in the field of medical research. Its Geneva headquarters and its six regional offices on Copenhagen, Alexandria, Brazzaville, Manila, New Delhi and Washington have a total staff of almost 5000.
The main building, a rectangular eight-storey block 150 m/492 ft long built of prefabricated elements, rests on 22 concrete piles and contains 550 rooms. In front of it is a lower structure containing the main assembly hall, surrounded by gardens. The building contains many works of art and other features presented by member nations, notably a large wall decoration (7 m/23 ft square) presented by Brazil.

International Labour Office

To the south of the World Health Organisation, on a previously undeveloped site at Le Grand Morillon rises the new headquarters of the International Labour Office (Bureau International du Travail ILO/BIT: 1969–73)
Designed by Beaudouin, Camenzind and Nervi, this has an 11-storey main building 190 m/623 ft long and 60 m/197 ft high on a biconcave ground plan borne on two supporting blocks (in the north one various services, in the south one conference rooms and the library). The outer walls (4000 windows) are of aluminium and glass, on a framework of steel and concrete.

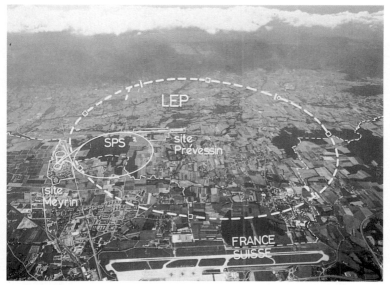

European atomic research centre CERN

The building has some 2500 telephone extensions, facilities for simultaneous interpretation, 23 passenger and 7 goods lifts, a system for the transmission of documents within the office and a four-storey underground garage for 1450 cars.

Surroundings

See entry

To the west of the town, at the "Jonction", the River Arve flows into the Rhône, its turbid yellowish water mingling with the clear greenish-blue water of the larger river. Beyond the Arve is the Bois de la Bâtie (woodland, meadows, animal enclosure; view of town).

To the south-east of this is an artificial ice-rink, the Patinoire des Vernets (partly roofed over; seating for 10,000). The suburb of Carouge, still farther south-east was incorporated in the city in 1816, with the large goods station and bonded warehouses of La Praille. Carouge, originally founded by Savoy as a rival to Geneva, has some attractive squares and old houses. 3 km/2 miles west of the city is the last of Geneva's eight bridges over the Rhône, the Pont Butin (built 1916–27, widened to eight lanes in 1970), spanning the valley at a point where it is 50 m/164 ft deep.

5 km/3 miles north-west of Geneva is Cointrin International Airport.

To the north-east, in the suburb of Grand-Saconneux, the New Exhibition and Congress Centre was opened in 1981. The Nouveau Palais des Expositions et des Congrès, abbreviated to "Palexpo", has 70,500 sq. m/84,318 sq. yards of floor space.

About 2 km/1 mile beyond this is the frontier town of Meyrin, a large residential suburb with an Alpine garden. Here, too, is the nuclear research

**Lake Geneva
Bois de la Bâtie

Carouge

*Cointrin airport
New Exhibition and Congress Centre ("Palexpo")

Meyrin, CERN

Schloss Coppet: once meeting-place of artists and poets

facility CERN (Conseil Européen pour la Recherche Nucléaire: partly on French territory), with a 600 MeV synchro-cyclotron, a 28 GeV proton synchroton, storage rings and a super proton synchroton (7 km/4 miles long ring tunnel).

4 km/2 miles west of the town, in a bend of the Rhône, is the residential development of Le Lignon, a striking example of modern architecture housing a population of 15,000.

Ferney-Voltaire   7 km/4 miles north-west, in French territory (bus services, on a road which passes under the runways of Cointrin airport in a tunnel), is Ferney-Voltaire (pop. 2000), once a potters' town. To the west of the little town is the château which Voltaire acquired in 1758 and later enlarged, where he held court until shortly before his death (mementoes). Above the former chapel is the inscription "Deo erexit Voltaire". In front of the Town Hall is a statue of Voltaire by Lambert.

Versoix   9 km/6 miles north (reached by rail or boat) is Versoix, an attractive little place on the west side of the Petit Lac, near the border between the cantons of Geneva and Vaud, with a beautiful lakeside promenade. The third Aga Khan, Head of the Ismaili sect, died here in his property of Le Barakat in 1957 (b. Karachi 1877; buried in Egypt). Near this house is the Château Rouge (the property of an Arab ruler).

Genthod   In Genthod, just south of Versoix (fish restaurant on lake), are a number of fine old 18th c. houses, including the Maison Ami-Lullin, built in 1723–30 by F. Blondel, which was occupied by the scientist H. B. Saussure. In the Maison de la Rive (1730), above the railway line, Goethe stayed in 1779 with the philosopher and naturalist Charles Bonnet (1720–93).

Coppet   14 km/9 miles north (reached by rail or boat), in the canton of Vaud, is Coppet, a little town on the west shore of the lake, founded in the 14th c., with old arcaded houses and a 15th c. Gothic church. Above the town, in an extensive park, stands a large château on a horseshoe plan, built in 1767–71 by G. de Smethe on the site of an earlier 13th c. castle and purchased in 1784 by the Geneva banker Jacques Necker (1732–1804), later French Finance Minister. In the early 19th c. Necker's daughter Anne-Loise-Germaine, who became the Baronne de Staël-Holstein, better known as the free-thinking Mme de Staël (1766–1817), made the château a meeting-place of the leading social and political personalities of the day. Necker and Mme de Staël are buried in the park, in a walled area west of the château (visitors not admitted). The château is open to the public from March to October.

4 km/2 miles north, away from the lake, is the pretty village of Céligny, in a little enclave belonging to Geneva.   Céligny

Cologny (alt. 450 m/1476 ft) 14 km/9 miles north-east (No. 9 bus or boat) on the hillside above the east shore of the Petit Lac, has a fine 17th c. country house and a number of modern villas. There is a magnificent view across the lake to the Palais des Nations and the Jura, particularly from the terrace between the Lion d'Or restaurant and the church and from the "Byron Stone" on the Chemin de Ruth. Byron stayed in the Villa Diodati in 1816 and met Shelley, then also living in Cologny.   Cologny
1.8 km/1 mile south at Chêne-Bougeries, is the modern residential development of La Gradelle, built since 1963.

6.5 km/4 miles north-east, on the lake (No. 9 bus or boat), is Bellerive, with the 17th c. Manoir de Bonvent (near the landing-stage) and a 17th c. château.   Bellerive

14 km/9 miles north-east, on the lake (No. 9 bus or boat), is Hermance, a pretty little place founded in 1245 close to the French frontier. 12th c. fortifications, château, 15th and 16th c. houses; Stone Age tombs.   Hermance

*Mont Salève

A good road and cableway ascend to Mont Salève, a long limestone ridge south of Geneva, in French territory (good rock-climbing): 16 km/10 miles to Monnetier, round trip 69 km/43 miles, maximum gradient 6%.
Leave Geneva by the Route de Florissant and road 42, which runs south-east via the suburb of Villette. 6 km/4 miles: Veyrier (alt. 422 m/1385 ft) on the French frontier (passport and customs control).   Veyrier
Straight ahead is the lower station of a cableway 1180 m/3872 ft long which runs up in 6 minutes to a height of 1143 m/3750 ft on Mont Salève. Alternatively turn left beyond Veyrier into road 206 and in 3.5 km/2 miles right into 206A. 7 km/4 miles: Mornex (572 m/1877 ft, a summer holiday resort on the southern slopes of the Petit Salève. Almost opposite the Protestant church is a house in which Richard Wagner lived in 1856.   Mornex

The road continues up the beautiful valley of the Viaison. 3 km/2 miles: Monnetier (696 m/2284 ft), a health resort on a cleft between the Petit and Grand Salève, from which it is a half-hour climb to the summit of the Petit-Salève (900 m/2953 ft: beautiful views).   Monnetier

4.5 km/3 miles above Monnetier, to the right, is the upper station of the cableway (1143 m/3750 ft; restaurant), with a magnificent panorama of Geneva, the lake and the Jura.   Télépherique
1.5 km/1 mile farther on a road branches off on the right to the Treize-Arbres inn (1184 m/3885 ft). Above the inn (1212 m/3977 ft; orientation table) there is a magnificent view of the Mont Blanc chain, Lake Geneva and the Jura. A footpath leads up (30 minutes) to the Crêt de Grange-Tournier (1308 m/4292ft), the highest point on the Grand Salève.   *Grand Salève

The road continues along the slopes of the Grand Salève. 5 km/3 miles: Col de la Croisette (1176 m/3858 ft; restaurant), with roads running down to

Lake Geneva

Grand Piton	Collonges on the right and La Muraz on the left. Then past the Grand Piton (1380 m/4528 ft), the highest point in the Salève range, and then downhill,
Cruseilles	with many bends. 16 km/10 miles: Cruseilles (781 m/2562 ft), on the road from Annecy to Geneva (N 201); then north on this road over the little pass
St-Julien	of Mont Sion (785 m/2576 ft) and through Le Châble and Saint-Julien to the Swiss frontier, 26 km/16 miles to Geneva.

*The Voirons

There are two alternative routes (each 37 km/23 miles) to this long ridge in French territory east of Geneva making an attractive round trip of 74 km/46 miles.

Leave Geneva on the Chamonix road. 7 km/4 miles: Annemasse (alt. 436 m/1431 ft). From here on N 507 to Bonne-sur-Menoge and Pont-de-Fillinges (10.5 km/7 miles), from which a road to the left climbs (fine views) via Boëge

Col de Saxel — to the Col de Saxel (12.5 km/8 miles: 945 m/3101 ft); then a road on the left which winds its way uphill, passing through wooded country. 7 km/4 miles: Grand Chalet (1400 m/4593 ft), sanatorium. From here it is a 30 minutes'

*Voirons — climb to the Calvaire or Grand Signal, on the summit of the Voirons (1486 m/4876 ft), with magnificent views (Savoy Alps, Jura, etc.).

8 km/5 miles: Bons (548 m/1798 ft), on the road from Thonon (N 203); then left along this road via Langin and Saint-Cergues to Annemasse (15 km/9 miles). 7 km/4 miles to Geneva.

Lake Geneva   B2

Within Switzerland and France
Cantons: Vaud (VD), Geneva (GE) and Valais (VS)

*Situation and general — Lake Geneva (in French Lac Léman or Lac de Genève), the largest of the lakes in the Alps, lies between the Savoy Alps, the Swiss Jura and the Vaud

Rolle Castle on Lake Geneva

Alps at a mean height of 371 m/1217 ft above sea level. Of its total area of 581 sq. km/224 sq. miles 60% falls within Switzerland and 40% within France. Its maximum depth is about 310 m/1017 ft. The lake, which the River Rhône enters at one end and leaves at the other, extends in a flat arc 72 km/45 miles long from east to west, with a maximum width of 14 km/9 miles. While the French southern shore of the lake (department of Haute-Savoie) is only thinly populated, with Evian and Thonon as its largest towns, the sunny northern shore in the canton of Vaud, with the vine-growing areas of Lavaux and La Côte, is the Swiss equivalent of the Riviera, a popular holiday and tourist region.

Regular steamer services between places on the lake, run by the Compagnie Genérale de Navigation sur le Lac Léman (CGN: head office Lausanne-Ouchy, branch office in Geneva at Le Bateau, Jardin Anglais); many round trips and cruises (evening trips with dancing on board); shuttle services and round trips in port and on the Petit Lac by the "Mouettes Genevoises "; short round trips on the motor-launches "Elma" and "Star of Geneva". A particular attraction is "Neptune", the last cargo-carrying sailing vessel on the lake, which can be chartered. Built in 1904 (length 24 m/78 ft, width 8.5 m/28 ft, weight 20 tonnes) it was used to transport stone blocks from Meillerie and gravel from Bouveret/Vieux Rhône to Geneva until 1968. Since 1976 it has been used for excursions.

Boat services

The north bank of the lake

For centuries the beauty of the northern shores of Lake Geneva has been lauded (e.g. by Byron, Voltaire and Rousseau), the luxuriantly fertile slopes rising gently above the lake, the picturesque towns and old castles, the magnificent backdrop of the Savoy and Valais Alps to the south and east. The climate has a southern mildness in which the vine flourishes.

The road along the shore of the lake from Geneva runs through Genthod (restaurant on lake) and the little town of Versoix, enters the canton of Vaud (8 km/5 miles) and comes to Coppet (see Geneva).

See entry.

Nyon

It then continues via the interesting little town of Nyon and Prangins (château of 1748) to reach the stretch of land along the lake known as La Côte,the fertile slopes descending from the Vaudois plateau, with flourishing vineyards, fruit orchards and farming land: a gentle prosperous landscape with many old castles and country houses.

La Côte

Rolle (alt. 376 m/1234 ft: pop. 3600) is a long straggling little town, an important wine-trading area, with a 13th c. castle (four towers) and old burghers' and vintners' houses lining the main street. On a small island in the harbour is an obelisk commemorating General de la Harpe (1754–1838), who played a part in securing the separation of Vaud from the canton of Berne in 1798. The local speciality is "petits pains au sucre" (sugar rolls).

Rolle

The road continues to Allaman (425 m/1394 ft): 16th c. castle with two towers) and St-Prex (373 m/1224 ft: pop. 2000), an old market town with a church which first appears in the records in 885. Cobbled streets; old street signs; Tour de l'Horloge (Clock Tower), the only gate-tower with loopholes in the canton of Vaud. Glassworks; beautiful lakeside gardens and villas.

St-Prex

Morges (381 m/1250 ft: pop. 12,700), on a site once occupied by a large village of pile-dwellings, is a town of fishermen, with the headquarters of the World Wildlife Fund. It was once the home of Paderevski and Stravinsky. There are handsome 18th c. burghers' houses, a church (1776) and 16th–17th c. Town Hall. In Blanchenay, an old patrician house which once

Morges

The "Neptune", a sailing-freighter   *Morges Castle*

belonged to the engraver Alexis Forel, is the Musée du Vieux Morges (furniture, sculpture, and pictures of the Renaissance and Gothic periods). The castle with its four round corner towers, typical of the "carré savoyard" style, (13th c.; alterations in 16th and 17th c.; restored 1948), today it houses the Vaudois arsenal containing a historical weapons collection and 10,000 lead soldiers.

L'Isle

From Morges an excursion can be made (10 km/6 miles) to L'Isle (666 m/2185 ft), with the little late 17th c. château of Chandieu, set in parkland. A visit to the Tine gorge on the southern slopes of La Sarraz is worthwhile.

* Vufflens-le-
Château

Near here are the châteaux of Chardonney (18th c.) and Vufflens-le-Château (14th–15th c.). The latter, of North Italian design, was built by Heinrich von Colombier (1395–1430) with a large cemetery and four towers which are characteristic of Savoy. It is privately owned and not open to the public.

St-Sulpice

The road continues through the select residential suburb of St-Sulpice (Romanesque conventual church, 12th c.) to enter Lausanne, capital of the canton of Vaud.

Lausanne

See entry.

* Corniche de
Lavaux

To the east of Lausanne is one of the most beautiful parts of Switzerland, with many features of interest. Between Lutry (380 m/1247 ft) and Vevey the road runs past the Monts de Lavaux, the slopes of which are entirely covered with vineyards. There is a magnificent stretch of road on the Corniche de Lavaux (Corniche Vaudoise), running high above the lake through the vineyards and affording views of the mighty peaks around the upper end of the lake. The road runs via Grandvaux (565 m/1845 ft) and the wine-growing villages of Riex (450 m/1476 ft) and Epesses to a superb viewpoint, the Signal de Chexbres (655 m/2149 ft), and the health resort of

* Signal de
Chexbres
Chardonne,
Corsier

Chexbres (559 m/1834 ft; pop. 1700) to the vine-growing village of Corsier (445 m/1460 ft; pop. 3030), which has a fine 12th c. church with a Romanesque tower, the device of the House of Savoy and old bells (1427, 1523). Charlie Chaplin (Sir Charles Spencer Chaplin, 1889–1977) is buried here.

From Lutry the lakeside road continues via Villette to Cully (380 m/1247 ft), a vine-growing village with picturesque old streets. Near the landing-stage is a monument to Major Davel, a native of the village, who made an unsuccessful attempt (1723) to free Vaud from Bernese rule.

Cully

The main road continues past the famous Dézaley vineyards to Rivaz, the castle of Glérolles (12th c., rebuilt in the Gothic period).

Rivaz

It continues past the vine-growing village of St-Saphorin (376 m/1234 ft: pop. 300), with beautiful old houses and a 16th c. church. This was originally a country seat of the bishops of Lausanne. In a house of 1705 opposite the church is the restaurant A l'Onde (old inn sign, 1750). The "traffic regulations for coaches" written on a "Pierre à sabot" (1812) in the Place du Peuplier make interesting reading.

St-Saphorin

See entry.

Vevey

See entry.

Montreux

The road then traverses the celebrated resorts of Vevey and Montreux and comes to Villeneuve (378 m/1240 ft; pop. 4500), a little harbour town at the end of the lake which was founded in the 13th c. on the site of earlier Celtic and Roman settlements. The triple-naved Romanesque parish church St-Paul) is of 12th c. origin.

Villeneuve

The south bank of the lake

Leave Geneva on road 37, which skirts the Parc des Eaux-Vives and passes below the hill of Cologny to Vésenaz, from which the main road to Thonon continues in long straight stretches through attractive rolling country, with the Yvoire peninsula to the left.

Beyond Corsier (a former Roman settlement), to the left of the road, the Swiss-French frontier is crossed (Swiss passport control). Then on N 5 through a customs-free zone to Douvaine (alt. 429 m/1408 ft: French frontier control).

Swiss-French frontier

The road continues below the vine-clad Mont de Boisy (735 m/2412 ft; on right) and in 5 km/3 miles reaches Sciez (408 m/1339 ft), where the lakeside road via Yvoire comes in on the left. Beyond Jussy, on a hill to the right of the road, is the village of Les Allinges, with two ruined castles and a pilgrimage chapel (beautiful view).

Les Allinges

10 km/6 miles beyond Sciez is Thonon-les-Bains (427 m/1401 ft; pop. 22,000), beautifully situated on the slopes above the lake (carbonated springs). Funicular down to the pretty harbour area and the fishing village of Rives.

Thonon-les-Bains

Beyond Thonon N 5 cuts across the delta of the Dranse. Interesting detour (2.5 km/2 miles) to the 15th c. castle of Ripaille, on the lake, where Duke Amadeus VIII of Savoy lived as a hermit before his election as Pope (Felix V, 1439–49).

Ripaille castle

2.5 km/2 miles beyond Thonon on N 5 is Vongy, where the road from Ripaille joins the main road which then crosses the Dranse and continues to Amphion, on the shores of the lake.

6.5 km/4 miles from Vongy is Evian-les-Bains (374 m/1227 ft; pop. 6000), a fashionable resort in a beautiful situation on the shores of the lake (alkaline thermal springs). On the broad Quai Baron-de-Blonay are the spa establishment and the Casino (gaming). From here a funicular ascends to a terrace above the lake, on which are the Pump room and the large hotels.

Evian-les-Bains

From Evian to St-Gingolph the road keeps close to the lake. It traverses Grande-Rive and Petite-Rive, on the outskirts of Evian, and at the Château de Blonay (16th c.) passes under the defensive walls. The hills alongside

Château de Blonay

Dent d'Oche | the lake now become steeper and higher; to the right is the Dent d'Oche (2225 m/7300 ft: from Evian by road to Bernex, 14 km/9 miles, then 4½ hours' climb with guide).

Meillerie | The road then comes to Meillerie (386 m/1266 ft), a picturesque fishing village in a magnificent situation, with large limestone quarries.
Beyond this , on the right, are the steep slopes of Mont Chalon (1058 m/3471 ft); to the left is a superb view across the Lake to Vevey and Montreux, with the villages and villas on the slopes above, and of the peaks of the Vaudois Alps (Pléiades, Dent de Jaman, Rochers de Naye); to the right, on the shores of the lake, is Chillon castle (see Montreux).

St-Gingolph | At Le Locum is the French frontier control. The road now crosses a customs-free zone at the foot of the Pic de Blanchard (1472 m/4830 ft) and comes to St-Gingolph (391 m/1283 ft), a picturesque little town straddling the River Morge, here flowing through a deep gorge, which marks the French-Swiss frontier (Swiss passport and customs control).

*Grammont

Bouveret | Then on road 37 beneath the steep slopes of Le Grammont (2178 m/7146 ft; wide views; 5-5½ hours from St-Gingolph, with guide). 4 km/2 miles from St-Gingolph is Bouveret (394 m/1293 ft), an attractively situated village near the inflow of the Rhône, which creates a wave effect (the "bataillère") reaching far out into the lake.
The road (SP Martigny) now leaves the lake and runs up the broad Rhône valley, keeping close to the foot of the hills. To the left of the road is Port-Valais, with the Hôtel de la Tour, a former 16th c. castle.
After passing through Les Evouettes the road comes to Porte-du Secx, a narrow passage (formerly fortified) between the rock face and the river where a road branches off on the left to Villeneuve (8 km/5 miles) and Montreux (see entry). The main road then continues to the large village of Vouvry (384 m/1260 ft, with a power station, and Martigny (see entry).

Glarus E1

Canton: Glarus (GL)

Situation | To the south of the picturesque Walensee the little canton of Glarus, occupies the basin of the River Linth, one of the most beautiful transverse valleys in the Alps, with the ridge of Glärnisch (2332 m/7651 ft) rearing above it on the west and the massive bulk of Tödi (3614 m/11,858 ft) closing its southern end. Surrounded on three sides by mountains, the canton is linked with the neighbouring canton of Uri by a road which runs south-west from Linthal over the Klausen pass.

General | The 37,000 inhabitants of the canton (area 685 sq. km/264 sq. miles), the land of St Fridolin, who appears on Glarus's coat of arms, are an independent-minded race, formed by this rugged mountain world. Industry (in particularly the cotton industry; spinning, weaving, coloured prints) established itself here at an early stage, using the water-power provided by the Linth. The main valley is served by a branch railway line from Rapperswil to Glarus and Linthal, connecting with the main line from Zurich to Chur at Ziegelbrücke. From Linthal there is a cableway to the traffic-free resort of Braunwald, and there is a bus service from Schwanden to Elm in the Sernf valley.

Specialities | Local culinary specialities are Schabzieger, a herb cheese, and Glarner Pasteten (fruit tarts).

History | From 1288 Glarus was under Habsburg jurisdiction, and after repeated threats to its independence became the sixth canton to join the Confeder-

In the Linth valley   *Renaissance doorway of the Freuler Palace*

ation. Since 1387 the cantonal meeting (Landesgemeinde) has been held every year in the Zaunplatz in Glarus on the first Sunday in May. In 1388 the men of Glarus finally shook off the Habsburg yoke by their victory in the Battle of Näfels. During the Reformation the canton was divided into two cantons, one Protestant and the other Catholic, but the two halves were reunited under the 1836 constitution.

Up the Linth valley

From the broad mouth of the valley at Ziegelbrücke (alt. 428 m/1404 ft) the road runs south to Linthal (alt. 651 m/2136 ft; 28 km/17 miles) and from there over the Klausen pass to Altdorf in the canton of Uri.

From Niederurnen (432 m/1417 ft; pop. 3500) there is a footpath up the Rebburg to the Schlössli (Burg Oberwindegg), with fine views of the Linth plain and the Walensee. The path then continues to Oberurnen (432 m/ 1417 ft) with a view of the Glarus Alps.

Niederurnen, Schlössli

In Näfels (440 m/1444 ft; pop. 3700) is the finest building in the canton, the Freulerpalast with a magnificent Renaissance doorway and Early Baroque interior. Built by Colonel Kaspar Freuler, commander of the Swiss guard in France (who was ennobled by Louis XIII), it has been occupied by the Cantonal Museum since 1942 and contains interesting collections (documents from Glarus's textile printing industry) and special exhibitions. The Roman Catholic parish church St Fridolin and Hilarius (1778–1781) is modelled on the parish church at Schwyz. The adjoining chapel commemorates the soldiers who died in the Battle of Näfels in 1388 against the Austrians. There is an interesting 17th c. Capuchin monastery Maria-Burg.

Näfels
*Freulerpalast

From here a steep road climbs to a charming little lake, the Obersee (989 m/3245 ft).

Obersee

Glarus

Freuler Palace, cantonal museum of Glarus

Mollis, Obstalden, Filzbach, Kerenzerberg	Näfels shares a railway station with its twin town of Mollis (444 m/1457 ft). In the Steinacker is the birthplace of the Glarus humanist Heinrich Loriti (1488–1563), who was crowned as poet laureate by the Emperor Maximilian. On the road up the Kerenzerberg are Obstalden and Filzbach (sports facility, with a public indoor swimming pool).
Netstal	Netstal (453 m/1486 ft; pop. 2800) is a long straggling village surrounded by hillocks formed by landslides of the past, with some industry and a hydroelectric power station (50,000 kW) built in 1909. The Late Baroque village church is a statutorily protected ancient monument.
*Klöntal	From Netstal a road (postal bus in summer) and footpath cross the Schwammhöhe (superb views of the Glarus mountains) into the Klöntal (850 m/2789 ft), one of the most beautiful and romantic of Alpine valleys, with the Klöntalersee and a series of tumultuous mountain streams. The lake was almost doubled in size by the construction of a dam. The road passes through Rhodannenberg (853 m/2799 ft; 5 km/3 miles; inn) and follows the lake, above the south side of which rear the
*Glärnisch	rock walls of Glärnisch (with the peaks of Vorderglärnisch, 2331 m/7648 ft, Vrenelisgärtli, 2904 m/9528 ft, Ruchen, 2905 m/9531 ft), to Vorauen (853 m/2799 ft; inn) and the Richisau (1095 m/3593 ft), an expanse of Alpine pasture at the beginning of the bridle-path over the Pragel pass (1554 m/5099 ft) to Muothal (5 hours' walk). The Klöntal is a popular resort with climbers and hill-walkers (e.g. over the passes into the Sihl and Wägi valleys).
*Glarus	Glarus (481 m/1578 ft; pop. 5700) lying at the foot of Glärnisch (Vorderglärnisch, 2331 m/7648 ft), is capital of the canton, rebuilt in 1861 on a regular grid plan after a devastating fire. The twin-towered Neo-Romanesque church (Protestant) was built in 1866; fine treasury. In the Town Hall is a relief model of the canton on a scale of 1:25,000. The Landesgemeinde (communal assembly) meets every year on the first Sunday in May in the Zaunplatz. In the courthouse are the cantonal archives and cantonal library, with a famous early map of Switzerland by Ägidius Tschudi (1570).

The Kunsthaus in the Volksgarten contains a natural history collection and mounts exhibitions of Swiss 19th and 20th c. artists (paintings and sculptures by F. Hodler, Ernst Ludwig Kirchner, Fritz Pauli), international graphics and the iconography collection of Hans Jenny-Kapers. Kunsthaus

Out of the town are some houses which survived the fire, examples of the architecture such as Leuzinger-Paravicini house (16th c.) and the "Haus in der Wies" ("house in the meadow"), built for Johann Heinrich Streiff (1746–1748), the founder of the Glarnus textile industry

Schwanden (528 m/1732 ft; pop. 2600) lies at the junction of the Sernf and the Linth, which provide water for the Sernf-Niederenbach hydro-electric scheme. It is a good starting-point for a walk into the Niederental, and from there by cableway to the Mettmenalp (mountain inn) and the artificial lake on the Garichte. Good climbing in the Karrenstock and Kärpf area (the oldest wildlife reserve in Switzerland, with numerous chamois, marmots and ibex). Schwanden

From Schwanden an attractive detour can be made into the Sernf valley (also known as the Kleintal); the road runs via Engi and Matt (oldest church in Glarus, 1261) and comes in 15 km/9 miles to Elm (977 m/3206 ft; pop. 800), in a quiet and secluded area which offers excellent walking. Sernftal

The last settlement in the main valley is Linthal (653 m/2142 ft; pop. 1400), with mighty mountains rearing above the little town. Selbsanft (3029 m/9938 ft) lies above the artificial lakes supplying the Linth-Limmern hydro-electric scheme, with the Gries glacier; the Bifertenstock (3426 m/10,722 ft) and Tödi (3614 m/11,858 ft). Tierfehd, 5 km/3 miles south is a good base for walks and climbs in the Tödi group. Linthal

From Linthal (parking garage) the Braunwaldbahn (length 1314 m/4311 ft, time 10 minutes) ascends to the only traffic-free mountain and holiday resort in eastern Switzerland, Braunwald (1256 m/4121 ft; pop. 500), an ideal jumping-off point for walking and climbing. Experimental rhododendron nursery. Musical festival in July. Chair-lift to Gumen mountain inn (1900 m/6234 ft). Braunwald

Over the Klausen pass to Altdorf

There is a magnificent drive over the Klausen pass from Linthal to Altdorf in the canton of Uri (48 km/30 miles) The road built in 1893–99 on the line of an old bridle-path, has a maximum gradient of 8.5% (1 in 12) and is usually open from June to November. *Klausen pass road

10 km/6 miles from Linthal the road crosses the Scheidbächli, a stream which has marked the boundary between the cantons of Glarus and Uri since 1196, and comes to the Urnerboden (1313–1400 m/4308–4593 ft), a meadow-covered high valley some 7 km/4 miles long through which flows the Fätschbach, following an almost level course for 4 km/2 miles. A series of well-engineered bends leads up to the Vorfrutt (1812 m/5945 ft), from which four further bends take the road to the Klausen pass (1948 m/6391 ft; chapel, kiosk), 23 km/14 miles from Linthal. The road then runs down 1.5 km/1 mile to the Klausenpasshöhe Hotel (1838 m/6030 ft) and continues down the Schächen valley, with the 93 m/305 ft high Stäubi falls. After passing through Urigen (1280 m/4200 ft) it reaches Unterschächen (994 m/3261 ft), at the mouth of the steep Brunni valley, with a view of the Grosse Windgälle (3192 m/10,473 ft) and the Grosser Ruchen (3136 m/10,289 ft). Between Spiringen and St Loreto is the Kinzigpass inn (640 m/2100 ft), with the 16th c. Loreto chapel. From Brügg a cableway (3.2 km/2 miles in two stages) runs up in 15 minutes to the Biel mountain inn (1634 m/5361 ft), below the Kinzig pass (2076 m/6311 ft) over which the Russian General Suvorov was compelled to retreat into the Muota valley in 1799 with 18,000 men suffering heavy losses. Urnerboden

*Klausen pass

Schächen valley

Bürglen	After passing through the village of Bürglen we arrive in Altdorf.
Altdorf	See entry.

Grindelwald D2

Canton: Berne (BE)
Altitude: 1050 m/3445 ft
Population: 3500

Situation and general

The "glacier village" of Grindelwald, one of the most popular health and winter sports resorts in the Bernese Oberland and a favourite base for climbers, straggles over a considerable expanse of Alpine meadows on the slopes of the Schwarze Lütschine valley. Three towering mountains enclose the valley on the south: the Eiger (3970 m/13,026 ft), with its sheer north face, the most dangerous mountain wall in the Alps (first climbed in 1938 by Heckmair, Vörg, Kasparek and Harrer, taking four days), on which the lights in the windows of the Eigerwand station of the Jungfraubahn can be seen twinkling after dark; to the left of the Eiger the Mettenberg (3104 m/10,184 ft), one of the subsidiary peaks of the Schreckhorn; and the Wetterhorn (3701 m/12,143 ft), the most characteristic landmark of the Grindelwald valley. Between the three mountains are the two Grindelwald glaciers.

Townscape

*Terrassenweg

The Talhaus, near the Protestant church, contains a local museum. The best general view is to be had from the Terrassenweg, which branches off the road 20 minutes' walk above the church, just before the Mühlbach bridge, and runs along the mountainside above Alpine meadows and through

The Wetterhorn . . .   *. . . Grindlewald's "local" mountain*

patches of forest to the hamlet of Duftbach (30 minutes), from which it is a 20 minutes' walk down to Grindelwald.

Wengernalpbahn and Jungfraubahn to Jungfraujoch (18 km/11 miles; see Jungfrau) via the Kleine Scheidegg. Cableway (1046 m/3432 ft long to Pfingstegg (upper station 1387 m/4551 ft; restaurant). Chair-lift (4354 m/14,285 ft in four stages) via Oberhaus, Bort and Egg in 30 minutes to First (2168 m/7113 ft; inn), with magnificent views and excellent skiing country (ski-lifts) on the Grindelalp, on the slopes of the Widderfeldgrätli, the ridge between the Faulhorn and the Schwarzhorn. The longest cableway in Europe is to the Männlichen (2343 m/7690 ft), a height difference of 1284 m/4214 ft in 30 minutes. *Mountain railways, cableways and lifts.*

Skiing at Grindelwald and on the First, Kleine Scheidegg and Lauberhorn; tobogganing; ice-rinks (indoor and outdoor); curling. *Winter sports*

Favourite walks include the Panorama Way to the First (round trip), Grosse Scheidegg–Schwarzwaldalp–Rosenlaui and the walk Pfingstegg–Marmorbruch–Gletschersch ucht and Pfingstegg–Oberergletscher (geological information; see below). *Walking, climbing*

The Grindelwald Mountain Guides Association organises guided climbs of the surrounding mountains over 4000 m/13,128 ft from the climbing centre, opened in 1985.

Surroundings

To the Upper Glacier (1½ hours): from the church take road (closed to cars) to the turn-off of the road to the Grosse Scheidegg, and continue to the end of the glacier, which has recently been advancing again, with an artificial cave hewn from the ice. There are eight walks providing geological information about the area: Pfingstegg–Milchbach, Pfingstegg–Stieregg, Milchbach–Sulz, Rubiweid–Sulz, Pfingstegg–Sulz, Pfingstegg–Uf der Halten, Pfingstegg–Fielewald–Uf der Halten, Pfingstegg–Marmorbruch. **Upper Glacier*

To the Lower Glacier (1½–2 hours): from the church go down to the bridge over the Lütschine (990 m/3248 ft), and from there either turn right and continue through the hamlet of Mettenberg to the entrance to the impressive Lütschine gorge (accessible through a gulley cut through the rock) and so to the end of the glacier; or turn left into a steep path leading up to the Lower Glacier or Unteres Eismeer (1650 m/5413 ft), a large expanse of ice covered with rock debris. **Lower Glacier, Lütschine gorge*

Up the Faulhorn (2681 m/8796 ft), one of the most renowned viewpoints in Switzerland, from which the giant peaks of the Bernese Oberland can be seen in all their magnificence: either by the chair-lift (30 minutes) to the First station and from there an hour's walk north to the Bachsee or Bachalpsee (2264 m/7428 ft), or a 3½ hours' walk from Grindelwald to the Bachalpsee; then 1½ hours' climb to the summit (Berghotel, summer only). **Faulhorn*

A climb of 2½-3 hours up the slopes above the Checklibach leads to the Grosse Scheidegg (1961 m/6434 ft). *Grosse Scheidegg*

See Jungfrau ***Jungfrau region*

Grisons E2

Canton: Grisons (GR)

The canton usually known in English by its French name of Grisons (German Graubünden, Romansch Grischun, Italian Grigioni), is a typica **Situation and landscape*

mountain region, with its valleys lying at heights of between 900 and 2000 m/2953 and 6562 ft and its highest peak, Bernina, rising to 4049 m/ 13,285 ft. Two-thirds of its boundaries lie along the frontiers of Italy and Austria. Within the canton are the sources of the Rhine (which receives the water of three-fifths of the rivers in the canton) and the Inn (Romansch En); the rivers in the south-facing valleys on the Italian side drain into the Po.

The climate of the Grisons reflects a variety of influences. In the catchment area of the Rhine a continental climate of northern type predominates, while the transverse valleys with a southern exposure show Mediterranean characteristics. Magnolias, chestnuts and vines flourish only a short distance away from the perpetual snow and ice.

Climate and vegetation

Grisons, the largest canton in Switzerland, owes its name to the Upper or Grey League (Ligue Grise, Grauer Bund) formed by the peasants of the region in 1395, like the League of the House of God and the League of the Ten Jurisdictions, to defend their interests against the Habsburgs.

Grey League

In 15 B.C. the Romans subjugated the Rhaetians and began to colonise the region, building roads over the Alpine passes which have not greatly altered their course since then. In 536 the Grisons fell under Frankish rule and, as Chur-Rhaetia, became part of the Duchy of Swabia. Later the people of the Grisons formed the three leagues mentioned above, which at the end of the 15th c. made common cause with Swiss Confederation. The Reformation was adopted by the region. During the Thirty Years War it was plunged into bitter internal strife by the conflict between the supporters of France, led by the Salis family, and of the Habsburgs, led by the Planta family. In the 17th c. Jürg Jenatsch freed the Grisons from foreign influence, but the region was not brought together in a single canton until the 19th c. Of the present population of the Grisons 54% speak German, 31% Romansch and 15% Italian.

History

From very early times the Alpine passes played a vital role in the life of the Grisons. The road over the Septimer pass (Pass da Sett), built in the 14th c., is believed to have been one of the first Alpine roads usable by vehicles. During the 19th c. ten pass roads were built, of which the Julier (Passo del o Guglia), Flüela, Splügen (Passo de lo Spluga) and Maloja passes, among others, are still of major importance. The opening of the San Bernardino tunnel in 1967 made available a north-south route open all year round.

Communications

The Rhätische Bahn (RhB), run by the canton of Grisons, is a narrow-gauge railway-system with a total length of 400 km/249 miles. The 6 km/4 miles long Albula tunnel is the highest tunnel in the Alps (1883 m/6178 ft).
The famous "Glacier-Express" (see Practical Information, Railways) came into operation in 1930, a communal project by the Rhätische Bahn, Furka–Oberalp Bahn and the Brig–Visp–Zermatt Bahn.

Rhätische Bahn

Gruyère   C2

Canton: Fribourg (FR)

The district of Gruyère (German Greyerzer Land), in the southern half of the canton of Fribourg, is a gently rolling Pre-Alpine region mainly devoted to intensive stock-farming and renowned as the home of Gruyère cheese. Its beautiful scenery, numerous remains of the past and vigorous folk traditions make it an attractive tourist region.

Situation and general

27 km/17 miles south of Fribourg, on the left bank of the Trême, is Bulle (alt. 769 m/2523 ft; pop.7700), chief town and commercial and cultural heart of the Gruyère district and one of the most important traffic junctions in the

Bulle

◀ The Inn valley, near Zernez

Bulle Castle

Gruyères, famous for its cheese

canton of Fribourg. From 1196 to 1537 this small market town belonged to the bishops of Lausanne, who built a massive castle here in the 13th c. The town was rebuilt after fires in 1447 and 1805. It has preserved a number of fine old buildings – the parish church (Protestant), rebuilt in 1751, the Capuchin friary and the Town Hall. The 13th c. Schloss Bulle, altered in the 16th c., is a typical example of the "carré-savoyard" design.

Musée Gruérien

In the castle is the Musée Gruérien, with a fine collection of local material; associated with it are the Tissot Collection (works by Corot, Courbet, Poussin, etc.) and a public library (closed Mondays).
In the public park is a monument to Abbé Bovet (1879–1952), a composer of lieder.

Château d'Oex

From Bulle there are roads over the Jaun pass into the Simmental and through the Sarine valley to Château-d'Oex in the Pays d'Enhaut. The local museum contains exhibits of the region's arts and crafts as well as local history.

*Gruyères

6 km/4 miles south-east of Bulle, on a green ridge of hills, is Gruyères (alt. 801 m/2628 ft; pop. 1200), famous for the cheese of the same name. Finely situated and still surrounded by its ancient walls, the town has largely preserved its old-world aspect. From 923 it was the capital of a county which was ruled by a succession of 19 counts; then in 1555 Fribourg and Berne divided the territory between them, and the castle (1493) became the residence of the governors until its acquisition by the Bovy family of Geneva in 1848. Since 1938 the castle has belonged to the canton of Fribourg, and now houses a museum (exhibits of particular interest being three mourning robes belonging to knights of the Golden Fleece, dating from the Burgundian wars). The town lies just off the main road from Bulle to Château-d'Oex but is closed to motor vehicles (car parks outside the town walls). The houses in the main street are statutorily protected as ancient monuments. At the entrance to the town is a Wax Museum (Musée de Cire; figures from Swiss history).

The commune of Gruyères also includes the villages of Epagny (712 m/2336 ft) and Pringy (746 m/2448 ft).

Adjoining the railway station is a famous model cheese-dairy making Gruyère cheese (open daily 6 a.m. to 6 p.m.; manufacture of cheese 9–11.30 and 1–3.30).

*Mocel cheese-dairy

4 km/2 miles south-west of Pringy is Le Moléson, a rounded hill in the midst of the Gruyère district which has become a popular walking and skiing area. From the holiday complex of Moléson-Village (1110 m/3642 ft) a cableway runs up in two stages to the summit of Le Moléson (2002 m/6569 ft), another to La Vudulla (1520 m/4987 ft).

*Le Moléson

Le Moléson has an observatory (open mid-December to mid-April and mid-June to mid-October) and a restaurant, from which there are far-ranging views, extending from Mont Blanc to Titlis; good walking and climbing.

Observatory

Between Bulle and Gruyères is the little industrial town of Broc (719 m/2359 ft; pop. 1870) with a chocolate factory established by F. L. Cailler in 1898 (conducted tours). Broc lies at the south end of the beautiful Lac de la Gruyère (alt. 677 m/2222 ft; area 9.6 sq. m/4 sq. miles, greatest depth 75 m/246 ft, capacity 180 million cu. m/6356 million cu. ft), formed by a dam on the Sarine (Saane).

Broc

Lac de la Gruyère

Gstaad

C2

Canton: Berne (BE)
Altitude: 1050 m/3445 ft
Population: 2500

The summer and winter resort of Gstaad in the high valley of the Saane, in the western part of the Bernese Oberland, has for many years enjoyed an international reputation, while still preserving its character as a village of holiday chalets. It is known for the Swiss International Tennis Championships, its Alpine golf-courses, the annual Menuhin Festival along with plays and concerts during the Alpine gala in September. The resort is a paradise for walkers and climbers, with cableways providing easy access to the mountains.

*Situation and general

River-rafting (white-water trips) on the river Saane and the Simme, to the south, is becoming increasingly popular.

The Montreux-Oberland railway (built 1910–11) and the adjacent pass roads make Gstaad easily accessible from both German-speaking and French-speaking Switzerland.

To Wasserngrat (2000 m/6562 ft; length 2585 m/8481 ft, height difference 826 m/2710 ft, time 20 minutes), Eggli (1580 m/5184 ft; length 1451 m/4761 ft, height difference 514 m/1686 ft, time 10 minutes) and Höhi Wispile (1940 m/6365 ft; length 3039 m/9971 ft, height difference 865 m/2838 ft, time 20 minutes).

Cableways

Together with Schönried, Saanenmöser and Château-d'Oex Gstaad has one of the most scenic skiing areas in the Bernese Oberland, the "Weisse Hochland" with 250 prepared runs and 69 cableways and ski-lifts. There are skiing areas in three directions: the Eggli with its southern slopes, the Wispile with its eastern slopes and the Wasserngrat to the north-east. A 25 km/15 miles long-distance course runs from Gsteig via Gstaad, Saanen, Rougemont to Château-d'Oex. On the Eggli and in Turbach there is toboganning, curling and ice-skating (ice stadium).

Winter sports

Surroundings

7 km/4 miles south-east is Lauenen (1259 m/4131 ft), a beautifully situated health resort with a Late Gothic church (1520). An hour's walk south is the Lauenensee (1379 m/4524 ft).

Lauenen

Gstaad in winter

Gsteig

The road to the Col du Pillon leads to the resort of Gsteig of the Saane valley, which has preserved the character of an Alpine farming village. The road continues over the Col du Pillon (1546 m/5072 ft) to Aigle in the Rhône valley.

Saanen

3 km/2 miles north-west of Gstaad is Saanen (1033 m/3389 ft), chief town in the Upper Saane valley, a climatic and winter sports resort (ski-lifts) surrounded by many isolated farms. Church (rebuilt in 15th c.) with a fine tower and 15th c. wall-paintings in the choir. A prosperous stock-farming and dairy-farming area, notable for its cheese (Saanen, a grating cheese). To the north of the town rises the Hugelirat (1902 m/6240 ft; 3 hours), from which there are superb views.

From Saanen it is possible to continue to Lausanne, by either the Col des Mosses or the Col du Pillon.

Ilanz   E2

Canton: Grisons
Altitude: 702 m/2303 ft
Population: 2200

Situation and general

Ilanz (Romansch Glion), the "first town on the Rhine", situated in the valley of the Vorderrhein, is the market town of the surrounding district of Surselva.

History

The town first appears in the records in 765, when the first church of St Martin was built. In 1395 it became the nucleus of the "Grey League" formed by the Abbot of Disentis together with the local feudal lords and peasants. The people of the Grisons were granted freedom of religious belief following a conference held in St Margaret's church in 1526.

Sights

Ilanz is a picturesque little town of winding streets with one or two buildings recalling its past greatness. The Late Gothic parish church of St Margaret (Protestant) has fine ceiling paintings, Gothic scrollwork and a Rococo organ-loft. There are a number of Baroque mansions, including the Casa Gronda (1677), in which the Fussian General Suvorov once stayed. The Casa Carniec houses the regional museum of Surselva (reopened 1988) with a comprehensive collection of folklore (including an Alpine dairy).

Surselva
Regional
Museum

Surroundings

A road runs west, climbing steeply up the northern slopes of Piz Mundaun (2067 m/6782 ft), to Flond (1075 m/3527 ft; toboggan run to Ilanz) and Meierhof (1302 m/4272 ft), the principal village in the extensive commune of Obersaxen, a German-speaking enclave (skiing). There is an interesting Catholic parish church (1904–1905) n Meierhof and a dozen chapels, such as the Chapel of St Georg (17th c.) with a Late Gothic winged altar.

Obersaxen

Through the Lugnez valley to Vrin (22 km/14 miles)

Leave Ilanz on a narrow road which goes through the Obertor and ascends the western slopes of the beautiful Lugnez valley (Romansch Lumnezia), through which flows the River Glenner. The road with a moderate gradient passes St Martin's church and below, to the left, can be seen the ruined castle of Castelberg; then beyond the Frauentor defile (formerly fortified), the St Moritzkapelle (St Maurice's chapel, 1068 m/3504 ft).
6 km/4 miles above Llanz a road goes off on the left to Peidenbad and the Vals valley. Beyond this point the main road climbs steeply for 1.5 km/ 1 mile to Cumbels (1145 m/3757 ft), a large village below the south side of Piz Mundaun. The church has 17th c. sgraffito painting.

2.5 km/2 miles: Villa (1244 m/4082 ft), with elegant 17th–18th c. houses and a Gothic church (16th c.; frescoes). Pleif, below the road on the left, has a church founded in the Carolingian period but much altered in later centuries. Opposite is the mouth of the Vals valley. The road continues along the side of the Lugnez valley. Below, to the left, is the village of Igels, with two Late Gothic churches. 6 km/4 miles: Lumbrein (1410 m/4626 ft. After a bend at the mouth of the Val Miedra (on right) the road enters the Vrin valley, the highest section of the Lugnez valley.

Villa

6 km/4 miles: Vrin (1454 m/4771 ft), a village with a Baroque parish church of 1675, a quiet summer holiday place and a good base from which to climb the numerous neighbouring peaks.

Vrin

From Ilanz to Bad Vals (21 km/13 miles)

The road follows the left bank of the Glenner below the road to Vrin. At the ruined 13th c. castle of Castelberg it crosses through two gorges, the Rieiner Tobel (road tunnel) and the Pitascher Tobel.

8 km/5 miles: Peidenbad (820 m/2690 ft), in a wooded setting (chalybeate spring). Above, to the right, is the village of Peiden.

Peidenbad

2 km/1 mile: Uors-Lumnezia (German Furth), where the road enters the beautiful Vals valley. To the right, on the mountain spur between the two valleys, is the picturesquely situated little village of Surcasti (German Oberkastels). 4 km/2 miles: St Martin (1000 m/3281 ft). the road now

Vals valley

Interlaken

traverses a magnificent rocky gorge, with the river surging and foaming over waterfalls far below; then through the villages of Lunschania (1200 m/3937 ft) and Bucarischuna (1170 m/3839 ft), along a defile and over the Valser Rhein on the Hohen Brücke (High Bridge).

Bad Vals

7 km/4 miles: Bad Vals (1248 m/4095 ft; pop. 1000; Therme Bad Vals and Häuser Zerveila/Tomül, 300b.) is a little spa frequented by holidaymakers, climbers and winter sports enthusiasts (cross-country skiing), with a church of 1669 and the "Stella Maris" spa establishment (spring containing calcium sulphate, 28° C/82° F; treatment facility, open-air thermal pool with artificial waves, indoor swimming pool).

Piz Tomül

The surrounding area has much of geological, botanical and entomological (butterflies) interest to offer. Piz Tomül (Weissensteinhorn, 2950 m/9679 ft) can be climbed in 4½ hours: panoramic views.

Zevreila

From Bad Vals the road ascends up the right bank of the valley for another 7.5 km/5 miles, passing through a number of tunnels, to the artificial lake of Zevreila (1862 m/6109 ft), beneath the towering bulk of the Zevreiler Horn (2900 m/9515 ft).

Interlaken

Canton: Berne (BE)
Altitude: 568 m/1864 ft
Population: 13,000

Situation and general

Interlaken, reached by way of the Berne motorway or the Brünig, Susten or Grimsel/Furka passes, lies between Lakes Thun and Brienz below the north side of the Jungfrau massif and offers an endless variety of walks, climbs and other excursions, particularly in the mountains of the Bernese Oberland, brought within reach by numerous mountain railways, cableways, etc. It is one of the oldest, best known and most popular summer holiday resorts in Switzerland, outstandingly well equipped to cater for the needs of visitors. Between the two lakes is an expanse of some 35 sq. km/14 sq. miles of alluvial soil, deposited over many millenia by mountain streams from the Bernese Oberland such as the Lütschine and the Lombach. On this green and level area, known as the Bödeli, live the 20,000 inhabitants of the

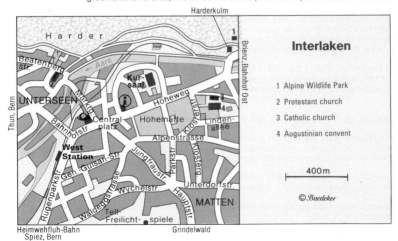

Interlaken

1 Alpine Wildlife Park
2 Protestant church
3 Catholic church
4 Augustinian convent

400m

© Baedeker

separate communes of Interlaken, Böningen, Matten, Unterseen and Wilderswil.

The fertile alluvial soil of the Bödeli was probably settled at an early stage by Celtic tribes. Later the main settlers were Alemanni, driven from their homeland by Burgundian incomers. A major influence on the economic and cultural development of the area was the Augustinian house founded here (inter lacus) in 1133, joined in 1257 by a nunnery. The monks were pioneers of urban development and soon became the largest landowners in the Bernese Oberland. After Berne's adoption of the reformed faith in 1528 the monastery was dissolved (and is now occupied by district administrative offices). The first visitors began to come here in the 17th c., and as transport facilities improved – with the coming of the railway, boat services on the lakes and most recently the motorway – Interlaken became the major tourist attraction of the Bernese Oberland. Among the great attractions of the area were its local folk traditions and art. In 1805 and 1808 the peasant stock-farmers of the Alpine pasturelands celebrated their first great pastoral festivals at Unspunnen, near Interlaken; and at this time, too, the painter Franz Niklaus König was living in Schloss Unterseen and painting the pictures of mountains which became so widely popular.

History

Sights

The Höhematte in the midst of the town is a remarkable example of farseeing town planning. The area of 14 hectares/35 acres which had belonged to the Augustinian convent was acquired in 1860 by a group of 37 hotel-owners and private persons and left as an open space, with the Höheweg, a splendid avenue running between the east and west stations and affording a magnificent view of the Jungfrau, surrounded by hotels and flower-beds. Here, too, is the Kursaal, with a theatre, a café, a gaming room and beautiful gardens (flower clock). At the east end is the former Augustinian convent (1133–1528; inner courtyard with cloister, restored), with a Late Gothic church (stained glass of 1950) and the adjoining Schloss added in 1750 (now housing cantonal offices).

*Höhematte

Höheweg

On the south-east side of Interlaken is Matten with its old timber houses.

Matten

The Marktgasse runs north-west from the post office over the Spielmatten islands to the little town of Unterseen (569 m/1867 ft; pop.4700), at the foot of Mt Harder, tourist museum. In the old part of the town stands the parish church, with Late Gothic tower (1471).

Unterseen

Tourist museum

On the right bank of the Aare opposite the Kursaal is the fresh water swimming-pool. There is an indoor pool, a golf course in Unterseen and trips on Lake Thun and Lake Brienz. For sporting enthusiasts there is sailing, windsurfing, riding and tennis.

Surroundings

Interlaken is an ideal base for day or half-day excursions in the surrounding area. A beginning can be made with the town's own hills, Harder and Heimwehfluh.

Beyond the bridge over the Aare on the road to Brienz, at the Harder Alpine Wildlife Park (Alpenwildpark; marmots, ibexes), is a funicular (length 1447 m/4748 ft, height difference 725 m/2379 ft, maximum gradient 64% (1 in 1½), time 8 minutes) up Harder (upper station 1322 m/4337 ft), with the Harderkulm restaurant magnificent views of the Jungfrau area and the lakes). The return can be made by forest paths, via the Hardermannli lookout pavilion (1116 m/3662 ft) and the Hohbühl pavilion (memorial to the composers Mendelsohn, Wagner and Weber).

*Harder

Interlaken: Kursaal   *Traditional carved façade in Bönigen*

*Heimwehfluh   From the south end of Rugenparkstrasse another funicular (length 167 m/548 ft, height difference 120 m/394 ft, time 3 minutes) runs up to the Heimwehfluh (676 m/2218 ft; café-restaurant, lookout tower; model railway layout), the north-west buttress of the Grosser Rugen (800 m/2625 ft).

*Schynige Platte   Another popular trip from Interlaken is to the Schynige Platte (2101 m/6893 ft; Hotel Kulm 40b.), reached from Wilderswil, 3 km/2 miles south of the town, on a rack-railway (cog-railway) opened in 1893 (7 km/4 miles, 50 minutes). From the top there is one of the finest panoramic views of the Alps. Alpine garden with 500 species of flowers.

Wilderswil   3 km/2 miles south of Interlaken is the little holiday town of Wilderswil (587 m/1926 ft). North-west of the town is the ruined castle of Unspunnen, with the Unspunnenwiese, a meadow on which herdsmen's festivals were held at the beginning of the 19th c.

Saxeten   From Wilderswil a road runs 6 km/4 miles up the Saxeten valley to Saxeten (1100 m/3609 ft), a picturesquely situated mountain village from which Sulegg (2412 m/7914 ft) can be climbed (about 4½ hours).

Bönigen   From the Höheweg a road goes east to reach the south shore of Lake Brienz at Bönigen (569 m/1867 ft; pop. 1900). The old part of the town has richly carved timber houses of the 15th to 18th c. The modern resort is well equipped with facilities for the entertainment of visitors.

Iseltwald   High above the south side of the lake is the village of Iseltwald (567 m/1860 ft; pop. 490), on a quiet little peninsula with no through road.

From Interlaken to Beatenberg (11 km/7 miles)

From Interlaken station take the Thun road, which crosses the Aare into Unterseen, where the road to Thun bears left: continue straight ahead up the Scheidgasse. 2 km/1 mile from Interlaken is a road junction, with a road on the right which runs up the Lombach valley to the prettily situated village of Habkern (6.3 km/4 miles, 1067 m/3501 ft). The road to Beatenberg, to the left, begins to climb through wooded country (attractive view of Interlaken to left) and then takes two sharp bends up the hillside. 3.5 km/2 miles Lueglibrückli restaurant (938 m/3078 ft; car park), with superb views. The road continues uphill on a moderate gradient (views of Lake Thun and the mountains to the left) and then takes another two sharp bends. Farther on it passes a number of children's homes under Amisbühl (1336 m/4383 ft; views) and then descends into the Sundgraben. 5.5 km/3 miles: Beatenberg (1150 m/3773 ft), a popular health and winter sports resort which spreads out along a sunny sheltered terrace high above the north side of Lake Thun, with magnificent views of the Bernese Alps, from the Schreckhorn to the Niesen.

From the Oberland Hotel (parking garage) a chair-lift runs up in 18 minutes to the Niederhorn (1957 m/6421 ft), on the Güggisgrat ridge, with still more extensive views. At the west end of the town is a funicular (1706 m/5597 ft, gradient 35–40%, 10 minutes) to Beatenbucht.

Habkern

Beatenberg

See Lake Brienz

Godswil

See Lake Brienz

Ringgenberg

Jungfrau

C2/D2

Cantons: Berne (BE) and Valais (VS)

The Jungfrau massif, with its group of three famous peaks, the Jungfrau (4158 m/13,642 ft), the Mönch (4099 m/13,449 ft) and the Eiger (3970 m/13,026 ft), has long had a powerful grip on men's imaginations. Originally difficult of access, this mighty range of mountains in the heart of the Bernese Oberland has now been brought within easy reach and attracts large numbers of visitors every year.

Situation and general

The Meyer brothers of Aarau first set foot on the summit of the Jungfrau in 1811; and a hundred years later, in 1912, the rack-railway to the Jungfraujoch was opened. The upper station (3454 m/11,333 ft) is the highest railway station in Europe.

The skiing area of the Jungfrau region around Grindelwald (see entry), Wengen, Lauterbrunnen (see Lauterbrunnen valley) and Mürren (see entry) offers 175 km/109 miles of pistes with 43 stations. The 10 km/6 miles long intermediate descent Lauberhorn–Grindelwald–Grund covers a height difference of 1450 m/4759 ft. The height difference between Männlichen and Grindelwald (6 km/4 miles; intermediate) is 1200 m/3938 ft. Schilthorn–Lauterbrunnen (12 km/39 miles; difficult) the height difference is 2170 m/7121 ft. The First, Eigergletscher and Lauberhorn all have deep snow.

Winter sports

Long-distance runs: Grindelwald–Bussalp (1800 m/5907 ft; length 4 km/2miles), Aspi–Grund (length 4 km/2 miles), Lauterbrunnen valley (12 km/7 miles), a circular course near Mürren and Lauterbrunnen–Stechelberg (12 km/7 miles).

Climbs from the Jungfraujoch (only to be undertaken with a guide): the Jungfrau (4158 m/13,642 ft; 4 hours, difficult), so named (the "Maiden") in honour of the Augustinian nuns of Interlaken; the Mönch (4099 m/13,449 ft; 4 hours, easier), the "Monk"; the Finsteraarhorn (4274 m/14,023 ft; 6½–8 hours), the highest peak in the Bernese Alps. There is also a popular glacier walk to Konkordiaplatz (2840 m/9318 ft), on the Aletsch glacier.

Climbs

Mountain railways and cableways

The area of most interest to visitors extends north from the 4000 m/13,124 ft peaks of the Bernese Oberland towards Lake Thun and Brienz (see entries).

Jungfraujoch
(3454 m ü.d.M.)

Section
schematic

© *Baedeker*

Mönch (4099 m)

Aufstieg zum Mönch

1 Jungfraujoch station	6 Road to plateau	11 Sphinx tunnel
2 Berghaus Hotel	7 Ice Palace	12 Sphinx elevator
3 Restaurant	8 Entrance to Sphinx tunnel	13 Sphinx lookout terrace (3573 m – 11,723 feet)
4 Restaurant	9 Tourist House	14 Exit from Sphinx tunnel
5 Cinema	10 Research station	15 Ski school and huskies

A railway line connecting the two lakes was opened between Därlingen and Bönigen in 1874 (the first steamer on Lake Thun having gone into service nearly 40 years earlier, in 1836). This was followed in 1888 by the Brünig-bahn between Lucerne and Interlaken, in 1893 by the Thuner-See-Bahn (Lake Thun railway) and in 1913 by the Lötschberg railway, which provided a link with Italy. The first mountain railways in the Jungfrau area had been built some years previously.

The Jungfrau mountain railways, all under the same management, now have a total length of more than 70 km/43 miles (all electric), with gauges of either 100 or 80 cm/39 or 31 inches.

History

Opened 1890; from Interlaken Ost (East station) to Lauterbrunnen (796 m/2612 ft) and from Interlaken Ost to Grindelwald (1034 m/3393 ft). Total length 23.5 km/15 miles; gauge 100 cm/39 inches; gradients up to 12% (1 in 8) (partly normal railway line, partly rack-railway).

Berner-
Oberland-
Bahnen (BOB)

Opened 1893 (associated with the Berner-Oberland-Bahnen since 1895); from Wilderswil (584 m/1916 ft) to the Schynige Platte (1967 m/6454 ft). Length 7.3 km/5 miles; gauge 80 cm/31 inches; gradients up to 25% (1 in 4) (rack-railway).

Schynige Platte
Bahn

Opened 1891; from Lauterbrunnen (796 m/2612 ft) to the Grütschalp (1487 m/4879 ft), cableway; Grütschalp-Mürren (1650 m/5414 ft), railway. Total length 5.7 km/4 miles; gauge 100 cm/39 inches; gradients up to 61% (1 in 1.6) (cableway).

Bergbahn
Lauter-
brunnen-Mürren
(BLM)

Cable railway opened 1912; from Mürren (1650 m/5414 ft) to the Allmend-hubel (1912 m/6273 ft). Length 536 m/1759 ft; gauge 100 cm/39 inches; gradients up to 61% (1 in 1.6).

Seilbahn
Mürren-
Allmendhubel
(SMA)

Opened 1893: from Lauterbrunnen (796 m/2612 ft) to Wengen (1274 m/4180 ft), the Wengernalp (1873 m/6145 ft) and the Kleine Scheidegg (2061 m/6762 ft), and from Grindelwald (1034 m/3393 ft) to the Kleine

Wengernalp-
bahn (WAB)

◀ *The Jungfrau, queen of mountains*

Jungfrau

Scheidegg (2061 m/6762 ft). Total length 10 km/6 miles (the longest single stretch track of rack-railway line in Switzerland); gauge 80 cm/31 inches; gradients up to 25% (1 in 4).

Jungfraubahn
(JB)

First section, from the Kleine Scheidegg (2061 m/6762 ft) to the Eiger glacier (2320 m/7612 ft), opened in 1898; from the Eiger glacier (2320 m/7612 ft) to the Eigerwand (2865 m/9400 ft) in 1903; from the Eigerwand (2865 m/9400 ft) to the Eismeer (3160 m/10,368 ft) in 1905; and from the Eismeer (3160 m/10,368 ft) to the Jungfraujoch (3454 m/11,333 ft) in 1912. Total length 9.3 km/6 miles; gauge 100 cm/39 inches; gradients up to 25%. Tunnel 7.1 km/4 miles long from the Eiger glacier to the Jungfraujoch. Rack-railway (cog-railway).

Drahtseilbahn
Interlaken-
Harder (HB)

Cable railway, opened 1908; from Interlaken (567 m/1860 ft) to the Harderkulm (1322 m/4337 ft). Length 1.4 km/1 mile; gauge 100 cm/39 inches; gradients up to 84% (1 in 1½).

Useful tip

The best starting-point for a trip into the Jungfrau area is the East station in Interlaken (Interlaken-Ost). It is possible to go by car to Grindelwald and Lauterbrunnen. The round trip from Interlaken to the Jungfraujoch and back (either via Lauterbrunnen and Wengen or via Grindelwald) takes between 4½ and 5 hours. It is important to choose a day with favourable weather conditions, to be stoutly shod and to take sun-glasses.

Information

Information from Bahnen der Jungfrau-Region (Jungfrau Railways), CH-3800 Interlaken, tel. (0 36) 22 52 52.

**To the Jungfraujoch

There are two routes from Interlaken to the Kleine Scheidegg, either via Lauterbrunnen or via Grindelwald: the best plan is to go one way and come back the other. The line to both places is the same as far as Zweilütschinen, at the junction of two streams, the Schwarze Lütischine (Black Lütischine) coming from Grindelwald and the Weisse Lütischine (White Lütischine) from the Lauterbrunnen valley.

Grindelwald

See entry

Lauterbrunnen

See Lauterbrunnen valley

The rail journey from Interlaken Ost to Grindelwald takes 40 minutes, from Grindelwald to the Kleine Scheidegg 35 minutes. The line runs below the dreaded north face of the Eiger, the most dangerous rock wall in the Alps, which claimed many deaths before it was finally climbed in 1938 by an Austrian team of four men (Vörg, Heckmayr, Harrer and Kasparek), who took four days for the ascent. The summit had already been reached by an Englishman, Christopher Berrington, in 1858, following a different route. The north face of the Eiger has since been climbed by over 700 men and women. A commemorative stone was unveiled in 1988 in memory of the first ascent.

The journey from Interlaken Ost to Lauterbrunnen takes 25 minutes, from Lauterbrunnen to the Kleine Scheidegg 42 minutes. There are parking facilities in Lauterbrunnen. The Wengernalpbahn runs up in 14 minutes to Wengen, on a sunny terrace, sheltered from the wind, high above the Lauterbrunnen valley (4 km/2 miles).

Wengen

Wengen (1275 m/4183 ft; pop. 1400), beautifully situated at the foot of the Eiger, Mönch and Jungfrau, is an ideal base for walks and climbs in the mountain world of the Bernese Oberland. There is a cableway up Männlichen (2343 km/7687 ft), and numerous attractive footpaths. Particularly

The Jungfrau railway to the "Top of Europe"

rewarding is the climb to the Wengernalp, either direct (1¾ hours) or by way of the Mettlealp (1700 m/5578 ft; immediately opposite the Jungfrau; 3 hours).

From Wengen the railway continues up for another 4 km/2 miles to the Wengernalp (1873 m/6145 ft; Hotel Jungfrau, November–April, C, 450.), from which there are splendid views of the Trümleten valley and the Jungfrau. There is a chair-lift from Wengernalp Wixi to the Lauberhornschulter (2310 m/7579 ft).

Wengernalp

11 km/7 miles farther on is the Kleine Scheidegg (2064 m/6772 ft; Scheidegg Hotels, open December–September), the terminus of the rack (cog)-railways from Lauterbrunnen and Grindelwald and the starting-point of the Jungfraubahn, with tremendous views of the nearby 4000 m/13,124 ft peaks of the Eiger, Mönch and Jungfrau. Magnificent walks; splendid skiing country (Arven, Honegg and Lauberhorn ski-lifts). Sight-seeing flights over the glaciers from Männlichen.

Kleine Scheidegg

**Jungfraubahn

The Jungfraubahn, built 1896–1912, runs up through Alpine meadows and an 87 m/285 ft long tunnel and after 2 km/1 mile arrives at the Eigergletscher (Eiger Glacier) station (2320 m/7612 ft; inn), in magnificently wild scenery and then enters the long tunnel (7.1 km/4 miles) which leads up towards the Jungfraujoch.

Eigergletscher

4.4 km/3 miles: Eigerwand station (2865 m/9400 ft), with a magnificent view of Grindelwald, 1800 m/5906 ft below. From here the line runs under the Eiger. 5.7 km/4 miles: Eismeer (Sea of Ice, 3160 m/10,368 ft) on the south face of the Eiger, 40 m/131 ft above the Upper Grindelwald-Fiescher Firn (névé, or frozen snow), with views over the much-crevassed surface of the

Eigerwand

Eismeer

glacier towards the Wetterhorn, the Schreckhorn, the Fiescherhörner and the great crevasse under the Mönchsjoch.

**Jungfrau-joch

After a journey of 50 minutes and 9.3 km/6 miles the rack-railway reaches the Jungfraujoch (3454 m/11,333 ft), the highest railway station in Europe, which together with the accommodation for visitors, the research stations, the underground passages and the elevators forms a little subterranean town of its own. An outer lobby (post office, shops, restaurants, lookout gallery) leads into the Ice Palace (Eispalast), a cavern hewn out of the glacier, with ice sculpture. Next to a self-service restaurant the first-class

*Top of Europe

Top of Europe restaurant opened in 1987, offers magnificent views of the mountains and in fine weather the Aletsch glacier. From the Sphinx Tunnel an elevator (112 m/367 ft) ascends to the summit of the Sphinx (3573 m/11,273 ft), with an lookout terrace, a research institute and a weather station. There is also an exit from the tunnel giving access to a summer ski school; here, too, visitors can have a sleigh ride, pulled by husky dogs.

The views from the Jungfraujoch itself, the saddle of firn (névé) between the Mönch and the Jungfrau, are breathtaking. To the south can be seen the Aletsch glacier, 22 km/14 miles long, to the north the mountain world of the Alps, the Mittelland and beyond this, on clear days, the Vosges and the Black Forest.

Jura Mountains   B2/B1/C1

Cantons: Jura (JU), Neuchâtel (NE) and Vaud (VD).

Situation and *landscape

The Jura is the range of folded mountains lying north-west of the Swiss Alps and extending from Geneva to Schaffhausen. This is the central area of the Swiss watchmaking industry; but, lying as it does on the periphery of the country, has so far played a relatively minor part in the Swiss tourist trade. For this reason is popular with nature lovers.

Canton Jura

The new canton of Jura, the 23rd to become a member of the Confederation, was established on 1 January 1979, following a popular referendum in September 1977. It has an area of 837 sq. km/323 sq. miles and a population of 65,000, 87.6% of whom are Roman Catholics. The capital is Delémont, and the canton is divided into three districts of Delémont, Porrentruy and Franches-Montagnes, with a total of 32 communes.

From Basle through the Jura to Lake Geneva

Delémont

The road runs through the beautiful Birs valley and after 41 km/25 miles arrives at Delémont (see entry). From here the road to Biel continues south through the picturesque narrow Val Moutier, which the River Birs has carved through the limestone rock.

Moutier

From Choindez the road continues to Moutier (alt. 532 m/1745 ft; pop. 8900), a former centre of medieval monastic culture with watchmaking and manufacture of machine tools. South-west of the town is the interesting Romanesque chapel of Chalières with ornate frescoes (c. 1020).

Tavannes

The road then runs through a picturesque defile, the Gorges de Court, and continues through the villages of Court, Malleray-Bévilard and Reconvilier (731 m/2398 ft; pop. 2600; important horse fair), birthplace of the famous clown known as Grock (Adrian Wettach, 1880–1959), to Tavannes (757 m/2484 ft; pop. 4000), near the source of the Birs.

Pierre Pertuis

From here the road ascends to the Pierre Pertuis, with a passage through the rock 12 m/39 ft high and 8 m/26 ft wide (Roman inscription), and then down to Sonceboz (656 m/2152 ft; pop. 1370), where the railway line from Biel to La Chaux-de-Fonds branches off.

Jura landscape

The route then continues through the Vallon de St-Imier, the valley of the River Suze, to St-Imier (814 m/2671 ft; pop. 6300), an important watchmaking capital, with a 12th c. Romanesque church and the Tour de la Reine Berthe, a remnant of the Romanesque church of St Martin. Cableway up the Mont Soleil (1290 m/4332 ft).

St-Imier

From here there is a direct road to Neuchâtel (30 km/19 miles), past Le Chasseral (1610 m/5282 ft; hotel), from which there are beautiful panoramic views. The main road continues to La Chaux-de-Fonds (see entry).

La Chaux-de-Fonds

From La Chaux-de-Fonds an attractive excursion can be made via Le Locle (9 km/6 miles) and the Col des Roches (917 m/3009 ft), 5 km/3 miles beyond which is the watchmaking village of Les Brenets (849 m/2786 ft; pop. 1200), situated above the Lac des Brenets (753 m/2471 ft). The lake (length 4 km/2 miles, breadth 100–200 m/328–656 ft, area 0.69 sq. km/0.27 sq. miles), enclosed by sandstone crags, is a natural formation on the River Doubs, which here forms the frontier between Switzerland and France. It is a 15 minutes' trip by motor-boat or a 45 minutes' walk to the Hôtel du Doubs, from which a 5 minutes' climb leads to a viewpoint opposite the Saut du Doubs, a waterfall 27 m/89 ft high. Immediately downstream from the Lac de Brenets is the Lac de Moron (4.5 km/3 miles long).

Lac des Brenets

Saut du Doubs

14 km/9 miles south-west of the Col des Roches we come to La Brévine (1046 m/3432 ft; pcp. 700), and a further 14 km/9 miles south, in the Val de Travers, Fleurier (743 m/2438 ft; pop. 4100). To the east of Travers it is a 30 minutes' round trip to former asphalt mines, (in operation until 1986), where natural asphalt, a mixture of bitumen and mineral (chiefly cha k), was mined.

Val de Travers, asphalt mines

14 km/9 miles south-west of Fleurier the town of Ste-Croix (1092 m/3583 ft; pop. 5300), famous for its musical boxes, lies in a valley on the slopes of Le Chasseron (1611 m/5286 ft). There is an interesting Musical Box Museum in

Ste-Croix

Hermitage of . . .　　　　　　　　　　　　　　　*. . . St Ursanne*

L'Auberson. Below the road from Ste-Croix to Vuiteboef wheel tracks can be seen in the rock of the old Roman road.

The road from La Chaux-de-Fonds to Neuchâtel (22 km/14 miles) runs past the Vue des Alpes (9 km/6 miles; 1283 m/4210 ft; inn), from which there is a beautiful panorama of the Alps (Mont Blanc).

Neuchâtel	See entry.
Yverdon	See entry.
La Sarraz	South-west of the Lac de Neuchâtel, via Orbe (see Yverdon), is La Sarraz (488 m/1601 ft; pop. 1000), with a massive 11th c. castle which was given its present form in the 16th c. The Musée Cheval has an exhibition of working, draught and riding horses as well as horses of the army and in art. As part of the project "Renovation 2000" the castle is undergoing extensive restoration. In the former parish church of St-Antoine (now the Town Hall) can be seen the tomb of Count François de la Sarraz (d.1363).
Romainmôtier, *Abbey of St-Pierre et St-Paul	North-west of La Sarraz, on a by-road to the left of road 9, is the old-world little town of Romainmôtier (658 m/2159 ft) which has a monastery founded in the 5th c. and dissolved in 1537. The Abbey Church of St-Pierre et St-Paul, built under the direction of St Odilo of Cluny in the 10th–11th c. and reconstructed in the 12th–14th c., is one of the oldest and most important ecclesiastical buildings in the country. The Romanesque monastery church has valuable 14th/15th c. frescoes.
Lac de Joux	The by-road continues to the north-east end of the Lac de Joux. An attractive road follows the south side of the lake, passing through the little village of L'Abbaye, dominated by the massive tower of its church.
Le Brassus	Just beyond the south-west side of the lake is Le Brassus (1024 m/3360 ft), a winter sports resort with excellent skiing terrain (ski-lifts up Molard, 1570 m/5151 ft).

From here it is possible to continue to Nyon (see entry), on Lake Geneva (see entry), either by way of the Col du Marchairuz (1467 m/4748 ft) or (passing through French territory) via La Cure, the Col de la Givrine (1228 m/4029 ft) and the winter sports resort of St-Cergue (1043 m/3422 ft); possible detour to the fine viewpoint of La Dôle, 1677 m/5502 ft.

From Delémont into the Ajoie

The so-called Pruntruter Zipfel (Porrentruy summit) is the name given to the hilly borderland with France, a chalk upland area which slopes down towards Burgundy. The road between Delémont and Porrentruy (German Pruntrut; 25 km/15 miles) is part of the main route Berne–Belfort–Paris.

Via Develier (church window by Bissière) along the beautiful "Corniche du Jura" (14 km/8 miles) the road reaches the Les Rangiers pass (alt. 858 m/2816 ft) with magnificent views of the mountain ridge Mont Terri. 1 km/ about ½ mile farther on the right is a war memorial, erected in 1924, in memory of the battles of the First World War.

Develier, Corniche du Jura

The "Corniche du Jura" continues via Les Malettes (inn) down through the Combe Maran and under a high railway viaduct (5 km 3 miles) to St-Ursanne (German St Ursitz; 440 m/1444 ft; pop. 1100), a romantic little medieval town on the River Doubs, which bends sharply through Swiss territory. St-Ursanne was founded on the site of the chapter-house, which dates back to the Irish monk Ursicinus (companion of Colomban). The church, a triple-naved basilica with buttresses and no transept (Romanesque choir, 12th c.; Gothic nave 13th–14th c.; front tower, 1441), is one of the most attractive buildings in the west of Switzerland and contains a cloister, Merovingian sarcophagi and a Romanesque crypt. Of particular note are the Romanesque south doorway, the towers, the old bridge and the castle ruins.
Motor enthusiasts will be interested in the International Rally St-Ursanne–Les Rangiers, the only Swiss motor race in the European Championships.

*St-Ursanne

The road to Porrentruy runs down from Les Malettes with views of the village and ruins of Asuel, through the village of Cornol 503 m/1651 ft), lying in a narrow valley into the hilly countryside of the Ajoie (German Eisgau). After 8.5 km/5 miles it comes to Courgenay (493 m/1618 ft), home of the legendary soldiers' mother "Gilberte de Courgenay".

Courgenay

5 km/3 miles to Porrentruy (426 m/1398 ft; pop. 7800), the commercial, industrial and cultural centre of the Ajoie. In 1988 it received the Wakker prize for its outstanding presevation of its medieval town centre.
The old town is dominated by the castle, which became the seat of the prince-bishops following Berne's conversion to the new faith (1529). The 13th c. round tower Tour Réfouse (refuge) is the oldest building with the Porte de France (1563) in the Faubourg as evidence of the former fortifications. Notable sights include the Catholic parish church of St-Pierre (1349), with Late Baroque side altars, the former Jesuit church which is now used as the hall of the cantonal school and several Baroque buildings such as the Hôtel de Ville (1761–1763; interesting bell towers), the Hôpital (now a local museum) with the Samaritan fountain by L. Perraud (564), the Late Baroque Hôtel des Halles and the Hôtel de Gléresse (c. 1750), houses the library. The Botanical Garden of the cantonal school, founded by Lémane in 1795, is open daily.

Porrentruy

From here it is 12 km/7 miles to the Swiss border town of Boncourt (375 m/1231 ft; pop. 1700), with a 12th/13th c. church, a traditional tobacco factory (1814) and caves with stalagtites.

Boncourt

From Delémont into the Franches-Montagnes

The road runs from Delémont via Saignelégier (33 km/20 miles) through the Jura to Neuchâtel and Geneva. First along the Sorne valley through the

Sorne valley

Préfecture in Saignelégier

villages of Courtételle and Courfaivre (bicycle factory; stained glass in the church by F. Léger) for 10 km/6 miles to the watchmaking village of Basse-court (478 m/1569 ft), then the road climbs the slopes of the wild Combe Tabeillon into the Franches-Montagnes, an upland chalk area from 1000 m/3282 ft to 1100 m/3610 ft, with a network of maintained walks (some suitable for mountain bikes). It is ideal for exploring on horseback or even in a hired Romany caravan. There are many long-distance tracks.

Montfaucon

Montfaucon (1006 m/3301 ft; pop. 450) has a Classical parish church (late 19th c.) and there are the "Grand Ceux" caves.

Saignelégier

5 km/3 miles farther lies Saignelégier (982 m/3222 ft), chief town of the Franches-Montagnes and horse-breeding centre with the National Horse Market ("Marché Concours") being held here the second weekend in August. The massive préfecture in the main street and its adjoining prison tower were built in the 16th c.

Noirmont, Les Bois

The village of Noirmont (970 m/3183 ft; pop. 1550) lies on the French border. In Les Bois (1087 m/3567 ft) there is a cheese dairy which is open to visitors ("Tête de Moine" = monk's head). Over the Col-de-Bellevue (1073 m/3521 ft) the road finally comes to La Chaux-de-Fonds.

Kandersteg   C2

Canton: Berne (BE)
Altitude: 1170–1200 m/3839/3937 ft
Population: 1000

Situation and general

Kandersteg is a popular summer and winter resort in the Upper Kander valley, in the Bernese Oberland. The village, with some attractive old peasants' houses and a small 16th c. church, spreads out along the mea-dows of the valley floor for almost 4 km/2 miles, enclosed by towering mountains.

To the north-east is the jagged Birrenhorn (2505 m/8219 ft), to the east the snow-capped Blümlisalp and the Doldenhorn, to the south-east the bare slopes of the Fisistöcke (2947 m/9669 ft) and to the south, closing the valley, the rugged Gellihorn (2289 m/7510 ft). At Eggenschwand, at the south end of the village, the Lötschbergbahn enters the Lötschberg tunnel, the third longest in the Alps (14.6 km/9 miles; cars carried).

Cabin railway from Eggenschwand to Beim Stock (1837 m/6027 ft) on the Gemmiweg (6 minutes); from there a chair-lift (12 minutes) to 1947 m/6388 ft on Sunnbühl.
Chair-lift from the mouth of the Oeschinental (5 minutes from the church) to Oeschinen (1700 m/5578 ft; 9 m nutes).
The Allmenalp cableway runs from Bütschels (10 minutes from the church) to Allmenalp station (1730 m/5678 ft) in 5 minutes.

Cableways and lifts

Surroundings

The Oeschinensee (1582 m/5191 ft) can be reached by a 1¼ hours' walk from the Victoria Hotel up the valley of the Oeschinenbach, or by taking the chair-lift to the Oeschinen station and walking down from there over the Im Lager meadows (extensive views 30 minutes). The lake lies below the Blümlisalp, mirroring the mountain's rugged shape in its clear water, in a setting of majestic beauty.

*Oeschinensee

From here it is a 3¾ hours' climb to the Blümlisalp hut (2837 m/9308 ft) and a 5 hours' climb (with guide) to the summit of the Blümlisalphorn (3664 m/12,022 ft), the highest peak of the mighty Blümlisalp.

Blümisalp

Into the Gastern valley

¾ hour to Klus, 2¼ hours to Selden; also possible to drive to Selden on payment of a toll.

The narrow road runs through a tunnel in the rock into the Klus, a gorge through which the River Gander rushes and tumbles, and then continues uphill through a second tunnel on the left bank and another on the right bank. In 15 minutes it arrives at a magnificent stretch of the valley at Gasternholz (1365 m/4479 ft; on the left bank the Waldhaus inn), with the mighty rock walls of the Tatlishorn and Altels towering up on the right.

*Kander-Klus

From here it is a 1¼ hours' walk along the right bank to the huts of Selden (1590 m/5217 ft), under a grand mountain screen formed by the Hockenhorn (3297 m/10,817 ft; 8 hours with guide), the Doldenhorn (3643 m/11,953 ft; 8 hours with guide, from Kandersteg) and the Balmhorn.

Selden
*Hockenhorn

*Balmhorn

To the Gemmi pass

To Schwarenbach Hotel 3 or 1½ hours, to Leukerbad 6½, 5 or 3½ hours depending on route taken.
First a 30 minutes' walk to Eggenschwand (road passable for cars for 2.5 km/2 miles to car park at lower station of Stock cableway); then either by cableway (6 minutes) or on foot (1¾ hours) to Beim Stock (1837 m/6027 ft; chair-lift to Sunnbühl).
Then a 1¼ hours' walk through wooded country high above the Gastern valley, and up the valley of the Schwarzbach and over the Spitalmatte (1900 m/6234 ft), an Alpine meadow littered with rock debris, to the Schwarenbach Hotel (2067 m/6782 ft), a good climbing base (climbing school), e.g. for the ascent of the Balmhorn (3709 m/12,169 ft; 6–7 hours with guide).
Then another 1¼ hours through a bleak and rugged region, past the Daubensee (2205 m/7235 ft; frozen for 8–10 months of the year) to the Gemmi

*Balmhorn

*Gemmi pass

pass (2316 m/7599 ft; Berghotel Wildstrubel, E), with astonishing views of the Rhône valley and the Valais Alps.

From the pass a cableway descends to Leukerbad (see entry). The walk down to Leukerbad on the old bridle-path (made in 1740) along a rock face which plunges precipitously down for almost 600 m/1969 ft, is to be recommended only to those with a good head for heights (2 hours).

Klosters   E2

Canton: Grisons (GR)
Altitude: 1127–1209 m/3698–3967 ft
Population: 3500

Situation and general

The popular health and winter sports resort of Klosters, made up of a number of separate groups of houses and hotels, lies in the wide Prättigau valley, through which flows the River Landquart, within a framework of high mountains. The first official reference to it was in 1222, the "Klösterli im Walt". The construction of roads and the Rhätische Bahn railway in the 19th c. linked it with the Rhine valley.

Sights

In the main part of the resort, known as Zentrum (formerly Klosters Platz, 1209 m/3967 ft) are the large hotels and the parish church (restored 1921), which originally belonged to the Premonstratensian (an order founded at Premonstré, France in 1119) monastery of St Jakob, dissolved in 1528: hence the name of the village (Kloster=monastery). Nearby a shopping centre has several small shops selling local crafts.

Local museum Nutli-Hüschi

A renovated 16th c. farmhouse houses a local museum "Nutli-Hüschi" with local historical exhibits.

Klosters: Nutli-Hüschi

244

In the Prättigau near Schiers

1.5 km/1 mile down the valley, at the mouth of the Schappin valley, is Klosters Dorf (1127 m/3698 ft).

Excellent ski-trails in the Parsenn area (several ski-lifts), in the Madrisa area and on the Saaseralp. The longest descent (14 km/9 miles) Weissfluhgipfel-Küblis (medium) covers a height difference of 2030 m/6662 ft. Chuecalanda has the deepest snow with bob-sleighing in the areas of Gotschna/Parsenn and Madrisa. There are over 40 km/25 miles of long-distance runs; ice-rink, curling, tobogganing. **Winter sports**

Surroundings

A cableway ascends from Kloster railway station by way of an intermediate station on the Gotschnaboden (1780 m/5840 ft) to the Gotschnagrat (2283 m/7491 ft; restaurant), with views of the Upper Prättigau and the Silvretta group. From here a footpath leads in 30 minutes to the Parsenn hut (2205 m/7235 ft; inn) from which it is another 2 hours' walk to the Höhenweg station on the Davos-Weissfluhjoch funicular (2215 m/7235 ft). There is also a cableway from the Parsenn hut (2400 m/7874 ft, 8 minutes) to the Weissfluhjoch (2663 m/8737 ft). **Gotschnagrat**
Another cableway (2280 m/7481 ft, 11 minutes) runs up from Klosters Dorf to the Albeina station (1884 m/6181 ft; restaurant) on the Saaseralp (several ski-lifts) below the Madrisahorn (2326 m/9272 ft; another 3–4 hours with guide).

The Prättigau (Romansch Val Partens or Portenz), extending north-west from Klosters is the narrow valley of the River Landquart. Although the neat little villages, situated among fruit orchards in the wider parts of the valley or on narrow terraces on the steeply sloping meadowland on the hillsides, have Romansch names dating from an earlier settlement they are inhabited by a German-speaking and mainly Protestant population. On the **Prättigau**

Rätikon	north side of the valley is the Rätikon chain (Scesaplana, 2967 m/9735 ft), along which runs the frontier with Austria (Vorarlberg). The numerous summer holiday resorts in the Prättigau are mostly some distance off the road on the hillside (Seewis on the north side. Fideris and Bad Serneus on the south side) or in the side valleys (Valzeina to the south, St Antönien to
Küblis, Schiers	the north). Küblis, with a late Gothic church, and Schiers, at the mouth of the Schraubach, are both worth a visit.
Prättigau Walk	A 5 hour walk through varied countryside with wonderful flora is marked from Madrisa station (1884 m/6183 ft) over the Jägglischhorn-Fürggli (2255 m/7401 ft), where there are marvellous views of Sulzfluh, Drusenfluh, Scweizertor and Scheseplana, to St Antönien (1420 m/4660 ft).
Alp Noval	From Klosters a narrow road climbs the right bank of the Landquart into the highest part of the Prättigau, with beautiful views of the Silvretta group. 3 km/2 miles: Monbiel (1313 m/4308 ft; restaurant). From here it is another 4 km/2 miles (road closed to cars) to the beautifully situated Alp Noval (1368 m/4488 ft), at the point where the Sardascabach and the Vereinabach join to form the Landquart. A bridle-path ascends the Vereina valley (to the
Berghaus Vereina	right) to the Berghaus Vereina (1944 m/6378 ft; inn, with beds), in a magnificent mountain setting (2¼ hours), a good base for climbers. 3½ hours' walk
Silvrettahaus	up the Sardasca valley, to the left, is the Silvrettahaus (2340 m/7677 ft; inn), in a magnificent situation under the Silvretta glacier (1 hour's climb). These are both good bases for climbs in the Silvretta group – the Silvrettahorn (3248 m/10,657 ft; 3½ hours, with guide), Piz Buin (3316 m/10,880 ft; 4½ hours, with guide).

Küssnacht am Rigi   D1

Canton: Schwyz (SZ)
Altitude: 440 m/1444 ft
Population: 6500

Situation and general	Küssnacht, chief town of the district of that name between Lake Lucerne and Lake Zug, famous for its associations with William Tell, lies at the farthest tip of the Küssnachter See, the most northerly arm of Lake Lucerne. It first appears in the records in 870, in connection with a gift to the monastery in Lucerne.

Sights

Hotel Engel	The Gasthaus Engel (Angel Inn) is a half-timbered building of 1552 with an old assembly hall and a Goethe Room. Parish church of St Peter and Paul (rebuilt in Baroque style 1708–10, enlarged 1968); Town Hall (1728).
William Tell	William Tell, the hero of Swiss legend who, the story goes, refused to recognise the authority of the Habsburg governor Gessler, won his freedom by shooting the apple on his son's head and later killed Gessler in the Hohle Gasse, is a symbolic figure who has been a powerful inspiration throughout Swiss history.
	The desire for freedom lay at the root of the striving by this people of herdsmen and forest-dwellers in the heart of Switzerland to achieve independence, and continued in subsequent centuries to inspire the Confederates in their struggle. Switzerland's develpoment into the well-ordered European state of today passed through many troubles and vicissitudes; but the "Perpetual Pact" between the three forest states in 1291 was strong enough to endure and form the basis of the present Confederation of 26 cantons.

Kussnacht: "Hohle Gasse", Tell Chapel . . .   . . . and Hotel Engel

Surroundings

2 km/1 mile north-east of Küssnacht on the road to Immensee is the Hohle Gasse ("Hollow Lane"), where tradition has it that William Tell shot the Austrian governor Gessler with his crossbow.

The spot is marked by the Tell chapel (built 1638, restored 1895, with paintings by H. Bachmann of "Gessler's Death" and "Tell's Death"). The Hohle Gasse was purchased by the young people of Switzerland and presented to the Confederation.

Above Küssnacht stands the ruined Gesslerburg ("Gessler's Castle"), the remains of a medieval stronghold which has no connection with Gessler. After visiting Küssnacht Goethe suggested the subject of William Tell to Schiller, and Schiller's play in turn inspired Rossini's opera.

5 km/3 miles above Küssnacht on a narrow and winding mountain road (or 7 minutes by cableway), on the slopes of the Rigi, is the Seebodenalp (1030 m/3379 ft), from which a footpath leads in 1½ hours to Rigi Staffel and Rigi Känzeli.

4 km/2 miles west of Küssnacht is Udligenswil, from which there is a footpath up the Rooterberg (798 m/2618 ft St Michaelkreuz chapel).

Just outside Küssnacht on the Lucerne road a Flemish-style memorial chapel is dedicated to Queen Astrid of Belgium, who was killed in a car accident here in 1935.

*Hohle Gasse

Tell chapel

Gesslerburg

Rigi

Rooterberg

Lausanne

B2

Canton: Vaud (VD)
Altitude: 380–530 m/1247–1739 ft
Population: 127,000

Lausanne

Lausanne, the lively capital of the canton of Vaud, is picturesquely situated on the north shore of Lake Geneva, on terraces rising above the lake which are broken by gorges. It ranks with Geneva as a focus of intellectual life in French-speaking Switzerland (Federal Court, University, College of Technology, Hotel School and many other technical colleges), and is also a popular convention and conference centre and the venue of important trade fairs (Comptoir Suisse in Autumn, International Tourism Fair in March). Major elements in the town's economy are the foodstuffs industries, vine-growing and the wine trade.

*Townscape

In the attractive townscape of Lausanne the modern office blocks and the high-level bridges spanning the gorges (now built over) of the Rivers Flon and Louve form a striking contrast to the narrow lanes and steep flights of steps which run up to the old town (Cité), dominated by the cathedral (530 m/1739 ft) and the Château, while to the south pleasant residential districts extend down to the port of Ouchy (380 m/1247 ft).

History

There was a Celtic settlement at the mouth of the River Flon which later became the Roman Lousonium or Lousonna. After the destruction of this town by the Alemanni about 379 a fortified settlement was built on the hill now occupied by the Cité, and after that the transfer of the episcopal see from Avanches to Lausanne (c. 590) this became a town of some size which, like Geneva, belonged successively to the Burgundians, the Franks and the second Burgundian Kingdom before becoming part of the Holy Roman Empire in 1033. In the 15th c. the Vaud region was conquered by the Bernese, who soon introduced the Reformed faith. In 1798, however, Vaud recovered its independence as the République Lémanique, and in 1803 it became the 19th canton to join the Swiss Confederation.

Boat services

On Lake Geneva (departures from Place de la Navigation, Ouchy) there are motor launches several times daily to lakeside towns in Switzerland and France; round trips and cruises.

Lausanne: capital of the canton of Vaud

Tour of the town

In the centre

The hub of the town's traffic is the Place St-François, surrounded by large office blocks and the Head Post Office. In the middle of the square stands the former Franciscan church of St-François (13th–14th c.; beautiful stained glass of 1907 in choir), with a tower of 1523. A little way east is the Derrière Bourg park (fine views).

St-François church

From Place St-François take Rue de Bourg (pedestrians only) and Rue Caroline and then turn left over the Pont Bessières (1910) to reach the cathedral (below).

The Grand-Pont (1839–44), an arched viaduct 180 m/591 ft long from which there is an attractive view of the old town and the cathedral, runs north-west from Place St-François into the busy imposing Bel-Air Métropole office block (1932; restaurant and café), crowned by a tower block 67 m/220 ft high (20 storeys).

Bel-Air Métropole

From Place Bel-Air, Rue Haldimand runs north-east, passing on the right the Protestant church of St-Laurent (1719; Baroque façade).

St-Laurent church

To the north-east is the spacious Place de la Riponne. On its east side stands the Palais de Rumine (1898–1906), which houses the University, originally founded as as Academy in 1537. (A new university complex is under consruction at Dorigny, 5 km/3 miles west of the town.) Also in the Palais de Rumine are the Cantonal and University Library (700,000 volumes, valuable manuscripts), the Cantonal Museum of Art (Musée Cantonal des Beaux-Arts; mainly pictures by 19th c. artists of western Switzerland), the Natural History Museum and the Archaeological Museum (bust of Marcus Aurelius).

Palais de Rumine

Museum of Art
Natural History
and Archaeo-
logical Museum

From the church of St-Laurent Rue de l'Ale runs north-west to the Tour De l'Ale, a round tower 21 m/69 ft high which is the only remnant of the town's 14th c. fortifications.

Tour de l'Ale

A little way south of Place de la Riponne (pedestrian precinct) is Place de la Palud, in which is situated the Hôtel de Ville (Town Hall, 15th and 17th c.; 16th c. stained glass). From here the Escaliers du Marché, a covered flight of steps, lead up to the cathedral, in the Cité (which can also be reached from Place de la Riponne by a flight of steps to the right of the University and Rue Pierre-Viret).

Hôtel de Ville

In the old town (Cité)

The Cathedral of Notre-Dame (Protestant), consecrated by Pope Gregory X in the presence of King Rudolf of Habsburg in 1275, is an Early Gothic building with five towers (central tower, 75 m/246 ft high, 1876; a watchman calls out the hours from the bell-cage during the night). The main doorway (16th c.) and the "Apostles' doorway" (13th c.) have very fine sculptured decoration (copies: originals under the rose-window). The restoration work, which has been taking place for years, should be completed by the end of the century.

*Cathedral

The interior is notable for its noble proportions. In the south transept is a large rose-window with beautiful 13th c. stained glass (the Universe); the south aisle has carved choir stalls of 1509; in the choir are remains of early Gothic stalls and (on left) the tomb of the Minnesinger Otto of Grandson (d. 1328); in the crypt are to be found remains of an 8th c. basilica, with old tombs.

*Rose-window

Lausanne

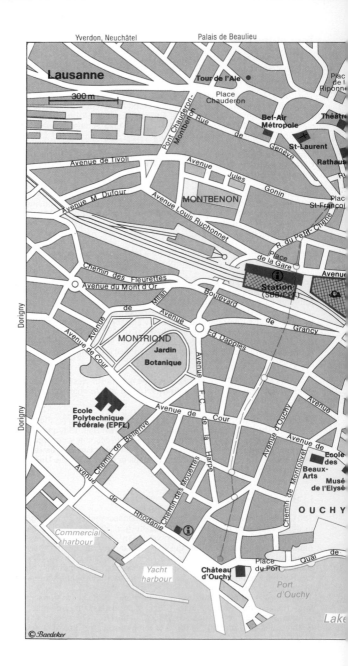

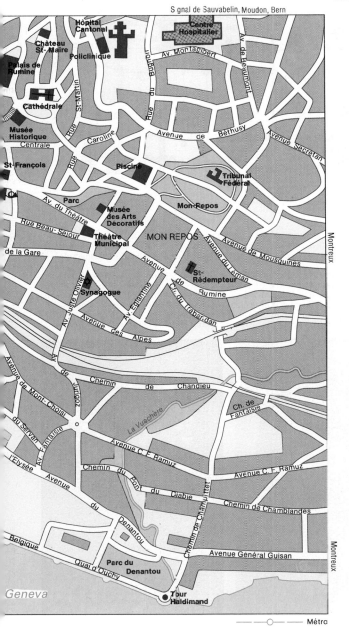

S gnal de Sauvabelin, Moudon, Bern

Hôpital Cantonal

Centre Hospitalier

Château St-Maire

Policlinique

Palais de Rumine

Av. Montagibert

Av. de Beaumont

Rue du Bugnon

Rue St-Martin

Cathédrale

Rue St-Martin

Caroline

Avenue de Béthusy

Avenue Secrétan

Musée Historique

Centrale

St-François

Rue

Piscine

Tribunal Fédéral

Parc

Av. du Théâtre

Musée des Arts Décoratifs

Mon-Repos

Rue Beau- Séjour

Théâtre Municipal

MON REPOS

Avenue de Mousquines

de la Gare

Avenue

Avenue du Léman

St-Rédempteur

Av. Juste Olivier

Synagogue

Av. Epinette

de

Rumine

Ch. du Trabandan

Avenue des Alpes

Av. de

Chemin de

Chandieu

Avenue de Mont-Choisi

Jomini

Ch. de Fantaisie

du Servan

Av. Fantaisie

La Vuachère

l'Elysée

Avenue C. F. Ramuz

Chemin du Pont du Diable

Avenue C. F. Ramuz

Avenue

du

Chemin de Chamblandes

Chemin de Chamblandes

Denantou

Belgique

Avenue Général Guisan

Quai d'Ouchy

Parc du Denantou

Geneva

Tour Haldimand

Montreux

Montreux

———○——— Métro

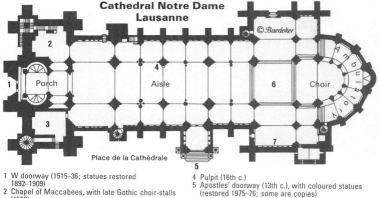

Cathedral Notre Dame Lausanne

© *Baedeker*

Ambulatory

2

1 Porch

Aisle

4

6 Choir

3

5

Place de la Cathédrale

7

1 W doorway (1515–36; statues restored 1892–1909)
2 Chapel of Maccabees, with late Gothic choir-stalls (1509)
3 S tower

4 Pulpit (16th c.)
5 Apostles' doorway (13th c.), with coloured statues (restored 1975–76; some are copies)
6 Central tower
7 Rose-window (c. 1240)

Musée Historique de l'Ancien Evêché

On the terrace to the south of the cathedral (beautiful view) is the tower (1373–83) of the old episcopal castle, which now houses the Musée Historique de l'Ancien Evêché and the Musée Permanent de la Cathédrale.

Ancien Academy

From the cathedral we go north, past the former Academy (1587), the forerunner of the University, where famous professors such as Sainte-Beuve and Adam Mickiewicz gave their lectures. In the Rue de l'Academie

Musée de la pipe
Château St-Maire

(No. 7) the Musée de la Pipe contains over 2500 examples documenting the history of the pipe. Farther to the north is the Château St-Maire (1397–1431), originally the bishop's palace, residence of the Bernese government

In Lausanne Cathedral . . .   *. . . is beautiful stained glass*

Cathedral of Notre-Dame   *Château St-Maire*

from 1536 to 1798, and now occupied by the cantonal government. This cubic building of sandstone and brick has 15th and 16th c. allegorical frescoes.

To the left, on the west terrace, is the Grand Conseil (the cantonal parliament; 1803–1806 by A. Perregaux), with its Classical façade.   Grand-Conseil

East of the Old Town

On the east side of the town is the beautiful old park of Mon Repos with an 18th c. palace of the same name rebuilt in the 19th c. by L. Damesme. Nowadays, the building where Voltaire staged his play "Zaïre", is used for official visits.   Mon Repos

On higher ground to the north of the park the Federal Court (Tribunal Fédéral; conducted tours) is housed in a building erected in 1922–27.   Federal court

North of the Old Town

Above the town to the north (20 minutes' walk) is the Signal de Sauvabelin (647 m/2123 ft; restaurant), with a famous view of Lausanne. On the Route de Signal (No. 2) the impressive Fondation de l'Hermitage, situated in beautiful parkland, has art exhibitions. Beyond this is a large wooded park, the Bois de Sauvabelin, with a small lake (restaurant) and a deer park. To the north of the park, on the far side of the motorway along the banks of the Flon, is the Vivarium, with reptiles, insects, birds of prey and small animals (combined admission ticket which covers also the Zoo at Servion, 15 km/ 9 miles north-west).   **Signal de Sauvabelin
Fondation de l'Hermitage
Bois de Sauvabelin
V varium
Zoo de Servion*

On the north-west side of the town (1 km/½ mile) from Place de la Riponne) stands the Palais de Beaulieu (1920; convention facility, restaurant, theatre), with the show and exhibition halls of the Comptoir Suisse, a sports complex and since 1987 the theatre of the "Béjart Ballett Lausanne".   **Palais de Beaulieu**

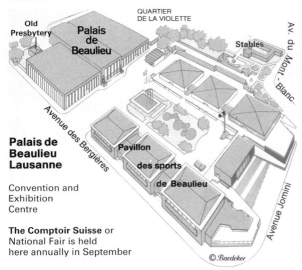

Old Presbytery

Palais de Beaulieu

QUARTIER DE LA VIOLETTE

Stables

Av. du Mont - Blanc

Avenue des Bergières

Palais de Beaulieu Lausanne

Pavillon des sports de Beaulieu

Avenue Jomini

© Baedeker

Convention and
Exhibition
Centre

The Comptoir Suisse or
National Fair is held
here annually in September

Château de Beaulieu, Collection de l'Art Brut	To the south, beyond the Avenue Bergières, the Château de Beaulieu (1756) houses a collection of marginal art ("Art Brut") donated by Jean Dubuffet.

Ouchy

Château d'Ouchy	On the lakeside 1.5 km/1 mile south of the town's central district lies the busy little port of Ouchy (380 m/1250 ft). Between the old and the new harbours is a 12th c. castle, the Château d'Ouchy, now a hotel and restaurant, in which the peace treaty between Turkey, Greece and the Allies was signed in 1923.

There is a statue in the square by Dönninger of General Guisan, the commander of the Swiss army during the Second World War.

Near the Hôtel de l'Angleterre a plaque commemorates Lord Byron, who wrote "The prisoner of Chillon" here (Montreux see entry). Several historical treaties were signed in the famous grand hotels, such as in the Beau-Rivage Palace, where the "Accord de Lausanne" was signed in 1932.

Port d'Ouchy	From Port d'Ouchy, the old harbour, a beautiful lakeside promenade affording attractive views runs 1 km/½ mile east to the Tour Haldimand and the pretty Parc Denantou. The Elysée Museum in the Avenue de l'Elysée presents the history of photography, from its beginnings to the present day.
Musée de l'Elysée	
Botanic Garden	Above Ouchy to the north-west is the Parc Montriond (fine views), with the Botanic Garden; of particular interest are the alpinum, the Pharmaceutical garden and the arboretum.

Vidy

To the west of the suburb is Vidy, in Gallo-Roman times the port of
Losonna. On the shores of the lake are a yacht harbour, a rowing facility,

Ouchy: Yacht harbour

extensive sports grounds and a camping site. A "Promenade Archéolo-
gique" is to be found at the beginning of the motorway.

North of the camping site is the Château de Vidy, headquarters of the
International Olympic Committee (founded 1894), where there is a
museum and an exhibition outlining the Olympic movement from the
original idea of Pierre de Courbertin. In the park the first of 20 planned
sculptures were handed over in 1988 by Prince Rainier of Monaco.

Musée
Olympique

To the north of the motorway, in the Chemin du Bois-de-Vaux, is the Vidy
Roman Museum (Gallo-Roman material).

Musée Romain

Pully

To the east of Ouchy the suburb of Pully has modern bathing facilities and
the remains of a Roman villa (destroyed in the 2nd c. A.D.). A monastery was
later built on its site and excavations have uncovered a 20 sq. m/215 sq. ft
wall-painting from the 1st c. A.D..

Roman villa

Surroundings

25 km/16 miles north-east, off the west side of E4 the little industrial town of
Moudon (alt. 513 m/1683 ft; pop. 300) occupies the site of the Roman
Minnodunum. In the lower town is the beautiful Gothic church of St-
Etienne, with richly carved choir-stalls of 1502, while in the upper town are
attractive old houses, the 12th c. Tour de Broye, the little château of Roche-
fort (1595; local museum) and the château of Billens (1677).

Moudon

20 km/12 miles east of Lausanne on the road to Romont, in Oron-le-Châtel
(above Oron-la-Ville), is the well-preserved Château Oron (13th c.;
museum).

Château Oron

Lauterbrunnen Valley   C2

Canton: Berne (BE)

Situation and general

The Lauterbrunnen valley to the south of Interlaken extends from Zweilütschinen to the foot of the Breithorn, in the Jungfrau massif. The Trogtal, a typical high Alpine valley through which the Weisse Lütschine flows down to join the Schwarze Lütschine at Zweilütschinen, is enclosed between sheer rock walls over which plunge a number of magnificent waterfalls. From Zweilütschinen the road climbs up the valley with a moderate gradient between limestone walls from 300 to 500 m/984 to 1641 ft high. On the right are the Sausbach Falls, and just beyond this, on the left, the Hunnenfluh (1334 m/4377 ft), rearing up like a semicircular tower.

Lauterbrunnen

Beyond this is Lauterbrunnen (800 m/2625 ft; pop. 1000), a popular summer resort and the starting-point of the funicular to the Jungfraujoch (see Jungfrau). Above the village are the Staubbach falls, which plunge down from an overhanging crag in a sheer drop of 300 m/984 ft. It was here, over 200 years ago, that the privy councillor Johann Wolfgang von Goethe found the inspiration for "Gesang der Geister über den Wassern" ("Song of the Spirits over the Water"), which was later set to music by Schubert. The Lauterbrunnen valley is renowned as a walkers' paradise offering beautiful climbs, while helicopter flights to the glaciers provide a bird's eye view of the mountains. There are also long-distance ski-runs (17.5 km/11 miles), tennis courts and two swimming pools. A collection of agricultural tools and equipment is on show in the museum.

Isenfluh

A rewarding excursion can be made on a mountain road which runs 3.5 km/2 miles north to the village of Isenfluh (1084 m/3557 ft), situated on a steep natural terrace affording a superb view of the mountain giants from the Grosshorn to the Eiger.

Lauterbrunnen – between the Jungfrau region and the Schilthorn

The road to Stechelberg branches off on the left at the Staubbach Hotel in Lauterbrunnen, bends to the left and runs down to cross the Lütschine; it then continues up the valley of the Breithorn, passing two camping sites and the Staubbach falls (on right).

In 4 km/2 miles it comes to the Trümmelbach Hotel (on left), from which there is a footpath (5 minutes) to the Trümmelbach Falls, which plunge down in five mighty cascades through the gorge carved out by the Trümmelbach (charge; electric elevator, stepped paths, floodlighting). There are breath-taking views of the falls, ten of which are accessible, thundering down through the mountain at 20,000 litres per second. They are fed by the giant ice walls of the Eiger, Mönch and Jungfrau. Almost hidden inside the Schwarze Mönch they are the only waterfalls in Europe inside a mountain which are accessible.

*Trümmelbach falls

From the hotel the road continues up the Lauterbrunnen valley. In 2 km/1 mile a side road goes off on the right to the lower station (867 m/2845 ft; car park) of the Schilthornbahn, a cableway 6967 m/22,859 ft long which ascends in 34 minutes, via the intermediate stations of Gimmelwand (1367 m/4485 ft), Mürren (1638 m/5374 ft; see entry) and Birg (2677 m/8783 ft; restaurant with observation terrace), to the Schilthorn (2970 m/9745 ft; revolving restaurant, sun terrace; summer skiing), from which there are magnificent views (telescope).

*Schilthornbahn

*Schilthorn

The road ends, 1 km/about ½ mile beyond the turn-off for the cableway station, at the little village of Stechelberg (922 m/3025 ft). From here it is a 45–60 minutes' walk to the group of huts at Trachsellauenen (1263 m/4144 ft), and from there another 1¼ hours' walk to the Schmadribach falls or a 1½ hours' walk to the Alp Obersteinberg (1770 m/5807 ft), which affords a superb panorama of the mountains and glaciers around the upper part of the Lauterbrunnen valley.

Stechelberg

*Schmadribach falls

Lenzerheide-Valbella

E2

Canton: Grisons: (GR)
Altitude: 1470 and 1540 m/4823 and 5053 ft
Population: 2400

In the park-like and wooded high valley of Lenzerheide (Romansch Planüra), the beauty of which has long attracted visitors, are the two resorts of Lenzerheide and Valbella, on either side of the Heidsee (the "Lei"; 1493 m/4899 ft; bathing beach).

Situation

Townscape

To the east of the two resorts, which are popular both in summer and in winter, rear up the Aroser Rothorn (2984 m/9791 ft), the Lenzerhorn (2911 m/9551 ft) and the ridges of the Parpaner Rothorn (2824 m/9266 ft) and Schwarzhorn (2683 m/8801 ft); on the west, Alpine meadows extend up the slopes of Piz Scalottas (2324 m/7625 ft) and the Stätzerhorn (2574 m/8445 ft).

These two resorts have expanded to form one town which is characterised by its Swiss chalet architecture. For the active holidaymaker there is golf, horse riding, tennis, water sports, walking and climbing to choose from as well as winter sports.

Chair-lift from Lenzerheide via Tgantieni (1730 m/5676 ft) to Piz Scalottas (2324 m/7625 ft); cableway from Valbella (Canois) via Alp Scharmoin (1900 m/6234 ft) to Parpaner Rothorn (2865 m/9400 ft; 15 minutes).

Cableways and lifts

The Val Sporz region saw the advent of "mechanised" skiing with the first sledge-railway as the forerunner of the ski-lift in 1936. Nowadays this

Winter sports

Lenzerheide

extensive area has over 50 prepared ski-lifts as well as numerous elevators below the Parpaner Weisshorn and Schwarzhorn (reached by cableway to Alp Scharmoin) and on the slopes of Piz Scalottas and the Stätzerhorn. Cross-country skiing, tobogganing, skating, curling, horse-drawn sleigh rides. Three ski schools.

Surroundings

*Schin gorge
A by-road runs south-west from Lenzerheide to Zorten and down into the wild Schin gorge on the River Albula.

Lenz
The main road runs south, past the golf course, a camping-site and the Bual nature park, to Lantsch or Lenz (1320 m/4331 ft), with a church dedicated to the Virgin (1505). 2 km/1 mile beyond Lantsch, below the road on the right, we see the farm of Vazerol (1130 m/3708 ft), where the three Rhaetian leagues agreed to unite in 1471.

Tiefencastel
8 km/5 miles farther on is Tiefencastel, a picturesquely situated village (parish church of 1660), at the confluence of the Julia and the Albula and at an important road junction. From here one road leads south over the Julier (Guglia) pass to Silvaplana and another goes east over the Albula pass to La Punt-Chamues-ch.

From Valbella the road runs north over the Acl' Alva pass (1549 m/5082 ft), also known as the Valbella saddle or the Lenzerheide pass, which marks the linguistic boundary between German and Romansch (fine view of the Oberhalbstein Mountains).

Parpan
The road then reaches Parpan (1511 m/4958 ft), another health and winter sports resort, with a number of fine old houses, including the "Schlössli" (16th–17th c.) of the Buol family, and a 16th c. church with a separate tower.

Churwalden
4 km/2 miles beyond this is Churwalden (1230 m/4036 ft), a rambling village with a former Premonstratensian abbey (15th c. church, tower-like abbot's

Heidsee – il Lei

lodging). Chair-lifts to the Alp Stätz (1824 m/5985 ft) and the Pradaschierer Alp (1817 m/5962 ft).

Leukerbad/Loèche-les-Bains   C2

Canton: Valais (VS)
Altitude: 1411 m/4629 ft
Population: 1500

The well-known spa of Leukerbad (in French Loèche-les-Bains) lies amid   Situation
the green Alpine meadows of a south-facing basin situated in a valley on
the north side of the Upper Rhône on the route to the Gemmi pass.
Leukerbad can be reached by the ordinary motor road from Leuk or by a
romantic little by-road which winds its way up from Sierre via Salgesch.
From the motor road a daringly engineered path with eight rough wooden
ladders up a 100 m/328 ft rock face leads to the mountain village of Albinen.

Townscape

This high-altitude resort was known to the Romans; in modern times the
earliest reference to the village – then known as Baden – dates from 1315.
The scattered settlement has grown up around its 20 or so thermal springs;
the old wooden houses of the village are on the right bank of the River Dala,
the hotels and spa establishments on the left.
The water (containing lime and sulphur, 51° C/124° F; temperature of baths
28–41° C/82–106° F) is efficacious in the treatment of rheumatism, gout and
paralysis; there is an open-air pool with thermal water as well as several
indoor pools; polio clinic. With its cableways and a magnificent sports
centre. Leukerbad is now popular both as a summer and a winter sports
resort.

259

Leukerbad; thermal baths

Surroundings

*Torrenthorn

The Torrentbahn runs from Leukerbad and the Albinen ladders to the Rinderhütte (2315 m/7596 ft). From the Hotel Torrenthorn (2462 m/8078 ft) it is a 1½ hours' climb to the summit of the Torrenthorn (2998 m/9836 ft), from which there is a superb panoramic view taking in twenty 4000 m/13,124 ft peaks.

Gemmiweg

The Gemmiweg, a path hewn from the rock in 1737–40, runs along a rock face with a sheer drop of 600 m/1969 ft, and is to be recommended only to those with a good head for heights. A cableway (length 1984 m/6510 ft, height difference 935 m/3068 ft, time 5 minutes) runs up to the Gemmi pass (2316 m/7599 ft), from which a bridle-path runs along the shores of the Daubensee and then down to Kandersteg in the Bernese Oberland.

Leuk Stadt

At the mouth of the Dala gorge, above the Rhône, is Leuk Stadt (725 m/2379 ft; pop. 2800), a little market town and district administratve capital which was once the summer residence of the Bishop of Sion. Features of interest include a Late Gothic tower (1541–43) once occupied by a local government official, the viztum; the bishop's castle (first mentioned in 1254); the late 15th c. parish church of St Stephan (R.C.); and the former residence of the de Werra family (16th–17th c.).

*Ringacker Chapel

The Ringacker Chapel, on a natural terrace south of the town, is the finest Baroque building in the Valais (1690–94). The interior of this single-naved church is richly decorated in stucco and its monumental altar was completed at the beginning of the 18th c.

Satellite station

At the Leuk satellite tracking station there is an exhibition on space communication with slide shows, demonstrations and models.

Principality of Liechtenstein

Prince's
arms

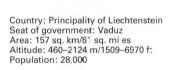

National Flag

Car
Nationality
plate

Arms on
car
number
plates

Country: Principality of Liechtenstein
Seat of government: Vaduz
Area: 157 sq. km/61 sq. miles
Altitude: 460–2124 m/1509–6970 ft
Population: 28,000

The Principality of Liechtenstein is an independent state in the Alpine region between Switzerland and Austria. It extends from the western slopes of the Rätikon ridge to the Rhine.

Situation

The most densely populated part of the country and the main agricultural area is the Rhine plain; the hillsides are mainly covered with forest, and in the high valleys Alpine meadows predominate. Its favourable tax laws have made it the headquarters of numerous holding companies. In proportion to its size Liechtenstein is the most highly industrialised nation in the world (metal-processing, chemical and pharmaceutical, textile and food industries), and its per-capita income is also one of the highest in the world. The language of the country is an Alemannic dialect of German.

General

History

The region of present-day Liechtenstein was already settled during the Early Stone Age. In the Roman period a road traversed the region from north to south.

Pre- and early history

The county of Vaduz, established in 1342, was acquired in 1712 by Prince Hans Adam of Liechtenstein and combined with the lordship of Liechtenstein. On 23 January 1719 Emperor Karl VI finally granted both counties the status of the Imperial Principality of Liechtenstein. In 1806 Liechtenstein was joined to the Rheinbund by Napoleon and subsequently the German Bund. With the dissolution of the German Bund Liechtenstein became an autonomous state. Prince Franz Josef II died in 1989, a week after his wife Gina, in his 51st year of office. He was succeeded by the Crown Prince Hans Adam II, who had already taken over the leadership of the government in 1984.

Foundations

From 1852 until after the First World War Liechtenstein was joined with Austria in a currency union, but in 1924 it formed an economic union with Switzerland (using Swiss currency and under Swiss customs and postal

Associations

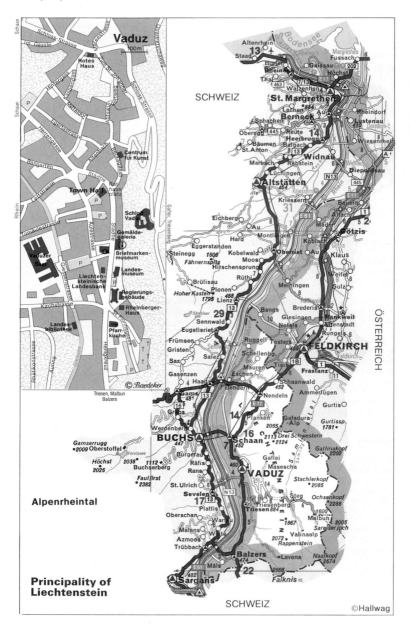

Vaduz

administration but with its own stamps). The Principality of Liechtenstein is
a member of the European Parliament and EFTA.

The Principality of Liechtenstein is a constitutional monarchy, inherited
through the male line. The Parliament consists of 15 delegates elected for
four years by secret ballot. Legislation may be changed by referenda.

Constitution

Vaduz

Vaduz, capital of the Principality of Liechtenstein, seat of its government
and parliament and its main tourist attraction, lies near the right bank of the
Rhine beneath the towering summit of the Rätikon.

General and
situation

To the east, above the town, rises Schloss Vaduz (no admittance), which
dates back to the 12th c. The cemetery and buildings on the east side form
the oldest part; the chapel is probably High Middle Ages. The round
bastions to the north-east and south-west were built in the 16th c. after it
was burnt down in 1499 by the Confederates. The west side was rebuilt in
the 17th c. and between 1901 and 1910 the castle was rebuilt in 16th c. style.

Schloss Vaduz

In the middle of the town is the Rathausplatz, with the Rathaus (Town Hall).
From here the town's main street, Städtle (one-way traffic in the opposite
direction), runs south for some 500 m/1641 ft to the Neo-Gothic parish
church (Pfarrkirche, 1869–73).

Rathausplatz,
Städtle, parish
church.

On the left-hand (east) side of the street, at No. 37, is the Engländerbau
("Englishmen's Building"), in which is housed the Art Gallery (Gemälde-
galerie), particularly notable for the permanent collection in the Prince's
Gallery (Rubens, Frans Hals, Van Dyck, Breughel, etc.), also the Postage
Stamp Museum (Briefmarkenmuseum) and the Tourist Information Office
(Fremdenverkehrszentrale).

*Art Gallery

Postal Museum

On the opposite side of the street is the Post Office.

Post Office

Then follows (No. 43) the Landesmuseum (relief model of the Principality
on a scale of 1:10,000; prehistory and the early historical period; weapons;
religious art).

Liechtenstein
Landesmuseum

Liechtenstein: Alpine Rhine Triesen . . .   *. . . and Vaduz Castle*

Principality of Liechtenstein

Government offices	At the south end of the street, on the left, stands the Regierungsgebäude (government offices, 1903–05).
Rotes Haus, Rheinberger-Geburtshaus	Other places of interest are the Rotes Haus (Schloss-Strasse), the Wine Cellar (17th c.) and the Rheinberger-Geburtshaus with the Liechtenstein music school.
Wildschloss ruins	The ruins of the Wildschloss (840 m/2756 ft) tower over Vaduz and are a popular place to visit.

Other places in Liechtenstein

Triesenberg	The little towns and villages on the hills and in the Upper Samina valley are popular both with summer visitors and winter sports enthusiasts. From Vaduz a hill road winds its way, with steep bends and extensive views, into the Samina valley (14 km/9 miles to Malbun), going either via the beautifully situated village of Triesenberg (884 m/2900 ft; Walser Museum), 6 km/4 miles from Vaduz, or via Rotenboden (1000 m/3281 ft), also 6 km/4 miles from Vaduz, to a road junction at Gnalp (8.5 km/5 miles from Vaduz); left to Gaflei, right to Malbun.
Masescha	1 km/½ mile past the above-mentioned junction, on the road to Gaflei, is the old Walser settlement of Masescha (1235 m/4053 ft; oldest Walser church, 14th c.; inn).
*Tourotel Gaflei, Kuhgrat, Drei Schwestern	About 2½ km/1½ miles beyond Masescha (12 km/7 miles from Vaduz) the road comes to the car park of the Tourotel Gaflei (1483 m/4866 ft), situated amid Alpine meadows, with extensive views. From here a footpath (the Fürstensteig or "Prince's Path") leads up in 2¼–2½ hours to the Kuhgrat (2124 m/6969 ft; magnificent views), the highest peak in the Drei Schwestern (Three Sisters) massif.
Kulm, Steg, Malbun	The road to Malbun, to the right, runs under the Kulm pass (1459 m/4787 ft) in a tunnel 850 m/2789 ft long to Steg (1312 m/4305 ft) in the Upper Samina valley, and continues along a side valley to Malbun, 14 km/9 miles from Vaduz (1650 m/5414 ft).
Sareiser Joch, Schönberg	From here a chair lift 850 m/2789 ft long ascends to the Sareiser Joch (2014 m/6608 ft), and the Schönberg (2104 m/6903 ft) can be climbed in 2½ hours.
Triesen	4 km/2 miles south of Vaduz is Triesen (463 m/1519 ft; pop. 3000), with old houses in the upper part of the village and chapels dedicated to St Mamertus and the Virgin. Walks and climbs on the Lavena, Rappenstein and Falknis hills.
Balzers	5 km/3 miles beyond Triesen we reach Balzers (476 m/1562 ft; pop. 3300), with Gutenberg Castle, the chapels of Mariahilf and St Peter, an old presbytery, a local museum and nature reserves.
Schaan	3 km/2 miles north of Vaduz, at the foot of the Drei Schwestern massif, is Schaan (450–500 m/1477–1641 ft; pop. 4700), a busy little industrial town with the foundations of a Roman fort. Idyllically situated above the town is the pilgrimage church Maria zum Trost ("Dux"; 18th c.). Various Roman remains have been excavated in the surrounding area of Schaan.
Planken	From here a good minor road runs north-east to the village of Planken (800 m/2625 ft), situated on a beautiful natural terrace, with good views of the Rhine valley and the Swiss Alps beyond. Planken is an excellent base for walks and climbs in the Drei Schwestern area.
Nendeln, Eschen	5 km/3 miles north-east of Schaan on road 16 is Nendeln. this little town and Eschen, a few kilometres west, are the principal places in the lowland part of Liechtenstein. In both towns remains of the past have been found (in Nendeln the foundations of a Roman villa). The main features of interest are the Pfrundhaus (prebend house), the Holy Cross chapel on the Rotenberg (formerly a place of execution and of assembly) and the chapels of St Sebastian and St Roch in Nendeln. There is also an interesting model pottery here.

To the west, on the western slopes of the Eschnerberg, lies the village of Gamprin-Bendern, from which the interesting "Eschnerberg History Trail" (Historischer Höhenweg Eschnerberg) runs to Schellenberg, with the ruined castle of Neu-Schellenberg.

Gamprin-Bendern
Schellenberg

At Ruggell, west of Schellenberg in the Rhine valley, is the Ruggeller Riet nature reserve, with interesting flora and fauna.

Ruggell

Locarno   D2

Canton: Ticino
Altitude: 205 m/673 ft
Population: 15,000

The old Ticenese town of Locarno is magnificently situated at the north end of Lake Maggiore, with country villas, gardens and vineyards rising up the hillsides; the newer parts of the town are laid out in a regular pattern on the flat ground of the swiftly flowing River Maggia. With its mild climate, in which figs, olives and pomegranates flourish and in August myrtles blossom, Locarno is particularly popular in spring and autumn.

Situation and
general

Boat services on Lake Maggiore. Motor ships (in summer also hydrofoils) to the islands and places on the lake (departure from Lungolago G. Motta).

Boat services

Sights

The town's main square is the broad Piazza Grande, which extends westwards from the landing-stage for some 400 m/1312 ft, with arcades containing shops on its north side. Along the south side are the Giardini Pubblici (Public Gardens) and the Kursaal (gaming rooms, restaurant). In Via della Pace, which runs south through the gardens to a fountain, is the

Piazza Grande

Public Gardens,
Kursaal

Locarno: Debarcadero (landing-stage)   *Mediterranean flora in public gardens*

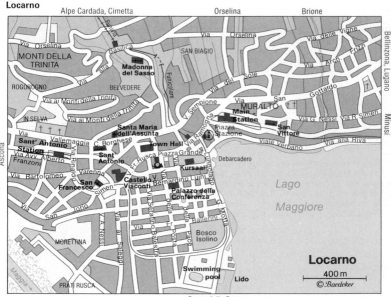

Locarno

Alpe Cardada, Cimetta   Orselina   Brione

Locarno

400 m

© *Baedeker*

Parco della Pace

Pretorio (Law Court) or Palazzo della Conferenza, in which the Locarno Pact was signed in 1925.

The Piazza Grande runs into curving Via Francesco Rusca, from which four narrow streets lead up to the Old Town. On the west side of Via Rusca is the Castello Visconti, the old castle of the Visconti Dukes of Milan, which was largely destroyed in 1518; it now houses the Museo Civico (closed Mondays), with Roman material recovered by excavations and the Hans Arp Collection (contemporary art).

Castello

To the south-west, on higher ground, is the conventual church of San Francesco, a basilica (1528–72) with massive granite columns and wall-paintings, now serving the German-speaking Catholics of the town.

San Francesco

To the north the 17th c. church of Sant'Antonio contains painting with perspective effect by G. A. F. Orelli. West of this are the cemetery and the former church of S. Maria in Selva and the tomb of Hans Arp (1887–1966), with sculpture.

Sant'Antonio

Santa Maria In Selva

To the east of Sant'Antonio is the small but fine Baroque church of Santa Maria dell'Assunta, also known as Chiesa Nuova (17th c.). Its façade is dominated by a large statue of St Christopher; the interior contains beautiful stucco work.

Santa Maria dell'Assunta

A beautiful lakeside promenade, the Lungolago Guiseppe Motta, skirts the bay. To the south this leads to the Lido (swimming pool, camping site), the Parco della Pace and the Trade Fair grounds on the Maggia delta. To the east is Rivapiana in the district of Minusio.

Lakeside promenade

In the Muralto distrct to the east of the station stands the parish church of San Vittore, originally Romanesque (12th c.) but much altered in later centuries (campanile, completed only in 1932; fine Romanesque crypt).

Muralto, San Vittore

Farther north-east is the outer district of Minusio, with the interesting old church of San Qurico. The bell tower (13th/14th c.) is a former watch tower.

Minusio, San Quirico

Santa Maria dell'Assunta

Piazza Statione

On the lakeside is the imposing 16th c. Cà di Ferro, once a barracks occupied by mercenaries in the employ of the Governor P etro à Pro. In the cemetery (north-east entrance in the wall on the right) is the grave of the German poet Stefan George (1868–1933).

Cà di Ferro

The pilgrimage church of the Madonna del Sasso, with a Capuchin friary on a wooded crag above Locarno (355 m/1165 ft) can be reached by funicular from Via Ramogna, between the station and the Piazza Grande, 825 m/2707 ft in 6 minutes; on foot, by a path with Stations of the Cross, in 30–45 minutes; or by road from Sant'Antonio via Monti or from Muralto via Orselina, 3.5 km/2 miles. The church, founded in 1480, was rebuilt in 1616 and overloaded with decoration in the 19th c. (restored in 20th c.). To the right of the entrance is a major work by Bramantino, the "Flight into Egypt" (1536), and in the second side chapel an "Entombment" by A. Ciseri (c. 1865). The notable collection of ecclesiastical art in the monastery museum includes valuable manuscripts. From the terrace there are superb views over Locarno and Lake Maggiore.

*Madonna del Sasso

On the hillside to the west and east of the Madonna del Sasso, commanding extensive views, are the residential suburbs of Monti (Monti della Trinità, 404 m/1326 ft and Orselina (456 m/1496 ft).

Surroundings

From the Madonna del Sasso a cableway 2 km/1 mile long ascends in 10 minutes to the Alpe Cardada (1350 m/4429 ft; hotel), with magnificent views. Chair-lift (869 m/2851 ft, 6 minutes) to Cimetta (1676 m/5499 ft; good skiing with several ski-lifts.

Alpe Cardada

From Monti a road (6 km/4 miles) runs steeply uphill through the forest, with many bends, to the little mountain village of Mont Bré (1004 m/

Monte Bré, San Bernardo

3294 ft). 1 km/about ½ mile beyond this along the mountainside is San Bernardo (1096 m/3596 ft), with a 16th c. chapel. From both villages there are splendid views.

To Mergoscia

(13 km/8 miles: narrow and winding road, but well worth it.)
The road runs north-east from the Madonna del Sasso along the hillside, with far-ranging views, via Orselina and Brione sopra Minusio (433 m/1421 ft). 8 km/5 miles: Contra (486 m/1595 ft), high above the mouth of the Val Verzasca. The road continues, through galleries and over bridges, along the west side of the valley.

Mergoscia   5 km/3 miles: Mergoscia (735 m/2412 ft), a beautifully situated village with a view of the Verzasca dam and Pizzo di Vogorno (2446 m/8025 ft). The church has 15th c. wall-paintings.

*From Locarno into the Val Verzasca

General   The Val Verzasca (30 km/19 miles) to Sonogno: resonably good road, but many bends; its attraction lies in the beauty of this remote and secluded Ticenese valley with its Italian-style houses and churches, many of them with campaniles; good footpaths.

Leave on the Bellinzona road. 4 km/2 miles: Tenero on the west bank of the Gordola   Verzasca. 1 km/about ½ mile: Gordola (206 m/676 ft, a neat village at the entry of the Verzasca into the Ticino plain (Piano di Magadino). The road now winds its way uphill to the left and continues along the left bank of the *Val Verzasca   river high up on the slopes of the deeply slashed Val Verzasca, an inhospitable valley which has been considerably changed by the construction of a

Lavertezzo in the Val Verzasca

dam. It has few inhabitants except in summer. 3 km/2 miles farther on is the mighty Verzasca dam, 220 m/722 ft high, built 1960–65, which has formed the Lago di Vogorno, an artificial lake with a capacity of 105 million cu. m/ 3708 million cu. ft. Beneath the dam is the hydro-electric power station (235 million kWh annually).

Verzasca dam

The road continues up the east side of the lake (6 km/4 miles long), passing through several tunnels, some of them or sharp bends. Mergoscia can be seen high up on the other side.
6 km/4 miles: Vogorno (490 m/16908 ft), a picturesque village with 13th c. frescoes of saints in the upper church. 2 km/1 mile: road on left (1 km/about ½ mile) to the little village of Corippo (565 m/1854 ft).

Vogorno

2 km/1 mile: Lavertezzo (548 m/1798 ft), at the mouth of the wide Val Lavertezzo, a charming village with a two-arched bridge and a quarry of excellent granite.
The road then climbs through the villages of Aquino (574 m/1883 ft), Motta (623 m/2044 ft) and Chiosetto (645 m/2116 ft) and crosses to the other bank of the river.

*Lavertezzo

8 km/5 miles: Brione-Verzasca (760 m/2494 ft), another picturesque village at the mouth of the Val d'Osola. The church is the finest in the valley, with a 14th c. figure of St Christopher on the outside and beautiful 14th–15th c. wall-paintings in the interior. The little castle with four towers belonged to the noble Marcacci family of Locarno.
The road continues through the straggling village of Gerra (826 m/2710 ft) and the closely huddled settlement of Frasco (885 m/2904 ft). 7 km/4 miles: Sonogno (920 m/3019 ft), a beautifully situated mountain village at the end of the post road. The valley forks into the Val Vigornesso (to the right), with a number of other villages, and the Val Redorta (to the left).

Brione-Verzasca

Sonogno

*From Locarno into the Maggia Valley

(45 km/28 miles to Fusio: a good road, almost level as far as Bignasco.)
Leave on the Centovalli road and in 4 km/2 miles, at Ponte Brolla (260 m/ 953ft), turn off to the right into a road which ascends the left bank of the Maggia, in a wide valley enclosed between steep wooded crags. 7.5 km/5 miles: church of Santa Maria della Grazie di Campagna, with a wooden ceiling and 16th c. frescoes (key in Ristorante Poncini, Maggia).

0.5 km/less than ½ mile: Maggia (347 m/1139 ft), among extensive vine-yards. In the village are charming old houses with arcades, picturesque courtyards and wooden balconies. Above the village the Baroque Parish church of San Maurizio, the oldest in the valley, has fine stucco work and 17th c. statues inside. It is a short walk to a beautiful waterfall.
5 km/3 miles: Giumaglio. Beyond the village, on the left, is the Sasso Trolcia, a rock wall over which the River Soladino plunges in a waterfall 100 m/328 ft high. 8 km/5 miles: Cevio (418 m/1371 ft), the chief place in the Maggia valley, with a 17th c. governor's house (pretorio), situated at the mouth of the beautiful Valle di Campo. A road runs up this valley to Cimalmotto (14 km/9 miles) and (in a side valley) Bosco-Gurin (15 km/9 miles), the only German-speaking village in Ticino.

*Maggia

Sasso Trolcia

Cevio

Bosco-Gurin

3 km/2 miles: Bignasco (441 m/1447 ft), delightfully situated at the mouth of the Val Bavona (characteristic local style of building, beautiful little churches; hydro-electric installations). 11 km/7 miles up the valley is San Carlo, with several cableways. Beyond this point the Maggia valley is known as the Val Broglio. 8 km/5 miles: Prato (750 m/2461 ft), at the mouth of the Val di Prato, which runs down from Pizzo Campo Tencia. 2 km/1 mile: Peccia (839 m/2753 ft), with a hydro-electric station. From here the road climbs in sharp bends to the upper part of the Maggia valley, the Val

Bignasco
Val Bavona

Val Broglio
Val di Prato
Val Lavizzara,
Fúsio

Lavizzara which has interesting flora. 7 km/4 miles: Fúsio (1281 m/4203 ft), picturesquely situated on the mountainside (parish church). Above the village lies an artificial lake Lago Sambuco.

*From Locarno to the Val Centovalli

(19 km/12 miles to Ponte Ribellasca.)
Leave Locarno on the Vai Vallemaggia, going north-west through Solduno. In 4 km/2 miles the road crosses a bridge (33 m/108 ft high) over a gorge on the tumultuous River Maggia. At Ponte Brolla (260 m/853 ft), at the mouth of the Valle Maggia (on right), the Centovalli road turns left into the fertile Pedemonte, a level area in a wider part of the Val Centovalli. After passing through the picturesque villages of Tegna (255 m/837 ft) and Verscio (274 m/899 ft) it comes in 2.5 km/2 miles to Cavigliano (296 m/971 ft), where a road branches off on the right into the beautiful Val Onsernone with a view to the rear of Lake Maggiore.

Ponte Brolla

Tegna
Vescio
Cavigliano

The road now passes under a railway bridge, over a road bridge (fine view), through a curving tunnel and over the Isorno to enter Intragna (342 m/ 1122 ft), a neat village situated among vineyards on a hill between the Isorno and the Melezza. Church of San Gottardo (1738), with a fine tower (1775) 70 m/230 ft high, the tallest in Ticino. 2 km/1 mile beyond the village is a parking place (view).

Intragna

Now begins the increasingly winding stretch of road through the beautiful Val Centovalli ("Valley of a Hundred Valleys"), between steep hillsides covered with chestnut trees and slashed by numerous gullies, with a series of picturesquely situated little villages. 2 km/1 mile along the road is another parking place (view). A road goes off on the left, crosses a dam over the river and continues for 1.5 km/1 mile to the village of Palagnedra which has vivid 15th c. frescoes in the church of San Michele.

*Centovalli
Valley

Palagnedra

Beyond this there are magnificent views down into the valley, with the river swollen into the form of a lake by the dam and Monte Limidario rearing above it. 9 km/6 miles from Intragna is Camedo (552 m/1811 ft), the last Swiss village (customs). The road then crosses a bridge (with parallel railway bridge) into the village of Ponte Ribellasca (562 m/1844 ft), on the Italian frontier (Italian customs).

Camedo

Ponte Ribellasca

An interesting alternative is to take the Centovallibahn, which crosses the frontier to Domodóssola.

*Cento-
vallibahn

Lötschental   C2

Canton: Valais (VS)

Situation and general

The Lötschental, surrounded by seventeen 3000 m/9843 ft peaks in the Bernese and Valais Alps, has preserved much of its traditional character and customs. It now lies just off one of the great traffic routes through the Alps, the Berne–Lötschberg–Simplon railway. The people of the valley have kept their old local costume and their distinctive dialect, which even their compatriots from other parts of Switzerland find difficult to understand. The subject of study by folklorists, historians and naturalists, the Lötschental now mainly appeals to visitors in quest of peace and seclusion.

Communications

From the north the valley is reached by way of Thun and the Kander valley (cars carried by train from Kandersteg to Goppenstein), from the south by way of the Rhône valley and Gampel (641 m/2103 ft), which lies at the mouth of the Lötschental.
From Gampel the road winds its way up through the wild gorge of the Lonza to Goppenstein (1220 m/4003 ft). The 2.4 km/1.5 miles Mittal-Tunnel to the car-loading station at Lötschberg is open all year round.

Winter sports

The Lötschental was made accessible with lifts and cableways at the end of the Seventies. Today there are about 30 km/19 miles of prepared descents of varying difficulty and long-distance courses along the Lonza.

Fafler Alp – base for touring in the high mountains

Through the Lötschental

The Lötschental proper is 10 km/6 miles long, with magnificent scenery.

Beyond Ferden (1389 m/4557 ft) the valley opens out into a wide basin dotted with picturesque villages and hamlets and enclosed by a splendid ring of mountains to the right the Bietschhorn, 3934 m/12,907 ft, to the left the Petersgrat, 3205 m/10,516 ft.   Ferden

Kippel (1376 m/4515 ft; pop. 430) is the chief place in the valley. In addition   Kippel
to the traditional single-storey houses characteristic of the Lötschental, it
has 17th and 18th c. houses of two or more storeys with inscriptions and
richly carved decoration. Several of the typical wooden granaries and
barns can still be seen. The single-naved parish church of St Martin dates
from 1779 with extension work at the beginning of the 20th c. It contains an
interesting 18th c. high altar and a Renaissance tabernacle. The adjoining
ossuary is of 16th c. origin. Kippel is the scene of colourful traditional
processions. Its history is documented in the local museum.
There are attractive walks on the Kummenalp, which can also be reached
by cableway.

Wiler (1421 m/4662 ft; pop. 410) is the only place in the valley with a modern   Wiler
aspect, the old church having been burned down. The little church has
beautiful stained glass by Richard Seewald.
Cableway to the Lauchernalp (1970 m/6464 ft), with good skiing and
walking.

The last place in the valley is Blatten (1542 m/5059 ft), lying a little off the   Blatten
road which continues up the valley and past the Baroque Kühmad chapel,
to the Fafleralp (1788 m/5866 ft), a good base for mountain walks and   Fafleralp
climbs.

Lucerne   D1

Canton: Lucerne (LU)
Altitude: 436 m/1431 ft
Population: 50,000

Situation and general

Lucerne (in German Luzern), capital of the canton of the same name, lies at the north end of Lake Lucerne (Vierwaldstätter See – Lake of the Four Forest Cantons) at the point where the River Reuss flows out of the lake. For more than a century the town, with its well-preserved medieval core and elegant historic old buildings, has been one of the great tourist attractions of Switzerland.

History

Lucerne first appears in the records in 840 as Luciaria. The name comes from the Benedictine monastery of St Leodegar, founded about 730. After the opening of the St Gotthard pass in the 13th c. it became an important trading town. In 1291 it fell into the hands of the Habsburgs, but in 1332 joined the Confederation. After the occupation of the whole of Switzerland by Napoleon in 1798 Lucerne was for a brief period capital of the Helvetian Republic.

Sights

*Kapellbrücke

The most characteristic feature of Lucerne is the Kapellbrücke (Chapel Bridge), a covered bridge running diagonally across the Reuss (1333); it is one of the best-preserved wooden bridges in the country. Hanging from the rafters of the roof are more than 100 17th c. pictures depicting local saints and scenes from the town's history. Beside it is the octagonal Water Tower (Wasserturm, 13th c.), once part of the town's fortifications.

Reussbrücke

The nearby Reussbrücke (Reuss Bridge) was built in 1877 on the site of the oldest "Pons Lucernensis" (first mentioned in 1246 and 1253). The steel diagonal construction is being replaced by a copy (1989/1990).

Lucerne:

Farther downstream is another covered wooden bridge, the Spreuerbrücke (1406), decorated with scenes from the "Dance of Death" (17th c.).

Adjoining the Spreuerbrücke, at 6 Kasernenplatz, is the interesting Nature Museum (including ecological exhibit with living animals).

The Old Town on the right bank of the Reuss, still preserves many old burghers' houses and little squares with fountains. In the Kapellplatz is the oldest church in Lucerne, St Peter's chapel (1178), which received its present form in the 18th c.

In the Kornmarkt is the Old Town Hall (Altes Rathaus, 1602–06), in Italian Renaissance style but with a very typical Swiss hipped roof. The adjoining tower dates from the 14th c. and is by P. A. Isenmann.

Immediately east of the Old Town Hall (entrance in Furrengasse) stands the Am Rhyn-Haus (17th–18th c.) which houses a collection of important works by Picasso (Rosengart Donation: closed Mondays).

To the west of the Kornmarkt is the picturesque Weinmarkt; the Late Gothic fountain (1481) by K. Lux is a copy (original in the courtyard of the Regierungsgebäude).

Along the north side of the old town runs the Museggmauer, a wall built between 1350 and 1408, with nine towers built in differing styles.

Along the north shore of the lake, to the east of Schwanenplatz, extends a series of broad tree-lined quays lined with shops and hotels – Schweizerhofquai, Nationalquai and Spittelerquai – from where there is a magnificent panorama of the Alps. To the left is the Rigi group, in the middle the Bürgenstock, to the right the Stanserhorn and Pilatus, and beyond, in the distance, the Glarus and Engelberg Alps. In Nationalquai are the Kurplatz and the Kursaal (restaurant, gaming rooms).

Kapellbrücke (chapel bridge)

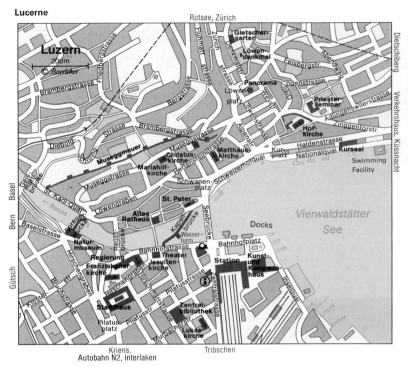

Hofkirche	Above the Nationalquai, on the site of the old monastery of St Leodegar, is the twin-towered Hofkirche (R.C.), which was rebuilt in 1634–39 but preserved the towers (1525) of the previous church. On the north tower a Late Gothic sculpture depicts the Agony in the Garden. The church has a carved pulpit and choir-stalls of 1639 and a famous organ (recitals in summer). In the picturesque arcades which surround the church are the tombs of members of old Lucerne families.
Löwenplatz	From the Kurplatz Löwenstrasse leads north to the Löwenplatz, to the right of which is the Panorama, a large circular painting (11,000 sq. m/118,360 sq. ft) by the Geneva battle painter Castres, with the collaboration of Hodler and other Swiss painters (1877–79). The painting depicts in highly realistic fashion the retreat of the French Eastern Army into Switzerland in 1871.
*Lion monument	A little way north, to the rear of the pool is the famous Lion Monument (Löwendenkmal), a huge figure of a dying lion hewn from the face of the living rock. The monument (1820–21), designed by Thorwaldsen, commemorates the heroic death of the Swiss Guards (26 officers and over 700 troops) who were killed during the attack on the Tuileries during the French Revolution (1792).
*Glacier Garden	Above the Lion Monument is the Glacier Garden (Gletschergarten), a remarkable relic of the Ice Age which was exposed between 1872 and 1875 (open March–October): glacier-polished rock, erratic boulders and 32 pot-holes, some of them of huge size, with a working model showing the process of formation of a pot-hole. Higher up are an early climbers' hut and a lookout tower. In the museum are relief maps of Switzerland, groups of Alpine animals, specimens of rock and old domestic interiors.

The Baroque Jesuit church *Spreuerbrücke*

On the outskirts of the town, 1 km/½ mile farther north, is an elongated lake, the Rotsee, on which a well-known regatta is held every year.

Rotsee

On the south bank of the Reuss, extending east to the lake and linked with the Schwanenplatz by the busy Seebrücke (Lake Bridge; 1935–36), is the Bahnhofplatz; here are the railway station and the docks used by the various boat services. A replacement bridge is planned for the end of 1991, along with a new railway station. In the gardens stands the Wagenbach fountain (1934).

Seebrücke

Railway station

At the east end of the square, adjoining the station, is the Kunst- und Kongresshaus (1932–33), which contains conference and concert halls and the Museum of Art (Kunstmuseum; closed Mondays), with a fine collection of Swiss painters of the 16th–20th c., 20th c. European painters and the Rieder Collection (also special exhibitions). A new congress centre with a concert hall, restaurants and a small art gallery is planned for the Nineties. The Museum of Art will be accommodated in the Panorama building, presently undergoing restoration, in the Löwenplatz.

Kunst- und Kongresshaus

As part of Lucerne's plans for cultural development a new music centre for the young jazz and pop scene is envisaged. Situated in the former Boa metal pipe factory, next to the old Sedel prison, which has recently been turned into a music club, it will create more space for concerts and plays.

In the part of the old town that extends west from the station along the left bank of the Reuss are the Municipal Theatre and the Jesuit church, a Baroque building (1666–77) with an elegant Rococo interior (1750).

Jesuit church

The Regierungsgebäude (Government Building) adjoining the church was formerly a Jesuit college, the core of which is the Ritter palace, a Renaissance mansion (1557–64 built by Lukas Ritter, a local dignitary who had grown rich in foreign service. In the handsome arcaded courtyard can be

Regierungsgebäude

Thorwaldsen's Lion Monument

Swiss Transport Museum

seen the original of the Weinmarkt fountain. To the rear of the building is the Neo-classical Chamber of the Great Council (1841–43). Closeby are the Cantonal Archives.

Franciscan church

South-west of the Regierungsgebäude stands the Franciscan church (13th–17th c.; completely restored 1988–1989), the nave walls of which have paintings of flags and banners (carved pulpit 1628, choir stalls 1647–51). In front of the church (also known as the Barfüsserkirche or Church of the Barefoot Friars) is the Barfüsserbrunnen, a copy of the original of 1651.

Central Library

South-west of the station, at 10 Sempacherstrasse, the Central Library (Zentralbibliothek) contains over 400,000 volumes and pamphlets, 2500 manuscripts and over 800 incunabula.

* Dietschiberg

Utenberg Costume and Folk Museum

On the north side of the lake, just off Haldenstrasse, is situated the lower station of the funicular to the Dietschiberg (632 m/2014 ft). There is a fine view of the town and the lake from the top. Near the upper station there are a café-restaurant, a golf-course and a miniature railway (scale 1:10). Below, to the south-west, is a park with the interesting Utenberg Costume and Folk Museum (Schweizer Trachten- und Heimat-museum Utenberg).

** Swiss Transport Museum

Beyond the funicular station Haldenstrasse continues to the fascinating Verkehrshaus der Schweiz (Swiss Transport Museum, Schweizerisches Verkehrsmuseum; entrance in Lidostrasse). The museum is a large complex of exhibition halls and outdoor exhibits covering all forms of transport, including air and space travel (cosmorama), communications and tourism, with railway locomotives and rolling-stock, ships, aircraft rockets and automobiles (originals or models), together with a Planetarium. By means of 150 projectors the sky can be seen through a 18 m/59 ft-wide dome.

The tourism department, opened in 1984, contains the largest pin-ball machine in the world and is an entry in the Guinness Book of Records.

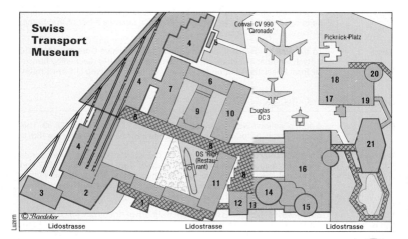

Swiss Transport Museum Lucerne
Schweizerisches Verkehrmuseum Luzern
Musée Suisse des Transports Lucerne
Museo Svizzero dei Trasporti Lucerne
Museum Svizzer da Traffic Luzern

1 Entrance, kiosk, transport archives
2 Model of St Gotthard Railway
3 Locomotive cab simulation
4 RAIL TRAFFIC HALL
    Normal and narrow gauge original rolling stock of
    Swiss railway companies of various dates on more
    than 1 km of track;
    Steam locomotives and historically interesting
    electrically driven vehicles;
    Wagons, railway equipment
5 SBB dining car of 1914 (restaurant)
6 Workshops
7 ROAD TRANSPORT HALL

Ground Floor:	Swiss cars, milestones of motoring history
First Floor:	Chassis and engines, fuel, accident prevention
Second Floor:	Coaches, history of land transport, bicycles, motorisation in the post-war period

8 Connecting halls
9 Lecture hall
10 POSTAL SERVICES HALL

Ground Floor:	Postal sorting centre, airmail travel post, film show, original postal coach
First Floor;	postage stamps

11 TELECOMMUNICATIONS HALL

Ground Floor:	International telephone network, Marconi radio transmitter, transmission of sound and pictures, TV studio
First Floor:	Amateur radio station, telephone service

12 Administration
13 Restaurant

14 "Longines" PLANETARIUM (Commentary through
    headphones in English, French, German and
    Italian)
15 Cosmorama (see No. 16, second floor)
16 HALL OF AIR AND SPACE TRAVEL

Ground	History of aviation
Floor:	"Lighter than air" flying, Swissair, airports
	Aircraft: Fokker VIIa, P 51 "Mustang"
	Heliswiss and rescue service
	Military aviation, Swiss aircraft industry
First	Flight safety, control tower
Floor:	Swiss Aero-Club, flight meteorology, Basis of flying
	Aircraft: Bücker "Jungmeister", Lockheed "Orion", Fieseler 'Storch', Blériot, Dufaux
Second	Gliders WF 7 and S 21, Piper seaplane,
Floor:	helicopters Bell 47G, Alouette III, Messerchmitt aircraft Me 108B COSMORAMA Mercury and Gemini space capsules, moonsuit, lunar rocks; multi-media show (on 18 canvas screens) on the history of space travel

17 SHIPPING Shipping on the Swiss lakes and rivers,
    models of historic and modern craft, dioramas
18 CABLE RAILWAYS Original cabins, including one
    from the Wetterhorn lift (first aerial cableway in
    Switzerland), scenes and models of various
    systems
19 TOURISM Swiss National Tourist Office
    Working models and equipment illustrating Swiss
    tourism
20 SWISSORAMA Multivision show about Switzerland
    (360° circular projection; 20 minutes)
21 HANS-ERNI MUSEUM About 300 works of the
    Lucerne artist Hans-Erni (b. 1909; in the auditorium
    can be seen his wall painting "panta rhei"
    (= 'everything flows"; 18×2 m), with personalities
    who have left their mark on western philosophy.
    'Hans Erni" video show (15 minutes).

Lucerne

At the east end of the complex is the Hans-Erni-Haus which contains paintings and graphic art by the well-known Lucerne artist of that name, and also a lecture hall.

Gütsch

To the west of the town, on the edge of the extensive Gütschwald, is the Gütsch, another hill which affords extensive views. It is reached by funicular from Baselstrasse or on foot by way of the Gütschweg (1.5 km/1 mile).

Surroundings

Emmen

A 16th c. gallows was excavated in the suburb of Emmen in 1988-89. This was the first to be found in Switzerland and had been in use until the 18th c.

Tribschen

On a hill south-east of the town, on the west side of the lake, stands Tribschen, a country house in which Wagner lived from 1866 to 1872 and composed the "Mastersingers" and other works. The house is now a museum, with original scores, pictures, prints and a collection of old musical instruments.

Kriens
Sonnenberg

South-west of Lucerne is the industrial suburb of Kriens (alt. 492 m/1614 ft), with the little castle of Schauensee (1595, with a 13th c. round tower). From here there is a funicular up the Sonnenberg (780 m/2559 ft), which affords superb views. Here too is the lower station of a cableway up Mt Pilatus.

*Maria Loreto
pilgrimage
chapel

5 km/3 miles south-west of Kriens at Hergiswald there is the beautiful 17th c. pilgrimage chapel of Maria Loreto (flight of 1000 steps; timber ceiling with more than 300 symbolic images of the Virgin by K. Meglinger, 1654). The road continues to the mountain resort of Schwarzenberg (831 m/ 2727 ft).

*Ascent of Mt Pilatus

A popular round trip going up by the cableway and down by the cog-railway.

Cableway from Kriens (4968 m/16,300 ft; 30 minutes) to the Fräkmüntegg (1415 m/4643 ft; skiing), and from there another cableway (1400 m/4593 ft; 7 minutes) to the Pilatus-Kulm (2070 m/6792 ft). Visitors can also travel by rail, boat or road (16 km/10 miles on the road to the Brünig pass) to

Alpnachstad

Alpnachstad (440 m/1444 ft). From there travel on the cog-railway (4.6 km/ 3 miles; 30 minutes, gradients up to 48% (1 in 2)), which runs up through Alpine meadows (orchards) and forests to the passing station at Ämsigen (1350 m/4429 ft) and then continues over the rock-strewn Mattalp and up the steep rock face, through four tunnels, to the upper station on Pilatus-Kulm (2070 m/6792 ft).

*Pilatus

From here it is a 6–10 minutes' climb to the summit (surrounded by a wall) of the Esel (2111 m/6962 ft), the central but not the highest peak of Pilatus, from which there are magnificent views of the Alps, from Säntis to the Blümlisalp, Lakes Lucerne and Zug, and the Swiss uplands. The name of the mountain probably comes from the Latin pileatus, "covered (with clouds)", although legend ascribes it to Pontius Pilate, said to have been buried in a former lake on the Upper Bründlenalp. Until the 17th c. Pilatus was known as Frakmunt (from fractus mons).

Tomlishorn

From the Pilatus-Kulm it is a 30 minutes' walk to the Tomlishorn (2132 m/6995 ft), the highest point in this rugged limestone massif.

Wolhusen,
Werthenstein
convent

To the west of Lucerne, in the valley of the Kleine Emme, is the industrial town of Wolhusen (568 m/1864 ft; pop. 3500). On a hill near the town is situated the convent of Werthenstein, which boasts a beautiful pilgrimage church (1608–16) and a fine cloister.

National Quay, with the "Stiftskirche am Hof"

From here road 2 runs north-west to the old-world little town of Willisau (557 m/1828 ft; pop. 2900) with well-preserved town walls and an upper tower dating from 1551. Nearby the 17th c. pilgrimage chapel of Heiligblut has a fine wooden ceiling with biblical decoration. The tower of the former governor's castle (17th c.) is part of the walls, built about 1400.

Willisau

To the Sempach, Baldegg and Hallwil lakes

North-west of Lucerne lie three beautiful lakes. Road 2 leads to the south end of the attractive Sempacher See (507 m/1663 ft), on the east side of which is the pretty little town of Sempach (520 m/1706 ft; pop. 1500), with a fine half-timbered town hall (1737; old coat-of-arms in council chamber). On the Kirchbühl north of the town stands St Martin's church (13th and 16th c.). By this lake, to the south of the town, the Swiss Bird-Watching Station (Schweizerische Vogelwarte), houses an ornithological museum.

Sempacher See

Sempach

2 km/1 mile north, above the town on the road to Hildisrieden, is the Schlachtkapelle (Battle Chapel), built in 1473 to commemmorate the Confederates' victory over Duke Leopold III of Austria on 9 July 1386, a victory traditionally attributed to the self-sacrifce of Arnold von Winkelried.

Schlachtkapelle

At the north end of the lake, from which the river Suhre flows north, is the tranquil little country town of Sursee (507 m/1663 ft; pop. 5000) which has a Baroque parish church (1641), a late Gothic town hall (1546) and 18th c. burghers' houses. Neat rows of houses and two towers surround the moated Mühlplatz (mill square). There is an interesting museum of mechanical toys and instruments (Retonios Mechanisches Musikmuseum). The old Roman road along the lake heading south is of interest to walkers.

Sursee

From here road 23 runs north-east to Bermünster (642 m/2106 ft; pop. 1700), with St Michael's church, which belonged to a monastic house

Bermünster

279

Lucerne

Sursee: St Martin's Church . . .   *. . . and Late-Gothic Town Hall*

founded by Count Bero of Lenzburg about 980. The church, originally Romanesque, was rebuilt in 1606 and remodelled in Baroque style in 1775; fine choir-stalls of 1609, rich treasury. Castle (local museum), in which the first book printed in Switzerland was produced in 1470.

Baldegger See, Hochdorf

To the east of Beromünster is the Seetal (Lake Valley) in which lie the Baldegger See and Hallwiler See. Hochdorf, at the south end of the Baldegger See, has a fine church of 1768. On a hill 3 km/2 miles east stands a former commandery of the Knights of St John, Hohenrain (614 m/2015 ft), now a special school.

Schloss Horben

Continue up the east side of the lake on road 26. On the Lindenberg, to the right of the road, is Schloss Horben (1701), from which there is a beautiful view of the Alps.

Gelfingen, Schloss Heidegg

At Gelfingen is Schloss Heidegg which has a massive 12th c. tower house, with a hall decorated by Ticinese artists.

Hitzkirch

From Gelfingen a road goes off on the right to Hitzkirch (473 m/1552 ft), with a former commandery of the Teutonic Order (main building 1749, church 1680), which now houses a teachers' training college and a lake-dwelling museum.

Hallwiler See, Beinwil

Road 26 continues to the south end of the Hallwiler See. Beinwil 9522 m/1713 ft), on the west side of the Hallwiler See, lies at the foot of the Homberg (792 m/2599 ft; inn), which commands extensive views.

Schloss Hallwil

1 km/½ mile north-east of Boniswil on the north bank of the lake stands Schloss Hallwil (9th–16th c. Museum; local collection). Countess Wilhelmine von Hallwyl had the moated castle restored at the beginning of the 20th c. with important items going to the Landesmuseum in Zürich, where they are now on display.

Schloss Brestenberg

The road back to Lucerne along the east side of the lake passes Schloss Brestenberg (462 m/1516 ft), a country house with a park built in 1625, which is undergoing redevelopment as a hotel, restaurant and museum (open 1990).

From Gelfingen road 26 returns to Lucerne.

Lugano   D2/3

Canton: Ticino (TI)
Altitude: 272 m/892 ft
Population: 29,000 (Greater Lugano 50,000).

Lugano, the "pearl of Lake Lugano", lies in a bay half-way down the lake, flanked by Monte San Salvatore and Monte Brè. It is the largest and most important town in Ticino, and the beauty of the town and its setting makes it one of Switzerland's most popular holiday resorts during the warmer months of the year. The architecture and way of life of Lugano show distinctly southern characteristics, as does the plant life.

**Situation and townscape

Lugano has a notably temperate climate, with plenty of sunshine of moderate intensity and mild air temperatures with little variation over the day.

Climate

Cars are best parked in the multi-storey parks in the middle of town (signs). Trolley service between Paradiso and Castagnola, from Pregassone to Breganzona, from the centre to Vezia, from the station to Viganello and Cornaredo. Local boat services to several destinations. Funicular (1½ minutes) from the station to the old town (Piazza Cioccaro). Bus from Lugano to Brè-Dorf.

Transport

The town and surrounding area lie directly on the important north-south

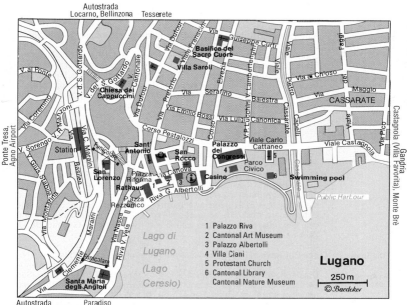

Autostrada
Locarno, Bellinzona   Tesserete

Ponte Tresa,
Agno Airport

Castagnola (Villa Favorita); Monte Brè
Gandria

1 Palazzo Riva
2 Cantonal Art Museum
3 Palazzo Albertolli
4 Villa Ciani
5 Protestant Church
6 Cantonal Library
   Cantonal Nature Museum

Lago di Lugano
(Lago Ceresio)

Lugano

250 m

© Baedeker

Autostrada   Paradiso
                  Monte San Salvatore

Lugano: the Municipio (town hall)   *Museo cantonale d'Arte*

traffic route, both road and rail, over the St Gotthard. Flights from Lugano-Agno airport to Zürich, Geneva, Basle, Berne, Paris, Nice, Venice and Florence.

History

Along the shores of Lake Lugano traces of the Etruscans and the Gauls have been found, together with remains of the Roman, Lombard and Frankish periods. During the Middle Ages the town was under the jurisdiction of the Bishop of Como and thus became involved in the conflicts between Milan and Como. After the conquest of Ticino by the Confederates Lugano was from 1512 to 1798 the seat of the district governor. The opening of the St Gotthard railway in 1882 gave fresh impetus to the development of the town, particularly as a tourist and holiday resort.

Sights

Municipio

The pulsating activity of Lugano revolves around three squares surrounding the Town Hall (Municipio, Palazzo Civico, Town Hall, 1844-1845 by G. Moraglia from Milan). To the north is the Piazza della Riforma, with the former Pretorio (Law Court; 15th–18th c.), now occupied by the Cantonal Bank, and a number of cafés. By the lake is the Piazza Riziero Rezzonico and the Piazza Manzioni (gardens), and in front of the 18th c. Palazzo Riva is the Debarcadero (dock). The long lakeside promenade from Cassarate to Paradiso has sub-tropical gardens with modern sculptures by G. Genucchi, O. Zadkine and P. Selmoni.

*Old Town

The Old Town of Lugano contains a number of historic buildings.

St Lawrence
Cathedral

Outstanding among the churches is the Cathedral of St Lawrence (San Lorenzo). Originally Romanesque, it was enlarged in the 13th–14th c. and underwent extensive alteration in the 17th and 18th c. It has an imposing Renaissance façade, rich fresco decoration and a Baroque interior.

Villa Ciani: Ticino art from the Baroque to the present

North-east of the Piazza della Riforma in the Via Canova the Museo cantonale d'arte in the Palazzo Reali has modern art exhibitions. The adjoining handsome Palazzo Albertolli was built in the 19th c.; in the Piazza Maghetti is the 16th c. church of St Roch (San Rocco) with its 20th c. façade and the new Centro Maghetti. Still further east we come to the Piazza Indipendencia, on the south side of which is the Kursaal.

Museo
cantonale d'arte

Centro Maghetti

The extensive and beautiful Parco Civico (Municipal Park) with old trees and sub-tropical plants is the site of the Palazzo dei Congressi (convention facility; 1965–1975 by Rolf Otto) and the Villa Ciani. The Palazzo houses the Museo delle Belle Arti (Ticinese art from Baroque to present day, European masters, special exhibitions).
From the Piazza della Riforma the Via Pretoria runs north into Viale Stefano Franscini. On the left-hand side stands the Villa Saroli and new building (Banca del Gottardo) by Mario Botta.

*Parco Civico
Congress centre
Villa Ciani

The conventual church of Santa Maria degli Angicli (1499–1515) on the south side of town contains a fine fresco of the Passion by Bernado Luini (1529).

Santa Maria
degli Angioli

The nearby pilgrimage church of the Madonna di Loreto (1524) has 17th c. frescoes.

Madonna di
Loreto

In Castagnola, to the east of the town, is the Villa Favorita, which boasts one of the finest private picture galleries in Europe, the Schloss Rohoncz Collection, belonging to Baron Heinrich von Thyssen-Bonemisza. Among the paintings are masterpieces by Italian, Flemish, Dutch, Spanish, German and French artists from the Middle Ages to the 20th c.

Castagnola
Villa Favorita
**Thyssen-
Bonemisza
collection

Surroundings

The town's two hills, Monte San Salvatore and Monte Brè, offer attractive day and half-day trips.

View of San Salvatore from Municipal Park

**Monte San Salvatore	Monte San Salvatore (912 m/2992 ft). From Paradiso, on the lake, a cableway 1658 m/5440 ft long, with gradients of 38–60% (1 in 2½–1 in 1½), ascends in 10 minutes to the upper station at 884 m/2900 ft (restaurant and viewing terrace). From the summit there are magnificent panoramic views of the town and the lake, the Bernese and Valais Alps (Monte Rosa) and the north Italian plain. Footpaths to Carona, Melide, Morcote and Figino; return by rail, postal bus or boat.
**Monte Brè	Monte Brè (933 m/3061 ft). From Cassarate, to the east of the little stream of the same name, a cableway 1621 m/5319 ft long, with gradients of 47–60% (1 in 2–1 in 1½) arrives in 15–25 minutes at the upper station (restaurant), from where there are fine views extending to the Valais Alps. This favourite viewpoint can also be reached by car on a narrow and winding road (11 km/7 miles) from Lugano, via Castagnola, Ruvigliana and Aldesago).
Holiday saver ticket	There are also a variety of possible excursions further afield. From 1 March to 31 October a reasonably priced holiday ticket covering travel on all train, boat and postal bus services for a period of 7 days can be obtained from travel agencies and tourist information offices. For trips on the lake, see under Lake Lugano, below.

From Lugano into the Malcantone

Agno Cademario Breno Monte Lema	An attractive drive through this area between Lugano and the Italian frontier, of about 50 km/31 miles, with Agno (8 km/5 miles west of Lugano) as its starting-point, might take in the health resort of Cademario (795 m/2608 ft), Breno (802 m/2631 ft; base for the ascent of Poncione di Breno, 1658 m/5440 ft, 3 hours) and Miglieglia (751 m/2464 ft), from which a chair-lift (2673 m/8770 ft, 18 minutes) goes up Monte Lema (1624 m/5328 ft; upper station 1550 m/5086 ft; inn, superb views). Also worth seeing are the villages of Novaggio (644 m/2113 ft), Banco (585 m/1919 ft) and Astano (633

m/2077 ft; surrounded by chestnut forests) as well as Caslano on Lake Lugano, from which the return road runs north-east to Agno.
South-west of Agno on the Swiss-Italian border lies Ponte Tresa.

From Lugano to Tesserete

An excursion (20 km/12 miles) into the densely populated valley of the Cassarate, running through romantic villages including Vezia, Cureglia and Tesserete (532 m/1745 ft), chief place in the hilly Capriasca district; then into the Val Colla, returning from Bogno (963 m/3160 ft via Sonvico, Dino and Cadro.

Tesserete

From Lugano to Gandria

(5 km/3 miles) via Cassarate and Castagnola to the Gandriastrasse (Gandria road), which runs south to Porlezza and Lake Como (Italy). The last part of the trip must be done on foot, to the picturesque village of Gandria (alt. 300 m/984 ft; pop. 196), a typical Ticinese settlement clinging picturesquely to a steep slope rising from the lake (narrow lanes, arcades, Baroque church) and surrounded by terraced vineyards.

*Gandria

On the other side of the lake (boat service), to the south is the Cantine di Gandria dock, with an interesting Customs museum, situated near the Italian frontier (containers for smuggled goods, weapons). To the south-east is the Italian village of Santa Margherita, from which there is a funicular to the Belvedere di Lanzo (887 m/2910 ft; good views).

Customs museum

Lake Lugano

D2/3

Within Switzerland and Italy
Canton: Ticino (TI)

Lake Lugano (in Italian Lago di Lugano or Ceresio), on the southern edge of the Alps, lies mainly within the Swiss canton of Ticino, the remainder being in the Italian province of Varese and Como. Lying at an altitude of 270 m/886 ft, it has an area of 48.7 sq. km/19 sq. miles, with a maximum depth of 288 m/945 ft. From the west end of the lake the River Tresa flows into Lake Maggiore. The climate already shows distinct Mediterranean characteristics.

Situation and general

Very pleasant round trips on the lake are run by the motor-ships of the Lake Lugano Shipping Company (SNL; head office in Lugano, information in harbour).

Boat services

Towns on **Lake Lugano

The principal town on Lake Lugano is Lugano (see entry), on the north shore of the lake.

**Lugano

From there a road runs south alongside the lake to Melide (alt. 277 m/909 ft), situated on a peninsula from which a causeway crosses the lake.

Melide

A feature of interest here is "Switzerland in Miniature", which reproduces many of Switzerland's principal tourist attractions (towns, castles, monuments, transport) on a 1:25 scale.

*Switzerland in miniature

Across the causeway, to the north, is the Italian enclave of Campione d'Italia, with the 14th c. church of the Madonna dei Ghirli and a gaming casino.

Campione d'Italia

Lugano, below Monte Brè

*Morcote	South of Melide, on the southern slopes of Monte Arbostora (839 m/2753 ft), a promontory projecting into the lake, is the old-world little town of Morcote (277 m/909 ft; pop. 650), one of the most picturesque places in Switzerland and a great tourist attraction, with its beautiful setting and its well-preserved old houses and streets. In a commanding situation above the village stands the pilgrimage church of the Madonna del Sasso (originally 13th c., rebuilt 1462, remodelled in Baroque style 1758), with a separate campanile; it contains fine 16th c. frescoes. From the church a flight of 408 steps goes down to the village on the shores of the lake. In the cemetery are the graves of Moissi, Eugen d'Albert and Balkanoff. There is a beautifully laid out park, the Parco Scherrer, with a collection of international art, culture and inspiration.
	Facing Morcote across the lake is Brusino-Arsizio, which can be reached from Melide by way of Melano and Capolago.
Bissone	From Melide we cross the causeway and go south along the far side of the lake to Bissone (274 m/899 ft; pop. 720), which dates back to Roman times. It has well-kept patricians' houses with impressive arcades and façades. The Tencalla museum contains ancient exhibits with an exhibition of painting and sculpture by local artists.
Melano	Melano (296 m/971 ft; pop. 875) at the foot of Monte Generoso, has patricians' houses including the Haus Fogliardi with fine Baroque decoration.
Capolago **Monte Generoso	At the south end of the lake is Capolago (277 m/909 ft), from which a rack-railway (cog-railway) serves Monte Generoso (1704 m/5591 ft; hotel-restaurant), with superb views of the Alps and the Lombard plain, including Milan.
Riva San Vitale *Baptistery, *Santa Croce	1 km/½ mile west of Capolago in the village of Riva San Vitale there is an octagonal baptistery (5th c.) and the church of Santa Croce (16th c.), one of the finest Renaissance churches in Switzerland.

Melide: "Switzerland in miniature"

Beyond this is Brusino-Arsizio (277 m/909 ft; pop. 380), which lies within the administrative district of Lugano, but from the tourist point of view belongs to the fertile and densely populated Mendrisiotto area. This picturesque village lies at the foot of Monte San Giorgio.

Brusino-Arsizio

A cableway runs to Serpiano (645 m/2116 ft; extensive views), reached by cableway or by road from Mendrisio.

Serpiano

Through the Mendrisiotto to Chiasso

The administrative district of Mendrisiotto (pop. 47,590), with a total area of 133.61 sq. km/51.6 sq. miles, lies at the southernmost tip of Switzerland (most southerly point in Chiasso-Pedrinate). The most easterly finger of Lake Lugano drives a wedge through this area which is in contrast to the more mountainous surroundings.

*Mendrisiotto

To the south of Brusino-Arsizio, surrounded by fertile fields and vineyards, lies the village of Meride (583 m/1913 ft; pop. 270). There are interesting 18th c. houses, such as the Haus der Oldelli with magnificent arcades and colonnades, and a local museum.

Meride

The chief town of the region Mendrisio (354 m/1162 ft; pop. 6900) has been an important political centre since the Middle Ages. Neolithic and Roman remains provide evidence of an earlier settlement. Its picturesque territory extends as far as Bellavista on Monte Generoso. Interesting sights include the church of SS Cosma and Damano (1875), Palast der Edelleute Rusca (mansion; former 15th c. courthouse), the Torrianische Palast (15th–16th c.) and the recently renovated Palast Pollini (1715). A former monastery houses an art museum where exhibitions, concerts and other cultural events are held.

Mendrisio

Not far to the west at Rancate (359 m/1178 ft; pop. 1200) are the Grosse Palast (Great Palace) and the Cantonal art collection, housed in a former church hall, which consists of around 200 paintings by Ticinese artists.

Rancate

Lake Maggiore

Bezasio
: Just before the Italian border we come to Bezasio (501 m/1644 ft; pop. 410), known for its "brocatello" red marble.

Ligornetto, Vela Museum
: Ligornetto (364 m/1194 ft; pop. 1300) lies at the junction of the roads to Stabio and Genestrerio. The Vela artists such as the sculptors Vincenzo and Apollonio Pessina are supposed to come from here. Exhibits relating to the family are on display in the Vela Museum.

Stabio
: Stabio (375 m/1230 ft; pop. 2800) dates back to Pre-roman times with evidence of Etruscan, Roman and Langobard settlements having been found. It was the chief town in the region under the Romans and contains interesting burghers' houses and a local museum.

Balerna
: The road from Mendrisio to the Italian border passes Balerna (310 m/1017 ft; pop. 3500), which joins up with the commercial centre of Chiasso. It was once an important religious centre. There is a ruined castle, Schloss Pontegana, which was built before the Langobard period.

Chiasso
: Chiasso (239 m/784 ft; pop. 8850) developed into an important centre for trade and transport due to its strategic location. First mentioned in 1127 Chiasso gained independence in 1416. Surrounded by hills it has long been a transit town, its status as a customs-point contributing to its economic growth. The Palast Züst (1906 by C. Brambilla) and the 18th c. Neo-classical Camponovo Palast (formerly Matti) are worth visiting.

Lake Maggiore   D2/3

Within Switzerland and Italy
Canton: Ticino (TI)
Altitude: 194 m/637 ft

Situation and general
: Lake Maggiore, known to the Romans as Lacus Verbanus, is the second largest of the north Italian lakes (area 212 sq. km/82 sq. miles, length 60 km/37 miles, breadth 3–5 km/2–3 miles, greatest depth 372 m/1221 ft). Less intricately patterned than Lake Como and without the sheer rock faces of the northern part of Lake Garda, it nevertheless offers scenery of southern splendour.

  The northern part of the lake, with the town of Locarno, is in Switzerland, but the greater part of it is in Italy, the east side belonging to Lombardy and the west side to Piedmont. The lake's principal tributaries are the Ticino and the Maggia to the north and the Toce on the west side. The river which flows out of the south end, having carved a passage through massive morainic walls, preserves the name of Ticino.
  The northern part of the lake is enclosed by mountains, for the most part wooded, while towards the south the shores slope down to the plain of Lombardy. In clear weather the water in the northern part of the lake is green, in the southern part deep blue.

Climate and vegetation
: The climate is mild. From midnight until morning the tramontana blows, usually coming from the north; from midday until the evening the inverna blows from the south. The plant life of Lake Maggiore, like that of Lakes Garda and Como, includes many sub-tropical species: figs, olives and pomegranates flourish in the mild climate, and in August the myrtle blossoms. On the Borromean Islands lemons, oranges, cork-oaks, sago-palms and carob-trees grow.

*Ascona, *Locarno **Borromean Islands
: The most popular tourist areas are around Ascona and Locarno (see entries), and on the western arm of the lake between Pallanza and Stresa, where the Borromean Islands with their sub-tropical gardens are the main attraction.

Locarno: Panorama with the pilgrimage church of Madonna del Sasso

One very attractive excursion is a boat trip from Locarno to Arona (service through the year, twice daily in summer; also hydrofoil services), calling alternatively at places on the east and west sides of the lake.

Boat services

Martigny   C2

Canton: Valais (VS)
Altitude: 477 m/1565 ft
Population: 13,000

The ancient little town of Martigny, the Roman Octodurum, situated on the great bend in the Rhône at the inflow of the River Drance, lies on the important through route from Lake Geneva to the Simplon pass and on the roads to the Great St Bernard pass and the Col de la Forclaz (Chamonix – Mont Blanc Tunnel).

Situation and general

Sights

In the newer part of the town, Martigny Ville, is the attractive Place Centrale, with the 19th c. Hôtel de Ville (Town Hall). Close by is the former inn La Grande Maison, where famous personalities such as J. W. Von Goethe and A. Dumas stayed. Haus Supersaxo (16th c.) at Rue des Alpes 1, is the oldest house in the town.
2 km/1 mile south is the old-world Martigny Bourg, with the Old Town Hall (17th c.) and the old residence (17th–19th c.) of the bishop's representatives.

The cantonal education department opened the Valais Film Centre in 1988, which specialises in films and photographs connected with Valais.

Valais Film Centre

On the vine-clad hillside above the town (30 minutes from Martigny Ville) can be seen the ruins of the 13th c. castle of La Bâtiaz (destroyed in 1518), which belonged to the Bishops of Sion; the tower was restored in 1898.

Burg La Bâtiaz

Martigny

La Bâtiaz Castle　　　　　　　　*Pierre Gianaddas' vintage-car collection*

**Fondation Pierre Gianadda　To the south-east, close to the remains of a Roman amphitheatre, around the foundations of a Gallo-Roman temple, stands the cultural centre of the Fondation Pierre Gianadda, the idea of Léonard Gianadda (in memory of his brother) and Umberto Guglielmetti. There is a Gallo-Roman museum, exhibition galleries and a veteran car collection of over 40 vehicles from 1897 to 1939. On display are Benz, Alfa 1750c, Rolls-Royce, Mercedes SSK, Bugatti, Pic-Pac and the famous Delaunay-Belleville owned by Tsar Nicholas II of Russia.

The upper gallery is reserved for Gallo-Roman exhibits. The main finds of the excavations at Martigny are on display here (bronze statues from Octodurum, discovered in 1883, the Roman forum Claudii Vallensium) and enjoy international acclaim.

The garden contains famous sculptures by famous artists such as A. Rodin ("La Méditation avec Bras", 1885), J. Miró ("Tête", 1979–1985), H. Moore ("Large Reclining Figure",1982) and C. Brancusi ("Grand Coq IV", 1949).

Every September as part of the Montreux-Vevey Festival concerts take place with international ensembles and soloists.

Surroundings

From the end of Martigny Bourg a narrow winding road runs east through the forest on the slopes of Mont Chemin. 3 km/2 miles: Chemin-Dessous (774 m/2539 ft). 3.5 km/2 miles: Col des Planches (1409 m/4623 ft), with fine views which is the starting point for the ascent of the Pierre à Voir (2476 m/8124 ft: 4 hours), the highest peak between the Rhône and the Drance and a commanding view-point. From here there is also a beautiful footpath along the mountainside, level for most of the way, to Isérables (4 hours).

Sembrancher　　From the Col des Planches the road descends steeply, with many sharp bends, to Sembrancher (9 km/6 miles), in the Drance valley, which has a parish church of 1676 with a fine Late Gothic tower.

Henry Moore: "Large reclining figure"   *Finds from the Roman Octodurum*

From Sembrancher (which can also be reached from Martigny on the   **Verbier**
excellent main road, No. 21) it is 15 km/9 miles to the well-known winter
sports resort of Verbier, situated on a natural terrace facing south, with
views of the Grand Combin and the Mont Blanc group (1420 m/4659 ft .

Access to the skiing area is provided by numerous cableways. It is a
popular area with skiers (over 80 lifts and 300 km/186 miles of pistes) as it is
still possible to ski up to 3300 m/10,830 ft in summer. There are well laid out
runs for long-distance skiing.

Into the Val de Trient

This is a short valley west of Martigny, gorge-like in places, through which
the Trient flows to join the Rhône

The steep and narrow mountain road runs north-west through La Bâtiaz,
crosses the Trient on the Gueroz viaduct and turns south-east.

7 km/4 miles: Salvan (927 m/3041 ft), a health resort, from which a daringly   **Salvan**
engineered road climbs by way of Les Granges (1044 m/3425 ft) to the Lac
de Salanfe (8 km/5 miles), an artificial lake 2 km/1 mile long formed between 1947 and 1952 (1914 m/6280 ft; hotels; skiing). From Les Granges
there is a footpath to the impressive Gorges du Dailly.   **Gorges du Dailly**

1.5 km/1 mile south-west of Salvan is the summer and winter resort of Les   **Les Marécottes**
Marécottes (1100 m/3604 ft; "Reno Ranch" Alpine Zoo, natural swimming
pool), from which a chair-lift 1470 m/4823 ft long (lower station 1140 m/
3740 ft) goes up to Creusaz (1780 m/5840 ft).

The Val de Trient road continues beyond Salvan to Le Trétien (4 km/2 miles),
from which it is possible to reach Finhaut, higher up the valley, but only
by rail.

Over the Col de la Forclaz to Chamonix (France)

Col de la Forclaz Mont de l'Arpille	Just south of Martigny on the road to the Great St Bernard (see entry) turn right into a road which winds its way up, with a number of sharp bends, through the villages of La Fontaine and Le Fays to the Col de la Forclaz (1527 m/5010 ft), between the Croix de Prélayes and the Mont de l'Arpille (2089 m/6854 ft; chair-lift; extensive views).
Trient	It then runs down with attractive views of the Trient valley and the Trient glacier, to Trient (1305 m/4282 ft), a summer and winter sports resort in a more open stretch of the valley.
Le Châtelard	After passing through Le Châtelard (1120 m/3675 ft) it comes to the French frontier, from which it continues over the Col des Montets to Chamonix.

Meiringen   D2

Canton: Berne (BE)
Altitude: 600 m/1969 ft
Population: 4000

Situation and general	Meiringen the chief town in the Hasli valley, lies on the Aare, which flows into Lake Brienz a few kilometres west of the town. It is a popular summer holiday resort and a good base for excursions into the Bernese Oberland, and has a long tradition of wood-carving and hand-weaving.

Sights

The parish church, on higher ground, was built in 1684 on the remains of an earlier church (13th c.), and has an 11th c. crypt. The tower, with round-arched windows, dates from the 14th and 17th c. There is also an interesting local museum, the Haslimuseum.

Sherlock Holmes Museum	The Neo-gothic English church (1893) became a museum for the famous English fictional detective Sherlock Holmes in 1989. Memorabilia relating to the immortal character is on show and a life-size statue by John Double-day, complete with deerstalker and pipe, stands in the tree-lined church square.

Surroundings

*Aare gorge	2 km/1 mile south-east is the Aare gorge, 1400 m/4593 ft long, through which there is a footpath (½ hour, through tunnels and galleries) to the Lammi inn, on the road to Innertkirchen.
*Upper Reichenbach Falls	From the left bank of the Aare (car park) a funicular takes 5 minutes to reach the Upper Reichenbach Falls. From the upper station there is a good view of the falls, which plunge down in two stages. This is the spot where Arthur Conan Doyle had Sherlock Holmes killed in a fight with his arch enemy Professor Moriarty. Footpath (20) minutes to the Zwirgi inn.

To the Schwarzwaldalp

Willigen	(13 km/8 miles to the Scwarzwaldalp). A narrow road branches off the Grimsel road in the hamlet of Willigen and winds its way up through the

Meiringen: Aare gorge   *Sherlock Holmes Museum*

forest. 3 km/2 miles Schwendi (779 m/2556 ft). 2 km/1 mile Zwirgi inn (976 m/3202 ft), with a fine view to the rear of Hasli valley and Hasliberg.

The road then continues high above the Reichenbach on the slopes of the Hohbalm (1371 m/4498 ft). Straight ahead is the Wellhorn, with the Wetterhorn and Eiger to the right.

4.5 km/3 miles Gschwandemaad (1298 m/4259 ft), from which there is a celebrated view of the Engelhörner (2781 m/9124 ft), the Rosenlaui (1330 m/4364 ft), in a magnificent setting. A footpath, largely hewn from the rock, winds uphill (½ hour) through the Rosenlaui gorge, carved out by the Weissenbach.

The road climbs in a sharp bend and comes in 2.5 km/2 miles to the Schwarzwaldalp (1467 m/4813 ft).

From here a bridle-path leads in 2–2½ hours to the Grosse Scheidegg or Hasli-Scheidegg (1961 m/6434 ft), from which there is a view of the Grindelwald basin (descent, 2 hours).

See Sarnen

Gschwande-maad

Rosenlaui,
*Rosenlaui
gorge

Schwarzwaldalp

Grosse
Scheidegg

Hasliberg

Montreux   B2

Canton: Vaud (VD)
Altitude: 375 m/1230 ft
Population: 20,000

With a magnificent situation and an unusually mild climate which make it the most popular resort on Lake Geneva, Montreux extends for some 6 km/4 miles along the shores of the lake, incorporating a number of smaller places which were formerly independent communes.

The charm of the town's setting depends on its variety of geography and vegetation, ranging from the gardens on the lakeside, through the Alpine meadows and forests around Caux and Les Avants, to the lofty peaks of the Rochers de Naye.

Situation and
general

Montreux Palace

Sights

Montreux Ville

The main part of the resort, Montreux Ville, lies on the steep slopes above the Baye de Montreux, a swiftly flowing mountain stream. On the shores of the lake is the Casino. From the terrace in front of the parish church (1507), higher up, there is a beautiful view of the lake.

To the west, in Vernex, stands the modern Maison des Congrès, and beyond this lies the attractive residential suburb of Clarens.

To the east the district of Territet is situated on a narrow coastal strip below the steep slopes of Glion. The Grand Hôtel (1887) by Maillard ranks among the great hotels built at the end of the 19th c. A museum for audio and video technology is planned to open here in 1990, documenting the history and development of information technology. At the station a marble monument (1902) commemorates the Empress Elisabeth of Austria, murdered in Geneva in 1898.

**Château de Chillon

General

1.5 km/1 mile beyond Territet, in the outlying district of Veytaux, is the popular tourist attraction of Chillon Castle, a stronghold of the Counts and Dukes of Savoy. Situated on a rocky islet close to the shore, it commanded the road from Burgundy over the Great St Bernard into Italy.

The castle, which now belongs to the canton of Vaud (conducted tours), was built in the 9th or 10th c., enlarged in the 11th–12th c. and given its present form in the 13th c. In the basement are large dungeons hewn from the native rock. Many Genevese were confined here for expressing their views too freely, among them François de Bonivard, Prior of St Victor's in Geneva. He was incarcerated here by the Duke of Savoy in 1530, fettered to an iron ring which is still shown to visitors, but was released in 1536 when Bernese conquered Vaux and, with the help of ships from Geneva, took the

Château de Chillon

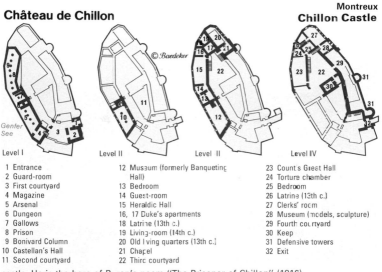

Level I

Level II

Level II

Level IV

1 Entrance
2 Guard-room
3 First courtyard
4 Magazine
5 Arsenal
6 Dungeon
7 Gallows
8 Prison
9 Bonivard Column
10 Castellan's Hall
11 Second courtyard

12 Museum (formerly Banqueting Hall)
13 Bedroom
14 Guest-room
15 Heraldic Hall
16, 17 Duke's apartments
18 Latrine (13th c.)
19 Living-room (14th c.)
20 Old living quarters (13th c.)
21 Chapel
22 Third courtyard

23 Count's Great Hall
24 Torture chamber
25 Bedroom
26 Latrine (13th c.)
27 Clerks' room
28 Museum (models, sculpture)
29 Fourth courtyard
30 Keep
31 Defensive towers
32 Exit

castle. He is the hero of Byron's poem "The Prisoner of Chillon" (1816). Other illustrious poets and writers such as Victor Hugo, Rodolphe Töpffer and Juste Olivier have written about the castle.

Nowadays it is hard to distinguish the 25 buildings that make up Chillon castle, closely grouped around three courtyards; the oldest being the keep and the Duke's Tower, which are linked by an internal wall, the square tower, which dominates the entrance and the living quarters.

Château de Chillon

Montreux

Montreux on Lake Geneva

St Pantaleon Chapel	Of interest is the small Chapel of St Pantaleon, of which only the St Tryphon crypt remains. The chapel contained the first Christian altar of the region, after that of St Maurice. A reliquary from the Carolingian period, which was discovered here is on display in the Weapons Room.
Basement	The imposing underground vaults, which are actually at water level and replaced the old timbers of the ground floor, are double-naved halls with mighty pillars and Gothic vaulting. The largest vault was Bonivard's prison.
Castle kitchen	On the ground floor are the large kitchen ("Grosse Bernerküche") with massive chestnut pillars and the courtroom.
Banqueting Hall Heraldic Hall	On the upper floor are the former Banqueting Hall, the adjoining Bernese Room decorated with pretty bird and floral motifs and the splendid Heraldic Hall, formerly known as "aula paramenti" or the Knights' Hall with an interesting gallery of shields bearing the coats-of-arms of the Bernese governors. In the old tower, in the Duke's apartments, traces of the rich 13th and 14th c. decoration with birds and flowers are still visible. There are
St Georg's Chapel	more living quarters and the little St Georg's Chapel where the ribbed vaulting on six low pillars is completely decorated with figures and tendrils.
Count's Great Hall	Crossing the upper courtyard we come to the Count's Great Hall (Grosser Grafensaal; "magna aula", "aula vetus") with a 15th c. coffered ceiling. Notable are the four windows with charming quatrefoils above two lanceolate 13th c. Gothic arches.
	Through the treasury, the former prison and Vaud arsenal with its magnificent arches and Gothic ribbed vaulting we come to the medieval main tower ("magna turris"), 26 m/85 ft high, and completed in three stages (12th–14th c.). From the top are marvellous views of the castle and the outline of the Alps. During the restoration work begun at the end of the 19th c. the original moat was restored.

Surroundings

To Les Avants

Les Avants (8 km/5 miles). From the station take Rue de la Gare; then left along Avenue de Belmont and into a road which climbs up in sharp bends (daffodils in flower in May).

On the left is the massive Château Châtelard, built by Jean de Gingins as a refuge for the people of Montreux in 1476. Partly destroyed by the Confederates it was later rebuilt; the large dungeon is of north Italian style.

Château
Châtelard

Cross N 9 and continue uphill in long bends, via the villages of Fontanivent (559 m/1834 ft), Chernex (603 m/1978 ft), Sonzier (664 m/2179 ft) and Chamby (752 m/2467 ft; Narrow Gauge Railway Museum; light railway to Blonay).

Chamby

The road continues to climb, along the east side of Mont Cubly, towering above the Gorge de Chauderon. 9 km/6 miles: Les Avants (974 m/3196 ft), a summer and winter resort high above the valley of the Baye de Montreux. 3 km/2 miles farther on is the Col de Sonloup (1158 m/3799 ft; hotel), which can also be reached from Les Avants by funicular.

Les Avants

Col de Sonloup

From Montreux to the Col de Jaman

To the Col de Jaman (14 km/9 miles). Leave by Rue de la Gare and the district of Les Planches; then a road which runs uphill in a wide curve. 3 km/2 miles: Glion (692 m/2270 ft), with beautiful views of the lake and the Alps; funicular down to Territet.

Glion

The road now climbs steeply, with numerous sharp bends. 3.5 km/2 miles: Caux (1054 m/3458 ft), a health resort in a magnificent situation, with extensive views; meeting-place of the "Moral Rearmament" movement. From here there is a cog-railway to the popular skiing area (ski-lift) on the Rochers de Naye, and from the upper station (1973 m/6473 ft; hotel) it is a 10 minutes' climb to the summit (2045 m/6710 ft), which has superb views of the Alps and Lake Geneva; Alpine garden.

Caux

*Rochers de Naye

From Caux a mountain road runs up 7.5 km/5 miles to the Col de Jaman (1516 m/4974 ft; restaurant), with far-ranging views.

*Col de Jaman

From Montreux to the Pléiades

To the Pléiades (15 km/9 miles to Lally; mountain road). Leave on the Lausanne road, and in Clarens turn right into a road which crosses the N 9 and winds its way uphill via Chailly (485 m/1591 ft) and comes in 6 km/4 miles to Blonay (623 m/2044 ft), where Paul Hindemith (1895–1963) spent his last years. The castle dates back from the 12th c. The town (which for administrative purposes is part of Vevey; see entry) is noted for its almost champagne-like wine. From here there is a cog-railway to the Pléiades (4.7 km/3 miles), 25 minutes.

Blonay

The road from Blonay to the Pléiades climbs in sharp bends, passing a side road on the right to the spa (sulphurous water) of L'Alliaz (1044 m/3425 ft). 9 km/6 miles Lally (1237 m/4059 ft), at the end of the road. From here it's 4 minutes on the cog-railway from Blonay or 20 minutes on foot to the Pléiades (1364 m/4475 ft; pension and restaurant), from which there is a beautiful view.

L'Alliaz
Lally

Pléiades

Mürren   C2

Canton: Berne
Altitude: 1650 m/ 5414 ft
Population: 430

The holiday and winter sports resort of Mürren lies on a sunny terrace   Situation
700 m/2297 ft above the Lauterbrunnen valley, with magnificent views of
the Jungfrau massif.

First mentioned in the records in 1257, Mürren developed during the 19th c.   History
into a popular resort, particularly favoured by the British. The Mürrenbahn
(narrow-gauge railway) was opened in 1891, the Allmendhubelbahn (funicular) in 1912.

Townscape

Mürren is traffic-free. Only vehicles from the hotels and shops are allowed
on the narrow streets of this rustic chalet village. Access is from Lauterbrunnen by funicular (6.5 km/4 miles) to Grütschalp (1490 m/4889 ft) and
from there by the narrow-gauge railway (5.5 km/3 miles), or from Stechelberg by cableway (the Schilthornbahn to Gimmelwald (1367 m/4485 ft) and
Mürren.

Wengen, situated on the rocky plateau opposite is also accessible by
cableway (see Grindelwald).

The British made this resort, lying at the foot of the Schilthorn, famous for
sport. The revolving restaurant "Piz Gloria" was inspired by a James Bond
film. The biggest amateur race in the world, the "Inferno Race", started by
the British, still takes place here annually. A new Alpine sports centre close
to the skiing area offers a wide choice of activities (indoor swimming pool,
tennis and squash courts, sauna, library and games room, etc.). Guided
glacier walks and helicopter skiing are popular.

Difficult slopes on the Schilthorn; medium to easy on the Gimmeln, Schilt-   Winter sports
grat and Winteregg slopes. The Jungfrau region also has 175 kilometres of
downhill slopes and a 2 km/1 mile circular course near Mürren.

Surroundings

To the north-west is a mountain commanding panoramic views, Allmend-   *Allmendhubel
hubel (1938 m/6359 ft; restaurant), which can be reached either by the
funicular or by walking (30 minutes).

From Gimmelwald (1367 m/4485 ft), which is accessible either by the   Gimmelwald
Schilthorn or on foot (30 minutes), there is a footpath (1½ hours) along a
mountain terrace into the Sefinental and to the Gspaltenhorn glacier.

The upper sections of the Schilthornbahn lead by way of Birg (2676 m/   *Schilthorn
8780 ft) to the Schilthorn (Piz Gloria, 2970 m/9745 ft; revolving restaurant),
from which there are ski trails (moderate and difficult) to Mürren. The
longest descent (12 km/7 miles) runs to Lauterbrunnen (height difference
2170 m/7122 ft).

◀ *Mürren, at the foot of the Schilthorn*

Murten/Morat   C2

Canton: Fribourg (FR)
Altitude: 450 m/1476 ft
Population: 4600

Situation and general

**Townscape

Murten (the German form: French Morat) lies on a ridge of hills marking the linguistic boundary between French and German, on the south-east side of the idyllic Murtensee (Lac de Morat). This beautiful little medieval town has preserved, more completely perhaps than anywhere else in Switzerland, the old-world character derived from its many surviving buildings of the 15th–18th c. The old town is still surrounded by its circuit of walls (with a wall-walk).

History

In 515 King Sigismund of Burgundy presented a property at Murten, on the road to Valais, to the monastery of St Maurice. In 1013 Murten was a stronghold held by King Rudolf III of Upper Burgundy. The real foundation of the town was the work of the Zähringen dynasty between 1157 and 1177.

Murten's main claim to fame is the battle fought here in 1476 in which the Confederates defeated the troops of Charles the Bold of Burgundy. The field of battle ranged from Cressier (572 m/1877 ft) to Greng (442 m/1450 ft), where a memorial now stands.

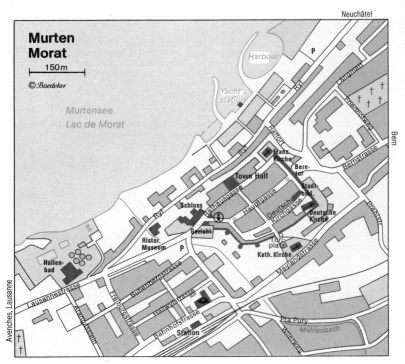

Murten/Morat: the main street . . .   *. . . and the medieval town fortress*

Sights

The town walls (12th–15th c.) are a remarkable example of a medieval defensive wall; access to the wall-walk is by flights of steps at the German church and the Käfigturm (Cage tower). From the walls there are fine views over the roofs of Murten.

*Town walls

At the western tip of the old town stands the castle, built by Peter of Savoy in the 13th c. Nowadays it serves as the prefecture with open-air concerts in the courtyard in summer. At the north-east end of the picturesque Hauptgasse, is the Berne gate (Berntor, 1777-78), a late Baroque reconstruction, with one of the oldest clocks in Switzerland (1712).

Schloss

*Hauptgasse

The Town Hall was rebuilt after 1416, and was given a Neo-classical façade in 1832. Also of interest are the Late Gothic French church (1478–80) and the German church (1710–13). Opposite the latter is the birthplace of the writer Jeremias Gotthelf (whose real name was Albert Bitzius, a pastor, 1797–1854).

Town Hall
French church
German church

One of the town's most picturesque old buildings is the Late Gothic Rübenloch, with a frontal gable. The old town mill now houses a Historical Museum, opened in 1978 (weapons, banners and uniforms from the Burgundian wars, and an old oil-mill). In Schulhausplatz a "world sundial" shows the time in different parts of the world.

Haus Rübenloch
Historical
Museum

There is a 1 hour round trip on the Murtensee (Lac de Morat) and trips encompassing three lakes: Murtensee, Neunburger See (Lac de Neuchâtel) and Bieler See. It is popular with water sports enthusiasts.

Boat trips

Surroundings

From the Bodenmünsi hill south of Murten there are magnificent panoramic views of the lake and the Jura mountains.

Lac de Morat

Murten-
Muntelier

Archaeologists have discovered what is thought to be the oldest village in Europe in the countryside around Murten-Muntelier. The settlement has been dated at 3867 B.C.

From Murten to Avenches

Monument to
the Battle of
Murten

Leave on the Lausanne road, which runs through the suburb of Meyriez and begins to climb. 2 km/1 mile from the middle of the town, at the junction with the bypass road (on right), is the monument to the Battle of Murten, an obelisk erected in 1823 on the site of an ossuary destroyed by the French in 1798. It commemorates the decisive victory of the Confederates over Duke Charles the Bold of Burgundy on 22 June 1476.

Murtensee or
Lac de Morat

The road runs close to the south-east shore of the Murtensee or Lac de Morat (alt. 433 m/1421 ft; area 27 sq. km/10 sq. miles, length 9 km/6 miles, greatest depth 46 m/151 ft), which is linked with the Lac de Neuchâtel by the River Broye (motor-boat traffic). To the right is the flat-topped Mont Vully or Wistenlacher Berg (657 m/2156 ft) which lies between the Murtensee and the Lac de Neuchâtel.

2 km/1 mile beyond the monument is Faoug (pronounced Foo; German Pfauen), from which a road descends on the right to a beach station and camp site (inn), 2.5 km/2 miles west on the wooded shores of the lake, and follows a fairly straight and level course to Avenches, passing the remains of the Roman town just before reaching the modern town.

Avenches
Castle, Aviation
Museum

Avenches (alt. 474 m/1555 ft; pop. 2000; bypass), a little town situated on a hill, with a medieval castle (remodelled in Renaissance style) and attractive old houses. The castle houses the Musée de l'AMVANAS, a museum of the history of flight in Switzerland, with documents, models and navigational instruments. It occupies the site of the old capital of the Helveti and the

Roman town of Aventicum, which had its heyday in the 1st and 2nd c. A.D., when it had a population of some 20,000; it was destroyed by the Alemanni about 260. The excavated remains of the Roman town can be seen to the east of modern Avenches: a theatre (semicircular in form, with a diameter of 106 m/348 ft) which could seat 10,000 spectators; the "Tornallaz", the only surviving remnant of the town's 6 km/4 miles circuit of walls; the remains of the Forum baths; and a 12 m/40 ft high Corinthian column, probably from the Forum, known as the Cigognier from the stork's nest which formerly crowned it. The numerous finds from the site are displayed in a museum adjoining the amphitheatre.

*Aventicum

Neuchâtel B2

Canton: Neuchâtel
Altitude: 430 m/1411 ft
Population: 33,000

Neuchâtel (German Neuenburg), capital of the canton of the same name, lies on the north shore of the Lac de Neuchâtel (Neuenburger See), below the Jura mountains. It is the seat of a University and has a Commercial College and the Swiss Watchmaking Research Laboratory. The public buildings are mainly on the shores of the lake around the harbour; the residential districts, with their houses of yellow Jurassic limestone, rise above the lake on the foothills of the Chaumont, surrounded by parks and vineyards.

Situation and general

The town first appears in the records in 1011 under the name of Novum Castellum, and in the course of the 11th c. t became part of the Holy Roman

History

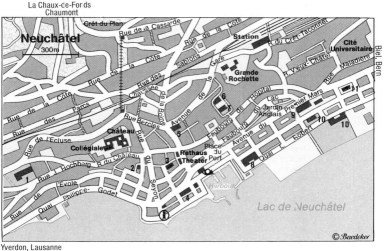

1 Museum of Ethnography
2 Market Hall
3 Temple du Bas/Music Salon
4 College Latin/Municipal Library

5 Natural History Museum
6 Archaeological Museum
7 Hôtel du Peyrou
8 Museum of Art and History

9 University
10 Commercial College
11 Catholic Church

Neuchâtel: near the harbour . . .   *. . . stands the Musée d'Art et d'Histoire*

Empire. Thereafter it changed hands several times. The Counts of Neuchâtel gave place to the Counts of Freiburg im Breisgau, who in turn were succeeded by the Counts of Hochberg. From 1504 to 1707 the town belonged to the the Dukes of Orléans-Longueville, and then passed to the Crown of Prussia. In 1848 a federal and republican constitution came into force, and in 1875 King William IV of Prussia renounced his claim to Neuchâtel. During the 18th c. the town developed into a commercial and industrial centre (watch-making, fabric printing) and in 1815 it became the cantonal capital.

Boat services
Motor boats ply between the other towns on the lakeside. The trip around the three lakes (Lac de Neuchâtel, Bieler See and Murtensee) is highly recommended.

Sights

On the long quays which extend on either side of the harbour are a series of fine late 19th c. buildings. In Place du Port is the Post Office and in Place Nume Droz (to the south) the Collège Latin (1835), with the Municipal Library.

Collège Latin

Musée d'Art et d'Histoire
At the near end of Quai Léopold-Robert, north-east of the harbour, stands the Museum of Art and History (closed Mondays), which houses a comprehensive collection of antiques, automata (mechanical figures) and clocks and watches.

University
Parallel to Quai Léopold-Robert is the broad Avenue du Premier-Mars, which runs past the Jardin Anglais to the University (1909), successor to an Academy founded by King Frederick William III of Prussia in 1838. Behind the University, on the shores of the lake, stands the Commercial College (Ecole Supérieure de Commerce).

Faubourg de l'Hôpital
To the north of the Jardin Anglais lies a select part of the town, the Faubourg de l'Hôpital, with handsome 18th c. patrician houses, including

Hôtel du Peyrou, in Louis XIV style

the Hôtel du Peyrou (1764–70; beautiful garden), which is now used for receptions and banquets, and the Grande Rochette (1730; private property). The adjoining Musée d'Histoire Naturelle (Natural History Museum) has important departments of zoology, mineralogy and geology. Behind the Hôtel du Peyrou the Archaeological Museum (Musée d'Archéologie) contains an interesting collection of excavated material from La Tène.

Hôtel du Peyrou

Musée d'Histoire Naturelle
Musée d'Archéologie

The Old Town lies north-west of the harbour, rising up the hillside towards the Château. On its east side are the Town Hall (Hôtel de Ville; 1784–90), with a pillared portico, and the Theatre (1775). The main street, Rue de Seyon, occupies the bed of a stream which was diverted in 1844. Side streets on the left lead to the elegant Renaissance Market Hall (Maison des Halles, 1570–75).

Old Town, Town Hall

Maison des Halles

There are a number of fine 16th and 17th c. fountains: the Banner Carrier fountain (1584), the Griffin fountain (1664), the Justice Fountain (1547) and the Lion fountain (1655; the lion itself 1664).

Fountains

© *Baedeker*

Collegiate Church Neuchâtel

1 St Guillaumes Chapel
2 St Michel's Chapel (Upper Storey)
3 14th century fresco
4 Remains of Romanesque Cloister

5 Seal of Farel
6 St Pierre's Doorway
7 Tomb of Counts of Neuchâtel
8 Reformation Inscription

Neuchâtel

Collegiate church . . .   *. . . with pointed vaulting*

Château	From Rue de Château a stepped lane and a street lead up to the château, which belonged to the Counts and Princes of Neuchâtel and is now occupied by cantonal government offices. The west wing dates from the 12th c., the remainder from the 15th to the 17th c.; the interior has undergone much alteration.
Collegiate Church *Monument of the Counts of Neuchâtel	The Collegiate church was built in the 12th–13th c. (west towers 1867–75). Until 1530, when it was taken over by the Reformed faith, it was the Catholic Collégiale Notre-Dame. In the very dark Romanesque choir the monument of the Counts of Neuchâtel (1372) has 15 painted effigies and is the finest Gothic memorial in the whole of Switzerland.
	On the north side of the church is a Romanesque cloister (restored). Outside the west front of the church stands a statue of the Reformer Guillaume Farel (1489–1565); from the terrace there are extensive views.
Museum of Ethnography	South-west of the park in Rue St Nicolas, is the Museum of Ethnography, with an excellent permanent collection and occasional special exhibitions from Asia, Africa and Oceania.
*Cret du Plan	From Rue de l'Ecluse, on the edge of the old town, a funicular ascends to the Cret du Plan (598 m/1962 ft), from which there are extensive views of the lake and the Alps.

Surroundings

*Chaumont	5 km/3 miles north-east, in La Coudre, is a funicular to the summit of Chaumont (1177 m/3862 ft), which can also be reached on a steep road from Neuchâtel. From the top there are far-ranging views of the Mittelland with its lakes, and a panorama of the Alps from Sântis to Mont Blanc.
La Tène	Near St-Blaise, at the end of the lake, in the hamlet of La Tène, is a famous Late Iron Age site first excavated in 1858.

In neighbouring Marin there is a butterfly garden where over 1000 species of butterflies, as well as fish and birds, are on show among the tropical plants of the Papillorama. An artificially created atmosphere maintains the ideal conditions necessary for the butterflies and moths.

Marin,
*Papillorama

*From Neuchâtel to Yverdon

The road (39 km/24 miles) skirts the north-west side of the Lac de Neu-châtel, the largest of the three Swiss lakes on the fringes of the Jura (39 km/24 miles long, up to 8 km/5 miles wide). The hillsides are mostly covered with vineyards.

Leave Neuchâtel by way of Quai L. Perrier and road 5. In the suburb of Serrières are the Suchard chocolate factory (1826) and a tobacco factory (visitors admitted).

Auvernier (alt. 460 m/1509 ft) is a vine-growing village with a school of viticulture. It has a number of elegant patrician houses (16th c.) with Renaissance doorways.

Auvernier

Colombier (alt. 460 m/ 1509 ft; pop. 4000) has a massive castle, built in the 12th c. on Roman foundations and rebuilt and enlarged in the 14th and 16th c. From 1754 it was occasionally used as a residence by the Prussian governor of Neuchâtel. It now contains a military museum and a collection of pictures. The surrounding vineyards produce an excellent wine.

Colombier

Boudry (470 m/1542 ft; pop. 3000) is a picturesque little town at the mouth of the Gorges de l'Areuse with a 16th c. castle which houses a museum of viticulture. Boudry was the birthplace of the French politician Jean-Paul Marat (1743–93) and of Philippe Suchard.

Boudry

The road continues, with beautiful views, to Bevaix (476 m/1562 ft), which has a Gothic church and a 1722 mansion-house. Gorgier (518 m/1700 ft) has a castle of the 14th and 16th c., restored in Romantic style in the 19th c. (view).

Bevaix
Gorgier

St-Aubin (474 m/1555 ft) is the most important town in the district of La Béroche which lies on the slopes of the Montagne de Boudry with many picturesque villages and country houses. Beyond this, to the right, stands the castle of Vaumarcus, and on the left the former Carthusian house of La Lance, with a beautiful Late Gothic cloister.

St-Aubin

La Lance
monastery

The road continues via Grandson (see Yverdon) to Yverdon (see entry), at the south-west end of the lake.

Nyon

B2

Canton: Vaud (VD)
Altitude: 404 m/1326 ft
Population: 14,000

The little old-world town of Nyon is beautifully situated on the north-west shore of Lake Geneva, at the end of a mountain road over the Col de la Givrine to La Cure.

Situation

There was a settlement of the Helvetii here (Noviodunum) and Julius Caesar established the Roman station of Civitas Iulia Equestris. The town enjoyed a period of prosperity under Bernese rule in the 16th c. when many fine burghers' houses were built. From 1781 to 1813 there was a porcelain factory in Nyon. It was the birthplace of the writer Edouard Rod (1857–1910) and the pianist Alfred Cortot.

History

Roman columns . . .   *. . . in Nyon*

Sights

Castle Museums *Roman columns	The town, with its old houses and its church (12th c.; Roman walling in substructure), is picturesquely situated on the slopes of a hill which is crowned by the five-towered castle (12th and 16th c.). The castle now houses the Historical Museum and the Musée du Léman, and contains an interesting collection of antiquities (including Roman material) and an exhibition of Nyon porcelain (1781–1813). From the castle terrace there is a magnificent view of the lake with the Alps and Mont-Blanc. In the Bourg-de-Rive are Roman columns.

Surroundings

Coppet, Crans- près-Céligny	8km/5 miles south-west of Nyon are two châteaux: Château Coppet and Château Crans-près-Céligny, an elegant 18th c. residence.
Bonmont Abbey	9 km/6 miles north-west is the former Cistercian abbey of Bonmont.

Oberhalbstein/Sursés   E2

Canton: Grisons (GR)

Situation and general	Oberhalbstein (Romansch Sursés) is the name given to the valley of the river Julia, which flows down from the Julier (Guglia) pass to join the Albula at Tiefencastel. There was already a road here in Roman times, runing from the Engadine over the pass and down the successive levels of the valley. The language of the valley is Romansch.

Over the Julier pass into the Engadine

Tiefencastel	The road from Chur and Lenzerheide (see entries) was built between 1820 and 1840 and later improved. At the north end of the Oberhalbstein valley is

Savognin, below the Piz Mitgel *Roman column on the Julier Pass*

Tiefencastel (Romansch Casti; alt. 851 m/2792 ft; pop. 350), situated at a road junction on the site of the Roman station of Imacastra. On a rocky hill between the rivers Julia and Albula stands the parish church of St Stephen (1660), with a richly decorated interior. To the south-west lies the village of Mon (1227 m/4026 ft); in the church are 15th c. frescoes.

Mon

A few kilometres before Tiefencastel, high above the Albula gorge, is St Peter in Mistail. Recently excavated remains of frescoes indicate it was built in the time of Charles the Great, around 800.

St Peter

The road continues to climb for 30 km/19 miles via the old village of Bergün (1376 m/4516 ft) to the Albula pass (2312 m/7588 ft).
The Rhätische Bahn railway line winds its way across the romantic countryside between Bergün and Preda through tunnels and viaducts. In early 1985 a "railway history walk" was opened with information boards at regular intervals.

Bergün, Albula pass

Railway history walk

The road to the Julier pass runs up from here to the limestone wall of Crap Sès, above which the next stage of the valley opens up – Oberhalbstein ("above the rock").

Julier road

Cunter (1182 m/3878 ft) is a beautifully situated village frequented both by summer visitors and by winter sports enthusiasts. From here a narrow road (8.5 km/5 miles) runs south-west via Riom up to Radons (1864 m/6116 ft; also reached by cableway from Savognin), from which Piz Caquiel (2970 m/9745 ft) can be climbed (4 hours).

Cunter

Savognin (1210 m/3970 ft; pop. 1000) is the primary town in the Oberhalbstein, situated at the mouth of the Val Nandro, which runs down from the south-west to join the Oberhalbstein. The village has three 17th c. churches and numbers of attractive houses. At the upper end of the village, on the left, is a tablet commemorating the residence of the painter Giovanni

Savognin

Segantini (1886–94). Savognin is also a popular winter sports resort (many ski-lifts; "snow cannon" for producing artificial snow for the ski trails). To the west of the village is Piz Curver (2972 m/9751 ft; 6 hours, with guide). Chair-lifts via Tigignas to Somtgant (2143 m/7031 ft) and via Malmigiucr to Radons (see above).

Tinizong

Farther up the valley is Tinizong (1232 m/4042 ft; pop. 360), on the site of the Roman station of Tinnetio. In the parish church (1647) is a carved altar (Late Gothic, 1512) by Jörg Kändel of Biberach in Swabia. At Rona (1420 m/4659 ft) the road reaches the next "step" in the valley.

Lai da Marmorera

The road continues via Mulegns to the step above this, on which is Lai da Marmorera (1680 m/5512 ft; car park), an artificial lake with a capacity of 60 million cu. m/2118 million cu. ft. Further along the road, on the left, the new village of Marmorera replaces the old village which was submerged by the lake.

Bivio

In the highest part of the valley is Bivio (1776 m/5827 ft; pop. 250), so called (Latin bivium, "roadfork") because a busy medieval road, now represented only by a bridle-path, branched off here and ran over the Septimer pass (Pass da Sett, 2311 m/7582 ft). In Bivio four different languages are spoken: German, an Italian dialect from the Val Bregaglia, Ladin and the Surmeirian dialect.

* Julier pass

Beyond the village the road climbs to the Julier pass (Passo dal Guglia, 2284 m/7494 ft), with the stumps of two columns which probably belonged to a Roman shrine on the pass. To the right, is a small lake.
The road now descends the rocky valley of the Ova, past Piz Julier (3385 m/11,106 ft), on the left, to a lookout with a magnificent view of the Bernina massif (4049 m/13,285 ft). It then continues down to Silvaplana, where it enters the Engadine (see entry).

Olten   C1

Canton: Solothurn
Altitude: 396 m/1299 ft
Population: 19,000

Situation and general

Olten, an important railway junction, with the main workshops of the Swiss Federal Railways, and a considerable industrial town (engineering), lies astride the river Aare at the foot of the Hauenstein (824 m/2704 ft), which commands extensive views.

History

The place was founded by the Froburg family on the site of a Roman castrum and first appears in the records as a town in 1201.

Sights

The handsome twin-towered parish church dates from 1806, the modern Stadthaus from 1966. An old covered wooden bridge leads into the Old Town, the most notable landmark of which is the Late Gothic tower of St Martin's church (demolished in 1844). The Old Town Hall (1701) now houses the municipal library. At Kirchgasse 10 is the Museum of Art (Kunstmuseum), with works by the Olten-born painter Martin Disteli (1802–44), and to the north, in Konradstrasse, the Historical Museum.

Surroundings

North of the town is the ruined castle of Froburg (excavations). Road 2 runs south up the Aare valley, enclosed between wooded hills.

Aarburg

It comes in 4 km/2 miles to Aarburg (415 m/1362 ft), a picturesque little town of 6000 inhabitants situated above the junction of the Aare and the Wigger,

Olten: Old Town on the Aare

with an 11th c. castle much altered in later centuries, now a penal establishment for young offenders.

On the Engelberg (667 m/2188 ft) is the "Säli-Schlössli", the ruined castle of Wartburg-Säli. A fire-watching post was established here in 1547, and remained the responsibility of the Säli family for 300 years.

Säli-Schlössli

South-west of Aarburg via Rothrist and Roggwil-Wynau stands the former Cistercian abbey of St Urban (founded 1184), in the north-west corner of the canton of Lucerne. The Baroque church (completed 1716) has a fine organ and richly carved choir-stalls, which were acquired by a foreign purchaser in 1854 but were later bought and returned to St Urban by the Gottfried Keller Foundation.

Cistercian
Abbey of St
Urban

Payerne

B2

Canton: Vaud (VD)
Altitude: 452 m/1483 ft
Population: 7000

The name of this charming little old town, on the River Broye, has its origins with the Roman family Paterni. From the 10th c. the town has been the home of the Burgundian kings. The Benedictine monastery founded by Empress Adelheid. wife of Otto I, in 962 is an outstanding example of Cluny architecture.

Situation and
general

Sights

Founded in the 11th c. on the ruins of a Roman villa the Abbey church is one of the chief examples of Romanesque architecture in the country. Con-

*Abbey Church

Abbey Church of Payerne

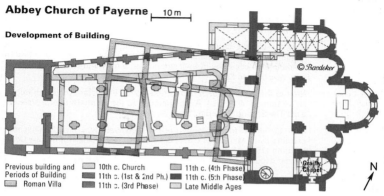

Development of Building

© *Baedeker*

Grailly Chapel

N

Previous building and Periods of Building	10th c. Church	11th c. (4th Phase)
Roman Villa	11th c. (1st & 2nd Ph.)	11th c. (5th Phase)
	11th c. (3rd Phase)	Late Middle Ages

12th c. frescoes in the abbey church

structed in the shape of a Latin cross this triple-naved pillared basilica has a large, semi-circular apse with apsides, a central nave with cross-vaulting in the lateral naves. The transept has notable 11th c. block capitals and chapels surround the choir, the capitals of which are of Burgundian influence. The yellow and grey stone blocks of the light interior are impressive, and 12th c. frescoes (Deesis) can be seen in the vestibule. Extensive renovations and excavations were carried out (including the grave of Queen Bertha, who died 1000 years ago) in the second half of this century.

Jean de Grailly, verger and later vicar of Payerne, had his own chapel built in Gothic style, to the right of the choir, in the middle of the 15th c. It suffered severe damage during the Reformation. Restoration work on the chapel's frescoes along with those of Romainmôtier, Moudon, Lausanne Cathedral and Château Chillon was completed in 1982. On the north wall are St Moritz, the Compassionate Virgin and Mary Magdalena, while on the south wall are St Martin and La Pietà. The outer wall is decorated with a

Grailly Chapel

◀ *Payerne: Nave of the abbey church*

representation of the Triple Throne with Jean de Grailly, dressed in the dark attire of the Cluny monks, kneeling before it.

Only the chapter-house (rebuilt in the 16th c.) remains of the convent building. There is a local history collection, an interesting exhibition of Romanesque churches in Switzerland and a museum to General Jomini who was born in Payerne.

Notre-Dame parish church

Next to the Abbey church is the triple-naved Protestant parish church of Notre-Dame (14/16th c.). A wall-painting in the southern lateral aisle depicts The Shroud of Christ (16th c.).

Law courts

Four 13–14th c. towers remain of the medieval town. Fine Renaissance painting by H. Maraschet (1576) can be seen in the Late Gothic Law Court building (1571–1572) next to the parish church. Close by are the Banner Carrier's fountain and the fountain of Serruriers (16th c.).

Pontresina   E2

Canton: Grisons (GR)
Altitude: 1800 m/5906 ft
Population: 1820

Situation

Pontresina (Romansch Puntraschigna), once a mere village on the road to the Bernina pass and now a popular health resort, climbers' base and winter sports capital, lies in a sheltered spot in the highest side valley of the Upper Engadine, on a natural terrace facing south-west. It is surrounded by forests of stone pines and larches and enclosed by the majestic peaks of the Alps.

General

The two famous skiing areas of Diavolezza and Piz Lagalp (see Bernina) make Pontresina a popular winter sports centre.

Pontresina, among stone-pines and larch woods

There are about 500 km/310 miles of walks in the region. Guided tours of the glaciers are popular with climbers as are the nature walks. Golf, fishing, tennis, ice-skating, long-distance skiing, curling and tobogganing as well as winter sports and summer skiing are some of the activities on offer.

Pontresina first appears in the records in 1129, but evidence has been found of human settlement here dating back to the Bronze Age. The name has been thought to derive from one Saracenus who built a bridge here. (Pons Sarasinae).

History

Sights

Pontresina has some elegant hotels from the Belle Epoque period, typical stone houses with sgraffiti and window grilles.

The Punt Ota bridge is of 12th c. origin. In the Laret district the village church (Protestant) was built in 1640. Between Piz Rosatsch and Piz Chalchagn a beautiful glimpse of the Roseg valley and Roseg glacier can be enjoyed. Near here is a plant reserve with an Alpine garden.

On the hillside above Ober-Pontresina are the ruins of the pentagonal Spaniola tower and the little Romanesque church of Santa Maria, with a ceiling of stone pine (1497) and frescoes of the 13th–15th c. The west wall was part of the previous building and retains wall-paintings from the 13th c. (God's appearance, The Baptism of Christ and the Last Supper). The life of Christ is depicted from the south wall to the north.

Church of Santa Maria

Surroundings

Ascent of Muottas Muragl: 3 km/2 miles from Pontresina on the St Moritz road a funicular (length 2200 m/7218 ft, gradient 13–54%) takes 15 minutes to reach Muottas Muragl (2453 m/8043 ft; restaurant), which commands the finest view of the Bernina group and the lakes of the Upper Engadine. A good return route is by a path which skirts the Schafberg to the Unterer Schafberg restaurant (1 hour; see below) and on to the Alp Languard (2250 m/7382 ft; 45 minutes); then by chair-lift (ski-lift) or on foot (45 minutes) to Pontresina.

**Muottas Muragl

*Alp Languard

The Schafberg (Munt della Bes-cha, 2731 m/8960 ft) is reached from Pontresina in 2¾ hours by way of the Unterer Schafberg restaurant (2230 m/7317 ft), from which there are magnificent views. On the summit, which has a prospect embracing the whole of the Bernina group, is the Segantini hut, with a tablet commemorating the painter Giovanni Segantini, who died here in 1899.

*Schafberg

Roseg glacier (Vadret da Roseg). A narrow road (6 km/4 miles; closed to traffic; horse-drawn carts) leads up the Roseg valley to the Roseg-Gletscher restaurant (2000 m/6562 ft) from which it is a 30–45 minutes' walk under a fine row of stone pines to the end of the glacier, now much reduced in size.

*Roseg Glacier

There are more extensive views from the Alp Ota (2257 m/7405 ft; 1¼ hours from the restaurant) and the Tschierva hut (2573 m/8442 ft; 2 hours). From the Roseg glacier it is a 2¼ hours' walk to the Fuorcla Surlej and the Murtel station on the Corvatschbahn (see St Moritz).

**Alp Ota

Morteratsch glacier (Vadret da Morteratsch). Leave Pontresina on the Bernina road and in 4.5 km/3 miles take a little road on the right to the Morteratsch Hotel (1908 m/6260 ft).
From here it is an hour's walk to the end of the glacier. A finer view of the

Morteratsch Glacier

*Chünetta

Boval hut	glacier can be had by climbing Chünetta (2096 m/6877 ft; 35 minutes). 2 hours beyond this is the Boval hut of the Swiss Alpine Club (2495 m/8186 ft; inn with beds), from which there is a superb view of the Bernina group.
Climbs	Possible climbs from the Boval hut (to be undertaken only with a guide) include Piz Morteratsch (3751 m/12,307 ft; 4½–5 hours; easy, for those with a good head for heights), with superb panoramic views; Piz Palü (3905 m/12,812 ft; 6–7 hours), a beautifully shaped peak; and Piz Bernina (4049 m/13,285 ft; 7–8 hours, very strenuous).
	Ascent of the Diavolezza (on foot from the Morteratsch Hotel or by cableway from Bernina-Suot; see Bernina.
	Another rewarding climb from Pontresina is the ascent of Piz Languard, to the east (3268 m/10,722 ft; 4 hours), with fine views. There is a restaurant 15 minutes below the summit.
Cableways	From the cableways to the Diavolezza (summer skiing) and Piz Lagalb (see Bernina).

Bad Ragaz   E1–2

	Canton: St Gallen (SG) Altitude: 517 m/1696 ft Population: 4000
Situation and general	Bad Ragaz, attractively situated in the Rhine valley at the mouth of the Tamina gorge, is one of Switzerland's leading spas. The warm radioactive springs (37° C–99° F), with a flow of 3000 to 10,000 litres/660 to 2200 gallons a minute, are used in the treatment of rheumatism, paralysis, metabolic disorders and injuries of all kinds. The springs rise in the Tamina gorge and the water has been piped down to Ragaz since 1840.

Sights

Catholic Church	On the left bank of the Tamina stands the parish church (1703) of St Pancras with 18th c. ceiling paintings. In the churchyard is the grave of the German philosopher Friedrich Wilhelm von Schelling.
Spa	On the right bank we find the Kurgarten with the Kursaal, baths, a restaurant and a golf course.
	North-west of the town are the Freudenberg ruins which were destroyed in the 15th c. by the Confederates. Close by stands the St Leonhard chapel with an Italian style choir. To the north is the Giessen Park, with a lake.

Surroundings

Sargans	8 km/5 miles to the north-west is the little town of Sargans (482 m/1581 ft), its old town was completely destroyed by fire in 1811. The 19th c. Town Hall (Gallatihaus) is built in Classical style. The parish church of St Oswald and Cassian is of 18th c. origin, restored and extended in the 19th and 20th c. There are two interesting chapels in the hamlet of Vild – St Sebastian and St Maria. In Züricherstrasse (No. 5) there is an interesting private collection of cars, motorcycles and accessories (visits by prior arrangement). Sargans is dominated by the castle, former seat of the Counts of Werdenberg-Sargans. First mentioned in 1282 and partly rebuilt in the 15th c. it was the official seat of the provincial governors until the end of the 18th c.; today the keep houses a local historical museum.
Bad Pfäfers	A road (4 km/2 miles; closed to motor vehicles) climbs the left bank of the Tamina between schist walls almost 250 m/820 ft high to Bad Pfäfers

The Tamina Gorge, near Bad Ragaz ▶

Bad Ragaz: Kursaal . . .   *. . . and evangelical church*

*Tamina gorge	(685 m/2247 ft; public baths), the buildings have the appearance of a monastery and date from 1704. In the spa (Badehaus) tickets are issued for admission to the Tamina gorge. Long passages run down to the gorge (500 m/1641 ft long), at the end of which is a narrow steam-filled gallery where the principal spring emerges from a deep chamber in the rock. In 1242 a gangway was constructed on the rock face, supported on projecting beams, and in about 1465 a chamber was excavated above the spring, from which patients were let down on ropes.
Bad Valens	Another road parallel to the Bad Pfäfers road runs west up the valley to the developing spa of Bad Valens (915 m/3002 ft).
Wartenstein	3 km/2 miles south-east of Ragaz we come to the Wartenstein (see below), with the Hotel Wartenstein (751 m/2464 ft), from which there is a beautiful view of the Churfirsten. Below the hotel are the ruins of Wartenstein Castle (13th c.) and St George's Chapel.
Guschakopf	West of Ragaz, above the right bank of the Tamina, is the Guschakopf (751 m/2464 ft; ¾ hour), from which there is a fine view.
*Pizol	South-west of Ragaz Pizol (2848 m/9344 ft), can be reached by way of a cableway (3.5 km/2 miles, 22 minutes) to Pardiel (1630 m/5348 ft; mountain inn), from which a chair-lift leads up to the Laufböden (2222 m/7290 ft), near the Pizol hut (2229 m/7313 ft; cableway from Wangs; first-rate ski trails).

From Ragaz to Vättis (15 km/9 miles)

Pfäfers	The road winds its way up to the Wartenstein. 4 km/2 miles: Pfäfers (822m/2697 ft; several inns), with the former Benedictine monastery of St Pirminsberg (founded *c.* 740, rebuilt 1672–93), now a cantonal home.

The road continues along the east side of the deep Tamina valley, via Ragol and Vadura. 11 km/7 miles: Vättis (951 m/3120 ft), a quiet and beautifully situated summer resort under the west side of the towering Calanda (2806 m/9206 ft). From here a very narrow road (excursions by minibus from Ragaz to St Martin, 1350 m/4429 ft, beyond this jeeps only: information from Verkehrsverein, Vättis) runs west up the beautiful Calfeisental to the Alp Sardona (1742 m/5716 ft; 12 km/7 miles), from which Piz Sardona (3059 m/10,137 ft) can be climbed (4¼ hours, with guide) by way of the Sardona hut (2161 m/7090 ft).

Vättis

Piz Sardona

Rapperswil   D1

Canton: St Gallen (SG)
Altitude: 409 m/1342 ft
Population: 7700

The old-world little town of Rapperswil is picturesquely situated on a peninsula on the north side of Lake Zurich, which is crossed at this point by a causeway 1000 m/3281 ft long.

Situation

The town appears to have been founded about 1200, and first appears in the records in 1229. The line of the Counts of Rapperswil died out at an early stage. In 1358 Duke Rudolf built a wooden bridge over the lake, which stood until 1878, when it was replaced by a masonry-walled causeway carrying the road and railway. From 1415 to 1464 Rapperswil was a free Imperial city and in 1803 it was incorporated in the canton of St Gallen.

History

Sights

In the main square stands the tall Town Hall (1471), with a richly carved door at the entrance to the council chamber. The town library and a cultural forum are housed in the adjoining Haus Zum Pfauen.

Main square

Rapperswil: rose garden of Capuchin friary   *Historic fresco on the Curti-Haus*

Rapperswil

Rapperswil: Yacht harbour and landing stage

Castle Polish Museum	From the square a broad flight of steps leads up to the Schlossberg (Castle Hill) or Endingerhügel (436 m/1431 ft), with the 15th c. parish church (restored 1887; two massive east towers) on the right and the imposing 13th c. castle on the left. The castle, on a triangular plan, with a keep and two other towers (restored 1988–89) was built by the Counts of Rapperswil and from the middle of the 15th c. was the seat of the Confederate governors. It houses the Polish Museum (Polenmuseum; the Renaissance, the Turkish wars, Copericus, Zeromski, Chopin, the struggle for freedom against Russia in 1868) and a small library.
Hintergasse	Three rows of houses run down to the lakeside, among them are Marktgasse and Hintergasse with attractive old arcades and neat little shops.
Lindenhof, Deer Park	From the tree-lined west bastion, the Lindenhof, there are charming views of the town and the lake. On the north side of the hill is the Hirschgarten (Deer Park), on the south side a vineyard.
Brenyhaus, Local Museum	On the Herrenberg, east of the parish church, is the Heimatmuseum (local museum), in the 15th c. Brenyhaus (formerly Haus Landenberg; restored).
Harbour Capuchin Friary	There is a pretty little harbour with a dock for the lake boat services. Two wall-paintings on "Curti-Haus" (private) in the Engadinergasse commemorate the destruction of the town by the Zurich mayor Rudolf Brun and later the town's entry into the Confederation. Close by the lakeside is the "Heilig Hüsli" (c. 1600) which was part of the wooden bridge built in 1358, replaced by a stone dam in the 19th c. On the western promontory is a Capuchin friary (founded 1605), with a rose-garden, and nearby is a small vineyard first referred to in 972.
Knie National Circus Children's Zoo	On the Strandweg (lakeside road) south of the station, is a Children's Zoo belonging to the Knie National Circus, which is based in the town (dolphin show).

Surroundings

A road runs over the causeway (Seedamm) along the Hurden peninsula, via the fishing village of Hurden (chapel of 1497), to Pfäffikon, on the south side of the lake (see Lake Zurich).

Hurden

It is a 10 minutes' trip by motor-boat or motor-launch to the island of Ufenau (nature reserve; restaurant in old farm), which belonged to Einsiedeln abbey from 965 onwards (church and chapel of 1141). On Zwingli's advice the humanist Ulrich von Hütten sought refuge here in 1523, but died two weeks later; he is buried in the churchyard of the old parish church.

Ufenau

A lakeside road (10 km/6 miles) runs south-east from Rapperswil through the commune of Jona to Busskirch, with an old church, and continues to Wurmsbach, which has a former convent of Cistercian nuns (16th–17th c.), now housing a girls' boarding school. The road then continues via Bollingen to Schmerikon, at the end of the lake.

Lakeside road

From Rapperswil road 8 runs east over the Ricken pass (805 m/2641 ft; beautiful view) into the Toggenburg district (see entry).

Toggenburg

The Rhine

D–E2–1

Cantons: Grisons (GR), St Gallen (SG), Thurgau (TG), Schaffhausen (SH), Zurich (ZH), Aargau (AG), Basel-Land (BL) and Basel-Stadt (BS).

The Rhine (a name probably of Celtic origin: Latin Rhenus, German Rhein, French Rhin, Romansch Reno, Dutch Rijn) is Europe's most beautiful river and most important waterway. The first 375 km/233 miles or its total length of 1320 km/820 miles are in Switzerland. Its source is in the eastern part of the St Gotthard massif, from which the two principal arms of the river flow separately westward for the first 60 km/37 miles.

Situation

Source

The Vorderrhein flows out of the Tomasee (2345 m/7694 ft), at the foot of Mt Badus (2928 m/9607 ft). The Hinterrhein originates in the névé of the Rheinwaldhorn (3402 m/11,116 ft). 10 km/6 miles west of Chur, at Reichenau, the two streams join to form the Alpenrhein (Alpine Rhine), which flows north into Lake Constance.

Vorderrhein and Hinterrhein

Alpenrhein

Emerging from the west end of the lake, the river plunges over the Rhine Falls at Schaffhausen and, as the Hochrhein (High Rhine) continues west to

Hochrhein, **Rhine Falls

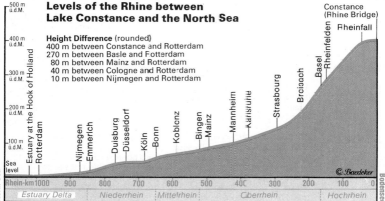

Levels of the Rhine between Lake Constance and the North Sea

Height Difference (rounded)
400 m between Constance and Rotterdam
270 m between Basle and Rotterdam
80 m between Mainz and Rotterdam
40 m between Cologne and Rotterdam
10 m between Nijmegen and Rotterdam

© Baedeker

The High Rhine at Zurzach

Basle. In its passage through Switzerland to this point the Rhine drains two-thirds of the country's total area, including 548 sq. km/212 sq. miles of glaciers.

Upper Rhine, Middle Rhine and Lower Rhine

At Basle the river leaves Switzerland, with an average flow of 1027 cu. m/36,263 cu. ft of water per second, and turns north, flowing through the Rhenish Uplands as the Middle Rhine. Below Bonn it is known as the Lower Rhine. In Holland it splits up into a number of arms which flow into the North Sea.

Sights along the Rhine

N.B.

In this section, for the convenience of visitors coming from the West, the routes along the Rhine valley are described from west to east, going upstream.

The High Rhine (Basle to Lake Constance)

*Basle

From Basle (see entry) the road runs along the north bank of the swiftly flowing High Rhine (navigable to above Basle), which supplies power to many hydro-electric stations. The pleasant valley is bounded on the north side by the Black Forest and on the south by the Swiss Jura.

Rheinfelden

The first place of any size is Rheinfelden (alt. 277 m/909 ft), a little town of 7000 inhabitants beautifully situated on the left bank of the river facing the southern slopes of the Black Forest. It is a popular salt-water spa, with two indoor salt-water baths. The water has one of the highest salt contents in Europe. The waters of the springs are drunk for medicinal purposes.
The attraction of Rheinfelden lies in its picturesque old town, with ancient walls and towers rising above the rapidly flowing river. Notable features

Zurzach: thermal baths

are the Town Hall (16th–18th c.) and St Martin's church (15th c., with Baroque interior). In the Haus zur Sonne (12 Marktgasse) is the Fricktaler Museum (local history).

At Rheinfelden we cross the Rhine and take a secondary road which runs north of the motorway to Möhlin and the village of Stein, where it joins road 7. Bad Säckingen, opposite on the north bank of the river, can be reached by the longest covered wooden bridge in Europe. This road continues east to Laufenburg (318 m/1043 ft; pop. 2000), opposite the German town, also called Laufenburg, on the north bank (bridge, with border control), at one of the most beautiful spots in the Rhine valley between Basle and Lake Constance, framed by wooded hills. The town has a tall Late Gothic parish church (1489) with a beautiful interior.

Stein, *Wooden Bridge

Laufenburg

After an attractive bend in the valley the road continues via Leibstadt (to the north of which a nuclear power station is under construction) to a bridge over the Aare (5.5 km/3 miles), just above its junction with the Rhine. Opposite, on the north bank, is the German town of Wadshut. Beyond the bridge a road goes off on the right to Brugg (Berne, Lucerne).

The Schaffhausen road continues to Koblenz (321 m/1053 ft), an important road junction near the confluence (hence its name – Latin Confluentia) of the Aare and the Rhine. From here road 7 runs via Winterthur and St Gallen to Rorschach. The Schaffhausen road turns left over the Rhine bridge (border control) into Germany.

Koblenz

In 6 km/4 miles road 7 reaches Zurzach (342 m/1122 ft; pop. 3500), on the site of the Roman fort of Tenedo, a little town which was formerly a considerable river port, noted for its fairs, and is now a well-known spa. The hot springs (40° C/104° F), the spa facilities (including three outdoor swimming pools) the Turm Hotel and the Rheumatic clinic lie west of the town. Zurzach has a number of fine old burghers' houses and a church of the 10th and 14th centuries (sarcophagus of St Verena, 1603, in crypt; tombstone of

Zurzach

Kaiserstuhl: Oberer Turm

a Roman legionary of 1st c. A.D. built into wall). Opposite Zurzach (bridge) is the German village of Rheinheim.

Kaiserstuhl

The road, signposted to Winterthur, continues along the left bank of the Rhine and in 12 km/7 miles reaches the old-world town of Kaiserstuhl (350 m/1148 ft), with a massive 13th c. tower and a Gothic church, picturesquely situated above the Rhine opposite the German village of Hohentengen (bridge).

Glattfelden

Road 7 then leaves the Rhine and comes to Glattfelden (359 m/1178 ft), on the River Glatt just above its junction with the Rhine. This was the home town of the Swiss writer Gottfried Keller and is frequently referred to in his novel "Der grüne Heinrich".

Eglisau

At a crossroads 2 km/1 mile farther on, where the right-hand road runs south to Zurich, turn left to cross the Rhine on a stone bridge into the picturesque old town of Eglisau (360 m/1181 ft), which has 18th c. church situated on a higher road.

The road then cuts across the Ratzer Feld, an area surrounded on three sides by Germany, and a projecting finger of German territory linked with the district of Waldshut only by a narrow corridor. To the east of the

Rheinau

German village of Jestetten is the small Swiss town of Rheinau, almost completely enclosed within a loop in the river, where there is a dam on the Rhine (motor-boats to the Rhine-Falls). The sumptuously appointed Baroque church (1705) belonged to a Benedictine abbey founded in the 9th c. and dissolved in 1862.

**Rhine Falls

From Jestetten the road runs north-east into Switzerland again to the industrial town of Neuhausen, at the Rhine Falls (see entry).

Schaffhausen
Diessenhofen

3 km/2 miles farther on is Schaffhausen (see entry). From Schaffhausen take road 13, which runs 10 km/6 miles east to Diessenhofen (416 km/1365

ft), a medieval town of 3000 inhabitants, once a free Imperial city, with handsome old burghers' houses, old town walls, the Siegelturm, a church of 1602 and conventual buildings of 1571. On the opposite side of the river is the German village of Gailingen.

Then along the river to Stein am Rhein (see entry).

Stein am Rhein

2 km/1 mile beyond this, at Eschenz, the Rhine opens out into the Untersee, the most westerly arm of Lake Constance (see entry).

Lake Constance

Along the Alpine Rhine

From the south-east end of Lake Constance road 13 leads up the wide valley of the Rhine to the village of Heerbrugg, with an old castle, and Altstätten (457 m/1499 ft; pop. 10,000), an ancient town with attractive arcaded houses (Marktgasse), a parish church of 1794 and a He matmuseum (local museum) in Prestegg, an old burgher's house (restaurant).

Altstätten

Here a road goes off on the right and over the Stoss pass to Gais (Appenzell, St Gallen), and another road crosses the Ruppen pass, through beautiful scenery, to Trogen (see Appenzell) and St Gallen (see entry).

The road continues through Oberriet and comes in 29 km/18 miles to Buchs (450 m/1476 ft; pop. 6000), chief town of a district and a road and rail junction. Buchs is a busy town (many haulage firms) on the route into Austria (Feldkirch–Innsbruck–Vienna).

Buchs

From Buchs the route continues either through the Principality of Liechtenstein (see entry) or on road 13, which runs along the west side of the valley to Balzers. Then either on the motorway via Bad Ragaz (see entry), or via Maienfeld (525 m/1723 ft; pop. 1500), an ancient Grisons town, with handsome patrician houses, the medieval Schloss Brandis ("Roman Tower"; inn) and Schloss Salenegg (17th–18th c.). In the cemetery is the grave of the writer John Knittel (1891–1970).

Principality of Liechtenstein
Bad Ragaz
Maienfeld

From Maienfeld there are two possible routes to Landquart. The direct road (expressway) traverses the Rhine plain in a straight line (5 km/3 miles) to the bridge which crosses the river Landquart into town. The alternative route, 2 km/ 1 mile longer, is on an attractive minor road which follows the hillside through the orchards and vineyards of the old "Bündner Herrschaft" (Grisons Lordship) to the old-world village of Jenins, famous for its wine, and then continues below the ruined castles of Aspermont, Wyneck and Klingenhorn and past the lower station (1 km/½ mile before Malans, on left) of a cableway which runs north-east to Aelpli (1802 m/5912 ft) under the summit of Vilan (2376 m/7796 ft; 1½ hours), to the vine-growing village of Malans (568 m/1364 ft), with handsome old patrician houses, under Burg Bothmar (16th and 18th c.).

Malans

Landquart (527 m/1729 ft) is a busy road and rail junction (paper-making). The motorway to Chur continues south between the railway and the right bank of the river (with strong side winds when the föhn is blowing).

Landquart

On the hillside to the east (not visible from the road) is Schloss Marschlins, with its four towers (538 m/1765 ft; 13th and 17th c.), commanding the entrance to the Prättigau. It can be reached by a side road (1 km/½ mile) off the old road via Zizers. Beyond this, to the east of the road, lies the village of Igis, with a college of agriculture in the Plantahof. In another 5 km/3 miles the road passes Zizers station, serving the old market town of Zizers, Romansch Zizras (540 m/1772 ft), which lies off the road to the left and has two churches and two 17th c. mansions which belonged to the Salis family (the Unteres Schloss and the smaller Oberes Schloss, in the upper part of the town).

Schloss Marschlins

Zizers

The road then comes to Chur (see entry) and continues, bearing west, to the village of Domat Ems (583 m/1916 ft), with a church of the Assumption in

Chur

Valley of the Vorderrhein

Italian Baroque style (1730–38). On a rocky hill are the Late Gothic St John's church (1515; carved high altar of 1504) and the Romanesque St Peter's chapel.

Reichenau   3 km/2 miles further on we leave the motorway at the Reichenau exit, just before it comes to an end. To the left is Reichenau (603 m/1978 ft), picturesquely situated on a rocky hill at the confluence of the Vorderrhein and the tumultuous Hinterrhein, with an old castle (altered in 1775 and 1820) belonging to the von Planta family; from the beautiful castle gardens there is a view of the junction of the two branches of the Rhine.

Along the Vorderrhein

Tamins   From Reichenau road 19 (signposted to Flims and Disentis), after crossing the Rhine, goes up to the village of Tamins (Romansch Tumein, "hill", alt. 668 m/2192 ft; bypass), dominated by the prominent spire of its 16th c. parish church. The road then curves round to cross the Lavoi-Tobel (gorge) and winds its way up the hillside, with views to the left of the Domleschg (valley of the Hinterrhein) and Schloss Rhäzuns, one of the many old castles in the valley, and of the gorge carved by the Vorderrhein through the great Flims landslide.

Shortly before Trin the highest point on this section of road (895 m/2936 ft) is reached. On a crag to the left is the old tower of Hohentrins castle.

Trin   4 km/2 miles from Tamins is Trin, German Trins (890 m/2920 ft), attractively situated on a terrace above the gorge of the Vorderrhein.

The road then continues downhill, with a view to the rear of the tower of Hohentrins. In 1 km/½ mile it bends to the right, and one can see on the left the hamlet of Digg, picturesquely situated on the hillside. Then follows a fairly level stretch of road under the sheer cliffs of the Porclas defile, with meadowland and forest on the valley floor below. At the Trinsermühle

Flims: "Schlössli"

(Romansch Trin-Mulin, 833 m/2733 ft; restaurant), an old mill, there are beautiful waterfalls. The road then climbs again, with many bends, along the edge of the gigantic masses of rock debris which tumbled down from the Upper Segnes valley during the Ice Age, covering some 52 sq. km/20 sq. miles of the Rhine valley. Off the road to the left is the little Cresta-See (850 m/2789 ft). Beautiful view of the valley below.

6.5 km/4 miles beyond Trin is Flims (see entry). The road then passes a **Flims** parking place (on right) for two cableways and bends to cross the Neue Stennabrücke (new Stenna bridge) over the Flembach (Segnesbach). After passing through the park-like landscape of the hotel settlement of Flims Waldhaus (see Flims) the road winds its way through a beautiful stretch of woodland and meadowland. 1 km/½ mile further on a side road goes off on the left to a camp site; then in another 1 km/½ mile, at Mulania (on right), is the lower station of a cableway 4045 m/13,272 ft long to Crap Sogn Gion (upper station 2220 m/7284 ft; large restaurant ski-lifts) and Crap Masegn (2477 m/8127 ft). The road then runs downhill and uphill again on a moderate gradient, crosses the Laaxer Bach and descends again above the deeply slashed Laaxer Tobel (gorge).

The road continues via Laax (see Flims) to Ilanz (see entry) and from here it **Ilanz** follows a fairly straight and level course to Disentis along the left bank of the Vorderrhein, close to the Rhätische Bahn, through a stretch of the valley known as the Pardella.
2 km/1 mile beyond Ilanz is Strada (720 m/2362 ft; bypass), with the charmingly situated little village of Schnaus higher up on the right. 2.5 km/1 mile farther on is Ruis station (736 m/2415 ft; the village is above the road on the right). The road crosses the Panixer Bach, with the ruins of Jörgenberg Castle (495 m/1624 ft) on a wooded crag on the right.

4 km/2 miles beyond Strada a road goes off on the right and winds its way **Waltensburg** up (3 km/2 miles) to Waltensburg (Romansch Vuorz, 1010 m/3314 ft), where

there is a church containing fine 14th and 15th c. frescoes. From Waltensburg a by-road, with extensive views, runs along a natural terrace to Brigels (5 km/3 miles; see below).

The main road continues along the left bank of the Vorderrhein, then crosses to the other bank and curves under the railway.

Tavanasa

It reaches Tavanasa (800 m/2625 ft), at the narrow mouth of the Tscharbach valley, above which are two ruined castles, Schwarzenstein to the left and Heidenberg to the right. Here a side road on the right crosses the river to

Brigels

Danis and winds its way up (6 km/4 miles north) to the village of Brigels, Romansch Breil (1283 m/4210 ft), a popular summer and winter sports resort in a sunny expanse of Alpine meadows, with the Late Gothic churches of St Maria (restored 1963–66) and St Martin. In the surrounding area (good walks with far-ranging views) are a number of pretty chapels, including the chapel of St Eusebius, with 14th c. frescoes on the exterior. Route over the Kisten pass (2638 m/8655 ft) to Tieffehd (9–10 hours).

Zignau

From Tavanasa the road to Disentis continues along the wooded slopes above the right bank of the Vorderrhein. Off the road to the left is Zignau, at the mouth of the wild Val Zavragia, and the ruins of Ringgenberg Castle. Then on a stretch of concrete road to a bridge over the Vorderrhein and past

St Anne's
Chapel

St Anne's chapel (1716, on right), on the spot where the "Upper" or "Grey" League of the people of the Grisons against the oppressions of the nobility was renewed in 1424.

Trun

6 km/4 miles from Tavanasa is Trun, German Truns (855 m/2805 ft), a village of 1600 inhabitants at the mouth of the Val Punteglias, which runs down from the Brigelser Hörner (3250 m/10,663 ft; 10 hours, with guide). In the village are the parish church of St Martin (1660–62), with a Romanesque tower, and the former residence of the Abbots of Disentis (1675), now housing the district court and a museum, with handsome rooms (interesting coat-of-arms of the communes belonging to the Grey League and of all district judges since 1424). Above the village stands the 17th c. church of St Maria della Glisch.

Rabius,
Val Sumvitg

The road now climbs gradually to the village of Rabius (955 m/3133 ft), where a road on the left crosses the Rhine to Surrhein (892 m/2927 ft) and climbs the wooded Val Sumvitg (Somvixer Tal to 6.5 km/4 miles south) Tenigerbad, Romansch Bagn Sumvitg (1273 m/4177 ft) (indoor pool). From Tenigerbad the road continues 1.7 km/1 mile to Runcahez (1300 m/4265 ft), on a small artificial lake.

Somvix

The main road continues from Rabius to Somvix, Romansch Sumvitg (summus vicus, "highest village"; 1050 m/3445 ft), with the Gothic chapel of St Benedict. Below, on the Rhine, lies the village of Compadials (965 m/3166 ft). Beyond this is a beautiful stretch of road high up on the hillside, running through a defile and then over a new bridge (to the right the old covered wooden bridge) spanning the deep gorge of the Val Russein, which runs down from Mt Tödi. The road then ascends the rocky hillside and comes to Disentis (see entry), 7.5 km/5 miles from Somvix.

Val Tavetsch

From Disentis road 19 leads up the Val Tavetsch on a moderate gradient, high above the river, with picturesque views of Disentis and its white abbey to the rear and the villages on the slopes of the valley downstream. Ahead can be seen, on the hillside to the right, the villages of Acletta (chapel), Segnes (1336 m/4383 ft) and Mompé Tujetsch (1397 m/4584 ft).

The road then continues, with expanses of coniferous forest, passes close to a high viaduct on the Furka-Oberalp railway and curves round to cross a mountain stream, the Bugnei.

Sedrun

9 km/ 6 miles from Disentis is Sedrun (1401 m/4597 ft), chief place in the Val Tavetsch (Val Tujetsch), beautifully situated on gently sloping Alpine mea-

Valley of the Hinterrhein

dows and popular both with summer visitors and winter sports enthusiasts (ski-lift); enclosed swimming pool. The church of St Vigilius (1693), has a Romanesque tower and a carved altar (1491). Chair-lift to the spring pastures of Cungieri (1900 m/6234 ft; restaurant).

To the south is Piz Pazzola (2582 m/8472 ft; 4 hours), from which there are magnificent views. Further up the valley there is a fine view of Mt Badus (Six Madun). At Camischolas the road crosses a stream flowing down from the Val Strim. From here a narrow road (closed to traffic) runs up 8 km/ 5 miles to the Lai da Nalps, an artificial lake (1909 m/6263 ft).

*Piz Pazzola

Rueras (1450 m/4757 ft) is a little village in the Val Milar, with a small church and fine wooden houses. The road then winds its way up again from the valley floor to the hillside and crosses streams flowing down the Val Milar and Val Giuf. To the left can be seen a tower of the ruined castle of Pontaningen (Pultmenga) and beyond this the chapel of St Brida. 1.5 km/ 1 mile before Tschamut a road branches off on the left via the village of Selva to the hamlet of Sut Crestas (1540 m/5053 ft) lying in the valley, and which has a charming little church.

Rueras

The road then comes to the beautifully situated hamlet of Tschamut (1648 m/5407 ft), opposite the mouth of the Val Curnera (on left), crosses the Gämmerrhein, which flows down from the Val de Val (on right), and bears right at the foot of Mt Calmot into the Val Surpalix. To the left the Vorderrhein flows out of the Tomasee, at the foot of Mt Badus.

Tschamut

Along the Hinterrhein

The road south from Reichenau, where the Vorderrhein and the Hinterrhein join, crosses the Hinterrhein and runs along a terrace above the left bank of the river to Bonaduz.

329

The Rhine

Bonaduz

From Bonaduz (660 m/2165 ft; pop. 1000) a road goes off on the right via Versam to Ilanz and Disentis. Here a road goes off on the right via Versam to Ilanz and Disentis. The main road (signposted to Thusis) continues south on the terrace above the river. High up on the left can be seen the Late Romanesque chapel of St George, with fine wall-paintings of the 14th–15th c. and a Late Gothic carved altar (key at Rhäzuns station).

Rhäzuns

The road then comes to Rhäzuns (648 m/2126 ft). To the right is the village, with the Romanesque church of SS Peter and Paul and another church of 1702. To the left, on a steep crag above the Hinterrhein, stands the imposing Rhäzuns Castle, the oldest parts of which date from the 13th c., and which commands the entrance to the Domleschg (below). At the end of the village, on left, is the lower station of a cableway, 2100 m/6890 ft long, to Feldis.

The road follows the railway on the wooded hillside above the Hinterrhein, whose broad stony bed is enclosed between massive levees. On the opposite bank is a tower of the ruined castle of Nieder-Juvalta.
2 km/1 mile beyond this, on the right, is the Rhäzuns mineral spring ("Rhätisana" table water; visitors can tour bottling plant). In another 2 km/1 mile, just before the Rothenbrunnen railway station (625 m/2051 ft; to left), the valley opens out and the road forks. The valley floor and the gentle lower slopes on the east side are known as the Domleschg, the steeper west slopes as the Heinzenberg. On both sides are vineyards, and cornfields reaching high up on the hillsides. The main road to Thusis skirts the left bank of the river under the Heinzenberg; the very attractive side road to the left passes through the numerous villages in the Domleschg and rejoins the main road at Thusis. The castles built on projecting spurs of rock were almost completely destroyed at the end of the 15th c.

Through the Domleschg to Thusis

(11 km/7 miles; well worth the extra 1.5 km/1 mile).
The road to the left crosses the Hinterrhein and comes to the village of Rothenbrunnen, under high rock walls, with the ruined castle of Ober-Juvalta. It has a chalybeate (iron-bearing) spring containing iodine (bottling plant).
Farther on, beyond the bridge over the Scheidbach (on right), is the large Ortenstein castle (754 m/2474 ft), with an early medieval keep and 15th c. domestic quarters. 350 m/1148 ft south is the ruined pilgrimage church of St Lawrence.

Tomils

3 km/2 miles from the road junction a mountain road (not dust-free, with some steep gradients; in winter open only as far as Scheid) runs up on the left via the village of Tomils or Tumegl (800 m/2625 ft; Late Gothic church with an altarpiece of 1490 and 16th c. wall-paintings) and continues with many bends, through Unterscheid and Oberscheid to (8 km/5 miles north-

Feldis

east) Feldis or Veulden (1472 m/4830 ft), a health resort in a sunny spot commanding extensive views (cableway from Rhäzuns).

Paspels

The Thusis road continues to Paspels, with St Lawrence's chapel (Romanesque wall-paintings) and Alt-Sins Castle (restored). Beyond this, higher up on left, is the ruined castle of Neu-Sins or Canova.

Rodels

Rodels (700 m/2297 ft) has attractive 17th and 18th c. houses. Above the village, to the east, can be seen the 12th c. castle of Rietberg or Rätusberg, which features in Conrad Ferdinand Meyer's "Jurg Jenatsch".
Beyond this is Pratval, with the ruins of Hasensprung castle.

Fürstenau

At Fürstenau are two castles which belonged to the Planta family; the Haus Stoffel has 15th and 16th c. wall-paintings. Higher up, on the left, is the beautiful village of Scharans (780 m/2559 ft), where Jürg (Georg) Jenatsch was pastor in 1617–18. The road then crosses the Zollbrücke over the Albula, which emerges from the Schin gorge a little higher up the hill and flows down to join the Hinterrhein. To the left are Baldenstein castle and St Cassian's chapel (13th c.).

Sils, Thusis

At Sils (Seglias, 683 m/2241 ft) we join the road from Tiefencastel through the Schin gorge and turn right along this to reach Thusis (722 m/2369 ft).

The main road to Thusis (No. 13) continues from Rothenbrunnen station along the left bank of the Hinterrhein under the Heinzenberg, with views of the villages and castles of the Domleschg. To the left are Alt-Sins castle and the ruins of Neu-Sins.

Heinzenberg, Rothenbrunnen

In 5.5 km/3 miles the road reaches Cazis (600 m/1969 ft) where we find an old Dominican nunnery (1504) (church with wall-paintings in choir) and the Romanesque chapel of St Wendelin.

Cazis

Beyond this is an attractive view, to the left, of the mouth of the Schin gorge, with the village of Scharans (on left) and Baldenstein castle (on right), the Tinzenhorn (3179 m/10,430 ft) rearing up above the gorge and in front of it the snow-capped Piz Curvèr (2972 m/9751 ft). 1 km/½ mile beyond Cazis a road goes off on the right to Präz. Farther on, above the road on the right, are the little villages of Masein and Tagstein castle. Ahead, barely discernible, is the entrance to the Via Mala, with the ruined castles of Hohen-Rhätien and Ehrenfels.

4 km/2 miles from Cazis we come to Thusis, Romansch Tusaun (722 m/2369 ft), a handsome market village at the junction with the road through the Schin gorge to Tiefencastel. The village was almost completely destroyed by fire in 1845. The Protestant parish church dates from 1506, the new Catholic church from 1965. All round Thusis are the ruins of medieval castles. On a steep crag at the entrance to the Via Mala, 246 m/807 ft above the river, perches the 12th c. castle of Hohen-Rhätien or Realta (950 m/3117 ft; 45 minutes' climb from the village); at Sils are Ehrenfels and Baldenstein; to the left, above the entrance to the Nolla valley, is Ober-Tagstein (1130 m/3708 ft; 1¼ hours on a forest track) from the slopes of the Heinzenberg stands the castle of Tagstein or Nieder-Tagstein (848 m/2782 ft; ½ hour).

Thusis

From Thusis the road to Splügen and the San Bernardino pass continues past the end of the Tiefencastel road, crosses the river Nolla, which flows into the Hinterrhein here.

The road then enters the Via Mala, a magnificent gorge on the Hinterrheir, enclosed between limestone walls 500 m/1641 ft high; the lowest section of the gorge, the Verlorene Loch ("Lost Hole"), is particuarly wild and has been passable only since the construction of a road in 1322. The medieval bridle-path bypassed the gorge, running up from the Nolla valley to the right of the wooded crag of Grapteig; the road follows the windings of the gorge. The present road runs through a short tunnel and soon afterwards, high up on the hillside, enters a gallery leading into the 500 m/1641 ft long Rongellen Tunnel. 2.5 km/2 miles from Thusis at the little hamlet of Ronge - len (863 m/2832 ft), the gorge opens out into a small basin. It then closes in again, and in this narrower section, the real Via Mala of medieval times, the old road branches off the new road (No. 18).

*Via Mala

In 1988 a signposted educational walk through the narrow Via Mala gorge between Thusis and Zillis was opened. Information boards and maps explain the geological history and hydrology of the area and highlight man's great feats of engineering.

Via Mala Walk

The new road (distances about the same as on the old road described below) runs through a gallery, beyond which the old road, going in the opposite direction, comes in on the left. It then traverses a winding tunne, crosses the Hinterrhein on a pre-stressed concrete bridge 170 m/558 ft long and runs through another curving tunnel 400 m/1313 ft long, beyond which the old road, with the bridge at Rania, can be seen lower down on the right. Then through a gallery and a short tunnel to an access road to the expressway, 5.3 km/3 miles from Rongeller and 1 km/½ mile north of Zillis.

N 13 expressway

The old road through the Via Mala (closed to large cars) branches off 1 km/½ mile beyond Rongellen, immediately before a gallery. 800 m/2625 ft

Old Via Mala road

Zillis: Panels Nos. 136/137 and 143/144

farther on, beyond the second gallery, is the Erste Brücke (First Bridge), built in 1941 on the site of an earlier bridge of 1738. Immediately beyond the bridge, on the right, are a parking place and a kiosk, from which a flight of 257 steps leads down to a gallery 120 m/394 ft long running above the tumultuous river (admission charge). 300 m/984 ft beyond this, after the third gallery, is the Zweite Brücke (Second Bridge: 800 m/2887 ft, built 1941), alongside the old bridge of 1739, 50 m/164 ft above the river. Above, to the right, can be seen the new road. In 1.3 km/1 mile is the Dritte Brücke (Third Bridge: 885 m/2904 ft), at the end of the Via Mala, beside the little restaurant at Rania (on right). The road now enters the pleasant open valley of Schams (Romansch Sassám), with the pointed summit of Hüreli or Hirli (2855 m/9367 ft) in the background. 1 km/½ mile before Zillis is an access road to the N 13 expressway.

Zillis St Martin's Church	1 km/½ mile south is the village of Zillis, Romansch Ciraun or Ziran (933 m/3060 ft), with the very interesting church of St Martin. The nave and tower are Early Romanesque, the choir Late Gothic; the whole structure was carefully restored in 1938–40. Its most notable feature is the 12th c.
*Wooden Ceiling	painted wooden ceiling, made up of 153 square panels depicting Biblical scenes – a unique example of very early figural painting. Under the ceiling is a Romanesque frieze revealed in 1940. Near the church in the Schams museum (Tgea da Schons) is a collection of tools, furniture and manuscripts from Schams, Avers and the Rheinwald.
Hinterrhein	From Zillis a narrow and winding road runs 2km/1 mile south-west up the Schamserberg, on the left bank of the Hinterrhein, to the village of Donath (1033 m/3389 ft). Above the village are the ruins of Fardün castle (1214 m/3983 ft), famous for the story of a 15th c. castellan who, during a peasant rising, spat into the dinner of a peasant named Johannes Calcar, who thereupon thrust his head into the bowl and suffocated him, with the words "Maglia sez il pult cha ti has condüt" ("You've salted the dish; now eat it!"). From Donath the road climbs another 6 km/4 miles west to the quiet

E (Chancel)

1	2	3	4	5	6	7	8	9
48	49	50	51	52	53	54	55	10
47	56	57	58	59	60	61	62	11
46	63	64	65	66	67	68	69	12
45	70	71	72	73	74	75	76	13
44	77	78	79	80	81	82	83	14
43	84	85	86	87	88	89	90	15
42	91	92	93	94	95	96	97	16
41	98	99	100	101	102	103	104	17
40	105	106	107	108	109	110	111	18
39	112	113	114	115	116	117	118	19
38	119	120	121	122	123	124	125	20
37	126	127	128	129	130	131	132	21
36	133	134	135	136	137	138	139	22
35	140	141	142	143	144	145	146	23
34	147	148	149	150	151	152	153	24
33	32	31	30	29	28	27	26	25

S (left)   N (right)

W (Entrance)

☐ 140 original panels   ☐ 13 panels restored 1939–40

Romanesque painted ceiling in St Martin's Church (12th c.)

Zillis (GR)

38 Dragon swallowing a winged fish
39 Dragon
40 Fish-tailed animal with small nereid
41 Two dragons biting one another
42 Fish-tailed unicorn
43 Fish-tailed elephant
44 Fish-tailed lion
45 Fish-tailed wolf
46 Fish-tailed boar
47 Fish-tailed ram
48 Sea-horse biting the tail of a fish-tailed roebuck

INNER PANELS

49–51 Kings David, Solomon and Rehoboam
52, 53 The Synagogue and the Church
54, 55 Annunciation
56, 57 Joseph's Doubts
58 Visitation
59 Annunciation to the Shepherds
60–62 Nativity
63–66 The Three Kings on their way to see Herod
67–69 The Three Kings before Herod; three horses in waiting
70–73 Adoration of the Infant Jesus by the Three Kings
74–76 The Three Kings returning home
77 The Three Kings
78 Purification of the Virgin
79 Presentation in the Temple
80 Joseph's Dream
81–83 Flight into Egypt
84 Holy Family
85–90 Slaughter of the innocents
91 The Child Jesus gives life to clay birds
92, 93 The 12-year-old Jesus in the Temple
94–97 John the Baptist preaching in the wilderness
98 Baptism of Christ
99–101 Christ tempted by the Devil
102 Christ with two angels
103, 104 Marriage in Cana
105 Christ and the centurion of Capernaum
106, 107 Christ healing the sick
108 Christ casts out a devil
109 Christ heals the Canaanite woman
110, 111 Christ heals the impotent man at the pool of Bethesda
112 Christ heals a paralytic
113–115 Raising of Lazarus
116 Christ and the woman of Samaria
117, 118 Christ teaching in the school of Nazareth
119 Christ and the children
120–122 Mission of the Apostles
123–125 Transfiguration
126–130 Entry into Jerusalem
131, 132 Cleansing of the Temple
133–134 Judas's betrayal
135 Washing of the feet
136, 137 Last Supper
138, 139 Agony in the Garden
140–143 Christ taken prisoner; Judas's kiss
144 Christ before Pilate
145 Mocking of Christ
146 Christ is crowned with thorns
147, 148 St Martin with the beggar
149 St Martin consecrated as an acolyte by St Hilary
150 St Martin raises a man from the dead
151–153 The Devil appears to St Martin in the guise of a king

MARGINAL PANELS (including some copies)

1 Auster, the S wind
2 Dragon
3 Fish-tailed cock
4 Nereid with horn
5 Nereid with harp
6 Nereid with fiddle
7 Eagle
8 Dragon
9 Aquilo (written in mirror script), the N wind
10 Fisherman
11 The prophet Jonah
12 Part of a ship
13 Naked woman riding on a fish-tailed bird
14 Fish-tailed goose
15 Fish-tailed fox swallowing a fish-tailed cock
16 Monkey riding on a fish
17 Siren and fish-tailed stag
18 Naked man with axe riding on a fish
19 Fish-tailed wolf
20 Fish-tailed bear
21 Fish-tailed camel
22 Fish-tailed wolf
23 Fish-tailed lion
24 Fish-tailed ram
25 Angel
26 Dragon-tailed bird with snake
27 Dragon
28 Nereid with horn
29 Nereid with harp
30 Nereid with fiddle
31 Fish-tailed goose
32 Dragon-tailed bird with snake
33 Angel
34 Fish-tailed cock
35 Dragon
36 Fish-tailed boar
37 Fish-tailed he-goat

little mountain village of Mathon (1521 m/4990 ft), from which Piz Beverin (2997 m/9833 ft) can be climbed in 5 hours.   Fiz Beverin

The N 13 expressway continues south up the Hinterrhein valley, coming in 3 km/2 miles to the village of Clug n, on the left bank of the river (to right of road), with a picturesque little Romanesque church. 500 m/1641 ft south-west of the village are the ruins of Cagliatscha castle.   Clugin

Beyond this, also on the right of the road, in the hamlet of Bad (Romansch Bogn), there is an alkaline chalybeate (iron-bearing) spring, the water of which is piped to Andeer. On the bridge over the Pignieuer Bach, which flows down from Piz Curvèr (2976 m/9764 ft), is a 15th c. Latin inscription.   Bad

5 km/3 miles from Zillis is the exit for Andeer (979 m/3212 ft; pop. 1000), chief town in the Schams area, in medieval times an important trading station and now a health resort (mineral swimming pool) and winter sports facility, with a large parish church (1673: Protestant) and a number of fine 16th c. houses with sgraffito decoration, notably the Haus Padrun.   Andeer

The old road continues through the Rofla gorge to join the new road (the distance is much the same). From Andeer there are rewarding and fairly easy climbs: to the west Piz Vizan (2472 m/8111 ft: 4½ hours); to the south-east Piz la Tschera (2632 m/8636 ft; 5 hours).

The new road (N 13) continues above Andeer in a wide curve, twice crossing the old road on bridges and passing below the village of Bären-burg (1042 m/3419 ft). Through the trees can be seen the ruined castle of the same name; to the right is an artificial lake.   Bärenburg

The road then traverses a tunnel of some length and crosses the Averser Rhein to reach the junction, at Avers, with the old road coming up from Andeer on the right, which gives access to the Rolfa gorge and the Avers valley.

For the Rofla gorge, bear right into the old road to Avers soon branches off on the left. 1 km/½ mile farther downhill is the Roflaschlucht inn (1097 m/3599 ft), at the entrance to the Rofla gorge (or Rofna: access to gallery hewn from rock, admission fee payable at the inn).   *Rofla gorge

Beyond this is a reservoir (maximum capacity 1 million cu. m/35 million cu. ft, a compensation basin for the reservoir at Sufers, from which water is carried down under pressure through a tunnel 13 km/8 miles long to a power station at Sils in the Domleschg. The old road then crosses under the new one twice and comes in 2 km/1 mile to Andeer.

A rewarding excursion can be made into the beautiful high valley of the tumultuous Averser Rhein, which is divided into two parts by a narrow defile – the Romansch-speaking Val Ferrera and the German-speaking Averser Tal (Avers valley). It is reached on a good minor road (18 km/11 miles to Cresta) which branches off the old road to the Rofla gorge, passes under the expressway and then continues up the wild Val Ferrera, first on the left bank and then on the right bank.   **Val Ferrera**

3.5 km/2 miles up this road is Ausserferrera (1321 m/4334 ft), in a wider part of the valley. The road then runs through the Ragn da Ferrera defile. To the right are the Ferrera turbine house (185,000 kW), hewn from the rock, and a compensation basin (230,000 cu. m/8 million cu. ft) for the reservoir in the Valle di Lei. Then, opposite the mouth of the Val d'Emet or Val Niemet, the village of Innerferrera (Romansch Canicül or Canlantgi, 1480 m/4856 ft) is reached. The road next crosses the Averser Rhein, runs through a tunnel   Ausserferrera   Innerferrera

◄ *The Rofla gorge of the Rhine, near Andeer*

The Rhine

(200 m/656 ft) and then another grandiose defile (natural rock arch), with a waterfall at the mouth of the Val Starlera on the left. After another tunnel (500 m/1641 ft) it comes to the new bridge (lower down, the old bridge) over the Reno di Lei. This river issues from the Italian Valle di Lei, in which a dam was built in 1957–61 as a joint Swiss-Italian enterprise (Valle di Lei-Hinterrhein hydro-electric scheme).

100 m/328 ft beyond the bridge the road goes through another tunnel (250 m/820 ft), and 1.3 km/1 mile farther on a road branches off on the right to the dam. This runs uphill, with two sharp bends, and in 2.5 km/2 miles reaches a tunnel 1 km/½ mile long (traffic lights; closed in winter), at the far end of which are the Swiss-Italian frontier, the Swiss customs (on right) and beyond this the dam (car park). The dam rises to a height of 138 m/453 ft above the foundations and is 635 m/2083 ft long at the top. The artificial lake formed by the dam, the Lago di Lei (alt. 1931 m/6336 ft, capacity 197 million cu. m/6956 million cu. ft), lies in Italian territory. The water is carried down under pressure in a tunnel 6.9 km/4 miles long to the Ferrera turbine house (above).

Lago di Lei

Avers valley

The main road continues past the turning for the dam along the Avers valley, whose German-speaking population originally came from the Valais (Wallis) and adopted the Reformed faith as early as 1530. After passing through the hamlet of Campsut (1670 m/5479 ft) the road comes to Cröt (1720 m/5643 ft: inn), at the mouth of the Madriser Tal, with the Cima di Lago (3082 m/10,112 ft) and Piz Gallgione (3135 m/10,286 ft) rearing up in the background.

It then climbs the wooded hillside in sharp bends, crosses the Rhine once again and after a number of other sharp bends reaches the highest part of the valley.

Cresta

Cresta (Avers, 1960 m/6431 ft), beautifully situated amid flower-spangled Alpine meadows, attracts many visitors as a mountain resort and a climbing base, and offers good skiing. Outside the closely huddled village of brown wooden houses is the picturesque little 17th c. church. On the east side of the valley are the three peaks of the Weissberg (3057 m/10,030 ft; 3 hours) and the bold pyramidal silhouette of Piz Platta (3398 m/11,149 ft; 4–5 hours).

Juf

From Cresta the road continues for another 6 km/4 miles, past the Podestatshaus (2042 m/6700 ft; built 1664), to Juf (2133 m/6998 ft), the highest permanently inhabited settlement in the Alps. From here it is possible to walk to Casaccia over the Septimer pass (Pass da Sett) or to Bovio.

Beyond the junction with the road to Andeer, the N 18 expressway to Splügen and San Bernardino continues through a long gallery above the Rofla gorge, and then through two tunnels, one fairly long, the other shorter. Below, to the right, is the Hinterrhein.

Sufner-See

Farther up the valley, on the left, is the Sufner-See (alt. 1401 m/4597 ft; capacity 18.3 million cu. m/646 million cu. ft), formed by a dam 58 m/190 ft high (viewing platform), which is linked with the reservoir in the Valle di Lei. Beyond this, on the right (exit road from expressway), is the little village of Sufers (1387 m/4551 ft).

Rheinwald Valley

The road continues through a beautiful expanse of forest. Soon afterwards the magnificent prospect of the Rheinwald valley opens up, with its backdrop of mountains: on the left the pyramid of Pizzo Tambo, to the right of this the blunt summit of Guggernüll (2886 m/9469 ft), beyond this the sharp peak of the Einshorn (2944 m/9659 ft) and in the background the Hohberghorn (3005 m/9859 ft).

Splügen

Farther on the exit for the Splügen pass and the village of Splügen (1450 m/4757 ft), in a wide valley at the foot of the Kalkberg, above which rears the

Teurihorn (2973 m/9754 ft). The village, with handsome stone-built houses and a parish church of 1690, is a popular summer and winter resort (ski-lifts to the Danatzhöhe, 2160 m/7087 ft), and also attracts considerable through traffic as a result of its location on the route to the Splügen and San Bernardino passes. From the "Burg" (1527 m/5010 ft: 15 minutes northeast), a remnant of the old fortifications of the village, there is a fine view of the valley and the Tambohorn.

There is an attractive walk (2½ hours south-east) to the three Surette lakes (2270 m/7448 ft), in a grandiose mountain setting at the foot of the Surettahorn (3031 m/9945 ft); and Guggernüll (2886 m/9469 ft) offers a rewarding climb (4½ hours, with guide). For the continuation of the road over the Splügen pass to Chiavenna (see San Bernardino Pass).

The road to the San Bernardino pass (see entry)) continues past the village of Splügen and runs up through the meadows of the Hinterrhein valley, following a fairly straight and almost level course, with beautiful views. In 2.5 km/2 miles it comes to the little village of Medels in Rheinwald (1533 m/5030 ft), consisting of three groups of houses (to right; exit from expressway). 4 km/2 miles beyond this, also on the right (expressway exit), is the trim village of Nufenen (1563 m/5145 ft), opposite the mouth of the Areuetal, which runs down from the Tambohorn, with Guggernüll (2886 m/9469 ft) to the left and the Einshorn (2944 m/9659 ft) to the right.

3.5 km/2 miles farther on, to the right, is Hinterrhein (1624 m/5328 ft), the last village in the Rheinwald valley, which comes to an end beneath the snow-capped peaks and glaciers of the Rheinwald or Adula Massif. There is a rewarding walk up the valley to the Zapport hut (2276 m/7468 ft; 4 hours), at the lower end of the Rheinwald glacier, the source of the Hinterrhein. From here there are many possible climbs (for experienced climbers only) – e.g. the Rheinwaldhorn (3406 m/11,175 ft; 4 hours), the Güferhorn (3395 m/11,175 ft; 3½–4 hours, with guide), the Zapporthorn (3149 m/10,332 ft; 4 hours).

Hinterrhein

Rhine Falls

D1

Cantons: Schaffhausen (SH) and Zurich (ZH)

The Rhine Falls (Rheinfall) at Schaffhausen, the mightiest falls in Central Europe, surge over a ledge of Jurassic limestone 150 m/492 ft across and

Situation and general

The Rhine Falls

between 15 and 21 m/49 and 69 ft high, with two higher rocks standing in the middle of the river. The flow of water is at its greatest in June and July, after the melting of mountain snow.

Schaffhausen   The falls can be reached from Schaffhausen (see entry) on either side of the river.

Neuhausen   To reach the north side, leave Schaffhausen by way of Mühlenstrasse and road 4, which runs south-west to Neuhausen. There is a fishing museum (37 Rosenbergstrasse) with a collection of equipment, models and photographs documenting amateur and professional angling.

**Rheinfall   A footpath leads from the car park to the Rheinfallbrücke (192 m/630 ft long), which carries the Schaffhausen–Winterthur railway line. From here it
Schloss Laufen   is a 15 minutes' walk to Schloss Laufen (16th c., restored; restaurant), on the south bank from where there is a good general view of the falls.

A short walk through the park leads down to a number of viewpoints – the "Pavillon", "Känzli" and the "Fischez", an iron structure which brings the spectator almost within touching distance of the surging river.

Schloss Wörth   From the lower gate of the park a ferry can be taken across the river to the little Schloss Wörth (restaurant), with the best general view of the falls. From here it is a 10 minutes' walk up the right bank of the Rhine, past the Park Restaurant and then up a flight of steps to the left, to the car park.

Rhône Valley   A–D2

Cantons: Valais (VS), Vaud (VD) and Geneva (GE)

Situation   The Rhône rises in the Bernese Oberland, flows through Swiss territory for 260 km/162 miles and then enters France, eventually reaching the Mediterranean after a total course of 810 km/503 miles.

*Rhône Glacier   The source of the Rhône is the Rhône glacier, which comes down from the Dammastock, near Andermatt (see entry). The river, also known as the Rotten in its passage through German-speaking territory, flows south-west along the southern margin of the Bernese Oberland, with the Valais Alps on its south side, draining both these massifs through tributaries on either bank. At Martigny (see entry) it turns sharply north-west, almost at a right
**Lake   angle, and flows into Lake Geneva (see entry). After passing along the
Geneva   whole length of the lake it emerges again at Geneva (see entry), leaves Switzerland and in a few kilometres makes its way into the French Jura.

Through the Rhône valley

The best way of seeing the Rhône valley is to travel upstream. In this direction the route passes through a great variety of scenery, rising to a culmination in the majestic landscapes of the High Alps.

Rhône Valley/   The Rhône valley, which with its lateral valleys occupies the whole of the
Vallée du Rhône   canton of Valais (German Wallis), is a longitudinal trough up to 3 km/2 miles wide between the steeply scarped southern slopes of the Bernese Alps, from which tumble a succession of short and swift mountain streams, and the main ridge of the Valais Alps, some 30–40 km/19–25 miles away, the deep side valleys of which originate for the most part on terraces above the Rhône valley. The valley floor, originally littered with rock debris, has mostly been brought into cultivation through the regulation of the river and is now covered with fields of maize and vegetables and fruit orchards. At the bottom and on the lower slopes of the hills are vineyards, on the higher

Birth of the Rhône near Gletsch   *The Rhône valley near Mörel*

slopes and terraces, fields, forests and Alpine meadows. Irrigation is necessary due to the shortage of rain and is provided by a network of channels (bisses), mostly fed by glacier water.

The Rhône valley road runs north-east from the old town of Martigny (see entry), from which roads run south to the Great St Bernard and the Col de la Forclaz, and then up the left bank of the river, traversing a region of fruit orchards on the valley floor, flanked by rocky hillsides, and often passing between long rows of poplars. It then crosses to the right bank and continues through a famous wine-growing region to the old episcopal and cantonal capital of Sion (see entry), dominated by its two old castles, and the little town of Sierre (see entry), situated amid a jumble of hills created by a huge prehistoric landslide, in an area offering numerous attractive excursions.

*Rhône Valley Road

Beyond Sierre the road returns to the left bank and enters the German-speaking Upper Valais (Oberwallis), passing within sight of the interesting little towns of Leuk (see Leukerbad) and Gampel on the sunny right bank. After passing through the picturesque little market town of Visp (see Brig), where the road to Zermatt branches off, we soon come to the old town and road junction of Brig (see entry), where the towers of the Stockalperschloss form a distinctive landmark at the beginning of the road over the Simplon pass.

The character of the landscape now gradually changes. Although there are still walnut-trees and chestnuts to give something of a southern air, the rock faces now come closer, wooded gorges and steeper gradients make it clear that we have entered the region of high mountains.

Then through the Alpine region of Goms (see below), and through Oberwald to Gletsch, with fantastic views of the famous Rhône glacier. From here there are magnificent passes over the Grimsel into the Bernese Oberland and over the Furka to the St Gotthard road (see Andermatt).

Typical Valais barn in the upper Goms valley

Goms

General

Beyond Fiesch the road leads through the thickly populated Goms valley, with its brown wooden houses and gleaming white churches, and after passing through Oberwald climbs up into the highest part of the valley, with the hotel complex of Gletsch, at the foot of the famous Rhône glacier (see Andermatt).

Topography

Seen longitudinally the Goms, whose name is derived from "Conches" (hollow, basin) is a series of steps. The wide glaciated basin of the Upper Goms valley slopes gradually, in contrast to the valley steps of Gletsch and Fiesch. The numerous side valleys formed during the Pleistocene period with the rivers subsequently eroding deeper into the valleys. Above Geschinen the subsoil of the wide plain consists of glacial debris from the Rhône. A series of alluvial deposits left by the streams from the side valleys adjoin the wide plain between Geschinen and Münster.

Settlement

Evidence of temporary settlements date back to the Stone and Bronze Age. The first permanent settlement is thought to have been in the early Iron Age (from the 5th c.) with large clearings being left by the Alemannic tribes in the 8th c. During the Middle Ages settlement spread from the valley floor to individual farms and hamlets on the upper slopes. The region flourished economically and culturally during the 16th c. with the cattle trade, traffic using the pass and high political office bringing prosperity. Many elaborately decorated churches and artistic craftwork are the result of the religious Baroque revival in the 17th–18th c.

Buildings

The traditional building, as elsewhere in the Inner Alps, is the Streuhof (barn). In contrast to the Mittelland, where living quarters, barn, threshing room and food store are all incorporated under one roof, the buildings here are single-purpose. The house is a high-walled block with a flat ridge roof. The oldest date from the Late Middle Ages and are colloquially referred to as "Heidenhäuser" ("Heathens' houses"). They are characterised by a ridge which holds together the grooved wall beams of the gable ends. In the 16th c. the wide "Renaissance houses" were built; in the 17th and 13th c. the multi-storey "Baroque house". The traditional functional building is the grain store, a towering block supported by typical stone "Mäuserp atten" ("mouse dishes") built on top of a lower construction, which served different purposes and in the Upper Goms even consisted of two floors. There is also a smaller store, of similar design, which was used as a food store and meat drying room. Due to the importance of cattle-rearing the most commonly found functional building is the cow stall or "Gade", as it is known in the Goms. Above the lower floor is the hay loft.

White water trips are very popular on the young Rhône between Oberwald (1371 m/4500 ft) and Gluringen (1313 m/4309 ft). The 14 km/8 mile-long journey takes in seven pretty villages of the Upper Goms (Information: Verkehrsverein Obergoms, CH-3985 Münster, Tel. 0 28/73 22 54).

White Water Trips

Rigi   D1

Cantons: Schwyz (SZ) and Lucerne (LU)

The Rigi, the most famous mountain viewpoint in Switzerland, 1800 m/5906 ft high, rises in isolation above Lake Lucerne, Lake Zug and the Lauerzer See, and is brought within easy reach by two cog-railways and a cableway. The roads from Küssnacht, Weggis and Gersau terminate halfway up the mountain.
The Rigi massif is an extensive range with a summit ridge some 50 km/31 miles long.
The most popular viewpoints are the Kulm (1800 m/5906 ft), the Rotstock (1662 m/5453 ft) and the Scheidegg (1665 m/5463 ft). The many attractive footpaths and the mountain air, however, make it well worth while spending more time on the Rigi than a brief period for the sake of the view. The best places for winter sports are the sheltered hotel settlements of Kaltbad, with the excellent facilities provided by the Hostellerie Rigi, and Klösteri (several ski-lifts).

Situation and general

The view from the Rigi-Kulm is impressive both for the nearer view of the three surrounding lakes and the more distant panorama of the Alps; this prospect extends for some 200 km/124 miles from end to end, with Säntis and Glärnisch, preceded by the Mythen, standing out with particular prominence in the east, Tödi in the south-east and the giants of the Bernese Oberland in the south-west; Pilatus closes the range of mountains in the west, and farther right one sees the Mittelland with its lakes, and beyond this the Jura and the Black Forest. On Rigi-Kulm, too, are the high tower antenna (the "Rigi-Nadel" or "Needle of the Rigi") and other installations of the Swiss Post Office.

**Landscape

Mountain Rail- and Cableways

Vitznau to Rigi-Kulm, the first cog-railway in Europe, built 1871 and electrified 1937 (length 7 km/4 miles), maximum gradient 25% (1 in 4), time 35 minutes). During periods of heavy snow in winter it runs only as far as Staffelhöhe.
The line climbs up through Alpine meadows, the views becoming more and more extensive. 4.5 km/3 miles: Rigi-Kaltbad (1440 m/4725 ft) lies in a sheltered hollow. Footpath to the First, and in 20 minutes to the Känzeli (1470 m/4823 ft), with fine views of the mountains and a prospect of Weggis, 1000 m/3281 ft below. 5 km/3 miles: Staffelhöhe (1552 m/5092 ft). Beyond this the view of Lake Zug appears. 6 km/4 miles: Staffel (1606 m/5269 ft), the station for the Rotstock (1662 m/5453 ft; 15 minutes), with a view similar to that from the Kulm. 7 km/4 miles: Rigi-Kulm (1750 m/5742 ft). In summer there are also some steam trains.

Vitznau-Rigi Line
Vitznau

Rigi-Kaltbad

*Känzeli

*Rotstock
Rigi-Kulm

Regina Montium towers over the Lauerzer See

Weggis-Rigi-Kaltbad	There is a cableway from Weggis to Rigi-Kaltbad (7 minutes). It is a beautiful walk by moonlight.
Arth-Rigi Line Arth-Goldau	Arth-Goldau to Rigi-Kulm: cog-railway, opened 1875, electrified 1906 (length 9 km/6 miles, maximum gradient 21% (1 in 5), time 35 minutes). The best views are on the right-hand side. The line runs uphill in a wide curve to the passing station at Kräbel (766 m/2513 ft: cableway to Scheidegg, 6 minutes) and then continues up the Kräbalwand, with views of the Rossberg and Lake Zug.
Klösterli	6 km/4 miles: Klösterli (1315 m/4315 ft), in a sheltered hollow, with the pilgrimage church of Maria zum Schnee (Our Lady of the Snow: founded 1689, rebuilt 1721; pilgrimages on 2 July and 8 September).
	1.8 km/1 mile: Staffel, where the view to the north and west opens up. The line then runs close to the Vitznau line, from where it is 9 km/6 miles to Rigi-Kulm.
Rigi-Kulm	Special trips by boat and Rigi cableway are organised to see the famous sunrises and sunsets over the Rigi.
Walks	There are rewarding walks from either Kaltbad or Klösterli to Rigi-Scheidegg (2 hours).
	The initial stage is to the Rigi-First (1454 m/4771 ft; 20 minutes); then by the "Felsenweg", with superb views, to Unterstetten (1440 m/4725 ft; 25 minutes); and from there either by way of the Nollen and Dossen (1688 m/5538 ft) in 1¼ hours or on the "Seeweg" (fine view down to the lake) to the ridge between the Dossen and Scheidegg (45 minutes) and from there another 30 minutes to the Scheidegg (1665 m/5463 ft; inn, with terrace café), from which there are good views to the south.
Scheidegg	

Rorschach   E1

Canton: St Gallen (SG)
Altitude: 398 m/1306 ft, Population: 10,800

Rorschach on Lake Constance

The old port of Rorschach, lying at the foot of the Rorschacher Berg in a wide bay, the most southerly in Lake Constance (Obersee), was once an important trading post for the town of St Gallen. Its principal industries are textiles, metalworking and piano manufacture ("Sabel").
The pumping station for the supply of Lake Constance water to St Gallen is here.

Situation and general

The development of Rorschach was closely bound up with economic prosperity of the abbey of St Gallen. As early as A.D. 947 it was granted the right to hold markets, coin money and levy tolls by the Abbot of St Gallen. The old dock was enlarged in 1484, enabling the town to carry on a considerable trade, particularly in corn. In the 18th c. the linen trade also flourished. In 1803, on the dissolution of the abbey, Rorschach passed to the canton of St Gallen.

History

Sights

At the federal harbour there is a harbour station and the Kornhaus (Granary: built 1746, restored 1956–58), now houses a local museum (closed in winter; well-displayed collection of prehistoric material).

Harbour, *Kornhaus

To the east of the park stretches the beautiful Seepark (fountains) with a lakeside promenade. Not far south of the park and the harbour the main road runs parallel to the lake with a number of prettily decorated 18th c. houses. Further south stands the Roman Catholic parish church of St Columban (Baroque, 1645–67; nave altered 1783).

Seepark

St Columban

On the hillside above the town is the former monastery of Mariaberg (alt. 440 m/1444 ft), a teachers' training college since 1805, with a beautiful cloister (1519) and a Gothic chapter-house (music room).

Mariaberg monastery

The cliffs "Grosser Schröntaler" and "Kleiner Schröntaler" can be seen from the easterly suburb of Staad.

Staad

Surroundings

St Anna Schloss, *Rossbüehel	Past the Mariaberg monastery turn left to reach, 2 km/1 mile from Rorschach, St Anna Schloss (568 m/1864 ft; private property), with extensive views.; then to the top of Rossbüehel (964 m/3163ft; 1 hour), with views of five countries.
Wilen, Schloss Wartegg	From Mariaberg monastery take the Goldach road which runs 3 km/2 miles east to Wilen, with Schloss Wartegg (1557: beautiful park) where the Austrian royal family took refuge after the First World War.
Goldach, Schloss Sulzberg	4 km/2 miles south-west of Rorschach by way of Goldach is Schloss Sulzberg or the Möttelischloss (550 m/1805 ft; private property), with a 13th c. tower.
Rorschach-Heiden Line	7 km/4 miles south of Rorschach in the canton of Appenzell are the holiday resorts of Heiden and Wienacht, which can be reached by cog-railway in 25 minutes.
Altenrhein	In the fishing village of Altenrhein (397 m/1302 ft), situated on the delta of the Alter Rhein (Old Rhine), is a nature reserve. The Altenrhein aircraft and vehicle manufacturing works (FFA, owned by Dornier since 1985) and Altenrhein airport, from where the legendary Dornier Flying Boats (including DO-X) took off in the Twenties, are to found here.
Altenrhein Marina	To the north-east of Altenrhein, on the left-hand finger of the Alter Rhein (Unterer Rheinspitz), is the Altenrhein marina or yachting harbour. A beautiful recreational park is in Buriet, to the south of Altenrhein.

Saas Valley   C2

Canton: Valais (VS)

Situation and general	The narrow Saas valley, through which the Saaser Vispa flows down to join the Rhône, extends for some 28 km/17 miles to the south of the little town of Visp, on the Rhône, at heights of between 1000 and 2000 m/3281 and 6562 ft, with the popular resorts of Saas Grund, Saas Fee and Saas Almagell. The starting-point of the valley is the village of Stalden, where the Zermatt and Saas valley roads separate.
History	The name of Saas Fee first appears in the records in 1217, in a document in which the Bishop of Sion disclaims responsibility for the protection of the Antrona pass road. About 1400 the commune of Saas became an independent parish, and in 1893 Fee was also made a separate parish. The local priest, Johann Josef Imseng (1806–69), began to experiment with skis in 1849, and is honoured as the pioneer of winter sports in Switzerland.

In the Saas valley

Saas Grund

	The lowest part of the commune of Saas is Saas Balen (1487 m/4879 ft; pop. 470), which has a round church (Baroque). 24 km/15 miles higher up is the chief place in the valley, Saas Grund (1562 m/5125 ft), situated in meadowland on the valley floor, with a large parish church (1939). Lying between
Mischabel Group, Fletschhorn Weissmies	the Mischabel group (the main peak of which is concealed behind lower mountains) to the west and the Fletschhorn (3996 m/13,111 ft; not visible from valley floor) and Weissmies (4023 m/13,199 ft) to the east, it is a popular base for climbers. Indoor swimming pool in Touring Hotel.

Saas Fee

From Saas Grund a minor road (4 km/2 miles long, gradient 8% (1 in 12) with two hairpin bends) runs up to the "road terminus", just below Saas Fee (car park, parking garage, service garages; no cars beyond this point). The village of Saas Fee (1798 m/5899 ft), in a magnificent location facing the great Fee glacier, with the peaks of the Mischabel group towering above it in a wide arc, is a popular health resort, with winter sports (indoor swimming pool, ski-lifts, ice-rinks, curling, toboggan run) and climbing. The modern church (1963), with a separate tower, is well adapted to its setting. In the churchyard is the grave of the writer Carl Zuckmayer (1896–1977), an honorary citizen of Saas Fee. The nearby Saas museum contains furniture, fittings and the original study belonging to him, along with the history of the glacier.

*Situation

Saas Museum

A cableway 3400 m/11,155 ft long runs south-west (23 minutes), via an intermediate station at Spielboden (2450 m/8038 ft; marmots), to the Längfluh (2865 m/9400 ft; restaurant, climbers' hostel), which can be reached on foot from Saas Fee via the Gletscheralp (2135 m/7005 f) in 2½-3 hours (from Gletscheralp chair-lift 560 m/1837 ft long, winter only).

Spielboden
*Längfluh

The Längfluh is the starting-point for the ascent of the Allalinhorn (4027 m/13,213 ft; 4 hours, with guide), the least difficult peak in the Mischabel group, the highest point of which is the Dom (4545 m/14,912 ft), the highest mountain entirely in Swiss territory.

*Allalinhorn

A cableway runs south-east from Saas Fee (12 minutes to the Plattjen (2567 m/8422 ft; restaurant, chair-lift; Berghaus Plattjen 30 minutes lower down), from which it is a 2½ hours' climb to the Britannia hut (3029 m/9938 ft). Cableway from Saas Fee to the Hannig-Alp (2400 m/7874 ft), to the west.

Plattjen

From Saas Fee to Kalbermatten a cableway 3652 m/11,982 ft long runs south (9 minutes) to the Felskinn (2990 m/9810 ft; restaurant, ice cave,

Felskinn,
Metro Alpin

Saas valley – chair-lift to the Felskopf

345

geological trail; skiing area, with summer skiing). The Metro Alpin, opened in 1985 (the highest underground funicular in the Alps), runs from Felskinn

Mittelallalin
to Mittelallalin (3500 m/11,487 ft), where the highest revolving restaurant in Central Europe has marvellous views.

Saas Almagell

From Saas Grund the road continues south-east up the valley, with moderate gradients, passing through Zenlauenen and Moos, and in 4 km/2 miles reaches Saas Almagell (1679 m/5509 ft), the highest village in the valley, a health resort, winter sports (ski-lifts, ice-rink) and climbing base. Chair-lift to 1950 m/6398 ft on the Furggstalden (good skiing; ski-lift). Walk to the

Almageller Alp
Almageller Alp (2225 m/7300 ft; 1¼ hours).

The road continues for another 7.5 km/5 miles, past the hamlet of Zermeiggern (1716 m/5630 ft) and the huge moraine of the Allalin glacier, to the dam (115 m/377 ft high, 780 m/2559 ft long at the top), completed in 1967,

Mattmarksee
which has formed the Mattmarksee. A massive fall of ice from the Allalin glacier crashed down on the construction site in August 1965, killing 88

Monte Moro
Pass
workmen. from the dam it is a 45 minutes' climb to the Monte Moro pass (2862 m/9390 ft), which until the construction of the Simplon road was the principal route from the Valais into Italy (Swiss-Italian frontier). From the

Macugnaga
pass a cableway (large cabins) descends to Macugnaga (1307 m/4288 ft), in the Val d'Anzasca.

Great St Bernard   C3

In Switzerland and in Italy
Canton: Valais (VS)
Height of pass: 2469 m/8101 ft

Situation and
general
The road over the Great St Bernard pass, between the Mont Blanc group and the Valais Alps, the highest pass road in the Swiss Alps after the Umbrail road, is for the most part excellently engineered (maximum gradient 11%), but is usually open only from the middle or end of June until October. The drive through the defiles of the Drance valley on the north side and above all the descent from the rugged world of the mountains into the southern beauty of the Aosta valley is a great scenic experience.

The construction of the St Bernard tunnel (5828 m/19,122 ft long, carriageway 7.5 m/25 ft; toll) in 1959–63 made the road passable throughout the year and shortened the distance between western Switzerland and Italy in winter by several hundred kilometres.

History
This ancient and historic traffic route was used by the Celts, from 105 B.C. onwards by the Romans, in 547 by the Lombards and later by many German emperors travelling to Italy (Charlemagne in 773, Henry IV on his journey to Canossa in 1077, Frederick Barbarossa in 1175). In May 1800 Napoleon led an army of 30,000 men over the pass to Aosta and Milan in order to expel the Austrians from Italy (Battle of Marengo).

Martigny
From Martigny the road climbs the wild narrow valley of the Drance, passing through the village of Sembrancher at the mouth of the Val de Bagnes, to Orsières, and then up the featureless Vallée d'Entremont to

Bourg-St-Pierre
Bourg-St-Pierre (1634 m/5631 ft), a little market town in a wider part of the valley at the mouth of the Valsorey. The parish church (1739) has an 11th c. tower. Beside the church is a Roman milestone (4th c. A.D.). From here a number of difficult climbs can be undertaken including Mont Vélan

*Grand
Combin
(3765 m/12,353 ft; 7–8 hours, with guide) and the Grand Combin (4317 m/ 14,164 ft; 11 hours, with guide).

On the Great St Bernard Pass

From Bourg-St-Pierre a covered concrete road (8 m/26 ft wide, maximum gradient 6% (1 in 16) runs up the east side of the valley above the Défilé de Saraire and past the Lac des Toules (1800 m/5906 ft), an artificial lake (capacity 20 million cu. m/706 million cu. ft) formed by a dam 80 m/262 ft high (short tunnel).

The road then reaches Bourg-St-Bernard, at the entrance (station, 1915 m/6283 ft; passport and customs control; toll charge) to the Great St Bernard tunnel. To the left are the Petit Vélan (3233 m/10,607 ft) and the snow-capped summit of Mont Vélan. Cableway (2530 m/8301 ft, 14 minutes) to the Col de Menouve (2753 m/9033 ft; Super-St-Bernard winter sports centre; magnificent ski trails).

*Great St Bernard Tunnel

From here the route continues either through the tunnel (maximum speed in tunnel 60 km p. h./37 m.p.h.) and on a covered road (9.5 km/6 miles long, 9 m/30 ft wide) to beyond St-Rhémy, or on the old road over the Great St Bernard.

The road over the Great St Bernard runs south-west over the Alpine meadows, strewn with rock debris, of the Plan de Proz to the Cantine d'en Haut (1905 m/6250 ft), and from there through a wild gorge, the Pas de Marengo, to the huts of Hospitalet (2100 m/6889 ft). After crossing the Drance on the Pont Nudry (2190 m/7185 ft) it winds its way up to the pass through the desolate Combe des Morts, which is filled with snow right into the height of summer.

Over the Great St Bernard

The Great St Bernard pass (2469 m/8101 ft), used since ancient times, crosses the main ridge of the Alps, between the Mont Mort (2867 m/9407 ft) on the left and the Pic de Drona (2950 m/9679 ft) on the right. In summer the Swiss customs control takes place here.

*Great St Bernard Pass

The famous Hospice founded about 1049 by St Bernard of Menthon (d. 1081) to succour distressed travellers is now occupied by Augustinian Canons. In the old buildings (16th c.) are the monks' quarters and the

Hospice

guest-rooms of the hospice, which now accommmodate only groups of young people. The new building (1898) has been occupied by a hotel since 1925. In the church (1676–78) is the tomb of the French General Desaix, who was killed in the Battle of Marengo. The Museum contains Celtic and Roman antiquities from the Plan de Jupiter, relics of Napoleon, a natural history collection and a library of 30,000 volumes. The Hospice is famous also for the St Bernard dogs bred by the monks and used to scent out travellers lost in the snow.

Chair-lift (10 minutes) to La Chenalette (2800 m/9187 ft) from which there are superb views.

The road to Aosta skirts a small lake, rarely ice-free even in summer, through which runs the Swiss-Italian frontier (Italian customs control in summer). To the right is the Plan de Jupiter, with a stone cross (1816) and a bronze statue of St Bernard (1905). The name Plan de Jupiter, like the earlier name of the pass, Mont Joux (Mons Jovis), recalls a Roman temple to Jupiter Poeninus which stood here.

Plan de Jupiter

The road now descends in a wide curve past the hamlet of La Baux and a large crag, the Gour des Fous, to the Cantine d'Aoste (2217 m/7274 ft; Italian customs), in a green hollow.

Vallée du Grand-St-Bernard

From here it winds its way down to Aosta. To the left is the exit from the tunnel (1875 m/6152 ft; Italian and Swiss passport and customs control for entry to Switzerland). The road then crosses the expressway coming from the tunnel and descends, with two sharp turns, to the left bank of the Torrente Artanavaz and the village of St Rhémy (1632 m/5355 ft) which is situated in a wooded defile. The expressway bypasses the village to the west. The road then bears right through the deeply eroded Combes des Bosses, and in another 2.5 km/2 miles is joined by the expressway from the tunnel exit (9.5 km/6 miles).

St Gallen   EJ

Canton: St Gallen (SG)
Altitude: 670 m/75,000 ft
Population: 75,000

Situation and general

St Gallen lies about 15 km/9 miles south-west of Lake Constance, in a narrow high valley of the Pre-Alps, here dissected by numerous streams (the Goldach, the Steinach, the Sitter) flowing through constricted gorges. The motorway and express trains connect the town with Zurich-Kloten airport and other important towns in Switzerland. St Gallen is the capital of the canton of the same name and the commercial hub (embroidery, textile and metal industries; largest shopping centre in Eastern Switzerland; trade fairs) and cultural centre of Eastern Switzerland as well as a popular congress resort.

History

The town takes its name from the Irish missionary monk Gall or Gallus who established a hermitage here about 612. This developed into the Benedictine abbey which became a flourishing seat of religion and scholarship in the 9th c.; its school and library made it one of the focal points of European culture north of the Alps.

In the 10th c. St Gallen, until then no more than a settlement of craftsmen and tradesmen which had grown up around the abbey, achieved the status of a town which in the 15th c. shook off the authority of the abbey and, in 1524, under a burgomaster named Vadian, adopted the Reformed faith.

In the 16th–18th c. the town became exceedingly prosperous through its linen industry and grew considerably in size. The craft of embroidery, introduced in the 18th c., developed about 1830 with the advent of the

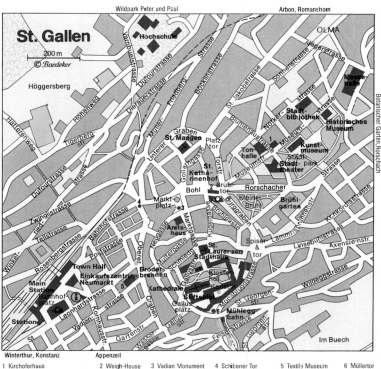

1 Kirchoferhaus   2 Weigh-House   3 Vadian Monument   4 Schibener Tor   5 Textile Museum   6 Müllertor

hand-operated embroidery machine and later the shuttle embroidery machine into a considerable export industry (Textile Museum). Other industries, in particular metal-working, were established later.

Sights

In the northern part of the old town, which has handsome 17th and 18th c. burghers' houses with oriel windows, is the Marktplatz. At the corner of Marktgasse and Neugasse stands a statue of the 16th c. burgomaster Joachim von Watt (Vadian).

Marktplatz

Heading south from the Marktplatz No. 23 Marktgasse houses the Labhart musical box cabinet.

Musical Box Cabinet

To the east of the Marktplatz is the broad street known as the Bohl, at the end of which is the 16th c. Weigh-House (Waaghaus); this houses the Council Chamber. Also here is the Hotel Hecht, the oldest inn in the town.

Bohl, Waaghaus

To the north of the Bohl is the St Katharinenhof, a relic of the former cloister of 1507. Still farther north is St Mangan's church (founded c. 900 but much altered in later centuries), with a 16th c. tower.

St Katharinenhof, St Mangan's church

From the Marktplatz the Marktgasse runs south – on the right Multergasse, a well known shopping street in the pedestrianised zone – to St Lawrence's church (St Lorenz; restored 1851–54).

Multergasse, St Lawrence's church

349

Plan of St Gallen Monastery

Carolingian idealised plan (*circa* 820)

1 Saint's tomb (beneath High Altar)
2 Scriptorium (below) Library (above)
3 Sacristy (below) Robing Room (above)
4 Chapter House
5 Clerical guests
6 School Master
7 Gatekeeper
8 Visitors' room
9 Old People's Warden
10 Heating room (below) Dormitory (above)
11 Provision store (cellar below)
12 Refectorium (below) Wardrobe (above)

W Business rooms
00 Lavatories

Generalised plan

To the south is the spacious Klosterhof (Abbey Yard), around which is the former Benedictine Abbey. The extensive range of buildings, dating from the 17th and 18th c., now accommodates the bishop's palace, the residences of the cathedral clergy and cantonal government offices.

✶✶Benedictine Abbey

The Late-Baroque three-aisled former collegiate church, now the cathedral, was reconstructed on the site of the earlier abbey church which had been pulled down. The most notable features are the colourful ceiling-paintings by Christian Wenzinger, the stucco work in the choir by the Gigi brothers, the ceiling-paintings by J. Wannenmacher (1722–80), the wrought-iron choir-stalls by Josef Feichtmayr, with carved scenes from the life of St Benedict. The interior of the cathedral was thoroughly restored and renovated in 1962–67 making the old ceiling paintings in the choir visible again. In the crypt, part of which dates from the 10th c. can be seen the tombs of all the bishops of St Gallen. The monastic treasury is also worth seeing.

✶Cathedral

◀ *St Gallen: the Late-Baroque cathedral*

Treasures of the famous . . .   *. . . Abbey library*

*Abbey Library	The Abbey Library, housed in a charming Rococo Library Hall by Peter Thumb (1758–67), with stucco work by the Gigi brothers and ceiling-paintings by Josef Wannenmacher, possesses works which belonged to the old abbey school, one of the leading European capitals of learning in the 9th–11th c., notable particularly in the fields of book illumination, poetry and the translation of Latin works into Alemannic. The finest items in the library are displayed in rotation and include the 9th c. "Psalterium Aureum", the "Casus Monasterii Sancti Galli" by Ekkehard IV (11th c.) and Manuscript of the Nibelungenlied (13th c.). The famous plan of St Gallen abbey in 820, displayed under glass, presents the model of a large monastic establishment, a plan which was followed until the end of the Middle Ages. A sarcophagus contains a mummy from Upper Egypt (700 B.C.).
Gallusplatz, Gallusstrasse, Haus zum Greif	In Gallusplatz and Gallusstrasse, to the west of the cathedral, are elegant old burghers' houses of the 17th and 18th c., such as the Haus zum Greif (House of the Griffin, Gallusstrasse 22), with a carved oriel window.
Karlstor	In Moosbruggstrasse, immediately south of the abbey, are two remnants of the old town walls, the Karlstor (reliefs of 1570) and a round tower.
Spisertor, Schlössli, St Gall Memorial Textile Museum	Next to the Spisertor stands the historic Schlössli. South-east of Gallusplatz, at the falls on the Steinach, is a terrace with a memorial to St Gall. North-west of Gallusplatz the Textile Museum (Vadianstrasse 2) has an important collection of embroidery and lace from the 14th to the 20th c., finds from Egyptian tombs (Coptic period, 4th–12th c.) and antique books.
Broderbrunnen Neumarkt	In the Oberen Graben is the Broderbrunnen (Broder fountain; 1896) commemorating the opening of Lake Constance waterworks in 1894. Along the Vadianstrasse is the modern shopping centre "Neumarkt" with an iron sculpture of St Gall by Max Oertli.
Tonhalle, *Municipal Theatre	North-east of the Bohl is Museumstrasse, in which are the Tonhalle (1907; concert hall) and, on the right, the Municipal Theatre (Stadttheater, 1966–68) in modern style.

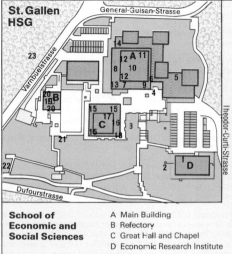

St. Gallen HSG

General-Guisan-Strasse

Varnbüelstrasse

Theodor-Curti-Strasse

Dufourstrasse

23 20 19 20 21 22 8 10 12 13 7 9 4 A 11 5 15 17 C 6 3 15 16 D 2

ART WORKS

1. Zoltan Kemeny: Brass relief
2. Umberto Mastroianni: Aluminium sculpture
3. Alicia Penalba: Reinforced concrete sculptures
4. Jean Arp: "Schalenbaum" (Bronze)
5. George Braques: "Oiseau" (Mosaic)
6. Soniatta: Wood Relief on ceiling
7. Etienne Hajdu: Beaten lead reliefs
8. Joan Miró: Ceramic frieze
9. Pierre Soulages: Tapestries
10. Alexander Calder: Mobile (Aluminium)
11. Alberto Giacometti: "Stehende" (Bronze)
12. Antoni Tàpies: Wal decoration
13. Ferdinand Gehr: Flower paintings
14. Max Gubler: "Nachtlandschaft" (Oil painting)
15. Coghuf (Ernst Stocker): three four-part reliefs (iron and glass)
16. Coghuf+Silvia Valentin: Tapestry
17. Coghuf: Ceiling relief
18. Otto Müller: interior of chapel with brass cross, bronze relief, lead relief, gilded glass sculpture
19. Walter Bodmer: iron and glass sculpture
20. Jean Baier: Coloured reliefs (enamelled aluminium)
21. Francois Stahly: Bronze sculpture
22. Carl Burckhardt: "Amazone" (Bronze)
23. Max Oertli: Bronze sculpture

School of Economic and Social Sciences

A Main Building
B Refectory
C Great Hall and Chapel
D Economic Research Institute

Farther to the left, at Museumstrasse 27, is the Kirchhoferhaus Museum (prehistoric material from caves; Züst collection of silver, 16th–19th c.).

Kirchhoferhaus Museum

Beyond this, on the right-hand side of the Stadtpark (Museumstrasse 23), stands the recently reopened (1987) Museum of Art and Natural History, which was built in Classical style in 1877. The Natural History section contains collections of minerals and precious stones and geology and holography exhibitions. The art collection includes works by Romanticists and Impressionists, paintings by Segantini, folk art and modern art.

Museum of Art and Natural History

Beyond this again (No. 50) is the Historical Museum or Neues Museum (New Museum), with prehistoric, historical and ethnographic collections, domestic interiors and utensils, porcelain, etc.)

Historical Museum

North-west of the Historical Museum, at Notkerstrasse 22, the Municipal Library (Stadtbibliothek Vadiana), founded in 1551, houses the Municipal Archives. To the north-east are the exhibition grounds where the annual Agricultural and Dairy Show (OLMA) is held.

Municipal Library Vadiana

OLMA

To the north of the town, on higher ground, is situated the School of Economic and Social Sciences (Hochschule für Wirtschafts- und Sozial-wissenschaften; conducted tours by appointment, tel. 23 31 35), a fine example of modern architecture (1960–63), with the Institute for Tourism and Transport, student residences and a sports hall. Within the buildings and grounds are numerous works by leading artists, including Jean Miró, Alexander Calder, Alberto Giacometti, Antoni Tàpies, Georges Braque, Otto Müller, Hans Arp and Carl Burckhardt.

School of Economic and Social Sciences Institute for Tourism and Transport

The Botanic Garden lies north-east of the town.

Botanic Garden

Surroundings

3 km/2 miles south of the town is the Freudenberg (887 m/2910 ft; restaurant), from which there is a magnificent view of the town, Lake Constance and Säntis.

Freudenberg

St Gotthard

Rotmonten,
*Wildpark
Peter und Paul

3.5 km/2 miles north is the Wildpark Peter und Paul (Wildlife Park; 800 m/2625 ft) with Alpine animals (chamois, ibex, marmots, etc.)

*Säntis Leisure
Park

In Abtwil, near the N 1 (St Gallen-Winkel exit), the Säntispark leisure and shopping centre was opened in 1987.

Teufen

7 km/4 miles south-east of St Gallen the village of Teufen (837 m/2747 ft), a desirable suburb of St Gallen, has an interesting museum.

Gossau

Gossau lies about 11 km/7 miles west of St Gallen between the rivers Glatt and Sitter in Fürstenland. It is the centre of agricultural production in the canton of St Gallen (butter and cheese dairies, mills) and has a variety of industries. There is a motorcycle museum and a small zoo.

Schloss
Oberberg

4 km/2 miles to the west is Schloss Oberberg (restaurant; museum) with a 13th c. tower.

Oberbüren

About 8 km/5 miles west of Gossau lies the district of Oberbüren. Its former castle, the Glattburg, which was later converted into the Benedictine monastery of St Gallusberg, is mentioned in a historical document from 788, making it the oldest castle site in the country.

Wil

27 km/17 miles (motorway) is Wil (574 m/1883 ft; pop. 16,000), an industrial town which at one time was a favourite summer residence of the Prince-Abbots of St Gallen. The beautiful old town lies around the Hofplatz (also known as the "Goldener Boden" or "Golden Ground"), with the former Abbot's palace (the Hof), now housing a local museum, and the Baronenhaus (1795). Nearby is the parish church of St Nicholas (1429–78) and to the south-west (originally Gothic) church of St Peter.

St Gotthard   D2

Cantons: Uri (UR) and Ticino (TI)
Height of pass: 2108 m/6916 ft

Situation and
general

The St Gotthard massif in central Switzerland is one of Europe's most important watersheds, with the sources of the Rhine, the Rhône, the Reuss and the Ticino (Tessin). This rugged mass of crystalline schists and granite was for many centuries an obstacle to transit through the Alps, and it was only the bold road-building operations of the 18th and 19th c. and the construction of the St Gotthard railway that opened up this shortest route from north to south for modern traffic. In 1980 after 11 years' work the St Gotthard road tunnel was completed.

History

There was already a bridle-path over the St Gotthard pass in the 13th c. The first section of the modern road, between Andermatt and Airolo, was constructed in 1819–30, and this was later extended farther south. The construction of the St Gotthard railway (Gotthardbahn) in 1874–82 was an outstanding technical achievement for its day, costing the lives of 177 men, including the engineer in charge, Louis Favre.

*Gotthardbahn

The railway tunnel (15 km/9 miles long) runs under the summit of the St Gotthard massif at a height of 1154 m/3786 ft. The Gotthardbahn from Basle or Zurich to Lugano takes 4 or 3 hours respectively through the Gotthard Tunnel.

*William Tell
Express

The William Tell Express (first stage by steamer from Lucerne to Flüelen) runs to Lugano from the end of May to the end of October (see Practical Information, Railways).

*Historic post
route

The Gotthard Post has a nostalgic route from Lucerne to Lugano using old post vans and horse-drawn carriages (five-day trip; information from Historische Reisepost, CH-6002 Lucerne; tel. 0 41/50 22 33).

The new St Gotthard Road Tunnel (toll-free) is the longest road tunnel in the world (16.3 km/10 miles), passing through the mountains at a height of 1175 m/3855 ft. Its completion means that the St Gotthard route is now open all year round. It runs from Göschenen, north of Andermatt, to Airolo in the canton of Ticino.

*St Gotthard Road Tunnel

The opening of the N 2 in 1986 means that it is possible to drive direct from Basle to Chiasso, leading to an increase in through-traffic along the valleys of the Reuss and Ticino. In view of the expected growth in the volume of traffic as a result of the single market in the European Community (EC) in 1992 plans for a 50 km/31 mile long tunnel, from Amsteg in the Reuss valley to Bodio in Ticino, are under discussion.

From Andermatt to Bellinzona over the St Gotthard Pass (85 km/53 miles)

From Andermatt (alt. 1444 m/4138 ft; see entry) the road to the St Gotthard at first follows an almost level course through the wide Urseren valley, with views of the Furka.

Andermatt

Hospental (1484 m/4869 ft), an old village (Lat. hospitium, "hospice") situated at the point where the Furka-Reuss and Gotthard-Reuss join to form the Reuss, is now a health and winter sports resort (ski-lift to 2000 m/6562 ft on the Winterhorn) with heavy through traffic. Church (1705–11); tower of 13th c. castle.

Hospental

The road to the Furka pass (see Andermatt) goes off on the right. The St Gotthard road, bearing left, now climbs up into the desolate valley of the Gotthard-Reuss with five hairpin bends. The view to the rear of the Urseren valley and the chain of mountains to the north, from the Spitzigrat (2560 m/8399 ft) to the Galenstock (3597 m/11,802 ft), like the later views towards the pass, reveals the landscape of the St Gotthard massif in all its austerity – bare gneiss and granite crags, sometimes containing rare minerals, which have been little affected by glacier action but have been worn smooth by earlier ice, with many small lakes gleaming between the hills.

St Gotthard Road

The road continues up the long stretch of valley known as the Gamsboden (1640 m/5381 ft), subject to dangerous avalanches in winter, climbing at a moderate gradient. To the left is the Guspis valley, below the Pizzo Centrale and the Guspis glacier.

Gamsboden

Guspis Valley

4 km/2 miles farther on we reach the Mätteli (1791 m/5876 ft; inn), at the foot of the Winterhorn of Piz Orsino (2661 m/8731 ft; 3½ hours' climb from Hospental), to the right. The road then climbs more sharply in a double hairpin bend. At the Brüggloch (1908 m/6260 ft) the cantonal boundary between Uri and the mainly Italian-speaking Ticino is crossed. Ahead can be seen La Fibbia (2742 m/8997 ft).

Mätteli

The road continues, following a fairly straight course, past the Capanna di Rodont (1966 m/6450 ft) to the Lucendro bridge (2015 m/6611 ft) over the Reuss, which flows out of the Lago di Lucendro (2077 m/6815 ft; 30 minutes up on the right; detour recommended), an artificial lake supplying a power station at Airolo. From the lake it is a 3½ hours' climb (with guide) to the summit of the Piz Lucendro (2964 m/9725 ft), from which there are superb views.

Lago di Lucendro

The road then climbs in a series of sharp bends to the St Gotthard pass (2108 m/6916 ft), a bare flat depression with a number of small lakes. To the left is Monte Prosa (2471 m/8107 ft; 2½ hours), to the right La Fibbia (2742 m/8997 ft; 2½ hours, with guide), sloping down sharply into Val Tremola. The St Gotthard group of mountains, forming a link between the Valais and the Grisons Alps, lies in the centre of Switzerland – the core around which the Confederation grew up. Here the valleys carved out by the Reuss and

*St Gotthard Pass

St Gotthard

St Gotthard Hospice by the lake

the Ticino have prepared the way for this magnificent route over the central ridge of the Alps.

100 m/328 ft beyond the pass is a fork at which the old road continues straight ahead and the new road bears right.

St Gotthard Hospice, Gotthard Museum

500 m/1641 ft beyond the pass, on the old road, is the St Gotthard Hospice (2095 m/6874 ft; founded in the 14th c. but frequently rebuilt and now a protected national monument) with a hotel of the same name, a weather station and the National Gotthard Museum (Museo Nazionale del San Gottardo). The collection records the development of the pass (relief models, minerals, weapons, uniforms, documents, etc.).

From here it is a 45 minutes' walk to the Sellasee (2231 m/7320 ft) and a 3½ hours' climb (with guide) to the summit of the Pizzo Centrale (3003 m/9853 ft).

*Val Tremola

Beyond the hotel the road descends the slopes of the wild Val Tremola ("Valley of Trembling") in 38 well-engineered bends, some of them supported on retaining walls. In 5.5 km/3 miles it comes to the Cantoniera Val Tremola (1695 m/5561 ft), from which the view down into the Val Bedretto and the Valle Leventina opens up.

The new road, 7.8 km/5 miles long, bypasses the Val Tremola on the west, with some remarkable examples of road engineering (three tunnels). It then crosses the old road and later joins it.

Airolo

Continuing down in 13 sharp bends, the road comes to Airolo (1154 m/3786 ft; pop. 2000), a summer and winter sports resort in a magnificent mountain setting in the upper valley of the Ticino, known above the town as Val Bedretto and below it as Valle Leventina. To the west is the Rotondo group (Pizzo Rotondo, 3192 m/10,473 ft). After a great landslide from the Sasso Rosso in 1898 the place was rebuilt and provided with a protective wall. In the Gotthardbahn station, just outside the tunnel, is a bronze relief commemorating the men killed during the construction of the tunnel. Above

View of Airolo

the bridge over the Ticino stands the Lucendro power station (completed 1945). South-west of Airolo is the lower station of a cableway up the Sasso della Boggia (2065 m/6775 ft; skiing area).

From Airolo a road, narrow in places, goes west up the Val Bedretto, passing through a number of small villages which offer quiet summer holiday accommodation. The road through Fontana is particularly constricted. Villa (1358 m/4456 ft) has a five-sided church tower designed to resist avalanches. 1 km/½ mile farther on we come to the picturesque mountain village of Bedretto (1405 m/4610 ft).

Val Bedretto

From All'Acqua (1605 m/5266 ft) it is a 3 hours' walk to the San Giacomo pass, which leads into the Toce valley (Domodossola).

All'Acqua

The road continues over the Nufenen (Novena) pass (2478 m/8133 ft; view) into the Rhône valley.

Nufenen Pass

From Airolo to Biasca the Bellinzona road descends the valley of the Ticino, here known as the Valle Leventina: a superb Alpine valley which drops down in a series of stages, its slopes at first clad with green meadows and mountain forests, which soon give way to chestnuts and walnut-trees (many waterfalls).

Valle Leventina

At the mouth of the wild Val Canaria the road traverses the Stretto di Stalvedro, passing under four natural rock arches.

Beyond Piotta (1012 m/3320 ft), in a wider part of the valley, to the left on the other side of the Ticino is the Ritom power station (50,000 kW), which supplies the St Gotthard railway. From here a funicular 1360 m/4462 ft long (average gradient 72% (1 in 1.3) serves the cantonal Gotthard Sanatorium (1177 m/3862 ft) the picturesque mountain village of Altanca (1346 m/4416 ft; also reached by road from Piotta; beautiful church of 1603) and Piora (1795 m/5889 ft; 24 minutes). From the funicular station it is a 15 minutes' walk to the Ritomsee (1830 m/6004 ft), an artificial lake which supplies the Ritom power station; from here it is a 3 hours' climb to the summit of Taneda (2670 m/8760 ft; magnificent views).

Piotta

Altanca
*Val Fiora

Ritomsee

*Taneda

357

Giornico: San Nicolao Church

From Ambri (980 m/3215 ft) a narrow mountain road winds up to a number of villages high in the mountains (1.5 km/1 mile to Quinto, 6 km to Ronco, 7 km/4 miles to Altanca).

Rodi-Fiesso

Rodi-Fiesso (945 m/3101 ft) is a double village beautifully situated between steep hillsides clad with larches and firs (summer holiday accommodation). From here there is a pleasant walk up to the Lago Tremorgio (1828 m/8998 ft; 2 hours), to the south-west, nestling picturesquely in a deep rocky hollow. There is also a narrow mountain road from Rodi to the little

Prato Leventina

village of Prato Leventina (1030 m/3379 ft; 2 km/1 mile south-east), on a natural terrace high above the Ticino valley, with a beautiful, Romanesque

Dalpe

campanile. 4 km/2 miles beyond this is the village of Dalpe (1140–1200 m/3740–3937 ft), above the Piumogna gorge, from which it is a 2¾ hours'

*Campo Tencia

climb to the Campo Tencia (3072 m/10,079 ft), the highest peak in Ticino.

*Piottino
Gorge

Just beyond Rodi-Fiesso, at the old customs post of Dazio Grande (949 m/3114 ft), the road enters the wild Piottino gorge, with a number of tunnels through the rock, between which (on right) the waterfalls on the river Ticino can be seen.

Faido

Faido (725 m/379 ft; pop. 1500), in a beautiful location, is the primary town in the Valle Leventina, and attracts many summer visitors. The stone-built houses of Ticinese type which now appear alongside the 16th c. timber houses with carved decoration, together with the first chestnuts and mulberry-trees, are the first imitations of a more southern landscape. On the western side of the valley the Piumogna plunges down in three beautiful waterfalls to join the Ticino.

Chiggiogna

In Chiggiona (668 m/2192 ft), beyond the railway line, stands the parish church of the Madonna di Ascente (13th c., rebuilt in the 16th c.).
The road continues through wooded country, with waterfalls on both sides. Just before Lavorgo, on the right, are the Cribiasca falls, pouring down in a cloud of spray.

Lavorgo (622 m/2041 ft) lies in a magnificent setting, with the long crest of the Monte di Sobrio on the left and a series of ridges running down from Campo Tencia and the Cima Bianca (2630 m/8629 ft) on the right.

Below Lavorgo a narrow road goes off on the right, crosses the Ticino and runs up (4 km/2 miles) to Chironico (800 m/2625 ft), a beautiful mountain village with a fine Romanesque church (12th c.) and the 14th c. Torre dei Pedrini.

Beyond this, in the Biaschina gorge, the Ticino bursts through into the lowest part of the Valle Leventina (beautiful waterfall).

Biaschina gorge

The village of Giornico (378 m/1240 ft) straddles the Ticino, with handsome old stone houses and two fine Romanesque churches on the right bank. To the right of the road the church of San Nicolao (12th c.), has a beautiful three-aisled crypt; higher up, amid vineyards, is Santa Maria di Castello. At the end of the village stands a monument commemorating a victory by 600 men of the Valle Leventina and the canton of Uri over a force of 10,000 Milanese on 28 December 1478.

Giornico

*San Nicolao
*Santa Maria
di Castello

Beyond this, after crossing the railway, a beautiful waterfall on the Cramosina is seen on the right. After the next crossing of the railway, also on the right, is the Biaschina power station (30,000 kW). The vegetation now takes on an increasing southern character (figs, mulberries); the vines are grown on pergolas, in the manner characteristic of the south.

Biasca (305 m/1001 ft; pop. 3500) lies in a fertile basin in the Ticino valley, at the mouth of the Val Blenio (the valley of the Brenno), through which a road descends from the Passo del Lucomagno (Lukmanier pass); granite quarries, timber trade, railway workshops. On the hillside is the beautiful Romanesque church of Santi Pietro e Paolo (11th-13th c.; interior remodelled in 1685), from which a path with Stations of the Cross runs up to the Petronilla Chapel (384 m/1260 ft) and a waterfall on the Frodalunga. To the east is the Pizzo Magno (2298 m/7540 ft).

Biasca

The road to Bellinzona now continues down through the wide and almost straight valley of the Ticino, which from here to Bellinzona is known as the Riviera, with purely southern vegetation (vines, chesnuts, walnuts, mulberries, figs). At Osogna (280 m/919 ft; bypass), above the village, is the chapel of Santa Maria del Castello (altar of 1494, 17th c. frescoes).

Riviera

Osogna

At Claro (253 m/830 ft), on the slopes of the Pizzo di Molinera (2293 m/7525 ft), to the left, stands the Benedictine monastery (founded in 1490), of Santa Maria (650 m/2133 ft).

Claro

4 km/2 miles beyond Claro the road from Chur over the San Bernardino pass (see entry) comes in on the left.

Arbedo (283 m/929 ft; bypass), which has a fine 15th c. parish church (the "Chiesa Rossa" or Red church), lies at the mouth of the Valle d'Arbedo (on left): there was a landslide here in 1929 from the Motto d'Arbino, which had been in gradual motion since 1888. In a battle at Arbedo in 1422, during the war with the Duchy of Milan, a force of 3000 Confederates was defeated by an army six times their number, 2000 of them being killed in the battle.

Arbedo

At Bellinzona (230 m/755 ft;) the road divides: straight ahead for Lugano, to the right for Locarno (see entries).

Bellinzona

St Maurice

C2

Canton: Valais (VS)
Altitude: 420 m/1378 ft
Population: 3500

The little town of St Maurice is picturesquely situated in a narrow pass in the Rhône valley, some 25 km/16 miles south of the end of Lake Geneva, at

Situation and
general

359

St Maurice

St Maurice: Rathausplatz

Augustinian abbey

the end of a road which runs via Monthey to Champéry. This was the site of the Celtic settlement of Agaunum, where the legend has it that St Maurice and his companions of the Theban Legion were martyred by Roman soldiers about the year 300.

Sights

Augustinian Abbey

At the north end of the town is an Augustinian abbey founded about 515 in honour of the martyrs, the oldest monastic house in Switzerland. The present church dates from 1611 to 1627; the beautiful Romanesque tower (11th c.) survives from an earlier building. The conventual buildings (now occupied by a secondary school and commercial college) were largely rebuilt in 1707–13. In the courtyard, between the cliffs, foundations and catacombs belonging to the earliest church on the site, including a 4th c. chapel, have been brought to light. The famous Treasury contains some outstanding works of art, largely of the Merovingian period, including several reliquaries, a gold-enamelled jug of Oriental origin and a Roman vessel of sardonyx.

*Treasury

The triple-aisled parish church of St Sigismond (18th c.) has beautiful Baroque side altars. The two-storeyed Town Hall, the Haus de la Pierre with an arcade of three storeys and the Haus de Bons date from the same period. Also of interest are the pilgrimage church of Notre-Dame-du-Scex and the 13th c. castle above the Rhône, built by the Savoyards and restored in the 16th c.; now houses a military museum.

Grotte aux Fées

To the north, above the town (footpath from the bridge over the Rhône), is a stalactitic cave, the Grotte aux Fées, with a restaurant and a view of the town.

Surroundings

At Bex, 8 km/5 miles north of the town is the only working salt mine in Switzerland (open to visitors: April – mid-Nov., c. 17° C/63° F). The labyrinth of tunnels and shafts, only part of which is accessible to visitors, stretches for up to 50 km/31 miles as far as the villages of Villars, Chesières and Arveyes. A film show of the development of the tunnels from 1684 to the present-day is held in a former salt water reservoir (1826). A "Bähnli" (small train) takes visitors to the mining area.

Bex, Saltmine

6 km/4 miles north-west is Monthey (428 m/1404 ft), a busy little town of 11,000 inhabitants with a medieval castle (rebuilt in the 16th and 18th c.; museum). From here a road runs south-west into the Val d'Illiez, first climbing up the steep hillside in sharp bends and then continuing up the slopes of the valley high above the left bank of the Vièze. Amid the vineyards and woods of chestnut-trees are many large boulders brought here by glacial action, including the Pierre à Dzo, resting on a base no bigger than a man's hand, and the Pierre des Marmettes, with a small house on the top.

Monthey

Val D'Illiez

In 6km/4 miles the road comes to Troistorrents (760 m/2494 ft), a prettily situated village at the mouth of the Val de Morgins, through which a road runs up to Morgins.

Val de Morgins

The road continues beyond Troistorrents ascending the beautiful valley (many waterfalls) alongside the cog-railway, with views of the Dents du Midi and the Dents Blanches. 3.5 km/2 miles farther on is Val d'Illiez (952 m/3124 ft), a village which attracts summer visitors.

Champéry

The road continues up the valley, dotted with huts, and in another 3.5 km/2 miles reaches Champéry, a village of 1000 inhabitants at the upper end of the Val d'Illiez, surrounded by forests and flanked by imposing peaks, popular as a health resort and especially for winter sports (heated swimming pool, tennis, golf, climbing school; curling with an indoor rink; cross-country skiing). Two cableways, one (1.7 km/1 mile long, 7 minutes) leaving from the south end of the village, the other (2.2 km/1 mile, 10 minutes) 1.5 km/1 mile north of the Monthey road, go up to the skiing area of Planachaux (1800 m/5906 ft; several restaurants, mountain inn; many ski-lifts; beautiful views).

Planachaux

There are many attractive walks and climbs from here. Walks: 1¼ hours south-west to the Chalets d'Ayerne (1473 m/4833 ft; good general view of the valley), 1¾ hours south to the Chalets de Bonaveau (1556 m/5105 ft; inn). Climbs: Croix de Culet (1966 m/6450 ft; superb views), 2½–3 hours west (30 minutes from Planachaux); Dents Blanches (2645–2764 m/8678– 9069 ft), 7 hours south (with guide); Dents du Midi (Haute Cime, 3260 m/ 10,696 ft), 7–8 hours east (with guide).

*Croix de Culet

*Dents du Midi

From St Maurice to Les Diablerets

Leave St Maurice on road 9 (E 2), which runs north down the Rhône valley, and in 13 km/8 miles turns right into a steep and winding but very beautiful mountain road which comes in 3 km/2 miles to Ollon (15th c. church). From here the road continues uphill, with beautiful views into the Rhône valley, curves round to enter the Gryonne valley and climbs in several sharp bends to the village of Huémoz.

Ollon

It then runs along the hillside, with a view of Villars, and climbs again in a double hairpin bend to the health resort of Chesières (1220 m/4003 ft). 10 km/6 miles from Ollon is Villars-sur-Ollon (1256 m/4121 ft), a popular health resort (salt-water swimming pool, golf-course, climbing school) and winter sports resort (several ski-lifts; cross-country skiing trail 25 km/16 miles long; ski-bobbing run; artificial ice-rink; curling; ski-flying school), magnificently set on a sunny terrace high above the Rhône valley, with views

Chesières

Villars-sur-Ollon

Les Diablerets in winter

extending to the Mont Blanc group. It is the terminus of an electric railway from Bex (1¼ hours), connecting with the line over the Col de Soud (1523 m/4997 ft) to the Col de Bretaye (1850 m/6070 ft), which is reached in 20 minutes: beautiful views and good skiing (lift to the Petit Chamossaire, 2030 m/6660 ft). From the Col de Bretaye a chair-lift (12 minutes; on foot ¾ hour) ascends Grand Chamossaire (2120 m/6956 ft), from where there is a famous panoramic view embracing the Bernese, Valais and Savoy Alps and Lake Geneva, and (summer only) a chair-lift to the Lac Noir and the Chaux Ronde (2027 m/6651 ft).

*Grand Chamossaire

The narrow road continues east over the Col de la Croix (1780 m/5840 ft) and comes in 16.5 km/10 miles to Les Diablerets (1163 m/3816 ft; pop. 1200), a magnificently situated health and winter sports resort (climbing school, ski-lifts, toboggan run) in the Vallée des Ormonts, a high valley surrounded by wooded hills and dotted with huts. The valley is bounded on the south by the Creux de Champ, a semicircle of rock under the peaks of the Diablerets (Teufelshörner, 3246 m/10,650 ft; 7–8 hours, with guide; cableway from the Col du Pillon), with numerous waterfalls which join to form the Grande-Eau (pleasant walk, 1½ hours, up the valley). Cableway (2.4 km/1 mile, 15 minutes) to Isenau (1770 m/5807 ft; ski-lift).

Les Diablerets

*Creux de Champ

From Les Diablerets it is possible to continue over the Col du Pillon (1546 m/5072 ft) to Gsteig, Gstaad and Saanen (see Gstaad).

Col du Pillon

St Moritz   E2

Canton: Grisons (GR)
Altitude: 1853 m/6080 ft
Population: 6000

Situation and general

The world-famed winter sports resort (Winter Olympics 1928 and 1948) of St Moritz (Romansch San Murezzan), in the midst of the Upper Engadine, is

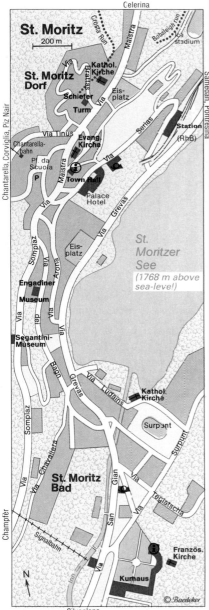

St. Moritz

200 m

St. Moritz Dorf

Celerina

Crosa Run

Maistra

Bobsleigh run

stadium

Kathol. Kirche

Schiefer

Turm

Eis- platz

Via Tinus

Via Maistra

Chantarella- bahn

Evang. Kirche

Pf. da Scuola

P

Town Hall

Palace Hotel

Serlas

Station (RhB)

St. Moritzer See

(1768 m above sea-level)

Eis- platz

Via Somplaz

Via Arona

Via Grevas

Engadiner Museum

Segantini- Museum

Via Dim

Via Grevas

Via Ludains

Kathol. Kirche

Surpunt

Via Somplaz

Via Chavallera

Via Bagn

Via Surpunt

St. Moritz Bad

Via San Gian

Via Teglatscha

Franzos. Kirche

Signalbahn

Kurhaus

N

Via Inn

© Baedeker

Silvaplana
(Julier pass, Maloja pass)

Chantarella, Corviglia, Piz Nair

Champfèr

Samedan, Pontresina

in two parts. St Moritz Dorf – a "village" which has all the appearance of a town, with its large and palatial hotels – is situated on a sunny terrace, sheltered from the north wind, above the St Moritzer See (Lake of St Moritz, 1768 m/5801 ft), through which the river Inn flows from south to north. St Moritz Bad, on the valley floor at the south-west end of the lake, has iron-bearing springs of high carbonic acid content which were already being used in Bronze Age times.

The beautiful scenery with 25 crystal clear mountain lakes, forests and glaciers, the legendary "Champagne climate" and intense sunshine provide an unforgettable setting for an action-packed holiday. Along with winter sports (see below) in the colder months, in summer there are watersports (sailing, windsurfing and rafting on the river Inn), summer skiing, tennis, horse-riding and golf.

The magnificent view from St Moritz embraces the mountains from Piz Languard in the east to Piz Julier in the west, the most prominent peaks being Piz Rosatsch with its glacier, above the lake, to the right of this Piz Surlej and Piz Corvatsch, and in the distance the beautiful Piz della Margna.

Transport

Access is from Chur, over the Julier pass or from Landeck. The airline companies Air Engadinia and Crossair fly regularly to Zurich. There are four memorable Alpine rail journeys to St Moritz with the Rhätische Bahn (see Practical Information, Railways): Glacier-Express (St-Moritz–Zermatt), Bernina-Express (St Moritz–Tirano/Italy), Engadin-Express (St-Moritz–Bad Scuol–Landeck) and the Palm-Express (St Moritz–Ascona–Zermatt).

Cableways * Corviglia

From St Moritz Dorf a funicular (2.1 km/1 mile) ascends in 20 minutes via an intermediate station at Chantarella (2005 m/6578 ft) to Corviglia (2486 m/8157 ft; restaurant), with fine views and excellent skiing; from there a cabin cableway (2450 m/8038 ft, 10 minutes) up Piz Nair (3057 m/10,030 ft; magnificent view).

From St Moritz Bad the Signalbahn (cabins; 1460 m/4790 ft, 5 minutes serves the Signalkuppe (2150 m/7054 ft; several ski-lifts).

Winter sports

The origins of winter tourism in St Moritz go back to the end of the last century. From those early days with the first ski-runs it has developed into a world famous skiing

363

St Moritz village

metropolis with 25 snow cannons. It features artificial and natural ice-rinks; curling, toboggan run, the famous Cresta Run or Skeletonbahn (1400 m/4593 ft); bobsleigh run to Celerina-Cresta (1600 m/5250 ft); Olympic ski-jump. Every year there are three international horse races on the frozen lake, as well as winter golf, polo and greyhound racing.

This excellent skiing country with descents of varying difficulty is easily accessible by the funicular, cableways and numerous lifts. The new slopes opened in 1988 and the glacier on Corvatsch and Diavolezza make skiing possible from November to May. There are cross-country trails to Majola and Zuoz.

Sights

*St Moritz Dorf

The heart of St Moritz Dorf is the Schulplatz (Pl. da Scoula), in which stands the Town Hall. To the south-east, lower down, is the Tourist Information Office, to the north, on higher ground, the Protestant church (1786), and beyond this, in the idyllic Old Cemetery, the Schiefer Turm (Leaning Tower), all that remains of the old Romanesque church of St Maurice.

Segantini Museum

In the Via Somplatz (towards Suvretta) is the Segantini Museum, a domed granite building (1911) containing pictures by Giovanni Segantini, including an unfinished triptych with an Alpine setting, "Coming into Being, Being and Passing Away" (1897–99).

Opposite the museum stands a monument commemorating the victors in the Winter Olympics of 1928 and 1948.

Engadine Museum

The Engadine Museum in the Badstrasse contains domestic interiors, embroidery, costumes, implements and utensils. Exhibits excavated in the Engadine from Neolithic and Bronze Age periods and Roman finds from the Septimer and Julier passes are on display.

Panorama of St Moritz in the Upper Engadine

In St Moritz Bad (1.5 km/1 mile south of St Moritz Dorf), with its high-rise buildings, is the Roman Catholic church (1867), with a separate tower. **St Moritz Bad**

On the eastern fringe of the forest are the Spa Establishment (1973–76), an open-air swimming-pool and the Kurhaus. Spa Establishment

Attractive paths run along the wooded slopes.

Surroundings

There are fine views from Oberalpina (1990 m/6529 ft; 30 minutes south-west of St Moritz Dorf), Alp Nova (2185 m/7169 ft; 1 hour west) and Alp Laret (2101 m/6893 ft; 1 hour north). From Oberalpina there is a ridge path by way of the Chantarella funicular station to the Alp Laret (1 hour). Oberalpina

2 km/1 mile from St Moritz Dorf on the east side of the lake are the Meierei hotel-restaurant and café. From there it is another kilometre to the Staz Hotel and restaurant on the eastern shore of the Lej Staz (Stazer See, 1808 m/5932 ft; swimming pool), from which it is an hour's walk on forest paths to Celerina or Pontresina. St Moritz Lake

From St Moritz Bad it is an hour and a half's walk on beautiful forest paths by way of the Quellenberg (1920 m/6300 ft) or the Johannisberg (2002 m/6569 ft) to the Hahnensee (2159 m/7084 ft; restaurant) and a further 2 hours along the slopes of Piz Surlej (3192 m/10,473 ft) to the Furocla Surlej (2755 m/9039 ft), from which there is a breathtaking view of the Bernina group and the Engadine lakes. From here a 2½ hours' climb brings the walker to the summit of Piz Corvatsch (3451 m/11,323 ft) cabin railway from Silvaplana; superb views; summer skiing on the glacier (3303 m/10,837 ft with two ski-lifts). Hahnensee

*Furocla Surlej

*Piz Corvatsch

To the west of St Moritz there is a rewarding climb (not difficult for experienced climbers) by way of the Alp Suvretta (2211 m/7254 ft) to the summit

Sils Maria, below the Piz Corvatsch   *Piz della Margna*

*Piz Julier	of Piz Julier (3385 m/11,106 ft; 5 hours), which offer magnificent distant views.
Silvaplana	7 km/4 miles south-west, at the junction with the road over the Julier pass, is Silvaplana (1815 m/5955 ft; bypass), a health and winter sports resort situated on the green alluvial fan of the Ova dal Vallun, with a Late Gothic parish church (1491). A bridge crosses the narrow neck of the lake on which it lies to a 19th c. baronial mansion, the Crap da Sass (private property), and
Surlej	the houses and chalets of Surlej ("above the lake"). 15 minutes' walk farther up is the lower station (1870 m/6135 ft; car park, restaurant) of the Corvatsch cableway.
Silvaplaner See Silser See	5 km/3 miles farther south-west on the road to the Majola pass, lying to the left of the road between the Silvaplana lake (Silvaplana See, 1794 m/5886 ft; area 2.6 sq. km/1 sq. mile, depth 77 m/253 ft) and the Silser See (Romansch Lej da Segl, 1797 m/5896 ft; area 4.2 sq. km/2 sq. miles), is the
Sils	popular summer and winter sports resort of Sils (Romansch Segl). This is in two parts: Sils Maria (the "Maria" is actually a corruption of a word meaning "farm"), the main tourist attraction at the mouth of the Val Fex, and Sils Baseglia at the outflow of the River Inn from the Silser See. In both parts of Sils there are elegant houses in the style of the Engadine. Sils Maria has a Baroque church (1764), and beside the Edelweiss Hotel is a modest museum devoted to Nietzsche, who spent the summer months here from 1881 to 1889 (commemorative tablet). Sils Baselgia has a church dating from 1448. From both parts of Sils there are pleasant footpaths (15 minutes) to the wooded peninsula of Chasté (1838 m/6030 ft; nature reserve), with scanty remains of an old castle and a Nietzsche quotation carved in the rock.
	On the south-east shore of the Silser See (45 minutes' walk) lies the hamlet of Isola (inn), which is abandoned in winter: behind it, in the gorge of the Fedozbach, is a beautiful waterfall. From here it is another 45 minutes' walk to the Majola pass.

From Sils Maria a narrow road (closed to cars) runs south up the Val Fex to Crasta (3 km/2 miles, alt. 1948 m/6391 ft) and Curtins (6 km/4 miles, alt. 1976 m/6483 ft), from which there is a beautiful view of the mountains framing the Fex glacier.

*Val Fex

East of Sils Maria (1¼ hours) is the Marmorè (2203 m/7288 ft; ski-lift), with a magnificent view into the Upper Engadine.

Marmorè

A good footpath (3½ hours) leads east to the Fuorcla Surlej (2756 m/9042 ft).

To the south of Isola (4–4½ hours, with guide) is the Piz della Margna (3159 m/10,365 ft; superb views).

*Piz della Margna

A cableway ascends to the Alp Präsura (2311 m/7582 ft), giving access to the Furtschellas (2800 m/9187 ft; ski-lifts).

San Bernardino Pass   E2

Canton: Grisons (GR)
Height of pass: 2065 m/6775 ft

The San Bernardino pass is the highest point on the San Bernardino road, a very convenient link between Lake Constance and Ticino. From Thusis onwards it is now mostly of expressway standard, and since the construction of the San Bernardino tunnel (1961–67) it has been the fastest all-year-round route from Lake Constance through eastern Switzerland to northern Italy.

Situation and general

From Chur the road follows the Rhine and Hinterrhein valleys to Thusis, and from there takes a new line by way of the famous Via Mala (see The Rhine) to Splügen (bypass).

Access

Splügen

From Splügen over the San Bernardino to Mesocco

The San Bernardino road to Bellinzona (69 or 76 km/43 or 47 miles) continues past Splügen, where the road branches off south over the Splügen pass (2113 m/6933 ft), on the Italian frontier, and continues to Chiavenna, from where one can drive east into the scenic Val Bregaglia (see entry).

San Bernardino Road
Splügen pass

The road to San Bernardino continues up the Hinterrhein valley. Beyond the valley of Hinterrhein the old road branches off to cross the pass, while the expressway (N 13) passes a parking place (on right kiosk-restaurant) and over the Hinterrhein, here still quite small, to the northern entrance (1613 m/5292 ft) of the San Bernardino tunnel (length 6.6 km/4 miles, width of carriageway 7.5 m/25 ft, highest point 1644 m/5394 ft; emergency telephones; maximum speed 80 km p. h./50 m.p.h., overtaking prohibited; toll-free). The tunnel runs in an almost straight line under the pass, emerging just to the west of the village of San Bernardino. The route through the tunnel is 7 km/4 miles shorter than the road over the pass.

San Bernardino Tunnel

The road over the pass climbs in 18 hairpin bends (maximum gradient 9% (1 in 11.1) up the steep slope below the Mittaghorn (2609 m/8560 ft; on left), with beautiful and constantly changing views to the rear of the Rheinwald valley and the peaks rising to over 3000 m/9843 ft on its north side. In 4 km/ 2 miles it reaches the bare valley of the Thälialp (1920 m/6300 ft) and then ascends in nine hairpins to the pass.

San Bernardino Pass Road

The San Bernardino pass (2065 m/6775 ft; simple hospice), which may have been used as early as the Bronze Age as a route through the Alps was originally known as the Vogelberg ("Bird Mountain"). It takes its present name from San Bernardino of Siena, who is said to have preached here in the early 15th c. On the pass, with its rocks worn smooth by the ice, is the Lago Moèsola, in which is a small rocky islet. To the east is the pointed

San Bernardino Pass

San Bernardino Pass

summit of Pizzo Uccello (Bird Mountain, 2716 m/8911 ft), to the west the blunt top of the Marschalhorn (2902 m/9521 ft), beside which the Zapporthorn, with the Muccial glacier, comes into view as the road continues south.

The road skirts the lake and then continues down in 21 hairpin bends, following the course of the River Moèsa, through a rugged landscape, with magnificent views of the surrounding peaks, particularly of the precipitous Pan de Zucchero (2600 m/8531 ft) and (to the rear, on the left) Pizzo Uccello, which towers up ever more imposingly as the road descends. To the east are Piz Lumbreda (2977 m/9768 ft) and Piz Curciusa (2875 m/9433 ft). After the last hairpin the southern exit from the tunnel (1631 m/5351 ft) is seen on the right.

San Bernardino

Just beyond this point is the village of San Bernardino (1607 m/5273 ft), the highest place in the Val Mesocco and now a developing holiday and winter sports resort. There are many attractive footpaths through the meadows and woodland of this high valley below Pizzo Uccello (3½–4 hours). Cableway from the Alpe Fracch (1630 m/5348 ft) to Confin (1953 m/6405 ft; restaurant), ski-lifts to 2500 m/8203 ft, ice-rink, cross-country skiing. 2 km/1 mile south, on the old road, is the Lago d'Osso (1646 m/5401 ft), surrounded by forest.

From the tunnel exit N 13 continues south over the moorland plateau, passing on the right an artificial lake (1604 m/5263 ft), curves round to cross the old road and then continues downhill, passing through two tunnels and two galleries. In 11 km/7 miles it passes (on right) the scattered houses of

Pian San Giacomo

Pian San Giacomo (1172 m/3845 ft), from which the old road runs down on the right to Mesocco.

N 13 then goes down in wide curves and several hairpins (beautiful views) into the Val Mesocco, which descends in a series of steep steps, with several hydro-electric stations. To the south-east are the twin peaks of Cima di Pian Guarnei (3015 m/9892 ft) and Piz Corbet (3026 m/9928 ft).

Just before Mesocco N 13 crosses the old road, which traverses the village, while N 13 passes above it (short tunnel) and then descends to the valley floor in a hairpin turn.

Mesocco or Misox (769 m/2525 ft; pop. 1500), formerly known as Cremeo, is a village of fine stone houses, the chief place in the Val Mesocco or Mesolcina (Misoxer Tal), and, like the Val Calanca which runs parallel to it on the west, belongs to the canton of Grisons but is inhabited by an Italian-speaking and Roman Catholic population. The two valleys together are known as the Moèsano (from the River Moèsa which flows down the Val Mesocco).

Mesocco

*Misoxer Tal

Below Mesocco the road passes under a crag crowned by the ruined Castello di Misox (748 m/2453 ft), the ancestral castle of the Counts Sax von Misox, which was purchased by the Trivulzi family of Milan in 1483, destroyed by the people of Grisons in 1526 and restored by Swiss students in 1922–26 (magnificent view of the deep trough of the Val Mesocco).

*Castello di
Mesocco

At the foot of the hill on which the castle stands is the 12th c. church of Santa Maria del Castello, with 15th c. wall-paintings.
Further down the valley is Soazza (bypass), where the expressway comes to an end.

Santa Maria del
Castello

Sarnen   D2

Canton: Unterwalden
Half-canton: Obwalden (OW)
Altitude: 476 m/1562 ft
Population: 7300

Sarnen, capital of the half-canton of Obwalden, lies at the north end of the Sarner See, on the road from Lucerne to Interlaken over the Brünig pass. The Landsgemeinde, the communal assembly, meets on the Landenberg here on the last Sunday in April.

Situation and
general

Sights

In the Town Hall (Rathaus, 1729–32) is kept the "White Book" (Weisses Buch), containing the earliest account (c. 1470) of the history of the Confederation. The neighbouring church of St Andreas dates from the 17th–18th c.

Town Hall

At the north end of the town at 12 Brünigstrasse is the Heimatmuseum (local museum) which surveys the cultural history of the canton of Oberwalden. The collect on includes prehistoric and early material, some from the Roman settlement of Alpnach, weapons, religious art of the 14th–18th c. (wooden statues, altars, liturgical items), pictures and sculpture by local artists from the 17th–20th c., furniture, coins, agricultural implements and a reconstructed alpine hut.

Local Museum

On a hill to the south-east stands the twin-towered Baroque parish church of St Peter (by the Singer brothers, 1739–42). It occupies the site of a earlier Romanesque building first mentioned in 1036. The interior contains rich stucco work

St Peter's
Church

The painted carving (1507) in the neighbouring charnel house (c. 1500) is the work of Peter Tischmacher from Uri.
To the west, on the Landenberg, is the Baroque Schützenhaus (Riflemen's Clubhouse, 1752) and nearby an armoury.

2.5 km/2 miles south-west, on the sunny western shore of the lake, lies the attractive outlying district of Wilen, from which a road follows the lake via Oberwilen to Giswil.

Wilen

Sachseln: Pilgrimage church of St Theodul

Surroundings

To Schwendi-Kaltbad

A beautiful road 11 km/7 miles long leads up the hillside (known as
Schwendi) above the lake, reaching Stalden (797 m/2615 ft), a small health
resort, after 3 km/2 miles. The road continues through the hamlet of Gassen
and over the Alpine meadows on the Schwendiberg; then road on right to
(8 km/5 miles) Schwendi-Kaltbad (1445 m/4741 ft), with an iron-bearing
spring. Beyond the turning for Schwendi the road goes on into the Entlebuch valley (see entry).

Stalden

From Sarnen into the Melchtal

(22 km/14 miles to Melchtal-Frutt). Leave Sarnen on the road to Stans,
which runs east, crossing N 8. 2 km/1 mile: Kerns (569 m/1867 ft), a village
frequented by summer visitors. Turn right into a road which climbs the east
side of the valley of the Grosse Melch-Aa. 3 km/2 miles: Zuben.

Kerns

Here a road branches off on the right, crosses the Melch on a bridge 97
m/318 ft high and reaches Flüeli (2 km/1 mile: road recommended as return
route from the Melchtal), a hamlet commanding extensive views, and
which boasts a pilgrimage chapel of 1618 and a house said to have
belonged to the 15th c. hermit Nikolaus von der Flüe. His hermitage is lower
down on the slopes of Mt Ranft (close by, a chapel of 1700).

Flüeli-Ranft

3 km/2 miles: St Niklausen (839 m/2753 ft), with a 14th c. chapel and the old
Heidenturm ("Heathens' Tower").

St Niklausen

4 km/2 miles: Melchtal (894 m/2933 ft), a beautifully situated mountain
village and health resort. Cableway (1200 m/3937 ft) to the Rütialp (1350

Melchtal

◀ *Sarnen: the parish church*

m/4429 ft; restaurant; view). The road continues uphill over the Balmatt, at the foot of the precipitous Rämisfluh (1866 m/6122 ft). 4 km/2 miles: Stöckalp (1070 m/3511 ft), from which there is a cableway (3333 m/10,936 ft) to Melchsee-Frutt.

Melchsee-Frutt   The road (alternate one-way traffic) continues, with many bends, up the valley of the Keselnbach, below the rock walls of the Brünighaupt (2315 m/7396 ft). 6 km/4 miles: Melchsee-Frutt (1920 m/6300 ft), a popular mountain resort and winter sports resort magnificently situated in a green valley on the shores of an Alpine lake, the Melchsee (1838 m/6030 ft), from where an unobstructed view of the whole Titlis chain may be enjoyed.

A good base for climbs, e.g. to the Erzegg (2176 m/7139 ft; 1¼ hours; ski-lift) and the Hochstollen (2484 m/8150 ft; 2–2½ hours); easy and pleasant footpath to the Engstlenalp (3 hours). Chair-lift from the southern end of the Melchsee (1900 m/6234 ft; 20 minutes) to the Balmeregghorn (2230 m/7317 ft).

Over the Brünig Pass to Brienz

Sachseln   Leave Sarnen on Road 4, which runs south along the east side of the Sarner See to Sachseln (475 m/1558 ft), a prettily situated lakeside village which is popular with summer visitors. In the choir of the church (rebuilt 1672–84; lower part of tower Romanesque) is a glass sarcophagus containing the remains of St Nikolaus von der Flüe (1417–87), popularly known as "Bruder Klaus", whose conciliatory approach brought about the admission of Fribourg and Solothurn to the Confederation in 1481.

A museum (Dorfstrasse 4), the former house of the Landamman P. Ignaz von Flüe, contains literature and paintings commemorating the mystic and politician Klaus von Flüe. It also has a collection of manuscripts and works by the writer Heinrich Federer (1866–1928).

Alp Älggi, Geographical Centre of Switzerland   In celebration of the 150th anniversary of the Federal Department of Topography the geographical centre of Switzerland was officialy marked. It is situated in the Kleiner Melchtal on Alp Äggli (district of Sachsen), where a resting-place has been built, surrounded by a stone wall in the shape of Switzerland. A pyramid stands in the centre as a symbol of land surveying.

Giswil   Giswil (488 m/1601 ft), in a green hollow in the valley surrounded by fine mountains, has a church (above the village) and ruins of an old castle. A winding mountain road runs west, affording fine views, over the Moerli-Alp (1100 m/3609 ft; restaurant), a popular skiing area.

Kaiserstuhl, Lungernsee   Kaiserstuhl (701 m/2300 ft): view on right of the picturesque Lungernsee (692 m/2270 ft). The road runs along the lake (viewpoints, on right), to which water is conveyed from the valleys of the Grosse and the Kleine Melch in a tunnel 10 km/6 miles long, producing some 50,000 kW of electricity (power station between Giswil and Kaiserstuhl). To the south can be seen the Schwarzhorn chain, to the left the three peaks of the Wetterhorn (3701 m/12,143 ft).

Lungern   Lungern (715 m/2346 ft), a popular summer holiday place beautifully situated at the southern end of the lake in a setting of steep wooded hills, with a neo-Gothic church above the village. In 1323 the town of Berne and the three original cantons of Uri, Schwyz and Unterwalden formed an alliance against the Habsburgs here (commemorative tablet at the near end of the village, on left). From Lungern-Obsee a cableway runs up west via the intermediate station of Turren (1531 m/5023 ft) to Schönbüel (2010 m/6595 ft; skiing), from which there is a path (4 km/2 miles) to the Brienzer Rothorn and a ski-lift to the Hohe Gumme (2209 m/7248 ft).

Brünig Pass   The road now comes to the Brünig pass (1007 m/3304 ft), on the wooded ridge between the Wilerhorn (2006 m/6582 ft; 3–3½ hours), to the west, and the Giebel (2039 m/6690 ft). To the left is the Brünig-Hasliberg station (restaurant). The view embraces the Engelhörner (2783 m/9131 ft) and the Faulhorn chain; below, to the left, is the Aare valley, extending west from Meiringen to Lake Brienz (see entries), with its beautiful waterfalls.

From the Brünig pass it is worth while taking a well-engineered panoramic road branching off on the left along the Hasliberg, a sunny mountain terrace high above the Aare valley which is a popular holiday area, with good skiing in winter. | Hasliberg

The road comes first to the health resort of·Hohfluh (1049 m/3442 ft), with far-ranging views, and then continues past the lower station (1150 m/3773 ft) of a cableway to Käserstatt (1826 m/5991 ft; restaurant; chair-lift to Hochsträss, 2120 m/6956 ft; ski-lift to Hochbühl, 2037 m/6683 ft) to Goldern (1053 m/3455 ft). It then passes through Alpine meadows and crosses the gorge of the Alpbach in a wide bend to reach the health resort of Reuti (1045 m/3429 ft; extensive views). From here there are cableways via Bidmi to Käserstatt or Planplatten (2245 m/7366 ft) and down to Meiringen (see entry). | Hohfluh ... Reuti

From the Brünig pass the road to Brienz leads down through wooded country, with attractive glimpses to the left of the Hasli valley (the valley of the River Aare) and the Faulhorn chain. 1.5 km/1 mile below the pass is a road junction, where an excellent road goes off on the left and winds its way down the slopes of the Hasliberg to Meiringen (8 km/5 miles; see entry), in the valley of the canalised Aare.

The Brienz road bears right and descends, with a very fine·view of the Aare valley, to the village of Brienzwiler (709 m/2326 ft), on a terrace above the Aare. | Brienzwiler

It then continues along the Aare valley below the Ballenberg (727 m/2385 ft; Swiss Open-Air Museum; see Lake Brienz) to the hamlet of Kienholz (570 m/1870 ft), where Lake Brienz comes into sight. Then beneath the Brienzer Rothorn to Brienz (see Lake Brienz), on the lake of the same name. | ***Ballen-berg, Open-Air Museum ... Brienz

---

Schaffhausen D1

Canton: Schaffhausen (SH)
Altitude: 404 m/1326 ft
Population: 34,000

Schaffhausen, capital of the canton of that name, situated close to the Untersee and north of the Rhine, is enclosed on three sides by Germany. | Situation

Its well preseved medieval town centre and the picturesquely situated Kastell Munot make it one of the most interesting towns in Switzerland. Schaffhausen is also an important hub of communications and industrial town (iron and steel works, chemical plants, engineering works, clocks, textiles and playing cards). | General

Schaffhausen grew up as a transhipment point for traffic on the Rhine, here interrupted by the Rhine Falls. In 1045 the Emperor Henry III granted Count Eberhard von Nellenburg the right to mint coins here, and about 1050 the Benedictine abbey of All Saints was founded. From 1330 to 1415 the town was mortgaged to the Habsburgs, and thereafter, until 1501, was a free Imperial city. In 1454 Schaffhausen concluded an alliance with the Confederation, of which it became a member in 1501. From 1798 to 1803 the town and canton were part of the Helvetian Republic. | History

Sights

In the heart of the old town is the Fronwagplatz, with the Fronwag tower and two fountains, the Moor's fountain (Mohrenbrunnes, originally 1520) | **Old Town

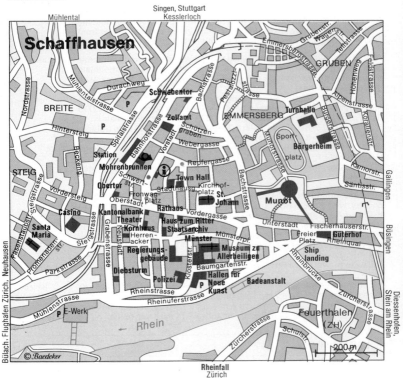

and the Metzgerbrunnen, 1524), which has a striking figure of a lands-knecht (mercenary).

To the north of the Fronwagplatz is the Vorstadt, with a whole series of houses with oriel windows and coats-of-arms on the façade, which ends at the Schwabentor (Swabian gate, 14th–16th c.); to the west the short Oberstadt, at the far end of which is the Obertor (upper Gate, originally 13th c.).

Rathaus
To the east of Fronwagplatz the long Vordergasse opens out into a square. On the right of the Vordergasse the 15th c. Rathaus (Council House), with the fine Chamber of the Great Council (Grossratssaal, 1632) and the Council Arcade (Ratslaube, 1586). In the nearby Sporrengasse (No. 7) the private Stemmler museum has stuffed birds and mammals from all over Europe.

Haus zum Ritter
Beyond this, at the corner of Münstergasse, is the colourful Haus zum Ritter (1485), with paintings on the façade by Tobias Stimmer (originals, 1570, removed in 1935, now in All Saints Museum; reproductions of 1938–39, restored 1943). Diagonally across the street the Late Gothic St John's church (Protestant) has an imposing tower.

Herrenacker, Arsenal
In a spacious square south of Fronwagplatz, Herrenacker, are the old Kornhaus (Granary, 1679) and the Municipal Theatre (rebuilt 1956). In a small square immediately east, the Beckenstube, is situated the Cantonal Government Building (Regierungsgebäude), a skilful conversion of the old Arsenal (17th c.), with a magnificent doorway.

Schaffhausen: Kastell Munot

The Minster (Münster), a pillared basilica with a single tower (1087–1150), was originally the church of the Benedictine abbey of All Saints and is now the Protestant parish church. The spacious nave, flat-roofed (restored 1950–58), is a fine example of Romanesque religious architecture. The sparse furnishings are modern; near the altar, a simple wooden table stand the bronze font and wooden pulpit. In the apse are three stained-glass windows and a large tapestry. The choir contains remains of old wall-paintings. Outside the Minster, on the north side, is a bronze figure of David with Goliath's head (by K. Geiser, 1959). On the south side the cloister (freely accessible) has delicate 12th c. arcades.

*Minster

In the forecourt of St Anne's chapel, adjoining it on the east, is the famous Hosanna Bell (Osannaglocke), cast in 1486, with a Latin inscription ("Vivos voco, mortuos plango, fulgura frango" – "I call the living, I mourn the dead, I quell the lightning") which inspired a well-known poem by Schiller, the "Song of the Bell" ("Das Lied von der Glocke").

Hosanna Bell

The handsome conventual buildings of the abbey now house All Saints Museum (Museum zu Allerheiligen), one of the richest local museums in Switzerland, with collections of prehistoric material (mainly from the Kesslerloch at Thayngen), works of religious art (the finest of them in the "Treasury" in the Abbot's Room), a series of rooms furnished in period style, weapons, relics of the old guilds, traditional costumes, etc., and a large picture gallery, notable in particular for the works by modern Swiss artists.

*All Saints Museum

Of the old conventual buildings St Erhard's chapel (1104), St John's chapel (1064), a Romanesque loggia (1200) and the Kreuzsaal (c. 1620) are noteworthy.

South of All Saints Museum, at Baumgartenstrasse 23, the Hallen für Neue Kunst, a museum for international contemporary art (1960s and 70s), has been built in a former textile factory.

Hallen für Neue Kunst

375

*Kastell Munot To the east, dominating the town on a vine-clad hill is Kastell Munot (1564–85), a circular structure designed in accordance with Dürer's principles of fortification, with walls more than 5 m/16 ft thick and vaulted gunports below. The principal tower has a ramp in place of a staircase to allow supplies to be carried up to the artillery. From the battlements there is a fine view of the town.

**Rhine Falls See entry

Rhine See entry

Surroundings

Diessenhofen About 10 km/6 miles to the east of Schaffhausen lies the old-world former Imperial town of Diessenhofen (416 m/1365 ft; pop. 3000), with its fine Gothic burghers' houses, old fortifications (Siegelturm, 1545), parish church of St Dionysis (1200; rebuilt 15th c.) and the Dominican convent of St Katharinental (1571; Baroque conventual church).

Gailingen An old wooden covered bridge crosses to the opposite bank of the Rhine to the health resort of Gailingen (pop. 2500; neurological rehabilitation centre), with a St Nikolaus chapel (1100) and an interesting Jewish cemetery (1676); in the 19th c. there were as many Jews as Christians in Gailingen.

Schwyz   D1

Canton: Schwyz (SZ)
Altitude: 517 m/1696 ft
Population: 12,000

Situation and general The old town of Schwyz, which gave its name to the whole country, is capital of the canton of the same name. It is charmingly situated on the edge of the orchard-covered plain between Lake Lucerne and the Lauerzer See, under the towering twin horns of the Mythen (1815 and 1902 m/5955 and 6259 ft).

Sights

Rathaus Schwyz has many beautiful 17th and 18th c. patrician houses. In the main square is the richly decorated Baroque parish church of St Martin (1774), and opposite it the Rathaus (1642–43), its façade decorated with frescoes (1891) of scenes from Swiss history. The Great Council Chamber contains a series of portraits of Landamänner (cantonal presidents) from 1544 to 1850; the Little Council Chamber has beautiful panelling and a carved ceiling of 1655 (restored 1989/90).

Turmmuseum In the tower south of the Rathaus is the Cantonal Historical Museum and a small geology collection.

Bundesbrief-archiv In the Bahnhofstrasse (the road to Seewen) can be seen the Bundesbriefarchiv, in which the original deed of confederation (Bundesbrief) between Schwyz, Uri and Unterwalden, signed on 1 August 1291, is displayed as well as other historic documents and mementoes.

Ital-Reding Haus The Ital-Reding Haus in Reckenbachstrasse offers an insight into 17th c. social history.

Haus Bethlehem On the same site is the Haus Bethlehem, the oldest wooden house in Switzerland (1287; restored 1988/89).

Above the town is the Kollegium Mariahilf, a large Roman Catholic seminary, rebuilt after a fire in 1910.

Surroundings

*Stoos Take the road which runs south-east up the Muota valley and arrives in 4 km/2 miles at Schlatti. From there a funicular (1.5 km/1 mile long, gradient

Schwyz: Rathausplatz . . .

. . . guarded by the statue of Justina

Federal archives of Switzerland in Schwyz

Fronalpstock	up to 77%, time 8 minutes) climbs the steep wooded hillside to Stoos (1290 m/4232 ft), situated on a terrace commanding extensive views, with a large area of excellent skiing terrain. 8 minutes' walk south-west of the Kurhaus a chair-lift (in winter a ski-lift) takes 15 minutes to reach the Karrenstöckli (1740 m/5709 ft). From here it is a 10 minutes' walk to the Luegi viewpoint. Another chair-lift goes to the summit of the Fronalpstock (1922 m/6325 ft; inn), from where superb views of Lake Lucerne and the mountains can be enjoyed.
*Grosser Mythen	From Schwyz it is a 4 hours' walk by way of the Holzegg inn (1407 m/4617 ft; cableway from Brunni) to the summit of the Grosser Mythen (1902 m/6240 ft), with a splendid view of central Switzerland.
Rickenbach	1.8 km/1 mile south-east of Schwyz is Rickenbach, from which a cableway 2466 m/8025 ft long ascends in two stages by way of Husernberg to the upper station (1565 m/5135 ft) on the Rotenfluh.
From Schwyz in the Muota valley Schlatti Muotathal, St Joseph nunnery	(20 km/12 miles to Bisisthal.) The road (in good condition as far as Bisisthal) climbs through flourishing fruit orchards to the foot of the Giebel (918 m/3012 ft), where it enters the wooded gorge of the Muota. 4 km/2 miles: Schlattli (573 m/1880 ft), with the lower station of the Stoos funicular. The road continues past a number of beautiful waterfalls, running through the hamlets of Ried (chair-lift via Illgau to the Oberberg, 1150 m/3785 ft) and Föllnis. 8 km/5 miles Muotathal (612 m/2008 ft) has a beautiful parish church (1792) and the picturesque nunnery of St Joseph (1684–93). 2 km/ 1 mile: Hinterthal, where a road goes off on the left into the Starzlenbach valley. 6 km/4 miles: Bisisthal (870 m/2854 ft), in a beautiful setting.
*Hölloch- grotten Gutentalboden	The road up the Starzlenbach valley comes in 1 km/½ mile to the entrance to the Höllochgrotten, a cave system with extensive branches (total length of passages about 93 km/58 miles; 1 km/½ mile open to visitors), and ends in 5km/3 miles at the Gutentalboden (1281 m/4203 ft), from which it is a 2¾ hours' walk on a bridle-path over the Pragel pass (1554 m/5097 ft) to Richisau in the Klöntal (see Glarus).
Brunnen	See entry
**Rigi	See entry
**Vierwald- stätter See	See entry

Bad Scuol/Schuls-Tarasp-Vulpera   F2

	Canton: Grisons (GR) Altitude: 1203–1268 m/3947–4160 ft Population: 1900
Situation and general	The village of Scuol, situated on the left bank of the Inn along the main road from St Moritz to Landeck bypass, combines with Bad Tarasp, only a short distance upstream, the summer holiday village of Vulpera, a little way south above the right bank of the river, and the village of Tarasp-Fontana below Schloss Tarasp to form the leading resort in the Lower Engadine. Scuol is a spa (recommended for liver and bile ducts, stomach disorders, etc.), a health resort and a winter sports resort.

Sights

Bad Scuol Oberschuls, Spa Quarter	The heart of the resort is the lively little town of Bad Scuol or Schuls (1244 m/4094 ft), in a beautiful sunny setting on a gently sloping area of Alpine meadows. In the spa quarter, Oberschuls (Scuolsura), is the Badehaus

Engadine house in Bad Scuol   *Schloss Tarasp*

(Pump room), to which water of Vi, Sotsass and Clozza springs (high carbonic acid content) is piped. Extensions and additions to the spa centre are planned under the scheme "Scuol 2000".

In the old village of Unterschuls (Scuol-sot) are richly decorated old Engadine houses, the Protestant parish church of St George (1516) and the Lower Engadine Museum.   Unterschuls
On the south-west side of Scuol the Inn gorge is spanned by the Gurlaina viaduct (40 m/131 ft high). From here it is a half-hour walk to Vulpera.

Bad Tarasp, 2 km/1 mile south-west of Scuol, has sodium sulphate and   **Bad Tarasp**
chalybeate (iron-bearing) springs which are similar in their action to those
of Karlsbad. On the left bank of the Inn stand the large Kurhaus and the
Kurhotel, on the right bank the Trinkhalle (Pump room).
From here a road climbs 1 km/½ mile, with sharp turns, to Bad Vulpera   **Bad Vulpera**
(1268 m/4160 ft), a quiet little place beautifully situated on a narrow terrace
above the river, amid attractive parks and woodland.
From Vulpera a road winds up for 3 km/2 miles to the little village of   Tarasp-Fontana
Tarasp-Fontana (1444 m/4738 ft), delightfully set on a small lake.
Perched on a high schist crag is an imposing medieval castle, Schloss   *Schloss
Tarasp (1505 m/4938 ft), which became the residence of Austrian governors   Tarasp
and was much altered during the 16th–18th c. (restored 1907–16 by a
Dresden industrialist and made habitable; private property).
To the east is the Kreuzberg (Munt la Crusch, 1477 m/4846 ft), from which   *Kreuzberg
the best view of the castle is to be had.

Surroundings

From Bad Scuol a cableway 2.3 km/1 mile long leads up the Motta Naluns
(2136 m/7030 ft; restaurant; winter sports area), to the north-west.

Val Sinestra	Val Sinestra (11 km/7 miles to Bad Val Sinestra).
Sent	From the east end of Bad Scuol a road on the left climbs to 4 km/2 miles Sent (1440 m/4725 ft), a village with fine Engadine houses and the picturesque ruins of St Peter's chapel (12th c.), originally belonging to the castle. It is also a winter sports resort (ski-lift, toboggan run). The road continues (turn left beyond the village) into the deep and narrow Val Sinestra, running high above the River Brancla. 7 km/4 miles: Bad Val Sinestra (1471 m/4826 ft), in a sheltered setting among beautiful forests, with arsenical chalybeate (iron-bearing) springs.
Ftan	Ftan (6 km/4 miles west). From Oberschuls a road runs up the valley past the open-air swimming-pool and the lower station of the cableway, and then climbs steeply, with many turns, to the village of Ftan or Fetan (1648 m/5407 ft), a summer holiday place and winter resort (chair-lift, ski-lift) on a high terrace of meadowland on the north side of the valley, opposite Tarasp.
Val da S-charl	Val da S-charl (12 km/7 miles south). After crossing the Gurlaina viaduct a narrow road, straight ahead, winds its way up through the forest. 2 km/1 mile from Scuol a road branches off on the left (1 km/½ mile) to the farm of San Jon (1469 m/4834 ft), with fine views of the Inn valley and the Lischanna group. The road to S-charl continues through the beautiful Val da S-charl, the eastern boundary of the Swiss National Park (see entry). 10 km/6 miles: S-charl or Scarl (1813 m/5948 ft), a tiny village in a remote and beautiful setting.

Sierre   C2

	Canton: Valais (VS) Altitude: 538 m/1765 ft Population: 11,000
Situation and general	The little town of Sierre (German name Siders) in the Rhône valley, lies near the linguistic boundary between French and German. It is set amid vine-clad hills formed by a gigantic rock-fall in prehistoric times, facing the gorge-like mouth of the Val d'Anniviers. On the left bank of the Rhône, at Chippis, is a large aluminium plant.

Sights

Château des Vidomnes	In the main street is the 16th c. Château des Vidomnes, with four corner turrets, residence of the episcopal bailiffs (vice domini). Close by stands the church of Notre-Dame-des-Marais, which dates in its present form from the 15th to the 16th c; the Baroque parish church is 17th c. (restored 1947). The Château de Villa (16th c.), in the north-west of the town, contains one half of the Valais Wine Museum (the other half is in Salgessch).
Hôtel Château-Bellevue	Close to the railway station, in the north-west of the town, is the Hôtel Château-Bellevue (Rue de Bourg; restaurant). Built in the 17th–18th c. and restored in the 20th c. it houses a collection of pewter and the Rilke room with mementoes of the poet Rainer Maria Rilke (1875–1926).
Tour de Goubing	On a commanding crag (590 m/1936 ft) above the town to the east is the massive Tour de Goubing (13th c.).
Carthusian monastery	To the south, on a rocky hill above the two Lacs de Géronde (bathing lido), stands the former Carthusian monastery of Géronde.

Surroundings

To the *Val d'Anniviers

(German Eifischtal: 26 km/16 miles to Zinai, on a good road.) Leave Sierre on the road up the Rhône valley to Visp and in 2 km/1 mile, at Pfynwald, turn right onto a road which climbs steeply uphill, with numerous hairpin turns. Below, to the right, is the Chippis aluminium plant.

(900 m/2953 ft), situated high above the River Navigenze or Navisence, which flows down through the Val d'Anniviers. The road then skirts the mouth of the Pontis gorge (short tunnel), beyond which is the Sentier de Sussillon viewpoint (1029 m/3376 ft). From here a steep and narrow road on the left climbs up (3 km/2 miles) to Susillon (1386 m/4547 ft), from which it is a 2 hours' walk to Chandolin (1936 m/6352 ft), one of the highest mountain villages in Switzerland, with a superb view (road from St-Luc). The road up the Val d'Anniviers continues to the hamlet of Fang (1095 m/3593 ft), above the road on the right. Beyond this Chandolin can be seen high up on the left.

Niouc

Susillon
Chandolin

Vissoie (1221 m/4006 ft) is the chief place in the valley (pop. 400); it has a square stone tower dating from the 14th c. From here it is worth making an excursion on a road to the left which runs steeply up in seven hairpin bends (gradients of up to 12%, 1 in 8) to the village of St-Luc, 6 km/4 miles east (1643 m/5391 ft), situated on a steeply sloping expanse of Alpine meadows. This is a popular health and winter sports resort (several ski-lifts) with magnificent views of the Val d'Anniviers and its ring of mountains and over the Rhône valley to the Bernese Alps. Above the village is the Pierre des Sauvages (1714 m/5624 ft), with prehistoric engravings.

Vissoie

St-Luc

Chair-lift to the Alm Tignousa (2050 m/6726 ft; restaurant). Rewarding climb (4 hours) to summit of Bella Tola (3028 m/9935 ft), with a superb view over the Bernese and Valais Alps to Mont Blanc. From St-Luc a road runs 5.5 km/3 miles north to Chandolin.

*Bella Tola

From Vissoie a side road on the right (8 km/5 miles) descends to a bridge over the Navigenze and continues along the left bank to the little village of

Grimentz

Sierre: Château des Vidomnes

Entrance to St Catherine's Church

Grimentz in the Val d'Anniviers

Grimentz (1570 m/5151 ft; bypass), picturesquely situated on a little mountain stream, the Marais, above the mouth of the Val de Moiry. The village is a popular summer vacation spot, and also attracts winter sports enthusiasts (ski-lift).

Lac de Moiry

The road continues south and in 5 km/3 miles reaches the artificial Lac de Moiry (capacity c. 75 million cu. m/2648 million cu. ft; parking place by the lake, beyond a short tunnel; restaurant near the dam). It then follows the east side of the lake to the Moiry glacier (2350 m/7710 ft), 4 km/2 miles from the dam. From here it is a 1½ hours' climb south-east to the Moiry hut (2850 m/9351 ft).

Quimet, Mission

The road up the Val d'Anniviers continues from Vissoie along the right bank of the Navigenze to the hamlets of Quimet and Mission (1307 m/4288 ft), opposite the mouth of the Val de Moiry.

Ayer

It then climbs with a double hairpin to Ayer (1484 m/4869 ft), a large village of Valais-style houses preserved intact, which is surrounded by forest and Alpine meadows.

Zinal

From here it is 5 km/3 miles up the highest section of the valley, the Val de Zinal, to Zinal (1678 m/5506 ft), a popular climbers' base, health resort, winter sports centre (ice-rink, toboggan run) in a magnificent mountain setting. At the head of the valley is the Zinal or Durand glacier (1¾ hours), and above it tower the Zinal-Rothorn (4221 m/13,849 ft; 12 hours, with guide), the jagged twin peaks of Besso (3668 m/12,035 ft; 9 hours, with guide), the Pointe de Zinal (3806 m/12,487 ft; 9 hours, with guide) and the Dent Blanche (4357 m/14,295 ft; 15 hours, with guide, very difficult).

Climbs

To the west of the Zinal-Rothorn is a Swiss Alpine Club hut, the Cabine du Mountet (2886 m/9469 ft; 5 hours from Zinal). Easier climbs are to the Alpe de la Lex (2188 m/7179 ft; 2 hours) and the Roc de la Vache (2587 m/8488 ft;

3 hours), which both afford splendid views; 1½–2 hours north-east of the Roc de la Vache is another SAC hut, the Cabane de Tracuit (3256 m/10,683 ft). From the near end of Zinal a cabin cableway (2000 m/6562 ft) ascends to the Alpe de Sorebois (2470 m/8104 ft; restaurant), a good skiing area (two ski-tows up to 2900 m/9515 ft).

From Sierre via Montana-Vermala to Crans

A funicular goes up via St-Maurice-de-Laques (change cars) to Montana (4.2 km/2 miles, gradient 39%, (1 in 2), 30 minutes).

There is also a well-engineered road to Crans (15 km/9 miles) which winds its way up the steep hillside through vineyards and forest. From the first bend there is a view of the little Château de Muzot (not open to the public), in which the German poet Rainer Maria Rilke lived at one time.
4 km/2 miles: Venthône (813 m/2667 ft), a picturesque village with a Gothic church. 5 km/3 miles: Randogne (1250 m/4101 ft), with the Montana sanatoria (pulmonary tuberculosis, tuberculosis of the bones and joints).

Venthône,
Randogne

4.5 km/3 miles: Montana (1500 m/4922 ft; see Crans-Montana). 1.5 km/1 mile north, higher up, is Vermala (1680 m/5512 ft; see Crans-Montana). 1.5 km/1 mile west of Montana is the separate resort of Crans sur Sierre (1480–1500 m/4856–5922 ft; see Crans-Montana).

Montana
Vermala
Crans sur Sierre

From here an excellent road, with extensive views, runs south-west to Lens (5 km/3 miles), a small health resort in a commanding situation, and from there to Sion (see entry).

Lens

Sion

From Sierre to Vercorin (18 km/11 miles)

The road runs south from Sierre and over the Rhône to Chippis (2 km/1 mile; 534 m/1752 ft), at the entrance to the Val d'Anniviers, where there is a large aluminium plant (Alusuisse).

Chippis

From here a road runs 3.5 km/2 miles down the Rhône valley to Chalais (521 m/1709 ft), at the near end of which, on left, is a cableway up to Vercorin (1820 m/5971 ft, 7 minutes).

Chalais

From Chalais a winding mountain road, with sharp bends and two tunnels, continues up 10.5 km/7 miles to Vercorin (1342 m/4403 ft), a beautiful old village 800 m/2625 ft above the Rhône valley. A cableway runs south to Sigeroula (1865 m/6119 ft). Still farther south is Mont Tracuit (2332 m/7651 ft).

*Vercorin

Simmental   C2

Canton: Berne (BE)

The Upper Simmental extends down from Lenk in the Bernese Oberland by way of Zweisimmen to Weissenbach, going almost due north; the Lower Simmental then turns east, bounded on the north-west by the steep limestone crags of the Fribourg Alps. At Spiez the valley opens out and the River Simme flows into Lake Thun. With its handsome timber houses, its typically "Oberland" church towers, its herds of cattle (the famous Simmentaler breed) and its Alpine meadows dotted with huts, the Simmental is a very characteristic stretch of Bernese farming country.

Situation and general

At the west end of Spiez (see Lake Thun) turn off the lakeside road to Thun into road 11 (on left), which climbs, with a fine view of the Niesen (2367 m/7766 ft), to Spiezwiler (652 m/2139 ft), where the Kandertal road goes off on the left via Mülenen (7 km/4 miles; funicular up the Niesen) to Kandersteg and Adelboden.

Spiez
*Niesen

Simmentaler Hof, near Därstetten

Road 11 continues straight ahead and then curves down to enter the valley of the Kander, which it crosses (to the left a view of the Blümisalp, 3671 m/12,045 ft).

Wimmis

It then continues through wooded country to Wimmis (631 m/2070 ft), below the north side of the Niesen, with attractive old wooden houses and a 10th c. church. Above the village on the Burgfluh stands the imposing Weissenburg Castle (14th c.), which now houses the Nieder-Simmental communal offices (on the ground floor a room furnished in Simmental style).

Weissenburg Castle

Beyond Wimmis the road passes the end of a section of motorway and crosses the Simme to join a road coming in from Thun on the right. It then continues alongside an artificial lake, the Simmensee, and through the Port, a narrow passage between the high rock walls of the Burgfluh (990 m/3248 ft) and the Simmenfluh (1456 m/4777 ft). Now in the Lower Simmental, it ascends on a moderate gradient, with a view of the Jungfrau area to the left, to Latterbach (703 m/2307 ft), in the commune of Erlenbach.

Lower Simmental

From here an attractive detour can be made on a narrow road to the left which runs through Oey and then 14 km/9 miles south-west up the Diemtigtal to the Grimmi-Alp (1222 m/4009 ft), with far-ranging views, from which the Seehorn (2283 m/7491 ft; 3 hours) and the Männifluh (2654 m/8708 ft; 4½ hours) can be climbed (fine views from both peaks).

Grimmi-Alp

Erlenbach

Erlenbach (707 m/2320 ft) is a typical Simmental village, with 18th c. timber houses. Situated on high ground is its old church (11th–13th c.), with an octagonal steeple (fine wall-paintings, mainly 15th c., with some late 13th c. work at the south-east corner of the nave). Important cattle markets. A cableway 4040 m/13,255 ft long runs north, via an intermediate station at Chrindi (1640 m/5381 ft; restaurant), to the Stockhorn (2190 m/7185 ft; upper station 2160 m/7087 ft: restaurant; mountain hut, magnificent view) in 15 minutes (on foot 4½ hours).

Därstätten

5 km/3 miles beyond Erlenbach lies the village of Därstätten, also with fine 18th c. timber houses on the south bank of the Simme (in particular Haus

Zweisimmen: Heimatmuseum

Knutti, 1756). 2.5 km/2 miles north-west in Nidfluh (920 m/3019 ft) is the oldest farmhouse in the Simmental (1642). · Nidfluh

Weissenburg (776 m/2546 ft). 1.5 km/1 mile north-west is Weissenburgbad (844 m/2769 ft), a former spa (sulphurous spring, 31° C/88° F) which no longer operates. From Weissenburg the main road continues steadily uphill through a wooded valley, with villages situated on a terrace higher up on the right. It then comes to Boltigen (830 m/2723 ft), in a wider part of the valley, with the precipitous limestone peak of the Mittagfluh (1890 m/6201 ft) rearing above it. · Weissenburg · Boltigen

Beyond this, at Reidenbach (840 m/2756 ft), a road goes off on the right over the Jaun pass to Bulle and Lausanne. · Reidenbach

The main road continues up through the green Alpine meadows of the Simmental to Weissenbach (846 m/2776 ft), and 2 km/1 mile beyond this through a narrow passage which separates the Lower from the Upper Simmental. Beyond the crag of Laubeggstalden (ruined castle; waterfall on the Simme) the valley opens out again. The road passes the ruined castle of Mannenberg (1016 m/3333 ft), on the left. · Weissenbach

It then comes in to Zweisimmen (954 m/3130 ft; pop. 3000), the chief place in the Upper Simmental, situated in a wide expanse of meadows at the junction of the Grosse and Kleine Simme. The little town attracts many summer visitors, but is particularly favoured by winter sports enthusiasts (30 km/19 miles of cross-country skiing; toboggan run; indoor tennis courts). It has a fine church with a typical Simmental tower (15th c.; 15th–16th c. stained glass). Cableway (5.1 km/3 miles, 30 minutes) up the Rinderberg. To the west is the Hundsrügg (2049 m/6723 ft; 4 hours), with extensive views. · Zweisimmen

From Zweisimmen the main road continues to Saanen (see Gstaad), while the road to Lenk through the Upper Simmental branches off on the left, · Upper Simmental running alongside the Grosse Simme to Betelried (960 m/3150 ft), with the 18th c. Schloss Blankenburg (local government offices).

It then continues to St Stephan (996 m/3268 ft; 15th c. church), with the Wildstrubel (3253 m/10,673 ft) in the background, and to Matten (1026 m/3366 ft), at the mouth of the Fermelbach valley.

Lenk

5 km/3 miles farther on (views of Wildstrubel) is Lenk (1068 m/3504 ft; pop. 2000), in a beautiful setting of woodland and meadows at the head of the Upper Simmental, with the grandiose bulk of the Wildstrubel closing the valley to the south. Lenk is a health and winter sports resort (ice-rink, curling, cross-country skiing) and also a spa (sulphurous springs). The spa establishment lies to the south-west of the village.

Mülkerblatten

Cableway (3698 m/12,133 ft, 26 minutes) via intermediate stations at Stoss and Betelberg (1650 m/5414 ft; restaurant) to the Leiterli station on the Mülkerblatten (2000 m/6562 ft), with beautiful views and good skiing. From the Wallbach a chair-lift (3241 m/10,634 ft, 28 minutes) also provides access to the Mülkerblatten via an intermediate station at Wallegg (1580 m/5184 ft).

*Iffigen Falls,
Iffigenalp
*Wildhorn

*Wildstrubel

A narrow road (8 km/5 miles; alternate one-way traffic) runs south from Lenk up the Pöschenried valley, past the Iffigen Falls (130 m/427 ft high) to the Iffigenalp (1618 m/5309 ft). From here there are rewarding climbs (not difficult for experienced climbers, with guide) by way of the Wildhorn hut (2315 m/7596 ft) up the Wildhorn (3248 m/10,657 ft; 6 hours) and by way of the Wildstrubel hut (2793 m/9164 ft) up the Wildstrubel (west peak 3251 m/10,667 ft, east peak 3253 m/10,673 ft; 7 hours), from both of which there are magnificent views of the Valais Alps and the Mont Blanc group.

Simme Falls
Siebenbrunnen

A new road (N 6) is planned to run through a tunnel 4 km /2 miles long into the Valais. Another road leads south-east from Lenk up the Simme valley, past a cableway to Metsch (1480 m/4856 ft), to Höhenhaus (5 km/3 miles; 1103 m/3619 ft), at the head of the valley. From here a footpath (1 hour) ascends past the Simme Falls to the huts on the Räzliberg (1404 m/4607 ft; restaurant), near which the Siebenbrunnen (1446 m/4744 ft), the main source of the Simme, gushes out of seven clefts in the rock walls of the Fluhhorn (2139 m/7018 ft).

Bühlberg,
Hahnenmoos

Finally a road running east from Lenk climbs with steep bends to the Bühlberg restaurant (6 km/4 miles; 1660 m/5446 ft), from which it is an hour's climb to the Hahnenmoos pass (1957 m/6421 ft).

Simplon Pass   D2

Canton: Valais (VS)
Height of pass: 2005 m/6578 ft

Situation and
general

The road to the Simplon pass (Italian Passo del Sempione), constructed on Napoleon's orders between 1801 and 1805, is the shortest route between Valais and southern Ticino or northern Italy. The road is usually open throughout the year; but it is always possible for motorists to avoid the pass by loading their cars on to the train which runs through the 19.8 km/12 mile long Simplon tunnel between Brig and Iselle (Italy).

Over the Simplon pass to Domodossola (Italy)

The road, which offers a tremendous scenic experience, ascends from the old town of Brig, at an important road junction in the Upper Rhône valley, with numerous turns and constantly changing views of the deep tributary valleys of the Saltina and the magnificent peaks of the southern Bernese Alps, and continues over the pass and down to Domodossola (Italy) and Locarno.

Simplon Pass road

The Simplon road (64 km/40 miles to Domodossola) branches off the Rhône valley road at Brig and winds its way up towards the towering Glishorn (2528 m/8294 ft), with beautiful views of Brig (see entry) to the rear. It then climbs the Briger Berg in the direction of the Klenenhorn (2695 m/8842 ft), affording an attractive view, to the left, of Brig and the Rhône valley. Ahead is the Belalp, with the Sparrhorn (3026 m/9928 ft) rearing above it; to the left the Nesthorn (3820 m/12,533 ft), and to the right, higher up, the conical peak of the Eggishorn (2934 m/9626 ft).

*Simplon road

Brig

Beyond Ried-Brig (938 m/3078 ft) the road continues uphill through wooded country, passing under a cableway to Rosswald (2000 m/6562 ft) to the south-east. At the Schallberg Refuge hut (Schutzhaus II, 1320 m/4331 ft) the view of the pass, with the Bellevue Hotel opens up. To the rear are the Bernese Alps, from the Bietschhorn to the Aletschhorn.

Schallberg
Refuge Hut

The road now curves round into the wooded Ganter valley, beyond which (from left to right) are the Bortelhorn (3194 m/10,480 ft), Furggenbaumhorn (2991 m/9813 ft) and Wasenhorn (3246 m/10,650 ft).

Ganter valley

Berisal (1526 m/5007 ft), a little hamlet with accommodation for summer visitors. The road continues to wind its way up the mountainside through forests of larch, with beautiful views of the Bernese Alps. At Rothwald (1750 m/5742 ft; inn) the magnificent summit of the Fletschhorn (3996 m/13,111 ft) comes into view above the pass (to right).
100 m/328 ft further on a side road on the left runs up through the forest (0.5 km/¼ mile) to the commandingly situated Taferna Hotel.

Berisal

Rothwald
*Fletschhorn

The main road now makes straight for the pass, running high above the Taverbach, with beautiful views down into the valley on the right. Schallberg Refuge Hut (Schutzhaus V, 1934 m/6345 ft). The Simplon pass (2005 m/6578 ft; Hotel Bellevue and Simplon-Blick) is a ridge covered with Alpine meadows at the foot of the glaciated Monte Leone (3553 m/11,657 ft;

*Simplon Pass

7 hours, with guide) and the black rock walls of the Hübschhorn (3192 m/10,473 ft), lying closer to the pass.

The road now crosses a fairly level stretch of ground, passing a large stone eagle on a mound to the right which commemorates the manning of the frontier by Swiss troops during the Second World War. Beyond this, on the left, is the Simplon Hospice (2001 m/6565 ft), established by Napoleon, which has been occupied since 1825 by monks from the Great St Bernard Hospice (see Great St Bernard).

Simplon
Hospice

The road then descends the wide valley of the Krummbach, enclosed by snow-covered mountains, with fine views of the magnificent Fletschhorn. Below the road on the right can be seen the tall building of the Altes Spital (Old Hospice; 1872 m/6142 ft), established about 1660 by Kaspar Stockalper, the great merchant prince of Brig (see entry).

At the Engeloch (1795 m/5889 ft) the road leads down to the valley floor, crosses the Krummbach (1617 m/5305 ft) to Eggen (1660 m/5250 ft), at the mouth of the Rossboden or Sengbach valley, from which there was a devastating rock fall and avalanche from the Rossboden glacier in 1901.

Eggen,
Rossboden
valley

Simplon Dorf
Simplon Dorf (Italian Sempione, 1479 m/4853 ft) is beautifully situated in an expanse of green Alpine meadows in a wider part of the valley. To the east is Monte Leone, to the south the Fletschhorn (3996 m/13,111 ft) and Weissmies (4023 m/13,199 ft).

Gabi or Gstein
Gabi or Gstein (1232 m/4042 ft) is situated at the confluence of the Krummbach and Laggienbach, forming the Diviera or Doviera River, which the road now follows downstream. Beyond the Gabi gallery is the rugged

*Gondo Gorge
Gondo gorge, one of the wildest and deepest ravine roads in the Alps. The road continues through the Gondo gallery and crosses the Alpienbach, which flows down from the Alpien glacier on Monte Leone, forming beautiful waterfalls.

Gondo
Gondo (858 m/2815 ft), picturesquely situated below the rock walls of the ravine opposite the mouth of the Zwischenbergen valley (waterfall), is the last village in Switzerland (customs; Swiss passport control). The church dates only from 1968, but has an older choir; the high square tower was built by the Stockalper family of Brig about 1660 for the protection of travellers.

Val Divedro
1 km/½ mile beyond this is the Swiss-Italian frontier (800 m/2625 ft; Italian passport and customs control). From here the road runs down the valley, now known as the Val Divedro, to Iselle (657 m/2156 ft). At Iselle station, 1 km/½ mile beyond the village, the railway emerges from the southern end of the Simplon tunnel; cars loaded here for Brig.

Iselle

Valle d'Ossola
After passing through Crévola d'Ossola the road runs in a long straight stretch through the wide and fertile valley of the Toce, here known as the Valle d'Ossola, in which the vegetation already has a southern character (chestnut, fig and mulberry trees, fields of maize, vineyards), and comes to

Domodossola
Domodossola (278 m/912 ft), a town of 20,000 inhabitants, with an attractive market square, the Piazza del Mercato. From here a road runs east through the Val Centovalli to Locarno (see entry).

Sion   C2

Canton: Valais (VS)
Altitude: 520 m/1706 ft
Population: 25,000

Situation and
general
Sion (German Sitten), capital of Valais, occupies the site of the Roman town of Sedunum and has been the see of a bishop since the 6th c. It is now an important market town for the wine (Provins Valais depot; conducted tours), fruit and vegetables of the fertile Rhône valley , with many features

Sion: Rue du Grand-Port   *Château de Tourbillon*

of interest. The old town is built on the detrital fan of the river Sionne, dominated by two picturesque castle-crowned crags. Here the river Borgne, coming from the Val d'Hérens to the south, flows into the Rhône, carrying down boulders and scree which the Rhône has thrust against its northern bank.

Sights

In the spacious Place de la Planta are the Palais du Gouvernement (cantonal offices) and a monument commemorating the centenary of Valais' adms sion into the Confederation (1815).

Place de la Planta

At 7 rue de Conthey stands the Maison Supersaxo, built by Georg Supersaxo, the provincial governor, in 1505; it has a fine hall with an elaborately carved and painted ceiling.

Maison Supersaxo

In the main street, Rue du Grand-Pont, which is built over the conduited river Sionne, is the Hôtel de Ville (Town Hall, 1660), with an astronomical clock. Built into the hall on the ground floor are a number of Roman inscribed stones, including one of A.D. 377 which is the earliest evidence of Christianity in Switzerland.

Rue de Grand-Pont
Town Hall

To the north-east the Cathedral of Notre-Dame-du-Glarier, was rebuilt in the 15th c. and has a 12th c. Romanesque tower. It contains 15th c. bishops' tombs and 17th c. choir-stalls; among the many valuable items in the treasury are a number of reliquaries of the 8th–10th c. In 1988 the great organ, a more than 100-year-old masterpiece by the famous organ builder Carlen of Reckingen, was brought back into service after being restored.

Cathedral Notre-Dame-du-Glarier

Facing the cathedral, to the south-west, is the church of St Théodule, a sober building of 1516. The Bishop's Palace (Evêché) on the west side of the square was rebuilt in 1840.

St Théodule's Church,
Bishop's Palace

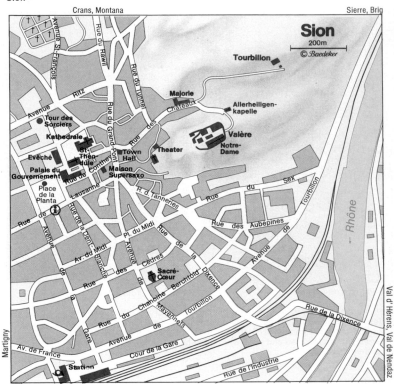

Crans, Montana   Sierre, Brig

Tour des Sorciers	From here the narrow Rue de la Tour runs north to the Tour des Sorciers (Wizard's Tower, 12th c.), a relic of the medieval fortifications. Close by, at the junction of Rue de Gravelone and Avenue St-François, stands the Muli (Mule) monument (by M.-E. Sandoz, 1966).
Grenette Cultural Centre	In 1988 a cultural centre was opened in the Grenette building (1860) with capacity for concerts, exhibitions and other performances.
Natural History Museum	At 40 Avenue de la Gare there is an interesting Museum of Natural History with geology, mineralogy, botany and zoological departments (dinosaur finds, 1979).

From the Town Hall another narrow street, Rue des Châteaux (No. 19 Cantonal Museum of Art), leads up to the castles. (It is possible to drive as far as the All Saints chapel and park there.) On the left are the remains of the

Valais Museum of Art — Château de la Majorie, which now houses the Valais Museum of Art. In front of the castle is a monument to St Theodulus (Bishop of Valais).

Museum of Antiquities — The Museum of Antiquities is at No. 12 Place de la Majorie with prehistoric finds and Gallo-Romanic exhibitions.

Beyond this is All Saints chapel (Tous-les-Saints), still in Romanesque style though it was built as late as 1325 (with some 17th c. rebuilding). From here it is a few minutes' walk to the Château de Tourbillon). The Château de

*Notre-Dame-de-Valère — Valère (621 m/2038 ft) and the former collegiate church of Notre-Dame-de-Valère (12th–13th c.), built on Roman foundations, combine to form an

Early-Romanesque architecture . . .   *. . . of the priory church of St-Pierre de Clages*

impressive architectural group (floodlit on summer evenings). The church is a three-aisled pillared basilica, with fantastically decorated capitals in the choir; the carved wooden altar is 16th c., the beautifully carved choir-stalls 17th c., the stone rood-screen 13th c., and the organ, in a painted loft, 15th c. (one of the oldest that can still be played). Beside the church is the cantonal Musée de Valère with Roman antiquities and medieval sculpture.

Musée de la Valère

On the higher of the two hills above the town (655 m/2149 ft) are the imposing ruins of the Château de Tourbillon (built 1294, destroyed by fire 1788), from which there is a view embracing the Rhône valley from Leuk in the east to Martigny in the west.

Château de Tourbillon

Surroundings

Road 9 runs down the Rhône valley via the wine-producing village of Vétrcz to St-Pierre-de-Clages (526 m/1726 ft), which has a church of the 11th-12th c. with an octagonal tower, one of the finest Romanesque churches in the country (stained glass of 1948).

*St-Pierre-de-Clages

Saint-Pierre -de-Clages

Nave   Crossing Tower   Choir

Plan of Romanesque Church
(Founded *c.* 407; first mentioned in 1152)

10 m   © *Baedeker*

Sion

To the Val de Nendaz

(16 km/10 miles to Haute-Nendaz, 27 km/17 miles to the Lac de Cleuson.) Leave Sion on the Val d'Herens road and after crossing the Rhône take a road on the right which gradually leads uphill and comes in 5 km/3 miles to

Arvilard
Baar

Arvilard (684 m/2244 ft), where a road branches off on the left to Mayens de Sion. 1 km/½ mile: Baar (738 m/2421 ft), beyond which the road turns south into the narrow Val de Nendaz. 2 km/ 1 mile: Brignon (895 m/2936 ft). 2 km/ 1 mile: Basse-Nendaz (992 m/3255 ft).

Haute-Nendaz

Haute-Nendaz (1370 m/4495 ft), a holiday and skiing resort high above the Rhône valley. Cableway (2270 m/7448 ft, 12 minutes) to Tracouet (2200 m/7218 ft; skiing), at the foot of the Dent de Nendaz (2463 m/8081 ft; 2–3 hours).

Le Bleusy
Siviez

The road continues south up the valley above an irrigation channel (bisse). 2km/1 mile: Le Bleusy (1412 m/4633 ft), with a chapel. 3 km/2 miles: L'Antie (1565 m/5135 ft). 3 km/2 miles Siviez (1758 m/5770 ft; several ski-lifts). From here a road (2 km/1 mile) runs to the Alpe de Tortin (2039 m/6690 ft), from which there is a cableway (2280 m/7481 ft, 12 minutes) to the Col de Chassoure (2734 m/8970 ft); from there a chair-lift to the Lac des Vaux. Cableway from Tortin-Col des Gentianes to Mont Fort.

Lac de Cleuson

Lac de Cleuson (2115 m/6939 ft), an artificial lake 1200 m/3937 ft long created in 1958.

Thyon 2000

From Beuson a steep and narrow mountain road climbs 3.5 km/2 miles to Veysonnaz (1233 m/4045 ft), from which a cableway ascends to the holiday and winter sports resort of Thyon 2000 (2068 m/6785 ft; blocks of flats; indoor swimming pool, ski-lifts), which can also be reached by road (13 km/8 miles) from Vex via Les Collons (1800 m/5906 ft).

To Mayens de Sion

Mayens de Sion

(15 km/9 miles.) At Arvilard (5km/3 miles) on the Val de Nendaz road turn left into a road which climbs in large bends via Salins (847 m/2779 ft) to (13 km/8 miles) Les Agettes (1030 m/3379 ft). 2 km/1 mile Mayens de Sion (1300–1400 m/4265–4593 ft), a summer village of chalets widely dispersed over the Alpine meadows, which are supplied with water by irrigation channels (bisses). Magnificent views of the Bernese Alps, in particular the Wildhorn (3248 m/10,657 ft), due north above Sion.

To the Lac de Tseuzier

(23 km/14 miles: the Rawil road.) The road runs up the Sionne valley and then climbs in sharp turns up the east side of the valley. 3.5 km/2 miles: Champlan (714 m/2343 ft), a village surrounded by vineyards. 2.5 km/2

Grimisuat

miles Grimisuat (881 m/2891 ft), on a rocky spur. From here a narrow mountain road ascends steeply to Arbaz (1146 m/3760 ft), immediately above Grimisuat to the north.

Ayent

3.5 km/2 miles: Ayent (978 m/3209 ft), a widely scattered settlement made up of a number of separate villages. Road to Crans via Lens. In neighbouring La Giète (1154 m/3786 ft) the road goes off on the left to Anzère (see below). The main road now climbs up through the forest in two large bends. 7 km/4 miles: Praz Combeira (1620 m/5315 ft), beyond which the

Lac de Tseuzier

road passes through three tunnels. 4 km/2 miles: Lac de Tseuzier (1777 m/5830 ft), an artificial lake (1956–58) 1 km/½ mile long and 600 m/1969 ft across, in wild and lonely country. A footpath follows the west side of the lake.

Anzère

From La Giète a road (5 km/3 miles) goes up to Anzère or Antsère (1500 m/4922 ft), a developing winter sports resort beautifully set on a mountain terrace (ski-lifts). Cableway (2180 m/7153 ft) to the Pas de Maimbré (2362

*Wildhorn

m/7750 ft; view; ski-runs). To the north is the Wildhorn (3248 m/10,657 ft),

Val d'Hérens: earth pillars near Euseigne

the highest peak in the western Bernese Oberland (5½ hours, with guide).
Several chair-lifts.

To the Col du Sanetsch

(27 km/17 miles; to the Sanetschsee 32 km/20 miles.) Road 2–6 m/7–20 ft
wide, maximum gradient 18% (1 in 5½); closed in winter. The winding road
runs north-west from Sion through vineyards. 5km/3 miles: St Germain
(820 m/2690 ft). The road then passes through the commandingly situated
villages of Granois (857 m/2812 ft) and Chandolin (818 m/2684 ft) and turns
north above the wild valley of the Morge 6 km/4 miles: Pont du Diable (919
m/3015 ft), where it crosses to the right bank. It then continues winding its
way uphill, crosses the Morge again and later the Nétage, and climbs, with
many turns to (16 km/10 miles) the Col du Sanetsch or Col de Senin (2243   Col du Sanetsch
m/7359 ft), on a ridge between the Arpelistock (3035 m/9958 ft) to the east
and the Sanetschhorn (Mont Brun. 2942 m/9653 ft) to the west. From both
of these peaks (respectively 3½ and 2½ hours' climb from the pass) there
are magnificent views. The road continues for another 5 km/3 miles to the
dam (42 m/138 ft high) at the north end of the Sanetschsee, a reservoir (2.7   Sanetschsee
million cu. m/95 million cu. ft) on the upper course of the River Saane
(Sarine).

The Val d'Hérens

(52 km/32 miles to Les Haudères) The road runs south-east from Sion,
turns right over the Rhône bridge towards Val d'Hérens.
Vex (957 m/3140 ft; pronounced Veh) is commandingly situated high above   Vex
the gorge of the Borgne, which flows down through the Val d'Hérens A
narrow road goes off on the right and ascends the Val d'Hérémence,
running from above the Val d'Hérens road to the picturesque village of

Sion

Hérémence

Hérémence (1236 m/4055 ft), with the church of St Nicolas (by W. M. Förderer, 1963–71).

Val
d'Hérémence
Motôt
Grand-Dixence
Dam

The road continues up the Val d'Hérémence via Pralong (1608 m/5276 ft) to Motôt (1925 m/6316 ft), with a parking place (1970 m/6464 ft). From here it is a 2 hours' walk (also private road, 5.5 km/3 miles) to the Grande-Dixence dam (2365 m/7760 ft; completed 1961; 284 m/932 ft high; top 748 m/2454 ft long, 15 m/49 ft wide, in the Val des Dix. Its water is carried in underground tunnels to the Fionnay power station and beyond this, under pressure, to the main power station at Nendaz in the Rhône valley. At the end of the road, beneath the dam, is a hotel and restaurant with a large car park. From here a cableway runs up to the lake (motor-boat). At the southern end of the lake is an iron suspension bridge. Prominent among the peaks forming the magnificent mountain setting of the lake are the Rosablanche (3336 m/10,945 ft), Mont Blanc de Cheilon (3871 m/12,701 ft) and the Aiguilles Rouges d'Arolla (3650 m/11,976 ft).
Walks: along the lake (2½ hours); to the Cabane des Dix (4 hours; by boat 2 hours); to the Col de Riematten (4 hours); to Arolla (6 hours).

*Val d'Hérens
*Earth Pillars

The road to Les Haudères continues along the hillside, following an almost level but winding course. On the opposite side of the valley is the pretty village of Vernamiège. After crossing the River Dixence, coming from the Val d'Hérémence, the road turns into the Val d'Hérens (German Eringertal) and passes through a tunnel under a series of earth pillars, columns of morainic debris which have been protected from erosion by a large boulder or capstone.

Euseigne

Euseigne or Useigne (970 m/3183 ft): road on right into Val d'Hérémence. On the opposite side of the valley is the village of St-Martin.

La Luette

Praz-Jean

La Luette (1020 m/3347 ft), beyond which the road crosses the grey waters of the Borgne on a high bridge, the Pont Noir de Lugnerez (1001 m/3284 ft). 1 km/½ mile farther up the valley, at Praz-Jean (1100 m/3609 ft), a narrow road goes off on the left and passes through a number of hamlets and the villages of St-Martin and Mase, standing high above the right bank of the Borgne and offering fine views. The road then runs down in steep bends to Bramois and across the Rhône to Sion (5 km/3 miles).

Evolène

*Sasseneire

The Val d'Hérens road continues to Evolène (1378 m/4521 ft), the chief town in the valley (pop. 1500) and a popular holiday resort, lying in the wide green stretch of valley between Sasseneire (3259 m/10,693 ft; 5½ hours with guide) to the east and the Pic d'Arzinol (3001 m/9846 ft; 5–5½ hours) and the Mont de l'Etoile (3372 m/11,064 ft; 6 hours, with guide) to the west. Higher up the valley the view is dominated by the bold outline of the Dents de Veisivi and the massive Dent Blanche (to left).

Les Haudères

The road continues along the right bank of the Borgne and in 4 km/2 miles reaches Les Haudères (1433 m/4702 ft), a health resort. It is the highest village in the Val d'Hérens, which divides at this point into the Val d'Arolla and the Combe de Ferpècle.

Arolla

A good road ascends the Val d'Arolla to Arolla, properly Mayens d'Arolla (1962 m/6437 ft), winter sports and mountain resort (ski-lifts, cross-country skiing, toboggan run, curling) magnificently set facing the Pigne d'Arolla (3801 m/12,471 ft; 5–6 hours) and Mont Collon (3644 m/11,956 ft; 7 hours, with guide).

Ferpècle

A narrow and sometimes steep road runs up the Combe de Ferpècle from Les Haudères to the huts of Ferpècle or Salay (6.5 km/4 miles, 1800 m/5906 ft), near the end of twin glaciers, the Glacier du Mont Miné and the Glacier de Ferpècle.

*Alp Bricolla

From here it is a 2 hours' climb to the Alpe de Bricolla (2462 m/7960 ft), with the Dent Blanche (4364 m/14,318 ft; 9–10 hours, with guide) rearing above it on the left, and the Glacier du Mont Miné, with the Dents de Bertol, the Aiguille de la Za (3673 m/12,051 ft) and the Dents de Veisivi (3425 m/11,237 ft; 5½–6 hours).

Solothurn/Soleure C1

Canton: Solothurn (SO)
Altitude: 442 m/1450 ft
Population: 15,800

Solothurn (French Soleure), capital of the canton of the same name, lies astride the river Aare at the foot of the Jura hills. Numerous Renaissance and Baroque buildings bear witness to the one-time splendour of the town, which in the 16th, 17th and 18th centuries was the residence of the French ambassadors to the Confederation.
The number 11 is significant for Solothurn. It was the 11th canton to join the Confederation in 1481, there are 11 churches and chapels, 11 historic fountains and 11 towers. St Ursen Cathedral has 11 altars and 11 bells and its staircase is divided into sections each with 11 steps.

Situation and general

The town of Salodurum ranked with Trier in Germany as one of the oldest Roman settlements north of the Alps. In A.D. 303 two members of the Theban Legion, Ursus and Victor, were martyred here. Solothurn joined the Swiss Confederation in 1481.

History

Sights

Just inside the Baseltor (Basle Gate, 1508), where the Baselstrasse enters the old town, stands the Cathedral of St Ursen (St Ursus: 1763–73), in Italian Baroque style, which has been the cathedral of the diocese of Basle since 1830.
On the ground floor of the 60 m/197 ft high tower is the rich Treasury containing goldsmiths' work, textiles of 15th–19th c. and papal coins. On

*St-Ursen Cathedral

*Treasury

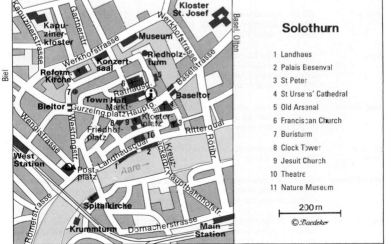

Solothurn

1 Landhaus
2 Palais Besenval
3 St Peter
4 St Ursen' Cathedral
5 Old Arsenal
6 Franciscan Church
7 Buristurm
8 Clock Tower
9 Jesuit Church
10 Theatre
11 Nature Museum

200 m

© Baedeker

395

Solothurn: St Peter's Chapel and cathedral   *Statue of St Ursen on a fountain*

the steps leading up to the cathedral are two fountains with figures of Moses and Gideon.

Old Arsenal   The Old Arsenal (Altes Zeughaus, 1610–14), north-west of the cathedral, houses the largest collection of arms and armour of Europe. The extensive arsenal has weapons and uniforms from the 16th and 17th c. to the present-day.

Town Hall   Almost opposite is the Rathaus (Town Hall), of the 15th and 17th c., with a fine Renaissance doorway; in the north tower a cantilevered winding staircase dates from 1632.

Market   In the nearby Marktplatz is the 12th c. clock tower (Zeitglockenturm), with mechanical figures (1545) of a king flanked by Death and a soldier. Close by is the Mauritius fountain decorated with a figure by the famous master Hans Gieng of Fribourg.

Jesuit Church   In Hauptgasse, which runs between the Marktplatz is the Jesuit church (1680–89) with an interior decorated with stucco work by Ticenese artists. In the cloister is an interesting lapidarium with Roman inscriptions.

St Peter's   This much-restored chapel contains the tombs of the Theban martyrs
Chapel   Ursus and Victor.

Nature Museum   At No. 2 Klosterplatz is the Nature Museum. From the Marktplatz the Gurzelngasse leads west to the Bieltor (Biel gate, originally 12th c.) and a 16th c. tower, the Buristurm.

Museum of Art   At No. 30 Werkhofstrasse, in the old town, is the Museum of Art, housing works by old masters (including a Madonna by Hans Holbein the Younger) and by 20th c. artists.

Old Armoury: collection of weapons from the Middle Ages to the present

Farther north, at Blumensteinweg 12, is the Schloss Blumenstein Historical Museum, with collections of applied art (patrician domestic interiors of the 18th c.).

Blumenstein Historical Museum

On the western outskirts of the town St Mary's church (1953), has the largest stained-glass windows in the country (some 100 sq. m/1076 sq. ft) by H. Stocker.

St Mary's Church

Surroundings

For Weissenstein (10 km/6 miles) leave Solothurn by the Bieltor and Bielstrasse and bear right along Weissensteinstrasse into a road which runs through the watchmaking town of Langendorf (artificial ice-rink in winter) to Oberdorf. 4.5 km/3 miles: Oberdorf station (658 m/2159 ft), from which a chair-lift (2369 m/7773 ft, 16 minutes) ascends to the Weissenstein (1284 m/4214 ft).
The road then climbs in steep bends up the Nesselboden (1051 m/3448 ft), with a celebrated view of the Alps extending as far as Mont Blanc. Marked footpaths lead to various viewpoints in the hills, which offer excellent skiing in winter.

To the Weissenstein

Oberdorf Weissenstein

There are numerous walks along marked paths, of which the Planetenweg (Planet Way) is recommended. It represents on a scale 1 to 1 billion the distance between the sun and the planet Pluto. Other walks encompass the flora (Botanical Garden) and geology of the Jura.

Planet Way

For safety reasons visitors to the "Nidenloch" caves must report to the Gasthaus Hinterweissenstein before and after visiting the caves. In the entrance are wire cable ladders; stout footwear is essential.

Nidenloch

The Weissenstein region is a popular skiing area in winter.

*Weissenstein

397

Solothurn: Rathaus . . .   *. . . and Mauritius Fountain*

Stork Colony, Altreu	Not far to the west at Altreu is the oldest and most well known stork colony in Switzerland with at present over 200 wild storks.
Schloss Waldegg	Schloss Waldegg, lying 4 km/2 miles from Feldbrunnen (north-east), is the headquarters of the organisation of the same name, which seeks to promote contact between the different linguistic areas of Switzerland.
Wangen on the Aare	About 10 km/6 miles north-east from Solothurn is the medieval little town of Wangen, with a very well-preserved medieval centre which is almost of a square design. The covered wooden bridge over the Aare was built in the 16th c. Worth seeing are the parish church of the Holy Cross and St Maria (1825; 14th and 15th c. frescoes) and the castle (restored 1680; Baroque ceiling paintings by J. Werners). The Gemeindehaus by the clock tower contains documents about the town's history and ceramics.
Wiedlisbach	The little picturesque town of Wiedlisbach was, like Solothurn, founded by the Counts of Fribourg (c. 1280). A corner tower remains from the old fortifications in the "Hinterstädtli", and in St Catherine's chapel (Katharinenkapelle; 1338) there are Late Gothic frescoes. The Kornhaus contains a small local collection of ceramics, glass and tin from Bernese and Solothurn studios.

Stein am Rhein   D1

	Canton: Schaffhausen (SH) Altitude: 405 m/810 ft Population: 3000
Location and ****Townscape**	The little town of Stein am Rhein, situated at the western tip of the Untersee, the arm of Lake Constance by which the Rhine leaves the lake, is, with Morat, one of the best-preserved medieval towns in Switzerland.

Stein on the Hochrhein

Sights

In the very picturesque Marktplatz (fountains) stands the Rathaus (Town Hall, 1539), which contains the town's historical collections, including weapons, heraldic crests and valuable stained glass.

*Marketplace/ Town Hall

From the Marktplatz the Hauptstrasse (with an old house, the Weisser Adler or White Eagle, at No. 14) runs north-west to the Untertor (Lower Gate). On the north side of the old town is the Obertor (Upper Gate).

Untertor/ Obertor

South-east of the Rathaus stands the former Benedictine Conventual Church of St George, a 12th c. Romanesque basilica which is now the Protestant parish church; it has old frescoes in the choir. The adjoining former Benedictine Monastery, founded by King Henry II and his consort Kunigunde *c.* 1005, was dissolved in 1524; the present buildings date from the 14th–15th c. and house the St George's Abbey Museum (Klostermuseum St Georgen) with original 15th and 16th c. furnishings. Associated with the museum is a local collection (closed in winter) of prehistoric finds from the Island of Werd and from the surroundings of the town.
The Great Hall of the abbey has fine wall paintings (1515–16) by Thomas Schmid and A. Holbein, and in the Late Gothic cloister are old tombstones.

St George's Abbey

Benedictine Monastery
*Abbey Museum

West of the Town Hall at Schwarzhorngasse 138 is a doll museum (closed in winter) containing more than 400 old dolls and automata from central Europe.

Doll museum

Near the landing stage for boats in the south-west of the Old Town is a miniature steam railway for children.

Landing stage
Miniature steam railway

On the left bank of the Rhine is the district of Burg. On the hill (views) are remains of the Roman castrum of Tasgaetium (A.D. 294). Within the castrum stands the parish church of St John (originally built *c.* 800) with frescoes of about 1400.

Tasgaetium

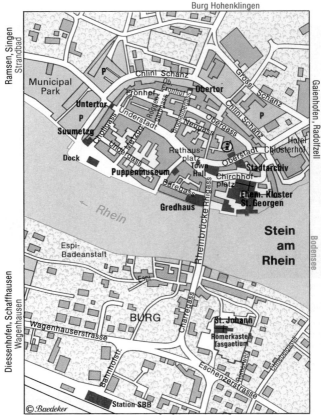

Eschenz, Stammheimertal, Frauenfeld, Konstanz

Benedictine abbey	1 km/¾ mile west of Stein am Rhein is the outlying district of Wagenhausen, with the remains of a former Benedictine abbey built 1090–92 and dissolved in 1529. The Romanesque pillared basilica (1083–87) has been preserved.

Surroundings of Stein am Rhein

Burg Hohenklingen	On the Klingenberg (593 m/1946 ft), a wooded hill north of the town, is a well-preserved 12th c. castle, Burg Hohenklingen (armoury, 16th c. stained glass; restaurant), once the home of the minnesinger Walther von Klingen (c. 1215–86). From the tower (worn steps) there is a fine view over the town and the Rhine.
Eschenz	Not far south of Stein am Rhein, at the end of the Untersee, lies the village of Eschenz (406 m/1332 ft; pop. 1300). It occupies the site of the Roman town of Tasgaetium (see above) from which the name of the village is derived.
Werd Island	Near the district of Untereschenz lies the little island of Werd, where more than 5000 years ago people dwelt in houses built on piles (excavation finds

in the local museum of the Benedictine monastery). The pilgrimage church
of St Othmar dates from the 15th c.

South-east of the village of Obereschenz (1.5 km/1 mile; narrow road)
stands Freudenfels castle (528 m/1733 ft).

Freudenfels
castle

On the far side of the Stammer Hill, south-west of Stein am Rhein, lies the
charming Stammheimer or Stammer valley which was formed during the
Ice Age. Idyllic lakes (Nussbaumersee, Hüttwilersee and Hasensee) nestle
in wooded hills of glacial moraine, with neat little villages of typical half-
timbered houses.

Stamm-
heimertal

The Gasthof zum Hirschen, an inn in Oberstammheim, built in 1684, with
oriel windows dating from 1730, is one of the finest half-timbered houses in
eastern Switzerland.

Ober-
stammheim

Swiss National Park

Canton Grisons (GR)

The Swiss National Park (Schweizerischer Nationalpark, Parc National
Suisse, Parco Nazionale Svizzero, Parc Naziunal Svizzer) lies in the Lower
Engadine to the north-west of the Ofen pass (Pass dal Fuorn), and covers an
area of 168.7 sq. km/65 sq. miles. In the south it borders on Italy for a
distance of 19 km/12 miles. It is a mountainous region of eastern Alpine
character, with some Dolomitic features. The highest peak in the National
Park is Piz Pisoc (2174 m/10,414 ft), to the north, closely followed, in the
south, by Piz Quattervals (3164 m/10,381 ft) from which radiate the four
valleys referred to in its name. The permanent snow level lies between
2900 m/9515 ft and 3000 m/9843 ft.

Location and
general

The only area of habitation in the park is the Il Fuorn Hotel on the busy Ofen
pass road (Ofenberg road), which runs from Zernez into Val Müstair. Along
this road are nine parking places, from which radiate a network of footpaths

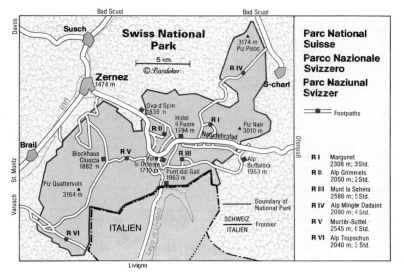

401

Nature reserve . . .   *. . . on the Ofen Pass*

(marked white–red–white) with a total length of 80 km/50 miles. Visitors must not leave the marked paths: the National Park is subject to strict regulations designed to ensure that the natural conditions are not disturbed in any way.

Information can be obtained from the Nationalparkhaus in Zermez (see below).

Flora

About a third of the park's area is covered by forest. The characteristic tree is the mountain pine; larches and stone pines, forest pines and spruces feature less prominently, and deciduous trees (birch, aspen, willow) play a very minor role. Above the tree-line dwarf shrubs predominate (rhododendrons, dwarf willows, junipers, crowberries, etc.). On the dry limestone crags the commonest form of grass cover is the brownish type of turf known in Switzerland as "crooked sedge turf" (Krummseggenrasen, Caricetum curvulae). On the sunnier hillsides the predominant vegetation is blue grass (Sesleria semperviretum). The type known as "milk-grass pasture" (Milchgrasweide), which includes a wide variety of species, prefers wetter ground, while on poor soil the mat grasses form a thick felt-like carpet. Particularly attractive flowers are found in small hollows on shaded slopes which become impregnated with melt-water. The brilliantly yellow Rhaetian Alpine poppy manages to find a foothold even on steep scree slopes.

Fauna

Reptiles and amphibians are represented by the grass frog, Alpine newt, viviparous lizard and adder. The commonest rodents are the marmot, the blue hare and the squirrel. Altogether thirty species of mammals are found – among the larger game are red deer, chamois, ibex and small numbers of roe-deer; among the predators the fox, the marten and the ermine. There are more than a hundred species of birds, the commonest being nutcrackers, ring ouzels, Alpine titmice and greater spotted woodpeckers; the game birds include capercaillie, black grouse, rock partridge, ptarmigan and hazel hen; and the crags provide nesting-places for ravens, Alpine choughs and, in many places, golden eagles.

**Walks in the Park

Marked footpaths run through some of the most beauti ul parts of the National Park, with opportunities for observing the wildlife. The animals are wary of man, so that they can usually be seen only at distances of 500 to 1000 m/550 to 1100 yds. Observers shou d therefore be properly equipped (field glasses, telephoto lens).

Note

From parking place 7 on the Ofen pass road through the wooded Val cal Botsch to the first rest area (Rastplatz), from which chamois can be observed; then on to the large rest area at Margunet (2308 m/7573 ft), with a beautiful view (Munt la Schera, P z Nair, Piz dal Fuorn; red deer); down from here to another rest area (red deer) and the Stabelchod hut (parkkeeper's house; colony of marmots); then back to the Ofen pass road and along a path parallel to the road, past parking places 9 and 8, to parking place 7. The path continues to Il Fuorn. Time about 3 hours.

Route I; to Margunet

From Il Fuorn north-west over Plan Posa and through Val Ftur; then climb to the Champlönch dry valley and the Alpine meadows of Grimmels (2050 m/6726 ft: marmots, sometimes in the early morning red deer hinds), w th a beautiful view (Ofen pass, Munt la Schera, Piz dal Fuorn). Then either back to Il Fuorn or down (west) to parking place 1, 2 or 3 on the Ofen pass road. An easy walk of 2–2½ hours.

Route II; to the Grimmels Alp

The route starts from Buffalora, just outside the National Park boundary: from there south through a forest of stone pines to Marangun, then west over the flower-spangled meadows of Fop da Buffalora to enter the park beneath Munt Chavagi. After about 2 hours' walking bear right up Munt la Schera (2586 m/8485 ft), with magnificent views of the Or ler group (3900 m/12,796 ft) in the south-east, of the snow-covered Bern na group (4000 m/13,124 ft) in the south-west and the whole area of the Nat onal Park. Then down the south side of the hill to the Alp la Schera (rest area: marmots; red deer may be seen on the southern slopes of Munt la Schera). From there on the upper forest path to Il Fuorn; then either back on the postal bus to Stradin Buffalora or on the footpath to the right of the road (1¼ hours). The day's outing occupies about 5 hours.

Route III; to Munt la Schera

The route starts from the parking place at the junction of the Mingèr with the Clemgia on the road from Scuol to S-charl. After crossing the Clemgia the path leads south-west through tall spruce forest to Min gèr Dadora, past a sandstone crag known as the Hexenkopf ("Witches Head") and on to the Alpine meadow of Mingèr Dadaint (2090 m/6855 ft): good opportunities for observing red deer and marmots. At the head of the valley are the precipitous peaks of Piz Plavna Dadaint (3166 m/10,388 ft). Return by the same route, or alternatively continue west to Il Foss and then via Alp Plavna to Tarasp. This half-day outing lasts about 3½ hours.

Route IV; to the Mingèr Dadaint Alp

Starting from Zernez, cross the covered bridge over the Spöl at the east end of the village and continue over the Selva meadows to a clearing at Al Pra (beautiful view from the Bellavista viewpoint). Then down to the valley floor and a short climb on the other side to the Cluoza hut (Blockhaus Cluoza, 1882 m/6175 ft: food, dormitory accommodation – to book, tel. 8 12 35). Then up the hillside to the left and by way of Alp Murtèr to the Murtèrgrat (2545 m/8350 ft), with fine v ews of Piz Quattervals and Piz del Diavel to the south and the Fuorn valley and Piz Terza to the north, with an opportunity to see chamois and marmots. Descend by way of Plan dal Poms to the Praspöl meadows, then over the Spöl and up to the Ofen pass road at Vallun Chafuol (postal bus stop). Time about 6 hours.

Route V; by way of the Cluoza hut to the Murtèrgrat

The Nationalparkhaus . . .   *. . . in Zernez*

Route VI; to Alp Trupchun

From the bridge over the Inn north-east of S-chanf make for Mulins Varusch; then continue along the stream in the direction of Val Casana and at the next junction take a path on the left through Val Trupchun. Along the park boundary and opposite the mouth of Val Müsschauns there are opportunities for observing wildlife (chamois, ibex, eagles' nests). Then climb to the hut on Alp Trupchun (2040 m/6693 ft), with numbers of animals (including ibexes) in almost every direction. Return along the right bank, past the mouth of Val Müschauns, to reach the National Park boundary at Chanels; then on to the Varusch hut (refreshments), and from there back to the parking place. The day's outing takes about 5 hours.

Over the Ofen pass into Val Müstair

Zernez

National- parkhaus

Ofen Pass road

La Serra

Val Cluozza

Wegerhaus Ova d'Spin

The village of Zernez (1474 m/4836 ft), situated in a broad valley basin, is the best base from which to visit the National Park (of which a good general impression can be had in the Nationalparkhaus). Part of the village was burned down in 1872 and rebuilt in rather urban style. In the older part, standing on higher ground, is the parish church (1607), with rich stucco decoration. Another old building that has survived is the Schloss Planta-Wildenberg (17th–18th c.). – From here take the Ofen Pass road, which runs E from the main road through the Engadine to St Moritz, following the Spölbach upstream through the wooded gorge of La Serra; then a well-engineered stretch of road up the rocky wooded hillside, passing through three galleries designed to provide protection from avalanches. In 3·5 km (2 miles) there is a fine view down to the right of the wild Val Cluozza, the oldest part of the National Park with the glacier descending the slopes of Piz Quattervals (3164 m/10,381 ft) in the background. The road then follows a fairly level course over the forest-covered Champ Sech, beyond which the Piz del Diavel (3072 m/10,079 ft) comes into sight, and then descends down in a wide curve to the Wegerhaus Ova d'Spin (on left: car park), at the W entrance to the National Park.

The road runs downhill, crosses the Ova d'Spin (parking place) and continues along the wooded slopes above the river, then above the Spölbach (parking place) and the Ova del Fuorn, flowing down from the Ofen pass, and comes to the Punt la Drossa (1710 m/5611 ft): Swiss customs; parking place), in a narrow pass, where the road crosses to the left bank of the Ova del Fuorn. On the right is the entrance to a road tunnel 3.3 km/2 miles long, belonging to the Munt la Schera hydroelectric complex, which reaches the Italian frontier at the Punt dal Gall (1963 m/6441 ft) over the River Spöl, at the N end of an artificial lake 8 km/5 miles long (dam, alt. 1805 m/5922 ft, 540 m/1771 ft long, 130 m/427 ft high, 10 m/33 ft thick; capacity 164 million cu. m/5791 million cu. ft). A road runs down the W side of the lake through a customs-free zone to Livigno (19.5 km/12 miles, alt. 816 m/2677 ft: large skiing area, four ski-lifts). Beyond the Punt la Drossa the road to the Ofen pass climbs gradually; then comes a fairly level stretch, in which the road emerges from the forest; and finally it returns to the right bank of the Ova del Fuorn and reaches the Park Naziunal Hotel, in the lonely high valley of Il Fuorn (German *Ofen*, 1804 m/5919 ft), named after an iron-smelting works which once stood here. From here a marked footpath ascends Munt la Schera (2590 m/8498 ft: 2½ hours), from the limestone summit plateau of which there is a fine general view of the National Park.

Punt la Drossa

Punt dal Gall

Livigno

Il Fuorn

Munt la Schera

From the hotel the road continues uphill through the coniferous forests in the high valley of the Ova del Fuorn, past the mouths of the wild Val dal Botsch and Val da Stabelchod, at the foot of Piz Nair (3010 m/9876 ft); several parking places. In 4.5 km (3 miles) it comes to the Alp Buffalora (1963 m/6441 ft), in a marshy valley bottom, with Val Nüglia running down from Piz Tavrü (3168 m/10,394 ft) on the left and Munt da Buffalora (2629 m/8626 ft) on the right. The road then climbs more steeply to the Ofen Pass (Romansch Süsom-Givè or Pass dal Fuorn, 2149 m (7051 feet: hotel), from which there is a view of the Ortler group. It then winds its way down, with three hairpin turns, first over Alpine meadows and then along the slopes of the valley, through stretches of forest, with fine views.

Alp Buffalora

Ofen Pass

Tschierv (1664 m/5460 ft: Hotel Sternen; camping site) is the highest village in Val Müstair, the valley of the Rom. Here the road crosses the river and runs down the S side of the valley, with patches of woodland, on a moderate gradient.

Val Müstair

Fuldera (1641 m/5384 ft: bypass) is a little hamlet at the foot of Piz Turettas (2958 m/9705 ft). Beyond this a road goes off on the left to Lü (3.5 km/ 2 miles, 1920 m/6300 ft), the highest village in its valley. The main road now runs down more steeply to Valchava (1435 m/4708 ft: bypass), where the first fruit-trees appear. Beyond this, on the right, is the mouth of the beautiful Val Vau.

Fuldera

Valchava

Santa Maria (1388 m/4554 ft), the chief town in Val Müstair (pop. 350; Prot.), lies at the mouth of Val Muraunza, which runs down from the Umbrail pass. It has pretty painted houses, a church of 1491 and a local museum. Down the valley the view embraces the castles of Taufers and the Ötztal Alps, with the snow-capped peak of the Weisskugel. From Santa Maria a road goes off on the right to the Umbrail and Stelvio (Stilfserjoch) passes. The main road continues down Val Müstair, through the village of Müstair, into the Upper Adige valley.

Santa Maria

Thun

Canton: Berne (BE)
Altitude: 557 m/1828 ft
Population: 39,000

The old-world town of Thun (French Thoune), which has belonged to the canton of Berne since 1384, lies on the River Aare just below its outflow

Location and general

Brahms Quay by Lake Thun

from Lake Thun. Charmingly situated on both banks of the swiftly flowing green river and on a 1 km/½ mile-long island in the middle, with its castle on a hill 30 m/98 ft high dominating the town, it is the gateway to the Bernese Oberland. An unusual feature of the old town is the flower-bedecked pedestrian walkways running along above the arcades containing the shops on ground level in the main street (Hauptgasse).

Sights

**Rathaus
Castle Historical
Museum**

From the Rathausplatz, with the handsome Rathaus (Town Hall: 1589, rebuilt 1685), a covered flight of steps leads up to the castle, whose massive keep with its corner turrets is a prominent landmark of the town. It was built in 1191 by Duke Berthold V of Zähringen; later it became the seat of the Counts of Kyburg, and in 1492 was enlarged by the addition of an official residence for the chief magistrate of Berne. Since 1888 it has housed the Historical Museum, with arms and armour and 14th and 15th c. tapestries in the large Knights' Hall, prehistoric and Roman materials, furniture and ceramics in the three lower rooms and a collection illustrating 19th c. Swiss military history in the upper hall. From the castle and from the Protestant parish church (rebuilt 1738, with an older tower) on the south-east slopes of the castle hill there is a superb view of Lake Thun and the Alps (the Stockhorn chain, the Niesen and, to the left, the snow-covered Blümlisalp).

Art Gallery

In the Thunerhof (Hofstettengasse 14) is the Municipal Art Gallery, containing painting and sculpture of the 19th and 20th c., particularly by Swiss artists, among them F. Hodler and C. Amiet. The paintings include Swiss and foreign work, both old and modern.

**Swiss Steam-
engine Museum**

On the site of the former Schadau market garden (c. 17,000 sq. m/183,000 sq. ft) a museum is being established (1991 "pre" Museum; 1994 actual museum), illustrating the history of the steam-engine. Exhibit No. 1 is the paddle-wheel steamer "Blümlisalp" which used to ply on Lake Thun. Other exhibits will include the steamship "Lötschberg" (from Lake Brienz) as well as steam-trains of the Schynige–Platte, the Brünig and the Brienz–Rothorn railways.

Brahms Quai

The Aare basin is lined by the Johannes Brahms Quai, where there is a bronze monument to the Late-Romantic musician who spent several summers in Thun and who dedicated a violin sonata to the lake.

Thun: the Castle dominating the town

A series of little wooded islands extend opposite the shoreline with a romantic path; to walk along this is called "Inseli-Kehr machen" (doing the round of the islands).

Surroundings

1½ km/1 mile south the village of Scherzlingen on the lake has a little 12th c. church (frescoes).

Scherzligen

Where the basin of the Aare broadens out into the lake and an unexpected wonderful panorama meets the eye, Schloss Shadau towers up on the shore. The castle, a smaller replica of the château of Azay-le-Rideau on the Loire, was built in 1852 for the de Rougemont family of Neuchâtel. Since 1988 it has housed the Swiss Museum of Gastronomy, with exhibits of crockery, cutlery and kitchen utensils; temporary exhibitions are an additional feature. In the library the visitor can find rare cookery books from Japan, Russia, China and South America, the oldest of which dates from the time of the Thirty Years War.

Schadau Castle
Gastronomic
museum

In the park of Schadau is the Wocher Panorama, a larger circular painting (38 × 7.5 m/125 × 25 ft) by Marquard Wocher (1760–1830) of the town of Thun as it was about 1810.

On the right, in Dürrenast can be seen the shipyard of the Lake Thun Shipping Company.

Shipyard of
Lake Thun

The pleasant promenade along the shore, which is part of the scenically beautiful Lake Thun circular route, leads to the outskirts of the village of Hilterfingen. Here stands Schloss Hünegg, another gem of the lovely lakeside landscape. The name recalls the early-Germanic tumuli ("giants' graves") which were discovered on a hill near the lake at the beginning of the 19th c. Hünegg Castle is also reminiscent of the French châteaux,

Hilter-
fingen/Schloss
Hünegg
Art Nouveau
Museum

particularly those of Blois and Chenonceaux. The industrialist G. Lemke-Schukkert of Wiesbaden gave the castle a new aspect at the turn of the century. Some rooms were carefully converted to reflect old styles, others in pure Art Nouveau. Since 1966 the building has been a museum of Historicism and Art Nouveau. From the park there is a wonderful view of the lake and the Alps.

Goldiwil — Some 5 km/3 miles north-east of Thun is the health resort of Goldiwil (1010 m/3314 ft).

Amsoldingen — About 6 km/4 miles south-west is the village of Amsoldingen (644 m/2113 ft) on the shores of a small lake. It has a castle and a fine Romanesque church (St Mauritius) of the 10th or 11th c. which shows Lombardian influence.

Kiesen — 8 km/5 miles north-west on the Berne road is Kiesen, where a visit to the dairy museum is highly recommended. Here can be seen apparatus used in cheese-making, and a village cheese dairy has been reconstructed (sound-film and slide show).

Lake Thun and Lake Brienz

Canton: Berne (BE)

Lake Thun

Location and general — Lake Thun (altitude 560 m/1837 ft) is 18 km/11 miles long and between 2 and 2.8 km/1 and 2 miles wide, with an area of 48 sq. km (19 sq. miles); its greatest depth is 217 m/712 ft. There are roads from Thun to Interlaken

Sailing regatta on Lake Thun

along both the north and south shores of the lake. Boat services operate during the season (Apr.–Sept.) from Interlaken-West via Spiez to Thun, and from Interlaken-Ost to Brienz (see Lake Brienz); there are also various round trips, cruises and excursions.

Along the north shore of Lake Thun

The road along the north side of the lake (23 km/14 miles), which affords a succession of beautiful views, leaves Thun by way of Hofstettenstrasse along the banks of the Aare, passing on the right the Municipal Art Gallery in the Thunerhof and on the left the Kursaal. It then follows the northern shore of Lake Thun (trolley-bus to Beatenbucht). Sheltered from north and east winds, the lake has an unusually mild climate. Many southern plants including laurels and fig-trees flourish in the gardens of the charming lakeside villages which attract many visitors in spring and autumn as well as in summer. Almost all the way along the lake there are magnificent views of the giants of the Bernese Alps. At the entrance to the Kandertal and Simmental the conical Stockhorn (2190 m/7185 ft) can be seen on the right and the pyramidal peak of the Niesen (2362 m/7750 ft) on the left, with the three peaks of the Blümlisalp (3664 m/12,022 ft) further to the left. To the right of the Blümlisalp a series of summits come gradually into view – from left to right the Fründenhorn (3369 m/11,054 ft), Doldenhorn (3709 m/12,169 ft), Altels (3629 m/11,907 ft) and Rinderhorn (3453 m/11,329 ft). In the direction of Interlaken the most prominent peaks are (from right to left) the Ebnefluh (3960 m/12,993 ft), Jungfrau (4158 m/13,642 ft), Mönch (4099 m/13,449 ft) and Eiger (3970 m/13,026 ft), and beyond these the Schreckhorn (4078 m/13,380 ft) and Wetterhorn (3701 m/12,143 ft).

*Shore Road
Thun

3.5 km/2 miles: Hilterfingen (562 m/1844 ft) has a small church of 1470 and the 18th c. Schloss Hünegg. Thuner See sailing school.

Hilterfingen
Schloss Hünegg

Adjoining Hilterfingen (575 m/1887 ft) the feudal castle of Oberhofen, picturesquely situated by the lake, can be seen from afar. The fortress was built in the 12th c. by the Lords of Oberhofen but had to be surrendered to the Austrians in 1306. After the Battle of Sempach in 1386 the castle was occupied by Berne; later it came into the possession of the Scharnachtal family. The western domestic wing, with its lipped roof, dates from the time of the Landvögte (governors; 1652–1798). In 1844 the Prussian Count Friedrich von Pourtales de Castellane Norante gave the castle a romantic aspect by adding numerous turrets, balconies and dormer windows. Regularly patterned flower-beds were laid out on the lakeside terrace and exotic trees were planted. An American, W. M. Measy, inherited the castle in 1926 and had a branch museum of the Bernese Historical Museum installed, which gives a graphic picture of the domestic life of the town and countryside including Bernese rural pottery of the 18th and 19th c., a Turkish smoker's saloon and a children's chalet.

Schloss
Oberhofen/
Historical
Museum

To the right there is a fine view of the Niessen before reaching Gunten, (567 m/1860 ft) a pretty health resort at the mouth of the Gunter stream which breaks through a gorge above the village. By the lake are a bathing beach and a water-skiing school.

Gunten

The by-road to the left goes inland and here the gentle hills suddenly end at the steep slopes of the Alpine foothills. In 3 km/2 miles we reach the well-known hill resort of Sigriswil on a sunny plateau.

Sigriswil

From here a narrow but very beautiful road (toll charge; alternate one-way traffic) leads to Beatenberg (12 km/7 miles: see Interlaken).

Beatenberg

Continuing along the shore of the lake we reach in 3½ km/2 miles the resort of Merligen (568 m/1864 ft) in a very sheltered situation at the mouth of the Justis valley.

Merligen

Schloss Oberhofen

Beatenbucht	The road goes on to Beatenbucht where the lake steamers call. This is the terminus of the trolley-bus line from Thun and from here a funicular takes passengers up to Beatenberg (1150 m/3773 ft; see Interlaken). The lakeside road now changes in character. The gently sloping shore with its villages and gardens gives way to a steep wooded scarp, along which the road climbs in a series of bends. 1.5 km/1 mile farther on it passes in two tunnels through a rocky promontory, the Nase. 1 km/½ mile beyond this, there is a beautiful glimpse of the lake to the right.
Beatushöhlen	The road now comes to the parking place for the Beatushöhlen or St Beatus's caves (623 m/2044 ft: 8 minutes' walk from the road), an extensive complex of stalactitic caves of which 2 km/1 mile are accessible to visitors. According to legend the caves were occupied by St Beatus (6th c.) and until the Reformation were a place of pilgrimage (conducted tour, 1 hour; Waldhaus restaurant). In the 8 km/5 miles of caves which have so far been explored, are several impressive waterfalls, lakes and stalactitic formations.
	The route continues through three tunnels and around a sheer rock face which, in places, actually overhangs the road, to Sundlauenen (615 m/2018 ft). It then runs along below the crag above the lake; in another 1.5 km/1 mile it passes a camping site and at the Neuhaus bathing station (on right; camping site on left) comes to the end of Lake Thun. 2 km/1 mile farther on the road passes the Hotel Beau-Site and crosses the "Bödeli", an area of alluvial soil deposited by the Lombach, to Unterseen (old church), an outlying district of Interlaken, where a road branches off on the left to Beatenberg (see Interlaken). The road then bears right and
Interlaken	crosses the Aare to enter Interlaken (see entry).

Along the south shore of Lake Thun

Shore road	The road along the south side of the lake offers two alternative routes between Thun and Interlaken. One way is to go south from the old town

Schloss Spiez

over the Aare and continue under the railway and then south-west for 3 km/2 miles to join the motorway from Berne (N 6), which runs at some distance from the lake to Spiez (10 km/6 miles). Alternatively, after passing under the railway, turn left along Frutigenstrasse and continue past the bathing beach at the end of the town (on left: beautiful gardens, camping site). This road, at some distance from the lake, comes in 4.5 km/3 miles to Gwatt (564 m/1850 ft), beyond which a turn on the right leads to the Simmental. Then over the River Kander and up a winding stretch of road, with beautiful views of the bay of Spiez and the Niesen. Below the road, on the left, is the village of Einigen with a Romanesque church (11th and 13th c.). 5.5 km/3 miles from Gwatt is Spiez (630 m/2067 ft). At the near end of the town a road goes off on the right to the Simmental (see entry) and via Mülenen (8 km/5 miles: funicular up the Niesen) to Frutigen (Kandersteg, Abelboden). The picturesquely situated town of Spiez (pop. 10,000) is a popular health and water sports resort (sailing school), and it is also an important junction for the roads and mountain railways into the Kandertal and Simmental.

Spiez

From an intersection in the upper part of the town near the parish church (1907) a street runs down to the medieval castle, delightfully situated in a cove. It has a massive 12th c. keep and fine buildings added in the 14th–18th c. This noble estate, which, in the time of the kings of Neuchâtel, bore the title of the "Golden Court on the Wendelsee", was for centuries owned by the Erlach family. Today the castle is the headquarters of the municipal council. It also houses a museum (drawing and reception rooms of the 13th–18th c., including Renaissance panelled rooms and an Early-Baroque hall).
The neighbouring little 11th c. church has three Romanesque apses and fine Gothic frescoes.
An attractive path leads along the lake from Spiez to Faulensee (30 minutes).

Schloss Spiez

Lake Thun and Lake Brienz

Aeschi   6 km/4 miles south-east of Spiez is the village of Aeschi (860 m/2822 ft), a popular summer resort on the hill between Lake Thun and the Kander valley. The Protestant church, dating in part from the 12th to the 13th c., has frescoes in the choir (probably 14th c.) which were exposed in 1966.

To the Niesen
**Niesen   From Spiez, take the Kandersteg road to Mülenen (8 km/5 miles), from which a funicular 3.5 km/2 miles), maximum gradient 68% (1 in 1·4), 30 minutes) serves the Niesenkulm Hotel (2362 m/7750 ft), a few minutes below the summit of Niesen (2362 m/7750 ft; see entry), with superb views of Lake Thun and Lake Brienz, the Jungfrau massif and the Blümlisalp. Descent to Wimmis on foot, 2 hours.

Kiental   To the Griesalp (22 km/14 miles): From Spiez take the Kandersteg road to Reichenbach (9 km/6 miles); then turn left into a narrow road which winds its way up to the village of Scharnachtal and continues through the narrow wooded Kiental (6 km/4 miles). Kiental (906 m/2973 ft), a village which attracts many summer visitors, with a beautiful view of the Blümlisalp. From here a chair-lift (1405 m/4510 ft: 18 minutes) ascends to a skiing area (1500 m/4922 ft) on the east side of the Gerihorn (2133 m/6998 ft).

Pochtenalp   Then on to the Tschingelalp (1151 m–3776 ft), and beyond this a series of narrow turns up the wooded hillside (gradients of up to 20% (1 in 5)) and past the Pochten Falls (curious rock forms resulting from erosion) to the Pochtenalp (1400 m/4593 ft).

Griesalp   Finally, continue (3 km/2 miles) to Griesalp (1407 m/4616 ft), which attracts summer visitors and skiers (interesting nature reserve). From here it is a 3 hours' climb to the Blümlisalp hut (2837 m/9308 ft) (see Blümlisalp) to the south. (See also Kandersberg).

*View   The Interlaken road continues straight ahead through the upper part of Spiez, with parking places 1 km/½ mile and 1.5 km/1 mile from the town which afford beautiful views of the bay of Spiez and its picturesque castle.

Faulensee   It then skirts a wooded promontory projecting into the lake and comes to Faulensee (587 m/1926 ft), attractively set in a bay (bathing beach). On the left, above the road, is the church of St Columban (1962).

There follows a beautiful but winding stretch of road closely following the lake (parking places). 2 km/1 mile farther on an expressway from Spiez comes in on the right. Just before Leissigen an attractive road branches off on the right to Aeschi (6.5 km/4 miles).

Leissigen   6.5 km/4 miles from Spiez is Leissigen (573 m/1880 ft), among beautiful orchards, with an old church.

The road now runs along above the lake, with a view of Beatenberg (see Interlaken) high up on the opposite side. The next place is Därligen (564 m/1850 ft) with a bypass to the south of the village.

Lake Brienz

Location and general   Lake Brienz (altitude 567 m/1860 ft) is 14 km/9 miles long and between 2–2.5 km/1–2 miles wide, with an area of 29 sq. km/ 11 sq. miles); its greatest depth is 259 m/850 ft. The lake, which is in effect an enlargement of the valley of the River Aare, lies between the limestone ridge of the Brienzer Grat and the Jurassic Faulhorn group.
Lake Brienz was originally connected with Lake Thun, but now lies 7 m/23 ft higher. The slopes of the surrounding hills are wooded and this gives the landscape an exceptionally charming aspect.

Along the north shore of Lake Brienz

From Interlaken the road along the north side of Lake Brienz crosses the Aare, on the banks of which to the right are a camping site and motel, and

Lake Brienz   *Brunnengasse in Brienz*

winds up the wooded slopes of the Harder (funicular: station on left), from which there are extensive views.

In 2 km/1 mile it comes to Goldswil (612 m/2008 ft), a prettily situated little village with a ruined castle surrounded by a beautiful cemetery. Beyond this, on the right, is the Burgseeli bathing beach.

Goldswil

The road now keeps rather closer to the water and comes to the village of Ringgenberg (599 m/1965 ft) in a sheltered situation on a terrace above the lake. Here are weathered brown timber houses and a church (1671–1674), with an Early Baroque interior, which stands above the village in the ruins of a castle.

Ringgenberg

An excursion (12 km/7½ miles) to the "Planet Path" is recommended. The walk, of about five hours, takes the visitor through the whole of the solar system at a scale of one to one billion. Walking at a normal pace corresponds to the five-fold speed of light.

Planet Path

Then on, through a short rocky defile, to Niederried (580 m/1903 ft), situated amid orchards at the foot of the Augstmatthorn (2140 m/7012 ft) and Oberried (592 m/1942 ft), before passing through the little village of Eblingen to Brienz.

Brienz is a town of 3000 inhabitants which attracts many summer visitors and has many more passing through on their way between Lucerne and Interlaken. It is beautifully situated on the lake, with steep wooded slopes rising above the town to the precipitous Brienzer Grat, which reaches its highest point in the Rothorn. The long, straggling little town is the centre of the Oberland craft of woodcarving, with a woodcarving school and the Swiss Violin-Making School (open to visitors). Beside the Protestant church, with an early 12th c. Romanesque tower, is the house in which the Swiss writer Heinrich Federer (1866–1928) was born. Other features of Brienz are the village museum in the Wiesplatz and the 19th c. wooden houses in the Brunnengasse, with beautifully carved friezes on the façades.

Brienz

Swiss Open-Air Museum of Rural Life

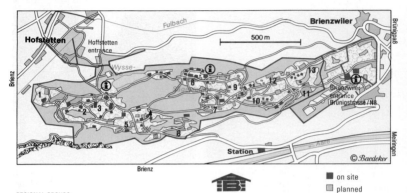

■ on site

□ planned

REGIONAL GROUPS
(as planned, numbered items are complete)

1 Jura
  No. 111 Farmhouse (1617) from La-Chaux-de-Fonds (Neuchâtel)

2 Central Mittelland
  No. 211 House (1617) from Villnachern (Aargau)
  No. 221 Farmhouse (1609) from Oberentfelden (Aargau)
  No. 222 Pigsty (19th c.) from Brugg (Aargau)
  No. 231 Farmhouse (1675) from Therwil (Basel-Land)

3 Bernese Mittelland
  No. 301 Cereal fields
  No. 302 Herb garden
  No. 303 Instructional garden of useful plants
  No. 311 "Alter Bären" inn from Rapperswil (Berne)
  No. 312 House with stove (1796) from Oberwangen (Berne)
  No. 321 Farmhouse from Madiswil (Berne)
  No. 322 Granary (18th c.) from Kiesen (Berne)
  No. 325 Textile worker's house from Herzogenbuchsee (Berne)
  No. 326 "Stöckli" with herb room (19th c.) from Köniz (Berne)
  No. 331 Farmhouse (1797) with collection of old clocks, and
  No. 332 Barn (18th c.) from Ostermundigen (Berne)
  No. 333 "Stöckli" from Detlingen (Berne)
  No. 334 Journeyman's house (1760) from Detlingen (Berne)
  No. 341 Barn (1702) from Faulensee (Berne)
  No. 351 Farmhouse (17th c.) from Eggiswil (Berne)
  No. 352 Granary (18th c.) from Wasen (Berne)

4 Rural Trades
  No. 411 Sawmill (c. 1841) from Rafz (Zurich)
  No. 421 Linseed press (18th c.) from Medel (Grisons)
  No. 491 Charcoal kiln
  No. 492 Lime burning oven
  No. 495 Refuge hut

5 Western Mittelland
  No. 501 Tobacco field
  No. 511 Farmhouse (17th/18th c.) from Tentlingen (Fribourg)
  No. 532 Farmhouse (1800) from Villars-Bramard (Vaud)
  No. 532 Granary (17th c.) from Ecoteaux (Vaud)
  No. 551 Farmhouse (1762, 1796, 1820) from Lancy (Geneva)

6 Eastern Mittelland
  No. 611 Half-timbered house (c. 1780) from Richterswil (Zurich)

  No. 612 Wash-house from Rüschlikon (Zurich)
  No. 613 Storehouse from Männedorf (Zurich)
  No. 615 Trotte (17th c.) from Schaffhausen
  No. 621 Half-timbered house (17th c.) from Uesslingen (Thurgau); bread museum on 2nd floor
  No. 622 Granary (1760) from Wellhausen (Thurgau)
  No. 631 Wine cellar from Schaffhausen with beam-press from Flesch (Grisons)
  No. 641 General purpose building (1680) from Wila (Zurich)
  No. 642 Granary (15th/16th c.) from Lindau (Zurich)
  No. 691 Sawmill (c. 1840) from Rafz (Zurich)
  No. 692 Bone-grinder (19th c.) from Knonau (Zurich)

7 Central Switzerland
  No. 711 House (17th, 19th c.) from Sachseln (Obwalden)
  No. 714 Bee-hive
  No. 721 House (17th c.) from Erstfeld (Uri)
  No. 722 Cold store (18th c.) from Unterschächen (Uri)
  No. 723 Hay barn (18th c.) from Spiringen (Uri)

8 Ticino

9 Eastern Switzerland
  No. 911 Appenzell cross-ridged house (16th c.) from Brülisau (Appenzell-Innerrhoden)
  No. 931 House (15th, 18th c.) from Wattwil (St Gallen)

10 Bernese Oberland
  No. 1011 Miner's house (1698) from Adelboden (Berne)
  No. 1012 Cheese store (1608) from Lütschental in the Grindelwald valley
  No. 1021 House (17th c.) from Matten (Berne)
  No. 1022 Granary (1656) from Niederried (Berne)
  No. 1024 Hay barn (19th c.) from Brienzwiler (Berne)
  No. 1031 House (1787) from Brienz (Berne)
  No. 1032 Drying oven (18th c.) from Brienzwiler (Berne)
  No. 1051 Pottery (19th c.) from Unterseen (Berne)
  No. 1052 Smithy (19th c.) from Bümpliz (Berne)
  No. 1061 Alpine cheese dairy (19th c.) from Kandersteg (Berne)
  No. 1062 Cheese store (18th c.) from Guttannen (Berne)
  No. 1063 Cheese store (1780) from Leissingen (Berne)

11 Valais
  No. 1111 House (1568) from Blatten (Valais)
  No. 1112 Hay barn (18th c.) from Blatten (Valais)
  No. 1121 Post-mill (19th c.) from Törbel (Valais)
  No. 1122 Mill (1872) from Naters (Valais)
  No. 1141–1145 Alpine buildings (16th–19th c.) from Bellwald (Valais)

12 Grisons

13 Alps

Traditional interior . . .   *. . . and exterior*

The Brienzer Rothorn (2350 m/7710 ft), with a magnificent prospect of the Appenzell, Uri, Engelberg, Berne and Valais Alps extending from Säntis to the Diablerets. There is a cableway from Sörenberg and a splendid four-hour mountain walk (stout footwear required) from the Brienzer Rothorn to the Brünig Pass, or to the mountain station of Schönbüel (1½ hours).   *Brienzer Rothorn

In 1988, the Brünig railway celebrated the centenary of the section between Alpmachstad and Brienz. Extensions to Lucerne and Interlaken were not built until 1916. This, the smallest rack-and-pinion railway of the Swiss federal network (length 74 km/46 miles; electrified 1941/42), crosses 124 bridges and climbs gradients up to 1 in 8 on its scenically attractive trip over the 1002 m/3289 ft-high Brünig Pass.   Brünigbahn

** Swiss Open-air Museum of Rural Life

The main entrance of the Swiss Open-air Museum of Rural Life, north-east of Brienz, is reached by road via Schwanden in Hofstetten (car park; bus service from Brienz; side-entrance in Brienzeiler.) The extensive grounds cover some 50 ha/124 acres of Alpine countryside on the Ballenberg. A series of regional groups, some still in course of construction, display the traditional way of life in different parts of Switzerland in old houses and other buildings brought here from their original sites, with appropriate furniture, utensils and implements. Old crafts and traditional customs have also been revived. A tour (guide available by prior arrangement) through the museum lasts 2½–3 hours; open daily 9 a.m.–5 p.m. April–October).

Along the south shore of Lake Brienz

To reach the Axalp (9 km/6 miles) you take a narrow road which branches off the Lucerne road on the right at the hamlet of Kienholz, 3 km/1 mile from   Axalp

415

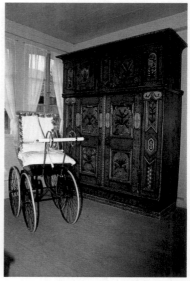

In Ballenberg open-air museum . . .   *. . . a farmhouse room from Ostermundigen*

Brienz. The road skirts the east end of the lake at the inflow of the Aare and climbs up the slopes on the south side of the lake, past a turning to the Giessbach (see below). It then winds its way up to the Axalp (1460–1549 m/4490–5053 ft; good walking and skiing, with ski-lifts) from which there are far-ranging views. From here there is a beautiful footpath into the Upper Giessbach valley, and also a 1¼ hours' walk to the Hinterburgsee, a beautiful mountain lake in the Hinterburg nature reserve.

*Giessbach Falls

The Giessbach (663 m/2175 ft) can be reached by the road referred to above or by boat to the Giessbach See landing-stage (15 minutes from Brienz) and from there either on foot (20 minutes) or by funicular (345 m/1132 ft). The best view of the Giessbach, which tumbles down from a height of 300 m/984 ft, to the lake in a series of falls over successive ridges of rock on the beautifully wooded hillside, is to be had from the terrace in front of the Park Hotel. There are footpaths up both banks to the highest of the three bridges, under which the stream emerges from a narrow gorge and plunges into a rock basin 60 m/197 ft deep.

Thurgau   D-E1

Canton: Thurgau (TG)

Location and general

The canton of Thurgau in north-east Switzerland lies on the south side of Lake Constance, occupying most of the Swiss shoreline of the lake. It is bounded on the west by the canton of Zurich and on the east by St Gallen. It has an area of 1006 sq. km/388 sq. miles and a population of 185,000. The canton is a region of markedly pre-Alpine character, with its highest points rising to barely 1000 m/3281 ft. The main source of income is fruit-growing.

History

There were many settlements in the canton in Roman times, as is shown by the results of excavation at Arbon (Arbor Felix) and Pfyn (Ad Fines). Later,

Frauenfeld: Old Town . . .   *. . . and castle above the Murg*

the area was occupied by Alemannic tribes. In medieval times, it was held by the Zähringen and Kyburg families and, from 1264, by the Counts of Habsburg. In 1460, Thurgau was taken over by the Confederates from the excommunicated Duke Sigismund and governed as a "common province". From 1798 to 1803 it was part of the Helvetian Republic; thereafter, it became an independent canton.

Frauenfeld

The cantonal capital is Frauenfeld (414 m/1359 ft; pop. 19,000, situated on the river Murg just south of its junction with the Thur. In the upper town, rebuilt to a rectangular plan after a fire in the 18th c., stands the castle high above the Murg. It was once the seat of the Confederate landvögte (governors) and has a massive 12th c. tower, from which there is a fine view. The tower was built by the Kyburgs of Findlingen in about 1227. Additions to the fortress were made at intervals. The castle now houses the Thurgau Cantonal Museum which has a rich collection of exhibits ranging from Neolithic times to the Early Middle Ages. Of particular interest are the furnished rooms of town and country dwellers (17th–19th c.), the exhibition illustrating the history of the town and a comprehensive collection of religious art, especially of the 14th c.

Castle

The Lucerne House which, like the Berne and Zürich Houses, has an impressive Baroque façade, is now the Cantonal Nature Museum, presenting the history of the development of our planet and its biospheres in a most vivid manner.

Luzernerhaus
Nature Museum

A few kilometres north-west of Frauenfeld, above the Thur, is the former Carthusian monastery of Ittingen, founded as an Augustinian house in 1152 and taken over by the Carthusians in 1461. Much of the monastery

*Ittingen
Monastery

417

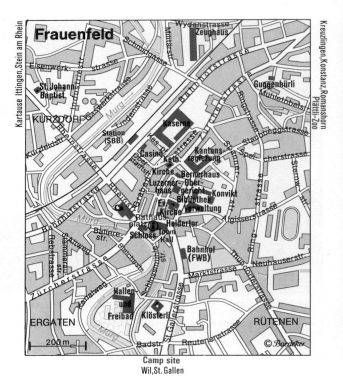

Camp site
Wil,St. Gallen

was destroyed by fire in 1524. The cloister dates from about 1540; the church was built in 1549–53 and re-modelled in Baroque style in the 18th c.

Tour of Thurgau

From Frauenfeld road 14 runs east to Wellhausen, where, on a hill 500 m/547 yds south, stands Wellenberg Castle (13th c.).

Weinfelden

The road now crosses the Thur and comes to the busy little town of Weinfelden (432 m/1417 ft; pop. 8500), seat of the cantonal parliament and court. Above the vineyards on the slopes of the Ottenberg is a castle of 1180 (restored c. 1860).

Bürglen
Amriswil Coach
Museum

The road continues through Bürglen (442 m/1450 ft), where a 16th–17th c. castle is a prominent landmark and comes to Amriswil (437 m/1434 ft; pop. 9200) a lively little industrial town. The private Sallmann Coach Museum has horse-drawn wagons and post coaches, including Napoleon III's battle wagon.

Schloss
Hagenwil

In Hagenwil, 3 km/2 miles south-east, can be seen a well-preserved moated castle, with a chapel and Gothic knights' hall.

Bischofszell

South-west of Amriswil, above a loop in the Thur, lies the ancient town of Bischofszell (510 m/1673 ft). The Gothic parish church of St Pelagius

(14th–15th c.) in the centre of the town has a notable treasury. The attractive Town Hall (1743) with its artistic iron balustrade, was designed by the architect Kaspar Bagnato. The former Bishop's Palace (13th–15th c.) is now the headquarters of the local public works department. At Marktgasse 4, the Bodenturm houses a museum of local history.

From Bischofszell we go south-west to join road 7 and follow it westwards to Münchwilen, from which a detour can be made a short distance south to Sirnach (550 m/1805 ft; pop. 4200), with attractive old half-timbered houses, and Fischingen (620 m/2034 ft) which has a church belonging to the former Benedictine abbey (rebuilt 1795; richly decorated 18th c. interior).

Sirnach
Fischingen

From Münchwilen, road 7 returns to Frauenfeld.

Frauenfeld

Ticino

Canton: Ticino (TI)

Ticino (German Tessin), the most southerly of the Swiss cantons, takes its name from the River Ticino, a left-bank tributary of the Po, which rises on the Nufenen pass (Passo della Novena), flows through Lake Maggiore and joins the Po after a course of 248 km/154 miles.

Location and general

The canton has an area of 2811 sq. km/1085 sq. miles and a population of some 250,000. Its capital is Bellinzona (see entry), situated near the junction of the roads from the St Gotthard (see entry) and the San Bernardino pass (see entry). The canton's main sources of revenue are agriculture and tourism. In the past, many German-speaking Swiss and Germans from the Federal Republic have settled in the canton, particularly by the lakes, which has led to a considerable change in the population structure. The indigenous population is almost exclusively Italian-speaking, but with a local dialect.

The "Paradise" of Lugano below Monte San Salvatore

Toggenburg

History   The territory of Ticino, occupied in the early historical period by Rhaetians and Lepontii, was later incorporated in the Roman province of Gallia Cisalpina. Between the 5th and 8th c. it was successively occupied by the Goths, the Lombards and the Franks. In the 15th c. the Confederates gradually wrested it from the overlordship of the Dukes of Milan. It became an independent canton in 1803.

Flora and Fauna Along the northern boundaries of Ticino are high-Alpine regions with their characteristic plants and animals. Farther south, Mediterranean vegetation increasingly predominates, flourishing particularly in the south-facing valleys. By the lakes, palms and citrus fruits are found. The animal life, particularly insects and reptiles, also shows clear Mediterranean characteristics.

Architecture   The markedly southern orientation and the protection against influences from the region north of the Alps, which result from Ticino's geographical situation, are reflected also in the architecture of the houses and public buildings. In many places, the churches are built of natural stone without any external rendering, as in northern Italy, and the canton has a rich heritage of Renaissance and Baroque architecture.

                 *Ascona; *Bellinzona; *Locano; **Lugano; **Lake Lugano; **Lake Maggiore; see entries.

Toggenburg   E1

                 Canton; St Gallen (SG)
                 Capital: Lichtensteig

Location and   The Toggenburg district, a region of varied scenery lying south of Thurgau,
general   comprises the Upper Thur valley and its tributary valleys. Once an independent county, it is now part of the canton of St Gallen.

Tour of Toggenburg from Wil to Buchs

Untertoggenburg

General   South of Wil (see St Gallen) the road passes through the pleasant area of Untertoggenburg. On the slopes of the hills are elegant farmhouses of Alemannic type and, in the villages, are 18th c. "manufacturers' houses" (Fabrikantenhäuser) dating from the period when the region's flourishing textile industry was established.

Flawil   The chief town and trading centre of Untertoggenburg is Flawil (610 m/2002 ft; pop. 9000), a village situated above the river Glatt, with a flourishing spinning and weaving industry. Flawil still has a few richly painted houses (Hof "Gupfen", "Dorfschmiede" village smithy) and an interesting museum.

Oberglatt   A little way to the east lies Oberglatt which was, for centuries, the ecclesiastical centre of the district. Every year in summer the "Musikzychus" (music cycle) takes place.

Burgau,   About 1½ km/1 mile south-east of Flawil lies the charming old village of
Magdenau   Burgau, with fine old houses (law court of 1639), and another 1½ km/1 mile
Convent   west is the Cistercian Convent of Magdenau, founded in 1244, which has 17th and 18th c. buildings.

Burg Landegg   Not far south-west of the convent stands the parish church of St Verena
(ruin)   and, to the west, the ruins of Landegg Castle.

Lichtensteig – chief town of Toggenburg

Further south-east, in Degersheim, is Retonio's Magic Casino, with mechanical organs, automata and magicians' equipment.

Retonio's Magic Casino

*Obertoggenburg

Beyond Neu-St Johann the road runs through the Starkenbach defile into Obertoggenburg, a beautiful mountain region between the limestone massifs of Säntis and the Churfirsten which is a popular health and winter sports area.

It then crosses the Wildhaus pass (1098 m/3602 ft; climbing frames for children) and through the beautifully wooded Simmigorge into the Rhine valley.

Wildhaus

By taking road 8 from St Gallen (see entry) or road 16 from Kreuzlingen via Wil, we reach Lichtensteig (618 m/2028 ft; pop. 2200), an old-world little town which is picturesquely situated on a rocky hill above the right bank of the Thur. It is the principal place in the Toggenburg region with some handsome old arcaded houses. In the Toggenburg Heimatmuseum can be seen a notable collection of rural crafts and popular art, including documentation of alpine husbandry as well as musical instruments and costumes. Also of interest is the church of St Gallus, a modern building (1966–72) by W. M. Förderer, and Freddy's Mechanical Music Museum in the Hans Zur Frohburg.

Lichtensteig

2 km/1 mile south of Lichtensteig on road 16 is Wattwil (617 m/2024 ft): pop. 9000), a long straggling town which is the economic hub of Toggenburg, with a variety of industry (Textile College). The popular Swiss writer Ulrich Bräker (1735–98) worked here as a weaver.

Wattwil

On the hillside to the right of the road can be seen the Franciscan nunnery of St Maria zu den Engeln (574 m/1883 ft: 17th c.) and, opposite it, to the

St Maria zu den Engeln

south, Iberg Castle (13th c., restored). A road on the right leads via Ricken to Surih or Glarus.

Ebnat–Kappel   The road to Buchs continues from Wattoril up the Thur valley, here wide and fertile, and in 5.5 km/3 miles reaches Ebnat–Kappel (633–650 m/2077–2133 ft), actually two towns with a combined population of 5500 inhabitants and a variety of industry. The twin towns attract summer visitors and winter sports enthusiasts. The Albert Edelmann Foundation has a notable exhibition concerning traditional Toggenburg customs.

Krummenau   Beyond this, the valley closes in. Ahead the Churfirsten (on right) and the Stockberg (on left) come into sight. At Krummenau (716 m/2349 ft) the valley briefly opens out again. At the far end of the village, on the right, is a large parking place near the chair-lift (2025 m/6644 ft) from Krümmenschwil (740 m/2427 ft) to Rietbach (1120 m/3675 ft), from which there is a ski-lift to the Wolzenalp (1456 m/4777 ft).

"Sprung"   Beyond Krummenau, the Thur flows under the natural rock bridge known as the Sprung and through the Kesseltobel gorge, with the road running on the hillside high above it.

Neu-St Johann   2.5 km/2 miles from Krummenau is Neu-St Johann (760 m/2494 ft), a village set amid meadows in a wider part of the valley (summer holiday accommodation, winter sports), with a fine 17th c. Baroque church belonging to a former Benedictine monastery.

From Neu-St Johann to the Säntis   A reasonably good road (12 km/7 miles to the lower station of the cableway) branches off the main road to Nesslau in Neu-St Johann and climbs the slopes above the Luternbach valley, with a fine view of the Säntis. Reaching the top of the hill in 1.5 km/1 mile, it runs level past the Ennetbühl and then descends gradually to cross the Luternbach gorge.

Rietbad   Beyond this, a good road winds its way up to Rietbad (927 m/3041 ft), with a well-known spring of sulphurous water (drinking fountain 100 m/328 ft beyond the Kurhotel), at the foot of the Stockberg (1784 m/5853 ft; 1 hour; extensive views).

Seeben Kräzeren pass   The road now follows a level course through the meadows of a high valley, passing in 1 km/½ mile the Kurhaus at Seeben. It then climbs over the meadows of the Alp Bernhalde (1283 m/4210 ft) and continues through forest to the Kräzeren Pass (1300 m/4265 ft). A short way downhill you arrive at the Schwägalp inn.

Schwägalp   In Schwägalp you pass the road from Umäsch coming in on the left and then it is a drive of 1 km/¾ mile up to the lower station (1350 m/4462 ft) of the Säntis cableway which was opened in 1935 and which has been renewed several times, most recently in 1974. It takes seven minutes to reach the

**Säntis   summit of the Säntis (upper station 2433 m/8116 ft, see Appenzell) from where there is a breathtaking panorama over the Vorarlberg, Bündner, Glarus and Uri alps, as well as across Lake Constance into Swabia. In good weather, the view even takes in the Vosges and the Jura.

Nesslau *Speer   From Neu-St Johann, road 16 continues through the adjoining village of Nesslau (762 m/2400 ft), frequented as a summer vacation and winter sports resort. Towering above it to the south-west is the Speer (1954 m/6411 ft), which offers a rewarding climb (5 hours).

Giessen Falls   Higher up the valley is Germen, where the road runs through a narrow wooded pass, with the two Giessen Falls on the Thur (hydro-electric station). It then winds its way uphill to the little vacation spot of Stein (860 m/2823 ft) and continues up through the Starkenbach Pass (894 m/2933 ft; on the right the ruins of Starkenstein castle) into the Alpine high valley of

Starkenstein Castle (ruin)

Unterwasser in Obertoggenburg

Obertoggenburg, with innumerable farms and huts dotting its green meadow-covered slopes. To the right is the jagged ridge of the Churfirsten; to the left is a first glimpse of the Wildhauser Schafberg.

*Obertoggen-burg

5 km/3 miles from Stein is Alt-St Johann (897 m/2943 ft), a popular health and winter sports resort, founded in the 12th c. as the monastery of St John.

Alt-St Johann

At the end of the village, on the right, is the lower station of a chair-lift (1.5 km/1 mile, 15 minutes) to the Alp Sellamatt (1390 m/4561 ft): panoramic views, near which are the Churfirsten hut (1450 m/4757 ft) and the Iltiosalp (30 minutes' walk). Good walking and cross-country trekking.

Sellamatt Alp

Road 16 continues to Unterwasser (927 m/3041 ft), a popular health resort (swimming pool) and winter sports resort in a beautiful sheltered setting between the Säntis chain and the Churfirsten, at the junction where the two streams combine to form the River Thur. In the Haus Rotenbrunnen in the village street is an alpine dairy museum, with exhibits illustrating milk processing and showing a kitchen and living-room.

Unterwasser

From Unterwasser a narrow mountain road climbs steeply up (2 km/1 mile north) to the Kühboden Alp (1050 m 3445 ft); from here it is an hour's walk to the charming little Gräppelensee (1302 m/4272 ft).

Kühboden

Gräppelensee

Another little road runs 3.5 km/2 miles south-east to the Schwendi (1165 m/3822 ft) from where there is a road 3.5 km/2 miles to Wildhaus.

Schwendi Lakes

A funicular 1.2 km/1 mile long goes up from Unterwasser in 6 minutes to the much visited Iltiosalp (1350 m/4429 ft), from where a magnificent view of the Säntis massif can be enjoyed. There is excellent skiing (ski-lift to Alp Stöfeli, 1480 m/4856 ft).

*Iltiosalp

Chäserrugg	From the Iltiosalp a cabin cableway (3450 m/11,319 ft, 8 minutes) runs up to Chäserrugg (2250 m/7382 ft); Stöfeli mountain inn).
*Churfirsten	Footpaths (extensive views) lead east to the Schwendi-Seen (30 minutes) and west to the Alp Sellamatt (30 minutes). The ascent of the Hinterrugg (2309 m/7575 ft), the highest peak in the Churfirsten chain, takes 3½ hours.
Lisighaus	The main road continues up from Unterwasser in a double hairpin bend and comes in 2.5 km/2 miles to the hamlet of Lisighaus (1056 m/3456 ft: commune of Wildhaus), with the modest house in which the reformer Ulrich Zwingli (1484–1531) was born.
Wildhaus	Barely 5 km/3 miles from Unterwasser is Wildhaus (1098 m/3603 ft), a widely scattered health and winter sports resort (indoor swimming pool; climbing school; holiday courses in hand-weaving; ice-ink, curling rink, cross-country skiing), magnificently situated on an open pass below the south side of the Wildhauser Schafberg (2384 m/7822 ft).
Oberdorf	From here an 800 m/2625 ft long chair-lift goes up to Oberdorf (1270 m/4167 ft) from which another chair-lift continues up to the Gamserrugg (1771 m/5811 ft) on the Gamsalp.
Gamplüt	There is yet another chair lift from Wildhaus north-westwards to the Gamplüt (1334 m/4377 ft).
Schönen-bodensee	1½ km/1 mile north of Wildhaus lies the little Schönen lake, with a bathing beach.
Simmitobel	From Wildhaus the road goes downhill on a moderate gradient over Alpine meadows flanked by mountains, then enters the forest and runs more steeply down through the wooded Simmi gorge to the Zolhaus inn (706 m/2316 ft).
*Gamser Berg	From here it winds its way down the slopes of the Gamser Berg, with extensive views (parking place in 200 m/656 ft, on right) and magnificent vistas of the Rhine valley and the Liechtenstein Alps.
Gams	Gams (504 m/1654 ft) is a neat village with a church above it on higher ground. From here there is a road east to Hagg.
Rhine Valley	Road 16 now turns south along the edge of the wide Rhine valley and comes to Grabs.
Grabs	Grabs (482 m/1581 ft) is a large village surrounded by orchards. Here a steep and narrow mountain road (10 km/6 miles) turns off on the right and winds its way up the Grabser Berg to the Kurhaus Voralp, below the
Voralpsee	beautiful Voralp Lake (1116 m/3662 ft).
Buchs Schloss Werdenberg	From Grabs the road continues along the densely populated valley to the straggling village of Buchs (450 m/1476 ft; see Rhine) to join the road from St Margrethen to Chur beneath Werdenberg castle. Chur is set picturesquely above a lake.

Valais Alps   C-D 2/3

Canton: Valais (VS)

Location	The Valais Alps (German–Waliser Alpen; French–Alpes Valaisiennes) lie between the Upper Rhône valley and the Italian river Dora Baltea. The Swiss-Italian frontier runs along the main ridge of the massif which forms part of the southern Swiss Alps.
**Landscape	The principal valleys in the Valais Alps are accessible on side roads opening off the main road along the Rhône valley (see entry). Two important north-

south routes run through the massif, over the Great St Bernard (see entry), in the west and the Simplon pass (see entry) in the east. Rising to well over 4000 m/13,124 ft, the range includes some of the mightiest peaks in Switzerland, including the Matterhorn (4478 m/14,692 ft) and the Monte Rosa group, with the Dufourspitze (4634 m/15,204 ft), the country's highest mountain. One notable man-made feature is the artificial lake of Grand-Dixence (see Sion) in a grandiose mountain setting.

Matterhorn
**Dufourspitze

The beauties of the Valais Alps were discovered by tourists relatively early. The best-known resorts are Zermatt (see entry) and Saas Fee (see Saas Valley), but in recent years a number of other resorts such as Verbier (see Martigny), Grimentz (see Sierre) and Zinal (see Sierre) have developed into popular winter sports areas.

**Zermatt
*Saas Fee

Vevey   B2

Canton: Vaud (VD)
Altitude: 383 m/1257 ft
Population: 16,000

Vevey, the chief town of the Canton of Valais, lies on Lake Geneva at the mouth of the river Veveyse and is dominated on the north by Mont Pèlerin (1084 m/3557 ft) and the Plèiades (1364 m/4475 ft). On the slopes to the north are the famous Lavanx vineyards. Every twenty-five years the "Fête des Vignerons", a unique vintners' festival is held here (last in 1977), which includes many folkloristic events.
Vevey lies on the Simplon railway line and is a motorway junction (N9 /E2 and N12 /E4).

Location and general

In Roman times, Vevey (Viviscus) was the most important port on Lake Geneva. The town received its municipal charter about 1200 and, during the Middle Ages it rose to prosperity as a trading station on the road from Burgundy to Piedmont. It began to develop into a major tourist attraction in the 19th c.

History

Sights

The finest feature of the town is the Grand' Place, an unusually large market square on the shores of the lake. At its north end is the colonnaded Grenette (Corn Exchange, 1808) and, beyond this, near the Theatre, is the Auberge de la Clef, in which Rousseau stayed in 1730 (commemorative plaque).
In house No. 5 is the Swiss Camera Museum which has an interesting collection of old cameras and photographic equipment. On the west side of the Grand' Place is the Jardin du Rivage (concerts during the season), with the beautiful Seahorse Fountain.

Grenette

Camera museum

From the market square and the Quai Perdonnet to the east there are magnificent views over the lake to the Savoy Alps, with Le Grammont (2172 m/7126 ft) in the foreground. In the middle of the quai stands the "Charlot Memorial" (John Doubleday) to the great film artist Charlie Chaplin.
Nearby is the Alimentarium, a museum of the history of food, a Nestlé foundation opened in 1985. At the east end of the quay (800 m/2625 ft long) in front of a small park is an amusing bronze sculpture group, "Première chevauchée de Bacchus" (1930) and a bust of the poetess Anna de Noailles (1876–1933).

Quai Ferdonnet

Alimentarium

No. 2 Avenue de la Gare, which leads east from the station square, houses the Musée Jenisch (established in 1897; closed Mon.). The collection includes pictures and sculpture by Swiss artists of the 19th and 20th c.,

Jenisch museum Kokoschka Foundation

Vevey: La Grenette, the former corn-hall

including Hodler, Steinlen and Gimmi, and also etchings and natural history exhibits. Temporary art exhibitions are also held here.

As a memorial to the Austrian painter and writer Oskar Kokoschka, an exhibition of his works was opened in 1988 in the Jenisch Museum. On view are paintings, watercolours, drawings and etchings by the artist. His literary works were left to the Zurich central library.

Musée du Vieux-Vevey et Musée de la Confrérie des Vignerons

In the Rue d'Italie, north of Quai Perdonnet, are the Musée du Vieux-Vevey (Museum of Old Vevey) and Musée de la Confrérie des Vignerons (Museum of the Confraternity of Vintners; closed on Mondays), housing pre-historic material, fine old furniture, weapons, costumes, and documents on the history of wine.

St Martin's Church

On a terrace above the railway line (fine views: orienteering tablet) stands the church of St Martin (14th–15th c., with 20th c. stained glass).

Palais Nestlé

On the north-western outskirts of the town, near the Lausanne road, is the Y-shaped Palais Nestlé (1960), headquarters of the famous Swiss firm.

**La Tour de Peilz
Castle, Museum of Games**

To the east, contiguous with Vevey, is the little town of La Tour de Peilz, dominated by a 13th c. castle, which, since 1987, has contained the Musée Suisse de Jeu. The interesting collection comprises games from all over the world and of various periods, and includes educational, strategic, simulated games, and games of chance. In the Place du Temple stands a "Freedom Monument" by Gustave Courbet, who died here in 1877. A walk along the shore of the lake by the fine yacht harbour is recommended.

Surroundings

*Mont Pèlerin

From the hotel colony (alt. 806 m/2644 ft) on the slopes of Mont Pèlerin (1084 m/3557 ft) there are fine views of Lake Geneva, the Rhône valley and

La Tour de Peilz: the yacht harbour

the Savoy Alps. It can be reached either by road (12 km/7 miles, via Corsier) or by funicular (1.6 km/1 mile, 10 minutes), via Corseaux (429 m/1480 ft: swimming pool), where there is a house built by Le Corbusier for his parents in 1924 (museum), and Chardonne. In summer a tourist railway runs between Vevey and Chamby. In 1988 the Dalai Lama, who was awarded the Nobel Peace Prize in 1989, opened a new cultural centre on Mont Pèlerin. This forms part of the Tibetan centre of 1977 in which live about a dozen monks. The centre is intended as a meeting-place for Tibetans who are exiled in Europe, and also to give interested Europeans the opportunity to learn something of Tibetan culture and Buddhism.

Tibetan Centre

The route (by road 5 km/3 miles, by electric railway 6 km/4 miles in 20 minutes, continuation to the Pléiades 12 km/7 miles in 45 minutes) passes the English church and continues up the Route de Blonay, turning left up the hill in 1 km/½ mile. After passing the 18th c. Château de Hauteville (off the road to the right: beautiful private gardens, with lookouts) it runs through the villages of St-Légier (champagne-style wine) and La Chiésaz, where the grave of the composer Paul Hindemith (1895–1963) can be seen in the cemetery and where there are a number of houses with humorous external paintings by A. Béguin. Finally, the road runs below the massive 12th c. Château de Blonay, which has remained in the possession of the Blonay family since it was built. 5 km/3 miles: Blonay (623 m/2044 ft). For description of village and continuation of road to the Pléiades: see Montreux.

From Vevey to Blonay

Hauteville Castle

*Blonay Castle

Vierwaldstätter See

D1/2

Cantons: Uri (UR), Schwyz (SZ), Unterwalden (NW) and Lucerne (LU)

The Vierwaldstätter See or Lake of the Four Forest Cantons (the three original cantons of Uri, Schwyz and Unterwalden together with the canton

Location and
**Landscape

of Lucerne) is commonly referred to in English as Lake Lucerne, but this is, in fact, only one of the lake's many arms. Lying at an altitude of 437 m/1434 ft, it is the fourth largest of the Swiss lakes (area 114 sq. km/44 sq. miles), length from Lucerne to Flüelen 38 km/24 miles; greatest depth 214 m/702 ft), but is second to none in magnificence and scenic variety.

General

The great mountains with their endless scope for walks and climbs are reflected in the spacious surface of the lake. The famous lookouts of the Rigi, Pilatus and the Stanserhorn are brought within easy reach by mountain railways and cableways. The beautiful shores of the lake with their southern vegetation offer numerous bathing places. The neat towns and villages provide luxurious or modest accommodation at the visitor's choice. These attractions, plus the lake's associations with the origins of the Swiss Confederation and the legend of William Tell all help make the Lake of the Four Forest Cantons one of the most popular tourist areas in Europe.

Lake Lucerne
Alpnacher See
Küssnachter See

The lake begins in the west as the beautiful Luzerner See (Lake Lucerne), with the Bucht von Stansstad (Stansstad Bay) and the Alpnacher See to the south and the Küssnachter See (Lake Küssnacht) to the north-east. Then come the Weggiser Becken (Weggis Basin) and, beyond the Rigi and Bürgenstock promontories, which reduce the width of the lake to only 825 m/902 yds, the Gersauer Becken (Gersau Basin) and the Buochser Bucht (Buochs Bay).

*Lake Uri

Running south from Brunnen is the Urner See (Lake Uri), a fjord-like strip of water enclosed between massive rock walls, scenically the most magnificent part of the lake.

Boat services

From Lucerne to Flüelen: 48 km/30 miles, 3–3½ hours.

The full beauty of the lake and its mountain setting can best be appreciated by taking a boat trip, which will provide a pleasant alternative to the journey by car. Even a one-way trip is worth taking if you can arrange to have your car driven to meet you.

There are also boat services from Lucerne to Küssnacht (15 km/9 miles, 1 hour) and from Lucerne via Kehrsiten–Bürgenstock and Stansstad to Alpnachstad (25 km/16 miles, 1¼–1½ hours). In summer, services between Lucerne and Flüelen operate in conjunction with the William Tell Express excursion; there are connections with the railway to Locarno or Lugano (see Practical Information: Railways).
Water-taxis (maximum 10 passengers) of the St Niklausen Schiffsgesellschaft run throughout the day, stopping at any place by request.

*Around the Vierwaldstättersee by road

From Lucerne to Flüelen along the northern and eastern shores

Lucerne

Lake Lucerne

Leave Lucerne (see entry: altitude 438 m/1437 ft) on the Haldenstrasse, going past the Kursaal (on right) and the beautiful lakeside gardens and continuing close to the shore of Lake Lucerne. In 2 km/1 mile a side road goes off on the right (0.5 km/¼ mile) to the public beach (park, camp site, restaurant). The road then runs past the Swiss Transport Museum (see entry) and the Liliputbahn (a miniature steam railway). Beyond this a road comes in on the right from the beach.

Seeburg

Then the hotels on the Bürgenstock and later the Rigi (see entries) come into view. The first place to be reached is Seeburg (440 m/1444 ft; beach), an outlying suburb of Lucerne. Beyond this, the road winds its way up to cross the Megger Berg (496 m/1627 ft), with fruit orchards and many houses, past the Meggenhorn, a little wooded peninsula on the right.

Meggen is a long straggling village (483 m/1585 ft). In Vorder-Meggen we find Schloss Neu-Habsburg (1869), with the tower of an older castle which Rudolf von Habsburg had built in 1240, but which was destroyed by the men of Lucerne in 1352. The mansion of Schloss Meggenhorn (1886–1899) was built by Viktor von Segesser on the model of French Renaissance Châteaux; the Neo-Gothic chapel is worth seeing. The parish church of Hinter-Meggen dates from the 18th and 19th centuries.

Meggen

The road now enters the canton of Schwyz and continues along the north-west side of the Küssnacher See. 2 km/1 mile beyond the village of Merlischachen (444 m/1457 ft), below the road on the right, is the Astrid Chapel (1936), moved here in 1960 from its previous position on the left of the road, commemorating Queen Astrid of the Belgians, who was killed in a car accident here (spot marked by a cross) on 29 August 1935.

Lake Küssnacht

The road now descends to Küssnacht (440 m/1444 ft; see entry), from which the main road (No. 2) continues via Arth to Brunnen (see entry). The more attractive road via Weggis and Gersau branches off on the right and follows closely to the east side of the Küssnachter See, passing through pleasant countryside below the west side of the Rigi. In 0.5 km/¼ mile. it passes the lower station of the cableway to the Seebodenalp (on left). In 5 km/3 miles, on right, is the village of Greppen (454 m/1490 ft). The road now climbs (beautiful view of the lake to the rear) over a hill, with the Hertenstein peninsula to the right, and runs down to a junction.

Küssnacht

Here a road on the right leads to the popular resort of Weggis (440 m/1444 ft), prettily situated on the lake. A pleasant detour can be made to the public beach and to the Hertenstein peninsula (8 km/5 miles) and to the east a narrow road climbs 5½ km/3 miles up the slopes of the Rigi (see entry; no road to the summit). The main road, bypassing Weggis, runs uphill again. 2.5 km/2 miles beyond the turning for Weggis, the old road comes in on the right. Nearby is the lower station of the Weggis–Rigi–Kaltbad cableway (see Rigi). Then follows a beautiful stretch of road, running close to the lake at the foot of the Rigi, with splendid views. To the right can be seen the Bürgenstock (see entry) and its well-known hotels. Further on, there is a charming view of the narrowest part of the lake between the two promontories, the Obere and the Untere Nase, and of the Bürgenstock, with the Buochsehorn and Stansehorn rearing up behind it.

Weggis

Vitznau (440 m/1444 ft): a popular summer holiday resort affording extensive views, from which a rack-railway ascends the Rigi (35 minutes: see entry). (There is another rack-railway up the Rigi from Arth-Goldau, to the east.) At the far end of the village, on the left, are two cableways, one to Hinterbergen, the other to Weissenfluh (Wissifluh, 936 m/3071 ft: hotel), both giving access to fine walking country. The road continues past the beach and then winds its way around the Obere Nase, skirting the shore of the lake or running a little above it, with extensive views. 5 km/3 miles from Vitznau is the terminal of a car ferry to Beckenried on the south side of the lake (service every hour, taking 15 minutes).

Vitznau
**Rigi

Gersau (440 m/1444 ft) is the oldest health resort on the Vierwaldstätter See, occupying a charming sheltered site. From here, a mountain road leads north (5.5 km/3 miles) to the lower station, at Gschwend (1012 m/3320 ft: inn), of a cableway which runs north-west to the Burggeist guest-house, 20 minutes below the Rigi-Scheidegg peak (1665 m/5463 ft).
Beyond Gersau, the road continues close to the shore or on the wooded slopes above the lake. It passes the old Kindlimord chapel (rebuilt 1708), at the foot of the Rigi-Hochfluh (1702 m/5584 ft), with a view of the two peaks of the Mythen. Soon after this, the Lake Uri comes into view beyond the

Gersau

Fronalpstock on Lake Uri

Treib promontory. 4 km/2 miles further on, to the left, is a cableway up the Urmiberg.

Brunnen

In Brunnen (440 m/1444 ft: see entry) we join the St Gotthard road, coming from Lucerne and Zurich via Arth. The lakeside route from Brunnen to Flüelen follows this road. At the Wolfsprung Hotel an attractive little mountain road (3 km/2 miles) goes off on the left via the health resort of Morschach and the holiday centre of Axenfels (turn left), past the Rütliblick

*Axenstein

Hotel to the Axenstein (708 m/2323 ft; see Brunnen), with a superb view of both arms of the Vierwaldstätter See.

*Axenstrasse
*Lake Uri

The road to Flüelen continues along the magnificent Axenstrasse, which runs above the steep east shore of the fjord-like Urner See (Lake Uri), passing through numerous tunnels and galleries blasted from the rock (it is possible to walk along some stretches of the old road, built in 1863–65). The St Gotthard railway running parallel to the road, sometimes below it, also passes through many tunnels. On the far side of the lake can be seen the crag known as the "Schillerstein" (named after the German dramatist whose works include "William Tell") and, higher up on the Seelisberg the Rütli meadow where the original Swiss Confederation was established. Just before Sisikon, the road enters the canton of Uri.

Sisikon

Sisikon (457 m/1499 ft), at the mouth of the Riemenstalden valley, has a modern church built in 1968. Beyond this, the road continues through more tunnels to the Tellsplatte Hotel (512 m/1680 ft), with a car park and beautiful gardens (view of the massive Urirotstock, 2932 m/9620 ft). From here, a

Tell's Chapel

footpath (7 minutes) leads down to the famous Tell's Chapel (known to have existed since at least 1500; restored 1881, with paintings by Stükelberg), on the spot where William Tell is traditionally supposed to have leapt out of Gessler's ship during a storm. From the hotel, a cableway runs up in 4 minutes to the Axen station (825 m/2707 ft). 1 km/½ mile further on the Axenstrasse enters its last tunnel, with an old gallery (lookout) on the right.

The Schnitzturm of Stansstad

Flüelen (440 m/1444 ft), a port and holiday resort at the south end of the   Flüelen
Lake Uri, is built on the delta at the mouth of the canalised river Reuss (see
below). Near the station, behind the old parish church of St George and St
Niklaus (1665) stands the little Schloss Rudenz, which once belonged to the
lords of Attinghausen, whose estate extended to the shore of the lake and
who controlled the customs station. Here stands an iron sculpture
"Schwurhände" which Witschi created for the 1964 exhibition. There is a
cableway up the Eggeberge (1440 m/4775 ft).
Flüelen is the landing-stage for boats from Lucerne. Passengers who have
booked the "William Tell Express" excursion transfer here to the railway to
continue their trip into southern Ticino (see Practical Information:
Railways).

The Reuss plain is the only large level area in the canton of Uri which does   Reuss delta
not form part of the mountainous region. In 1966, work was begun to   project
reform the Reuss delta, which had been partly canalised between 1850 and
1863 and from 1939 provided with flood protection. An opening in the dam
on the left permits the water to flow into the plain and thus create a new
shallow water zone; a new channel is to be created on the right. The mouth
of the river which has hitherto extended far into the lake will be restricted
and, eventually, previously inaccessible supplies of gravel for quarrying
will be made available.

For the continuation of the road via Altdorf to Isenthal (see Altdorf).   Altdorf

From Lucerne to Seelisberg along the western and southern shores (37 km/23 miles)

Leave Lucerne (altitude 438 m/1437 ft; see entry) by Pilatusstrasse and   Lucerne
Obergrundstrasse (to left). Just after Paulusplatz a road goes off on the left
to Horw (445 m/1460 ft) from which it is possible either to travel south-east

431

Vierwaldstätter See

to Winkel, attractively situated in a bay on the lake, or to continue along the shores of the lake to Hergiswil.

The main road continues straight on past the turning for Horw. In ½ km/550 yds, we bear left on to the N2 motorway which we follow, at first running

*Pilatus
below Pilatus (see Lucerne) at some distance from the lake, and then above the lake, a beautiful view of the Rigi, the Bürgenstock and the Stanserhorn.

Hergiswil
To the left (motorway exit) is the summer holiday resort of Hergiswil, on the lake (445 m/1460 ft; bathing beach). At Brunni (825 m/2707 ft) 1.5 km/1 mile farther on, is a cableway which takes 6 minutes to reach the Gschwänd Alp (1216 m/3990 ft) on the north side of Pilatus.

*Lopperberg
The motorway continues on a beautiful stretch of road above the lake, running along the slopes of the Lopperberg (965 m/3166 ft), an outlier of Pilatus, and comes to a junction where the road diverges on the right to the Brünig Pass (see Sarnen; which can also be reached by taking the Sarnen exit after Hergiswil).

Alpnacher See
Stansstad
The N2 continues over the channel, only 150 m/492 ft wide, between the Vierwaldstätter See and the Alpnacher See to the exit for Stansstad (438 m/1437 ft: bathing beach), the port for Stans, a summer holiday resort and the beginning of the road to the Bürgenstock and the road and railway to Engelberg. On the shores of the lake stands the Schnitzturm, a relic of old fortifications. 1 km/½ mile north-east on the Harissenbucht (restaurant and night-club) is a funicular (382 m/1253 ft) which climbs in 4 minutes to the Kurhaus Fürigen (650 m/2133 ft).
From Stansstad a very attractive road runs east, climbing through the forest, then through the meadows of a high valley and finally through another stretch of forest to the parking place (fee) at the great complex of

**Bürgenstock
fine hotels on the Bürgenstock (878 m/2881 ft).

Stans
The motorway continues through the fertile valley (fruit orchards) between the Bürgenstock and the Stanserhorn to the exit for Stans (455 m/1493 ft), a little market town (population 6000), the capital of the half-canton of Nidwalden, the eastern half of the canton of Unterwalden. In the main square are the parish church (rebuilt in Baroque style 1641–47) and a monument to Arnold von Winkelried, hero of the Battle of Sempach (1386). To the right of the church is a double chapel of 1482 (charnel-house); to the left, above the church, stands the Town Hall (1715) where can be seen an interesting collection of paintings of Swiss cantonal officials. The Höfli is a restored medieval secular building. To the east of the centre the Kollegium St Fidelis has a small natural history collection. The former salt and corn store (1700) on the Stansstad road near the Stanserhorn funicular houses the Historical Museum, with a collection of weapons, uniforms, flags and official robes of the 16th–19th c., as well as costumes, religious art and paintings from the canton of Nidwalden.

*Stanserhorn
A combined funicular and cableway ascends in 25 minutes to the pan-oramic restaurant on the Stanserhorn–Kulm (1849 m/6067 ft) 5 minutes below the summit of the Stanserhorn (1901 m/6237 ft), from which there are superb views of the Uri, Unterwalden and Bernese Alps, the Vierwald-stätter See and the Alpine foreland.

Engelberger Aa
From Stans, the road to Seelisberg (Treib) branches off on the left and rejoins the N2 motorway, which crosses the fertile open valley of the Engelberger Aa and then the river. To the left is the Bürgenstock, to the right the Buochsehorn, ahead the Rigi.

Buochs
The next motorway exit leads to Buochs (440 m/1444 ft), a village, beauti-fully situated on the bay of the same name, which attracts many summer visitors; it has a church prominently located on higher ground.

Ennetbürgen
From here, a good road runs north to Ennetbürgen, below the east side of the Bürgenstock (road only as far as the Kurhaus Honegg: beyond this

Beckenried

Haus Treib

point no through traffic). Beyond Buochs, the road to Seelisberg skirts the lake, with a beautiful view of the Rigi.

At the near end of Beckenried, on the left, is the departure point of the car ferry to Gersau. Beckenried (440 m/1444 ft), a long straggling village at the end of the lakeside road, also popular as a quiet holiday resort.

Beckenried

A cableway runs up to the Klewenalp (1600/5250 ft) from which there is a beautiful view embracing the lake, the Rigi, the Mythen, the Glarus Alps and the Alpine foreland area with its lakes (good skiing; ski-lifts).

Klewenalp

Beyond Beckenried, the road to Seelisberg leaves the lake and crosses the motorway to Emmetten (762 m/2500 ft), another straggling village and summer holiday resort in a sheltered setting. The road continues uphill for a short distance before descending steeply near the church into a beautiful green Alpine valley and then climbing again on a moderate gradient to the Niederbauen (1927 m/6322 ft: on right, a cableway from Emmetten) and the Stutzberg.

Emmetten

Niederbauen

From Emmetten there is a cableway to the Stockhütte (1236 m/4219 ft).

Stockhütte

In another 3 km/2 miles, the road winds its way up through forest and then runs down and passes through a tunnel, beyond which there is a picturesque view of the Seelisberger See far below (736 m/2415 ft; bathing beach).

Seelisberg Lake

Beyond the lake a road branches off on the right to the Rütli meadow in the middle of the forest, where tradition has it that the Swiss Confederation was established. Here, in 1291, the three "forest cantons" of Schwyz, Uri and Unterwalden joined in an alliance which became the foundation of the "Perpetual League" against the Habsburgs. The Tell legend, which received its classical form in Schiller's drama "William Tell" (1804), was a later addition to the traditional story.

Rütli

Rütli meadow, where the Swiss Federation was traditionally founded

Seelisberg

The road continues to the health resort of Seelisberg (804–845 m/2638–2772 ft), situated on a wooded terrace high above the Vierwaldstätter See. The road passes the pilgrimage chapel of Maria-Sonnenberg (1667) and the funicular to Treib, and then descends through the forest, after which there is a superb view of the Vierwaldstätter See and the Rigi.

Treib

Treib (440 m/1444 ft), picturesquely set on the tongue of land between the Vierwaldstätter See and the Urner See, was formerly a little trading town and a haven for shipping on the lake. A funicular goes up to the Seelisberg (1149 m/3770 ft, 8 minutes) where there is a charming inn, built in 1903 in imitation of the previous inn (1658). Treib, where the road ends, has a landing-stage for the lake ships.

Seelisberg
Tunnel

The motorway south-east of Beckenried, opened in 1980, passes through the 9.3 km/5.8 miles long Seelisberg Tunnel to the south bank of Lake Uri and thence to the St Gotthard road.

Walensee

E1

Cantons: St Gallen (SG) and Glarus (GL)

Location

The Walensee (15 km/9 miles long, up to 2 km/1 mile wide and up to 151 m/495 ft deep) lies at an altitude of 423 m/1388 ft between the Glarus Alps to the south and the Churfirsten, which tower up on the north to a height of almost 1000 m/3281 ft above the light green waters of the lake (Hinterrugg 2309 m/7576 ft).

Weesen

At the west end of the lake is Weesen (431 m/1414 ft), a charming little town (population 1500) and holiday resort. From the shady lakeside promenade

Walensee, on the south flank of the Churfirsten ▶

Mollis: Hatli-Haus . . .　　　　　　　　　*. . . and orangery of the Höfli-Haus*

there are very beautiful views. 1 km/½ mile east, beyond the wooded detrital fan of the Flibach, is the hamlet of Fli or Fly.

A little road which branches off the road to Amden at Fli (alternate one-way traffic) runs along the north side of the lake. The road is cut from the rock for most of the way, with two tunnels. After passing the Muslen falls and the ruins of Strahlegg castle it comes to the little village of Betlis, 5 km/3 miles east of Weesen (520 m/1707 ft; boat service from Weesen), from which a footpath (15 minutes) leads up to the Seerenbach falls.

Betlis

A road, north-east from Weesen via Fli (6 km/4 miles: views), winds steeply up from the lake with two hairpin turns to the summer and winter sports resort (several ski-lifts) of Amden (911 m/2989 ft), lying high above the lake on sunny Alpine meadows between the Mattstock (1939 m/6362 ft: chair-lift, 1400 m/4593 ft in 15 minutes to the Alp Walau, 1285 m/4216 ft) and the Leistkamm (2105 m/6907 ft: 5 hours).

Amden

There is a rewarding climb from Amden to the summit of the Speer (1951 m/6401 ft: 3 hours).

*Speer

The N3 motorway follows the south side of the lake from the Glarus exit to Walenstadt, with viaducts (electrically heated in winter to prevent icing) and numerous tunnels and galleries.

There is also a slightly longer route via Näfels and the old road over the Kerenzerberg. 3.3 km/2 miles south of Niederurnen (see Glarus) is Näfels (440 m/1444 ft), a busy little market town of 4000 inhabitants (mainly Roman Catholic) at the mouth of the Linth valley. The richly appointed Freulerpalast contains the Glarus Cantonal Museum (see Glarus).

Detour via Näfels and the Kerenzerberg
Näfels

A steep road runs 6 km/4 miles west from Näfels to a charming little lake, the Obersee (989 m/3245 ft).

Obersee

In Näfels, take a road which branches off the Glarus road on the left and crosses the Linth. The first place on the road to the Kerenzerberg is Mollis

Mollis

(448 m/1470 ft), below the mighty Fronalpstock. It has a number of fine old burghers' houses, including the Zwickyhaus (1621), in the Kreuzgasse which has a fine gable-roof and, on the Kerenzerberg road, the former mansion of Haltli (1772–1784) which was designed by Konrad Schindler; it is now a special school. Hans Hof and the neighbouring Höfli, which were built in the second half of the 18th c., now form part of an old people's home. In the garden is an orangery, framed by beautiful beds of roses. The Fabrikhof on the Netstal road, built about 1760, has three fine curved gables.

Beyond Mollis, road 3, of excellent quality, climbs with many bends and sharp turns but with a moderate gradient. To the rear there are beautiful views of Näfels and over the Linth plain, bounded by the Hirzli, as far as Lake Zurich; to the left are the Weggis chain, the Glämisch and the Tödi. In 2 km/1 mile the Talblick inn is passed on the right, after which the road turns through the forest, with the first glimpses of the Walensee.

5½ km/3 miles from Mollis, on the left, is the Café Kerenser Berghaus (730 m/2395 ft), on the Kerenzerberg (1375 m/4511 ft), with a beautiful view of the Walensee and the Churfirsten; to the left, below the Mattstock, is Amden and, at the west end of the lake, the village of Weesen. Here, the road reaches its highest point and begins to descend.

Kerenzerberg

*Churfirsten

Filzbach (720 m/2362 ft) is a village and health resort, magnificently located on a terrace of meadowland 270 m/886 ft above the Walensee, below the pyramidal summit of the Mürtschenstock (2442 m/8012 ft). 1¼ hours' walk south is the little Talalpsee (1100 m/3609 ft). A chair-lift (1650 m/5414 ft; 14 minutes) ascends from Filzbach to the Habergschwänd Alp (1280 m/4200 ft; restaurant).

Filzbach

From Filzbach, the road continues gently uphill and circles the Sallerntobel gorge, with beautiful views at the Café Seeblick (1.5 km/1 mile) just before reaching Obstalden.

Obstalden (700 m/2297 ft), in a beautiful setting similar to that of Filzbach, has an old church. The road on the right leads into the Hüttenberge (5 km/ 3 miles) and then winds its way down (views) into the Merenbach valley and passes through a short tunnel to join the road along the Walensee at Mühlehorn.

Obstalden

5 km/3 miles beyond the Glarus exit the N3 motorway comes to a parking place and just beyond this, on the left, is the Walensee restaurant. 1 km/½ mile further on is an exit (cars only) to the village of Mühlehorn (423 m/1398 ft), at the inflow of the Merenbach into the Walensee. The road continues along above the lake, traversing two tunnels, and past the Mühlehorn/Kerenzerberg junction where the road from the Kerenzerberg comes in.

*Along the Walensee shore
Mühlehorn

The motorway now begins to climb a little. In another 1.5 km/1 mile it comes to the village of Murg (430 m/1411 ft), situated below the road (exit only on left) on the alluvial cone of the river Murg, which forms a promontory projecting into the lake. There is a pleasant walk (4–5 hours) up the quiet Alpine valley of the Murg to the three beautiful Murg Lakes (1673–1825 m/5489–5988 ft). On the north side of the lake opposite Murg (motor-boat service), beneath the Leistkamm (2105 m/6907 ft) at the west end of the Churfirsten massif, is the very attractive little village of Quinten (All inn), with beautiful southern vegetation. Like Terzen and Quarten, the village takes its name from the Latin numbering of ecclesiastical properties in the Middle Ages.

Murg

Quinten

The road continues past parking places on either side and then descends towards the shore of the lake. In another 1 km/½ mile, on the left is the Rössli hotel and restaurant, and 1.5/1 mile beyond this, on the right, the Mühle hotel.

Flums, at the mouth of the Schils valley

Unterterzen	Then comes Unterterzen (429 m/1408 ft), a little industrial town (cement works, match factory, etc.) of 8000 inhabitants. A road goes off on the right and runs up 3 km/2 miles via Quarten (574 m/1883 ft) (convalescent home) to Oberterzen.
Oberterzen	Oberterzen (662 m/2172 ft) is a health resort and a cross country-skiing base. From here it is a 2½ hours' walk to the three Seeben lakes (1643 m/5391 ft). At the far end of Unterterzen, the Chur road passes the lower station of a cableway which ascends via Oberterzen to the Flumserberge.
Mols	About 2 km/1 mile from Unterterzen is Mols (432 m/1417 ft), after which the road curves to the right under a wooded spur with the ruins of Bommerstein Castle. It then passes a camping site on the left and the Walenstadt bathing beach at the end of the lake.
Walenstadt	Crossing the Seez Canal you reach Walenstadt (430 m/1411 ft): population 3500; another popular summer holiday spot, it lies 1 km/½ mile from the east end of the Walensee below the steep rock-faces of the Hinterrugg.
Walenstadtberg	From here, an attractive mountain road winds its way up to the health resort of Walenstadtberg (800–900 m/2625–2953 ft), 4 km/2 miles north-west, on a terrace of meadowland above the north side of the lake, beneath the jagged peaks of the Churfirsten. 1.5 km/1 mile farther on is the Knoblishühl sanatorium (982 m/3222 ft) from where a narrow little road runs up another 2 km/1 mile to the Schrina-Hochrugg restaurant (1313 m/4308 ft), near which is a temple-like monument to Peace by Karl Bickel.
Seez valley	From Walenstadt, the Chur road continues up the broad Seez valley below the Alvier massif (on left). To the right, on a projecting spur above Flums, stands the ruined castle of Gräpplang.
Berschis	Berschis (446 m/1463 ft: bypass). On a wooded crag above the village to the left (easy climb) the pilgrimage chapel of St George (592 m/1942 ft: 12th and 15 c.) has wall-paintings (key from priest's house in the village).

Stalden in the Mattertal   *Monte Rosa massif*

Beyond Berschis, at the beginning of the motorway to Chur, a road branches off on the right, crossing the railway and the Seez canal, to the neat village of Flums (444 m/1457 ft) at the mouth of the Schils valley, with the Weissmeilen (2490 m/8137 ft) and the curiously shaped Spitzmeilen in the background. By the Seez canal is the church of St Justus, the nave of which was altered in the 17th c. (painted timber ceiling); under the Late Gothic choir (tabernacle of 1488) are the remains of an earlier Carolingian structure. Above the village are the ruins of the 13th c. Gräpplang castle (469 m/1539 ft) and 15 minutes south-west of this is St James's chapel (St Jakob), which is partly Romanesque.

Flums

From Flums two attractive little roads lead up to the Flumserberge, a region of Alpine meadows dotted with huts, visited both in summer and during the winter sports season (several ski-lifts, ice-rink, indoor swimming pool). To the south-east, above the east side of the Schilsbach valley, is the Kleinberg, with the Frohe Aussicht restaurant (900 m/2953 ft), 4.5 km/ 3 miles from Flums; higher up are the Sässliwiese (1200 m/3937 ft) and Schönhalden hotels (1494 m/4902 ft): hotel cableway from Saxli.

Flumser Berge

To the south-west, above the west side of the valley, is the Grossberg. A good road (11 km/7 miles) climbs up, passing a number of inns, to Tannenheim (1220 m/4003 ft; chair-lift via the Prodalp, 1576 m/5171 ft, to Prodchamm, c. 2000 m/6562 ft), with restaurant and the Tannenboden A p (1400 m/4593 ft; cableway from Unterterzen, with several hotels and many chalets). From here a cableway ascends via the Kreuz hotel (1610 m/ 5282 ft) to the Maschgenkamm (Maschgenlücke inn, 1960 m/6931 ft), on the Spitzmeilen (2505 m/8219 ft).

Tannenheim

Tannenboden Alp

Winterthur
D1

Canton: Zurich (ZH)
Altitude: 449 m/1473 ft
Population: 87,000

Location and
general

Winterthur, the second largest town in the canton of Zurich, lies in a wide basin near the river Töss in the pre-Alpine region, half-way between the Rhine and Lake Zurich. It is widely renowned for its engineering industry (Gebrüder Sulzer, Schweizerische Lokomotiv and Maschinenfabrik, etc.) and its textile factories and institutions, such as the Cantonal Technical College.

History

Winterthur was founded by the Kyburgs about 1150 as a market village, and received its municipal charter from Rudolf of Habsburg in 1264. Pottery, watchmaking and weaving were early local industries, followed in the 19th c. by engineering.

Sights

Old Town

Art treasure and a cultural inheritance bearing witness to the thriving craftwork of former times are good reasons for paying a visit to Winterthur. The little triangular Old Town still preserves streets with rows of old burghers' houses. Of special interest are the Waaghaus (weigh house) in Moorish-Gothic style, the former Early Classical Stadthaus, also the Oberes Spital (upper hospital, 1790) and the old Unteres Spital (lower hospital, 1806–1814), now an old people's home. The semi-detached house "Zur Geduld" with an Early Baroque façade was built between 1690 and 1717; the "Hans zum Adler" at the Obertor (upper gate) is an elegant example of Rococo. The fascinating graffiti on the Hans zum Hinteren Waldhorn where the Winterthur painter Hans Haggenberg lived from 1440 to 1494, have also partly survived.

Stadtkirche

The town church, a three-aisled basilica, was built 1264–1615; its two 65 m/213 ft-high towers were added in 1659 and 1794.

Gewerbe-
museum

At Kirchplatz 14 the industrial museum houses a fine collection of applied and decorative art and occasionally special exhibitions.

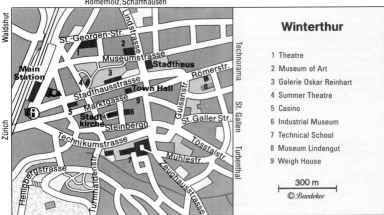

Römerholz, Schaffhausen

Winterthur

1 Theatre
2 Museum of Art
3 Galerie Oskar Reinhart
4 Summer Theatre
5 Casino
6 Industrial Museum
7 Technical School
8 Museum Lindengut
9 Weigh House

300 m
© Baedeker

Winterthur: parish church   *Fortuna fountain*

In the Marktgasse stands the Early-Classical town hall (18th–19th c.); in its assembly hall can be seen a magnificent stucco ceiling by Lorenz Schmid. On the ground floor, Josef Bösch created a shopping arcade in Italianate style at the end of the 19th c. and this links the Marktgasse with the Stadthausstrasse.

Rathaus

In a rear wing (No. 20) can be seen the Kellenberger Collection of Watches and Clocks (sundials, sand and oil timepieces and especially mechanical clocks of 16th–19th c. In the same building is the Jakob Brimer Collection of paintings by minor Dutch masters of the 17th c., together with miniatures by English, French, German and Swiss artists of the 16th to the 19th c.

Kellenberger collection of watches and clocks; Briner bequest

The old town is bounded on the north by the Stadthausstrasse, which runs east from the station. At No. 7 is the Galerie Oskar Reinhart, with a fine collection of works by Swiss, German and Austrian artists of the 18th–20th c., including many Romantics (C. D. Friedrich, K. Blechen, F. Hodler, A. Böcklin, L. Richter, R. G. Kersting, P. O. Runge, R. F. Wasmann, etc), and modern Swiss artists, including F. Hodler, C. Amiet, G. Segantini and G. Giacometti. At the east end of the Stadthausstrasse stands the Stadthaus a prestigious building of 1865–1869, built by Gottfried Semper and enlarged 1932–34; inside is the concert hall of the Collegium Musicum (1629); the hall extends over three storeys.

*Oskar Reinhart Bequest

Stadhaus

Not far from the town park can be seen the theatre (Theater am Stadtgarten), opened in 1965. The building, in echelon form, was designed by Frank Krayenbühl.

Theater am Stadtgarten

The Museum of Art at Museumstrasse 52, north-west of the Stadthaus, contains pictures by Swiss painters of the 16th–20th c. (including 25 portraits by Anton Graff of Winterthur), works by French artists from the Impressionists onwards (Van Gogh, Bonnard, Vuillard, Maillol) and by German artists (Marées, Corinth, Hofer). Also to be seen are works by

*Kunstmuseum

Museum of Art and scientific collection

modern artists (including M. Tobey, N. de Staël, F. Glarner and H. Antes and a large collection of drawings.

In the same building is the municipal Natural History Museum (palaeontology, zoology and reliefs of Swiss landscapes).

Coin Collection

Nearby at Lindstrasse 8 the Villa Bühler houses the municipal coin collection, mainly Greek coins and examples of Graeco-Roman artwork.

Lindengut Museum

In the mansion of Lindengut, at Römerstrasse 8, is the Lindengut Museum with exhibits illustrating the history of the town from Roman times to the 19th c., including the collections of the Winterthur Historical and Antiquarian Society (arts and crafts, textiles, toys). The aviary (1958, extended 1988) in the adjoining part is worth seeing.

* Oskar Reinhart Collection

To the north of the town at Haldenstrasse 95 in Römerholz is the celebrated private collection of the great art patron Oskar Reinhart. It includes works by a large number of old masters, including Cranach the Elder, Breugel the Elder, Grünewald, Rubens, Rembrandt, El-Greco and Goya, and paintings by 19th c. French artists, including Corot, Courbet, Daumier, Delacroix, Renoir and Cézanne.

Schloss Wülflingen

Decorative painting and carving can be seen in the rooms of Schloss Wülflingen (Wülflingerstrasse 214) which is now a restaurant. Ch. Kuhn painted the panels in the law court; the Salomon-Langholt Room has 17th c. decoration; the "Rose Room" is Rococo style. In almost all the rooms can be seen examples of stoves decorated in the Winterthur style.

Oberwinterthur

The Frauenfeld road (N 1) leads to the suburb of Oberwinterthur (445 m/ 1450 ft), on the site of the Celto-Roman settlement of Vitodurum. The 14th c. wall-painting in the Romanesque church (12th c.) is interesting.

* Technorama

In Frauenfelderstrasse, near the motorway exit, is the Technorama of Switzerland, opened in 1982. Science and technology are presented in a vivid manner to the visitor in the fields of energy, processing of materials, textile technology, measurement, building, home and hobbies, information, physics, safety at work. Apparatus, materials and experiments which visitors can do for themselves form an intrinsic feature of the complex.

In the grounds of the museum there is also a miniature steam railway and a laboratory for young people.

Surroundings

In the neighbouring village of Hegi stands a notable moated mansion dating from the 15th–18th c. Since 1947 the estate has been owned by the town of Winterthur; in addition to a collection illustrative of the history of rural and urban life of eastern Switzerland, there is also a youth hostel.

Schloss Hegi

To the south of the town rises the wooded Eschenberg (585 m/1919 ft) with a lookout tower and the "Bruederhus" game park. An instruction trail explains the origins of the district.

Eschenberg

Road 15 (the Rapperswil road) leads south to Sennhof (485 m/1591 ft), from which a road runs west to the Kyburg, splendidly situated on a hill (634 m/2080 ft). The castle, first mentioned in the 11th c., was restored in 1925 and now houses a historical museum; there is a fine view from the keep.

Kyburg

Road No. 1 runs beneath the motorway and passes the village of Sulz, from where a detour should be made to Mörsburg Castle. This contains a Romanesque chapel (1250) and a museum of the Historical and Antiquarian Society of Winterthur (weapons, ceramics and a knights' hall).

Schloss Mörsburg

Yverdon-les-Bains

B2

Canton: Vaud (VD)
Altitude: 435 m/1477 ft
Population: 21,000

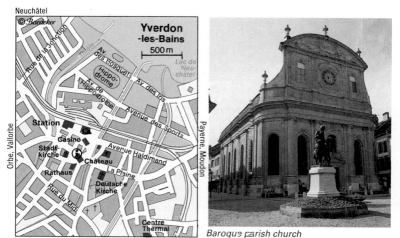

Baroque parish church

443

Yverdon Castle

Location and general	The old-world town of Yverdon, capital of northern Vaud, lies at the south-west end of the Lac de Neuchâtel. From ancient times this has been an important traffic junction.
History	Yverdon-les-Bains occupies the site of the Roman camp of Eburodunum. Traces of the earliest inhabitants were found when the inland waters of the Jura sank in the flood plain of the Orbe in the 19th c. According to the most recent excavations, the first settlements built on piles are dated to about 2800 B.C. At the beginning of the 5th c. Burgundians invaded the area. In the 13th c. the Dukes of Savoy built the massive castle in which the famous educationalist Pestalozzi ran his school from 1805 to 1826.

Sights

Castle	The town centre is dominated by the mighty château, with four towers, once surrounded by water. It was originally the property of the Dukes of Savoy and it was Peter II who built it in the characteristic "Savoy square" form. Later, the castle came into the hands of the Bernese governors (Landvögte) and, from 1805, it was the headquarters of the Pestalozzi Institute, where Johann Heinrich Pestalozzi ran his school for twenty years. The two rooms in which he lived (Salle Pestalozzi) contain the furniture and memorabilia of the pedagogue. Since 1912, the castle has housed a library and a historical museum, with interesting finds from the locality and an ethnographical collection.
Science Fiction Museum	Nearby in the Maison d'Ailleurs (5 rue du Four), the Science Fiction Museum, originating from the collection of Pierre Versin, encompasses the whole gamut of Utopian fantasy, ranging from books to magazines, comics, pictures, games, video-tapes and films.
Hôtel de Ville Parish Church	In the "Place" (the main square) stands the Hôtel de Ville (town hall), built 1769–1773 by A. D. Burnand, and on the west side of the square the parish

Grandson Castle by Lake Neuchâtel

church (1755–1757), designed by the Geneva architect J. M. Billon. The curved gable end of the façade has as its decoration an allegory of faith. The choir-stalls (1499–1502) by C. Chapius and B. Bottolier are of considerable merit. Outside the church stands a monument to Pestalozzi by A. Lanz (1889).

The Musée de l'Habillement, opened in 1982, exhibits in contemporary setting several thousand handmade articles of clothing and accessories from 1850 to the present day.

Museum of Clothing

The Centre Thermal (reconstructed 1977) contains the sulphurous spring (34°C–93°F) which was used for curative purposes from Roman times.

Centre Thermal

Surroundings

Some 19 km/12 miles west in Ste-Croix an interesting collection of musical automata, musical boxes and mechanical musical instruments can be seen in the Centre International de la Méchanique d'Art CIMA, at 2 rue de l'Industrie.

Ste-Croix, Museum of Musical Automata

About 7 km/4 miles south-east in the village of Ursins is the medieval church of St Nicolas, built on the foundations of a 2nd century Roman temple.

Ursins

South-east of Yverdon you pass the castle of Champvent, an imposing four-towered 13th c. castle (no admission).

*Château de Champvent

In 14 km/9 miles you reach Orbe (479 m/1572 ft; population 4000) occupying the site of the Roman settlement of Urba. In the Ferme de Boscéaz (Route d'Yverdon), to the north of the town, the visitor should not miss the collection of Roman mosaics which were discovered in 1841. They came

Orbe

Church of Saint-Jean-Baptiste in Grandson

Capitals

1 Thorn Motif
2 St Michael and the Dragon
3 Hell
4 Virgin Mary
5 Lions
6 Lions with Common Head
7 Eagle

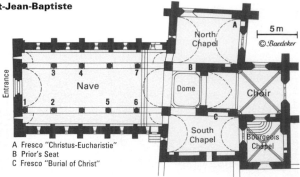

A Fresco "Christus-Eucharistie"
B Prior's Seat
C Fresco "Burial of Christ"

from a Roman villa and display representations of divinities and animals. From the 7th to the 15th c., Orbe was a fortified Burgundian residence. Of interest is the medieval church of Notre-Dame, with a magnificent Gothic doorway. Its richly decorated arch is adorned with wonderfully carved keystones. In the 13th c. Amadeus III of Montfalcon built a fortress on a hill overlooking the town, but only the round keep and a rectangular tower remain. The two-storeyed town hall (1785–1789) has a ballustrade decorated with the arms of the town. Local history is featured in the Musée du Vieil Orbe in the Rue Centrale.

Church of Notre-Dame

Grandson
*Castle

On the west bank of the Lac du Neuchâtel, north of Yverdon, lies the old little town of Grandson (439 m/1440 ft; population 2000). It has a mighty five-towered castle on a hill on the bank of the lake. The 13th and 15th c. fortress, the ground plan of which is an adaptation of the "carré savoyard" form, is now in private ownership. Of special interest here are the Knights' Hall (choir stalls of 1620), the collection of weapons and the museum of vintage cars.

*Church of St-Jean-Baptiste

Capital motif

The Romanesque church of St-Jean-Baptiste is all that remains of the former Benedictine monastery which was founded in 1049. From 1140, the priory was made subordinate to the Abbey of La Chaise-Dieu in the Auvergne, and the influence of the abbey can be seen in the Romanesque architecture. There was also a close connection to the abbots of Cluny. After the Burgundian wars, Grandson was ruled by Berne and Fribourg and, as a consequence of the Reformation, the monastery was finally dissolved in 1554. Relics of the first church are the remains of the walls in the north chapel. The building of the cornered cupula and the reconstruction of the former nave into a basilica with three arched aisles can be attributed to the monks of La Chaise-Dieu. The beauty of the church is mainly due to the lightness of its architecture. As in the church of St-Aimable-de-Riom in the Auvergne, the side aisles have half-barrelled or double-barrelled roofs. The nave has a round-barrelled roof of tuft, supported by beautiful marbled pillars, with capitals full of fanciful decoration. The seat of the priors (who included St Hugo, a former monk of the "Grande Chartreuse") has a representation of his swan and is considered the finest carving of its kind in Switzerland. A special mention should be made of the frescoes of the 15th c. tomb in a niche in the south chapel and the wall tabernacle (1470) by Pierre Chapuiset in the north chapel. The great Romanesque capitals of the main aisle form a unity of the highest artistic work. In spite of their varied inspirations, they form a unified synthesis of spiritual themes concerning the tragedy of human existence and the mystery of Christ.

Chenaux Castle

In the Battle of Grandson the Confederates gained their first victory on 2nd March 1478 over Duke Karl the Bold of Burgundy, who lost all his artillery and a great deal of treasure wh ch can now be seen in the Historical Museum of Berne.

From Yverdon to Payerne (30 km/19 miles)

Leave on a road going east along the south-east side of the Lac de Neuchâtel at some distance from the shore (marshy in p aces), from wh ch there is an attractive view across the lake to Grandson. 19 km/12 miles from Yverdon is the old-world little town of Estavayer-le-Lac (448 m/1470 ft: pop. 2500; bathing beach; youth hostel; camping site), with arcaded houses, gate towers and the Late Gothic church of St Laurent. The three-ais ed collegiate church has beautifully carved choir-stalls of 1572 which were the work of the Geneva artist J. Mattelin. A visit is recommended to the Dominican monastery (14th and 18th c.) in the Grand Rue; the monastery has a magnificent three-aisled church and a number of notable buildings, of which the Hôtel du Cerf (16th c.) and the Maison de la Dime (15th c.) in the Rue du Musée should be mentioned. The latter houses the museum of local history (including prehistoric finds, medieval kitchen utensils and a collection of old railway lanterns). The house at No. 142 rue Châtel dates from the 15th c. and was the last residence of the lords of Estavayer.

The great Château Chenaux was originally also a foundation by the Savoyards (13th c.). It was partly destroyed in the 15th c. and re-erected after the Burgundian wars, later being restored and rebuilt on several occasions.

The road now turns south-east and comes to Payerne, where the Benedictine abbey is one of the major Romanesque buildings in the country.

Estavayer-le-Lac

Château Chenaux

Payerne
*Benedictine Abbey

447

Zermatt

Canton: Valais (VS)
Altitude: 1820 m/5973 ft
Population: 4200

**Location
and general**

The mountain village of Zermatt (from "zur Matte", "on the mountain pasture") is the leading climbing and winter sports capital in the Valais and one of Switzerland's great international resorts. Nestling in a green valley enclosed between steeply scarped mountains, it is dominated by the "mountain of mountains", the huge and gracefully curved pyramid of the Matterhorn. The Nikolai valley, at the head of which Zermatt lies, is open to cars only as far as Täsch; Zermatt itself is without motor cars (local transport is by electric vehicles and horse-drawn cabs). Among the old timber houses, weathered brown with age, are numerous hotels, all built in a style adapted to the setting. A rack-railway, several long cableways and numerous ski-lifts bring the various walking, climbing and winter sports areas within easy reach. There are magnificent long ski-runs of all grades of difficulty.

Leisure activities include tennis, swimming, walking and mountain-climbing (mountaineering tuition). Visitors who would like to have a bird's eye view of the area can have a circular flight in a helicopter. The landing place ("heliport") is situated at the north end of the village. Since 1988, there has been a mountain trail for cyclists which runs from the Winkelmatten beyond Zermatt up to the Furi.

History

Until the end of the Middle Ages the glaciers were higher up and the tree-line was at about 2600 m/8531 ft so that the Theodul pass offered a fairly easy route through the mountains, and this was used from Roman times onwards. Zermatt itself is first recorded in 1218 under the Latin name of Pratoborgno. By the 17th c. its hundred or so families had purchased

Zermatt: Bahnhofstrasse

Gorner glacier

their freedom from the landowners of the Rhône valley and formed a citizen body, to which after 1618 only the 19th c. hotelier Alexandre Seiler was admitted. The mountains around Zermatt were first mastered from 1830 onwards almost exclusively by British climbers, who were the first to climb 31 out of the 39 principal peaks (Breithorn 1830, Monte Rosa 1855, Matterhorn 1865). The famous climbers' hotel, the Monte Rosa, was opened in 1854, the railway from St Niklaus in 1891, the Gornergrat rack-railway in 1898. 1898 also saw the appearance of the first skier, but Zermatt's rise into a great winter sports resort did not really begin until 1927.

The road from Visp, in the Rhône valley, is open to cars only as far as Täsch (30 km/19 miles), which has a large parking area (fee) at the station. In winter, depending on weather conditions, it may be advisable to take the railway from Visp or St Niklaus. The railway from Visp to Zermatt (the Brig–Visp–Zermatt or BVZ narrow-gauge electric line; 35 km/22 miles, journey time 1¼/1½ hours) runs alongside the road into the Nikolai valley.
Access to Zermatt

In 7 km/4 miles we come to Stalden-Saas (803 m/2635 ft), at the junction of the Saas valley (through which flows the Saaser Vispa) and the Nikolai valley (Matter Vispa). The old timber houses in Valais style cluster around the white parish church on high ground. A cableway ascends the east side of the valley to Staldenried and the Gspon plateau (1893 m/6211 ft); a road on the west side leads to the mountain village of Törbe (1491 m/4892 ft, 8 km/5 miles north-west).
Stalden-Saas

The Zermatt road now climbs up the Nikolai valley through the Kipfen gorge and in another 8 km/5 miles reaches St Niklaus (1130 m/3708 ft), the largest village in the Nikolai valley which is closely hemmed in by mountains. It has a fine parish church of 1964 with a medieval tower and three beautiful Baroque altars.
St Niklaus

From St Niklaus, a narrow and winding road climbs 8 km/5 miles north-east to Grächen (1617 m/5305 ft), which stands on a commanding mountain terrace traversed by irrigation channels (bisses). It is a village which attracts both summer visitors and winter sports enthusiasts and it has an indoor swimming pool. There is a cableway to the Hannigalp (2110 m/6923 ft; skiing). 26 km/16 miles further on you pass through Randa (1410 m/4626 ft) at the foot of the Mischabel group, before reaching Täsch in 29 km/18 miles, a picturesque little village. The peak of the Matterhorn now comes into view.
Grächen

Täsch

Sights

The life of the resort is primarily on the main street, which runs from the station to the market square, with a charming contrast between hotels and elegant shops and old village houses.
Bahnhofstrasse

In the gardens of the Mont Cervin Hotel is a stone pyramid (1902) with marble plaques of Alexandre Seilder and his wife, to whom the development of Zermatt as a resort was due.
Mont Cervin Hôtel

Here, too, is the very interesting Alpine Museum, with an extensive display of material concerning the climbing of the mountains around Zermatt (local guides and famous alpinists). The cartographic and folkloristic exhibits are also notable and include furniture, minerals, indigenous flora and fauna.
Alpine Museum

Above this are the guides' and ski school office and the English church (1871), built by the Alpine Club (founded 1857), which has the graves of climbers in the churchyard. Farther up the village is the Monte Rosa Hotel (1852), for 30 years the headquarters of all climbers in Zermatt, which has preserved much of its original character. A bronze plaque (1925) commemorates Edward Whymper, who made a series of attempts on the Matterhorn between 1860 and 1865. The neat little parish church to the left of the hotel dates from 1576.
English church

Zermatt

The Matterhorn

Market Square
: Around the market square are the Gemeindehaus (communal council house) and six characteristic old village houses, on one of which is a tablet commemorating Whymper's guides, the two Taugwalders (father and son). Here, too, is the charming Marmot Fountain (1902). The handsome church of St Maurice, rebuilt in 1914, has a tower modelled on that of the earlier church.

Cemetery
: At the bridge over the Vispa, on a strip of land between that river and its tributary the Triftbach, is the cemetery, with the graves of many climbers who met their death on the mountains, including Whymper's guide Michel Croz and his companion Hadow. Higher up in the village a few of the old larch-wood storehouses still survive, with large circular slabs of stone on the supporting posts to deter mice.

**Matterhorn
: The Matterhorn (French Mont Cervin, Italian Monte Cervino: 4478 m/ 14,692 ft) was first climbed on 14 July 1865 by a British team consisting of Edward Whymper, Charles Hudson, Lord Francis Douglas and Douglas Hadow, with Michel Croz and the two Peter Taugwalders, father and son, as guides. On the way down, 400 m/1312 ft below the summit, Hadow slipped and fell on to the Matterhorn glacier, dragging Hudson, Douglas and Croz with him: Whymper and the Taugwalders were saved by the breaking of the rope. The ascent of the Matterhorn from Zermatt is no longer considered to be particularly difficult, as it is achieved by some 3000 people every summer, but it should be attempted only by experienced climbers (4½–6 hours from the Hörnli ridge; the Italian or southwest ridge was climbed a few days later by a guide named Carrell, the Zmutt ridge in 1879, the difficult Furgg Ridge in 1911. The west face was climbed in 1927, the ice-covered north face and the south face in 1931 and the east face in 1932; the first winter climb of the north face was made in 1962.

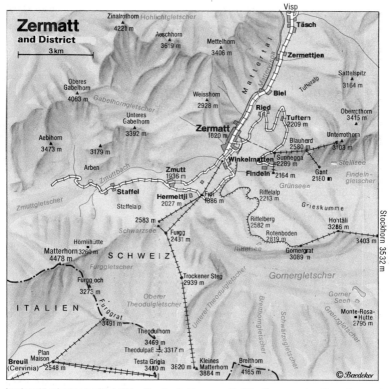

Zermatt
and District

3 km

Visp

Zinalrothorn 4221 m · *Hohlichtgletscher* · Täsch · Zermettjen · Aeschhorn 3619 m · Mettelhorn 3406 m · *Mattertal* · *Matter Visp* · *Tuftertal* · Sattelspitz 3164 m · Oberes Gabelhorn 4063 m · *Gabelhorngletscher* · Weisshorn 2928 m · Biel · Ried · Unteres Gabelhorn 3392 m · Zermatt 1620 m · Tuftern 2209 m · Oberrothorn 3415 m · Aebihorn 3473 m · 3179 m · Blauherd 2580 m · Unterrothorn 3103 m · Arben · *Zmuttbach* · Zmutt 1936 m · Winkelmatten · Sunnegga 2289 m · *Stellisee* · Findeln 2164 m · Gant 2160 m · *Findeln- gletscher* · Staffel · Hermettji 2027 m · Fluh 1886 m · Grünsee · Riffelalp 2213 m · *Grieskumme* · Staffelalp · *Zmuttgletscher* · 2583 m · Furgg 2431 m · Riffelberg 2582 m · Rotenboden 2819 m · Hohtäli 3286 m · *Schwarzsee* · Hörnlihütte · Matterhorn 3260 m / 4478 m · *Furggletscher* · SCHWEIZ · *Riffelsee* · Gornergrat 3089 m · 3403 m · *Stockhorn 3532 m* · Furgg Joch 3275 m · *Oberer Theodulgletscher* · *Gornergletscher* · *Gorner Seen* · ITALIEN · *Furggrat* · Trockener Steg 2939 m · *Unterer Theodulgletscher* · *Breithorngletscher* · *Schwärzegletscher* · Monte-Rosa- Hütte 2795 m · *Grenzgletscher* · Theodulhorn 3469 m · Theodulpaß 3317 m · 3491 m · Plan Maison · Breuil (Cervinia) 2548 m · Testa Grigia 3480 m · Kleines Matterhorn 3884 m · 3820 m · Breithorn 4165 m

© *Baedeker*

It takes 45 minutes to climb 10 km/6 miles to the summit of the Gornergrat by the Gornergratbahn, the highest mountain-railway in Europe running over open country (see Surroundings of Zermatt). A cableway from the upper station (restaurant) crosses the Hohtälligrat (3286 m/10,785 ft; restaurant) to the Stockhorn (3532 m/11,592 ft; upper station 3407 m/11,182 ft). There are also cableways from Zermatt–Winkelmatten via Furri (or Furi; 1886 m/6190 ft; restaurant; to the south at 1955 m/6416 ft is a glacier garden) to the Schwarzsee (black lake; restaurant) and via Furri and Furgg (2431 m/7979 ft) to the Trochenen Steg (2939 m/9646 ft: large restaurant) at the upper Theodul Glacier. From the Trochenen Steg a ski-lift (open also in summer) goes up to the Furgg saddle (3365 m/11,044 ft) on the Italian border. Another ski-lift runs via Gandegg to the Theodul Pass (3317 m/ 10,886 ft) from where there is a further lift to the Testa Grigia (3480 m/ 11,421 ft).

Mountain Railways
*Gornergrat-bahn

There is a spectacular trip on the highest cableway in Europe from the Trochenen Steg to the north face of the Kleines Matterhorn (3820 m/12,537 ft). From the upper station there is a lift to the summit of the Kleines Matterhorn (3884 m/12,747 ft).
A cableway from Furgg leads to the Schwarzsee (restaurant).

*Cableway to the Kleines Matterhorn

The so-called "Alpine-Metro", a funicular in a tunnel, runs from the centre of Zermatt to the Sunnegga sun-terrace (2289 m/7512 ft; restaurant) from where a cableway goes via Blauherd (2580 m/8468 ft) to the Unterrothorn

Alpine Metro

451

(3103 m/10,184 ft). From Blauherd, yet another cableway runs to Gant (2180 m/6155 ft); ski-lift to the skiing-ground (2814 m/9236 ft). You can also go down from Sunnegga by a winter chair-lift to Findeln (2164 m/7102 ft).

Winter sports

Zermatt provides facilities for skiing throughout the year, with skiing grounds all lying at an altitude between 2500 m/8250 ft and 3900 m/12,800 ft. They are accessible by numerous lifts: Schwarzsee–Trockener Steg–Theodul, Riffelberg–Gornergrat–Stockhorn, Sunnegga–Blauherd–Unterrothorn; in summer it is possible to ski on the Breithorn plateau (cableway to the Kleines Matterhorn) and on the Plateau Rosa (3500 m/11,487 ft) near the Theodul Pass. A special thrill can be had with heli-skiing or by taking part in a high-altitude ski-tour. There are delightful cross-country ski-runs (including a night-track of 3 km/nearly 2 miles, from Winkelmatten to Tutra) and about 50 km/30 miles of ski-tracks. In addition there are two natural-ice skating rinks and several curling rinks.

Surroundings

*Ascent of the Gornergrat

*Gornergrat-bahn

The rack-railway climbs the east side of the valley, crosses the Findelnbach on a high bridge and then runs through the curving Unteralp tunnel. 4 km/2 miles): Riffelalp (2213 m/7261 ft), with a superb view of the Gabelhorn group. The line continues up the slopes of the Riffelberg in a wide curve, with ever more impressive views of the Matterhorn. (6 km/4 miles): Riffelberg (2582 m/8472 ft) with the hotel of the same name. 7.5 km/5 miles from Zermatt lies Rotenboden station (2819 m/9249 ft). A few minutes' walk below the station is the Riffelsee, with the pyramidal peak of the Matterhorn mirrored in its water (particularly fine in the morning). The line then runs high above the Gorner glacier to the summit station (9 km/6 miles, 3089 m/10,135 ft), from which it is only a five-minute climb to the famous

Gornergrat

Gornergrat (3130 m/10,270 ft: observatory), a rocky ridge rearing above the Gorner glacier. From here there is one of the most magnificent panoramas in the whole of the Alps: in the middle the Matterhorn, with the Breithorn, the Zwillinge ("Twins" – Castor and Pollux), the Lyskamm and Monte Rosa to the left; to the north the peaks of the Mischabel group, including the Dom (4545 m/14,912 ft), the highest purely Swiss mountain; and to the west the mountains between the Zermatt and Zinal valleys.

Walks

The return walk from the Gornergrat to Zermatt is highly recommended; the path at first drops steeply (1½ hours) to the Findel Glacier Restaurant.

*Findeln Glacier

From here, a detour can be made uphill in ¾ hour to the steeply inclined Findeln Glacier (2298 m/7542 ft). From the restaurant the walk continues via the summer village resort of Findeln (2164 m/7102 ft) where cereals are grown (in winter a chair-lift goes down to the Sunnegga cabin) and, in another hour, Zermatt is reached.

Gorner Gorges

About ½–¾ hour south of Zermatt lie the Gorner Gorges through which thunders the Matter Vispa, the outflow of the Gorner Glacier.

*From Zermatt to the Schwarzsee

This tour on foot, an alternative to the cableway trip, lasts about three hours. The route follows the left bank of the Vispa and then the Zmuttbach, in ¼ hour it crosses the stream (magnificent view of the Matterhorn), and continues by way of the Sum See (1763 m/5784 ft) and Hermettji huts to the Schwarzsee hotel (2583 m/8475 ft) from which there are superb panoramic views. A few minutes' walk below the hotel is the little Schwarzsee (2552

Schwarzsee hotel
*Panorama

m/8373 ft), with the guides' chapel of Maria zum See (18th c.). 2½ hours higher up are the Belvédère mountain inn (3263 m/10,706 ft) and the Hörnli hut (3260 m/10,696 ft: 50 sleeping places), starting-point for the ascent of the Matterhorn. An hour's walk to the north-west is the Staffelalp.

To the Staffelalp

20 minutes above the Zum See huts on the road to the Schwarzsee take a road on the right which ascends through beautiful mountain forests, high up on the right bank of the Zmuttbach, to the Staffelalp (2206 m/7238 ft: restaurant), with a magnificent view of the Matterhorn and the Zmutt glacier, littered with rock debris. The Smuttbach has been dammed and harnessed to produce electric power.

*Staffelalp

To the Theodul pass

This tour lasts 5–5½ hours with a guide, but you can also use the cableway. First, in 1¼ hours to Hermettji then, in a further 2¼ hours at the moraine of the Upper Theodul glacier (Oberer Theodulgletscher, 2713 m/8901 ft), either with a rope directly across the much-crevassed glacier to the pass (2 hours) or via the Gandegg hut (3029 m/9938 ft: 1 hour) and over the glacier to the pass.

*Theodul
Glacier

The Theodul pass (Matterjoch, 3317 m/10,883 ft), which was already in use before the 4th c. A.D. lies on the frontier with Italy (magnificent views). From nearby Testa Grigia, a cableway runs down to Breuil (Italians' Cervina). Popular tours from the Theodul pass include the ascent of the Breithorn (4165 m/13,665 ft; magnificent views) with a guide; to the Kleines Matterhorn (3884 m/12,743 ft; cableway); from Rotenboden station on the Gornergrat railway in two hours to the Monte Rosa hut (2795 m/9170 ft) and from there in 6–6½ hours with a guide to the Dufourspitze (4634 m/15,204 ft), the highest peak in the Monte Rosa massif and in Switzerland, with one of the most breathtaking panoramas in the Alps.

Theodul pass

*Breithorn

*Dufourspitze
*Monte Rosa

Zofingen   C1

Canton: Aargau (AG)
Altitude: 437 m/1434 ft
Population: 10,000

The great road and rail cross-country routes of Switzerland, Basle–St Gotthard–Ticino, and Lake Constance–Lake of Geneva, intersect in the lower Wigger valley, the most westerly point of the canton of Aargau.

Location and
general

Of the twelve historic towns of Aargau, the old town of Zofingen is the most extensive. It was founded by the Counts of Frohburg who, in the third quarter of the 12th c., began to secure their lands to the north and south of the upper Hauenstein with eight new towns and several castles. The first known mention of the place was in 1175 or 1179; in 1201 the "Canonici de Zovingen" were acknowledged. As early as the 1st c. A.D. a Roman estate existed outside the line of the walls which were built later. During the Bernese domination, which lasted a most 400 years, the town was granted a certain measure of self-government and, in 1803, it was raised to the status of a district capital. From 1830, increasing industrialisation (printing, processing of textiles, chemical works and engineering, etc.) took place. Important educational buildings followed from the 19th to the mid-20th c., including, in 1974–78, the modern educational centre, embracing six schools, in the Wigger plain between Zofingen and Stengelbach.

History

Zofingen: Niklaus-Thut-Platz

Sights

*Thut Square

The very well maintained Old Town contains many attractive features. The broad Niklaus Thut Square, originally called "Am Spitzberg", forms the town centre. A fountain of the same name (1894) commemorates Mayor N. Thut who carried the town banner in 1386 at the Battle of Sempach.

Town Hall
Butchers'
Guildhall

Also to be seen here are the Baroque Town Hall (1792–1795) by N. E. Ringer, with a Classical assembly hall, and the impressive former Butchers' Guildhall (c. 1602), the restoration of which was completed in 1985. Of the former steward's house at the north-east corner of Thut Square, only a small part (dated 1595) now remains. In its top storey is a glockenspiel of sixteen bells which has been working since 1985. The Neuhaus, built by Ringer in 1770, is now the headquarters of the Swiss Banking Union. The hand of the architect Antoni Stal can be recognised in the former municipal Assistance Office (1598–1599).

Market Hall

The Market Hall (once the headquarters of the butchers) and a cloth-hall, later to become the library, form links to the Vorderer Hauptgasse (outer main street). The last named is a narrow Baroque building with a hipped roof and open arcades. Since reconstruction in 1984, the weekly market is accommodated here, together with banqueting and conference rooms.

Old Chancellery

The old 18th c. town chancellery, which adjoins on the west, was restored in 1982; it has a huge hipped roof and now serves as a local administration building.

Town church

The oldest parts of the Reformed Church of St Mauritius (restored 1981–83) are Romanesque but the building was greatly altered in the 14th and 15th c. In 1979, the roof of the church collapsed and this necessitated the reconstruction of the nave with a wooden roof, as well as making the west gallery smaller.

Interesting features of the church are the 16th c. choir, the crypt and the west tower. The last named was built in 1649 to a design by Antoni

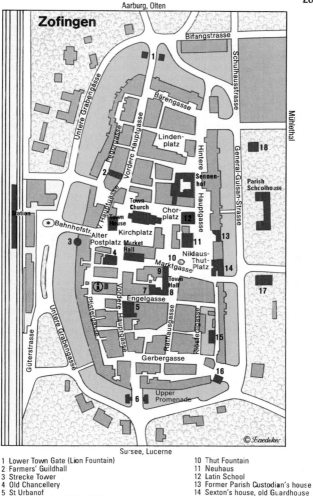

Aarburg, Olten

Sursee, Lucerne

1 Lower Town Gate (Lion Fountain)
2 Farmers' Guildhall
3 Strecke Tower
4 Old Chancellery
5 St Urbanof
6 Upper Town Gate (Officials' houses)
7 Weibelhaus
8 Archive Tower
9 Butchers' Guildhall

10 Thut Fountain
11 Neuhaus
12 Latin School
13 Former Parish Custodian's house
14 Sexton's house, old Guardhouse
15 Klösterli (little convent)
16 Powder Tower
17 Old Guardhouse
18 Museum

Tierstein; it is a prominent landmark and its oldest bell is dated 1409. Inside the church are six gallery windows of 1518, Late-Gothic choir-stalls, a new organ (1983) and fine stained glass (the middle window of the choir depicts a passion cycle in 12 parts, dating from about 1400). Near the church stands the Hans Bögli which was completely restored in 1985.

The old Schützenhaus (1825), built in mid-18th c. style, in which the municipal art collection is housed, is worth a visit, as is the museum in General   Schützenhaus   Museum

455

Guisan Strasse 18 which has a comprehensive historical and natural history collection. Also of interest are the funeral hall of the old cemetery in the Schützenmasse, which dates from 1873 and which was restored internally in 1983/1985, the 19th c. Gemeindeschulhaus (parish schoolroom), the Küstorei (sexton's house). "Loffelberg" (now a regional centre), the St Urbanhof (which once served the established monastery of St Urban as a sexton's house), and the Lateinschulhaus (Latin school house) by A. Stab (1600–1602), in which the civic library (established in 1693) has been housed since 1974 are all noteworthy.

| Sennerhof | In the Hintere Hauptgasse (outer main street) where the nobility once lived, the silk manufacturer J. A. Senn set up an alpine dairy, completed in 1732. In the domestic wing on the south side can be seen fine linen tapestries showing panoramic scenes and genre landscapes. |

Town fortifications

Remains of an encircling wall, mentioned in the 13th c., are the Schwarz or Pulvertum (black or powder tower) a well-known landmark in the south-east of the town, and the Strecke or Folterturm (rack or torture tower), now part of the Jelmoli department store. In the area of the Oberer Tor (upper gate) which was demolished in 1846 stand two original cottages in the Classical style.

Zoo

Lovers of nature can relax in the nearby zoo above the town or they can enjoy walks in the neighbourhood (there is an excellent nature trail). From the hill known as the "Bergli" there are good views over the upper Wigger valley and the Alps.

Lindengeviert

From the Lindengeviert in the Heiternplatz the view embraces the whole of the Old Town and extends to the Jura.

Roman finds

Where the Hotel Römerbad now stands, there was in the middle of the first century a Roman villa rustica. During excavations in 1826–1827, three Roman mosaic pavements were discovered; these were dug up and provided with protective covers in the style of Grecian temples. The pavements were re-protected in 1974. Finds from excavations can be seen in the museum.

Zug   D1

Canton: Zug (ZG)
Altitude: 426 m/1398 ft
Population: 24,000

Location and general

Zug, capital of the canton of the same name, lies at the north-east end of the Zuger See (Lake Zug), above which rises the flat-topped ridge of the Zugerberg. The local kirsch (Zuger Kirschwasser) is famous.

History

Zug was founded in 1242 by the counts of Kyburg. In 1283, it was inherited by the Habsburgs and became an important stronghold against the forest cantons which, in 1352, founded the confederation. In 1415, Zug was given a charter as a free imperial town and when the canton was formed in 1803 Zug was made the capital.

Sights

Lakeside

From the lakeside promenade, there is a fine view of the Rigi, Pilatus and the Bernese Alps (Eiger, Mönch and Jungfrau). The Landsgermeindeplatz (citizens' assembly area), near the Stadt landing-place, was laid out to a new plan at the beginning of the 1980s; there are cafés and restaurants where visitors can relax.

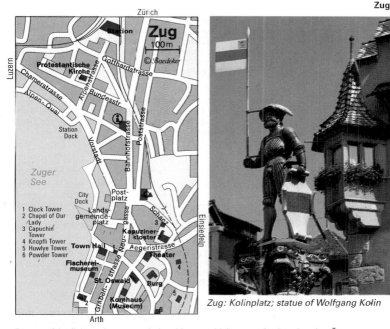

Zug: Kolinplatz; statue of Wolfgang Kolin

By way of the fish market we reach the old town with its attractive burghers' houses and fountains. Several buildings are noteworthy: the Baroque gabled building of the municipal planning office (18th c.), the 16th–17th c. mint and the nearby Rococo Glorietti Pavilion, and the 16th c. Brandenberg House which has a Rococo façade.

*Old Town

The Late Gothic Rathaus (town hall) was completed in 1505; in a council room on the top floor fine carvings of 1507 have been preserved. Also of interest are the Renaissance doorway and the panelling in the Small Council Chamber.

Rathaus

From here a gateway under the picturesque Zytturm ("Time Tower", with an astronomical clock) into the Kolinplatz where there is a fountain bearing the figure of the standard-bearer Wolfgang Kalin, who fell at the Battle of Arbedo against the Milanese.

Kolinplatz

To the south, stands the Late-Gothic St Oswald's church (1478–1545) a three-aisled basilica; the main doorway ("King's Portal") is decorated with beautiful sculptures depicting St Oswald and St Michael on either side of the Virgin Mary.

St Oswald's Church

Nearby (Kirchgasse 11) the so-called "Burg" (castle), once the official headquarters of the Kyburg and Habsburg governors, houses the historical and cultural museum of the town and the canton. The collection includes items of pre- and early history, stained glass, clocks, weapons, uniforms and implements used in agriculture and crafts. North-east of the Kolinplatz on a hill stands the Capuchin friary (1595–1597) with a church dating from 1676.

Museum in the Castle

At Aegeristrasse 56 is the Cantoral Museum of Pre-history, containing finds from the canton of Zug, dating from the Mesolithic era to the early Middle Ages. Among the exhibits are objects excavated from a Neolithic lakeside settlement and from the Roman estate of Cham-Hagendorn.

Cantonal Museum of Pre-history

Zug

Fischerei-museum	The Fishery Museum at Untergasse 16 houses a small collection of fish and birds which inhabit Lake Zug (open only by appointment).
Kunsthaus	The former 15th c. Corn Exchange at Untergasse 14 has been converted into a museum of art which mounts temporary exhibitions, specialising in 19th and 20th c. art of Zug and the heartland of Switzerland. Four watch-towers and remains of the walls of the old town fortifications can still be seen.
Bee collection	Those interested in bee-keeping should pay a visit to the Hotel Rosenberg, where the collection of the German-Swiss Bee-keeping Association is on display. The collection covers bee-keeping, the life and anatomy of bees and the production of beeswax.

Surroundings of Zug

Zugerberg	To the south-east of the town is the Zugerberg (988 m/3242 ft), with pleasant woodland walks and views of the Alps, particularly from the Hochwacht. It can be reached either by the direct road up the hill (9 km/6 miles) or by driving via Guggithal to Schönegg (3 km/2 miles) and taking the funicular (2 km/1 mile, 8 minutes). On the top stands the Zugerberg Hotel.
Cham	5 km/3 miles west on the Lucerne road (No. 4) we come to Cham (421 m/1381 ft; pop. 6500), at the junction of several roads. The church, built in 1786, has a slender steeple added in 1853. By the lake is the Schloss St Andreas, with a chapel of 1488 built on Carolingian foundations. The smart Villa Villette has, since 1988, been a meeting place and cultural centre.
Baar	3 km/2 miles north of Zug is the little industrial town (textiles) of Baar (447 m/1467 ft). In the main street are the fine parish church of St Martin (14th c., rebuilt in 1771) with a massive Romanesque tower with a Baroque helm roof, and the Town Hall (1676). In the cemetery stands a Late Gothic chapel (1507). An attractive excursion (7 km/4 miles south-east) can be made over a hill covered with fruit-trees and the deep Lorzentobel gorge to the Höll-grotten ("Caves of Hell") with magnificent stalactitic formations.

From Zug to the Ägerisee

	The distance to Oberägen is 13 km/8 miles, to Schwyz 29 km/18 miles, 4 km/2 miles more than by the main road via Arth.
	Leave Zug on a secondary road which runs east to Thalacker and crosses the Lorze gorge on a high bridge. In 5 km/3 miles we reach Nidfurren (654 m/2146 ft). The road continues along the east side of the Lorze valley. 5
Ägerisee	km/3 miles: Unterägeri (729 m/2393 ft), a busy little village and holiday spot at the north end of the charming Ägerisee (725 m/2379 ft; 5.5 km/3 miles long). The road runs along the north east side of the lake.
Oberägeri	About 3 km/2 miles further lies Oberägeri (737 m/2418 ft), a village of 3500 inhabitants which is also a holiday resort. The road then crosses a low ridge which forms the boundary between the cantons of Zug and Schwyz, where, on 15 November 1315, the Battle of Morgarten was fought, marking the Swiss Confederates' first victory over the Habsburgs. On the shores of the lake is the Morgarten monument (1908), and on the pass are the Schlacht-kapelle (battle chapel) of 1603 and a defensive tower of 1320.
Sattel Schwyz	Then comes Sattel (827 m/2713 ft), on the road from Pfäffikon, which continues south to Schwyz (9 km/6 miles; bypass; see entry). Alternatively, take a road which branches off on the right in Sattel and winds its way down the southern slopes of the Rossberg (fine views of Rigi and the Mythen), passing through the hamlet of Ecce Homo (735 m/2412 ft; chapel of 1667) and the village of Steinerberg (629 m/2064 ft; pilgrimage church of 1570),

and then continues past the scene of a great landslide at Goldau to Arth
(11 km/7 miles).

*Zuger See

The beautiful Zuger See or Lake Zug (alt. 417 m/1368 ft, length 14 km/9
miles, area 38 sq. km/15 sq. miles, greatest depth 198 m/650 ft), extends
south from Zug, its northern end surrounded by gentle hills, its southern
end enclosed between the steep scarps of the Rossberg and the Rigi (see
entry).

2½ km/1½ mile south of Zurich, on the east shore of the lake is Zug-Oberwil   East shore
(420 m/1378 ft), attractively situated at the foot of the Zürichberg, along the
foothills of which the road now runs. To the right, on the west shore, can be
seen Schloss Buonas (15th and 17th c.) and the little village of Risch; then
comes the Kiemen peninsula jutting out into the lake. After 4 km/2½ miles
you pass the Restaurant Lothenbach, where the stream of the same name
flows into the lake (waterfall), then the road passes through two short
galleries and finally reaches the summer resort of Walchwil, a popular   Walchwil
lakeside resort in a picturesque situation amid chestnut groves and
vineyards.

Beyond Walchwil the boundary between the cantons of Zug and Schwyz is
crossed, and you continue along the foot of the Rossberg, with fine views
across the lake to the Rigi; to the right is Immensee near the "Hohle Gasse"
(hollow road), and straight ahead is Arth.

At the southern end of Lake Zug lies Arth (420 m/1451 ft; pop. 3000), a little   Arth
town which has grown up around an important road junction. It has a
Baroque church dating from the late 17th c. The station of Arth-Goldau is
the starting point of a rack railway up the Rigi (see entry).   **Rigi

For the south-west shore of Lake Zug and Immensee, see Küssnacht am
Rigi.

Zurich   D1

Canton: Zürich (ZH)
Altitude: 410 m/1345 ft
Population: 353,000

Zurich (German spelling Zürich), Switzerland's largest city and capital of   **Townscape
the canton of Zurich, is also the country's economic and cultural hub; but   and general
with all its bustling activity it is still one of the finest Swiss towns, with
carefully cherished traditions and much to attract and interest the visitor.
The town lies at the lower north-western end of Lake Zurich astride the river
Limmat which flows out of the lake at this point, between the Uetliberg on
the west and the Zürichberg on the east. It has both a University and the
Federal College of Technology. Three of the five major Swiss banks have
their head offices in the famous Bahnhofstrasse, one of the finest shopping
streets in Europe. Zurich is also a great financial and industrial capital
(mainly textiles, engineering and electrical equipment). In addition it is the
country's leading tourist attraction, with about a million visitors a year. A
fifth of the country's total national income is earned in Zurich.

Zurich is also the most important focus of communications in Switzerland.   Communica-
It has the country's largest airport; its railway station is on the great   tions
international through routes from Vienna and Munich to southern France
and Spain and from Stuttgart to Milan; and a number of motorways meet at
the city. The motorways all end, however, at the city boundary, since the
citizens of Zurich – who have a large say in the matter – have been unable to
agree on the line of an urban motorway. As a result, all through traffic has
to find its way through the city, which can be very time-consuming. The
suburban railway in course of construction is scheduled to be completed in
1994.

Zurich

Zurich: city centre astride the Limmat

Area and Population	The city of Zurich has a total area of 92 sq. km/36 sq. miles. The population in 1892, before the incorporation of suburban communes, was 87,400. In 1960 the population of the enlarged city had risen to 440,170 – its highest point – but by 1987 it had fallen to 353,000 (840,320 for the whole urban area). Less than half the resident population belong to the canton of Zurich. Until the end of the 18th c. the population of Zurich was almost entirely Protestant but by 1979 the proportion of Roman Catholics had reached almost 40%, giving Zurich the largest number of Catholics of any town in Switzerland.
Canton of Zurich	Since 1830 Zurich has been capital of the canton of Zurich, the seventh largest of the Swiss cantons in terms of area (1729 sq. km/668 sq. miles) and the largest of them all in terms of population (1,131,000 (1987)). Situated in the Swiss Mittelland, it has a green and gentle landscape, reaching its lowest point in the Rhine valley (330 m/1083 ft) and its highest in the Schnebelhorn (1292 m/4239 ft). It has much to offer the visitor, with its charming little towns and neat villages, its beautiful countryside and well-kept vineyards.
History	The earliest traces of human occupation on the site of Zurich were a Neolithic settlement excavated on the Bauschänzli, the little island in the River Limmat. The Roman fortified settlement of Turicum was established on the Lindenhof, where there had been a Roman military station as early as 15 B.C. According to the legendary story the town's patron saints Felix and Regula fled to Zurich with the Theban Legion and were beheaded there; their remains were preserved in the Grossmünster (begun not later than the 9th c.). The works of Hartmann von er Aue and the poems by other medieval minnesingers preserved in the Manesse Manuscript (written in Zurich but now in the University Library of Heidelberg) are a reminder of the great days of chivalry. The development of Zurich into a city state was given a considerable stimulus when the guilds obtained equal rights with the nobility after an assault on the Town Hall in 1336 and, in 1351, it became

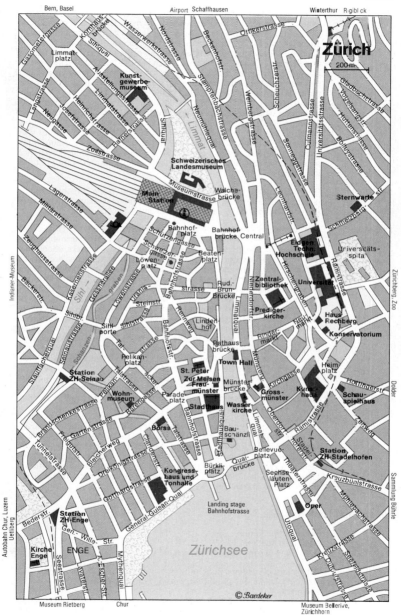

Zurich

a member of the Confederation. In 1523 Ulrich Zwingli (1484–1531) established the Reformation in Switzerland and made Zurich one of the great cities of the Reformed faith, ranking equally with Wittenberg and Geneva. The town rose to prosperity through its silk and cotton industries; but when a federal state was established in the 19th c. the status of capital passed from Zurich to Berne. In the 18th c. Zurich became influential in intellectual life, with such figures as the theologian Johann Caspar Lavater, the educationalist Heinrich Pestalozzi, the great scholar Johann Jakob Bodmer and the writer Salomon Gessner. During the 19th and 20th c. the town continued to be a pivotal point of liberal thought, and among the notable personalities who stayed here were Gottfried Keller, Conrad Ferdinand Meyer, Georg Büchner, August Bebel, Lenin, James Joyce, C. G. Jung, Ludwig Klages and Thomas Mann. In 1916 the Dadaist school was founded in Zurich. In 1980 and 1981 serious confrontations occurred between young people and police (including the occupation and clearance of a youth centre). In June 1982 the autonomous Youth Centre of Zurich was closed.

Newspaper

One of Europe's most important newspapers, the "Neue Zürcher Zeitung", is published in Zurich. Founded in 1780 by Salomon Gessner, it now has an editorial staff of 100 and a circulation of some 145,000.

Shopping

The Bahnhofstrasse in Zürich is one of the most attractive streets in Europe for shopping. Here there are fashion houses, boutiques, department stores and specialist shops (especially jewellery, watches and clocks, shoes, furs and fashion accessories). Small boutiques and antique dealers can be found mainly in the old town to the south of the Lindenhof (Rennweg, Strehlgasse, Augustinergasse, St Petershof, Münsterhof) and north of the Grossmünster. The Limmatquai (right bank), with its fine guild houses, is also a favourite shopping street. Unusual articles and curiosities can be found in the side streets of the old town, in Oberdorf and Niederdorf, where there are many bars, cafés and restaurants. The Löwenstrasse district and the adjoining "Shopville" in the station subcourse is another popular shopping area. The pedestrian zone around the Oerlikon market place is only a few steps from the exhibition centre.

Local souvenirs are sold by the Schweizer Heimatwerk at Rudolf-Brun Bridge, Bahnhofstrasse 2, Rennweg 14 and at the airport.

A large flea-market is held every Saturday between 6 a.m. and 4 p.m. on the Bürkliplatz from May until October and many handmade and exotic articles are on sale at the Rosenmarkt curiosities market (Thur. 10 a.m.–9 p.m.; Sat. 10 a.m.–4 p.m.).

Leisure and Sport

Among the sports and recreational activities available in Zurich are sailing on Lake Zurich and boating on the Limmat. There are football stadia in Letzigrund and Hardturm, a covered stadium and a race-track in Oerlikon. The Allment indoor sports complex is in Zurich-Wiedikon. Other facilities include a swimming bath with wave-making equipment and an artificial ice-rink in Dolde. There are covered municipal swimming baths at the Silhporte and in Oerlikon.

Museums, Galleries, etc.

Architectural Forum
Neumarkt 15;
Tue.–Fri. 1–6 p.m., Sat. 11 a.m.–4 p.m.

Art Gallery (Kunsthaus Zürich)
(Painting, sculpture, graphic art, mainly 19th and 20th c.)
Heimplatz 1;
Mon. 2–5 p.m., Tue.–Fri. 10 a.m.–9 p.m. Sat. and Sun. 10 a.m.–5. p.m.
Library: Tue.–Fri. 10 a.m.–noon and 2–6 p.m., Sat. 10 a.m.–4 p.m.;
closed Sun. and Mon.

Bärengasse Museum of Domestic Life (Wohnmuseum)
(Zurich domestic interiors of the 17th and 18th c.;
Sasha Morgenthaler Doll Museum)
Bärengasse 22;
Tue.–Fri. and Sun. 10 a.m.– noon and 2– 5 p.m., Sat. 10 a.m.–noon and
2–4 p.m.; closed Mon.

Bellerive Museum
(Applied and decorative art of the past and present)
Höschgasse 3;
Tue., Thur. and Fri. 10 a.m.–5 p.m., Wed. 10 a.m.–9 p.m., Sat. and Sun.
10 a.m.– noon and 2–5. p.m.

Beyer Museum of the Measurement of Time
(Clocks from antiquity to the present)
Bahnhofstrasse 31;
Mon.–Fri. 10 a.m.– noon and 2–4 p.m., Sat. 10 a.m.– noon.

E. G. Bührle Collection
(Dutch and Italian painters, French Impressionists, medieval sculpture);
Zollikerstrasse 172;
Tue. and Fri. 2–5 p.m., 1st Fri. in month 2–8. p.m.

Central Library
Zähringerplatz 6;
Mon.–Fri. 8 a.m.–8 p.m., Sat. 8 a.m.–5 p.m.; closed Sun.;
Exhibitions in choir of Predigerkirche
Predigerplatz 33;
Tue.–Fri. 1–5 p.m., Thur. until 9 p.m., Sat. 10 a.m.–5 p.m.
closed Sun. and Mon.

Federal College of Technology (Eidgenössische Technische Hochschule)
Geological and mineralogical collections;
Sonneggstrasse 5;
Mon.–Fri. 10 a.m.–7 p.m., Sat. 10 a.m.– 4 p.m.; closed Sun.
Collection of graphic art, ETH main building, entrance in Künstlergasse
Mon.–Sat. 10 a.m.–noon and 2–5 p.m.; during exhibitions also Sun.
10 a.m.– noon.

Foundation for Constructive and Concrete Art
(special exhibitions)
Seefeldstrasse 317;
Sat. and Sun. 10 a.m.–5 p.m.

Haller Atelier
(sculptures by Hermann Haller, 1890–1950);
Corner of Höschgasse/Bellerivestrasse;
June–Sept. Tue.–Sat. 3–6 p.m.

Haus zum Kiel
(special exhibitions)
Hirschengraben 20;
Tue.–Fri. 2–7 p.m., Thur. until 9 p.m., Sat. and Sun. 2–5 p.m.

Helmhaus
(special exhibitions)
Limmatquai 31;
Tue.–Sun. 10 a.m.–6 p.m., Thur. until 9 p.m.; closed Mon.

Jacobs–Suchard Museum
(history of coffee)
Seefeldquai 17;
Fri. 3–6 p.m., Sat. and Sun. 10 a.m.–5 p.m.; closed on public holidays.

James Joyce Foundation
(manuscripts, books)
Augustinergasse 28;
Tue.–Thur. 2–6. p.m.

Kulturama
(paleontological collection)
Rote Fabrik, Seestrasse 409;
Mon.–Fri. and 1st Sun. in month 10 a.m.–5 p.m.

Kunsthalle (modern art)
Hardturmstrasse 114
Tue–Fri. noon–6 p.m., Sat. and Sun. 11 a.m.–5 p.m.

Municipal Archives
(archives and literature on the history of the town)
Neumarkt 4;
Mon.–Fri. 8 a.m.–5.30 p.m., Sat. 8–11.30 a.m.

Municipal Collection of Succulents
(cactuses and other succulents)
Mythenquai 88;
Daily 9–11.30 a.m. and 1.30–4.30 p.m.; guided tours by arrangement.

Municipal Gardens Department – Show Houses
(Schauhäuser der Stadtgärtnerei)
Sackzeig 25–27;
Daily 9–11.30 a.m. and 2–5 p.m.

Museum of Decorative Arts
(Kunstgewerbemuseum für Gestaltung)
(Collection of Swiss and foreign posters)
Ausstellungsstrasse 60;
Tue.–Fri. 10 a.m.–noon and 2–6 p.m., Wed. 10 a.m.– noon and 2–9 p.m., Sat.
and Sun. 10 a.m.–noon and 2–5 p.m.; closed Mon.

Museum of Ethnology, (Völkerkundemuseum)
Pelikanstrasse 40, in "Zur Katz" Park;
Tue.–Fri. 10 a.m.–noon and 2–5 p.m., Sat. and Sun. 11 a.m.–4 p.m.;
closed Mon.

Museum of the Indians
(Culture of the North American Indians)
Schulhaus, Feldstrasse 89;
Sat. 2–5 p.m., Sun. 10 a.m.–noon.

Museum of Masks
(Swiss wooden masks by Paul Strassmann); Obere Waldstrasse
(opposite No. 9);
May–October, 1st Sun. in month 10 a.m.–noon, and by prior arrangement.

Museum of Tin Figures
(toys, Gottstein–Blum model collection)
Obere Zäune 19;
Tue.–Fri. 2–4 p.m., Sat. 2–5 p.m., Sun. 10 a.m.–noon and 1–4; closed Mon.

Mühlerama
(museum in the historic Tiefenbrunnen mill)
Seefeldstrasse 231;
Tue.–Sat. 2–5 p.m.; Sun. 1.30–6 p.m.

Palaeontological Museum
Künstlergasse 16.

Pestalozzi Memorial Rooms
(manuscripts, original editions, personal possessions)
Beckenhofstrasse 33;
Tue.–Fri. 2–5 p.m.

Rietberg Museum
(non-European art, especially Indian, Chinese and African)
Villa Wesendonck, Gablerstrasse 15;
Tue. and Thur.–Sun. 10 a.m.–5 p.m., Wed. also 8–10 p.m.

Johanna Spyri Foundation
(manuscripts, book illustrations and personal possessions)
Zeltweg 13;
Wed. 2–6 p.m.

Stadthaus
(special exhibitions)
Stadthausquai 17;
Mon.–Fri. 8 a.m.–6 p.m.; closed Sat. and Sun.

Strauhof Municipal Gallery
Augustinergasse 9;
Tue.–Sun. 10 a.m.–6 p.m., Thur. 10 a.m.–9 p.m.; closed Mon.

Swiss National Museum
(Swiss culture, art and history)
Museumstrasse 2;
Tue.–Fri. and Sun. 10 a.m.–noon and 2–5 p.m., Sat. 10 a.m.–noon and
2–4 p.m.; closed Mon.

Thomas Mann Archives (ETH)
(manuscripts, memorial room with library from the Kirchberg study)
Schönberggasse 15;
Wed. and Sat. 2–4 p.m.

Toy Museum of Zurich
(toys from 18th to 20th c.)
Corner of Fortunagasse 15/Rennweg 26;
Mon.–Fri. 2–5 p.m.

University of Zurich
Anthropological Collection,
Mensagebäude, Winterthurerstrasse 190;
Tue.–Fri. 9 a.m.–5 p.m.
Archaeological Collection
Rämistrasse 73;
Tue.–Fri. 1–6 p.m.
Botanical Garden
Zollikerstrasse 107;
Mon.–Fri. 7 a.m.–7 p.m., Sat. and Sun. 8 a.m.–6 p.m.
Greenhouses – daily 9.30–11.30 a.m. and 1–4 p.m.
Medical Collection
Rämistrasse 71;
Wed. and Thur. 2–5 p.m., Sat. 10 a.m.–noon; and by prior arrangement.

Zoo
Zürichbergstrasse 221;
March–October 8 a.m.–6 p.m.; November–February 8 a.m.–5 p.m.

Zunfthaus zur Meisen
(Swiss ceramics of the 18th c.)
Münsterhof 20;
Tue.–Fri. and Sun. 10 a.m.–noon and 2–5 p.m., Sat. 10 a.m.–noon and
2–4 p.m.; closed Mon.

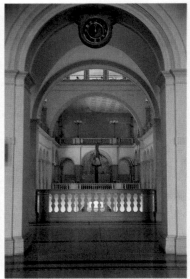

Pestalozzi Memorial

Federal College of Technology

Sightseeing in Zurich

Zurich is a town for sightseeing on foot, since the principal places of interest are on both sides of the river Limmat and on the north shore of Lake Zurich.

West of the Limmat

*Bahnhof-strasse

The pulsating activity of the city is focused on the Bahnhofstrasse, a street 1200 m/3937 ft long (most of it pedestrianised) which extends from the main station to the lake (landing stages). The middle section of the street was built in 1867 after the filling in of an old moat, the Fröschengraben; the lower part, towards the lake, was built from 1877 onwards, the upper part towards the station from 1885.

Among the interesting buildings in the lower part, dating from the turn of the century are the Weber business premises (Nr. 75), built in 1899 by R. Kuder and A. Müller (re-built 1912–1913 and 1928) and the Jelmoli department store (Seidengasse 1) a complex of buildings which has been reconstructed several times; it was originally designed in 1897 by H. A. Stadler and J. E. Usteri with a skeleton in iron. The historic façade (1913–1916) of the Peterhof and Leuenhof premises was the work of the brothers O. and N. Pfister.

Beyer Museum of the Measurement of Time

In the basement of Nr. 21 can be seen a comprehensive collection of timepieces belonging to the Beyer watch and clock business. The exhibits range from sun, oil and water-clocks to Swiss clocks with wooden wheels and Nuremberg pendulum clocks. There are also automata, navigational instruments and clocks from the Far East.

Paradeplatz

In the lower part of the Bahnhofstrasse lies the Paradeplatz, with the palatial headquarters of the Schweizerischen Kreditanstalt (1876) and the Hotel Savoy Baur en Ville, built in 1838 and reconstructed in 1978. In

Swiss National Museum . . .   *. . . cannon of 1678*

the 18th c., there was a cattle market on the Paradeplatz and, later, as its name suggests, it was used as a parade ground.

The Konditorei Sprüngli is the heart of a chocolate empire which has its chief factory in Kilchberg. The Sprüngli firm, the largest confectionery concern in Switzerland was divided about a century ago to form the chocolate factory Lindt and Sprüngli (Rudolf Sprüngli) and the Sprüngli Confectionery, now headed by Richard Sprüngli. As well as the main shop in the Paradeplatz (renovated in 1985), there are seven other shops belonging to the firm. Well-known confectionery specialities are: mouth-watering gâteaux, the delicious "Luxemburgerli" and Sprüngli's chocolate cubes "number one".

* Konditorei Sprüngli

Towards the upper end of the Bahnhofstrasse, on the corner of Uraniastrasse, stands the Urania Observatory and, to the west, are the Pestalozzi gardens with a bronze statue (1899) of the famous pedagogue Heinrich Pestalozzi (1746–1827).

Urania Observatory Pestalozzi Gardens

To the west of the Bahnhofstrasse, extending to the Sihlporte, is a district containing many commercial offices and the Börse (Stock Exchange). To the east, towards the Limmat, is the "Kleine Stadt" ("Little Town"), the western half of the old town.

The main railway station (Hauptbahnhof), built 1865–187 on the site of Zurich's old station, is still equal to present-day needs. On its south side is the Bahnhofplatz, now reserved exclusively for traffic. In the square can be seen a monument (1990) to the Swiss statesman Alfred Escher (died 1882) by R. Kissing. Beneath the square is a pedestrian concourse with a modern shopping area ("Shopville"). The west façade of the station is being given an artistic "facelift". On the north side of the station is the Air Terminal (buses to Zurich airport 20 minutes).

Main Railway Station

Immediately north of the station is the Swiss National Museum (Schweizerisches Landesmuseum), a large castellated building with Gothic elements

** Swiss National Museum

Swiss National Museum

Schweizerisches Landesmuseum Zürich

Musée National Suisse Zürich

Museo Nazionale Svizzero Zurigo

Museum Naziunal Svizzer Zürich

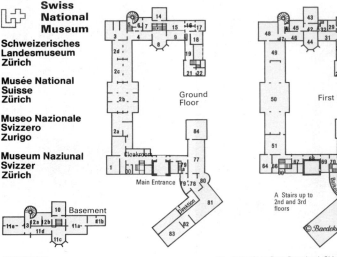

Ground Floor

First Floor

Main Entrance

Basement

Direktion

A Stairs up to 2nd and 3rd floors

© Baedeker

BASEMENT

10 Special exhibitions
11–13 Old trades and crafts
11a Milling: wine-growing (19th c.)
11b Coachbuilding and blacksmithing (19th c.)
11c Part of a Zurich armoury (16th–17th c.)
11d Casting of non-ferrous metals
11e Bells (12th–18th c.); tower clocks (16th–17th c.)
12a Comb-maker's workshop (19th c.)
12b Cooper's workshop (19th–20th c.)
13 Shoemaker's workshop (19th c.)

GROUND FLOOR

1a–3 Carolingian and Ottonian art (9th–10th c.); Gothic art, religious and secular (13th–14th c.)
4–9 Heraldry and geneaolgy; Zurich Arms Roll, etc.; Swiss pewter (16th–19th c.)
14 Council chamber from Mellingen (1467)
15 Cloister (c. 1240)
16–18 Rooms from Fraumünster abbey, Zurich (c. 1500)
19, 21 Transition from Gothic to Renaissance: portraits, furniture (16th c.)
22 Pharmacy (18th c.)
77–80 Temporary exhibitions of pre-history and early history
81 Objects of the Bronze Age (1800–800 B.C.)
82–83 Neolithic material (4th millennium to c. 1800 B.C.); bust of Ferdinard Keller (1800–81), founder of Neolithic archaeology and the theory of pile-dwelling

FIRST FLOOR

23 Stained glass, in particular from Tänikon convent (1557–59); clocks (16th–17th c.); globe from St Gallen abbey (c. 1569); keyed instruments (17th–18th c.)
24 Small room from Valais (15th c.)
25 Drawings, in particular sketches for stained glass (16th c.); bas-relief carving from the Dominican nunnery of Oetenbach, Zurich (1521)

26 Room from Casa Pestalozzi, Chiavenna (1585)
27 Room from Rosenburg, Stans (1602)
28 "Winter room" (bedroom) from Schloss Wiggen, Rorschach (1582); coats of arms (c. 1600)
29 Room from Alter Seidenhof, Zurich (1620)
30 Stained-glass panels (16th c.); wool embroidery; furniture (16th–17th c.); portraits by Samuel Hofmann (1624–32)
31 Painting of the alliance between Louis XIV and the Confederates in 1663; stained glass from the cloisters of the Cistercian nunnery at Rathausen (1591–1623); coin collection from the monastery of Rheinau (1745)
32 Zurich interior (18th c.); Zurich stove (c. 17th c.)
42 Door surround from Zurich (17th c.); special exhibitions
43 "Summer room" from the Lochmann-Haus, Zurich (c. 1660); celestial globe by Jost Bülgi (1594)
44 Upper Chapel: special exhibitions
45 Secular silverware of the late medieval period (to about 1700); gilded drinking-bowls from the convent at Sarnen (14th–15th c.)
46 Stained glass from the cloisters of the former Cistercian nunnery of Rathausen (1591–1623); painted furniture (18th c.); views of Zurich by Conrad Meyer (c. 1656)
47 Special exhibitions of graphic art; tiled stoves (18th c.)
48 Winterthur china (17th c.) and stoves; portraits and stained-glass panels
49 Items of historical interest, canton of Zurich (17th c.); pair of globes by Vincenzo Coronelli (1688); coats of arms (17th c.)
50 Armoury: development of arms and armour in Switzerland from 800 to 1800; Burgundian war: diorama of the battle of Murten (22.6.1476) with about 6000 tin figures
51 Uniforma of the federal arms (1815–60)

64 The Swiss in foreign service (1799–1859): uniforms, weapons, orders and decorations; pictures, etc.
66 Late 14th c. helmet (the "Hundsgugel"); Swiss Guards (17th–19th c.)
67 The federal army since 1898
68 Model of the Second Battle of Polotsk during Napoleon's Russian campaign (tin soldiers)
69–70a Military material of the Roman period (1st–4th c. A.D.)
71 Weapons and implements of the Late Iron Age (La Tène, 5th–1st c. B.C.)
72 Domestic objects of the Roman period
73 Cult object of the Roman period (reconstructions of domestic altars)
74 Models of early medieval refuge forts; jewellery, etc.
75 Coin collection

SECOND FLOOR
(Rooms 33–41 are reached from the first floor by the stairs at Room 47, Rooms 53–57 by the stairs at Rooms 24 and 32)
33 Liturgical utensils: monstrances, chalices, etc. (17th–18th c.)
34 Secular silverware (18th–19th c.)
35–39 Large cases with groups of figures in period costume (18th c.)
35 Furniture, domestic equipment, costumes (Zurich, 18th c.)
36 Music-making in a house of the Rococo period (c. 1760)
37 A reception, c. 1770–80; clockwork model in the form of a bird-cage from western Switzerland
38 Spinning-room from eastern Switzerland; rural costumes and painted furniture
39 Market scene, Zurich (c. 1800)
40–41 Scenes of 19th c. life
40 "Gift temple" with riflemen's cups; table-setting with gold ornaments; sewing-room
41 Large cases with two drawing-rooms of the 1870s
53–57 Town dress of the 18th and 19th c.; collection of footwear, jewellery and fans; smoking and sewing equipment

THIRD FLOOR
(Rooms 59–63, reached from the first floor by the stairs at Rooms 24 and 32)
59–61 Swiss costumes (18th–19th c.), the canton of Zurich being particularly well represented (Room 59)
62 Toys, dolls' houses
63 Toys, particularly dolls; picture showing Glarus costumes by Joseph Reinhart (c. 1790) and watercolour of costumes by Ludwig Vogel (19th c.)

which was built 1893–1898 to designs by Gustav Gull. It contains the most important collection of material on the history and culture of Switzerland. The main departments in this richly stocked museum are as follows: pre-history and the early historical period; weapons, flags and militaria; goldsmiths' and silversmiths' work; articles in non-ferrous metals and pewter; ceramics and glass; textiles, costume and jewellery; coins and medals; seals; stained glass; sculpture; furniture and domestic interiors; painting and graphic art; clocks, watches and scientific instruments; musical instruments; rural life; craft and industrial antiquities; library; special exhibitions. Of particular interest among the scientific instruments are the celestial globe by Jost Bürgi (1552-1632), the works of religious art and medieval wall paintings (including works by Hans Fries), the unique collection of old stained glass, the Armoury, with the celebrated murals by Hodler, a series of period rooms of the Gothic to Baroque periods, the most important antiquities in Switzerland of pre- and early history, and the largest collection of coins and medals in the country.

Behind the National Museum we find the Platzpromenade, a public garden on the triangular spit of land between the Limmat and its tributary the Sihl. To the north-west extends the city's large industrial zone.

Platzpromenade

North-west of the station on the left bank of the Sihl, at Ausstellungsstrasse 60, is the Museum of Decorative Arts (Kunstgewerbemuseum) which, from time to time, puts on special exhibitions of graphic art, design, architecture and applied art. The museum has drawings and prints from the 16th c. to the present day (including book-illustrations, commercial art, popular art) and a notable collection of posters with some 70,000 examples, including posters by Toulouse-Lautrec. The applied art collection is housed in the Bellerive Museum (see p. 474).

Museum of Decorative Arts

Zurich

Old Town (west)

Lindenhof

Between the Bahnhofstrasse and the left bank of the Limmat extends the western half of the old town. In this area is to be found the quiet tree-shaded Lindenhof, the site of a Roman fort and later of an Imperial stronghold and, today, a popular place for a short excursion. From the terrace there is a fine view of the old town.

St Peter's Church

To the south, on a little hill, stands St Peter's Church, the oldest parish church in Zurich. It has an early 13th c. Romanesque choir under the tower and a Baroque nave (three-aisled, with galleries) of 1705. In 1538 the church acquired the largest clock dials in Europe, 8.7 m/29 ft in diameter. The great preacher and writer J. C. Lavater (1741–1801) was pastor here for 23 years; his former house was the Hans zur Armbrust (Nr. 6) on the square outside the church.

Münsterhof

To the south is the Münsterhof, a pleasant square in the Old Town, with a long history. On the Münsterbrüche (1838) over the Limmat stands a bronze equestrian statue (by H. Haller, 1937) of Burgomaster Waldmann (beheaded in 1489), under whose rule Zurich reached the peak of its power in the 15th c.

Fraumünster Kirche

On the south side of the square is the Fraumünster (restored 1965), a three-aisled pillared basilica with a Gothic nave (13th–15th c.), an Early Gothic transept and a pointed spire. The Fraumünster was given by the Emperor Ludwig (Louis) the German to his daughter Hildegard in 853 and, from that time until the high Middle Ages, the head of the convent was also governor of the town.

*Stained glass

In the imposing Late Romanesque choir are five stained-glass windows by Marc Chagall (1970). The undercroft contains remains of the crypt of the abbey church founded by the Emperor Ludwig (Louis) the German in 853. The abbey itself was demolished in 1898 to make way for the Stadthaus, but the Romanesque and Gothic cloister survives, with paintings of old Zurich legends by P. Bodmer (1928).

*Zunfthaus zur Meisen
Ceramic collection

On the north side of the Münsterhof (No. 20) is the Zunfthaus zur Meisen, a magnificent Late Baroque guild-house (by D. Morf, 1752–57) in the style of a French hotel (town mansion) with a cour d'honneur, which now houses the Swiss National Museum's ceramic collection of the 18th c., (including Zurich work from the porcelain factory in the Schooren) near Kilchberg and a court of honour.

Zunfthaus zur Waag

On the west side of the square is another old guild-house (No. 8), the Zunfthaus zur Waag (1636; restaurant) with a stately Baroque doorway and Late-Gothic window-frames in the guild-hall.

*Bürkliplatz Quaibrücke

From here the Stadthausquai leads south past the Bauschänzli summer restaurant to Bürkliplatz and the Quaibrücke, which crosses the outflow of the Limmat to Bellevue Platz on the opposite bank. In Bürkliplatz is the landing stage for the lake steamers on which visitors can take delightful trips on the lake (see Lake Zürich). To the south, in good weather, there is a splendid view over the lake to the Glarus Alps.

Weinplatz

From the Weinplatz, with the Weinbauer fountain (1909), we cross the Limmat on the Rathausbrücke (1878), successor to a seies of earlier bridges which for centuries provided the only crossing. Along the banks of the Limmat are well-preserved old Burghers' houses, such as the "Schipfe" housing complex on the west bank which dates from the 17th–18th c.

Old Town (east)

Rathaus

At the east end of the bridge, overhanging the river on the right, is the Rathaus (Town Hall, 1694–98), a massive Later Renaissance building, with

Grossmünster: statue of Charlemagne   *Kunsthaus (art gallery)*

rich sculptured decoration, in which the cantonal and communal councils meet in public. The tastefully furnished Baroque ceremonial hall is well worth seeing.

Along the Limmatquai, a popular shopping street, are a number of elegant old guild-houses with richly appointed interiors reflecting the wealth of the guilds which governed the town until 1789: at No. 54 the Haus zur Saffran (1719–23), at No. 42 the Haus zur Rüden (1660) and at No. 40 the two-storeyed Haus zur Zimmerleuten (1709: extended 1783–1785; with a beautiful oriel window), all now housing restaurants. No. 62 is the Haus der Museumsgesellschaft (1866–1868; rebuilt in 1965).

Limmatquai

On the south side of the Münsterbrücke stands the Late-Gothic single-aisled Wasserkirche ("water church"), once entirely surrounded by the Limmat. It was not connected to the land until 1839 when the Limmat quay was constructed. In front of the choir is a bronze statue of 1885 to Ulrich Zwingli (1484–1531) Zurich's great Reformer. Built on to the north side of the church is the Helmhaus (1794). with an open fountain hall, in which special exhibitions are put on by the municipal authorities.

Wasserkirche

Helmhaus

On an open terrace above the river stands Zurich's principal church, the Grossmünster (Protestant), which dominates the city with its twin towers (domed tops added in 1782). Built between the 11th and the 13th c., it is a Romanesque three-aisled galleried basilica with an aisleless chancel over a crypt of about 1100. The upper levels of the towers date from 1487. On the upper part of the south tower, on the side facing the river, is a seated figure of Charlemagne (copy: original in the crypt), who is believed to have founded the house of secular canons to which the church originally belonged; on the north side of the north tower is a figure of the Reformer Heinrich Bullinger. notable features of the church are the two modern bronze doors (1935–36), the sculptured Romanesque capitals, remains of Gothic wall-paintings and the Late Romanesque cloister (c. 1200). In the

Grossmünster

choir are three vividly coloured stained-glass windows designed by Augusto Giacometti (1933) and in the crypt is the badly weathered statue of Charlemagne.

From 1519 until his death in the Battle of Kappel in 1531 the great Reformer Ulrich Zwingli was a secular priest in the Grossmünster. His residence was close by, at Kirchgasse 13. The Neo-Gothic Grossmünster chapel (1858-1859) was designed by J. J. Breitinger, the minster terrace is by A. Negrelli.

*Streets in the Old Town
Napfgasse

A walk through the eastern part of the the old town is full of charm and interest, with many excellent antique shops adding to its attractions. Going north up Münstergasse, we come to the Napfgasse, with the Brunnenturm, headquarters of the Lombard money-changers in the 14th and 15th c. The most interesting house is No. 6, the Haus zum Napt, which has fine interior furnishings, including rooms in Renaissance and Regency styles.

Spiegelgasse

In the Spiegelgasse is a house (No. 17) in which Lenin lived in 1917. In this street, too, was the cabaret in which Hans Arp and Tristan Tzara launched the Dadaist movement in 1916.

Neumarkt

The Spiegelgasse runs east into the Neumarkt in which are the Shoemakers' Guildhouse (No. 5), now the Theater am Neumarkt. The Hans zum

Town archives

Rech (No. 4), which dates from the High Middle Ages, now houses the town archives. The 13th c. Grimmenturm, (No. 27, restored in the mid 60s) was originally a residence.

Keller Haus

Set back from the street, this house was the birthplace of the great Swiss writer Gottfried Keller (commemorative plaque); he was the first Chief Clerk of the canton of Zurich. Close by, at Rindermarkt 12, is the Oepfelchammer restaurant, a favourite haunt of his.

Zeltweg

The house in which he died is at Zeltweg 27, south-east of the Heimplatz. Also in the Zeltweg lived the young authoress Johanna Spyri for 15 years;

Spyri Foundation

some of her work can be seen at No. 13, where the Spyri foundation is housed.

Predigerkirche
Town archives

To the north of Neumarkt stands the Predigerkirche (1611-1614), the Preachers' (i.e. Dominicans') church, an Early Baroque building with a Neo-Gothic tower. In 1917 the Gothic choir, which was added in the 14th c., became the home of the cantonal archives. Adjoining the church is the

Zentral-
bibliothek

Central Library, on the site of a Dominican monastery. The buildings are in process of extension (completion envisaged in 1995); the restored main house in the Zähringerplatz will house a special collection and the North American Library; there will also be a public wing with reading rooms along the Mühlgasse, an administration block between the Seilergraben and the Chorgasse. The High-Gothic choir of the Predigerkirche will be freed from its present additions and once again will be revealed in its full splendour. Between the Chorgasse and the inner courtyard of the choir a new pedestrian precinct will be a welcome addition to the Old Town.

Hirschengraben
Haus zum
Rechberg

To the east of the Neumarkt is the Haus zum Rechberg, Hirschengraben 40 (at the corner of Künstlergasse), which was built by D. Morf for the guild master J. C. Werdmuller amid terraced gardens between 1759 and 1790. It is Zurich's finest Rococo building and the most important secular building of the 18th c. In 1799 the house was occupied by French and allied generals and, in 1815, by the Emperor Francis I of Austria. Also of interest is the Hans zum Neuberg (No. 59/60) which dates from 1733 but rebuilt in 1818; Alfred Escher, the Zurich statesman, was born here. On the upper floor of No. 42, the Haus zum Krönli, built in 1739 and restored in the 19th-20th c., can be seen fine panelling.

To the south-east is the Conservatory of Music.

Heimplatz
*Kunsthaus

A short distance south of the Conservatoire is the Heimplatz, on the south-west side of which we find the Art gallery (Kunsthaus), with an important collection of pictures and sculpture from antiquity to the present day. To the right of the entrance can be seen a large piece of bronze sculpture, the

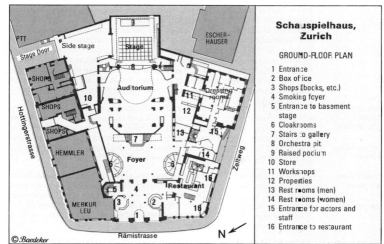

Schauspielhaus, Zurich

GROUND-FLOOR PLAN

1 Entrance
2 Box office
3 Shops (books, etc.)
4 Smoking foyer
5 Entrance to basement stage
6 Cloakrooms
7 Stairs to gallery
8 Orchestra pit
9 Raised podium
10 Store
11 Workshops
12 Properties
13 Rest rooms (men)
14 Rest rooms (women)
15 Entrance for actors and staff
16 Entrance to restaurant

"Porte de l'Enfer" ("Gate of Hell") by Auguste Rodin (1880–1917). The institution, run by the Zurich Society of Arts with the aid of a public subsidy, goes back to a society of artists, founded in 1787; the "Künstlergüetli" gallery was established in 1847. The buildings were extensively enlarged in 1925, in 1954–1958 and in 1976.

In addition to Swiss painters of the 19th and 20th c., such as J. H. Füssl , F. Buchser, R. Koller, A Böcklin, F. Hodler, C. Amiet, A. and J. Giacometti, M. Gubler and M. Bill, there are important works by E. Munch, O. Kokoschka and M. Beckmann. Also to be seen are paintings by French Impressionists, including Manet, Monet and Cézanne, international avant-garde artists of the 20th c. such as Klee, Mondrian, Picasso, Chirico, Matisse, Chagall, and many exhibits in a Dadaist collection. The department of modern sculpture since the time of Rodin has works by Moore, Picasso, Barloch, Maillot, Rodin, Segal, Caler and Tinguely. The graphic collection has about 80,000 drawings and prints by J. H. Füssli, S. Gessner, F. Hodler, F. Hegi, L. Corinth, A. Dürer, Raffael and Rembrandt, P. Klee, F. Glarner, C. Amiet, M. Klinger and the Zurich "concrete" movement.

Facing the Art Gallery, on the south-east side of the square, is the Haus zum Pfauen (House of the Peacock: built 1888–89, reconstructed 1976–78), with the Schauspielhaus (theatre), one of the most renowned of German-language theatres, completely remodelled in the recent rebuilding (see plan above).

Schauspielhaus

From 1642 to 1833 Zurich was surrounded by a ring of ramparts and bastions. After the demolition of these fortifications the moats were filled in, and the town was able to expand beyond its former limits. The monumental complexes of the University and the College of Technology are the result of this wave of building activity in the 19th and 20th centuries.

Colleges

From the Heimplatz, the Rämistrasse, coming from the Bellevueplatz, continues up to a terrace on which stands the University (founded 1833, rebuilt 1911–14), with a 64 m/210 ft high tower. The University buildings contain a number of museums and collections. Extensive new university buildings on the Irschel, in the Unterstrasse district, were brought into use in 1978. Zurich is the largest Swiss university – in 1988 there were some 19,000 matriculated students.

University

Immediately north of the University is the Federal College of Technology (Eidgenössische Technische Hochschule), founded in 1855, which now has

Federal College of Technology

473

some 11,000 students. The two-storeyed building with wings was constructed by Gottfried Semper in 1860–1864 in the Historism style, and extended in 1915–1925 by Gustav Gull. Semper was also responsible for the Federal Observatory (Sternwarte; Schmelzbergstrasse 25). In the main building of the College of Technology is a comprehensive collection of graphic art (exhibitions). Geological and mineralogical collections are housed at Sonneggstrasse 5. Extensions to the college were built on the Hönggerberg to the north-west of the town. From the north-west corner of the main complex a funicular decends to the Limmatquai.

Haus zum oberen Schönenberg	To the south of the University, at Schönbergstrasse 15, is the Haus Zum oberen Schönenberg, built about 1665 and occupied from 1756–83 by Johann Jakob Bodmer (1697–1783), a leading Swiss representative of the Enlightenment, who entertained Goethe, Klopstock and Wieland here.
Thomas Mann archives	Since 1960 it has housed the Thomas Mann Archives, containing all the papers left by the north-German novelist who died in 1955.
*Lake Zurich, east shore	At the junction of the Rämistrasse with the Utoquai is the spacious Bellevueplatz, from which a lakeside promenade offering extensive views runs south along the east side of Lake Zurich under the name of Utoquai and,
Opera House	farther on, Seefeldquai. To the left stands the neo-Baroque Opera-House (Oper), designed by the Viennese architects Fellner and Helmer and built within the space of 20 months in 1890–91.
Zürichhorn Park	About 1½ km/1 mile from the Bellevueplatz is the beautiful Zürichhorn Park (landing stage; restaurant).
Höschgasse Bellerive Museum	At Höschgasse 3 is the Bellerive Museum, with temporary exhibitions of craftwork from the Zurich Museum of Arts and Crafts (textiles, glass, ceramics). Of particular interest are exhibits in Art-nouveau style, modern Swiss ceramics, and musical instruments from the Hug collection.
Le Corbusier Centre Pavilion	Hochgasse 6 is the Centre Le Corbusier (1967; Heidi Weber Haus), which is now used as a forum for community action.
Haller-Atelier	At the junction of Höschgasse and Bellerivestrasse we find the studio of the sculptor Hermann Haller (1880–1950), with a collection of his work and the urn containing his ashes.
Heureka	Near the Zürichhorn restaurant is a gigantic piece of mechanical sculpture by Jean Tinguely, "Heureka" (1964: operates in summer at 11 and 5).
E. G. Bührle Foundation	800 m/½ mile east of Zürichhorn Park, at Zolliherstrasse 172, is the E. G. Bührle Foundation, founded in 1960. The villa houses one of the richest private collections of European art, mainly assembled by the industrialist Emil G. Bührle (died 1965) and notable particularly for its 19th and 20th c. French pictures, including the Impressionists, E. Delacroix, G. Courbet, Carot, E. Manet, C. Monet, E. Degas, A. Renoir, P. Bonnard, as well as medieval 15th c. wooden sculptures.
Botanical Garden	To the north (entrance at Zolliherstrasse 107) extends the new botanical garden, belonging to the university, it contains more than 1½ million plants.
Lake Zurich, west shore	The lakeside promenade, which follows the west shore of the lake from the Bürkliplatz, bears the names of General-Guisan Quai and, further south, Mythenquai. Near the landing-stage used by the lake steamers stands the
Kongresshaus Tonhalle	Congress hall (Kongresshaus), opened in 1939, which is built on to the older Tonhalle (1895) and is one of the major focal points of the social life of Zurich, with concerts, conferences and festive occasions of all kinds.
Belvoir Park	On the Mythenquai are the headquarters of a number of large insurance corporations, and above it lies Belvoir Park, with old trees, subtropical plants and a restaurant.
Rieter Park *Rietberg Museum	Above this again, beyond the Seestrasse, we find Rieter Park, at the north end of which, in the Gablerstrasse, is the Rietberg Museum, housed in a Neo-classical villa modelled on the Villa Albani in Rome. It was built in 1857

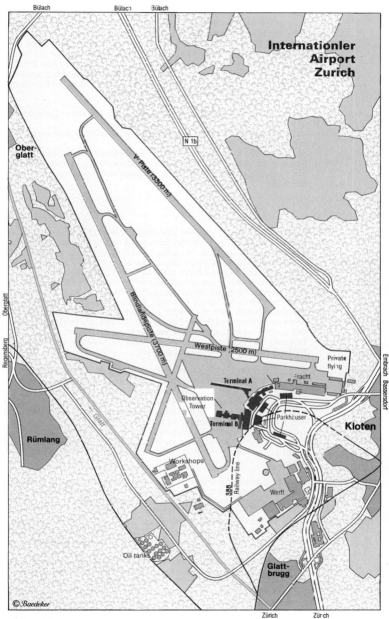

Internationler Airport Zurich

for a German industrialist, Otto Wesendonck and is reputed to be an exact copy of the Roman Villa Albani. The villa originally served as a meeting place for the intellectual elite of Zurich, including Wagner and Conrad Ferdinand Meyer. In 1952 it was acquired by the city of Zurich and now contains the fine collection of Baron Eduard von der Heydt. The exhibits of non-European art include Indian sculpture, temple pictures and bronzes from Tibet, Chinese grave decorations, Buddhist steles, ceramics and jade, as well as carvings, masks and bronzes by African tribes, and craftwork from the Pacific, the Near East and North America.

Municipal Collection of Succulents

Farther along the Mythenquai at No. 88 is the Municipal Collection of Succulents.

Muraltengut

At Seestrasse 203, the Muraltengut has reception rooms which are used by the Zurich Town Coucil.

Rote Fabrik Cultural Centre

Seestrasse 409 houses the popular Rote Fabrik Cultural Centre; concerts by rock groups, salsa, Reggae and other modern musical movements take place here. In addition, there is a small palaeontological collection in the building.

Surroundings

Zürichberg

To the east of the city rises the Zürichberg (679 m/2228 ft), a wooded hill with houses reaching far up its slopes and a number of restaurants commanding extensive views. From the Central Station and the Paradeplatz there are tram services (respectively Nos. 5 and 6) to the Zoo, one of the finest in Europe (opened 1929), with more than 2000 animals.

*Zoological Garden

Fluntern Cemetery

Near here are various sports facilities and the Fluntern Cemetery, with the grave of the Irish writer James Joyce (1882–1949).

Dolder

From the Römerhofplatz a funicular 1328 m/1453 yds long serves the Waldhaus Dolder (548 m/1798 ft), an hotel from which it is possible to continue on foot to the Dolder Grand Hotel, the golf course, the artificial ice rink and the swimming pool with wave-making equipment.

Rigiblick

From the Winterthurerstrasse another shorter funicular ascends to the Rigiblick (586 m/1923 ft; view of the Rigi).

*Uetliberg
Uetlibergbahn

To the south-west of the city rises the Uetliberg (871 m/2858 ft) the most northerly summit in the Albis ridge. The Uetlibergbahn, a mountain railway, runs from Selnau station to the upper station at 816 m/2677 ft, from which it is a ten-minute walk to the summit (restaurant). In clear weather there is a superb view from the lookout tower over the Vallais, Bernese and Glarus Alps, with the Black Forest to the north and the Säntis to the east. From here there is an easy ridge walk of just over one hour to the Felsenegg

Sihltalbahn

(790 m/2592 ft), from which a cableway descends to Adliswil (see Lake Zurich). The return to Zurich is by the Sihltalbahn (Zürich-Selnau to Sihlbrugg).

Forchbahn

From the Stadelhofen station in Zurich another electric railway, the Forchbahn, runs south-east via Forch to Esslingen in the Zurich Oberland. There are many marked trails in the countryside around Forch.

*Zurich Airport

11 km/7 miles north of the city centre (reached by rail – holiday card valid – or by bus from the Central Station), at Kloten (432 m/1417 ft) is Zurich Airport, one of the ten largest airports in Europe. It is the headquarters of Swissair, the Swiss National Airline.

The total area of the airport is some 800 ha/1977 acres. Construction began in 1945, and by 1948 two runways were ready for service. There were major extensions in 1958, 1971 and 1980. There are now three runways in service each 60 m/197 ft wide; the longest is the blind-landing runway (3700 m/4048 yds). There are two terminals equipped with shops, restaurants and service facilities: terminal A (with multi-storey car park A) for European flights and services by Pan-Am/TWA; terminal B (with multi-storey car park

B) for intercontinental and charter flights. On the second floor of car park B is a large shopping area with a bank and a post office Under the airport plaza lies the railway station concourse and below this (18 m/59 ft below ground level) four railway lines with 420 m/1378 ft of platforms. Adjoining car park B is the bus station. On the radiating arm of terminal B is an observation deck, and also the departure point for bus tours of the airport and sightseeing flights. On the busiest days there are more than 500 aircraft arrivals and departures. For flight information: tel. (01) 8 12 71 11.

South-east of Zurich Airport, on the Hegnau road, lies Dübendorf military airfield, with the museum of the Swiss Airforce. The museum has been extensively enlarged and was reopened in 1988; the exhibits include aircraft, engines, power plants, photographs, documents, navigational instruments and models illustrating the development of military aviation since 1910.

Dübendorf, Airforce Museum

West of Zurich, to the south of the Berne motorway are two small industrial towns, now part of the city. 8 km/5 miles west is Schlieren (pop. 12,500), with factories making trucks and elevators, and 12 km/7 miles west is Dietikon (pop. 25,000).

Schlieren, Dietikon

18 km/11 miles north-west of Zurich, on an eastern spur of the Lägern hills lies Regensberg (612 m/2008 ft; pop. 500), one of the best preserved medieval towns in the country which was founded about 1245 by the Barons of Regensberg. The round tower (21 m/69 ft high) of the old 16th–17th castle and the 57 m-/187 ft-deep draw-well (the deepest in the country) in the upper ward date from the time of its building. The church, originally 13th c., was rebuilt in 1506. Among the carefully restored old burghers' houses the half-timbered "Rote Rose" house (1540), with the Rose Museum of the painter Lotte Günthard, is particularly notable.

*Regensberg

The sleepy old town of Greifensee (437 m/1434 ft; pop. 5500) lies 15 km/ 9 miles east of Zurich on the north-eastern shore of the lake of the same name (area 8.6 sq. km/3 sq. miles; depth 34 m/112 ft; nature reserve). The castle was once the seat of the provincial governor Salomon Landolt. The church (c. 1330), in High Gothic style, has an unusual triangular plan. Trips on the Greifensee can be made in the motor ship "Heimat" or in the steam ship "Greif" which was restored in the mid 1980s.

Greifensee

About 5 km/3 miles south-east of Greifensee is the town of Uster (pop. 23,000).

Uster

Lake Zurich

D1

Cantons: Zürich (ZH), St Gallen (SG) and Schwyz (SZ)

Lake Zurich (in German Zürichsee), which was gouged out by the Linth glacier during the last Ice Age, extends for a total length of 39 km/24 miles in a beautiful pre-Alpine setting. With a maximum width of 4 km/2 miles, it has an area of 88 sq. km/34 sq. miles (Unterer See 68 sq. km/26 sq. miles, Obersee 20 sq. km/8 sq. miles) and a depth of up to 143 m/469 ft. Its principal tributary, the Linth, rises in Glarus, flows through the Walensee and continues into Lake Zurich as a canal. The lake is drained at the north-west end by the Limmat which flows into the Aare. Although the lake lies in a densely populated region, with about a million inhabitants of the cantons of Zürich, St Gallen and Schwyz living on its shores, a third of its shoreline is still freely accessible.

*Situation and general

The passenger boat services on Lake Zurich (Mythenquai 33, CH-8038 Zürich; tel. (01 482 10 33) are operated with modern motor vessels and also old steamships. They serve both shores as far as Rapperswill from Easter to October and, in the high season, also the Obersee.

Boat Services

Old steamer on Lake Zurich

North-east shore

The north-east shore of the lake, with an almost continuous succession of attractive towns and villages lying below vineyards and orchards and a whole string of beaches, is popularly known as the "Gold Coast" because of the many wealthy people who have houses here.

Küsnacht
The first place beyond Zurich is Küsnacht (427 m/1401 ft; see Zurich), a town of 12,000 inhabitants, with a church first mentioned in the records in 1158. The present building dates from the 15th c. and has wall-paintings in the choir. Also of interest are the "Höchhus", a 15th c. tower house, and a former commandery of the Knights of St John, now a teachers' training college.

Erlenbach
3 km/2 miles south-east lies Erlenbach (415 m/1362 ft), beautifully set at the foot of the vineyards belonging to the "Zur Schips" estate (sumptuous banqueting hall in the house) with Mariahalde, an elegant country house in Neo-Classical style (1770).

Meilen
5 km/3 miles beyond this we come to the chief town of the district, Meilen (423 m/1388 ft; pop. 10,000). The Protestant church by the lake was given to Einsiedeln Abbey by the Emperor Otto the Great in 965; the choir in its present form dates from 1493–1495.
From Meilen a steep road (5 km/3 miles) goes up to the Pfannenstiel (853 m/2799 ft), the highest peak on the north side of the lake, from which there are extensive views. There is a car ferry to Horgen on the south side of the lake.

Stäfa
About 7 km/4 miles south-east is Stäfa (417 m/1368 ft; pop. 7000) the largest commune on the north side of the lake, taking in Uerikon, Oetikon and many small hamlets. The reformed church, restored in the 1980s, stands on a hill overlooking the village. The origins of the Classical parish church go back to the period before the end of the first millenium and show that the

church, dedicated to St Verena, was owned by Einsiedeln Monastery. In Uerikon, on the lake, are two interesting old manor-houses and a 16th c. chapel.

9 km/6 miles east of Stäfa is Rapperswill (see entry), where the Winterthur road comes in on the left. From here a causeway (930 m/1017 yards long) crosses between the main part of Lake Zurich and the Obersee on the left to the peninsula of Hurden. Here there is a fishing village popular with summer visitors (chapel of 1497), and Pfäffikon, from which it is possible to return to Zurich either by the lakeside road or by the motorway.

Rapperswill

Hurden peninsula

North shore

From Rapperswill the route continues along the north shore of the Obersee into the canton of St Gallen, to the industrial district of Jona in the fertile area at the mouth of the river Jona. Here also are the former Cistercian nunnery of Wurmsbach (16th–17th c.), now occupied by a girls' boarding-school, and the 15th c. church of St Dionys, with wall-paintings of the same date. At the east end of the lake lies the village of Schmerikon (415 m/1362 ft).

Jona

Wurmsbach

At the east end of the lake in the Linth plain we reach the neat little town of Uznach (414 m/1358 ft), with the Kreuzkirche (1494–1505) and a cemetery chapel of 1679. Quite near the town stands the modern Benedictine missionary house of St Otmarsberg. From the road junction at Kaltbrun, to the south-east, it is possible to continue either north via Ricken to Wattwil or south via Näfels to Glarus (see entry).

Uznach

South-west shore

From Zurich (see entry) road 3 follows the south-west shore of the lake past a long string of old villages and modern villas surrounded by gardens, with many beaches. In 6 km/4 miles it reaches Kilchberg (427 m/1401 ft) on the hillside to the right of the road. This was the home of the Swiss writer Conrad Ferdinand Meyer (1825–1898) from 1875 onwards, and the German novelist Thomas Mann (1875–1955) and his wife (d. 1980) spent the last years of their lives here. Their graves are in the churchyard on the south side of the little church.

Kilchberg

Beyond this is the village of Rüschlikon (435 m/1427 ft), with the well-known IBM works near the Zurich–Sargans motorway. The research centre of the International Business Machines Corporation is one of the leading laboratories of the American multi-national concern. In 1986 the two IBM researchers G. Binnig and H. Rohrer received the Nobel prize for physics for their raster-tunnel microscope which was developed in Rüschlikon, and one year later two other physicists working in the laboratory, J. G. Bednorz and K. A. Müller, won the Nobel prize for their super-conductor for electric current.
In the local cemetery lies the Swiss industrialist G. Duttweiler (1888–1962), who founded in 1925 the Migros food company.

Rüschlikon
IBM Research
Centre

3 km/2 miles further on is Thalwil, a small town of 13,000 inhabitants with an old-established silk industry.

Thalwil

5 km/3 miles beyond Thalwil is Horgen (411 m/1348 ft; pop. 16,000) a long straggling industrial township with a Baroque church of 1782 containing fine frescoes of 1875. In the local museum by the lake (Alte Sust, Bahnhofstrasse 27) can be seen prehistoric finds from the lakeside settlement of Horgen as well as exhibits of local handicraft. There is a car ferry to Meilen on the north shore of the lake.

Horgen

The road then passes the village of Käpfnach (415 m/1362 ft) on the right, and the attractive Au Peninsula on the left. In the first house on the left past the bridge a museum of viticulture has been established, presenting

Au Peninsula
Museum of
Viticulture

479

⊛ visually the work of vintners (care of vines, cellarage, bottling, marketing) with the appropriate equipment and a complete cooper's workshop.

Wädenswil	In another 5.5 km/3 miles is Wädenswil (411 m/1348 ft), an industrial town of 15,000 inhabitants. Above the town the Neues Schloss (1518) houses the Federal Fruit-Growing Viticultural and Horticultural Research Station.
Mostorama	In Wädenswiler Grüntal the first Swiss fruit-liqueur museum (Mosterama) was opened in 1988. Here the refining of local-grown fruit and the development of its use is explained from its inception up to the present.

From here a road branches off to the right over the Hirzel-Höhe (750 m/ 2461 ft) to Sihlbrugg (18 km/11 miles).

Richterswil	About 4 km/2 miles further on is Richterswil (411 m/1348 ft), beautifully situated in a cove of the lake. Above the village are two churches from the terraces of which there are fine views.
Wollerau	A road on the right climbs 3 km/2 miles south-east to Wollerau (507 m/ 1663 ft) with a neo-Classical church (1787), and then winds its way steeply up, with fine views, for another 3 km/2 miles to Schindellegi.

The road to Pfäffikon beyond Richterswil enters the canton of Schwyz and continues along the side of the lake which here attains its greatest width (4 km/2 miles).

Freienbach	In 1.8 km/1 mile it reaches Bäch beyond which is Freienbach (416 m/1365 ft) with a Baroque church. Then the islets of Ufenau and Lützelau come into view and straight ahead can be seen the peaks of the Tuggenburg range.
Pfäffikon	Then in 2 km/1 mile the road reaches Pfäffikon (415 m/1362 ft; pop. 4000) at the southern end of the causeway across the lake, with the castle (13th c. tower) which belonged to Einsiedeln Abbey. At the northern end of the causeway is Rapperswil (see entry).

South shore

The road continues along the south side of the lake, known beyond the causeway as the Oberer Zürichsee or Obersee (upper lake), passes the Etzelwerk power station and comes to Altendorf (430 m/1411 ft). 1.5 km/1 mile beyond this off the road to the left is Lachen. On a hill to the right (505 m/1657 ft; road half-way up) stands the 15th c. St John's Chapel, which was built on the ruins of the old castle of Alt-Rapperswil (destroyed 1350).

Lachen 3 km/2 miles further on is Lachen (420 m/1378 ft; bypass), attractively situated on the Obersee; it has a fine twin-towered Rococo church (1700–1710), designed by the Thumb brothers of Vorarlberg.

North-east of Lachen at the east end of the lake is Uznach.

Alphorns ▶

Practical Information

Accommodation

Hotels	See Information
Holiday homes, Chalets	Holiday homes and chalets can be rented through such agencies as Interhome, Buckhauserstrasse 26, CH-8048 Zürich, and Utoring, Beethovenstrasse 24, CH-8022 Zürich or through the Swiss automobile clubs. Information is provided (but no reservations) by the Swiss National Tourist Office (see information) which produces a free leaflet "Ferienwohnungen und Chalets" (Holiday Homes and Chalets).
Holidays on the farm	This relatively new kind of holiday is now becoming popular in Switzerland, as in other countries. Information about farmhouses providing holiday accommodation can be obtained from the Swiss National Tourist Office.
Youth Hostels	See Information
Student Accommodation	The Swiss Student Travel Service offers inexpensive overnight accommodation at the following places: Davos, Klosters, St Moritz, Bad Scuol, Wengen and Lucerne. Information brochures "Studentenunterkünfte" (Student accommodation), "Universitäten in der Schweiz" (Universities in Switzerland) can be obtained from the Swiss National Tourist Office (see Information) or from SSR-reisen (Hotel Dept, Postfach, CH-8026 Zürich; tel. (01) 242 30 00).
Accommodation in Castles	Visitors who have never before tried a holiday in a traditional historic setting should consult the information leaflet "Hotels und Restaurants in Schlössern" (Hotels and Restaurants in Castles) and "Hotels in historischen Bauten" (Hotels in Historic Buildings), available from the Swiss Tourist Office (see Information).
Camping	See entry
Accommodation for the Handicapped	See Help for the Handicapped
Youth Hostels	See entry

Air Lines

Swiss Air	Swissair (Schweizerische Luftverkehr AG) Zentralverwaltung Balsberg CH-8058 Zurich-Flughafen Tel. (01) 812 12 12
Crossair	Agents at all Swiss airports Crossair AG CH-8058 Zürich-Flughafen Tel. (01) 816 43 43
	Agents in Basle (tel. 061 57 35 25), Berne (tel. 031 54 55 33), Geneva (tel. 022 98 88 31), Lugano (tel. 091 50 50 01)
British Airways	Central Bahnplatz 3–4 CH-4000 Basle Tel. (reservations) (061) 22 40 11

13 rue de Chantepoulet
CH-1200 Geneva
Tel. (reservations) (022) 31 40 50

Bahnhofstrasse 100
CH-8000 Zürich
Tel. (reservations) (901) 2 11 40 90

Air travel

Switzerland is linked to international air services through the airports of Zurich (Kloten) and Geneva (Cointrin). The airport Basle/Mulhouse is shared by France and Switzerland. There are excellent connections between Zurich (Kloten) airport (rail station directly beneath the airport) and Zurich main station. Geneva and Basle rail stations can be reached from the corresponding airports by a regular service of Swissair buses. Since 1937 there has also been a direct rail connection with Geneva (Cointrin) airport.

Airports

Since 1988 passengers travelling by Swissair and/or Swiss rail can effect all the customs formalities at the stations of Zurich, Geneva, Berne, Lausanne, Lugano, Lucerne, Neuchâtel and St Gallen.

Fly luggage

Swissair not only flies international routes but also some internal stretches. The regional airline Crossair provides inland air connections and also flights into neighbouring countries. There are air services between the following towns in Switzerland:
Basle–Geneva, Basle–Zurich; Berne–Lugano; Geneva–Basle, Geneva–Lugano, Geneva–Zurich; Lugano–Berne, Lugano–Geneva, Lugano–Zurich; Zurich–Basle, Zurich–Geneva, Zurich–Lugano.

Air connections

The regional airfields of Berne-Belp, Birrfeld, Grenchen, La Chaux-de-Fonds/Le Locle, Lausanne-Blécherette, Lugano-Agno, Gstaad-Saanen, Samedan-St Moritz and Sion are only used by charter companies.

Regional
airfields

Geneva-Cointrin International Airport

Airlines

—— Swissair
—— Crossair

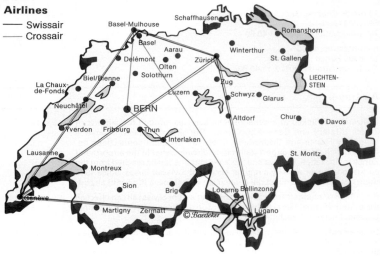

Pleasure flying   Information about pleasure flying can be obtained from the Aero-Club der Schweiz (AeCS), Lidostrasse 5, CH-6006 Lucerne.

Banks

See Currency

Boat Excursions

General   There are boat services on the larger lakes and rivers. All ships have restaurants and provide full meals as well as evening round trips (often with dancing). The leaflet "Viel mehr aufs Schiff" and timetables both for special trips and trips on steamships can be obtained from the Swiss tourist bureaux (see information).

Inland Shipping Services   See map page 571. A selection of special excursions and trips operated by the various shipping companies (with addresses) are given below:

Baseler Rhein-schiffahrt   See The Rhine

Lake Bienne (Bieler See)   Three-lake trip (Lake Bienne, Lake Neuchâtel and Lake Morat) at a special price with lunch; visit to St Peter's Island; trip on the River Aare from Bienne to Solothurn. Special features include breakfast and fondue trips.

Information: Bieler-See-Schiffsahrt-Gesellschaft (BSG)
Badhausstrasse 1
CH-2500 Biel/Bienne
Tel. (032) 22 33 22

Other excursions and further information see Lac de Neuchâtel (Neuen-berger See).

Lake Constance   Excursions by the SBB ships of the "White Fleet", for example on the flagship "St Gallen", the motorship "M/S Thurgau", Zürich or "Säntis", to places on Lake Constance.

Special attractions: In the high season on Tuesdays from Romanshorn whole day Folklore cruise on the "Schwäbischen Meer"; Trips on the car ferry Romanshorn–Friedrichshafen; Fondue (Sundays), Advent, and New Year trips.

Information
Bodensee-Flotte SBB
Bahnhof-Romanshorn
CH-8590 Romanshorn
Tel. (071) 63 14 23.

Schweizerische Schiffahrtsgesellschaft on the Untersee and Rhine – see Rhine.

See Lake Thun and Lake Brienz. Lake Brienz

The shipping company of Lake Geneva (CGN) has the largest paddle-wheel fleet in Western Europe, (four steam ships and four with diesel-electric motors). Lake Geneva (Lac Léman)

Special Attractions:
Whole day cruises, for example with a visit to Geneva, Lausanne, Montreux, Evian, Chillon Castle and Yvoire; midday cruises; firework cruises; cruises with special entertainment and a programme changing each year.

Information:
Compagnie Générale de Navigation sur le Lac Léman (CGN)
17 Avenue de Rhodaie
CH-1000 Lausanne 6
Tel. (021) 26 35 35

Geneva Office:
Jardin Anglais
CH-1204 Geneva
Tel. (022) 21 25 21

Round trips from Maur, Fällenden, Greifensee, Uster and Mönchaltdorf. Greifensee

Information:
Schiffahrtgenossenschaft Greifensee (SGG)
Verwaltung
CH-8124 Maur
Tel. (019) 80 01 69

Cruises on the Hallwil Lake Hallwilersee

Information:
Schiffahrtgesellschaft des Hallwiler Sees (SGH)
Delphinstrasse 224
CH-5616 Meisterschwanden
Tel. (057) 27 12 56

Day trips, etc., from Locarno to Stresa and to the Italian markets of Luino, Cannobio and Verbania-Intra. Connections (also by hydrofoil) between the Swiss Brissago Islands and the Borromean Islands of Italy. Lake Maggiore

Information:
Navigazione Lego Maggiore
c/o Fart
CH-6600 Locarno
Tel. (093) 31 61 40

Cruises without break of journey; cruises with stops in Gandria, Campione, Morcote, Swissminiature. Lake Lugano

Boat Excursions

Special attractions: Ticino evenings.

Lac de
Neuchâtel and
Lac de Morat

The shipping company of Lake Neuchâtel and Lake Morat operate principally on Lake Neuchâtel; numerous round trips are organised however, on Lake Morat and Lake Bienne.

Information:
Société de Navigation sur les Lacs de Neuchâtel et Morat SA
Case postale 1460
CH-2001 Neuchâtel
Tel. (038) 25 40 12

and Bieler-See-Schiffahrtgesellschaft (BSG).

The Rhine

The vessels of the Schweizerische Schiffahrtgesellschaft Untersee und Rhein ply between Konstanz–Stein am Rhein–Schaffhausen and vice versa. The river between Schaffhausen and Stein am Rhein is considered one of the most beautiful stretches of water in Europe.

Information:
Schweizerische Schiffahrtgesellschaft Untersee und Rhein
Freier Platz 7
CH-8202 Schaffhausen
Tel. (053) 25 42 82

Throughout the year the Basler Personen-Schiffahrts-Gesellschaft Kurs operates regular services and special trips. There are also day trips to Mulhouse and Breisach on the programme.

Particular attractions: Fondue-Ländler (dancing) and Spaghetti trips.

Information:
Basler Personen-Schiffahrts-Gesellschaft AG
Blumenrain 2
CH-4001 Basel
Tel. (061) 25 24 00

Lake Thun and
Lake Brienz

From Spring to Autumn there are regular trips on Lake Thun and Lake Brienz every day.

Special attractions: Midday round trips from Thun; evening round trips in summer; special trips for groups, firms, wedding parties; day tickets and season tickets on the lakes. All valid tickets issued both in Switzerland and abroad can be used on the regular ships.

Information:
Thuner See und Brienzer See
Schiffsbetrieb der Lötschbergbahn (BLS)
CH-3604 Thun
Tel. (033) 36 02 58

Untersee (Lake
Constance) and
the Rhine

See the Rhine

Lake of the Four
Forest Cantons
(Vierwaldstätter
See)

The shipping company of the Lake of the Four Forest Cantons (Lake Lucerne) has a large fleet of nostalgic paddle-wheel steamers in which you can visit well known holiday spots and historic sites dating from the foundation time of the Swiss Federation around the lake.

Special attractions: Midday and evening trips with Folklore and dancing. Wilhelm Tell Express (See Railways): You travel by steamer from Lucerne to Flüelen; and here you change into the train (saloon cars) to Lugano/

Steamer trip on Lake Lucerne

Locarno. The connection can be made daily in both directions from May to October.

Special attractions in winter: Every Friday at 7 p.m. a fondue ship operates; New Year cruises with a gala dinner or a Spaghetti fiesta. During the winter season there are several regular services daily between Lucerne and Brunnen.

Information:
Schiffahrtgesellschaft des Vierwaldstätter Sees (SGV)
Werftestrasse 5
CH-6002 Luzern
Tel. (041) 40 45 40

The Lake Zug Shipping company provides both breakfast trips (Schiffs-Zmorge) and an interesting evening circular programme from May to November; on Wednesdays and Fridays (at 8 p.m from Zug): Chinese Fondue, Risotto and Spaghetti Plausch, summer nights buffet, dance trips, raclette and fondue parties and the Lake Zug Metzgete.

Lake Zug

Information:
Schiffahrtgesellschaft für den Zuger See (SGZ)
ZVB-Haus an der Aa
CH-6304 Zug
Tel. (042) 21 02 95

There are regular services by steamship on Lake Zurich.
Further attractions: from May to October every Tuesday there are culinary evening trips (e.g. a "fondue cruise"); a cruise with dancing to a live orchestra from June to September, and many more.

Lake Zurich

Trips on the river Limmat: There are daily timetabled services from the Schweizerisches Landesmuseum (near the main station) to Zurichhorn–See–restaurant Enge and back to the Schweizerisches Landesmuseum.

Information for trips on Lake Zurich and on the River Limmat:
Zürichsee-Schifffahrtgesellschaft (ZSG)
Mythenquai 333
CH-8038 Zürich
Tel. (482) 1033

A car ferry between Horgen and Meilen makes it easy to cross from the west to the east bank of the lake (or vice versa) in a few minutes.

Information for ferry services:
Zürichsee–Fähre Horgen–Meilen
Schulhausstrasse 7
CH-8706 Meilen
Tel. (019) 23 27 77

Business Hours

Banks
Banks in the larger towns are usually open from Monday to Friday from 8.30 a.m. to 4.30 p.m. They are closed on Saturday. Elsewhere banks have the same opening hours, but generally close from noon until 2 p.m. Some remain open until 5.30 p.m. In important business centres banks often remain open during lunch time.
At airports and rail stations exchange offices may be open from 6 a.m. to 9 p.m. and often until 11 p.m.

Offices
Offices of all kinds are normally open on Monday to Friday from 8 a.m. to noon and from 2 to 5 or 6 p.m.

Shops
Shops are usually open on Monday to Friday from 8 or 8.30 a.m. to 6.30 p.m. On Saturday they close at 4 p.m. Stores and some other shops in large towns are closed on Monday morning; once a week they remain open until 9 p.m.

Outside town centres and in smaller places shops and offices are generally closed for one or two hours at lunch time. In most holiday centres there are often exceptions to general business hours, and shops remain open longer in the evenings and for an hour or two on Sunday.

Camping

Switzerland has at present over 450 camping sites, of which 90 remain open in winter. Most sites are administered by the Swiss Touring Club (see Information), the Swiss Camping and Caravan Association (SCCV), Habsburgerstrasse 35, CH-Lucerne 4; tel. (041) 23 48 22 or by regional camping clubs.

Information can also be obtained from the Verband Schweizer Campings (Sydefsdeli 40, CH-8037 Zurich 10; tel. (01) 44 57 13).
For motoring regulations for caravanners see Motoring.

Spending a night other than on an approved camping site, with the exception of a single night spent at a motorway rest area, is generally not allowed.

Car Rental

Avis
Basel
Basel-Mulhouse Airport; tel. (061) 57 28 40
Hotel Hilton, Aeschengraben 31; tel. (061) 22 22 62

Berne
Wabernstrasse 41; tel. (031) 46 13 13

Geneva
Geneva-Cointrin Airport; tel. (022) 98 23 00
Rue de Lausanne 44: tel. (022) 31 90 00

Lausanne
Avenue de la Gare 50; tel. (021) 20 66 81

Lugano
Hotel Europa, Quai Guisan; tel. (091) 54 36 41

Lucerne
Zurichstrasse 35; tel. (041) 51 32 51

Zurich
Zurich-Kloten Airport; tel. (018) 13 00 84
Gartenhofstrasse 17; tel. (012) 42 20 40

Basle   InterRent
Basle-Mulhouse Airport; tel. (061) 57 29 03
P. Merianstrasse 58; tel. (061) 23 85 55

Berne
Laupenstrasse 22; tel. (031) 25 75 55

Crans-Montana
Garage-Continental; tel. (027) 41 51 51

Davos
Davos-Platz, Garage Misucar, Talstrasse 43; tel. (083) 3 84 85

Fribourg
Garage Lehmann, Avenue Beauregard 16; tel. (037) 24 26 26

Geneva
Geneva-Cointrin Airport; tel. (022) 98 11 10
Rue de Lausanne; tel. (022) 31 51 50

Lausanne
Place de la Ripone; tel. (021) 23 71 42

Locarno
Via Trevani; tel. (091) 22 88 44

Lucerne
Garage Epper, Horwerstrasse 81; tel. (041) 41 11 23

St Moritz/Samedan
Airport Garage, C, Geromini; tel. (082) 6 56 01

Zurich
Zurich-Kloten Airport; tel. (018) 13 20 44
Josefstrasse 53; tel. (01) 42 56 56

Basle   Hertz
Gertenstrasse 120; tel. (061) 22 58 22

Berne
Kasinoplatz; tel. (031) 22 33 13

Geneva
Rue de Berne 60; tel. (022) 32 68 00

Lausanne
Parking de Montbenon; tel. (021) 20 66 51

Lugano
Via San Gottardo 13; tel. (091) 23 46 75

Lucerne
Maihofstrasse 101; tel. (041) 36 02 77

Zurich
Zurich-Kloten Airport; tel. (018) 14 05 12

Castles and Châteaux

1 Coppet: Castle (17th c.)

2 Crans: Castle (18th c.)

3 Nyon: Castle (12th c./16th c.)

4 Prangins: Castle (18th c.)

5 Rolle: Castle (13th c.)

6 Morges: Castle (13th/16th c.)

7 Vufflens-le-Château: Castle (14th c./15th c.)

8 Lausanne: Episcopal Castle (14th c./15th c.)

9 La Tour de Peilz: Castle (13th c.)

10 Montreux: Chillon Castle (11th c./13th c.)

11 Aigle: Castle (13th c.)

12 St-Maurice: Castle (15th c.)

13 La Sarraz: Castle (11th c./16th c.)

Castles and Châteaux in Switzerland

14 Oron-le-Châtel: Castle (13th c.)

15 Gruyères: Castle (13th c./15th c.)

16 Bulle: Castle (13th c.)

17 Romont: (13th c./16th c.)

18 Lucens: Castle (15th c./16th c.)

19 Yverdon: Castle (13th c.)

20 Grandson: Castle (13th c./15th c.)

21 Estavayer-le-Lac: Castle Chenaux (13th c./15th c.)

22 Murten/Morat: Castle (13th c.)

23 Gorgier: Castle (14th c./19th c.)

24 Boudry: Castle (16th c.)

25 Neuchâtel: Castle (12th c./15th c./17th c.)

26 Valangin: Castle (12th c./16th c.)

27 Erlach: Castle (13th c.)

28 Nidau: Castle (16th c./17th c.)

29 Porrentruy: Castle (13th c./14th c./16th c.)

30 Delémont: Castle (18th c.)

31 Rotberg: Castle (14th c.)

32 Erschwil: Thierstein ruined rastle (13th c.)

35 Dornach: Dorneck ruined castle (14th c.)

36 Prattein: Castle (14th c.)

37 Farnsburg: Ruined castle (14th c.)

38 Sissach: Ebenrair Castle (18th c.)

40 Balsthal: Ruined castle of Neu-Falkenstein (13th c.)

41 Oensingen: Bechburg Castle (14th c.)

42 Wangen an der Aare: Castle (17th c.)

43 Landshut: Castle (14th c.)

44 Hindelbank: Castle (18th c.)

45 Burgdorf: Castle (12th c./13th c.)

46 Jegensdorf: Castle (13th c.)

47 Worb: Castle (14th c.)

48 Oberdiessbach: Castle (17th c.)

49 Burgisten: Castle (16th c.)

50 Thun: Castle (12th c./15th c.)

51 Oberhofen: Castle (12th c./18th c.)

52 Spiez: Castle (12th c./16th c.)

53 Sion: Valère Castle (12th c.)

54 Sion: Tourbillon ruined castle (13th c.)

55 Interlaken: Castle (18th c.)

56 Brig: Alpine Castle (17th c.)

57 Hospental: Ruined castle (13th c.)

Castles and Châteaux

58 Attinghausen: Ruined castle (13th c.)

59 Altdorf: A Pro Castle (16th c.)

60 Schwanau: Ruined castle (13th c.)

61 Küssnacht: Gesslerburg ruins (12th c.)

62 Kriens: Schauensee Castle (13th c./16th c.)

63 Willisau: Castle (17th c.)

64 Gelfingen: Heidegg Castle (12th c.)

65 Hallwil: Castle (9th c./16th c.)

66 Horben: Castle (18th c.)

67 Aarburg: Castle (11th c.)

68 Aarau: Schlössli (13th c./15th c.)

69 Lenzburg: Castle (11th c./16th c.)

70 Wildegg: Castle (12th c./17th c.)

71 Bad Schinznach: Habsburg (11th c./13th c./16th c.)

72 Baden: Landvogteischloss (15th c.)

73 Baden: Stein ruined castle (13th c.)

74 Regensburg: Castle (16th c./17th c.)

75 Schaffhausen: Castle Munot (16th c.)

76 Walaltingen: Schwandegg Castle (14th c./17th c.)

77 Stein am Rhein: Burg Hohenklingen (12th c.)

78 Mammern: Liebenfels Castle (13th c./16th c.)

79 Steckborn: Turnhof Castle (14th c./17th c.)

80 Mannenbach: Arenenberg Castle (16th c.)

81 Märstetten: Altenklingen Castle (16th c./19th c.)

82 Frauenfeld: Castle (14th c./15th c.)

83 Winterthur: Hegi Castle (12th c./16th c.)

84 Sennhof: Kyburg (11th c.)

85 Hagenwil: Wasserburg (13th c.)

86 Arbon: Schloss (13th c.)

87 Nottwil: Schloss Wartensee (16th c.)

88 Gossau: Schloss Oberberg (13th c.)

89 Uster: Schloss (16th c.)

90 Rapperswil: Schloss (13th c.)

91 Näfels: Freulerpalast (17th c.)

92 Werdenberg: Schloss (13th/16th/17th c.)

93 Sargans: Schloss (12th c.)

94 Maienfeld: Schloss Salenegg (17th/18th c.)

95 Haldenstein: Schloss (16th c.)

96 Klus: Burg Fragstein (ruined: 13th c.)

97 Zizers: Schloss Marschlins (13th/17th c.)

98 Trimmis: Burg Liechtenstein (ruined: 14th c.)

99 Chur: Bishop's Palace (13th c.)

100 Rhäzüns: Schloss (13th c.)

101 Rothenbrunnen: Schloss Ortenstein (15th c.)

102 Rodels: Schloss Rietberg (12th c.)

103 Strada: Burg Jörgenberg (ruined: 12th c.)

104 Brigels: Burg Kropfenstein (ruined: 12th c.)

105 Zignau: Burg Riggenberg (ruined: 13th c.)

106 Mesocco: Ruined castle (11th/12th c.)

107 Bellinzona: Castello Grande (13th c.)

108 Bellinzona: Castello di Montebello (13th c.)

109 Bellinzona: Castello di Sasso Corbaro (14th c.)

110 Locarno: Castello Visconti (15th c.)

111 Promontogno: Ruined castle (13th c.)

112 Sils: Burg Ehrenfels (ruined: 12th c.)

113 Thusis: Burg Hohen-Rhätien (ruined: 12th c.)

114 Mulegns: Burg Marmels (ruined: 11th c.)

115 Filisur: Burg Greifenstein (ruined: 13th c.)

116 Surava: Burg Belfort (ruined)

117 Zernez: Schloss Wildenberg (17th/18th c.)

118 Ardez: Burg Steinsberg (ruined: 13th c.)

119 Tarasp: Schloss (16th/18th c.)

For further details see entries in A–Z section.

Caves open to the public, Zoos and Alpine Gardens

● Caves open to the public (selection)

1 Grotte de Milandre in Boncourt north-west of Porrentruy. Sinter formations, underground river.

2 Grotte de Réclère, near Réclère south-west of Porrentruy. Stalagtites.

3 Grotte de l'Orbe, near Vallorbe. Sinter formations, underground river.

4 Grotte aux Fees, near St-Maurice. Sinter formations, underground river.

5 Grotte de St-Léonard, in St-Léonard. Gypsum cave, underground river

6 Beatus Caves, west of Interlaken. Sinter formations, underground river.

7 Sandstone Cave, near Göschenen. Mountain crystal cave with quartz, calcite and chloride strata

8 Höllgrotten, north-east of Zug. Sinter formations.

9 Hölloch, near Muotathal, south-east of Schwyz. Sinter formations, fossils and an underground river.

10 Kristallhölle, near Oberriet. Limestone crystals, underground lake.

○ Zoological Gardens and Mini-Zoos (a selection)

11 Basle. Zoological Gardens. Animals from all over the world; terrarium, aquarium.

Caves open to the public, Zoos and Alpine Gardens

Caves, Zoos and Alpine Gardens in Switzerland

12 Basle. Tierpark, Lange Erlen. Deer, llamas, etc.

13 Reinach. Tierpark. Deer, birds.

14 Roggenhausen. Hirschpark. Red deer, wild pigs.

15 Zofingen. Hirschpark. Red deer.

16 Langenthal. Hirschpark. Red deer, wild pigs.

17 La Chaux-de-Fonds. Parc au Bois. Wild pigs, ibex, etc., vivarium.

18 Biel. Tierpark Bözingenberg. Ibex.

19 Studen. Tierpark Seeteufel (Zoo). Beasts of prey, aquarium, etc.

20 Berne. Tierpark Dählhölzi. European animals; aquarium, terrarium.

21 Le Vaud. Zoo la Garenne. European animals, birds of prey.

22 Lausanne. Vivarium (reptiles).

23 Lausanne. Sauvabelin Deer Park. Red deer, etc.

24 Servion. Zoo. Beasts of prey, red deer, etc.

25 Les Mareecottes. Reno Ranch. Mountain animals, wolves, bears.

26 Mitholz. Alpine Wildlife Park. Mountain animals.

27 Interlaken. Alpine Wildlife Park. Ibexes, marmots.

28 Brienz. Wildlife Park. Mountain animals.

29 Zurich. Zoological Gardens. Animals from all over the world, aquarium, terrarium.

30 Langnau am Albis. Langenberg Wildlife Park. Red deer, wild pigs, bears, etc.

31 Zug. Deer and Bird Park. Red deer, exotic birds.

32 Goldau. Nature and Animal Park. Red deer, wild pigs.

33 Hoch-Ybrig. Wildlife Park. Native animals.

34 Rapperswil. Children's Zoo. Mini-Zoo with dolphinarium. Deer Park near the castle.

35 Wald. Zoological Gardens. Kurhaus Tenne with a private Zoo.

36 Winterthur. Wildlife Park. Bruderhaus/Eschenberg.

37 Frauenfeld. Zoo plättli. Beasts of prey, monkeys, etc.

38 Oberglatt. Vivarium Python. Reptiles.

39 Gossau. Walter-Zoo. Beasts of prey, monkeys, etc.

40 St Gallen. Peter and Paul Wildlife Park. Native animals.

41 Piz Lagalb. Alpinarium. Alpine animals.

● Alpine Gardens

42 Basle. University Botanical Gardens.

43 Weissenstein. Juragarten.

44 Aubonne. Arboretum.

45 Lausanne. Botanical Garden.

46 Geneva. Conservatoire et jardin botaniques.

47 Rochers de Naye. Jardin alpin Rambertia (Botanical Garden).

48 Pone-de-Nant. Jardin botanique alpin La Thomasia (Alpine Botanic Garden).

49 Champex. Jardin Alpine Floralpe (Alpine Garden).

50 Bourg-St-Pierre. Linnea Alpine Garden.

51 Riederalp. Aletschwald.

52 Neuchâtel. University Botanic Garden.

53 Fribourg. University Botanic Park.

54 Berne. University Botanic Garden.

55 Schynige Platte. Alpine Garden.

56 Grüningen. Botanic Garden and Arboretum.

57 St. Gallen. Botanic Garden.

58 Braunwald. Alpine Rose Garden.

59 Vaduz (Liechtenstein). Nature Park.

60 Davos. Alpine Garden.

61 Alp Grüm. Alpine Garden.

Congresses and Conferences

Eighteen places in Switzerland have facilities for congresses. These are Basle, Berne, Biel/Bienne, Bürgenstock, Davos, Engelberg, Flims, Geneva, Grindelwald, Interlaken, Lausanne, Leysin, Lugano, Lucerne, Montreux, St Gallen, St Moritz and Zurich.

Congresses

Details can be obtained by sending for the information brochure "Swiss Congress" of the Swiss Tourist Bureaux (see Information).

Dates of trade fairs open to the public are in the annual calendar "Messeplatz Schweiz" which can also be obtained from the Swiss Tourist Bureaux.

Trade Fairs

Currency

The unit of currency in Switzerland and Liechenstein is the Swiss franc (German, Schweizer Franken; French, franc suisse; Italian, franco svizzero)

Currency

of 100 rappen or centimes. There are banknotes for 10, 20, 50, 100, 500 and 1000 francs and coins in denominations of 5, 10 and 20 rappen/centimes and ½, 1, 2 and 5 francs.

Rates of Exchange	Rates of exchange frequently vary and can be found in national newspapers, at banks and at tourist bureaux.
Currency regulations	There are no restrictions on the import or export of either Swiss or foreign currency.
Eurocheques	It is advisable to take Eurocheques or travellers' cheques. Eurocheques can be made out up to an amount of 300 Swiss Francs.
Credit Cards	Banks, many hotels, restaurants, shops and car rental firms accept most international credit cards (Diners Club, American Express, Visa, Access, etc). The most widely used credit card in Switzerland is the Eurocard.

Customs Regulations

Visitors to Switzerland may take in duty-free personal effects such as clothing, toiletries, sports gear, cameras and amateur movie cameras with appropriate films, musical instruments and camping equipment, provisions for one day's requirements, other goods taken in as gifts up to a value of 100 Swiss francs (with the exception of meat and certain other foodstuffs), and (if over 17 years of age) 2 litres/3½ pints of alcoholic beverages up to 15%, 1 litre/1½ pints over 15% and 200 cigarettes or 50 cigars or 250 grammes/9 ozs of tobacco (double these quantities for visitors from outside Europe).

Diplomatic and Consular Offices in Switzerland

United Kingdom

Embassy

Thunstrasse 50,
CH-3000 Berne
Tel. (031) 44 50 21-26.

Consulates

37–39 rue de Vermont (6th floor),
CH-1211 Geneva
Tel. (022) 34 38 00 and 33 23 85.

Via Maraini 14A, Loreto,
CH-6900 Lugano
Tel. (091) 54 54 44.

15 Bourg Dessous,
CH-1814 La Tour-de-Peilz/Montreux
Tel. (021) 54 12 07.

Dufourstrasse 56,
CH-8008 Zurich
Tel. (01) 47 15 20-26.

United States of America

Embassy

Jubiläumstrasse 93,
CH-3005 Berne
Tel. (031) 43 70 11.

Consulates

80 rue de Lausanne,
CH-1200 Geneva
Tel. (022) 32 70 20.

Zollikerstrasse 141,
CH-8008 Zurich
Tel. (01) 55 25 66.

Embassy   Canada

Kirchenfeldstrasse 88,
CH-3005 Berne
Tel. (031) 44 63 81.

Electricity

Current in Switzerland is supplied at 220 volts AC; 50 Cycles. Since English
plugs will not fit Swiss sockets an adaptor is necessary and can be obtained
from a suitable dealer.

Emergencies

There are emergency telephones on all Swiss motorways and on the more
important mountain roads.

Tel. 117	Police
Tel. 118	Fire Brigade
Tel. 144	Medical Service
Tel. 140	Breakdown

In urgent cases the Swiss radio transmitters will broadcast SOS calls.
Police and automobile clubs have details.   SOS on Radio

Zurich, tel. (01) 47 47 47   The Swiss Air
                                    Rescue Service
                                    (SRFW)

Geneva, tel. (022) 35 80 00   Alarm Head-
                                     quarters (TCS)

Events

Many places: **January**
"Greiflet" and "Dreikönigssingen" (Three Kings Singing) – Fertility Rite 6th
January.
Basle: Vogel Gryff
Hallwil: Bärzelitag (Bärzeli's Day).
Kandersteg: Fur Market.
Lausanne: Ballet Prize of Lausanne (international competition for late-
developing artists).
Lauterbrunnen: Inferno-Rennen (Ski-ing from the Schilthorn Summit)
Meisterschwanden: Meitlisunntig.
Mürren: Inferno ski-run (12 km); Swiss Curling Championship.
Pontresina, Samedan, St Moritz: Schlitteda.
Schwanden: Bärzelitag (Bärzeli's Day).
Solothurn: Film Festival.
Umäsch: Silvesterkläuse (New Year Celebrations).

"Basler Morgenstraich" – an annual festival

**January/
February**

Gstaad: International Ski Jumping.

February

Carnival and Lent: processions and masquerades (at many places).
Altdorf: Cat Music in Lent.
Ascona: Risotto eating on the Piazza of Ascona, Losone and Arcegno (this is Shrove Tuesday).
Basle: Basle Carnival beginning on the Monday after Ash Wednesday at 4 a.m. with the "Morgenstraich" der "Cliquen", "Guggenmusiken" and "Schnitzelbänke" (parade through the old town by the Carnival Guilds accompanied by fifes and drums).
Bellinzona: Carnival with risotto eating in the open air.
Bienne/Biel: Carnival.
Einsiedeln: Carnival with distribution of bread.
Lugano: Carnelvale (Carnival) with risotto eating in the open air for everybody.
Lucerne: Carnival with masquerades.
Morat/Murten: Carnival with processions.
Bad/Scuol/Schuls-Tarasp-Vulpera: Hom Strom (Chasing Winter away: first weekend in February).
Solothurn: Carnival with processions.

**Holy Week and
Easter**

Processions (at many places).

March

Basle: Trade Fair
Geneva: Salon Internationale de l'Automobile (10 days)
Glarus: Fridolinsfeuer (St Fridolin's Fire 6th March)
Grisons: many places Chalandarmarz (Spring Festival 1st March)
Lausanne: International Festival of Tourism.

March-July

Lugano: Primavera Concertistica di Lugano (Spring Concerts).

Appenzell: Landsgemeinde (Communal Assembly).
Basle: Art and Antiques Fair; Clocks and Jewellery fair; "Eiermarkt" (Egg Market) before Easter.
Glarus Canton: Näfelserfahrt (Memorial Festival for the victory over the Austrians in 1388).
Hundwil, Trogen; Landsgemeinde (Communal Assembly).
Sarnen: Landsgemeinde (Communal Assembly).
Stans: Landsgemeinde (Communal Assembly).
Zurich: Sechseläuten (Six o'clock ringing). **April**

Processions (at many places). **Corpus Christi**

Many places, May Day Celebrations (First Sunday). **May**
Berne: International Jazz Festival; Geranium Market.
Baden: Swiss Amateur Film Festival.
Escholzmatt, Entlebuch, Schüpfheim: Wyberschiessen (Women's Shooting).
Glarus: Landsgemeinde (Communal Assembly).
Lausanne: International Opera Festival.
Montreux: "Golden Rose" Music Festival.
Zurich: Summer Festival.

Lausanne: International Music weeks. **May—June**
Wallis: Cow fights (at many places).

Alpine processions (at many places). **June**
Baar: Costume Festival.
Basle: ART (International Arts Exhibition); Town Festival.
Berne: Small Stage Festival.
Bienne/Biel: 100 km run from Biel (Braderie, Folk Festival).
Geneva: Jazz Festival (summer jazz concerts in the "Jardin Anglais", 1 week).
Locarno: Floral Parade.
Lucerne: Nocturnal Festival with fireworks on the lakes.
Morat/Murten: Battle Festival (Youth Festival with floral procession, 22nd June); Shooting Festival commemorating Battle of Mürten.
Neuchâtel: Drum and Fife Festival of Western Switzerland.
Wallis: Midsummer Eve Bonfire (at many places).
Zurich: International Festival Weeks; Night Festival on the Lake.

Dornach: Faust Pagen Play (every three to four years, next planned for 1991). **June—July**
Lugano: New Orleans and Estival Jazz Festivals.
Montreux: Jazz Festival.
Mürren: International High Alpine Ballooning.
Spiez: Concert in the Castle.
Yverdon-les-Bains: Horse Racing.

Interlaken: William Tell Festival Play. **June—September**

Fribourg: Triennial Photographic Exhibition (next 1991). **June—October**
Interlaken: Folklore Evenings in the Kursaal.
Winterthur: Albani Festival (Traditional Club Festival of Music and Theatre; last weekend in June).

Aarau: Aarau Youth Festival (1st Friday in July). **July**
Braunwald: Music week.
Davos: Swiss Alpine Marathon.
Dornach: Commemoration of Battle of Dornach (every 5 years).
Gstaad: International Tennis Championships of Switzerland.
Klosters: Summer Festival.

"Hornussen"

Kreuzlingen: Nocturnal Festival on the Lake.
Lausanne: Festival de la Cité (Old Town Festival).
Loèche-les-Bains/Leukerbad: Shepherds' Festival on the Gemmi (Folk Festival).
Lugano: Nocturnal Festival on the Lake with Fireworks.
Lucerne: Federal Rifleman's Festival.
Meiringen: International Festival Music Weeks.
Mürren: Inferno Berglauf (Mountain Run); Country Festival.
Sempach: Commemoration of the Battle of Sempach.
Vevey: Rhône Festival (Popular events on Lake Geneva).
Villars: Folklore Meeting.

**July–
August**

Bienne/Biel: Bieler Braderie; Chess Festival.
Brig: Film performances in the castle courtyard, every Thursday Brig Mountain evenings in Ried-Brig.
Interlaken: Music Festival Weeks.
Lausanne: "Pour un Eté" (Concert, theatre and ballet performances free for guests.
Pontresina: Engadin Concert Weeks.
Rigi: Alpine Parade and Schwinger Festival (Wrestling).
Swiss Lakes: Evening trips on the Lakes.

**July–
September**

Altdorf: William Tell Plays.
Ascona: New Orleans Music Fiesta; Street Concerts by Tessine Wind Band "Bandella".
Vevey: Marché folklorique (Market with wine tasting and local specialities every Saturday).

August

Everywhere: National Festival 1st August.
Many places: Herdsmen's and Alpine Farmers' Festival.
Assumption (15th August): Processions at many places in the Catholic parts of the country.

Bienne/Biel: Old Town Chilbi.
Brunnen: Federal festival on the Rütli (1st August).
Fribourg: International Folklore Meeting (end August); performances by
yodlers, wrestlers and hornusser (propelling disks with a long club and
catching them by the opposition).
Gstaad: Yehudi Menuhin Festival.
Klosters: Children's Festival.
Loèche-les-Bains: 1st August Shepherds' Festival with illumination of the
slopes of the Gemmi.
Mürren: Village Festival.
Rigi: 1st August, Federal Festival on the Rigi, with bonfires on the summit
and folklore events.
Saignleégier: Horse Market.
Spiez: Castle Plays.
Vevey: International Festival Film Comedies.

Basle: Kleinbaslerfest.   August–
Langenthal: Federal Hornuss Festival.   September
Lucerne: International Music Festival.
Winterthur: Music Festival.

In many places: Hornuss matches.   August–
Ascona: Summer-night concerts on the Island of Brissago; International   October
Music Festival.

Aarau: Teenagers and Children's Lantern Procession (2nd Friday in   September
September).
Basle: Reformation Feast and Folk Festival.
Berne: Mineral Exchange.
Brig: Castle Concerts, Theatrical Performances.
Oberwalliser: Applied Art Exhibition.
Einsiedeln: Blessing of the Angels (14th September).
Geneva: Concours International d'Execution Musicale (2 weeks).
Gstaad: Alpine Gala (Theatre, Concerts).
Hasliberg: Chästeilet (Division of Cheese) and Popular Festival.
Lausanne: Comptoir Suisse (National Fair).
Locarno: Grape Festival.
Lucerne: Rowing Regatta; International horseracing.
Montreux: "Septembre".
Neuchâtel: Fête de Vendanges (Vintner Festival; last weekend in
September).
Zurich: Boys' shooting matches; Jazz Festival.

Many places: Wine Festivals.   September–
Basle: Basle Altenfair, the oldest fair in Switzerland.   October

Bienne/Biel: Grape-gathering Sunday on Lake Bienne; Onion Market.   October
Châtel-St-Denis: Harvest Thanksgiving.
Lausanne: Olympia Week (Various concerts).
Locarno: Chestnut Festival.
Lugano: Vine Growers' Festival Procession (1st Sunday in October).
Morat/Murten: Commemorative run Morat-Fribourg.

Basle: Autumn Fair (24th October to 2nd November).   October–
Berne: "Ziberle-Märit" (Onion Market, Folk festival; 4th Monday in   November
November).
Geneva: Foire International d'Inventions (Inventors' Fair).
Lausanne: Salon des Antiquaires (Antique fair).
Rütli: Rütli shooting.
Sursee: Gansabhauet (Cutting down the Goose).
Zurich: International Mineral Exchange.

December Many places: Lichtkläuse (around 6th December); Masquerades, Silversterkläuse, etc.
Geneva: Fête de l'Escalade (12th December, anniversary of the abortive attack by the Savoyards).

Food and Drink

General   Swiss restaurants are noted for the excellence of their cuisine, which is as varied as the ethnic composition of the country. The cuisine of the various parts of Switzerland is strongly influenced by that of the neighbouring countries – in the German-speaking cantons by German cooking, in the French-speaking cantons by the "Cuisine Française", in the Italian-speaking cantons by the "Cucina Italiana". In addition, however, there are a number of specifically Swiss dishes, mostly using locally produced ingredients such as dairy produce and fish.

The midday meal is usually eaten about 12.30 p.m., called either "dîner" and followed in the evening (7 p.m. onwards) by "souper", or "lunch" when the main meal is taken in the evening. Even quite small restaurants provide attentive service, using hot-plates (réchauds) to keep the food warm. The station buffets are usually excellent.

The cost of lunch or dinner will range between 10 and 20 francs in the more modest establishments to 20-50 francs in high-class restaurants. To eat à la carte is usually more expensive than to take the fixed price menu, which always provides a very satisfying meal. Many restaurants offer one-course meals which are very good value.

Swiss Menu

Meat   The Berner Platte is a very nourishing plate of ham and sausages with sauerkraut or beans. The Mittelland has another very substantial dish, Gnagi (slightly salted pigs' trotters), so tender that it is said to melt in the mouth. Favourite Geneva dishes are pied de porc au madère (pigs' trotters in madeira sauce) and gigot d'agneau (leg of lamb). Zurich has Gschnetzeltes (veal stewed with cream) and Leberspieler (calf's liver cooked on a spit, with bacon), Schwyz excellent Gegmsenbraten (roast chamois), the cantons on the Rhine Mistkratzerli or Güggeli (young chickens).

Sausages   Switzerland has a rich assortment of excellent sausages. Basle has Klöpfer (succulent cervelat sausages), St Gallen Schüblige and Bratwürste, Appenzell Pantli and Knackerli. Grisons has a particularly wide variety – Salsiz (a small salami), Beinwurst, Engadinerwurst, Leberwurst (liver sausage) and Tiges as well as Bündnerfleisch (air dried beef). The canton of Vaud also produces some excellent sausages, including boutefas, saucissons de Payerne, liver sausages and sausages made with vegetables. Then there are the longeoles of Geneva (pork sausages spiced with caraway and aniseed) and the Walliser Platte or "Valais dish" (cold meat including dried raw beef). The popular types of sausage in Ticino are coppa and zampone.

Fish Dishes   Fish dishes play a large part in the Swiss menu. The country's many lakes and rivers yield a variety of species: pike are found in Lake Constance, Lake Geneva, the Lac de Neuchâtel and the Lauerzer See, trout in the mountain streams around Arth-Goldau, in Lake Geneva, the Areuse and the mountain streams and lakes of southern Switzerland, barbel in Lake Zug, blue char in Lake Constance, dace, char and perch in Lake Geneva, bondelles and palées in the Lac de Neuchâtel. Further variety is added by various species of perch and barbel and by the eels of the mountain lakes. Blausee trout are regarded as a particular delicacy.

Among the favourite Swiss vegetables to accompany meat are Berner Rösti (sliced potatoes, lightly browned with bacon cubes), gratiné potatoes, aubergines and artichokes. There are also a variety of attractively seasoned salads.

Vegetables

This is eaten mainly in northern Switzerland, where the influence of German cuisine makes itself felt. In addition to Spätzli or Knöpfli there is a Zurich speciality, the Zürcher Topf (macaroni with minced meat and tomato sauce, cooked in the oven). In southern Switzerland various forms of pasta are popular, including ravioli. Notable among the egg dishes are the chucheôles of Fribourg which are eaten with sweet mustard.

Pasta

The Swiss are particularly good at making cakes and sweets. Among the most tempting are Basler Leckerli (a kind of gingerbread), Schaffhauser Zungen (Schaffhausen tongue), Zuger Kirschtorte, the cream filled meringues (from Meiringen) of the Bernese Oberland, the bagnolet crème of the Jura (eaten with raspberries and aniseed biscuits), the délices (soda rolls), croissants, rissoles (pear tarts), nougat and pralines of Geneva and the zabaglione of Ticino. Vermicelli, not the Italian pasta dish but a dessert made of chestnut mousse, is popular all over Switzerland.

Desserts

A Swiss speciality world renowned for its quality is chocolate, in a variety of flavourings.

Chocolate

Cheese

The excellent dairy products of Switzerland are famed world-wide, and the Swiss menu includes a variety of cheese dishes, varying from region to region. Cheese soups are particularly popular in central Switzerland; cheescakes (gâteau or salée au fromage, ramequin) are found all over the country.

General

Swiss cheeses

Food and Drink

Appenzeller (Appenzell): A semi-hard cow's-milk cheese, treated with spiced white wine during the maturing process.

Bagnes (Valais): A hard cow's-milk cheese, used in the making of raclette (see below).

Brienzer Mutschli (Berne): a hard cow's-milk cheese, usually made on the mountain pastures in summer.

Chaschöl chevra (Grisons): a soft goat's-milk cheese.

Emmentaler (Central Switzerland): A hard cow's-milk cheese, used in raclette.

Formaggelli (Ticino): A soft cheese made from ewe's or goat's-milk, usually eaten after several days' maturation.

Formaggini (Ticino): A small soft ewe's or goat's-milk cheese.

Goms (Valais): A semi-hard cow's-milk cheese, much used in the making of raclette.

Gruyère (Fribourg): A hard cow's-milk cheese, used in fondue.

Petit Suisse (Geneva): A fresh cow's-milk cheese.

Reblochon (Geneva): A soft cow's-milk cheese.

Saanen-Hobelkäse (Berne): A hard cow's-milk cheese, used in various cheese dishes or served by itself in thin slices.

Sbrinz (Central Switzerland): A hard cow's-milk cheese, mainly used in the preparation of various cheese dishes.

Schabzieger (Glarus): A hard cow's-milk cheese, with herbs.

Tête de Moine (Jura): A soft cow's-milk cheese.

Tilsiter (Thurgau): A semi-hard cow's-milk cheese.

Toggenburger Ploderkäse (Obertoggenburg): a soft cow's-milk cheese.

Tomme Vaudoise (Vaud): A fresh soft cow's-milk cheese.

Urserenkäse (Bernese Oberland): A mild soft cow's-milk cheese.

Vacherin Fribourgeois (Fribourg): A semi-hard cow's-milk cheese. There are two types, Vacherin à fondue and Vacherin à la main.

Vacherin Mont d'Or (Fribourg): A soft cow's-milk cheese, usually eaten after six weeks' maturation.

Vero Piora (Ticino): A semi-hard cow's-milk and goat's-milk cheese.

There are also a large number of regional varieties of cheese. Alpkäse is made on the mountain pastures in summer, and often toasted at an open fire (Bratkäsli). The process of cheese-making can be observed in the demonstration cheese dairy at Gruyère.

Two cheese dishes which are particularly popular in western Switzerland are fondue and raclette, both of them invariably accompanied by white wine.

Fondue (from French "fondre", to melt) is made by melting cheese and white wine, flavoured with kirsch and spices, in a special one-handled dish known as a caquelon. The dish is then set in the middle of the table over a flame to keep it hot, and each member of the party helps himself by dipping a piece of white bread on a special fork into the common bowl.

Fondue

In raclette (from French racler, to scrape), a large cheese is cut in half and heated until it melts, when the melted cheese is scraped off onto the plate and eaten with a potato in its jacket and various tasty accompaniments.

Raclette

Wine

Vines are grown in almost all the Swiss cantons, but particularly on the slopes above Lake Geneva and the lakes of the Jura and Ticino and in the wide valleys of the Rhône and the Rhine. Wine has been made in western and southern Switzerland since the 1st century B.C., in northern Switzerland only since the 7th or 8th c. A.D. Since the end of the 19th c. the area under vines has been considerably reduced. The present output of wine is about 1 million hectolitres, two-thirds of the total being white and the remaining third red (maximum strength 13% of alcohol by volume). Only small quantities of Swiss wine are exported, the imports of wine being significantly greater.

Vine growing

Lake Geneva, particularly in the Lavaux area (Vaud) between Lausanne and Montreux (from the Chasselas/Gutedel grape): Dézaley and St-Saphorin (the best), Pully, Lutry, Epesses; Aigle and Yvorne, from the Chablais area between Montreux and Martigny; and wines from the "Petite Côte" around Morges, the "Côte" from Rolle and the Mandement area (Geneva).
Valais: Fendant (from the Chasselas/Gutedel grape), in many different sorts; red Dôle (from a mixture of Pinot Noir/Blauburgunder and Gamay grapes); Johannisberg (known as "Rhin" or "petit Rhin", being made from Riesling/Sylvaner grapes); Ermitage, Amigne, Arvine, Humagne, Oeil de Perdrix (rosé); Muscat and Malvasier, two dessert wines made from the Pinot Gris grape ("Strohwein" or "straw wine"); and the very unusual

Varieties of wine

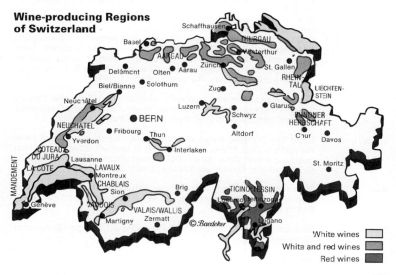

Wine-producing Regions of Switzerland

© Baedeker

White wines ☐
White and red wines ▨
Red wines ■

Food and Drink

Vineyards . . .   *. . . and the Aigle Museum of Wine*

Heidenwein, made from the highest vineyards (700–1200 m/2297–3937 feet) around Visperterminen; after maturing in the cellar for 10–20 years it yields the precious golden-brown Glacier.

Lac de Bienne and Lac de Neuchâtel: the slightly sparkling "Bernese lake wines" Schaffiser and Twanner; Cortaillod, Auvernier.

Ticino: Nostrano (red, from the Merlot grape); particularly good from Gordola.

Grisons: red wines - Veltliner (Vatellina), Malanser, Jeninser, Maienfelder, Fläscher (in the Bündner Herrschaft region).

Northern Switzerland: Meilener, Stäfener, Herrliberger from Lake Zurich; Neftenbacher, from the Töss Valley; Karthäuser (Ittinger), Steiner, Bachtobler from Thurgau; Bernecker, Melser, Wiler from St Gallen; Hallauer, Osterfinger, Rheinhalder from Schaffhausen; Villiger Schlossberger, Geissberger from Aargau; Riehener Schlipfen from Basle.

In Switzerland white wine is served in small tumblers. Soon after the wine harvest unfermented "must" (German "most", French "moût") appears in bars and restaurants. In Vaud there are numerous "wine trails".

Spirits	Swiss fruit brandies are of excellent quality. Kirsch (the best of which comes from Zug), Enzian (from the roots of gentian), Birne (from pears), grappa and marc (from the skins of pressed grapes), Bätzi (from apples), etc. Alpenbitter, Kräuterlikör (Chrüter: a herb liqueur).
Beer	The two leading Swiss brands are Feldschlösschen (Rheinfelden) and Cardinal (Fribourg). Beer is often mixed with lemonade to produce shandy. Ex-bier is non-alcoholic.
Table waters	Passuger (Grisons), Henniez (Vaud), Elmer (Glarus), Eptinger (Basle-Land), Weissenburger (Berne).
Restaurants	See entry

Getting to Switzerland

There are regular flights from major airports in Great Britain, USA and Canada to Zurich and Geneva. Swissair has international services between Switzerland and nearly 60 other countries. The Swiss National Tourist Office and other tourist bureaux provide information leaflets (and "Fly-Rail", "Welcome-pack" and "Fly-pack") as well as details of the facility for checking in at a rail station for flights by Swissair.
By air

From London (Victoria) to Basle, via Calais, takes about fourteen hours and from London (Liverpool Street) to Basle, via the Hook of Holland, about twenty hours.
By rail

The distance from London to Basle is about 940 km/585 miles. Practically the whole journey can be done on motorways from Ostend or Calais.
By road

Health resorts

● Spas

1 Rheinfelden (Alt. 280 m/919 ft)

2 Ramsach (Alt. 720 m/2263 ft)

3 Schwefelbergbad (Alt. 1400 m/4595 ft)

4 Lenk im Simmertal (Alt. 1105 m/3636 ft)

5 Saillon (Alt. 510 m/1510 ft)

6 Breiten (Alt. 900 m/2954 ft)

7 Andeer (Alt. 1000 m/3282 ft)

8 Serneus (Alt. 1031 m/3384 ft)

9 Bad Scuol and Bad-Tarasp-Vulpera (Alt. 1250 m/4103 ft)

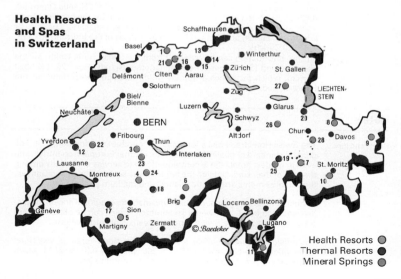

Health Resorts and Spas in Switzerland

Health Resorts ○
Thermal Resorts ●
Mineral Springs ●

10 St Moritz Bad (Alt. 1775 m/5826 ft)

11 Stabio (Alt. 347 m/1139 ft)

● Thermal baths

12 Yverdon-les-Bains (Alt. 435 m/1428 ft)

13 Zurzach (Alt. 344 m/1129 ft)

14 Baden-Ennetbaden (Alt. 388 m/1273 ft)

15 Bad Schinznach (Alt. 350 m/1149 ft)

16 Lostorf (Alt. 525 m/1725 ft)

17 Lavey-les-Bains (Alt. 417 m/1369 ft)

18 Leukerbad/Loèche-les-Bains (Alt. 1411 m/4631 ft)

› 19 Vals (Alt. 1250 m/4102 ft)

20 Bad Ragaz (Alt. 525 m/1723 ft)/Valens (Alt. 915 m/3003 ft)

● Mineral springs

21 Eptingen

22 Henniez

23 Weissenburg

24 Adelboden

25 Vals

26 Elm

27 Rietbad

28 Passugg

Help for the Handicapped

The Schweizerische Invalidenbund (Froburgstrasse 4, CH-4600 Olten; tel. (062) 21 10 37) issues a list of Swiss hotels suitable for the handicapped. Town guides for the handicapped (Basle, Berne, Lausanne, Lucerne, St Gallen and Zurich) are obtainable from the offices of Pro Infirmis (Box 129, CH-8023 Zurich).
Further information can be obtained from the Swiss Trade Union for the Handicapped (Schweizerische Arbeitsgemeinschaft; Box 129, CH-8023 Zurich), which publishes a holiday guide through Switzerland for the Handicapped.

Hotels

Hotels and Inns

The Swiss Hotel trade has a long and honourable tradition behind it. The general standard of quality is higher than in other European countries, and even in modest hotels the accommodation and service are usually among the best of their kind. Outside the larger towns such as Zurich and Geneva, the establishments are mostly of small and medium size.

Further details, with prices, can be found in the free regional and local hotel lists and also in the "Schweizer Hotelführer" which can be obtained from travel bureaux and the Swiss Tourist Bureaux (see Information).

The official information office is the Schweizer Hotel-Verein (Swiss Hotel Association), Monbijoustrasse 130, CH-3001 Bern; tel. (031) 50 71 11, which however, will not undertake the booking of accommodation.

Official category in this guide		Room rate per night in francs		Categories
		one person	two persons	
*****	A	150–380	200–550	
****	B	100–180	160–360	
***	C	60–150	100–260	
**	D	50– 90	80–160	
*	E	35– 60	65–100	

These are inclusive charges (i.e. with service and taxes). In purely tourist and holiday resorts the rates may be higher, particularly at the height of the season; and it is quite common in such places for hotels to let rooms only with half or full board.

Sb = Indoor pool; Sp = Outdoor pool;

A list of hotels and inns which provide good value can be found in the brochure "Check-in-1*-Hotels", "Preiswerte Unterkünfte in der Schweiz" and "Berggasthöfe in der Schweiz", published by the Swiss Tourist Bureau (see Information).   Reasonably Priced Hotels

Aarauerhof, B, 98 b; Stadtturm (no rest), C 24 b; Anker (no rest), D, 50 b.   **Aarau**

Parkhotel Bellevue, B, 100 b, Sb; Beau-Site. B. 65 b; Huldi & Waldhaus, C, 80 b; Crystal, C, 68 b; Bristol (no rest), C, 50 b; Bären, D, 18 b.   **Adelboden**

Du Nord, C, 30 b.   **Aigle**

Goldener Schlüssel, C, 50 b; Bahnhof, E, 40 b.   **Altdorf**

Alpina, C, 30 b; Drei Könige & Post, C, 40 b; Ideal-Hotel Krone, C, 85 b; Monopol-Metropol, C, 70 b; Helvetia, D, 65 b; Schweizerhof, D, 56 b; Löwen, E, 36 b.   **Andermatt**

Grand Hotel & Kurhaus, C, 100 b; Du Glacier, C, 35 b; Du Pigne d'Arolla, D, 20 b; Aiguille de la Tza, D, 35 b.   **Arolla**

Near both lakes: Valsana, B, 157 b, Sb, SP; Eden (only open in winter), B, 150 b; Seehof, B, 100 b; Waldhotel-National, B, 180 b, SB; Raetia, B, 70 b; Mariposa-Residence (no rest), B, 32 b; Obersee, C, 40 b; Carmenna, C, 45 b; Astoria, C, 56 b.   **Arosa**

Near the Kursaal: *Park Hotel, A, 180 b, Sb; *Savoy, A, 220 b, Sb; Hohenfels, B, 90 b; Cristallo, B, 70 b; Kaiser, C, 54 b; Merkur, C, 65 b; Belvédère-Tanneck, C, 70 b; Quellenhof, E, 40 b.

On the south-east slope of the Tschuggen: *Tschuggen Grand Hotel, A, 235 b, Sb; Bellavista (only open in winter), B, 160 b, Sb; Excelsior (only open in winter), B, 130 b, Sb; Streiff, C, 73 b; Panarosa, C, 50 b.

Inner-Arosa: *Arosa Kulm, A, 250 b, Sb; Des Alpes (only open in winter), B, 70 b; Bellevue (only open in winter), B, 110 b; Alpensonne, C, 62 b.

Above the town on the north: Berghotel Prätschli, B, 160 b; Golfhotel Hof Maran, B, 110 b.

*Eden Roc, on the lake, A, 100 b, Sp, Sb; *Delta, near the airfield, A, 90 b, Sp, Sb; *Castello del Sole, A, 125 b, Sb, Sp; *Losone (no rest), A, 135 b, Sp; Casa Berno, high above Lake Maggiore, B, 100 b, Sp; Europe, by the lake, B, 80 b, Sb, Sp; Ascolago, on the lake, B, 45 b, Sp, Sb; Acapulco, on the lake, B, 86 b, Sb; Ascona, on the hills, B, 120 b, Sp; Sasso Boretto, B, 83 b, Sb; Tamaro, by the lake, C, 78 b; Al Porto (no rest), by the lake, C, 65 b; Schiff (no rest), by the lake, C, 30 b.   **Ascona**

Hotels

Baden Du Parc, B, 150 b; Kappelerhof, C, 55 b.
Spa hotels on the left bank of the Limmat: *Staadhof, A, Sb, and Verenahof-Ochsen (adjoining), B, together 160 b; Blume, C, 45 b; Schweizerhof, D, 60 b.
Spa hotel on the right bank of the Limmat in Ennetbaden: Hirschen, D, 80 b.

Bad Ragaz See Ragaz

Basle Near SBB station: *Basel Hilton, Aeschengraben 31, A, 354 b, Sb; *Euler, Centralbahnplatz 14, A, 100 b; *Schweizerhof, Centralbahnplatz 1, A, 100 b; Bernina Basel, Innere Margarethentrasse 14, B, 75 b; Metropol (no rest), near Elisabethenpark, B, 70 b; Victoria by the station, Centralbahnplatz 3-4, B, 150 b; Helvetia, Küchengasse 13, C, 34 b; Bristol, Centralbahnstrasse 15, D, 55 b; Gotthard-Terminus, Centralbahnstrasse 13, D, 80 b.

In the town: *Drei Könige am Rhein, Blumenrain 8, A, 145 b; *International, Steinentorstrasse 25, A, 350 b, Sb; Basel, Münzgasse 12, B, 108 b; Drachen, Aeschenvorstadt 24, B, 65 b; City-Hotel, Henric-Petri-Str. 12, C, 130 b; Spalenbrunnen, Schüzenmattstrasse 2, C, 45 b; Steinschanze (no rest) Steinengraben 69, E, 60 b.

On the right Rhine bank: *Le Plaza, Riehenring 45, A, 450 b, Sb; Europe, Clarastrasse 43, B, 250 b; Merian am Rhein, Rheingasse 2, B, 100 b; Alexander, Riehenring 85, B, 100 b; Krafft am Rhein, Rheingasse 12, C, 78 b; Basilisk, Klingentalstrasse 1, C, 100 b; Admiral, Rosentalstrasse 5, C, 220 b, Sp; Du Commerce (no rest), Riehenring 91, C, 60 b; Hecht am Rhein (no rest), Rheingasse 8, D, 53 b.

Beatenberg Kurhaus Silberhorn, B, 55 b; Beatus, C, 30 b; Beau-Regard, C, 30 b; Gloria, C, 30 b; Jungfraublick, C, 25 b.

Beckenried *Sternen am See, A, 82 b, Sp; Nidwaldnerhof, B, 40 b, Sp; Edelweiss, C, 40 b, Sp; Mond, C, 50 b, Sp; Rigi & Villa Linde, C, 30 b.

Bellinzona Unione, Via General Guisan 4, C, 67 b; Internazionale, Piazza Stazione, C, 45 b.

Berne Near the main station: *Schweizerhof, Bahnhofplatz 11, A, 157 b; Alfa, Laupenstrasse 15, B, 60 b; City, Bubenbergplatz 7, B, 73 b; Bristol (no rest), Schauplatzgasse 10, B, 136 b; Savoy (no rest), Neuengasse 26, B, 95 b; Bären, Schauplatzgasse 4, B, 85 b; Wächter-Mövenpick, Genfergasse 4, C, 59 b; Krebs (no rest), Genfergasse 8, C, 80 b; National, Hirschengraben 14, D, 66 b.

Between the Käfig tower and the Nydegg Bridge: *Bellevue-Palace, Kochergasse 3-5, A, 280 b; Metropole, Zeughausgasse 28, B, 100 b; Kreuz, Zeughausgasse 41, C, 180 b; Continental, Zeughausgasse 27, C, 65 b; Nydeck, Gerechtigkeitgasse 1, C, 23 b; Hotel Bern, Zeughausgasse 9, D, 170 b; Hospiz zur Heimat, Gerechtigkeitgasse 50, D, 70 b; Goldener Schlüssel, Rathausgasse 72, E, 48 b.

South-west and north-west of the main station: Astor-Touring, Eigerplatz, C, 120 b; Regina-Arabelle, Mittelstrasse 6, C, 70 b.

Bettmeralp Waldhaus, B, 40 b; Bettmerhof, B, 45 b; Alpfrieden, B, 48 b; Aletsch, C, 40 b, Sp.

Biel/Bienne In the station district: Elite, B, 100 b; Continental, C, 146 b; Club-Hotel, C, 70 b.

In the old town: Atlantis, C, 32 b; Bären-en-ville, C, 24 b; Dufour, C, 60 b; Goya (no rest), C, 32 b; Royal Bienne (no rest), D, 40 b.

Braunwald *Bellevue, A, 100 b, Sb; *Niederschlacht, A, 80 b, Sp; Alpenblick, B, 100 b; Cristal, B, 40 b; Ideal-Hotel Alpina, B, 40 b; Tödiblick, B, 25 b; Rubschen, C, 21 b.

*Salina, A, 55 b, Sp: Im Grünen (no rest), B, 100 b, Sb, Sp. **Breiten ob Mörel**

Bären, B, 50 b, Sp; Krone, B, 60 b; Lindenhof, B, 80 b, Sb; Weisses Kreuz, B, **Brienz**
30 b; Brienzerburli, C, 50 b: Schönegg (no rest), C, 29 b; Löwen, D, 10 b;
Bellevue, E, 6 b.

Victoria, C, 72 b; Schlosshotel (no rest), C, 45 b; Alpina, C, 50 b; Londres & **Brig**
Schweizerhof (no rest), C, 33 b; Europe (no rest), C, 42 b; Ambassador, D,
50 b; Elite-Touring, D, 90 b; Sporting (no rest), D, 57 b; Simplon, E, 60 b;
Du Commerce, E, 18 b.

*Villa Cäsar, A, 62 b. Sb, Sp; Mirto au Lac, B, 45 b, Sp; Parkhotel Brenscir o, **Brissago**
B, 170 b; Bellavista, D, 26 b, Sp; Camelia, D, 50 b; Graziella am See, D, 21 b,
Sp; Collina (no rest), D, 19 b.

By the Lake: *Seehotel Waldstätterhof, A, 160 b, Sp, Sb; Bellevue au Lac, B, **Brunnen**
90 b; Schmid am See (no rest), B, 45 b; Elite-Aurora, C, 110 b; Eden au Lac,
C, 80 b; Hirschen am See, C. 50 b; Alfa au Lac (no rest), C, 40 b; Metropol au
Lac, C, 25 b; Brunnerhof, C, 90 b.

Away from the Lake: Parkhotel Hellerbad, B, 140 b; Cabana (no rest), C,
30 b, Sp; Weisses Rössli, C, 50 b; Alpina, D, 40 b.

Outside Brunnen: Hotel Waldhaus Wolfsprung, on Axenstrasse; Hotel
Bergfluh on the Gersau Road.

*Grand Hotel, A, 10 b; *Palace Hotel, A, 144 b; Park-Hotel, B, 116 b; All three **Bürgenstock**
hotels open only from May to October, Sp.
Waldheim, C, 70 b, open all year.

*Cresta Palace, A, 160 b, Sb; *Cresta-Kulm, A, 76 b, Sp; Saluver, B, 36 b; **Celerina**
Misani, C, 75 b; Posthaus, C, 100 b; Bellaval (no rest), E, 12 b; Stüvetta
Veglia (no rest), E, 16 b.

*Hotel de Champéry, A, 138 b; Beau-Séjour, B, 40 b; Suisse, C, 80 b; Du **Champéry**
Parc, C, 50 b; Des Alpes, C, 45 b; De la Paix, C, 35 b; Rose des Alpes, C, 45 b;
Buffet de la Gare, D, 18 b; Souvenir Pension, D, 32 b; Berra, D, 30 b.

*La Rocaille, A, 26 b; Beau Séjour et Taverne, B, 70 b; Bon-Accueil, B, 40 b; **Château d'Oex**
De L'Ours, B, 86 b; Ermitage, B, 48 b; Richemont, B, 23 b; Alpina-Rosat, C,
80 b; Bouquetins, C, 20 b; Roc et Neige, C, 200 b; Buffet de la Gare, D, 14 b;
De la Poste, D, 30 b; Hôtel de Ville, D, 20 b; Florissant, D, 15 b; La Printanière, D, 12 b; Le Vanil, D, 20 b.

Club, B, 80 b; Moreau, B, 60 b; Fleur-de-Lys, B, 66 b; Motel du Jura, C, 21 b; **La Chaux-de-**
De la Balance, D, 22 b; De France, E, 40 b. **Fonds**

Centro (no rest), B, 33 b; Corso, B, 50 b; Touring-Mövenpick, B, 120 b. **Chiasso**

Duc du Rohan, B, 60 b, Sp; Chur, B, 75 b; ABC-Terminus (no rest), B, 55 b; **Chur**
Romantik-Hotel Stern, C, 90 b; Sommerau, C, 185 b; Posthotel, C, 80 b;
Freieck, C, 80 b; Drei Könige, D, 60 b; Marsöl, D, 24 b.

Many hotels are closed during the months of October, November and May. **Crans-Montana**
In Crans: *Du Golf & Des Sports, A, 120 b, Sb, *Grand Hotel Rhodania, A,
80 b, Sp; Alpina & Savoy, B, 100 b, Sp; De l'Etrier, B, 200 b, Sp, Sb; Grand
Hôtel Beau-Séjour, B, 100 b, Sb; Eurotel-Christina, B, 100 b, Sb; Royal, B,
100 b; Alpha-Résidence, B, 110 b; Belmont, C, 50 b; Carlton, C, 66 b; City, C,
45 b; Serenella, C, 40 b; Central, D, 38 b.

In Montana-Vermala: *Crans Ambassador, A, 135 b, Sb; *La Tour de Super-
crans, A, 50 b, Sb; Le Hauts de Crans, B, 70 b, Sb; St Georges, B, 80 b, Sp;
Grand Hôtel du Parc, B, 135 b; Aïda-Castel, C, 100 b; De la Forêt, C, 140 b;
Primavera, C, 50 b; Vermala, C, 65 b; Cisalpin, D, 50 b.

Hotels

Davos
In Davos Dorf: *Flüela, A, 130 b, Sb; Derby, B, 100 b; Montana, B, 80 b; Meierhof, B, 130 b; des Alpes, C, 100 b; Parsenn, C, 70 b; Bristol, C, 57 b; Sonnenberg, C, 60 b, Sb; Stolzenfels, D, 60 b; Hermann, D, 40 b; Concordia, D, 40 b.

In Davos Platz: *Steigengberger Belvédère, A, 238 b, Sb; National, B, 100 b; Morosani's Pöstli, B, 160 b, Sb; Schweizerhof, B, 150 b, Sb; Sunstar-Park, B, 401 b, Sb; Central, B, 180 b, Sb; Cresta Sun, B, 90 b, Sb; Europe, B, 110 b, Sp, Sb; Bellavista, C, 50 b; Terminus, C, 95 b; Kongress, C, 150 b; Lohner, C, 65 b; Bündnerhof, C, 48 b.

On the Schatzalp: Berghotel Schatzalp, B, 173 b, Sb.

Delémont
City, C, 30 b; National, C, 54 b; La Bonne Auberge, D, 20 b; Motel Gros-Pré, D, 56 b.

Les Diablerets
*Ermitage, A, 150 b, Sb; *Eurotel, A, 220 b, Sb; Hostellerie-Les-Sources, B, 100 b; Mon Abri, B, 48 b; Alpin, C, 22 b; Les Lilas, C, 28 b; Auberge de la Poste, D, 18 b; Diablotins, D, 198 b; Le Terminus, D, 8 b; Hôtel d'Isenau, E, 15 b.

Disentis/Mustèr
La Cucagna, B, 90 b, Sp; Cristallina, C, 22 b; Oberalp, C, 25 b; Bellavista, C, 44 b.

Einsiedeln
Drei Könige, B, 100 b; Storchen, B, 60 b; Bären, C, 70 b; Linde, C, 46 b; Sonne, C, 50 b; Löwen, C, 40 b; St Georg, D, 105 b; St Johann, D, 70 b; Schiff, D, 62 b.

Engelberg
Dorint-Hotel Reg. Titlis, B, 256 b, Sb; Hess, B, 84 b; Ring-Hotel, B, 110 b; Bellevue-Terminus, C, 70 b; Europäischer Hof, C, 140 b; Edelweiss, C, 80 b; Schweizerhof, C, 77 b; Central, C, 80 b, Sb; Engel, C, 74 b; Hoheneck, C, 70 b; Engelberg, C, 42 b; Crystal, C, 45 b; Eden, D, 22 b; Alpenklub, D, 16 b; Hostatt, E, 24 b.

Fiesch
Derby (no rest), B, 36 b; Des Alpes, B, 40 b; Fiescherhof, B, 44 b; Ideal Hotel Christania, B, 44 b; Kristall, B, 50 b; Schmitta (no rest), B, 24 b.

Flims
In Flims Dorf: Crap Ner, B, 96 b, Sb; Albana, C, 78 b; Bellevue, C, 60 b; Vorab, C, 65 b; Meiler-Prau da Monis, C, 100 b.

In Flims-Fidaz: Fidazerhof, C, 30 b; Berghotel Haldenhaus, 16 b.

In Flims-Waldhaus: *Park-Hotel Waldhaus, A, 300 b, Sp, Sb; Adula, B, 180 b, Sb; Schweizerhof, B, 80 b; Sunstar Surselva, B, 144 b; Des Alpes, B, 130 b, Sb; Schlosshotel, C, 70 b; National, C, 46 b.

Flüelen
Flüelerhof - Grill Rustico, B, 50 b; Hostellerie Sternen, B, 31 b; Tourist, C, 70 b; Weisses Kreuz, C, 60 b; Tell & Post, E, 20 b.

Flumserberg
*Gauenpark, A, 64 b; Alpina, B, 51 b; Cafrida, B, 24 b; Edy Bruggmann, B, 50 b; Gamperdon, C, 52 b; Mätzwiese, C, 28 b; Schwendiwiese, E, 34 b; Kabinenbahn (no rest), E, 25 b.

Frauenfeld
Falken (no rest), B, 27 b; Libelle (no rest), C, 30 b.

Fribourg (Freiburg)
Eurotel, B, 200 b, Sb; De la Rose, B, 80 b; Duc Bertold, B, 60 b; Elite, C, 72 b; Alpha, C, 60 b; Touring, D, 26 b.

Geneva/Genève
North of the Lake and the Rhône, with views of the Alps: *Président, Quai Wilson 47, A, 360 b; *Noga-Hilton, Quai du Mont Blanc 19, A, 693 b, Sb; *Le Richemont, Jardin Brunswick, A, 200 b; *Beau-Rivage, Quai du Mont-Blanc 13, A, 180 b; *Des Bergues, Quai des Bergues 33, A, 185 b; *Angleterre, Quai du Mont-Blanc 17, A, 110 b; *Du Rhône, Quai Turrettini, A, 330 b; *Ramada, rue de Zürich 19, A, 337 b; * De la paix, Quai du Mont-Blanc 11, A, 152 b; *Bristol, rue du Mont-Blanc 10, A, 170 b; Ambassador, Quai des Bergues 21, B, 126 b.

Near the Station: *Rotary-PLM, rue du Cendrier 18-20, A, 139 b; Warwick, rue de Lausanne 14, B, 325 b; Rex, Avenue Wendt 44, B, 143 b; Californria (no rest), rue Gevray 1, B, 100 b; Amat-Carlton, rue Amat 22, B, 190 b; Cornavin, Boulevard James-Fazy 33, B, 175 b; Grand-Pré (no rest), rue du Grand Pré 35, B, 130 b; Royal, rue de Lausanne 41, B, 300 b; Epsom, rue Butini 9, B, 330 b; Excelsior, rue Rousseau, B, 100 b; Suisse (no rest), Place Cornavin 10, B, 100 b; Auteuil (no rest), rue de Lausanne 33, B, 204 b; Alléves, Passage Kléberg 13, B, 80 b; Balzac (no rest), Place Navigation, Ancien-Port 14, B, 70 b; Epoque, rue Voltaire 10, B, 100 b; Windsor (no rest), rue de Berne 31, B, 90 b; De Berne, rue de Berne 26, C, 160 b; International & Terminus, rue des Alpes 20, C, 83 b; Astoria (no rest), Place Cornavin 6, C, 95 b; Moderne, rue de Berne 1, C, 70 b; Savoy, Place Cornavin 8, C, 100 b; Rivoli (no rest), rue des Pâquis 6, C, 100 b; Chantilly (no rest), rue Naviga-tion 27, C, 125 b; Montana, rue des Alpes 25, C, 70 b; Strasbourg & Univers, rue Pradier 10, C, 100 b; Bernina (no rest), Place Cornavin 22, C, 110 b; Pâquis-Fleuris, rue des Pâquis 23, D, 20 b; De l'Union, rue Chovet 7, D, 80 b.

In the international organisations district: *La Réserve, Route de Lausanne 301, A, 225 b, Sp; *Intercontinental, Petit-Saconnex 7-9, A, 680 b, Sp; Eden, rue de Lausanne 135, C, 80 b; Mon Repos, rue de Lausanne 131, C, 180 b.

Near Cointrin Airport: Penta, Avenue Louis-Casaï 82, C, 496 b; Air Escale (no rest), Avenue Louis-Casaï 81, C, 50 b.

On the south bank: *Arbalète, rue de la Tour-Maîtresse 3, A, 70 b; *Les Armures, Puits-Saint-Pierre 1, 52 b; Adriatica (no rest), rue Sautter 21 (Plainpalais), B, 70 b; Century (no rest), Avenue de Frontenex 24, B, 177 b; Touring-Balance, Place Longermalle 13 (lower town), C, 100 b.

Glanerhof, B, 53 b; Sonne Terminus, C, 180 b; Stadthof, C, 17 b.	**Glarus**

Grächerhof, B, 42 b; Elite, B, 45 b; Gaedi, B, 50 b; Des Alpes, B, 40 b; Désirée, B, 40 b; Hannigalp, B, 50 b, Sb; Waldheim, B, 36 b; Walliserhof, B, 50 b; Beau-Site, B, 50 b, Sb; Alpha (no rest), C, 30 b; Alpina, C, 27 b; Sonne, C, 30 b; Abendruh, C, 20 b; Bellevue-Romantica, C, 70 b; Eden, C, 34 b; Touring (no rest), C, 46 b; Allalin (no rest), D, 18 b; Alpenrose & Chalets, D, 40 b; La Collina, E, 120 b, Sb; Ausblick, E, 23 b. — **Grächen**

Alpina, B, 60 b; Marenda, B, 74 b; La Cordée, C, 40 b; Les Becs-de-Bosson, C, 20 b; De Moiry, D, 38 b; Le Mélèze, D, 18 b; Bouquetin, E, 70 b. — **Grimentz**

*Grand Hotel Regina, A, 180 b, Sb, Sp; Belvédère, B, 85 b, Sb; Parkhotel Schoenegg, B, 85 b, Sb; Schweizerhof, B, 96 b, Sb; Silberhorn, B, 85 b; Sunstar-Adler, B, 345 b, Sb; Weisses Kreuz & Post, B, 85 b, Sb; Alpina, C, 60 b; Central Wolter, C, 70 b; Crystal, C, 55 b; Cabana (no rest), C, 32 b; Bel Air Eden, D, 40 b; Gletschergarten, D, 50 b; Blümlisalp, E, 12 b. — **Grindelwald**

*Gstaad Palace, A, 207 b, Sb, Sp; Grand Hotel Bellevue, B, 85 b; Parkhotel, B, 180 b, Sp; Grand Hotel Alpina, B, 60 b, Sp; Arc-en-Ciel, B, 65 b; Berner-hof, B, 90 b; Alphorn, C, 42 b, Sb; Posthotel Rössli, C, 36 b; Victoria, C, 40 b. — **Gstaad**

Haus Sunnermatt, B, 36 b; Kurhotel Heiden, B, 75 b, Sb; Krone, B, 50 b, Sp; Linde, B, 30 b; Park, C, 25 b; Santé (no rest), C, 20 b; Papillon, E, 12 b. — **Heiden**

Oberalp, C, 65 b; Casutt, D, 30 b; Eden-Montana, D, 105 b. — **Ilanz**

On the Höheweg: *Grand Hotel Victoria-Jungfrau, A, 400 b, Sb; Métropole, B, 180 b, Sb; Grand Hotel Beau Rivage, B, 170 b, Sb; Royal St. Georges, B, 170 b; Du Lac, B, 70 b; Carlton, C, 80 b; Oberland, C, 180 b; Du Nord, C, 90 b; Interlaken, C, 100 b; Weisses Kreuz, C, 90 b; Europe, C, 70 b; Hirschen, D, 36 b. — **Interlaken**

North of the Höheweg: Harder-Minerva, D, 50 b.

In the Marktgasse: Bellevue-Garden-Hotel, B, 90 b; Löwen, E, 35 b.

Hotels

By the Station: Krebs, B, 80 b; Bernerhof, C, 65 b; Merkur, C, 60 b; Crystal (no rest), C, 75 b; De la Paix, D, 40 b; Touriste (no rest), E, 28 b.
In Unterseen: Goldey, C, 65 b; Beau-Site, C, 80 b; Central, C, 70 b; Chalet Swiss, C, 90 b; Hardermannli, D, 50 b; Rössli, D, 50 b.

In Matten: Sonne, D, 40 b; Alpina, D, 60 b.

On the road to Lauterbrunnen: Park-Hotel Mattenhof, C, 120 b, Sp.

Kandersteg
*Royal Hotel Bellevue, A, 60 b, Sb, Sp; Victoria & Ritter, B, 130 b, Sb; Adler, C, 44 b; Blümlisalp, C, 45 b, Sb; Alfa-Soleil, C, 60 b, Sb; Alpenrose, D, 50 b; National, E, 20 b.

Klosters
*Pardenn, A, 110 b, Sb; Vereina, B, 160 b, Sb; Chesa Grischuna, B, 42 b; Alpina, B, 50 b; Kaiser (no rest), B, 50 b; Kurhotel Bad Serneus, C, 68 b, Sb; Surval, C, 30 b, Sp; Sport-Ferienzentrum, C, 96 b; Bündnerhof, D, 36 b.

Küssnacht am Rigi
Hirschen, C, 65 b; Engel, D, 20 b; Seehof du Lac, D, 30 b; Hörnli, D, 60 b.

Laax
In Laax: *Arena Alva, A, 160 b; *Rancho Sporthotels, A, 250 b, Sb, Sp; *Sporthotel Laax, A, 180 b; *Sporthotel Signina, A, 154 b, Sb; Bellaval, B, 50 b, Sp; Motel Rustico, B, 85 b; Sporthotel Larisch, B, 70 b; Capricorn, C, 32 b; Cap Sogn Gion, C, 75 b, Sb; Laaxerhof-Vallarosa, E, 250 b, Sb.

Lake Maggiore
See Ascona and Locarno

Lausanne
Place St-Francois and town centre: *Lausanne-Palace, Grand Chêne 7-9, A, 270 b; Del la Paix, Avenue Benjamin Constant 5, B, 210 b; Jan, Avenue de Beaulieu 8, B, 110 b; City, rue Caroline 5, C, 110 b; Crystal, rue Chaucrau 5, C, 80 b; Voyageurs, Grand-St-Jean 19, C, 52 b.

Near the station: Alpha, Petit Chêne 34, B, 270 b; Continental, Place de la Gare 2, B, 180 b; Mirabeau, Avenue de la Gare 31, B, 100 b; A la Gare-Transit, Avenue de la Gare 46, B, 100 b; Elite, Avenue Ste-Luce 1, C, 57 b; A la Gare-Transit, rue de Simplon 14, D, 92 b.

In Ouchy, on the lake: *Beau-Rivage Palace, A, 320 b, Sp, Sb (large park); Aulac, Place Navigation 4, B, 150 b; Château d'Ouchy, Place du Port 2, B, 85 b; La Résidence, Place du Port 15, B, 94 b, Sp; Navigation, Place Navigation, B, 50 b; Angleterre, Place du Port 9, D, 55 b.

In Croix-d'Ouchy: Royal-Savoy, Avenue d'Ouchy 40, B, 170 b, Sp; Carlton, Avenue de Cour 4, B, 80 b; Bellerive, Avenue de Cour 99, B, 80 b.

In Bussigny (5 miles northwest of the town centre): Novotel, Route de Soullens, B, 300 b.

Lenk
Kurhotel Lenkerhof, B, 120 b; Parkhotel Bellevue, B, 70 b; Crystal, B, 55 b; Kreuz, B, 140 b; Wildstrubel, B, 78 b; Krone, C, 60 b; Sunnestübli, C, 21 b; Waldrand, C, 50 b; Sternen, D, 25 b; Alpenruh (no rest), D, 24 b.

Lenzerheide-Valbella
In Lenzerheide: Schweizerhof, B, 200 b, Sb; Grand Hotel Kurhaus, B, 160 b, Sb; Guarda Val Sporz, B, 70 b; Sunstar, B, 170 b, Sb; Central (no rest), B, 50 b; La Palanca, C, 70 b; Sporthotel Dieschen, C, 84 b; Park-Hotel, C, 70 b, Sp.

Les Diablerets
See Diablerets

Leukerbad/ Loèche-les-Bains
Spa hotels (all with thermal baths): *Les Sources des Alpes, A, 60 b; *Bristol, A, 150 b; Maison-Blanche, B, 75 b; Regina Therme, B, 100 b; Grand-Bain, B, 75 b; Badnerhof, C, 28 b; Grichting, C, 60 b.

Other hotels: Astoria, B, 75 b; Alpenblick, B, 60 b; Alex, C, 46 b; Walliserhof, C, 50 b; Heilquelle, C, 52 b; Escher, C, 35 b; Waldrand, D, 30 b; Gemmi, D, 27 b.

Hotels without restaurants: De France, C, 78 b; Dala, C, 50 b; Victoria, C, 35 b; Paradis, D, 30 b; Chamois, E, 11 b.

Mountain hotels: Wildstrudel, 36 b; Torrenthorn, 30 b.

*La Palma au Lac, A, 128 b, Sb; Reber au Lac, B, 140 b, Sp; Esplanade-Hotel, **Locarno** B, 120 b, Sp; Muralto, B, 145 b; Grand Hotel, 160 b, Sp; Quisisiana, B, 110 b, Sb; Remorino (no rest), 44 b, Sp; Beau-Rivage, C, 90 b; Du Lac, C, 53 b; Excelsior Parco-Lago (no rest), C, 40 b; Schloss-Hotel, D, 62 b, Sp; Navegna au Lac, D, 30 b; Alexandra, E, 36 b.

In Monti: Olanda, 15 b.

In Orselina: Orselina, C, 140 b, Sp; Stella, D, 58 b; Migration, D, 55 b; Mon Désir, E, 46 b.

On the north shore of the lake: *Grand Hôtel National, A, 144 b, Sb; **Lucerne** *Palace, A, 296 b (bathing beach); *Schweizerhof, A, 214 b; *Carlton-Hotel Tivoli, A. 180 b (bathing beach); Montana, B, 120 b; Europe Grand Hôtel, B, 300 b; Luzernerhof, B, 116 b; Rebstock (no rest), B, 58 b; Eden du Lac, C, 70 b; Beau Séjour, C, 50 b; Royal, C, 80 b; De la Paix, C, 70 b, Sb; Kolping, D, 180 b.

North of the Reuss (old town): Balances & Bellevue, B, 100 b; Des Alpes, C, 80 b; Schiff, D, 32 b; Pickwick (no rest), D, 23 b; Gambrinus, E, 50 b.

South of the Reuss, near the station: Monopol & Métropole, B, 183 b; Schiller, B, 120 b; Flora, B, 280 b; Continental, C, 70 b; Park, C, 60 b; Diana, C, 70 b; Alpina, C, 55 b.

Near Pilatusplatz: Astoria, B, 230 b; Anker, C, 64 b.

Near Hirschengraben: Wilden Mann, B, 80 b; Rütli-Rheinischer Hof, C, 100 b; Drei Könige, C, 110 b; Rothaus, C, 85 b; Lige, C, 62 b, Sp.

Near the Bundesplatz: Johanniterhof, C, 90 b.

On the road to Basel: Untergrund, C, 90 b.

In Gütsch: Château Gütsch, B, 75 b, Sp.

In St Niklausen (on the lake, 4.5 km from the town centre): St Niklausen am See, D, 40 b (bathing beach).

On the lake: *Splendide-Royal, A, 204 b, Sb; Pullman Commodore, B, **Lugano** 130 b, Sp; Excelsior, B, 147 b; International au Lac, C, 120 b; Walter au Lac, C, 66 b; Plaza (no rest), C, 56 b; Felix, D, 40 b.

In the old town: Cristallo-Centro, C, 120 b; Lugano-Dante (no rest), C, 102 b; Ticino, C, 43 b; Lux-Centro (no rest), D, 70 b; Cattedrale (no rest), E, 30 b.

Near the station (elevated position): Holiday Select, C, 100 b; Arizona, C, 100 b, Sp; Scandinavia, C, 68 b; Kocher's Washington, C, 70 b.

In Paradiso: *Eden Grand, A, 230 b, Sp; Europa au Lac, B, 170 b, Sp; Du Lac-Seehof, B, 90 b, Sp; Admiral, B, 145 b, Sp; Meister, B, 130 b, Sp; Bellevue au Lac, B, 120 b, Sp.

In Cassarate: Villa Castagnola au Lac, B, 120 b, Sb; Strandhotel Seegarten, C, 130 b, Sp.

In Castagnola: Belmonte, B, 80 b, Sp; Carlton-Villa Moritz, C, 100 b, Sp.

In Origlio: Country Club, B, 110 b, Sp.

In Agno: *La Perla, A, 256 b, Sb, Sp.

Du Rhône, C, 100 b; Central, C, 50 b; De la Poste, C, 65 b; Forclaz-Touring, C, **Martigny** 120 b; Du Forum, C, 60 b; Kluser, D, 100 b; Du Grand St-Bernard, E, 65 b.

*Park-Hotel Sauvage, A, 123 b; *Alpin Sherpa, A, 96 b; Sherlock Holmes, B, **Meiringen** 110 b; Rebstock, C, 30 b; Löwen, C, 30 b; Victoria, C, 25 b; Adler, C, 24 b; Weisses Kreuz, C, 64 b; Hirschen, C, 41 b.

Hotels

Montana   See Crans-Montana

Montreux   *Le Montreux Palace, A, 500 b, Sp; *Hyatt Continental, A, 326 b, Sb; *Excelsior, A, 132 b, Sb; Eden au Lac, B, 210 b, Sp; Eurotel Riviera, B, 270 b, Sb; Suisse et Majestic, B, 250 b; Golf-Hôtel René Capt, C, 100 b; Bon-Port, C, 59 b.

In Clarens: L'Ermitage, C, 15 b; De Chailly, C, 62 b.

In Veytaux-Chillon: Bonivard, B, 180 b.

In Caux: Hostellerie de Caux, D, 10 b; Les Rosiers, E, 27 b.

In Glion: Victoria, B, 80 b, Sp; Des Alpes Vaudoises, C, 90 b, Sp; Righi Vaudois, C, 100 b.

Morges   *Fleur du Lac, Quai J Stravinsky/Route de Lausanne 70, A, 47 b, Sp; Du Mont-Blanc au Lac, Quai du Mont-Blanc, C, 80 b; De la Couronne, Grand-Rue 88, C, 68 b; De Savoie, Grand-Rue 7, 38 b.

Mürren   Résidence Sporthotel Mürren, B, 98 b; Eiger, B, 85 b; Jungfrau Lodge, C, 90 b; Bellevue, C, 30 b; Edelweiss, C, 50 b; Alpina, D, 50 b; Alpenblick, D, 30 b.

Murten/Morat   Schiff, B, 30 b; Krone, C, 65 b; Weisses Kreuz, C, 60 b; Murtenhof, C, 30 b; Enge, C, 60 b; Bahnhof, D, 13 b.

In Murten-Meyriez: Vieux Manoir au Lac, B, 40 b.

In Murten-Muntelier: Bonne Auberge des Bains, C, 52 b.

Neuchâtel/Neuenburg   Beaulac, B, 92 b (bathing beach); Eurotel, B, 94 b, Sb; City, C, 70 b; Touring au Lac, C, 80 b; Des Beaux-Arts, D, 46 b.

In Thielle: Novotel, B, 120 b.

Neuhausen   Bellevue (100 m above the Rhine Falls), C, 55 b; Löwenbräu, in Neuhausen, D, 60 b.

Nyon   Beau-Rivage, B, 100 b; Du Clos de Sadex, C, 30 b; Des Alpes, C, 70 b; Du Nord, C, 40 b; De Nynon, D, 50 b; Hostellerie du 16ième siècle, D, 21 b.

Oberhofen   Moy, B, 25 b, Sp; Parkhotel Oberhofen, B, 50 b; Kreuz, C, 30 b; Elisabeth, D, 43 b; Niesenblick, D, 13 b, Sp.

Olten   Astoria, C, 55 b; Schweizerhof, D, 60 b; Löwen-Zunfthaus, D, 10 b.
In Hauenstein: Froburg, D, 9 b.

Pontresina/Puntraschigna   *Grand Hotel Kronenhof, A, 180 b, Sp, Sb; Walther, B, 130 b; Schweizerhof, B, 130 b; Rosatch Residence, B, 90 b; Sporthotel Pontresina, C, 160 b; Bernina, C, 70 b; La Collina & Soldanella, C, 70 b; Engadinerhof, C, 140 b; Müller-Chesa Mandra, C, 65 b; Post, C, 70 b; Rosatch, C, 70 b; Atlas, C, 150 b; Steinbock, C, 53 b; Chesa Mulin Garni, C, 50 b.

Porrentruy   Belvédère, C, 15 b; Suisse, C, 21 b; Terminus, C, 92 b.

Bad Ragaz   *Quellenhof, A, 200 b; Grand Hotel Hof Ragaz, B, 180 b (thermal baths); Cristal, B, 90 b, Sb; Lattmann Royal, B, 140 b; Sandi, C, 86 b; Residence Tamina, C, 150 b (thermal bath).

In Pfäfers: TM Schloss Ragaz, C, 115 b, Sp; Wartenstein, C, 50 b; St Gallerhof, D, 50 b; Rössli (no rest), D, 36 b.

Rapperswil   Schwanen, B, 38 b; Speer, C, 24 b.

Rheinfelden   *Eden Solbad, A, 60 b, Sp; *Park-Hotel am Rhein (spa hotel), A, 115 b, Sp; Schwanen-Solbad, A, 75 b, Sb; Schützen-Seminar, B, 35 b, Sb; Schiff am Rhein, B, 80 b; Ochsen, C, 12 b; Bahnhof-Terminus, E, 20 b.

Hotels

*Art Furrer, A, 100 b, Sb; Walliser Spycher, B, 30 b; Adler, B, 36 b; Rieder-   **Riederalp**
hof, B, 31 b; Bergdohle-Riederalp, C, 30 b; Riederfurka, D, 15 b; Valaisia, E,
40 b, Sp.

In Rigi-Kaltbad: Hostellerie Rigi, B, 80 b, Sb; Bellevue, B, 80 b; Bergsonne,   **Rigi**
C, 35 b; Edelweiss, D, 35 b.

In Rigi-Scheidegg: Rigi-Scheidegg, D, 12 b.

On the Rigi summit: Rigi-Kulm, C, 100 b.

*Rivesrolle, A, 64 b, Sb, Sp; De la Tête Noire, C, 30 b.   **Rolle**

*Parkhotel Waldau, A, 70 b, Sp, Sb; Anker, C, 71 b (bathing beach); Mozart   **Rorschach**
(no rest), C, 66 b; Jud, D, 48 b.

Atlantic, C, 40 b; Kristall, C, 55 b; Mattmarkblick, C, 80 b; Portiengrat, C,   **Saas Almagell**
60 b; Christiania, D, 50 b; Lärcherheim, D, 35 b.

La Collina (no rest), B, 30 b; Saaserhof (apartments), B, 100 b; Beau-Site, C,   **Saas Fee**
106 b; Grand Hotel, C, 100 b; Derby, C, 60 b; Alphubel, C, 70 b; Eden, C,
40 b; Europa, C, 55 b; Etoile, C, 57 b; Mistral, C, 15 b; Waldhotel Fletschhorn, C, 20 b; Du Glacier, D, 100 b; Gletschergarten, D, 48 b; Soleil, D, 48 b.

Touring, C, 50 b, Sb; Adler, D, 45 b; Sporthotel, D, 45 b, Sb; Alpha, D, 45 b;   **Saas Grund**
Bergheimat, D, 40 b; Primavera, D, 40 b; Rodania, D, 57 b; Moulin, D, 30 b;
Eden, D, 30 b.

*Bernina, A, 105 b; *Quadratscha, A, 60 b, Sb; Donatz, B, 55 b; Golf-Hotel   **Samedan**
des Alpes, 64 b; Sporthotel Luzi, B, 55 b; Engiadina, C, 30 b; Chalet Rüesch
(no rest), D, 25 b; Terminus, D, 36 b; Berghaus Muottas Muragl, E, 50 b;
Central, E, 11 b; Post (no rest), E, 15 b.

*Silvretta, A, 70 b, Sb; Montana, B, 50 b, Sb.   **Samnaun**

*Albarella, A, 130 b, Sb; Brocco & Posta, 60 b, Sb; Lumbreida, B, 150 b;   **San Bernardino**
Ravizza-National, C, 70 b; Bellevue, E, 35 b.

Einstein, B, 117 b; Metropol, B, 52 b; Walhalla, B, 80 b; Continental, C, 62 b;   **St Gallen**
Ekkehard, C, 50 b; Jägerhof, C, 39 b; Sonne Rotmonten, C, 40 b; Weissenstein, D, 33 b.

Ecu de Valais, D, 35 b; Dents-du-Midi, E, 18 b; Motel Inter-Alps (no rest), E,   **St-Maurice**
80 b.

*Badrutt's Palace, A, 380 b, Sb; *Suvretta-House, A, 360 b, Sb; *Carlton, A,   **St Moritz**
180 b, Sb; *Kulm, A, 300 b, Sb; Schweizerhof, B, 150 b; Monopol-
Grischuna, B, 120 b, Sb; Park-Hotel Kurhaus, B, 250 b; Crystal, B, 160 b;
Europa St Moritz, B, 200 b, Sb; La Margna, B, 100 b; Belvédère (no rest), B,
118 b, Sb; Hauser (no rest), B, 70 b; Neues Posthotel, B, 110 b; Steffani, B,
120 b. San Gian (no rest), B, 94 b; Edelweiss, C, 100 b (kosher cuisine);
Waldhaus, C, 60 b; Salastrains, C, 45 b; Chesa sur l'En, D, 30 b; Sonne (no
rest), E, 100 b.

See Sils Baseglia, Sils Maria and Silvaplana.

Krone, B, 100 b; Seehotel Wilerbad, C, 90 b; Hirschen, E, 16 b.   **Sarnen**

Cresta, B, 90 b; Alpina, C, 100 b; Bela Riva, C, 28 b; Danilo, C, 70 b; Arlos, D,   **Savognin**
22 b.

Bahnhof, C, 80 b; Bellevue ü. d. Rheinfall, C, 55 b; Kronenhof, C, 54 b;   **Schaffhausen**
Park-Villa, C, 35 b; Rheinhotel Fischerzunft, C, 20 b; Tanne, E, 20 b.

Schwägalp, C, 60 b; Säntisgipfel, E, 22 b.   **Schwägalp**

Hotels

Schwyz Wysses Rössli, B, 46 b; Hirschen, D, 26 b.

Bad Scuol Parkhotel Tarasp, B, 220 b; Romantik Guardaval, B, 80 b; Belvédère, B, 90 b; Astras, C, 38 b; Bellaval, C, 50 b; Filli, C, 37 b; Collina, D, 12 b; Gabriel, D, 28 b; Quellenhof, E, 70 b.

Sierre/Siders Atlantic Manotel, C, 64 b; Casino, C, 60 b; Terminus, C, 55 b; Central, D, 28 b; La Grotte, D, 20 b; Victoria, E, 20 b.

Sils Baselgia Margna, B, 110 b; Chesa Randolina, C, 65 b; Chasté, E, 26 b.

Sils Maria *Waldhaus, A, 220 b, Sb; Edelweiss, B, 125 b; Maria, C, 65 b; Seraina, C, 50 b.

Silvaplana Albana, B, 60 b; Chesa Guardalej, B, 210 b; Sonne, C, 80 b; Julier-Chesa Arsa, C, 105 b; Arlas, D, 24 b.

Sion/Sitten Du Rhône, rue du Scex 10, C, 80 b; Touring, Avenue de la Gare 6, C, 40 b; Du Cerf, rue des Remparts 10, 42 b; Du Castel (no rest), rue du Scex 38, 60 b; Du Midi, D, 25 b.

Solothurn Krone (Couronne), B, 60 b; Ambassador (no rest), B, 46 b; Roter Turm (Tour Rouge), C, 40 b; Astoria, C, 80 b.

Spiez Belvédère Silence, B, 55 b; Edenhotel, B, 80 b, Sp; Alpenhof (Des Alpes), C, 60 b; Bellevue, D, 30 b.

Stans Stanserhof, B, 55 b; Zur Linde, B, 18 b; Motel Rex (no rest), E, 55 b.

Stansstad *Schutzen, A, 40 b; Seehotel Acheregg, B, 50 b, Sp.

Stein am Rhein Klosterhof, B, 140 b, Sp; Adler, C, 42 b; Zur Rheingerbe, D, 16 b.

Sursee *Sursee, A, 56 b; Hirschen (Landgasthof SHV), E, 27 b.

Susten Tenne, B, 36 b.

Bad Tarasp Schlosshotel Chasté, B, 35 b; Tarasp, C, 45 b.

Teufen Säntis (no rest), B, 24 b; Hotel zur Linde, E, 25 b.

Thun Elite, Bernstrasse 1, B, 72 b; Freienhof, Freienhofgasse 3, B, 98 b; Holiday, Gwattstrasse 1, B, 114 b; Krone, Rathausplatz, B, 60 b; Alpha, Dürrenast, C, 60 b; Beau-Rivage, Aare-Quai, C, 50 b.

Tiefencastel Albula, B, 85 b; Posthotel Julier, B, 85 b.

Vaduz *Park-Hotel Sonnenhof, A, 50 b, Sp; *Real, Städtle 21, A, 17 b; Engel, Städtle 13, B, 34 b; Schlössle, Schloss Strasse 68, B, 55 b; Vaduzerhof, Städtle 3, C, 54 b.

Verbier Rosalp, B, 40 b; Vanessa, B, 135 b; Grand Combin & Golf, B, 52 b; Les 4 Vallées (no rest), B, 40 b; Verluisant (no rest), B, 50 b; Le Mazot, C, 62 b; Rhodania, C, 75 b; L'Auberge, D, 40 b.

Vevey *Trois Couronnes, A, 109 b, Sp; *Le Mirador & Country Club, A, 135 b, Sp; Du Lac, B, 90 b, Sp; Du Parc, B, 130 b, Sp; De Famille, C, 100 b; Du Léman, C, 85 b; Pavillon de la Gare (no rest), C, 70 b; Touring et Gare, C, 52 b; Des Négociants, D, 45 b; Bahyse, D, 25 b.

Villars *Grand Hotel du Parc, A, 110 b, Sb; *Eurotel, A, 250 b, Sb; *Bristol, A, 220 b, Sb; *Panorama, A, 200 b, Sb; Alpe Fleurie, B, 30 b; Du Golfe & Marie

Louise, B, 110 b; Ecureuil, B, 48 b; Sunstar-Elite, B, 106 b; La Renardière, B, 40 b; Curling et Bellevue, C, 50 b; Montesano, C, 60 b, Sb; Les Papillons, D, 18 b.

*Park-Hotel Vitznau, A, 158 b, Sp; Seehotel Vitznauerhof, B, 90 b; Rigi, C, 61 b; Waldheim, D, 26 b. **Vitznau**

Waldhaus, B, 300 b, Sp; Schweizerhof, B, 24 b, Sp, Sb; Villa Maria, C, 30 b. **Bad Vulpera**

Churfirsten AG, B, 60 b. **Walenstadt**

Parkhotel Schwert, B, 40 b, Sp. **Weesen**

*Albana, A, 100 b; *Alexander, A, 30 b, Sp; *Beau-Rivage, A, 80 b, Sp; **Weggis**
Gerbi (no rest), A, 50 b, Sp; *Park-Hotel, A, 105 b, Sp; Waldstaetten, B, 72 b; Frohburg, B, 30 b, Sp; Schweizerhof, B, 50 b; Central am See, B, 70 b, Sp; Du Lac Seehof, B, 50 b, Sp; Friedheim, B, 40 b; Gotthard am See, 40 b, Sp; National, B, 64 b; Rössli, B, 80 b; Kurhaus Seeblick, B, 50 b, Sp; Rigi am See, C, 60 b, Sp; Seehotel Lützelau, C, 100 b, Sp.

*Parkhotel Beausite, A, 110 b, Sp; Sunstar, B, 150 b, Sp; Berghaus, B, 33 b; **Wengen**
Regina, B, 150 b; Silberhorn, B, 140 b; Am Waldrand, B, 70 b; Alpenrose, C, 80 b; Bellevue, C, 65 b; Eiger, C, 62 b; Jungfraublick, C, 65 b.

Garten-Hotel, Stadthausstrasse 4, B, 90 b; Winterthur, Meisenstrasse 2, B, **Winterthur**
83 b; Zentrum Töss, Zürcherstrasse 106, B, 32 b; Hotel zur Krone, Marktgasse 49, B, 55 b; Motel Wülflingen (no rest), Riedhofstrasse 51, B, 64 b; Römertor, Guggenbühlstrasse 6, C, 35 b; Wartmann am Bahnhof, Rudolfstrasse 15, C, 120 b.

*Hotel de la Prairie, A, 70 b; Motel des Bains, B, 90 b; Expo, B, 210 b; Don **Yverdon-Les-**
Camillo, C, 14 b; Maison Blanche, C, 37 b; Hôtel de l'Ange, D, 35 b; Ecusson **Bains**
Vaudois, E, 15 b.

*Mont Cervin, A, 228 b, Sb; *Grand Hotel Zermatterhof, A, 155 b, Sb; *Alex, **Zermatt**
A, 110 b, Sb; *Alex Schlosshotel Tenne, A, 60 b; *Allalin (no rest), A, 60 b; *Alpenhof, A, 110 b, Sb; *Alpenroyal, A, 60 b, Sb; *Ambassador, A, 220 b, Sb; *Astoria (no rest), A, 36 b, Sb; *Beau-Rivage (no rest), A, 31 b; *Christiania (no rest), A, 62 b, Sb; *Eden (no rest), A, 52 b, Sb; *Parkhotel/Beau-Site, A, 120 b, Sb; *Mirabeau, A, 72 b, Sb; *Monte Rosa, A, 89 b; *National, A, 108 b, Sb; *Pollux, A, 65 b; *Simi (no rest), A, 45 b; *Walliserhof, A, 60 b; *Adonis (no rest), B, 35 b; Admiral, B, 44 b; Albana (no rest), B, 52 b; Alfa (no rest), B, 41 b; Alpenblick, B, 56 b; Antares (no rest), B, 60 b; Antika (no rest), B, 40 b; Arca-Soleschwimmbad (no rest), B, 50 b, Sb; Aristella, B, 42 b; Artemis (no rest), 44 b; Atlanta, B, 46 b; Bellerive (no rest), B, 40 b; Bijou, B, 32 b; Biner (no rest), B, 80 b, Sb; Bristol, B, 80 b; Butterfly, B, 70 b; Carina, B, 36 b; Chesa Valese, B, 50 b; Continental, B, 50 b; Darioli, B, 40 b; Derby, B, 45 b; Dom, B, 70 b; Dufour (no rest), 30 b; Elite (no rest), B, 43 b; Europe, B, 50 b; Excelsior, B, 32 b; Gornergrat, B, 100 b; Hemizeus, b, 100 b; Holiday, B, 60 b; Jägerhof, B, 62 b; Julen, B, 72 b; Metropol (no rest), B, 44 b; Orion, B, 35 b; Parnass, B, 50 b; Perren, B, 120 b; Plateau Rosa (no rest), B, 32 b; Romantica (no rest), B, 25 b; Sarazena (no rest), B, 38 b; Sporthotel, B, 33 b; Tschugge, B, 60 b; Alpina, C, 42 b; Bella-Vista (no rest), C, 32 b; Blauherd (no rest), C, 38 b; Burgener Pension, C, 26 b; Cristal (no rest), C, 38 b; Malva (no rest), C, 42 b; Primavera, C, 30 b; Rhodania, C, 42 b; Seilerhaus (no rest), 22 b; Tannenhof (no rest), C, 35 b; Testa Grigia (no rest), C, 45 b, Sb; Touring, C, 38 b; Schönegg, B, 70 b; Welschen Pension, C, 24 b; Bahnhof (no rest), D, 30 b; Breithorn (no rest), D, 29 b; Gabelhorn (no rest), D, 20 b; Le Mazot (no rest), D, 13 b; Mischabel, D, 55 b; Weisshorn (no rest), D, 30 b; Urania (no rest), E, 38 b.

Bettini, B, 45 b; Kreuz/Crusch Alba, B, 32 b; Bär-Post, B, 80 b, Sb; Filli, B, **Zernez**
40 b;

Hotels

Engel (no rest), B, 75 b; Zofingen, B, 60 b; Römerbad, E, 15 b.

*City-Hotel Ochsen, Kolinplatz, A, 72 b; *Parkhotel Zug, A, 214 b; Central, Grabenstrasse 9, B, 45 b; Guggital, Zugerbergstrasse, B, 52 b; Rosenberg, Rosenbergstrasse 33, B, 62 b; Swiss-Motel Kollermühle, Kollerstrasse 1, B, 85 b; Zugertor, Baarerstrasse 97, B, 52 b; Löwen au Lac, Landsgemeinde-platz, C, 40 b; Rössli, Vorstadt 8, C, 30 b.

On or near the Lake: *Baur au Lac, Talstrasse 1, Bürkliplatz, A, 210 b, Sp; *Eden au Lac, Utoquai 45, A, 75 b; *Europe (no rest), Dufourstrasse 4, A, 65 b; Glärnischhof, Claridenstrasse 30, B, 130 b; Bellerive au Lac, Utoquai 47, B, 80 b; Splügenschloss, Splügenstrasse 2, B, 75 b; Schifflände, Schifflände 18, B, 40 b; Opéra (no rest), Dufourstrasse 5, B, 100 b; Excelsior, Dufourstrasse 24, B, 63 b; Helmhaus (no rest), Schiffländeplatz 30, B, 50 b; Ascot, Tessinerplatz 9 (near Enge station), B, 110 b, Sp; Ambassador, Falkenstrasse 5, C, 70 b; Neues Schloss, Stokkerstrasse 14, C, 89 b.

In the inner city: *Savoy Baur en Ville, Poststrasse 12, Beim Paradeplatz, A, 150 b; Carlton Elite, Bahnhofstrasse 41, B, 115 b; Zum Storchen, Weinplatz 2, An der Limmat, B, 110 b; Glockenhof, Sihlstrasse 31, B, 170 b; Kindli (no rest), Pfalzgasse 1, B, 30 b; Ammann (no rest), Kirchgasse 4, B, 53 b; Zürcherhof (no rest), Zähringstrasse 21, B, 50 b; Alexander (no rest), Niederdorfstrasse 40, B, 82 b; Scheuble (no rest), Mühlgasse 17, B, 110 b; Chesa Rustica, Limmatquai 70, C, 45 b; Franziskaner, Niederdorfstrasse 1, C, 40 b; City, Löwenstrasse 34, C, 100 b; Seidenhof (no alcohol), Sihlstrasse 9, C, 70 b; Goldenes Schwert, Marktgasse 14, C, 85 b; Krone Limmatquai, Limmatquai 88, D, 40 b.

At and near the main station: Schweizerhof, Bahnhofplatz 7, B, 150 b; St Gotthard, Bahnhofstrasse 87, B, 200 b; Central Plaza, Central 1, B, 135 b; Pullmann Continental, Stampfenbachstrasse 60, B, 330 b; Simplon (no rest), Schützengasse 16, C, 115 b; Trümpy, Limmatstrasse 5, C, 130 b; Du Théâtre (no rest), Seilergraben 69, C, 85 b; Montana (no rest), Konradstrasse 39, C, 140 b; Limmathof, Limmatquai 142, D, 100 b.

East of the main station and in the university district: Florhof, Florhofgasse 4, C, 56 b; Rigihof, Universitätstrasse 101, C, 110 b; Arc-Royal (no rest), Leonhardstrasse 6, C, 72 b; Leoneck, Leonhardstrasse 1, C, 90 b; Poly (no rest), Universitätstrasse 63, C, 65 b; Rlette, Stampfenbachstrasse 26, C, 44 b; Bristol (no rest), Stampfenbachstrasse 34, D, 100 b.

North of the main station: *Zürich, Neumühlequai 42, A, 500 b, Sb; Astor, Weinbergstrasse 44, C, 80 b; Rex (no rest), Weinbergstrasse 92, C, 58 b.

West of the main station: Nova-Park, Badenerstrasse 420, B, 800 b; Stoller, Badenerstrasse 357, C, 130 b; Goldener Brunnen, Rotachstrasse 33, C, 40 b; Olympia, Badenerstrasse 324, C, 70 b; Limmat (Congress Centre), Limmatstrasse 118, D, 106 b; Rothaus, Sihlkellenstrasse 1, D, 80 b.

At the exit-road to Schaffhausen: Krone-Unterstrass, Schaffhauserstrasse 1, C, 89 b; Coronado, Schaffhauserstrasse 137, D, 69 b.

At the exit-road to Chur (N3): Engematthof, Engimattstrasse 14, C, 120 b, (tennis).

In Oriklon: *International, In Marktplatz, A, 700 b, Sb; Sternen Oerlikon, Schaffhauserstrasse 335, C, 80 b.

On the Zürichberg: *Dolder Grand Hotel, Kurhausstrasse 65, A, 300 b, Sp (tennis, golf); Waldhaus Dolder, Kurhausstrasse 20, B, 160 b, Sp (tennis golf); Sonneberg, Aurorastrasse 98, C, 70 b; Zürichberg (no alcohol), Orellistrasse 21, D, 86 b.

At the foot of the Uetliberg: *Atlantis Sheraton, Döltschiweg 234, A, 310 b, Sb; Guesthouse Atlantis (no rest), Döltschiweg 234, B, 100 b.

At the airport: *Hilton International, Hohenbühlstrasse 10, A, 550 b, Sb; Mövenpick Hotel Airport, Mittelholzerstrasse 8, B, 570 b, Sb; Airport, Oberhauserstrasse 30, B, 62 b; Welcome-Inn, Holbergstrasse 1, C, 196 b, Sp.

In Regensdorf (about 5 miles north-west): Mövenpick, Waterstrasse, B, 262 b, Sb.

*Kurhotel Bad Zurzach, A, 134 b, Sp; *Park-Hotel Bad Zurzach, A, 335 b, Sb;   **Zurzach**
*Zurzacherhof Bad Zurzach, A, 73 b; Post Bad Zurzach, B, 44 b; Turmhotel
Bad Zurzach, B, 44 b, Sp; Gasthaus zur Waag, C, 29 b; Turmpavillon Bad
Zurzach, C, 135 b, Sp; Ochsen, E, 10 b.

Residence Simmental, C, 28 b; Sonnegg Rel. D. Silence, C, 20 b; Krone, D,   **Zweisimmen**
50 b; Sport Motel, D, 50 b.

Information

Swiss National Tourist Office (Schweizerische Verkehrszentrale – SVZ)

Bellariastrasse 38
CH-8027 Zürich
Tel. (01) 202 37 37

Swiss National Tourist Office   In GB
Swiss Centre, 1 New Coventry Street
London
W1V 3HG
Tel. (071) 734 1921

Swiss National Tourist Office   USA
Swiss Center, 608 Fifth Avenue
New York
NY 10020
Tel. (0212) 757 5944

Swiss National Tourist Office
250 Stockton Street
San Francisco
CA 94108
Tel. (0415) 362 2260

Swiss National Tourist Office   Canada
Commerce Court West, Suite No 2015
P.O. Box 215, Commerce Court Postal Station
Toronto, Ont. M5L 1EB
Tel. (0416) 868 0584

Regional Tourist Offices

Verkehrsverein, Alexanderstrasse 24, CH-7001 Chur,   Grisons
tel. (081) 22 13 60

Verkehrsverband, Bahnhofplatz 1a, CH-9001, St Galler,   East Switzerland
tel. (071) 22 62 62   and the
Principality of
Liechtenstein
Verkehrsverein, Bahnhofbrücke 1, CH-8023 Zürich,   Zurich
tel. (01) 211 12 56

Verkehrsverband, Alpenstrasse 1, CH-6002 Lucerne,   Central
tel. (041) 51 18 91   Switzerland

Verkehrsverein, Blumenrain 2, CH-4001 Basle,   North-west
tel. (061) 25 50 50   Switzerland

Information

Bernese Oberland	Verkehrsverband, Jungfraustrasse 38, CH-3800 Interlaken, tel. (036) 22 26 21
Bernese Mittelland	Verkehrsverband (at the station), CH-3001 Berne, tel. (031) 22 12 12
Fribourg	Union Fribourgeoise du Tourisme, rue de la Carrière 4, CH-1700 Fribourg 3, tel. (037) 24 56 44
Neuchâtel	Fédération Neuchâteloise du Tourisme, Place des Halles, CH-2001 Neuchâtel, tel. (038) 25 17 89
Jura	Office Jurassien du Tourisme, Place de la Gare 12, CH-2800 Delémont, tel. (066) 22 97 77
Berne Jura	Office du Tourisme du Jura Bernois, Avenue de la Poste 26, CH-2740 Moutier, tel. (032) 93 64 66
Lake Geneva District	Office du Tourisme, Avenue de Mon-Repos 3, CH-1005 Lausanne, tel. (021) 22 77 82
Valais	Union Valaisanne du Tourisme, rue de Lausanne 15, CH-1951 Sion, tel. (027) 22 31 61
Ticino	Ente Ticinese per il Turismo, Villa Turrita, CH-6501 Bellinzona, tel. (092) 25 70 56.

Information Offices in Towns and Communities

Aarau	Verkehrsbüro, Bahnhofstrasse 20, CH-5000 Aarau, tel. (064) 24 76 24
Adelboden	Kur- und Verkehrsverein, CH-3715 Adelboden, tel (033) 73 22 52
Aigle	Office du Tourisme, Avenue de la Gare 4, tel. (025) 26 12 12
Altdorf	Verkehrsbüro, Tellspielhaus, CH-6460 Altdorf, tel. (044) 228 88
Andermatt	Verkehrsbüro, Bahnhofplatz, CH-6490 Andermatt, tel. (044) 6 74 54
Appenzell	Verkehrsbüro, Hauptgasse 19, CH-9050 Appenzell (AI), tel. (071) 87 41 11
Apenzeller Land	Appenzell-Ausserrhoden: see Appenzell (AI) Appenzell-Innerhoden: Verkehrsbüro, Oberdorfstrasse 29, CH-9100 Herisau (AR), tel. (071) 51 44 60
Arbon	Verkehrsbüro, Bahnhofstrasse 25, CH-9320 Arbon, tel (071) 46 55 77
Arolls	Office du Tourisme, CH-1961 Arolla, tel. (027) 83 10 83
Arosa	Kur- und Verkehrsverein, opposite the Kursaal, CH-7050 Arosa, tel. (081) 31 16 21
Ascona	Ente turistico di Ascona e Losone, Via B Papio, CH-6612 Ascona, tel. (093) 35 55 44
Bad	See main name
Baden	Kur- und Verkehrsbüro, Bahnhofstrasse 50, CH-5400 Baden, tel. (056) 22 53 18
Basle	Verkehrsverein, Schifflände 5, CH-4001 Basle, tel. (061) 25 50 50 Central information offices: Bahnhof SBB, CH-4051, Basle, tel. (061) 22 36 84 Messeplatz 7, CH-4021 Basle, tel. (061) 691 77 00

Kur- und Verkehrsverein, CH-3803 Beatenberg, tel. (036) 41 12 86	**Beatenberg**
Verkehrsbüro, CH-6375 Beckenried, tel. (041) 64 31 70	**Beckenried**
Ente Turistico di Bellinzona e Dintorni, Via Camminata, CH-6500 Bellinzona, tel. (092) 25 21 31	**Bellinzona**
Verkehrsverein "Pro Bregaglia", CH-7605 Stampa, tel. (082) 15 55	**Bergeli**
Verkehrs- und Kongressbüro (at the station), P.O.B. 2700, CH-3001 Berne, tel. (031) 22 76 76	**Berne**
See Interlaken	**Berner Oberland**
See Pontresina	**Bernina**
Verkehrsbüro, CH-3981 Bettmeralp, tel. (028) 27 12 91	**Bettmeralp**
Verkehrsbüro, Bahnhofplatz, CH-2500 Bienne/Biel, tel. (032) 22 75 75	**Bienne/Biel**
Internationaler Bodensee-Verkehrsverein (IBV), Schützenstrasse 8, D-7550 Konstanz, tel. (075) 31 2 22 32	**Lake Constance**
See Arbon	
See Kreuzlingen	
See Rorschach	
Kur- und Verkehrsverein, CH-3784 Braunwald, tel. (058) 84 11 08	**Braunwald**
Verkehrsbüro, CH-3983 Breiten ob Mörel, tel. (028) 27 13 45	**Breiten ob Mörel**
Verkehrsbüro, CH-3855 Brienz, tel. (036) 51 32 42	**Brienz am See**
Verkehrsbüro, Marktplatz, CH-3900 Brig, tel. (028) 23 19 01	**Brig**
Ente Turistico di Brissago e Ronco, CH-6614 Brissago, tel. (093) 65 11 70	**Brissago**
Kur- und Verkehrsverein, Bahnhofstrasse 32, CH-6440 Brunnen, tel. (043) 31 17 77	**Brunnen**
Bürgenstock-Hotels, CH-6366 Bürgenstock LU, tel. (041) 61 55 45	**Bürgenstock**
Verkehrsbüro, CH-7505 Celerina, tel. (082) 3 39 66	**Celerina**
Office du Tourisme, CH-1874 Champéry, tel. (025) 79 11 41	**Champéry**
Office du Tourisme, La Place, CH-1837 Château d'Oex, tel. (029) 4 77 88	**Château-d'Oex**
Office de Tourisme, CH-2300 La Chaux-de-Fonds, tel. (039) 28 13 13	**La Chaux-de-Fonds**
Office du Tourisme, CH-1605 Chexbres, tel. (021) 346 22 31	**Chexbres**
See Mendrisio	**Chiasso**
Verkehrsverein, Ottostrasse 8, CH-7000 Chur, tel. (081) 22 18 18	**Chur**
Office du Tourisme Crans sur Sierre, CH-3985 Crans, tel. (027) 41 21 32 Office du Tourisme Montana-Vermala, CH-3962 Montana, tel. (027) 41 30 41	**Crans-Montana**
Verkehrsverein, Promenade 87, CH-7270 Davos Platz, tel. (083) 3 51 35 Informationsbüro, Bahnhofstrasse 7, CH-7270 Davos Dorf	**Davos**

Information

Delémont
Office du Tourisme, Place de la Gare 12, CH-2800 Delémont,
tel. (066) 22 97 78

Les Diablerets
Office du Tourisme, Bâtiment BCV, CH-1856 Les Diablerets,
tel. (025) 53 13 58

Disentis/Mustér
Kur- und Verkehrsverein, CH-7180 Disentis, tel. (086) 7 58 22

Einsiedeln
Verkehrsbüro, CH-8840 Einsiedeln, tel.(055) 53 44 88

Emmental
Verkehrsverband Emmental, Mühlgässli 2,
CH-3350 Langnau im Emmental, tel. (035) 2 42 52

Engadin/
Engiadina
Oberengadiner Verkehrsverein, CH-7504 Pontresina,
tel. (082) 8 85 75; See Zernez

Engelberg
Kur- und Verkehrsverein, Dorfstrasse 34, CH-6390 Engelberg,
tel. (041) 94 11 61

Entlebuch
Verkehrsverein Zentralschweiz, Pilatusstrasse 14, CH-6002 Lucerne,
tel. (041) 23 70 45

Fiesch
Verkehrsverein Fiesch-Fiescherthal, CH-3984 Fiesch, tel. (028) 71 14 66

Flims
Kur- und Verkehrsverein Flims, CH-7018 Flims-Waldhaus, tel. (081) 39 10 22

Flüelen
Verkehrsbüro, near the old church, CH-6454 Flüelen

Flumserberg
Kur- und Verkehrsverein Flumserberg, CH-8898 Flumserberg,
tel. (085) 3 32 28

Frauenfeld
Verkehrsbüro, Rathausplatz 1, CH-8500 Frauenfeld, tel. (054) 21 31 28

Fribourg/
Freiburg
Office du Tourisme, Square-des-Places 1, CH-1700 Fribourg,
tel. (037) 81 31 75

Geneva
Office du Tourisme, Gare Cornavin, CH-1201 Geneva, tel. (022) 738 52 00

Lake Geneva
Office du Tourisme du Canton de Vaud (OTV), Avenue d'Ouchy 60,
CH-1000 Lausanne-Ouchy, tel. (021) 27 72 02

See Chexebres

See Geneva

See Morges

Glarner Land
Verkehrsverein Glarner Land und Walensee, Info-Stelle, Raststätte N3,
CH-8867 Niedermann, tel. (058) 21 21 25

Glarus
Verkehrsbüro, Kirchweg 18, CH-8750 Glarus, tel. (058) 61 13 47

Grächen
Kur- und Verkehrsverein, CH-3925 Grächen, tel. (028) 56 13 00

Graubünden
Verkehrsverein Graubünden (WGR), Alexanderstrasse 24,
CH-7000 Chur, tel. (081) 22 13 60

Gruyère
Office du Tourisme, CH-1661 Pringy, tel. (029) 6 10 36

Grimentz
Office du Tourisme, CH-3961 Grimentz, tel. (027) 65 14 93

Grindelwald
Verkehrsbüro, CH-3818 Grindelwald, tel. (036) 53 12 12

Verkehrsbüro, CH-3780 Gstaad, tel. (030) 4 10 55 — **Gstaad**

Verkehrsbüro, Seeallee, CH-9410 Heiden, tel. (071) 91 10 96 — **Heiden**

Verkehrsbüro, CH-7130 Ilanz, tel. (086) 2 20 70 — **Ilanz**

Verkehrsverein, Höheweg 37, CH-3800 Interlaken, tel. (036) 22 21 21 — **Interlaken**

See Interlaken — **Jungfrau Region**

Bahnen der Jungfrau Region, CH-3800 Interlaken, tel. (036) 22 52 52

Office Jurassien du Tourisme pro Jura, rue de l'Hôtel de Ville 16, CH-2740 Moutier, tel. (032) 93 18 24 — **Jura**

Verkehrsbüro, CH-3718 Kandersteg, tel. (033) 75 12 34 — **Kandersteg**

Kur- und Verkehrsverein, CH-7250 Klosters, tel. (083) 4 18 77 — **Klosters**

Verkehrsbüro, Haupstrasse 1a, CH-8280 Kreuzlingen, tel. (072) 72 38 40 — **Kreuzlingen**

Verkehrsbüro, CH-6403 Küssnacht. tel. (041) 81 33 30 — **Küssnacht am Rigi**

Verkehrsbüro, Center Communal, CH-7031 Laax, tel. (086) 3 43 43 — **Laax**

See Ascona — **Lake Maggiore**

See Grissago

See Locarno

Office du Tourisme et des Congrès, Avenue de Rhodanie 2, CH-1000 Lausanne 6, tel. (021) 617 73 21.
Branches: Hauptbahnhof (Zentralhalle, tel. (021) 617 14 27).
Geneva Cointrin Airport (Auskunfthalle, tel. (022) 98 45 73).
Palais de Beaulieu, Centre des Congrès et Expositions,
Avenue des Bergières 10, CH-1000 Lausanne, tel. (021) 45 11 11.
Office du Tourisme du Canton de Vaud, Avenue d'Ouchy 60,
CH-1000 Lausanne, tel. (021) 27 72 02. — **Lausanne**

Verkehrsverein, CH-3822 Lauterbrunnen, tel. (036) 55 19 55 — **Lauterbrunnen**

Kur- und Verkehrsverein, CH-3775 Lenk im Simmental, tel. (030) 3 15 95 — **Lenk**

Kur- und Verkehrsverein, CH-7078 Lenzerheide, tel. (081) 34 34 34 — **Lenzerhide-Valbella**

Verkehrsverein, CH-3954 Leukerbad, tel. (027) 62 11 11 — **Leukerbad/ Loèche-les-Bains**

See Vaduz — **Liechtenstein**

Ente Turistico di Locarno e Valli, Via F Balli 2, tel. (093) 31 86 33 — **Locarno**

Verkehrsverein Lötschental, CH-3903 Kippel, tel. (028) 49 13 88 — **Lötschental**

See Lugano — **Lake Lugano**

Ente Touristico del Ceresio, Via Pocobelli 14, CH-6815 Melide, tel. (091) 68 63 83

Ente Turistico Lugano e Dintorni, Riva Albertolli 5, CH-6901 Lugano, tel. (091) 21 46 64 — **Lugano**

Information

Lucerne	Verkehrsverein, Frankenstrasse 1, CH-6002 Lucerne, tel. (041) 51 71 71
Martigny	Office Régional du Tourisme, CH-1920 Martigny, tel. (026) 22 10 18
Meiringen	Verkehrsverein Meiringen-Haslital, CH-3860 Meiringen, tel. (036) 71 43 22
Mendrisio	Ente Turistico del Mendrisiotto e Basso Ceresio, Via Zorzi, CH-6850 Mendrisio, tel. (091) 46 57 61
Montreux	Office du Tourisme, Grand-Rue 42, CH-1820 Montreux, tel. (021) 963 12 12
Morges	Office du Tourisme, Grand-Rue 80, CH-1110 Morges, tel. (021) 71 32 33
Mürren	Kur- und Verkehrsverein, CH-3825 Mürren, tel. (036) 55 16 16
Morat/Murten	Verkehrsbüro, Schlossgasse 5, CH-3280 Morat/Murten, tel. (037) 71 51 12
Neuchâtel	Office du Tourisme de Neuchâtel et environs, rue de la Place d'Armes 7, CH-2001 Neuchâtel, tel. (038) 25 42 42
Nyon	Office du Tourisme, Avenue Viollier 7, CH-1260 Nyon, tel. (022) 61 62 61
Oberhalbstein/ Sursée	See Savognin
	See Tiefencastel
Oberhofen on Lake Thun	Verkehrsbüro, CH-3653 Oberhofen am Thuner See, tel. (033) 43 14 19
Olten	Verkehrsbüro, Bahnhofpassage, CH-4600 Olten, tel. (062) 26 16 16
Pontresina	Kur- und Verkehrsverein, CH-7504 Pontresina, tel. (082) 6 64 88
Porrentruy	Syndicat d'Initiative Régional d'Ajoie du Clos-du-Doubs (SIR), CH-2900 Porrentruy, tel. (066) 66 18 53
Bad Ragaz	Kur- und Verkehrsverein, Haus Schweizerhof, CH-7310 Bad Ragaz, tel. (085) 9 10 61
Rapperswil	Verkehrsbüro, Am Seequai, CH-8640 Rapperswil, tel. (055) 27 70 00
Rhine	See Aarau
	See Basle
	See Frauenfeld
	See Graubünden
	See St. Gallen
	See Schaffhausen
	See Zürich
Rheinfall	Verkehrsbüro, Industriestrasse 39, CH-8212 Neuhausen am Rheinfall, tel. (053) 2 74 55
Rheinfelden	Kur- und Verkehrsverein, Marktgasse 61, CH-4310 Rheinfelden, tel. (061) 8 55 20

Union Valaisanne du Tourisme, Lausanne 15, CH-1950 Sion, tel. (027) 22 31 61; Office du Tourisme du Canton de Vaud, Avenue de la Gare 10, CH-1002 Lausanne, tel. (021) 22 77 82. **Rhônetal/ Vallée du Rhône**

See Geneva.

Verkehrsverein, CH-3981 Riederalp, tel. (028) 27 13 65 **Riederalp**

Verkehrsbüro, CH-6356 Rigi-Kaltbad, tel. (041) 83 11 28 **Rigi**

Association des Intérêts du Cœur de la Côte et Office du Tourisme, Grand-Rue 6, CH-1180 Rolle, tel. (021) 825 15 35 **Rolle**

Verkehrsbüro, Neugasse 2, CH-9400 Rorschach, tel. (071) 41 70 34 **Rorschach**

Verkehrsverein, CH-3908 Saas Fee, tel. (028) 57 14 57 **Saas Fee**

See Saas Fee **Saas Tal**

Verkehrsverein, CH-6549 San Bernardino, tel. (092) 94 12 14 **San Bernardino**

Verkehrsverein, Bahnhofplatz 1a, CH-9001 St Gallen, tel. (071) 22 62 62 **St Gallen**

See Andermatt **St Gotthard**

Office du Tourisme, Grand-Rue 48, CH-1890 St-Maurice, tel. (025) 65 27 77 **St-Maurice**

Kur- und Verkehrsverein, CH-7500 St Moritz, tel. (082) 3 31 47 **St Moritz**

Kur- und Verkehrsverein, Plazzet, CH-7503 Samedan, tel. (082) 6 54 32 **Samedan**

Verkehrsbüro, Hofstrasse 2, CH-6060 Sarnen, tel. (041) 66 40 55 **Sarnen**

Kur- und Verkehrsverein, CH-7460 Savognin, tel. (081) 74 22 22 **Savognin**

Verkehrsverein, Vorstadt 12, CH-8202 Schaffhausen, tel. (053) 5 51 41 **Schaffhausen**

Säntisbahn (Urnäsch), tel. (071) 53 19 21 **Schwägalp**

Nationalparkhaus Zernez, CH-7530 Zernez, tel. (082) 8 13 78 **Schweizer Nationalpark**

Verkehrsverein, Postplatz 9, CH-6430 Schwyz, tel. (043) 21 34 46 **Schwyz**

Kur- und Verkehrsverein, CH-7550 Bad Scuol, tel. (084) 9 94 94 **Bad Scuol**

Office du Tourisme, Max-Huber Strasse 2, CH-3960 Sierre, tel. (027) 55 85 35 **Siders/Sierre**

See Lenk **Simmental**

See Zweisimmen

Verkehrsverein, CH-3901 Simplon-Dorf, tel. (028) 29 11 34 **Simplon/ Sempione**

Office du Tourisme de Sion et Environs, Planta 3, CH-1950 Sion, tel. (027) 22 85 86 **Sion/Sitten**

Information

Solothurn/ **Soleurs**	Verkehrsbüro, Hauptgasse 69, CH-4500 Solothurn, tel. (065) 22 19 24
Spiez	Verkehrsverein, Bahnhofstrasse 12, CH-3700 Spiez, tel. (033) 54 21 38
Stans	Verkehrsverein Stans und Umgebung, Stansstaderstrasse 19, CH-6370 Stans, tel. (041) 61 32 17
Stansstad	Verkehrsbüro, Dorfplatz 13, CH-6362 Stansstad, tel. (041) 61 13 77
Stein am Rhein	Verkehrsbüro, Oberstadt 4, CH-8260 Stein am Rhein, tel. (054) 41 28 35
Sursee	Verkehrsbüro, Oberstadt 7, CH-6210 Sursee, tel. (045) 21 19 77
Ticino	Ente Ticinese per il Turismo, Piazza Nosetto, CH-6501 Bellinzona, tel. (092) 25 70 56. See Bellinzona, Locarno, Lugano
Teufen	Verkehrsverein, Bahnhof, CH-9053 Teufen, tel. (033) 38 73
Thun	Verkehrsverein, Bahnhofplatz, CH-3600 Thun, tel. (033) 22 23 40
Lake Thun	Verkehrsverband Thuner See, Thunstrasse 4, CH-3700 Spiez, tel. (033) 54 72 56. See also Brienz, Interlaken, Thun
Thurgau	See Frauenfeld
Tiefencastel	Verkehrsverein, Julierstrasse 42, CH-7450 Tiefencastel. tel. (081) 71 12 71
Vaduz	Liechtensteinische Fremdenvehrkehrszentrale, Städtle 37, FL-9490 Vaduz, tel. (075) 2 14 43
Verbier	Office du Tourisme, CH-1936 Verbier, tel. (026) 31 62 22
Vevey	Association des Intérêts de Vevey et environs, Place de la Gare 5, CH-1800 Vevey, tel. (021) 921 48 25
Villars-sur-Ollon	Office du Tourisme, CH-1884 Villars-sur-Ollon, tel. (025) 35 32 32
Vitznau	Verkehrsbüro, CH-6354 Vitznau, tel. (041) 83 13 55
Vierwaldstätter **See**	Verkehrsverband Zentralschweiz, Alpenstrasse 1, CH-6002 Lucerne, tel. (041) 51 18 91
Bad Vulpera	Kur- und Verkehrsverein, CH-7552 Bad Vulpera, tel. (084) 9 09 44
Walensee	See Walenstadt, Weesen.
Walenstadt	Verkehrsbüro, Seestrasse, CH-8880 Walenstadt, tel. (085) 3 55 45
Wallis	Union Valaisanne du Tourisme, rue de Lausanne 15, CH-1950 Sion, tel. (027) 22 31 61
Weesen	Verkehrsverein, Kirchgasse, CH-8872 Weesen, tel. (058) 43 12 30
Weggis	Kur- und Verkehrsverein, CH-6353 Weggis, tel. (041) 93 11 55
Wengen	Verkehrsbüro, CH-3823 Wengen, tel. (036) 55 14 14
Winterthur	Verkehrsbüro, Bahnhofplatz 12, CH-8400 Winterthur, tel. (052) 22 00 88

Kur- und Verkehrsverein, Place Pestalozzi, CH-1400 Yverdon-les-Bains, **Yverdon-les-**
tel. (024) 21 01 21 **Bains**

Kur- und Verkehrsverein, Bahnhofplatz, CH-3920 Zermatt, **Zermatt**
tel. (028) 66 11 81

Verkehrsbüro, CH-7530 Zernez, tel. (082) 8 13 00 **Zernez**

Verkehrsbüro, Sternengasse 3, CH-4800 Zofingen, tel. (062) 51 65 22 **Zofingen**

Verkehrsverband des Kantons Zug, Bahnhofstrasse 23, CH-6300 Zug, tel. **Zug**
(042) 21 00 78

Schweizerische Verkehrszentrale, Bellariastrasse 38, CH-8023 Zürich, **Zürich**
tel. (01) 202 37 37.
Offizielles Verkehrsbüro (Auskunft, Zimmernachwies), Bahnhofplatz 15,
Hauptbahnhof, CH-8023 Zürich, tel. (01) 2 11 40 00.
Verkehrsverein Zürich, Direktion, Kongressbüro, Bahnhofbrücke 1,
CH-8023 Zürich, tel. (01) 2 11 12 56

Kur- und Verkehrsverein, Quellenstrasse 1, CH-8437 Zurzach, **Zurzach**
tel. (056) 49 24 00

Verkehrsverein, Lenkstrasse, CH-3770 Zweisimmen, tel. (030) 2 11 33 **Zweisimmen**

Additional Useful Addresses

See Breakdown Services — Automobile Clubs

See Diplomatic and Consular Information — Embassies

See relevant town — Airlines

Handelskämmer Deutschland-Schweiz — Swiss-German Chamber of Commerce
Talacker 14
CH-8001 Zürich
Tel. (01) 22 37 02

See Diplomatic and Consular Information — Consulates

See entry — Emergencies

Schweizer Kulturstiftung Pro Helvetia — **Swiss Cultural Information**
Hirschgraben 22, CH-8024 Zürich

See Railways, Schweizerische Bundesbahnen (SBB) — SBB

Information Services for Switzerland: tel. 111 — **Telephone Services**

Road Conditions: tel. 163

Snow Forecast (Dec.–March): tel. 120

Tourist Bulletin (April–November): tel. 120

Avalanche Bulletin (November–May): tel. 187

Weather Forecast: tel. 162.

Insurance

Since there is no national health service in Switzerland and medical treat- General
ment must be paid for, it is advisable to take out insurance cover against

personal accident and sickness, as well as loss of, or damage to, luggage and personal effects. Special winter sports policies are obtainable.

Vehicles   Visitors to Switzerland who travel in their own vehicles should be in possession of an international insurance certificate ("Green Card") which can be obtained from the vehicles' normal insurers. The insurance effected in the United Kingdom normally only covers third party risks abroad and it is very desirable to have the fuller protection which the "Green Card" affords.

Motoring

Roadside Assistance

Automobile Club of Switzerland (Automobil Club der Schweiz, Automobile Club de Suisse (ACS)

Headquarters:
Wasserwerkgasse 39
CH-3000 Berne 13
Tel. (031) 22 47 22

Branch offices in the larger Swiss towns.

Traffic information: tel. 163

Touring Club of Switzerland (TCS) (Touring-Club der Schweiz, Touring Club Suisse (TCS)

Headquarters:
Touring Club Suisse
9 rue Pierre-Fatio
CH-1211 Genève 3
Tel. (022) 7 37 12 12

Branch offices and information bureaux in the larger Swiss towns.

Emergency headquarters and traffic information: tel. (022) 35 80 00

Breakdown   Touring Breakdown Service (24 hours a day): tel. 140.
If you are in a rented vehicle (see entry) it is best to contact the firm from which the vehicle was rented.

Emergencies   See entry.

Accidents in Switzerland. What to do

Immediate measures   However careful a driver you are an accident can always happen; even when you are very angry keep calm and be polite. Keep a cool head and take the following steps in order:

Security   1 Make the scene of the accident as safe as possible. Turn on your hazard lights, put out your warning triangle at a suitable distance.

Injured   2 Take care of anyone who is injured, and send for an ambulance if necessary.

Police   3 If there are any injured it is best to inform the police who will take charge of things for you.

Information   4 Make sure that you obtain a copy of a certificate from the police on which all possible information about the other driver or drivers is given. Make a note of the names and addresses of the other people concerned in the accident, take details of the number and make of the vehicles involved as well as the names and numbers of the insurance companies concerned. It is also important to make a note of the place and time of the accident and the address of the police station from which the officer concerned is stationed.

5 Make sure you have all the evidence possible. Write down the names and addresses of, if possible, independent witnesses. Make sketches of the situation at the scene of the accident, or better still if you have a camera, take several snaps from various directions.

6 If possible fill in a European accident report (obtainable from your insurance company) and get it countersigned by any other driver involved. Do not sign any admission of guilt and especially do not sign any paper in a language which you do not understand.

After an accident repairs should be undertaken as soon as possible. Note the following:

1 If a claim is made against you inform your own insurance company. You can also get in touch with the Swiss insurance company whose name and address are on your Green Card.

2 Make your own claims for repair against the person who caused the accident and against his own insurance company. The Green Card is not much help here. To take care of the costs of your own claims a full comprehensive insurance is essential.

Traffic Regulations

In Switzerland and Liechtenstein as in the rest of continental Europe vehicles travel on the right and overtake on the left.

Traffic signs correspond with the international norm. In built up areas trams and other vehicles on rails have priority at crossings and also at the junction of roads of equal status; otherwise traffic coming from the right has full priority. On mountain stretches, vehicles ascending have priority. In tunnels and rock galleries dipped headlights must be used. In the case of an accident on a main road the warning triangle must be set up at least 150 m/165 yards from the vehicle, and on other roads 50 m/55 yards away, after which the hazard lights must be switched off. Motorcyclists are recommended to have dipped headlights on while travelling and must wear a helmet.

On motorways 120 kmph/75 mph, On main roads 80 kmph/50 mph, In built up areas 50 kmph/35 mph. Drivers are earnestly advised to keep strictly to speed limits as even minor infringements attract heavy fines.

Seat belts are compulsory in Switzerland; non-compliance leads to fines.

The maximum blood alcohol level permitted is 0.8 per cent.

Caravans exceeding 2.1 m/6.9 ft in width and 6 m/19.7 ft in length must obtain a special permit at the frontier. With this they are allowed up to 2.2 m/7.2 ft wide and 7 m/23 ft on normal roads but only up to a length of 6.5 m/21.3 ft on mountain roads. The speed limit for caravans is 80 kmph/50 mph.

There are various limits for motor caravans over 3.5 tonnes permitted weight. The regulations should be obtained before leaving for Switzerland. Information can be obtained from the Federal Customs Headquarters (Eidgenössische Oberzolldirektion: see Customs Regulations).

Snow chains are essential in winter in the mountainous areas of Switzerland. They are not allowed in long road tunnels.

Private vehicles with spiked tyres are only permitted from the 1st November to 31st March (maximum speed 80 kmph/50 mph). With the exception of the N2 between Göschenen and Airolo (The Gotthard Road Tunnel) and the N13 between Thusis and Mesocco spiked tyres are not allowed on motorways and main roads.

Accidents   In the case of accidents where there are casualties the police must be called. If there is an accident causing damage the police need not be informed but in many cases this is strongly recommended.

See also Emergencies.

Mountaineering

Switzerland is the classic country for mountaineering, which has become increasingly popular as a sport since the middle of the 19th c., when it was pioneered by British climbers at Zermatt. The Swiss Alpine Club, founded in 1863, has built up a network of paths and huts to facilitate access to the mountains; and the central Alps, with numerous peaks rising to over 4000 m (13,124 ft), offer the most magnificent glacier walks and climbs in the whole of the Alps.

Equipment   There is sometimes a tendency nowadays to underestimate the importance of proper equipment; but this is essential for safe and enjoyable climbing or mountain walking. It is important to have weather-proof (and not too light) clothing, warm underwear, woollen socks, a light waterproof windbreaker and good climbing boots, which must have treaded rubber soles. The rucksack, which should have broad straps, should contain only the most essential requirements (the guides are not required to carry more than 7 kg (15 lbs) in addition to their own equipment). A small reserve of food (biscuits, chocolate, dried fruit, etc.) should always be carried. Other indispensable items are sun-glasses, sunburn cream (and for many people also a lip cream) and adhesive bandages.

Guides   The guides are subject to control by the Swiss Alpine Club and the cantonal authorities, who issue guides' licences only after testing their competence. The regulations on charges, food, carrying of luggage, etc., may vary from canton to canton, it is desirable, therefore, before engaging a guide to ask to see the list of charges and the local regulations and to check that the guide is insured.

Climbing without a guide is now very common; but it should be attempted only by climbers whose own competence on rock and ice, judgment and fitness are not much below those of the professional guides, or who are climbing with experienced Alpine mountaineers. Many accidents occur through a climber's ignorance of the hidden dangers in an apparently easy route, through losing the way when there is a sudden change in the weather or as a result of inadequate equipment. In the high mountains no one should climb alone; but it is also necessary to be wary of uninvited companions, who may give rise to grave difficulties or dangers. In the climbs mentioned in this Guide the need for a guide is indicated where appropriate.

Glaciers   Glaciers must be crossed early in the day, before the sun softens the snow covering the crevasses. Even experienced climbers should never tackle a glacier without a guide and a rope.

Mountain   At altitudes above 4000 m (13,124 ft) or so, and for some people even below
Sickness   this, mountain sickness can be a problem. The symptoms are palpitations, dizziness, loss of consciousness and bleeding from the mouth and nose. The best remedies are rest, stimulants and, most effective of all, an immediate descent to a lower altitude.

In the high Alps

Weather conditions in the Alps, particularly on their north-western and northern slopes, are unreliable and full of potential danger for the climber. Two generally accepted indications of good weather are a fall in temperature in the evening, when the wind blows down into the valley after blowing up on to the mountains during the day, and a fresh fall of snow on the peaks. The "föhn" which makes the mountains appear nearer and dark blue in colour, often brings a long period of beautiful weather, though this may change suddenly at any time. Signs of bad weather are the appearance of cirrus clouds moving from W to E (even though they may disappear in the early afternoon), swirls of dust on the roads and driving snow on the ridges and peaks when the weather is otherwise good. In rainy weather there is increased danger of rock falls. In the event of a thunderstorm do not stand under isolated trees, haystacks, etc., in view of the danger of being struck by lightning; come down from the peaks and ridges at once, and keep away from running water.

Weather conditions

Weather forecasts are posted up at stations and post offices and given daily on the radio. They can also be obtained by telephone (dial 162).

Alpenglow (German Alpenglühen) is the reddish light cast by the setting sun on the rocky and snow-covered summits; in particular it is the after-glow of yellow, purple and violet hues which occurs 5-10 minutes after sunset when there is a slight build-up of clouds in the west and twilight has already fallen in the valleys.

Alpenglow

The international Alpine distress signal, for climbers who need help, is a series of six signals given at regular intervals within a minute by whatever means are available (blasts on a whistle, shouts, flashes of a torch, waves of some conspicuous article), followed by a minute's pause, a repetition of the signals, and so on until an answer is received. The answer takes the form of three signals at regular intervals within a minute.

Alpine Distress Signal

Mountaineering

The Swiss Alpine Club has established a large number of rescue stations and reporting posts to ensure that in the event of an accident help can be summoned quickly.

The Swiss
Alpine Club
(SAC)

The Swiss Alpine Club, founded in 1863, maintains some 150 mountain huts, which are open to non-members as well as members of the club. In some of them there are limited facilities for obtaining food during the summer; in most of them, however, there is no warden, and it is therefore, necessary to inquire in the valley below about the means of gaining access, and sometimes to take the key with you. The charges for overnight accommodation are posted up in the huts.

Climbing
Schools

There are a number of excellently run climbing schools in Switzerland, providing instruction both for beginners and for those who want to learn specialised techniques. In most schools it is also possible to obtain guides. There are such schools, for example, at Wildhaus, Andermatt, Davos, Les Diablerets, Fiesch, La Fouly/Verbier, Grindelwald, Klosters, Pontresina, Meiringen, Kandersteg/Schwarenbach, Arolla and Villars-Chesières.

Information

Swiss Federation of Climbing Schools (Schweizerische Verband der Bergsteigerschulen)
c/o Ecole Suisse d'Alpinisme
CH-1874 Champéry
tel. (025) 79 14 30

Mountain Railways, Cableways

These various forms of mountain transport are of great importance in Switzerland, and of particular value to tourists. Apart from the services they provide for winter sports enthusiasts they also enable the older or less strenuously inclined visitor to enjoy the experience of the mountain world.

Brienz-Rothorn railway

There are in all some 400 mountain railways and cableways, supplemented in winter by over 1200 ski-lifts. Some of the railways and cableways climb to heights of over 3000 m/9843 ft, such as those up the Kleines Matterhorn (3820 m/12,533 ft), Jungfrau (3457 m/11,342 ft), Gornergrat (3407 m/11,178 ft), Corvatsch (3298 m/10,820 ft), Piz Nair (3025 m/9925 ft) and Mont Gelé (3028 m/9938 ft).

There are the following types: Funicular (German Standseilbahn, French Funiculaire), in which the cars run on rails and are drawn by cable. Rack (Cog) Railway (Zahnradbahn, chemin de fer à crémaillère), with a middle rail fitted with a cog which engages with a pinion on the locomotive. Cableway (Seilschwebebahn or Luftseilbahn, téléférique or télécabine), with cabins for anything from 4 to 100 passengers suspended from a continuous cable. Chair-lift (Sesselbahn or Sessellift, télésiege), with open chairs (sometimes double) suspended from a continuous cable. Ski-lift (Skilift or Schlepplift, monte-pente), in which skiers are pulled uphill on their skis attached to a moving cable. Sledge-lift (Schlittenseilbahn, funiculaire à traîneaux), in which sledges are attached to a cable and drawn uphill. Many of these facilities operate for only part of the year.

Price reductions such as regional season-tickets (e.g holiday or winter sports season tickets) of the various Swiss cable-car undertakings can be obtained.

Reductions

Schweizerische Verband der Seilbahnunternehmungen
Dählhölzliweg 12,
CH-3006 Berne,
Tel. (031) 44 24 16

Information

Museums

Visitors who like the unusual will certainly find a museum to their taste in Switzerland. A selection of the many specialised museums is indicated on the map on page 536. Detailed descriptions can be found under the corresponding heading in the A-Z section.

● Specialist Museums

1 Geneva. Car and Motorcycle Museum

2 Geneva. Museum on the History of Science

3 Geneva. Watch-making Museum

4 Geneva. Museum of Historic Musical Instruments

5 Geneva. Professor F. Peus' Flea Collection

6 Geneva. Swiss Mercenary's Museum

7 Geneva. Philatelic Museum of the United Nations

8 Nyon. Porcelain Museum

9 Morges. Alexis Forel Doll and Toy Museum

10 Morges. Vaudois Military Museum

11 Morges. Armaments Museum

12 Lausanne. Pipe Tobacco Museum

13 Lausanne. Museum of the Olympic Games

14 Vevey. Food Museum

15 Vevey. Collection of Photographic Apparatus

Speciality Museums
in Switzerland

Selection
of museums ●

Ballenberg Open-air
Museum ●

16 La Tour de Peliz. Games Museum

17 Blonay. Railway Museum

18 Roche. Organ Museum

19 Aigle. Swiss Wine Museum

20 Bex. Le Bouillet Salt Mine with Museum

21 St-Maurice. Military Museum

22 Martigny. Car Museum of the Gianadda Foundation

23 Château d'Oex. Silhouette Museum

24 Rougemont. Fossils Museum

25 Gruyères. Cheese-making

26 Gruyères. Waxworks

27 Lucens. Sherlock Holmes Museum

28 La Sarraz. Horse Museum

29 Vallorbe. Gyger Railway Museum

30 L'Auberson. Baud Musical Automata

31 Ste-Croix. Musical Automata and Musical Instruments

32 Grandson. Vintage Cars

33 Yverdon. Science Fiction

34 Estavayer-le-Lac. Frogs

35 Avenches. Aircraft

36 Salavaux. Musical Automata

37 Boudry. Wine production

38 Colombier. Military Museum

39 Neuchâtel. Automata

40 Le Locle. Clock and watches

41 La Chaux-de-Fonds. Rural Life and Crafts

42 La Chaux-de-Fonds. Watches and Clocks

43 La Chaux-de-Fonds. Care of the Hair

44 Ligerz. Viticulture

45 Biel/Bienne. Buildings on Stilts

46 Biel/Bienne. Omega Watches and Clocks

47 Rizenbach. Jerisberghof Museum of Rural Life

48 Mühleberg. BKW Power-station

49 Fribourg. Marionettes

50 Romont. Church Windows

51 Spiez. Regional and Vine Growing Museum

52 Interlaken. Model Railway (Large Layout)

53 Kiesen. National Milk-production

54 Toffen. Old-timer Museum

55 Berne. Swiss Alpine Museum

56 Berne. Swiss Postal Museum

57 Berne. Swiss Riflemen's Museum

58 Berne. Bank Museum

59 Utzenstorf. Swiss Hunting Museum

60 Solothurn. Artillery Museum

61 Solothurn. Kreuzen Mineral Museum

62 Solothurn. Arsenal

63 Porrentruy. Apothecary Museum

64 Seewen. Musical Automata

65 Basle. Films

66 Basle. Rhine Shipping

67 Basle. Swiss Fire Service

68 Basle. Collection of Musical Instruments

69 Basle. Swiss Historic Paper Collection

70 Basle. Museum of the History of Pharmacy

71 Basle. Sports

72 Basle. Collection of Caricatures and Cartoons

73 Binningen. Automobile Collection

74 Münchenstein. Coaches and Sledges

75 Riehen. Toys

76 Riehen. Cats

77 Rheinfelden. Old-timer

78 Rheinfelden. Model Castles

79 Schönenwerd. Bally Shoe Museum

80 Zofingen. Ringier Printing Museum

81 Langenthal. Linen Museum

82 Altishofen. Woodwork Museum

83 Alberswil. Farming Museum

84 Baden. Power Station Museum

85 Baden. Toys

86 Buchs. Quartz Mining Museum

87 Wohlenschwil. Museum of Rural Life

88 Wohlen. Straw Museum

89 Sursee. Retonios Mechanical Music Museum

90 Lucerne. Transport Museum

91 Lucerne. Glacier Garden Museum

92 Lucerne. Wagner Museum in Tribschen

93 Lucerne. Swiss Costume and European Harmonica Museum

94 Lucerne. Museum of Contemporary Glass

95 Guttannen. Wirzen Crystal Museum

96 Bürglen. William Tell Museum

97 Schwyz. Tower Museum (Weapons, etc.)

98 Goldau. Rockfall Museum

99 Zug. Bee Museum

100 Affoltern. Model Railway and Cycle Museum

101 Wädenswil. Brewery Museum

102 Freienbach. Printing Museum

103 Wolfhausen. Bühler Cycle Museum

104 Zimmerwald. Museum of Wind Instruments

105 Volketswil. Corkscrew Museum

106 Zurich. Criminal Museum of the Cantonal Police

107 Zurich. Museum of Measurement of Time

108 Zurich. Sasha Morgenthaler Doll Museum

109 Zurich. Doll and Toy Museum

111 Zurich. Typewriter Museum

112 Zurich. Tiefenbrunnen Tramway Museum

113 Zurich. Indian Museum

114 Zurich. Swiss Country Museum

115 Zurich. Kulturama Anatomical Museum

116 Zurich. Railway Paradise Museum

117 Zurich. Coffee Museum

118 Zurich. Tiefenbrunnen Mill Museum

119 Zurich. University Medical History Collection

120 Au (Peninsular). Museum of Viticulture

121 Dübendorf. Museum of the Swiss Flying Troop

122 Winterthur. Kellenberg Watch and Clock Collection

123 Winterthur. Technorama

124 Winterthur. Coin Museum

125 Neftenbach. Museum of Viticulture

126 Eglisau. Fishing Museum

127 Schleitheim. Plaster Museum

128 Diessenhofen. Museum of Printed Materials

129 Stein am Rhein. Appenzell Cheese Factory (open to the public)

130 Stein am Rhein. Doll Museum

131 Steckborn. Bernina Sewing Machine Museum

132 Kreuzlingen. Fire Service Museum

133 Kreuzlingen. Radio and Communications Museum

134 Güttingen. Jeannine Doll Museum

135 Kradolf. Fire Service Museum

136 Amriswil. Collection of Coaches

137 St Gallen. Museum of Industry and Crafts

138 St Gallen. Textile Museum

139 St Gallen. Musical Box Museum

140 Teufen. Grubenmann Collections

141 Berneck. Radio Museum

142 Appenzell. Retonios Mechanical Music and Magic Museum

143 Appenzell. Retonios Museum of Rarities

144 Gossau. Hilti Motorcycle Museum

145 Degersheim. Retonios Magic Museum

146 Lichensteig. Fredys Museum of Mechanical Music

147 Unterwasser. Alpine Dairy Museum

148 Sargans. Old-Timer Museum

149 Sargans. Gonzen Mining Museum

150 Jenins. Museum of Viticulture

151 Pfäfers. Bath Museum

152 Chur. Collection of Coaches

153 Davos. Mining Museum

154 Lottigna. Military Museum

155 Melide. Swiss Miniatures

156 Meride. Fossil Museum

157 Gandria. Smugglers Museum

158 Bosco/Gurin. Walserhaus Museum

159 Riederalp. Alpine Museum

160 Zermatt. Alpine Museum

161 Leuk Stadt. Satellite Museum

162 Sierre. Tin Museum

Opening Times

See Business Hours

Passes and Tunnels

Pass Roads

Switzerland has many roads leading over passes, some of them among the most fascinating mountain roads in Europe. The main N–S connections are magnificently engineered, but some of the minor pass roads are closed in winter.

Information on the current road conditions and the opening times of Alpine passes can be obtained from the Automobil Club der Schweiz by telephoning 163.

Passes in Switzerland

See map below.

Alpine Road Tunnels

For travelling through the Great St Bernard, San Bernardino and St Gotthard tunnels which are open throughout the year, a toll is charged.

● Mountain passes over 1000 m/3282 ft

Altitude, maximum gradient/descent, and months when normally open are given after the name of the pass.

Mountain Passes in Switzerland

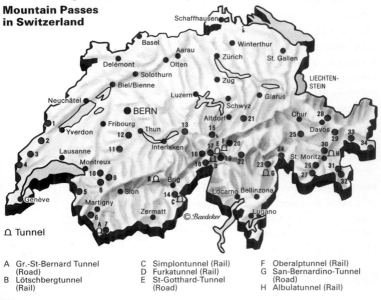

Ω Tunnel

A Gr.-St-Bernard Tunnel (Road)
B Lötschbergtunnel (Rail)
C Simplontunnel (Rail)
D Furkatunnel (Rail)
E St-Gotthard-Tunnel (Road)
F Oberalptunnel (Rail)
G San-Bernardino-Tunnel (Road)
H Albulatunnel (Rail)

1 Col des Etroits. 1153 m/3783 ft. Ste-Croix to Pontarlier (France).
Maximum gradient 10%. Open all year

2 Col de Mollendruz. 1180 m/3872 ft. Morges to Vallorbe.
Maximum gradient 7%. Open all year

3 Col du Marchairuz. 1447 m/4748 ft. Nyon to Le Brassus.
Maximum gradient 15%. Open all year

4 Col de la Givrine. 1228 m/4029 ft. Nyon to Morez (France).
Maximum gradient 14%. Open all year

5 Pas de Morgins. 1333 m/4492 ft. Monthey to Evian-les-Bains (France).
Maximum gradient 14%. Open all year

6 Col de la Forclaz. 1527 m/5010 ft. Martigny to Chamonix (France).
Maximum gradient 9%. Open all year

7 Grand St Bernard Pass. 2469 m/8010 ft. Martigny to Aosta (Italy).
Maximum gradient 11%. Open June to October. Road tunnel available

8 Col de la Croix. 1780 m/5340 ft. Villars to Les Diablerets.
Maximum gradient 13%. Open all year

9 Col du Pillon. 1546 m/5072 ft. Gstaad to Aigle.
Maximum gradient 11%. Open all year

10 Col des Mosses. 1445 m/4741 ft. Château d'Oex to Aigle.
Maximum gradient 10%. Open all year

11 Jaun Pass. 1509 m/4951 ft. Spiez to Bulle.
Maximum gradient 10%. Open all year

12 Selibühl Pass. 1587 m/5207 ft. Thun to Fribourg.
Maximum gradient 11%. Open all year

13 Brünig Pass. 1007 m/3304 ft. Lucerne to Brienz.
Maximum gradient 8%. Open all year

14 Simplon Pass. 2005 m/6578 ft. Brig to Domodóssola (Italy).
Maximum gradient 13%. Open all year

15 Susten Pass. 2224 m/7297 ft. Innertkirchen to Wassen.
Maximum gradient 9%. Open June to November

16 Grimsel Pass. 2165 m/7103 ft. Innertkirchen to Gletsch.
Maximum gradient 11%. Open June to October

17 Furka Pass. 2431 m/7976 ft. Gletsch to Andermatt.
Maximum gradient 14%. Open June to October

18 Nufenen (Novena) Pass. 2478 m/8130 ft. Ulrichen to Airolo.
Maximum gradient 10%. Open June to October

19 St Gotthard Pass. 2108 m/6916 ft. Andermatt to Airolo.
Maximum gradient 10%. Open May to October

20 Oberalp Pass. 2044 m/6706 ft. Andermatt to Disentis.
Maximum gradient 10%. Open May to November

21 Klausen Pass. 1948 m/6391 ft. Altdorf to Linthal.
Maximum gradient 10%. Open May to November

22 Lukmanier (Lucomagno) Pass. 1916 m/6286 ft. Disentis to Biasca.
Maximum gradient 10%. Open May to November

23 San Bernardino Pass. 2066 m/6779 ft. Splügen to Bellinzona.
Maximum gradient 15%. Open May to October

24 Splügen (Spluga) Pass. 2113 m/6933 ft. Splügen to Chiavenna (Italy).
Maximum gradient 13%. Open May to October

Passes and Tunnels

Wonderful Swiss scenery over the Nufenpass

25 Lenzerheide Pass. 1549 m/5082 ft. Chur to Tiefencastel.
Maximum gradient 10%. Open all year

26 Julier (Güglia) Pass. 2284 m/7494 ft. Tiefencastel to Silvaplana.
Maximum gradient 13%. Open all year

27 Maloja Pass. 1815 m/5955 ft. St Moritz to Chiavenna (Italy).
Maximum gradient 13%. Open all year

28 Wolfgang Pass. 1633 m/5358 ft. Klosters to Davos.
Maximum gradient 10%. Open all year

29 Flüela Pass. 2383 m/7819 ft. Davos to Susch.
Maximum gradient 10%. Open all year

30 Albula Pass. 2312 m/7586 ft. Filisur to La Punt-Chamues-ch.
Maximum gradient 12%. Open May to November.

31 Forcola di Livigno. 2315 m/7596 ft. Bernina Pass to Livigno (Italy).
Maximum gradient 12%. Open June to October

32 Bernina Pass. 2323 m/7622 ft. St Moritz to Tirano (Italy).
Maximum gradient 12%. Open all year

33 Ofen (Fuorn) Pass. 2149 m/7051 ft. Zernez to Santa Maria.
Maximum gradient 10%. Open all year

34 Umbrail Pass. 2501 m/8206 ft. Santa Maria to Bormio (Italy).
Maximum gradient 12%. Open May to November

Great St Bernard	Toll for cars: 15–34 sfr; if return journey is made within three days there is a reduction of 34%.
San Bernardino	Vignette required; no tunnel toll.
St Gotthard	Vignette required; no tunnel toll.

The Munt-la-Schera Tunnel (3.5 km/2 miles; open 8 a.m.–8 p.m.) from Zernez to Livigno (Italy) is subject to toll.

Munt-la-Schera Tunnel

Loading of cars at alpine passes

Several alpine passes have rail tunnels. Sometimes it is possible to transport vehicles by rail.

Loading stations: Thusis and Samedan
Duration: 1¼–1¾ hours
Prior reservation at the loading stations recommended
Thusis, tel. (081) 81 11 13; Samedan, tel. (082) 6 54 04.

Albula

Loading stations: Kanderstag and Goppenstein/Brig
Duration: 15 minutes.

Lötschberg

Loading stations: Kandersteg and Iselle di Trasquera (Italy)
Duration: about 1½ hours; change trains at Brig.

Lötschberg–
Simplon

Loading stations: Brig and Iselle di Trasquera (Italy)
Duration: 20 minutes.

Simplon/
Sempione

Loading stations: Oberwald and Realp
Duration: 15 minutes.

Furka

Loading stations: Andermatt and Sedrun
Duration: about 1 hour
Prior reservation at the loading stations recommended
Andermatt, tel. (044) 8 72 20; Sedrun, tel. (086) 9 11 37.

Oberalp

Post

Letters:
Within Switzerland (up to 250g), 0.5 sfr
Abroad (up to 20g including air mail):
In west European countries (in the International Postal Union), 0.9 sfr
To the rest of Europe and Mediterranean countries, 1.10 sfr
To other countries, 1.70 sfr

Postal rates

Postcards:
Abroad (including airmail):
To Europe and Mediterranean countries, 0.8 sfr
To other countries, 1.10 sfr

Express letters (inland and abroad), surcharge 4.0 sfr
Registered letters abroad, surcharge 2.0 sfr

Swiss Postbox

Post Offices are open from Monday to Friday 7.30 a.m.–noon, 1.30 p.m.– 6 p.m. and Saturday 7.30–11 a.m.

Opening times

Public Holidays

January 1st	New Year's Day	Holidays with
January 6th	Epiphany	fixed dates
May 1st	Labour Day	
August 1st	National Festival	
November 1st	All Saints	
December 25th/26th	Christmas	

Good Friday
Easter Monday
Ascension Day
Whit Monday

Movable Feasts

Corpus Christi (only in the Cantons with a large Catholic population)
Day of Atonement and Prayer

Local Festivals   See Events

Public Transport

Buses   The bus services run by the Swiss post office (PTT) play an important part in the Swiss transport system, particularly in the mountainous regions with more limited rail services. The postal buses serve even the highest Alpine roads. Tickets are sold at all the larger post offices.

Reduced fares are available on the Swiss postbus holiday ticket which is valid on all regular routes at present over a distance of 7500 km/4660 miles. There are also regional tickets.

Car Rental   See entry

Taxis   Taxis are relatively expensive in Switzerland, prices varying from place to place. Fixed prices for extras (e.g. luggage) are displayed in the vehicle.

Railways   See entry

Air Travel   See entry

Ships   Passengers holding a rail ticket which is valid along Lake Geneva, Lac de Neuchâtel, Lac de Bienne (including the river Aare), Lakes Thun, Brienz, the Vierwaldstätter See and Lake Zurich as well as the Untersee and the Rhine can use a ship even when this is not expressly stated on the ticket.

Boat excursions   See entry

Railways

Schweizerische Bundesbahn/ Swiss Federal Railways

◼ ⟨⊕⟩

(SBB/CFF/FFS)

The network of the Swiss Federal railways, which has been fully electrified since 1960, comprises about 2900 km/1800 miles. There are also many private railways which complement the lines of the SBB so that the total network is some 5000 km/3100 miles. There are no ticket barriers; tickets are inspected in the trains. No supplements are charged for express trains except for TEE trains. Children travel free up to 6 years of age, between 6 and 16 they pay half fare.

Central administration of the SBB

Zentralverwaltung
Hochschulstrasse 6, CH-3030 Berne
Tel. (031) 60 11 11

Representation in Great Britain

In Great Britain the Swiss Railways have an agency at:

Swiss Centre
1 New Coventry Street
London W1V 8EE
Tel. (071) 734 1921

In the USA:

Swiss Centre
608 Fifth Ave
New York
NY 10020
Tel. (212) 757 5944

250 Stockton Street
San Francisco
CA-94108
Tel. (415) 362 2260

PO Box 215
Commerce Court
Toronto
Ontario
M5L 1E8
Tel. (416) 868 0584

There are reduced fares for families and parties, young people and pensioners. Especially advantageous is the half-price season ticket (1 month or 1 year: which can be combined with the family ticket), the 6-day ticket at half-price, the Swiss Pass (formerly the Swiss Holiday Ticket). The Swiss Pass is a network ticket for rail, ship and post bus routes, as well as for the local transport facilities in 24 Swiss towns. There are combined day tickets including a visit to a trade fair or an exhibition, tram/bus day tickets, the "Schweizer Städteplausch" (a weekend ticket in 15 Swiss cities and on the William Tell Express), "Schweizer Bummler" (an Alpine train/flight combination valid for one month) and regional holiday reductions.

Information can be obtained from the Swiss National Tourist Office (see Information).

Express Services

Before taking any of the following rail trips visitors should assure themselves about frontier crossings and customs regulations in the countries concerned. Information concerning timetables, reduced fares (children, students, groups, pensioners; Swiss Holiday Ticket) and reservations can be obtained from the Swiss Travel Office (see Information), from local travel bureaux and the Information Offices given below.

Railways
— Main lines
— Branch lines

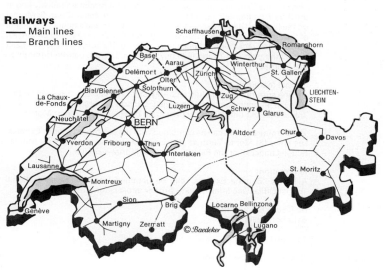

Basle main station

| Bernina Express | Route: Chur (Grisson)–Albula–St Moritz (Engadin)–Bernina–Poschiavo–Tirano (Italy) or in the reverse direction.
Length: 145 km/90 miles; duration 4 hours. |

Highlights:
The Bernina Express travels on Europe's highest mountain railway line in the Alps. It begins with one of the most beautiful stretches (Chur–St Moritz) on the famous Glacier Express (see entry) and with a gradient of 7% is one of the steepest railways in the world operated without rack and pinion. All the zones of vegetation between the glaciers of Piz Bernina (4049 m/13,289 ft) and the palms of Tirano (429 m/2695 ft) in Italy are passed through on this journey.

Special features:
On fine summer days in July and August it is possible to travel on certain trains in an open panorama carriage ("Carozza panoramica").
Trains with old-time dining cars operate between Chur and St Moritz.

The Bernina Express can be combined with the celebrated Glacier Express, see entry (St Moritz–Zermatt), the Engadin Express, see entry (St Moritz–Scuol–Landeck), or the Palm Express (St Moritz–Ascona).

Information:
A leaflet "Bernina Express" can be obtained from the Swiss National Tourist Office (see Information); further information from:

Rhätische Bahn (RhB)
Bahnhofstrasse 25
CH-7002 Chur
Tel. (081) 21 91 21

| Centovalli Railway | Route: Domodóssola–Locarno.
Length: 52 km/32 miles; duration 2 hours. |

Highlights:
This railway links the great European lines of the Simplon and the Gotthard
on narrow gauge. It traverses the wildly romantic Centovalli past idyllic
gorges and over numerous bridges with a maximum gradient of 17%.

Special features:
Visitors who have a complete day at their disposal should combine the
Centovalli railway with a return trip (Zurich–St Gotthard–Centovalli–Sim-
plon–Lötschberg–Brig–Zurich).
Information from the Swiss National Tourist Office (see Information).

The Engadin Express links the Tirol with the Engadin, the Arlberg Railway
with the Albula Railway; the Engadin Express Vienna–Salzburg–St Moritz
runs throughout the year daily in each direction. The gap between Landeck
and Bad Scuol is filled by Swiss or Austrian postal buses (PTT). The stretch
between St Moritz and Landeck is 122 km/76 miles long.

Engadin Express

Highlights:
During the trip there are views of green alpine pasture, snow covered
mountains, castles and the mighty fortress of Tarasp; in the background lie
the woods and valleys of the Swiss National Park.

Features:
The Engadin Express also has connections with three other attractive trains
– the Bernina Express, the Glacier Express and the Palm Express (see
entries).

A leaflet "Engadin Express" can be obtained from Swiss Tourist Offices
(see Information); further information is available at the tourist offices at St
Moritz and Bad Scuol (See A to Z), also from:

Rhätische Bahn (RhB)
Bahnhofstrasse 25
CH-7002 Chur
Tel. (081) 21 91 21

Schweizer Reisepost
CH-7000 Chur
Tel. (081) 22 38 23

Route: Zermatt–Andermatt–Chur–Davos/St Moritz or in reverse direction.
Length: 243 km/151 miles; duration 7¼ hours to Davos, 7¾ hours to St
Moritz.

Glacier Express

Highlights:
A trip on the Glacier Express – the "slowest express in the world" – is a
memorable experience for every railway enthusiast. Using meter-gauge
stretches of the Rhätische Bahn (RhB), the Furka–Oberalp Bahn (FO) and
the Brig–Visp–Zermatt Bahn (BVZ), the express provides an east–west

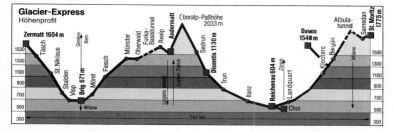

The "Glacier Express"

connection in the High Alps for tourists, and not only passes through magnificent mountain scenery but also makes use of real masterpieces of railway engineering. The train crosses 291 bridges and viaducts, goes through 91 tunnels including the longest meter-gauge tunnel in the world at the Oberalp pass (2033 m/6672 ft).

Features:
The Glacier Express carries first and second class coaches. Tickets for sections of the route only can also be obtained. Early reservation in all cases is necessary.

In connection with the centenary of the Rhätische Bahn a "Glacier Pullman Express" and a "Glacier Gourmet Express" were brought into service in 1989.

Information:
Information can be obtained from any railway station in Switzerland and from Swiss Tourist Offices (see Information) where a leaflet on the "Glacier Express" is also available. Most railway stations and travel agents in Switzerland and abroad can offer interesting package holidays which include travel on the "Glacier Express". Further information:

Rhätische Bahn (RhB)
Bahnhofstrasse 25
CH-7002 Chur
Tel. (081) 21 91 21

Furka-Oberalp Bahn (FO)
Box 97
CH-3900
Brig
Tel. (028) 23 66 66

Brig–Visp–Zermatt and Gornergrat Bahn (BVZ)
CH-3900 Brig
Tel. (028) 23 13 33

Since reservation for lunch in the dining car is compulsory, passengers should book in good time with the:

Schweizerische Speisewagen Gesellschaft
CH-4601 Olten
Tel. (062) 26 10 26

Route: Lucerne–Interlaken–Zweisimmen–Montreux and vice versa. The Golden
Length: 237 km/147 miles; duration 5½ hours. Pass Route

Highlights:
The Golden Pass route is one of the classic rail journeys in Switzerland. Passing through magnificent scenery, it runs from the banks of the Lake of the Four Forest Cantons as far as the Swiss Riviera.

Special Points:
You first travel by the narrow gauge Brünig line to Interlaken, and then continue on the Lötschberg Railway (administration in Berne); previously belonging to the BLS; as far as Zweisimmen and then continuing on a narrow gauge railway of the Montreux–Oberland Railway (MOB) to Montreux. This last stretch is particularly enjoyable since panorama coaches (Panoramic and Super-panoramic Express) were introduced.

Information from the Swiss Travel Bureaux (see Information) and from Railways (see Railways).

Route: Zermatt (1620 m/5317 ft)–Gornergrat (3089 m/10,138 ft). Gornergrat
Length: 9.34 km/5¾ miles; duration: 45 minutes. Railway

Highlights:
During the trip on the Gornergrat rack railway you will have magnificent views of the Gabelhorngruppe and the Matterhorn, which, especially in the morning, is beautifully mirrored in the waters of the Riffelsee; you will also see the Gorner Glacier (see A to Z "Surroundings of Zermatt"). Information from the Swiss Travel Bureaux (see Information) and from Railways (see Railways), and the:

Brig–Visp–Zermatt and Gornergrat-Bahn (BVZ)
CH-3900 Brig
Tel. (028) 23 13 33.

Route: Basle or Zurich–Gotthard Tunnel–Lugano or vice versa. Gotthard
Length of route: Basle–Lugano about 300 km/186 miles; Zurich–Lugano Railway:
216 km/134 miles. Duration of journey: from Basle 4 and from Zurich 3 hours.

Highlights:
The Gotthard Railway (built between 1874 and 1882) gives the Swiss railways the quickest North–South connection over the Alps. The summit of the Gotthard Massif is pierced by a railway tunnel with a length of 15 km/6 miles and a maximum height of 1154 m/3,787 ft. Since 1961 the Trans-Europa Express (TEE) "Gotthardo" has made the journey from Zurich to Lugano (First class with supplement) and this is the finest way of making this trip.

Special Points:
Sections of route can be booked using regional and express trains in second class.

Railways

Information from the Swiss Travel Bureaux (see Information) and from Railways (see Railways).

The Jungfrau Railway

Route: This railway, which, with the Gornergrat Railway, is probably the best-known mountain stretch in Switzerland operates throughout the year from the Kleiner Scheidegg to the highest railway station in Europe, the Jungfraujoch (3454 m/11,336 ft). The maximum gradient is 1 in 4. The Jungfrau Railway (JB; rack-railway, metre gauge) was built between 1896 and 1912.

Length of Route: 9.3 km/5.8 miles (7.1 km/almost 4½ miles are in tunnel); duration 50 minutes.

Highlights and Special Attractions:
See A–Z "Jungfrau Region".

Information from the Swiss Travel Bureaux (see Information) and from Railways (see Railways).

Head Office of the Jungfrau Railways is at:
Höheweg 37
CH-3800 Interlaken
Tel. (036) 22 52 52.

Palm Express

Route: St Moritz–Lugano–Locarno–Ascona (one night's accommodation)–Domodóssola–Brig–Visp–Zermatt or vice versa (at present only runs in summer).

Length of journey: about 300 km/186 miles; total duration of journey 2 days (travel by postal bus from St Moritz to Ascona or vice versa about 5 hours).

Highlights:
This journey by the Palm Express which links the Engadin and Upper Valais with Ticino, or St Moritz and Zermatt with Ascona (overnight accommodation) and Locarno and Lugano, provides wonderful views of Swiss mountains and glaciers as well as sub-tropical lakeside scenery.

Special features:The Palm Express is a combination of postal bus and railway; the various stretches are operated by the Swiss Postal Bus Service, the "Ferrovie Autolinee Regionali Ticinese (Centovalli Railway, FART) and the Brig–Visp–Zermatt–Gornergrat Railway (BVZ).

Further information can be had from Swiss Travel Bureaux (see Information) where you can also obtain the leaflet "Palm Express"; the relevant authorities in Ascona, St Moritz and Zermatt (see A–Z) and Swiss Railways can also provide information.

Postautodienst
CH-3900 Brig
Tel. (028) 23 77 77

Postautodienst
CH-7500 St Moritz
Tel. (082) 330 72

Rhätische Bahn (RhB)
Bahnhofstrasse 25
CH-7002 Chur
Tel. (081) 21 91 25

Schweizer Reisepost
CH-7000 Chur
Tel. (081) 22 38 23

Route: Alpnachstadt–Pilatus Summit and vice versa (at present only during summer).

Length of journey: 4.6 km/3 miles; duration 30 minutes.

Highlights:
See A–Z "Surroundings of Lucerne".

Special Details:
With a gradient of almost 1 in 2 the stretch of the Pilatus rack railway (gauge 800 mm) is the steepest in the world (in 1989 the Pilatus Railway celebrated it's centenary).

Information from the Swiss Travel Bureaux (see Information) and from Railways (see Railways).

Direction and Administration of the Pilatus Railway:
Inseliquai 8
CH-6002 Luzern
Tel. (041) 23 93 63

Route: Konstanz–Wil–Arth-Goldau and vice versa (at present only during summer).

Length of route: 158 km/98 miles; duration 2½ hours.

Special Details:
From Arth-Goldau Station there is a rack railway, opened in 1875 and electrified in 1906, up the Rigi. The maximum gradient is 1 in 5 (you are recommended to sit on the right); the journey of 9 km/5.6 miles takes 35 minutes.

Information from the Swiss Travel Bureaux (see Information) and from Railways (see Railways).

Reisedienst der Schweizerische Bundesbahnen
Bahnhofstrasse
CH-5322 Koblenz
Tel. (056) 46 18 00

Route: Ilanz–Disentis–Lukmanier Pass–Blenio Valley–Ascona along Lake Maggiore (from the beginning of July to the beginning of September every Tuesday; and in the high season also on Thursdays).

Return from Ascona–Gotthard Pass–Andermatt–Surselva.

Duration of journey: 10 hours.

Information from:

Postautodienst
CH-7130 Ilanz
Tel. (086) 2 16 50

Schweizer Reisepost
CH-7000 Chur
Tel. (081) 22 38 23

Information from the Swiss Travel Bureaux (see Information) and from Railways (see Railways).

Route: Lucerne–Flüelen–St Gotthard–Locarno–Lugano and vice versa.

Highlights:
The William Tell Express links two of the most attractive districts of the

country: Central Switzerland with Ticino. From May to September you can travel by paddle-wheel steamer (out of season by a diesel motor boat) from Lucerne on the Vierwaldstätter See to Flüelen (a three-course meal is served in the ship's saloon); then follows a rail trip in a club car or panorama car of the SBB through the impressive Gotthard massif as far as the towns of Locarno and Lugano.

Special Details:
During the boat trip the route is explained in several languages, and for the rail section a written description is provided. The kernel of the trip is the journey on the Gotthard Railway. The William Tell Express excursion can be combined with several other trips and excursions. Because of limited accommodation reservations and booking should be made in good time.

Information from the Swiss Travel Bureaux (see Information) and from Railways (see Railways).

Schiffahrtsgesellschaft des Vierwaldstätter Sees (SGV)
Werftestrasse 5/Postfach 4265
CH-6002 Lucerne
Tel. (041) 40 45 40

Grand Canyon Express (Postal Coach) An alternative to the railway is the postal coach of the Grand Canyon Express.
Route: Chur–Laax and vice versa.

Highlights:
From June to October a postal coach runs daily from Chur through the "Grand Canyon" of the Vorderrhein to Laax or vice versa. Between Bonaduz and Laax the road, which is little used, winds its way along the ravine to the Vorderrhein Gorge. There are views of the white calcite pinnacles and of the river glistening far below. The night is spent in the Sporthotel "Rancho" in Laax (address, see below).

Special features:
There are four coaches at the disposal of visitors, each having room for eight passengers and the driver. In good weather the roof is opened, but even if it rains the coach is perfectly comfortable. In the price quoted for this trip the rail journey from most Swiss stations to Chur or Laax (and return) as well as the coach trip from Chur to Laax and vice versa and accommodation at the Sporthotel "Rancho" are included. For information and booking:

Sporthotel Rancho
CH-7031 Laax
Tel. (086) 3 01 31

Museum trains and "Fitness Railway" Information concerning "Museum trains" with old-time steam engines, old-time trams and other special trains (for example the Bernese Oberland railway, the Rhätische Bahn) as well as the "Fitness Bahn" programme can be obtained direct from Swiss Railways (see entry) or from Swiss Travel Bureaux.

Bicycle Rental It is possible at most Swiss railway stations to rent bicycles ("Velo am Bahnhof": 5 gear ordinary bicycles, mountain bikes, tandems, etc.). Holders of valid rail tickets receive a reduction. Information at all Swiss railway stations.

Fly-Gepäck See Air Traffic.

Restaurants

Note for vegetarians Those who prefer vegetarian cuisine can obtain an information leaflet "Vegetarische Restaurants" from the Swiss National Tourist Office (SVZ; see Information). Most of these vegetarian restaurants are in the larger towns; there are a few in the spas. Many hotels, etc., offer a vegetarian menu and in this case it is better to get the information on the spot.

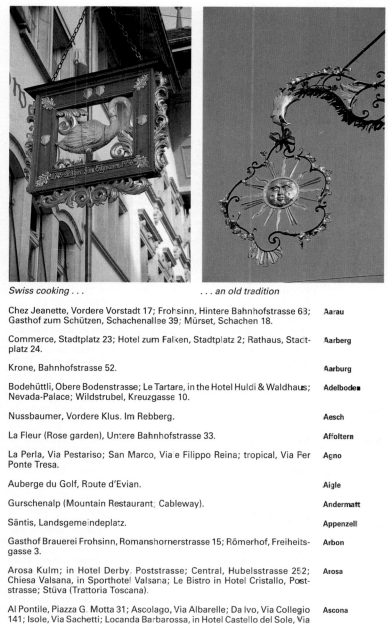

Swiss cooking . . .   *. . . an old tradition*

Chez Jeanette, Vordere Vorstadt 17; Frohsinn, Hintere Bahnhofstrasse 63; **Aarau**
Gasthof zum Schützen, Schachenallee 39; Mürset, Schachen 18.

Commerce, Stadtplatz 23; Hotel zum Falken, Stadtplatz 2; Rathaus, Stadt- **Aarberg**
platz 24.

Krone, Bahnhofstrasse 52. **Aarburg**

Bodehüttli, Obere Bodenstrasse; Le Tartare, in the Hotel Huldi & Waldhaus; **Adelboden**
Nevada-Palace; Wildstrubel, Kreuzgasse 10.

Nussbaumer, Vordere Klus. Im Rebberg. **Aesch**

La Fleur (Rose garden), Untere Bahnhofstrasse 33. **Affoltern**

La Perla, Via Pestariso; San Marco, Via e Filippo Reina; tropical, Via Per **Agno**
Ponte Tresa.

Auberge du Golf, Route d'Evian. **Aigle**

Gurschenalp (Mountain Restaurant; Cableway). **Andermatt**

Säntis, Landsgemeindeplatz. **Appenzell**

Gasthof Brauerei Frohsinn, Romanshornerstrasse 15; Römerhof, Freiheits- **Arbon**
gasse 3.

Arosa Kulm; in Hotel Derby, Poststrasse; Central, Hubelsstrasse 252; **Arosa**
Chiesa Valsana, in Sporthotel Valsana; Le Bistro in Hotel Cristallo, Poststrasse; Stüva (Trattoria Toscana).

Al Pontile, Piazza G. Motta 31; Ascolago, Via Albarelle; Da Ivo, Via Collegio **Ascona**
141; Isole, Via Sachetti; Locanda Barbarossa, in Hotel Castello del Sole, Via

553

Restaurants

Muraccio 142; Michelangelo, Via Collina 81; Osteria Nostrana, Piazza Ascona; Otello, vl. Papio; Ristorante Giardino, Via Segnale.

In Losone: Grotto Broggini, V.S. Materno 18.

Baden

Atelier, Bäderstrasse 17a; Badener Hof, Bahnhofplatz 1; Bodega, Cordulaplatz 6; Du Parc, Römerstrasse 24; Herstenstein-Panorama-Restaurant, Hertensteinstrasse 80; Wilden Mann, Obere Gasse 33.

Bad Ragaz

See Ragaz

Bad Tarasp

See Tarasp

Basel

In the centre, on the left of the Rhine: Au Premier, Aeschenvorstadt 24; Basler Keller, Münzgasse 12; Börse, Marktgasse 4; Brauner Mutz, Barfüsserplatz 10; Charolaise & Steinenpick, Steinentorstrasse 25; Chez Donati, St Johann-Vorstadt 48; Fischstube zum Pfauen, St Johann Vorstadt 13; Golden Gate, Steinengraben 42; Kämpf Centralhallen, Streitgasse 20; Kunsthalle, Steinenberg 7; La Popote, Elsässerstrasse 89; Le Bourguignon, Bachlettenstrasse 1; Löwenzorn, Gemsberg 2/4; Méditerranée, Blumenrain 12; Safranzunft, Gerbergasse 11; Schlüsselzunft, Freie Strasse 25; St Alban-Eck, St Alban-Vorstadt 60; Stadtcasino, Steinenberg 14; "Stucki" Bruderholz, Bruderholzallee 42; Zum Goldenen Sternen, St Alban-Rheinweg 70; Zum Schnabel, Trillengässlein.

Near the SBB Station: Bahnhofbuffet Basel SBB, Centralbahnstrasse 14; Euler, Centralbahnplatz 14; Heumattstube 25; Jeffrey's Indian Restaurant, Centralbahnstrasse 17; L'Escargot, Centralbahnstrasse 10; Markthalle, Viaduktstrasse 8; Wettstein Grill, Aeschengraben 31; Zoo-Restaurant, Bachlettenstrasse 72; Zum Schützenhaus, Schützenmattstrasse 56.

On the right bank of the Rhine: Café Spitz, Rheingasse 2/Greifengasse; Fischerstube, Rheingasse 45 (Brewery); La Marmite du Beaujolais, Klybeckstrasse 15; Le Petit Bâle, Rheingasse 12; Le Plaza Club, Messeplatz; Le Provençale, Riehenring 85; Les Quatre Saisons, in Hotel Europe, Clarastrasse 43; Terrasse, Haltingerstrasse 104; Zem Schnooggeloch, Rheingasse 12.

At the Basel-Mulhouse airport: Airport Restaurants.

Bellinzona

Delcò Raffaele, Carasso; Della Rocca, Carasso; Grotti; Torcett, Pedevilla; Grottino Ticinese, Bellinzona; Osteria Castello, in Unterwalden Castle.

Berne

Near the main station: Aarbergerhof, Aabergergasse 40; Bahnhofbuffet, Bahnhofplatz 10; Börse, Bärenplatz 27; Café Bubenberg Vegi, Bubenbergplatz 8; Della Casa, Schauplatzgasse 16; Hirschegrabe, Bubenbergplatz; Le Beaujolais, Aarbergergasse 50-52; Le Mazot, Bärenplatz 5; Old Inn, Effingerstrasse 4; Pizzeria Pinocchio, Aarbergergasse 8.

Between the Käfigturm and Nydegg Bridge: BZ-Bistro, Zeughausgasse 14; Casino Restaurant-Betriebe, Casinoplatz; Chindlifrässer, Kornhausplatz 7; Commerce, Gerechtigkeitsgasse 74; Du Théâtre, Theaterplatz 7; Ermitage, Amthausgasse 10/Marktgasse 15; Fédéral, Bärenplatz 31; Galleria, Bar-Restaurant, Marktgasse 37; Grosser Kornhauskeller, Kornhausplatz 18; Lorenzini, Marktgasse-Passage 3; Mistral, Kramgasse 42; Räblus, Zeughausgasse 3; Ratskeller, Gerechtigkeitsgasse 81; Schmiedstube, Zeughausgasse 5; Settebello, Gerechtigkeitsgasse 6; Thurm, Waisenhausplatz 13; Zimmermania, Brunngasse 19; Zum Rathaus, Rathausplatz 5.

On the right bank of the Aare: Brasserie Bärengraben, Muristalden 1; Kongress & Kursaal Bern, Schänzlistrasse 71-77; Rosengarten, Alter Aargauerstalden 31b, (pleasant views); Schönau, Sandrainstrasse 68.

On the left bank of the Aare: Innere Enge, Engestrasse 54 (1 mile north).

In Langenthal: Various restaurants and rôtisseries in the Hotel Bären.
In Roggwil near Langenthal: Landgasthof Kalten Herberge.

Gondelbahn (Views: 2700 m above sea level); Sportzentrum Bachtla (Views). **Bettmeralp**

Albergo Della Posta, over the road from the station. **Biasca**

Amphytrion, in Hotel Elite, Bahnhofstrasse 14; Bahnhofbuffet, Bahnhofplatz 4; Bielstube, Rosius 18; Cardinal, Kanalgasse 29; Kongresshaus, Zentralstrasse 60; Paradisli, Seevorstadt 19; Raffaele, Spitalstrasse 26; Restaurant Français, In Palace Hotel Club, Wyttenbachstrasse 2; Schöngrün, Madretschstrasse 102; Rüschli, Zentralstrasse 2; Sporting, Brasserie, Neumarktstrasse 14. **Biel/Bienne**

In St Niklaus: Waldschenke "au Provençale", 3½ miles from Biel.

In Worben: Worbenbad.

Il Roseto; Ticino, Piazza Borromini 21. **Bissone**

Weiherschloss, Schlossgasse 9. **Bottmingen**

Wildbach **Brienz**

Pizzeria Metropol, Axenstrasse 9. **Brunnen**

La Fleur de Lys, Rue de Gruyères 31. **Bulle**

Warteck, Bahnhofstrasse 11a; Zur Hofstatt. **Burgdorf**

Da Candida, Viale Marco da Campio 4. **Campione d'Italia**

Albergo Vetta, Monte Generoso. **Capolago**

Stüvetta Veglia. **Celerina**

Le Levant; Le Nord. **Champéry**

Hostellerie du Bon Accueil, La Frasse. **Château d'Oex**

Hure d'Argent, Rue Numa-Droz 1; La Fleur-de-Lys, Ave. Léopold-Robert 13; La Pinte Neuchâteloise, Grenier 8; Le Cafignon, Rue des Arêtes 35; Le Provençale, Rue Jacquet-Droz 60. **La Chaux-de-Fonds**

Speciality and snack restaurant in Corso, Via Valdani 1; Vecchia Osteria, Seseglio. **Chiasso**

Bahnhof-Buffet, Duc de Rohan, Masanserstrasse 44; Hofkellerei; Kornplatz; Mandarin, Malixerstrasse 3; Marsöl, Hofstrasse 5; Obelisco, Vazerolgasse 12; Rätushof, Bahnhofstrasse; Steinbock, across from the station; Stern, Reichsgasse 11; Ticino, Mühleplatz 3; Zunfthaus zur Rebleuten, Pfisterplatz 1. **Chur**

In Rheichenau: Speciality restaurant in Adler Hotel on the San-Bernardino Road.

Rotisserie du Lac, in Hôtel du Lac, Grand Rue. **Coppet**

In Crans-sur-Sierra: Le Cave, Le Chamois d'Or, in Hotel Les Hauts-de-Crans; Le Plaza; Le Régent; Snack Pic-Bois. **Crans Montana**

Restaurants

In Montana: Café de la Poste, Rue de la Gare Montana; Café Restaurant du Centre; Centre de Tennis, Au Lac Moubra; Cervin; Dancing le Mazot; De la Plaine Morte; Des Violettes; La Jeanne d'Arc; La Potinière; La Rôtisserie de la Reine; Le Vieux Moulin; Steakhouse le Ranch.

In Richtung Bluche: Auberge de la Diligence.

Crans-sur-Sierre
See Crans Montana

Davos
In Davos Town: Bündnerstübli, Dischmastrasse 8; Derby; Flüela-Stübli, in the Hôtel Flüela, Bahnhofstrasse 5; Meierhof, Promenade 135; Trattoria Toscana, in Hôtel des Alpes, Promenade 136.

In Davos Platz: Bergrestaurant Schatzalp; Davoserstübli, in Davoserhof, In Postplatz; grill Ferme, in Hôtel Steigenberger Belvédère, Promenade 89; Jenatschtube, in Davershof, In Postplatz; Pöstli, in the Hôtel Morosani Post, Promenade 42; Waldhuus, in Golfhotel Waldhuus; Zauberberg, in Hôtel Europe, Promenade; Zum Goldenen Drachen, in Hôtel Terminus. Talstrasse 3.

In Laret: Hubli's Landhaus, Kantonsstrasse.

Delémont
Du Midi, Place de la Gare 10.

Les Diablerets
De la Couronne; La Printanière; Les Vioz; Locanda Livia; L'Ormonan, in Ortszentrum; Mazots.

Einsiedeln
Krone-Bar, Hauptstrasse 69.

Engelberg
Alpstübli (ski restaurant), Trübsee, Eden, Bahnhofstrasse 7; Spannort-Stübli;Titlis-Bergrestaurants, Neuschwändi 8; Tudor-Stübli in Hôtel Hess, Dorfstrasse 50.

Epesses
Auberge du Vigneron.

Ermatingen
Adler (Auberge Napoléon), Dorfplatz; Hirschen, Obere Seestrasse 60.

Euthal
Burehof, Hauptstrasse.

Fiesch
Dancing Happyland.

Flims
In Flims-Fidaz: Fidazerhof

In Flims-Waldhaus: Barga, in Hôtel Adula; Prau la Selva, Sportzentrum; Schweizerhof; Segnes and Post.

Flüelen
Hostellerie Sternen, Axenstrasse 6; Unerhof, Axenstrasse 4.

Frauenfeld
Gasthof Zum Goldenen Kreuz, Zürcherstrasse 144; Roter Ochsen, Zürcherstrasse 224.

In Ortsteil Erzenholz: Hoffnung, Schaffhauserstrasse 266.

Fribourg
Boccalino, Route du Pont Muré 151; L'Aigle Noir, Rue des Alpes 58; Le Bistrot, Route de Beaumont 16; Le Singapour, Route Joseph-Chaley 29a; Le Vieux-Chêne, Route de Tavel 17; Pizzeria le Frascati, Rue de Romont 3; Plaza-Chalet Suisse, Rue de Lausanne 91; Restaurant de la Gare (Brasserie), Place de la Gare 1; Winebar, Rue de l'Hôpital 39.

Gandria
Descanso (Cantine)

Genf/Genève
On the north bank: Auberge "A la Mère Royaume", Rue des Corps-Saints 9, near the station; Au Fin Bec, Rue de Berne 55; Buffet Cornavin, Place

Cornavin 3; Fleur de Ming (Chinese), Rue de Prince 8, Rue du Port 7; La Cascade, Quai des Bergues 19; L'Amphitryon, Quai des Bergues 33; Mövenpick Cendrier, Rue du Cendrier 17.

On the south bank: Brasserie International (Speciality: Sauerkraut), Place du Cirque (Plainpalais); Buffet de la Gare des Eaux-Vives-Bahnhof; Café de la Pointe, Rue de Villereuse 5; Café du Centre, Place du Molard 7 (lower town); Palais de Justice (old Geneva atmosphere), Place du-Bourg-de-Four 8; Le Bateau, floating restaurant at the Jardin Anglais; Le Catalan (Spanish), Route Florissant 175; Le Chandelier, Grand'Rue 25 (old town); Les Armures (fondue, raclette, pizza), Puits-St-Pierre 1 (old town), with knights' hall 17th century; Mövenpick Fusterie, Place Fusterie (lower town).

Outside the town: Auberge du Lion d'Or, 2 miles north east in Cologny on the Lake; Creux-de-Genthod (speciality fish), 4 miles north in Genthod, Chemin du Creux-de-Genthod 21, on the Lake; Du Parc des Eaux-Vives, in the park of the same name, Quai Gustave-Ador 82; La Perle du Lac (only in summer) in the park of the same name, Rue de Lausanne 128, with views of the Lake and the Alps.

At the airport: De l'Aéroport (Canonica); Le Plein Ciel; etc.

Henessenmühle; Ochsen, St-Galler-Strasse 31; Schloss Oberberg.	**Gossau**
Krone.	**Gottlieben**
Désirée; Speiserestaurant Couronne.	**Grächen**
Au Rendez-Vous & Le Mignon, Hauptstrasse; Oberland; Spinne, in the town centre; Sportzentrum.	**Grindelwald**
Hostellerie des Chevaliers.	**Gruyères**
Bellevue Grill, Hauptstrasse; Eggli, at the Bergbahnstation; La Chesery, Cheseryplatz; Oleden, Hauptstrasse; Rialto, Hauptstrasse.	**Gstaad**
Restaurant in Hotel Gotthard.	**Gurtnellen**
Seemöwe, Hauptstrasse.	**Güttingen**
Gehren, Einsiedlerstrasse 263; Restaurant Taverne, in Hôtel Schwan, Zugerstrasse 9	**Horgen**
Arena Bar, Rugenparkstrasse 2; Barbarella, Cabaret, Höheweg; Bodega; Burestube, Höheweg 57a; Casino, Kursaal, CCCI, Höheweg/Strandbadstrasse; Chez Pierre, Bahnhofplatz 39; De la Promenade Schuh, Höheweg 56; Im Gade, in Hotel Du Nord, in Höheweg; Jungfrau-Stube, in Hotel Victoria-Jungfrau, Höheweg 41; La Bonne Fourchette, in Hotel Beau-Rivage, Höheweg 211; La Terrasse, in Hotel Victoria-Jungfrau; Le Bistro "Chez Pierre", Bahnhofplatz 39; Le Charolais, in Hotel Metropole, Höheweg 37; Piz Paz, Bahnhofstrasse 1; Pizzeria Horn, Strandbadstrasse; Zum Goldenen Anker, Marktgasse 57.	**Interlaken**
Alpina, Bahnhofstrasse 1; Chesa Grischuna; Greeness, in Aaba Hotel, Alte Bahnhofstrasse 1; Grillroom Pardenn, Monbielerstrasse; Walserstube, in Hotel Walserhof.	**Klosters**
In Klosters-Aeuja; Alte Post.	
In Klosters-Dorf: Dorfstube, in Hotel Albeina.	
Gasthaus Engel, Bachstrasse 11; Jakobshöhe, Bergstrasse 46.	**Kreuzlingen**

Restaurants

Küsnacht   Ermitage, Seestrasse 80; Petermann's Kunststuben, Seestrasse 160.

Küssnacht am Rigi   Adler, Dorfplatz 9.

Laax   Posta Veglia, Hauptstrasse; Teglia Larnags; Trattoria Toscana, in Sporthotel Laax, Via Pattadiras.

La Chaux-de-Fonds   See Chaux-de-Fonds

Lausanne   Place St François and town centre: Bonne Auberge, Ave. Druey 5; Chat Noir, Beau Séjour 27 (popular with artists); La Grappe d'Or, Cheneau-de-Bourg 3; Le Mandarin, Ave. de Théâtre 7 (Chinese); Le Relais (Hotel Lausanne Palace), Grand-Chêne 7-9; Le Vaudois, Place de la Riponne; Manuel, Place St François 5; Théâtre, in the theatre.

Around the station: Buffet de la Gare in the station; L'Agora, Ave du Rond-Point 9; Le Beaujolais, Place de la Gare 2; San Marino, Avenue de la Gare 20.

At the Botanical Gardens: Chinois Kwong Ming, Ave de Cour 74.

An the Lake: La Voile d'Or, Ave. E-J. Dalcroze, Vidy.

In Ouchy, on the Lake: Grand Café in Beau Rivage Palace; White Horse Pub, Ave. d'Ouchy 66.

In St Sulpice: Au Petit Port, Chemin Petit-Port; Le Débarcadère, Chemin du Crêt 7.

To the north on the hills: Auberge du Lac de Sauvabelin, in Sauvabelin Forest; Le Chalet Suisse, Signal de Sauvabelin, etc.

Lenzerheide   In Lenzerheide: Bündnerstübli, in Post Hotel; Grotto-Pizzeria Da Elio, Voa Sporz; Nino's Pub, Voa Principala 51; Rothorn (views).

In Sporz: Guarda Val; La Palanca, Val Sporz.

In Valbella: Romana, Voa Principala 12.

Les Diablerets   See Diablerets

Leukerbad/ Loèche-les-Bains   Jägerstube, Obere Maressen; La Malvoisie, in Hôtel Les Sources des Alpes; Die Rinderhütte, Torrent ob Leukerbad; Tannenheim, Vieux Valais.

Liestal   Bad Schauenburg; Restaurant Neuhaus, Kasernenstrasse 3.

Locarno   Al Parco, Via San Gottardo 8; Caffé-Bar Paolino, Pal. Jelmoli Largo Zorzi; Centenario, Muralto, Lungolago 17; Coq d'Or, in Hôtel La Palma au Lac, Muralto, Viale Verbano 29; Grillraum, in Réber au Lac, Muralto, Viale Verbano 55; Saleggi, Via Angelo Nessi 38; Yang Guan, by the Lake.

In Minusio: Le Petit Champignon.

In Muralto: Centenario, Lungolago 13.

Lucerne   Arbalète, Pilatusstrasse 1; Belle Epoque, in Hôtel Astoria, Pilatusstrasse 29; Bistro du Théâtre, Theaterstrasse 5; Chez Marianne – Restaurant zum Raben, Kornmarkt; Drü Chünge Stube, Klosterstrasse 10; Eichhof, Obergrundtstrasse 106; Flora – La Marmite, in Hôtel Flora, Seidenhofstrasse 5; Galliker, Schützenstrasse 1; Kunst – and Kongresshaus, Bahnhofplatz; Kursaal-Casino AG, Haldenstrasse 6; Kyoto, Baselstrasse 31; La Vague, in Hôtel des Balances, Weinmarkt 7; La Manoir, Bundesplatz 9; Mandarin,

Weinmarkt 3; Mignon Grill, in Palace-Hôtel, Haldenstrasse 10; Old Swiss House, near Löwendenkmal, Löwenplatz 4; Schwanen, Schwanenplatz 4; Stadt München, Metzgerrainle 9, on the Reuss; Von-Pfyffer-Stube, in Grand Hôtel National, Haldenstrasse 4; Zum Raben, Kornmarkt 5.

In Kastanienbaum: Restaurant Chreuztrichter, in Seehotel Kastanienbaum. Restaurant in the saloon of the luxury paddle-steamer "Wilhelm-Tell-Express" (see Railways and Boat Excursions).

Al Portone, Viale Cassarate 3; Baron de la Mouette (Mövenpick Luganella), **Lugano** Viale Cattaneo 25; Bianchi al Cenacolo, Via Pessina 3; Del Cassarate, Via Fusoni 18; Europa au Lac, Via Cattori 1; Excelsior-Rivera, Riva Vincenzo Vela 4/Via Nassa 15; La Tinera, Via del Gorini 2 (Tessiner Küche); Locanda del Boschetto, Via Casserinetta 40 (Italian); Oasis (Eden Grand Hotel), Riva Paradiso 1; Orologio, Via Nizzola 2; Osteria al Porto, Via Foce 9; Tavernetta Colorado, Via Maraini 19; Ticino, Piazza Cioccaro 1; Veranda, in Hôtel Splendide-Royal, Riva Caccia 7; Vil a Principe Leopoldo, Via Montalbano 5.

In Sorengo: Ristorante Santabbondio, Via al Grotti.

Surroundings of Lugano: Many "grotti" (country inns).

Le Gourmet, in Hotel Forum, Ave du Grand-St-Bernard 72. **Martigny**

In Martigny Croix: Le Grognard, La Toscana, La Pinte, all three in Hôtel La Porte d'Octodure.

Albergo Milano, Piazza della Stazione. **Mendrisio**

See Crans Montana **Montana**

Casino de Montreux, Rue du Théâtre 9; Caveau du Museum, Rue de la Gare **Montreux** 40; Hungaria, Ave. Nestlé 19; La Régence, in Hotel Hyatt Continental, Grand Rue 97; La Terrasse, in Hôtel Eden Au Lac, Rue du Théâtre 11; Le Breton, Ave. de Belmont 31; Le Clou, Place de la Paix 1; Le Pavillon du Palace, in Montreux Palace; Restaurant Français, in Hôtel Montreux Palace, Grand-Rue 100.

In Brent: (2 miles north-west): Le Pont-de-Brent.

In Territet: François Doyen (Le Bistro de Paris), Ave. de Chillon 82; T. du Château de Chillon, Territet-Veytaux.

Carina Carlton; Grotto del Parco, Parco Scherrer; Olivella au Lac; Voile **Morcote** d'Or, in Hôtel Olivella au Lac, Lungolago.

In Vico Morcote; Alpe di Vicania.

Restaurant in Hôtel Fleur du Lac, Route du Lausanne 70. **Morges**

Bären, Bernstrasse 3; Moospinte; Schützenhaus, Oberdorfstrasse 10. **München-buchsee**

Piz Gloria, Schilthorn (300 m above sea level; revolving restaurant, views). **Mürren**

Channe Valaisanne, Hauptstrasse 51; Chinese Dynasty, Grand-Rue 51; **Murten/Morat** Lord Nelson, in Hôtel Schiff; Schwarzer Adler, Hauptgasse 45.

In Meyriez: Le Vieux Manoir au Lac.

Beaulac, Quai L-Robert 2; Buffet de la Gare, Hauptbahnhof; China Town, **Neuchâtel** Rue des Chavannes 5; City and La Porte du Bonheur, in Hôtel City, Place A-M Piaget; Le Vieux Vapeur, Port de Neuchâtel; Restaurant des Halles, 4 du Trésor (Place du Marché).

Restaurants

Nyon	Clos de Sadex, Route de Lausanne 131; Du Lac, Rue de Rive 13; La Véranda, in Hôtel Beau-Rivage, Quai des Alpes; Le Léman, Rue de Rive 28.
Olten	Station buffet; Felsenburg, Aarauerstrasse 157; Swiss Restaurant Car Company; Zollhaus, Bahnhofstrasse 4; Zunfthaus zum Löwen, Hauptgasse 6.
Payerne	Night-Club Le Central, Grand-Rue.
Pontresina	Kronenstübli, in Hotel Kronenhof; Sarazena.
Porrentruy	Restaurant Romano du Buffet de la Gare, Place de la Gare 4.
Porto Ronco	Della Posta
Pully	La Prieuré, Avenue du Prieuré 1.
Bad Ragaz	Äbtestube Grill, in Grand-Hotel courtyard; Kursaal-Casino; Quellenhof.
	In Flappe: Paradies, off the road from Ragaz to Landquart.
Rapperswil	Eden, Seestrasse 3.
Rheineck	Landhaus, Rheineck, Appenzellerstrasse 73; Wirtschaft zur Alten Mühle, Töbelimülistrasse 15.
	In Rheineck-Thal: Schiff Buriet country inn.
Rheinfelden	Zum Goldenen Drachen (Chinese restaurant), Habich-Dietschistrasse 10; Taverne zum Zähringer, Robertenstrasse 95.
Rolle	Auberge de Bugnaux. Restaurant in Hotel Rivesrolle.
Rorschach	Pfeffermühle, Bellevuestrasse 1b.
Saanen-Gstaad	D'Halte-Beiz, in Steigenberger Hotel, on the Halten.
Saas Fee	Britannia-Hütte, ob Saas Fee; Café Central; Chämi-Stuba; Dreh-restaurant, Metro-Alpin; Feeloch; Waldhotel Fletschhorn.
Saignelégier	Restaurant in the Hôtel de la Gare et du Parc, Rue de la Gruyère 4.
Samedan	Donatz (Padella), Via Plazzet; Restaurant in Hotel Bernina.
St Maurice	Au Philosophe; La Charbonnière.
St Gallen	Alt Guggeien, Kesselhaldenstrasse 85; Bahnhof-Buffet SBB, Bahnhofplatz 2; Baratella, Untere Graben 20; Galetto, St Jakobstrasse 62; Gaststuben Zum Schlössli, Zeughausgasse 17; Kongresshaus Schützengarten, St Jakobstrasse 35; Mövenpick-Restaurant/Caféteria in Hotel Einstein, Berneggstrasse 2; Restaurant au Premier, in Hôtel Métropol, Bahnhofplatz 3; Rôtisserie am Gallusplatz, Gallusstrasse 24/26; St Leonhard, Burgstrasse 26; Schnäggehüsli, Hagenbuchstrasse 31; Schwarzer Bären, Speicherstrasse 151; Stadtkeller, in Spisermarkt, Spisergasse 17; Walhalla, Bahnhofplatz; Zum Goldenen Schäffli, Metzergasse 5.
	In St Gallen-Winkeln: Rôtisserie Kreuz, Letzistrasse 3.
St-Moritz	Albana; Badrutt's Palace (Grill); Chesa Veglia; Corviglia (Marmite); Restaurants in Carlton, Via Joh. Badrutt; Grotto, in Hotel Crystal, Via Traunter Plazzas 1; Restaurant in Hotel Kulm, Via Maistra; Restaurant in Hotel Neues Posthotel; Restaurant in Hotel San Gian; Restaurant in Hotel Suvretta

House, Via Chasellas 1; Stüvetta, in Hotel Margna; Veltlinerkeller, Via dal Bagn 11.

Sarnerhof, Brünigstrasse 154. **Sarnen**

Tagmon, Hauptstrasse 54. **Savognin**

Fischerzunft, Rheinquai 8; Musikhof, Posthof 5. **Schaffhausen**

In Dachsen: Schloss Laufen am Rheinfall.

In Herblingen: Hirschen, Schlossstrasse 20; Schloss-Taverne.

In Neuhausen: Park am Rheinfall, Rheinfallquai 5; Schlössli-Wörth.

Ratskeller, Strehlgasse 3. **Schwys**

Belvédère, Pizzeria "Chez Ernest"; De la Grotte, Lac de Géronde; Relais du Château de Villa, Rue Ste-Cathérine 4. **Sierre**

Chesa Marchetta; Waldhaus. **Sils Maria**

Albana, Hauptstrasse; Corvatsch, centre and station. **Silvaplana**

Brasserie Romande, Ave. de France 15; Buffet CFF, Bahnhof; Des Mayennets; Le Mandarin, Rue de Conthey 17; Le Prado, Place du Midi 29; Pub de la Bourse, Ave. de la Gare 28. **Sion/Sitten**

Bahnhofbuffet, Dornacherstrasse 48; Berntor, Berntorstrasse 9; Chez Deron, Hauptgasse 79; Krebs, Bettlachstrasse 29; Krone, Hauptgasse 64; Löwen, Löwengasse 15; Zunfthaus zu Wirthen, Hauptgasse 41. **Solothurn**

Belvédère **Spiez**

Linde, Dorfplatz **Stans**

Three speciality restaurants in Acheregg Seehotel **Stansstadt**

Frohsinn am See, Seestrasse 62; Seehotel Feldbach, Seestrasse 123. **Steckborn**

Badstube, Schifflände; Chlosterhof; Sonne, Rathausplatz 127. **Stein am Rhein**

Chaste (castle), Sparsels; Hotel-Restaurant National. **Bad Tarasp**

Sternen, in Niederteufen, Hauptstrasse 55. **Teufen**

Bahnhofbuffet, Seestrasse 2; China-Restaurant, in Elite Hotel Thun; Restaurant in Hotel Krone, Rathausplatz; Kursaal Casino, Hofstettenstrasse 35; Schloss Schadau, Seestrasse 45. **Thun**

Witschi's Restaurant, Zürcherstrasse 55. **Untereng-stringen**

Restaurant Au Premier im Real, Städtle 21; Torkel, Hintergasse 9 (speciality restaurant in the court cellar of the Prince of Liechtenstein). **Vaduz**

Café La Grange; L'Ecurie; Restaurant Pierroz, in Hotel Rosalp, Route de Medran. **Verbier**

Le Raisin, Place du Marché 3; Restaurant du Rivage, Ls. Meyer (lake terrace) 1; Trois Couronnes, Rue d'Italie 49. **Vevey**

In Oron-le-Châtel: Château d'Oron.

Restaurants

Villars-sur-Ollon Grand Restaurant du Parc; La Renardière (mountain restaurant with grill and bar), Route de Layeux; Le Sporting, Rue Centrale.

Vitznau Lakeside Restaurant in Parkhotel, Kantonstrasse.

Wädenswil Eichmühle, Neugutstrasse 933; Zum Letten, Neudorfstrasse 30.

Wangen Ochsen.
(near Olten)

Wengen Falken.

Wil Schwanen-Stube, Obere Bahnhofstrasse 21; Zum Wilden Mann, Marktgasse 35.

Winterthur Restaurant in Garten-Hotel, Stadthausstrasse 4; Strauss, Stadthausstrasse 8.

In Wülfingen: Sporrer, Im Sporrer 1.

Yverdon-les-Bains Buffet de la Gare, Ave. de la Gare; De L'Isle, Rue des Moulins 30; La Prairie, Ave. des Bains 9.

Zermatt Bahnhofbuffet; Dam Mario, in Hotel Schweizerhof, Bahnhofstrasse; Mont Cervin, Bahnhofstrasse; Monte Rosa; Selerhaus.

Zofingen Fédéral, Vordere Hauptgasse 57; Schmiedstube, Schmiedgasse 4.

Zug Aklin, Am Zytturm; Glashof, Baarerstrasse 41; Hecht am See, Fischmarkt 2; Hirschen, Zeughausgasse 11; Ochsen, Kolinplatz 11; Rathauskeller, Ober-Altstadt 1; Rosenberg, Rosenbergstrasse; Seerestaurant Casino, Artherstrasse 4; Trattoria Mamma Leone, Aegeristrasse 58.

Zürich Accademia Piccoli (Italian), Rotwandstrasse 48; Agnes Amberg, Hotingerstrasse 5; Augustiner (good plain cuisine), Augustinergasse 25; Au Premier (station buffet; 10 restaurants with 2000 places), Main Station; Baron de la Mouette, Mövenpick-Dreikönigshaus, Beethovenstrasse 32; Baur au Lac, Talstrasse 1; Bauschänzli (only in summer), Limmatufer, near Bürkliplatz; Bellerive, Utoquai 47; Blaue Ente, in the Tiefenbrunnen Mill, Seefeldstrasse 233; Bolognese , Seegartenstrasse 14; Braustube Hürlimann, Bahnhofplatz 9; Camino, Freischützgasse 4; Casa Ferlin (Italian), Stampfenbachstrasse 38; Chesa da Seoul, Klingenstrasse 33; Commercio, Mühlebachstrasse 2; Conti (theatrical folk, French cuisine), Dufourstrasse 1; Da Bianca (Rosenhof), Weberstrasse 14; Da Capo, Main Station, Bahnhofplatz 15; Da Cesare Augustus, corner of Zurlindenstrasse 21/ Erlachstrasse; Da Leone, Zähringerstrasse 28; Du Pont, Bahnhofquai 7; Elephant d'Or, Vetlibergstrasse 166; Emilio (Spanish), Müllerstrasse 5; Zürichhorn (fish restaurant), Bellerivestrasse 160 (only in summer); Fisherman's Lodge, Mythhenquai 61; Flühgass, Zollikerstrasse 214; Gasometer, Gasometerstrasse 24; Gleich (Vegetarian), Seefeldstrasse 9; Haxenstube (good plain cuisine), Schweizergasse 2; Hitli Vegi (vegetarian), Sihlstrasse 28; Hong Kong (Chinese), Seefeldstrasse 60; Lobster and oysterbar, in Hotel St Gotthard, Linth-Eschergasse 14; Jacky's Stapferstube, Culmannstrasse 45; Kongresshaus, Gotthardstrasse 5; Korea Pavillon, Badenerstrasse 457; Kronenhalle (frequented by artists, Swiss specialities), Rämistrasse 4, near the Opera House; Kropf, In Gassen 16; La Provence, Vogelsangstrasse 33; La Rotonde, in Dolder Grand Hotel, Kurhausstrasse 65; La Soupière, in Hotel Schweizerhof; Le Dézaley (specialities of the canton of Vaud), Römergasse 7 & 9 near the Minster; Le Jardin, in the Seiler Hotel Neues Schloss, Stockerstrasse 17; Leo's Bistro, Horneggstrasse 15/Seefeldstrasse 220; Lian Hua, Winterthurstrasse 698; Lindenhofkeller, Pfalgasse 4; Mère Catherine (rustic), Rüdenplatz 8; Mövenpick Paradeplatz, on Paradeplatz; Muggenbühl, Muggenbühlstrasse 15; Neuklösterli, Zürichbergstrasse 231;

Nostalgie-Restaurant, Wilder Mann, Forchstrasse 185; Nouvelle, Erlachstrasse 46; Oepfelchammer, Rindermarkt; Raja Bongo, Zwinglistrasse 3; Ravi's Indian Cuisine, Rütschistrasse 29;
Ribo, Luisenstrasse 43; Riesbächli, Zollikerstrasse 157; Rothus and Goldenes Schwert Restaurationsbetriebe, Marktgasse 14-17; Roxy, Beatengasse 11; Rüden, Limmatquai 42; Sala of Tokyo, Limmatstrasse 29; Schalom (kosher), Lavaterstrasse 33-37; Spazzacamino, Martastrasse 145; Storchen, am Weinplatz 2; Taverna Syrtaki, Werdstrasse 66; Tübli, Schneggengasse 8; Urania, Uraniastrasse 9; Valencia, Sihlfeldstrasse 141; Waldhaus Dolder, Kurhausstrasse 20; Widder (old fashioned), Widdergasse 8; Zeughauskeller, Bahnhofstrasse 28a, Paradeplatz; Zum Groben Ernst, Stüssihofstatt 16; Zum Roten Gatter (French cuisine), Schifflände 6; Zunfthaus am Neumarkt, Neumarkt 5; Zunfthaus zum Rüden, Limmatquai 42; Zunfthaus zur Saffran, Limmatquai 54; Zunfthaus zur Schmiden, Marktgasse 20; Zunfthaus zur Waag, Münsterhof 8; Zunfthaus zur Zimmerlauten, Limmatequai 40, all high quality.

In Buchenegg: Panorama Restaurant Buchenegg.
In Gattikon-Thalwil: Sihlhalde, Sihlhaldenstrasse 70.
In Horgen: Taverne, in Hotel Schwan, Zugerstrasse 9.
In Kilcherberg: Obere Mönchhof.
In Kloten: airport restaurants Top-Air Terminal A.
In Regensberg: Krone.
In Rorbas: Adler.
In Wädenswil: Eichmühle, Neugustrasse 933.

Cafés: Grand Café, Limmatquai and Löwenstrasse; In Gassen, In Gassen 8; Schober, Napfgasse 4; Sprüngli, Paradeplatz.

Road Traffic

In the relatively heavily populated Swiss Alpine foreland the road network is exceedingly dense; roads through villages and small towns are often narrow and require special care and attention. The mountainous regions   *Road Network*

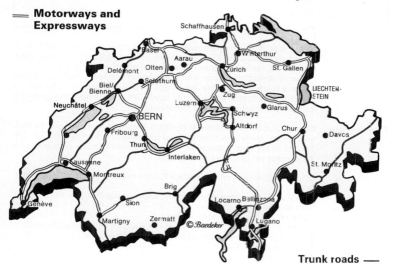

Road Traffic

	Zürich	Zug	Schaffhausen	St. Moritz	St. Gallen	Porrentruy	Olten	Montreux	Luzern	Lugano	Locarno	Lausanne	Kreuzlingen	Interlaken	Genève	Fribourg	Chur	Chiasso	Chaux-de-Fonds, La	Buchs/SG	Brig	Bern	Basel
Andermatt	117	78	170	162	155	204	125	200	75	111	102	234	164	93	296	186	92	135	220	133	78	154	169
Basel	85	113	93	291	166	68	41	182	94	267	258	198	139	147	264	127	196	291	98	188	236	91	
Bern	123	117	170	315	206	114	69	86	91	262	253	106	187	60	165	31	238	286	69	230	177		
Brig	195	156	247	240	228	306	190	123	153	146	113	153	242	117	215	180	170	170	244	211			
Buchs/SG	111	107	124	129	52	251	172	316	130	187	178	333	85	194	395	261	42	211	265				
Chaux-de-Fonds, La	158	164	206	360	239	62	101	122	160	316	307	98	225	129	142	68	273	340					
Chiasso	239	200	294	131	272	326	248	297	197	26	61	327	286	215	389	304	170						
Chur	119	115	171	77	94	257	180	324	138	146	137	341	125	185	403	266							
Fribourg	151	157	200	333	232	125	96	58	123	278	269	63	218	78	137								
Genève	288	295	334	424	366	204	234	93	262	361	324	62	352	215									
Interlaken	118	88	144	255	182	168	123	136	64	191	182	153	195										
Kreuzlingen	71	101	46	212	34	207	139	273	132	262	253	290											
Lausanne	226	232	272	378	304	157	172	26	200	299	262												
Locarno	206	167	258	163	252	293	215	246	164	37													
Lugano	215	176	267	126	261	302	224	283	173														
Luzern	55	25	107	237	118	130	52	183															
Montreux	189	215	255	363	287	183	155																
Olten	61	66	106	262	136	88																	
Porrentruy	144	150	158	346	222																		
St. Gallen	85	95	80	190																			
St. Moritz	206	202	258																				
Schaffhausen	53	82																					
Zug	30																						

Distances in Switzerland (Kilometres)

have a less closely meshed road network and the most important valleys are easily accessible. The Swiss road network consists of motorways (French – autoroutes; Italian – autostrade) which are subject to tolls, and motorists need to display an annual vignette on their cars. There are official national roads 1st class, national roads 2nd class which are equivalent to English main roads, and national roads 3rd class (important pass and valley roads), main roads and minor roads.

Road conditions
In general road conditions are excellent. Mountain stretches are, by their very nature, somewhat narrower and sometimes have steep descents and curves; in summer because of the considerable number of coaches on these roads extreme care is necessary.

Europa Routes
On the following stretches Europa Routes cross the territory of Switzerland:
E2: Vallorbe–Lausanne–Martigny–the Rhône Valley–Simplon Pass–Domodóssola (Italy).
E4: Basle–Berne–Lausanne–Geneva.
E9: Basle–Lucerne–Arth–Andermatt–St Gotthard–Bellinzona–Lugano.
E17: Basle–Zurich–Winterthur–St Gallen–St Margrethen.
E21A: Martigny–Great St Bernard–Aosta (Italy).
E60: Zug–Arth.

E61: St Margrethen–Chur–Splügen (village)–San Bernardino–Bellinzona.
E70: Bargen–Schaffhausen–Winterthur.

Since 1985 motorways and roads of motorways standard have been subject to toll and the signs on them are white and green. The motorway vignette which acts as a receipt for the toll can be obtained at frontiers, at post offices, filling stations and garages in Switzerland and from the Automobile Association in Great Britain. It costs 30 Swiss Francs and lasts for 14 months from 1st December to the 31st January of the following year.

As well as super and diesel, lead-free petrol is widely available in Switzerland, the cost varies considerably.

Fuel (Petrol/ Gasoline/ Diesel)

Outside business hours cars can obtain fuel at filling stations in towns and at automatic pumps on the motorways which take bank notes of 10 and 20 Swiss Francs and which are open 24 hours a day.

Emergency fuel in cans can only be carried up to 25 litres/approximately 5 gallons.

See Motoring

Tel. 163.

Traffic regulations Road conditions

Shopping and Souvenirs

The best known Swiss products are watches, clocks and jewellery. Also popular are lace and embroidery from St Gallen and the multi-bladed Swiss Army knives.

Souvenirs

There is a good selection of craft articles at the "Schweizer Heimatwerk" which has showrooms in Zurich and other large towns. Here mounted crystal, painted porcelain, wooden articles and vessels, musical boxes, dolls in traditional costume, carvings in wood, and other characteristic work of a particular district can be obtained.

Craftwork

Food of excellent quality can be bought. Among the most popular items are chocolate, cheese and spirits (cherry brandy from Zug and herbal liqueurs called "Chrüter") also wine, meat, and cherry bread. Coffee, conserves and ready-made dishes can be obtained in many varieties especially in chain stores such as Migros, Co-op, etc.

Food

Sport

A good survey of the facilities for sport, accommodation, evening entertainment, etc., during the summer can be found in the leaflet "Die Schweiz – eine ganze Ferienwelt" which can be obtained from the Swiss Tourist Office or from Swiss Travel Bureaux (see information). Also the brochure "Sportferien à la Carte", with 14 selected week-long holidays for different (summer) sports, can be obtained from the above mentioned information bureaux on request. For information about winter sports in Switzerland see "Winter Sports" below.

General

Switzerland has some 135,000 hectares/334,000 acres of lakes in which angling is allowed. Since the regulations for fishing and the conditions for a fishing permit vary from canton to canton, anglers are recommended to obtain information from the police or from the fishing supervisory organisation in the place where they wish to stay, or from the cantonal fishing administration before their holiday begins.

Angling

Bad Ragaz Golf Club

A brochure giving details of the most important fishing areas and the place from which fishing permits are available in the various cantons can be obtained from the Swiss Tourist Bureaux (see Information).

Ballooning

On 5th May 1788 Jean-Pierre Blanchard made the first ascent in a balloon in the history of Swiss air travel only five years after the Montgolfier brothers. Today ballooning is not only a popular sport but is also a pleasurable pastime and holiday activity. Further information can be obtained from the Aeroclub der Schweiz in Lucerne (see flying below).

Mountaineering

See entry

Boat rental

See Water sports

Flying

Information about all kinds of flying is obtainable from the:

Aeroclub der Schweiz
Lidostrasse 5
CH-6006 Luzern
Tel. (041) 312121

Special departments for gliding and parachuting.

The club also gives information about circular flights in Switzerland, the Alps, towns and other trips in aircraft. A leaflet about the most important aerosports and also details of schools for motor-boaters and parachutists and about organisations offering circular flights can be obtained from the Swiss Travel Bureaux (see Information).

Hang gliding and parasailing (for example in Engelberg) are becoming increasingly popular. Information from the:

Schweizerische Hängegleiterverband (SHV)
Postfach
CH-8620 Wetzikon
Tel. (01) 932 43 53

At present Switzerland has more than 30 golf courses and others are in course of construction or planned. Some of the golf clubs are near the Swiss border, even on French or German territory (for example the Lake Constance Golf Club), since they are easy to reach from Switzerland and are therefore included in the following list. Details concerning registration formalities (proof of handicap, fees, etc.) can be obtained from the various golf clubs under the telephone numbers given. Information can also be obtained from the Swiss Travel Bureaux (see Information) and the Swiss Golf Union (ASG).

Association Suisse de Golf (ASG)
En Ballègue
Case Postale
CH-1066 Epalinges-Lausanne
Tel. (021) 21 77 01

The Swiss golf card "Golf in der Schweiz" can be obtained from the above address on payment.

Bernese Mittelland: Blumisberg Golf Club, CH-3184 Wünnewil, tel. (037) 36 13 80. Alt. 605 m/1986 ft; 18 holes.

Bernese Oberland:
Interlaken-Unterseen Golf Club, CH-3800 Interlaken, tel. (036) 22 60 22. Alt. 556 m/1825 ft; 18 holes.
Gstaad-Saanenland Golf Club, CH-3777 Saanenmöser, tel. (030) 426 36. Alt. 4595 ft; 9 holes.

Lake Constance Area:
Bodensee Golf Club: this Swiss golf club is situated on German territory in D-8995 Weissenberg/Lindau, Lampertsweiler 5, tel. (033 89) 89 190. Alt. 500 m/1641 ft; 18 holes.

Lake Geneva Area:
Montreux Golf club, CH-1860 Aigle/Montreux, tel. (025) 26 46 16. Alt. 395 m/1296 ft; 18 holes.
Bonmont Golf Club, CH-1261 Chéserex/Nyon, tel. (022) 69 23 45. Alt. 590 m/1936 ft; 18 holes.
Geneva Golf Club, 70 Route de la Capite, CH-1223 Cologny/Geneva, tel. (022) 35 75 40. Alt. 400 m/1313 ft; 18 holes.
Golf & Country Club du Domaine Impérial, CH-1196 Gland, tel. (022) 62 10 72 and 62 10 73; Alt. 400 m/1313 ft; 18 holes.
Lausanne Golf Club, Chalet-à-Gobet, Route du Golf 3, CH-1000 Lausanne 25, tel. (021) 91 63 16. Alt. 853 m/2799 ft; 18 holes.
Golf et Country Club de Bossey; this Swiss golf course is on French territory in F-74160 St-Julien-en-Genevois, tel. (050) 43 75 25. Alt. 1376 m/4513 ft; 18 holes.
Villars Golf Club, Route Col de la Croix, CH-1884 Villars, tel. (025) 35 35 98. Alt. 1601 m/5251 ft; 18 holes.

Graubünden:
Arosa Golf Club, Clubhouse Maran, CH-7050 Arosa, tel. (081) 31 22 15. Alt. 1851 m/6072 ft; 9 holes.
Davos Golf Club, CH-7260 Davos, tel. (083) 5 56 34. Alt. 1561 m/5120 ft; 18 holes.
Lenzerheide-Valbella Golf Club, CH-7078 Lenzerheide, tel. (081) 34 13 16 Alt. 1501 m/4923 ft; 18 holes.
Engadin Golf Club/Samedan Golf Club, Golfhaus Samedan, CH-7503 Samedan, tel. (082) 6 52 26. Alt. 1721 m/5645 ft; 18 holes.
Vulpera Golf Club, CH-7552 Bad Vulpera, tel. (084) 9 96 88. Alt. 1280 m/4200 ft; 9 holes.

Neuchâtel/Bernese Jura:
Club de Golf de Neuchâtel, CH-2072 Voëns-sur-St-Blaise, tel. (038) 33 55 50. Alt. 580 m/1904 ft; 18 holes.

Northwest Switzerland (and the adjoining Alsace in France):
Basle Golf & Country Club, CH-4007 Basle, tel. (061) 6 95 11 11; the golf
course lies in French territory, in F-68220 Hagenthal (Hegenheim)/
Geisberg, tel. (089) 68 50 91. Alt. 400 m/1312 ft; 18 holes.
Golf Club de la Largue; this Swiss golf course lies on French territory, in
F-68580 Mooslargue, Chemin du Largweg, tel. (089) 25 60 62.
Alt. 450 m/1477 ft; at present 9 holes (extension to 18 holes planned).
Mittelland Golf Club, CH-5036 Oberentfelden, tel. (064) 43 85 85;
Alt. 400 m/1313 ft; 9 holes.
Schinznach-Bad Golf Club, CH-5116 Schinznach-Bad, tel. (056) 43 12 26.
Alt. 350 m/1149 ft; 9 holes.

Eastern Switzerland:
Bad Ragaz Golf Club, CH-7310 Bad Ragaz, tel. (085) 9 15 56.
Alt. 520/1707 ft; 18 holes.
Eastern Switzerland Golf Club, CH-9246 Niederbüren – St Gallen,
tel. (071) 81 18 55. Alt. 497 m/1631 ft; 18 holes.

Ticino:
Golf Club Patriziale Ascona, CH-6612 Ascona, tel. (093) 35 21 32.
Alt. 200 m/656 ft; 18 holes.
Lugano Golf Club, CH-6983 Magliaso/Lugano, tel. (091) 71 15 57.
Alt. 290 m/952 ft; 18 holes.

Valais:
Golf Club Crans-sur-Sierre, Postfach 138, CH-3963 Crans-sur-Sierre,
tel. (027) 41 21 68. Alt. 1500 m/4923 ft; 9 and 18 holes.
Riederalp Golf Club, CH-3981 Riederalp, tel. (028) 27 14 63.
Alt. 1950 m/6400 ft; 9 holes.
Approach Golf Club, CH-1936 Verbier, tel. (026) 7 49 95.
Alt. 1500 m/4923 ft; 18 holes.

Central Switzerland:
Bürgenstock Golf Club, CH-6366 Bürgenstock, tel. (041) 61 24 34.
Alt. 900 m/2954 ft; 9 holes.
Lucerne Golf Club, CH-6006 Dietschiberg-Lucerne, tel. (041) 36 97 87.
Alt. 670 m/2199 ft; 18 holes.

Zurich:
Breitenloo Golf Club, CH-8309 Oberwil/Bassersdorf, tel. (91) 8 36 40 80.
Alt. 560 m/1838 ft; 18 holes.
Hittnau Golf and Country Club, CH-8336 Dürstelen/Pfäffikon,
tel. (01) 9 50 24 42. Alt. 800 m/2625 ft; 18 holes.
Schönenberg Golf and Country Club, CH-8821 Schönenberg,
tel. (01) 7 88 16 24. Alt. 680 m/2232 ft; 18 holes.
Zurich Golf and Country Club, CH-8126 Zumikon-Zürich,
tel. (01) 9 18 00 51. Alt. 685 m/2248 ft; 18 holes.
Dolder Golf Club, CH-8032 Zürich, tel. (01) 47 50 45. Alt. 600 m/1969 ft;
9 holes.

There are at present more than 80 mini golf courses in Switzerland.

Cycling

Bicycles, whether private or rented can be carried by the railways and
inported into Switzerland without any difficulty. Four types of bicycles can
be rented at about 200 stations of the Swiss Federal Railways (SBB-CFF-
FFS) and a number of private railways:

Basic bicycles (Normal bicycles; with a child's seat provided free).
Children's bicycles
Mountain-bicycles
Tandems

Bicycles which are hired for a whole day or even by the week can normally
be handed back at any station; however if you hire bicycles and tandems

for only half a day then they must be returned to the station from which they were obtained. It is advisable to reserve a bicycle by telephone or personally at the appropriate SBB station, at the latest the evening before it is required.

In numerous places there are specially marked bicycle or mountain-bicycle tracks. The length of the total marked cycle network in Switzerland is over 5000 km/1070 miles. Seven day individual cycle tours, for example from "Berne to Lucerne", "High Points of Central Switzerland" or "Around Lake Constance" with a special service for conveying luggage are ideal for those who would like to book an active cycling holiday. Information can be obtained from local travel offices, and an information leaflet about the most important cycle paths can be obtained from Swiss Travel Bureaux (see Information).

In Switzerland there are more than 100 riding centres where horses for riding either in the open-air or in covered riding schools can be rented. The riding centre of Haslital in the Bernese Oberland has offered riding holidays for more than 20 years; a week spent trekking on horseback is also very popular.

Riding

Information:
Reitzentrum Haslital/Meiringen
CH-3860 Meiringen
Tel. (036) 71 16 53

The Blatten-Belalp Tourist Union offers on weekends in summer three-day trekking on a mule in the Aletsch glacier region. The route is Natters–Blatten–Belalp–the Great Aletsch Glacier and Riederalp.

Information:
Verkehrsbüro
CH-3914 Blatten-Belalp
Tel. (028) 23 13 85

In many places there are riding courses for children; for example beginners can learn to ride in Einsiedeln. Riding holidays can also be combined with language courses.

The brochure "Reitferien in der Schweiz" can be obtained at Swiss Travel Bureaux (see Information). It is produced in association between the Swiss Tourist Office (SVZ) and the Swiss Horse Magazine.

Another attraction is a holiday in a horse-drawn wagon, for example through the Valais

Les Roulottes du Bonheur
CH-1349 Eclépens (19 km/12 miles north of Lausanne)
Tel. (021) 8 66 77 50

Tennis enthusiasts will find in Switzerland more than 700 tennis courts and more than 200 covered courts at their disposal; there are squash courts in more than 40 places. To avoid bottlenecks tennis holidays should not be booked during the high season. Tennis in covered courts is recommended for the period before the beginning of the high season.

Tennis and
Squash

Many of the larger hotels have their own tennis courts. The hotel management and the relevant tourist bureaux will have the necessary details. The brochure "Tennis Squash Guide Indoor and Tennis Holidays" as well as the information leaflet "Tennishallen in der Schweiz" (covered courts in Switzerland) can be ordered from Swiss Travel Bureaux.

See entry

Walking

Sport

Silvaplaner Lake   Lake Geneva

Water Sports   There are over 1400 lakes and large rivers, including the Rhine, Rhône, Inn, Ticino, Aare, Reuss and Limmat, which have excellent facilities for water-sports enthusiasts.

Rowers and canoeists (even with collapsible canoes) can carry on their sport in most lakes and rivers. The finest water for rowing in the world is considered to be the Rot See (Red Lake) near Lucerne where international competitions take place every year.

Extended trips in canoes can be made for example on the Rhine, the Aare and the Reuss; canoeists are particularly fond of the Birs in the Jura and the Muota (Canton of Schwyz). Kayak trips can be made on the Inn, the Rhine, Reuss, Doubs, Broye, Venoge, Versoix, Ticino, Moesa and on Lake Lucerne. "River Rafting" (wild water canoeing) is possible on the Inn, Rhine, Simme, Saane, Aare and Rhône.

Visitors can swim from more than 170 bathing beaches on lakes and rivers, in more than 200 covered and public swimming pools, in over 380 open-air pools and in over 200 pools belonging to hotels.

Good wind conditions for sailors and wind surfers can often be found on lakes surrounded by mountains (Lake Geneva, Lac de Neuchâtel, Lac de Bienne, Lac de Morat, Lake Thun, Lago Maggiore, Lake Lucerne, Lake Uri, the Walensee, Lake Zurich and Lake Constance). Over 60 sailing and 100 wind surfing schools and 30 water-skiing schools provide instruction in these various forms of sport. Information and a list of schools can be obtained from the Swiss Tourist Office or from Swiss Travel Bureaux (see Information) where the leaflet "Schweizer Wasserstimmen heiter" with notes for boat hire is to be obtained.

Water Sport
Districts   See map above

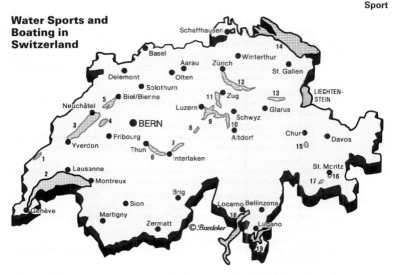

Water Sports and Boating in Switzerland

Water Sports and Inland Boat Services

Boat Excursions: see entry

Regions for Water Sports

1 Lac de Joux (Alt. 900 m./2953 ft)
Sailing, wind-surfing, fishing

2. Lake Geneva/Lac Léman (Alt. 372 m/1221 ft)
Regular boat services between many places on the lake. Rental of sailing-boats and rowing-boats; water-skiing, fishing, sailing, wind-surfing and water-skiing lessons.

3. Lac de Neuchâtel/Neuenberger See (Alt. 432 m/1417 ft)
Regular boat services between many places on the lake. Rental of sailing-boats and rowing-boats; water-skiing, fishing. Sailing, wind-surfing and canoeing lessons.

4. Lac de Morat/Murtensee (Alt. 433 m/1420 ft)
Rental of sailing-boats and rowing-boats, wind-surfing, angling. Sailing and wind-surfing lessons.

5. Lac de Bienne/Bieler See (Alt. 432 m/1417 ft)
Regular boat services between many places on the shores. Rental of sailing-boats and rowing-boats; water-skiing, fishing. Sailing and wind-surfing lessons.

6. Lake Thun (Thuner See) (Alt. 560 m/1837 feet)
Regular boat sevices between many places on the lake. Rental of sailboats and rowboats; water-skiing, wind-surfing, fishing. Sailing and wind-surfing lessons.

7. Lake Brienz/Brienzer See (Alt. 567 m/1860 ft)
Regular boat services between many places on the lake. Rental of sailing-boats and rowing-boats; water-skiing, wind-surfing and fishing. Fishing lessons.

8. Sarner See (Alt. 473 m/1552 ft)
Regular boat services between most places on the lake. Rental of sailing-boats and rowing-boats; fishing, wind-surfing. Sailing and wind-surfing lessons.

9. Lake Lucerne/Vierwaldstätter See (Alt. 437 m/1434 ft)
Regular boat services between many places on the lake. Rental of sailing-boats and rowing-boats; wind-surfing. Sailing lessons.

10. Lake Uri/Urner See (Alt. 437 m/1434 ft)
Regular boat services between many places on the lake. Rental of sailing-boats and rowing-boats; wind-surfing.

11. Lake Zug/Zuger See (Alt. 437 m/1434 ft)
Regular boat services between Zug and Arth. Rental of sailing-boats and rowing-boats; wind-surfing.

12. Lake Zurich/Zürichsee (Alt. 410 m/1345 ft)
Regular boat services between many places on the lake. Rental of sailing-boats and rowing-boats; wind-surfing. Sailing and wind-surfing lessons.

13. Walensee (Alt. 423 m/1388 ft)
Regular boat services between Weesen and Walenstadt. Rental of sailing-boats and rowing-boats; fishing. Sailing and fishing lessons.

14. Lake Constance/Bodensee (Alt. 395 m/1296 ft)
Regular boat services between many places on the lake. Rental of sailing-boats and rowing-boats; wind-surfing and fishing. Sailing, wind-surfing and fishing lessons.

15. Heidsee (Alt. 1493 m/4899 ft)
Rental of sailing-boats; wind-surfing, fishing. Sailing, wind-surfing and fishing lessons.

16. St Moritzer See (Alt. 1771 m/5811 ft)
Rental of sailing-boats; wind-surfing, canoeing. Sailing, wind-surfing and fishing lessons.

17. Silser See and Silvaner See (Alt. 1795 m/5889 ft)
Regular boat services between certain places on the lake. Sailing, wind-surfing. Wind-surfing lessons.

18. Lake Maggiore/Lago Maggiore (Alt. 194 m/637 ft)
Regular boat services between many places on the lake.

19. Lake Lugano/Lago di Lugano (Alt. 274 m/899 ft)
Regular boat services between many places on the lake. Rental of sailing-boats and rowing-boats; wind-surfing, water-skiing. Sailing, wind-surfing and water-skiing lessons.

Tourists can bring their motor- or sailing-boats, provided they are registered in the country from which they come and are re-exported at the latest three months after their arrival, without particular customs formalities; there are no tolls for the boats. Kayaks, canoes, dinghys and surfboards are considered as tourist luggage and technically are not subject to duty.

The driver of a motor boat must be at least 14 years old. A foreign driving permit is required (it suffices for a temporary stay in Switzerland), when the motor of the boat exceeds 6 kW or the sail area is more than 15 sq. m. For both a compulsory insurance is required. The permit for a boat, which can be obtained from any cantonal authority, is valid for one month on all Swiss waters.

Smaller lakes such as the Greifensee, Pfäffikersee, the Aargau lakes and the lakes of Grisson are not available for sailing boats.

Boats, etc., below 2.5 m/8 ft in length which are not subject to a permit can only be used in an area of 150 m/164 yds from a shore (exceptions are racing shells and surfboards). On all Swiss lakes there is a speed limit of 10 km/6 miles per hour within an area 300 m/328 yds from the shore.

Winter Sports   Switzerland is a paradise for winter sports with especially attractive skiing areas; these include the Jungfrau region with its mountain areas and the

Winter-sports enthusiasts in the Alps

mighty Aletsch Glacier, the Engadine, where St Moritz is the best-known winter-sports resort in the world, and Zermatt, with the impressive rock pyramid of the Matterhorn in its unique valley.

Hundreds of prepared and marked pistes at heights between 1000 m/3200 ft and 3200 m/10,500 ft (Little Matterhorn) are at the disposal of skiers. For ascents there are more than 1600 ski-lifts, rack-railways, funiculars and cableways with an hourly capacity of 1.2 million persons.

About 4000 ski instructors, both male and female, give lessons in more than 200 Alpine skiing schools; and in addition there are more than 160 schools for cross-country skiing. There is a great deal of advertising material, for example a general survey ("Schweiz – (w)international") with details of tracks, activities, sports schools, as well as facilities for sport, entertainment and accommodation. Various information leaflets, such as "Snowboard" (including the snowboard camp in Wildhaus) and monoski; details of organisers of ski safaris, (white weeks, as in Villars), deep snow weeks, Langlauf weeks for pensioners (for example in Stalden), ice and "Schlittelplausch" for holiday makers, as well as ski kindergartens. Details can be obtained from any Swiss Travel Bureaux.

Various high-lying ski territories can guarantee snow throughout the year so that they can be used throughout summer.

Winter-Sports Areas

1. Morgins. Alt. 1343 m/4406 ft. Cableways to 1922 m/6306 ft

2. Champéry. Alt. 1052 m/3452 ft. Cableways to 1800 m/5906 ft

3. Gruyères-Moléson. Alt. 1110 m/3642 ft. Cableways to 2002 m/6569 ft

Winter Sports Areas in Switzerland

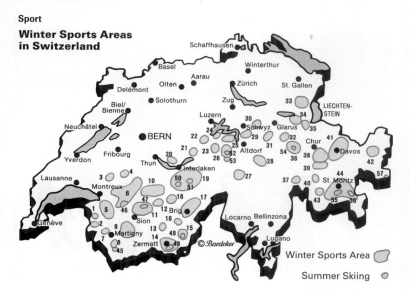

4. Charmey. Alt. 890 m/2920 ft. Cableways to 1630 m/5348 ft

5. Villars-sur-Ollon. Alt. 1256 m/4121 ft. Cableways to 2118 m/6949 ft

Leysin. Alt. 1256-1450 m/4150-4757 ft. Cableways to 2326 m/7632 ft

6. Saanen. Alt. 1033 m/3398 ft. Cableways to 2200 m/7218 ft

Gstaad. Alt. 1050 m/3617 ft. Cableways to 2000 m/6562 ft. Helicopter service

Saanenmöser. Alt. 1269 m/4164 ft. Cableways to 1950 m/6398 ft

Zweisimmen. Alt. 945 m/3101 ft. Cableways to 2079 m/6821 ft

Château-d'Oex. Alt. 990 m/3248 ft. Cableways to 1630 m/5348 ft

Les Diablerets. Alt. 1163 m/3816 ft. Cableways to 2950 m/9679 ft

7. Salvan/Les Marécottes. Alt. 927–1100 m/3041–3609 ft. Cableways to 1780 m/5840 ft

8. Champex. Alt. 1472 m/4830 ft. Cableways to 2374 m/7789 ft

9. Verbier. Alt. 1420 m/4659 ft. Cableways to 3026 m/9931 ft

Haute-Nendaz. Alt. 1370–1736 m/4495–5696 ft. Cableways to 2734 m/8972 ft

10. Lenk. Alt. 1068 m/3504 ft. Cableways to 2098 m/6885 ft

Adelboden. Alt. 1357 m/4452 ft. Cableways to 2200 m/7218 ft

Kandersteg. Alt. 1170 m/3839 ft. Cableways to 1947 m/6388 ft

11. Crans-Montana. Alt. 1500–1680 m/4922–5512 ft. Cableways to 2943 m/9656 ft

12 Leukerbad. Alt. 1411 m/4629 ft. Cableways to 2240 m/8006 ft

13. Zinal. Alt. 1678 m/5506 ft. Cableways to 2900 m/9515 ft

14. Zermatt. Alt. 1630 m/5315 ft. Cableways to 3820 m/12,533 ft

15. Saas Fee. Alt. 1562–1679 m/4926–5509 ft. Cableways to 3100 m/10,171 ft

16. Stalden. Alt. 803 m/2635 ft. Cableways to 1893 m/6211 ft
    Grächen. Alt. 1617 m/5305 ft. Cableways to 2110 m/6923 ft

17. Fiesch. Alt. 1062 m/3484 ft. Cableways to 2870 m/9416 ft

18. Wiler im Lötschental. Alt. 1419 m/4656 ft.
    Cableways to 2700 m/8859 ft

19. Lauterbrunnen. Alt. 796 m/2612 ft. Cableways to 1800 m/5906 ft
    Wengen. Alt. 1276 m/4187 ft. Cableways to 3454 m/11333 ft
    Mürren. Alt. 1634 m/5361 ft. Cableways to 2971 m/9748 ft
    Grindelwald. Alt. 1034 m/3393 ft. Cableways to 3454 m/11333 ft

20. Beatenberg. Alt. 1150 m/3773 ft. Cableways to 1950 m/6398 ft

21. Sörenberg. Alt. 1165 m./3822 ft. Cableways to 2320 m/7612 ft

22. Melchtal. Alt. 894 m/2933 ft. Cableways to 1350 m/4429 ft

23. Melchsee-Frutt. Alt. 1920 m/6300 ft. Cableways to 2230 m/7317 ft

24. Stans. Alt. 455 m/1493 ft. Cableways to 1850 m/6070 ft

25. Beckenried. Alt. 440 m/1444 ft. Cableways to 1600 m/5250 ft

26. Engelberg. Alt. 1020 m/3347 ft. Cableways to 3020 m/9909 ft

27. Andermatt. Alt. 1444 m/4738 ft. Cableways to 2961 m/9715 ft

28. Disentis. Alt. 1140 m/3740 ft. Cableways to 3000 m/9715 ft

29. Muotathal. Alt. 600–870 m/1969–2854 ft. Cableways to 1922 m/6306 ft

30. Hoch-Ybrig. Alt. 1038 m/3406 ft. Cableways to 1856 m/6090 ft

31. Braunwald. Alt. 1300 m/4265 ft. Cableways to 1910 m/6267 ft

32. Elm. Alt. 962 m/3156 ft. Cableways to 2036 m/6680 ft

33. Alt St Johann. Alt. 897 m/2943 ft. Cableways to 1390 m/4561 ft
    Unterwasser. Alt. 927 m/3041 ft. Cableways to 2250 m/7382 ft
    Wildhaus. Alt. 1098 m/3603 ft. Cableways to 1771 m/5811 ft

34. Flumserberge. Alt. 1220–1400 m/4003–4593 ft.
    Cableways to 2222 m/7290 ft

35. Wangs/Bad Ragaz. Alt. 502–520 m/1647–1706 ft.
    Cableways to 2227 m/7307 ft

36. Flims. Alt. 1070–1103 m/3511–3619 ft. Cableways to 2678 m/8787 ft

37. Splügen. Alt. 1450 m/4757 ft. Cableways to 2160 m/7087 ft

38. Arosa. Alt. 1740–1890 m/5709–6201 ft. Cableways to 2653 m/8704 ft

39. Lenzerheide/Valbella. Alt. 1470–1540 m/4823–5053 ft.
    Cableways to 2865 m/9400 ft

40. Savognin. Alt. 1173 m./3849 ft. Cableways to 2713 m/8901 ft

41. Klosters. Alt. 1124–1206 m/3688–3957 ft. Cableways to 2300 m/7546 ft
    Davos. Alt. 1508–1563 m/4948–5128 ft. Cableways to 2844 m/9331 ft

42. Bad Scuol/Tarasp/Vulpera. Alt. 1203–1268 m/3947–4160 ft.
    Cableways to 2900 m/9515 ft

43. Bivio. Alt. 1776 m/5827 ft. Cableways to 2660 m/8727 ft

44. Silvaplana. Alt. 1815 m/5955 ft. Cableways to 3300 m/10,827 ft
    St Moritz. Alt. 1822 m/5978 ft. Cableways to 3057 m/10,030 ft
    Celerina. Alt. 1725 m/5656 ft. Cableways to 2955 m/9695 ft
    Pontresina/Bernina. Alt. 1805 m/5922 ft. Cableways to 2973 m/9754 ft

Summer Skiing Areas

45. Bourg St Pierre. La Chenalette

46. Les Diablerets. Diablerets Glacier

47. Crans-Montana. Glacier de la Plaine Morte

48. Zermatt. Theodul Glacier Breithorn Plateau.

49. Saas Fee. Egginer Felskinn

50. Mürren. Schilthorn

51. Jungfraujoch. Jungfraujoch

52. Engelberg. Titlis

53. Meiringen. Susten Pass

54. Laax. Vorab 3000

55. St Moritz. Corvatsch

56. Pontresina. Diavolezza

57. Münstertal. Stilfser Joch

Winter Sports (continued)	In many winter sports resorts there are complimentary buses in which guests can be taken to the stations or to the proximity of the skiing areas.
Telephone Information	Snow and tourist reports: Tel. (01) 120

Telephone and Telegraph

Telephone	Telephone calls to places abroad can be made from public telephone boxes. First 00 must be dialled, then there will be a shrill whistle. To make a call to Great Britain dial 44 followed by the number without the first 0 of the area code; for Canada and America dial 1 followed by the number excluding the area code.
	From the United Kingdom to Switzerland and Liechtenstein dial 010 41 followed by the number required less the 0 in the code.
	From the United States and Canada to Switzerland and Liechtenstein 011 41, etc.
Telephone Information	Inland 111 International 191
Telephone Service	See Information

Time

Switzerland and the principality of Liechtenstein observe Central European Time: i.e. one hour ahead of Greenwich Mean Time (six hours ahead of New York time). Swiss Summer Time, first introduced in 1981, is one hour ahead of Central European Time (two hours ahead of GMT, seven hours ahead of New York time).

Travel Documents

A valid passport is required. No visa is needed by holiday and business visitors from the United Kingdom (British subjects and British protected persons), Ireland, Commonwealth countries, the United States and many other countries.

Personal Papers

Visitors can take a private car, motor cycle or motor scooter into Switzerland for a temporary stay without customs documents, provided a valid national driving licence can be produced. An international insurance certificate ("green card") should be obtained from the vehicle's normal insurers: visitors from the United Kingdom and Ireland, as members of the EC, are not required to produce a green card, but since their own insurance covers only the minimum legal requirements it is very desirable to have the extra protection which the green card affords. Foreign cars must display an oval international distinguishing sign of the approved type and design. Failure to comply with this regulation is punishable by a heavy on-the-spot fine.

Vehicle documents

Pets (dogs, cats) can be taken to Switzerland and Liechtenstein provided they have a rabies inoculation certificate from a veterinary surgeon. The inoculation must not have been shorter than 30 days and not longer than a year before the animal is imported. Of course, visitors from the United Kingdom would be foolish to take an animal with them since the animal would have to spend six months in quarantine on their return.

Pets

Walking

Switzerland is a veritable paradise for anyone who likes walking. There are approximately 50,000 km/31,000 miles of marked footpaths and many other tracks which can be explored individually. Destinations and the time taken to reach them are displayed on yellow signposts, not only for long walks but also for shorter ones. Suitable maps for walkers are available from the "Bundesamt für Landestopographie" on a scale of 1:25,000. Visitors who are particularly interested in flora and fauna will find beautiful walks through unspoilt countryside and protected areas, and there are many opportunities for guided walks. Food can be obtained either at simple kiosks or at country inns or mountain restaurants (see mountaineering). More than 150 huts and bivouacs of the Swiss Alpine Club (SAC; see Mountaineering) provide shelter and accommodation for those on mountain walks. Among the very many impressive upland walks are those through the sunny Ticino heights, across the Bergel, Prättigal or Schächental mountain paths, through the parched Saas Valley, the karst area of Leysin, or the Kiental with its abundant water. There are also classic paths across the Rigi, the Simplon or a walk at altitude over the Hörnli. Information brochures can be obtained from the Swiss Tourist Offices (see Information).

General

Walking

Hiking Passes   Hiking passes, such as the Reka Pass of the Schweizer Reisekasse (Neuen-gasse 15, CH-3001 Berne, tel. (031) 22 66 33), include free trips on public transport and mountain railways as well as accommodation and breakfast in a hotel of your own choice.

Mountaineering   See entry.

When to go

The best time to visit the pre-Alpine regions is from mid-May to the beginning of July; the best season for the mountains is during July, August and the first half of September, when all the passes are open. The summer resorts usually have a season beginning in May and ending about the end of September. The lakes in the south attract their greatest numbers of visitors in spring and autumn. Those who go to Switzerland in May can enjoy the contrast between the spring blossoms in the warmer pre-Alpine valleys and the wintry conditions still prevailing in the mountains. The winter-sports regions are at their busiest from the end of January to March; the season extends from December to the beginning or end of April, depending on altitude.

Climate   See Facts and Figures.

Youth Hostels

Switzerland has some 120 youth hostels (German: Jungendherberge, French: Auberge de Jeunesse, Italian: alloggio per giovani) providing modestly priced accommodation, particularly for young people (with priority for those under 25). During the main holiday season it is advisable to book in advance; the maximum period of stay permitted in any one hostel will vary according to the demand for places. Youth hostellers must produce a membership card issued by their national youth hostel association.

Information   Schweizerische Bund für Jugendherbergen
Postfach 265
Engestrasse 9
CH-3012 Berne
Tel. (031) 24 55 03

Zoos and Alpine Gardens

See Caves open to the public

Index

Index